CRIMES OF PERCEPTION

AN ENCYCLOPEDIA OF HERESIES AND HERETICS

LEONARD GEORGE

At most times during the history of Western civilization, mere possession of this book would have earned the reader a visit from the town magistrate or the local Inquisitor; the publisher's hands would have been cut off; and the book itself, along with its author, would have been righteously consigned to the flames! *Crimes of Perception* is an encyclopedic collection of the ideas, persons, and practices that, over the centuries, have been judged by the arbiters of religious orthodoxy to be too dangerous for laypeople to know about.

Contained herein are fas of the history of heresy and th Meet Abraham Abulafia, the t Spanish messiah who marche order to convert the Pope to Ju acquainted with the Abbe Guib   , ringleader of a Satanic group that conducted magic rituals (including human sacrifices) in an attempt to control King Louis XIV's love life; and be enthralled by Brother Twelve, a charismatic mystic who established an Aquarian community (complete with personal harem and heavily armed fortress) on the West Coast during the 1920s. Discover unorthodox views of Christ, who has been variously depicted as an angel, a tattooed Egyptian magician, a reincarnation of the serpent from the Garden of Eden, a strict vegetarian, a voracious cannibal, and a hologram. And marvel at the transformation of some well known heretics—such as Joan of Arc,

(continued on back flap)

Crimes of Perception

AN ENCYCLOPEDIA
OF HERESIES AND HERETICS

Leonard George

PARAGON HOUSE

New York

First Edition, 1995

Published in the United States by

Paragon House
370 Lexington Avenue
New York, NY 10017

Library of Congress Cataloging-in-Publication Data
George, Leonard.
   Crimes of perception : an encyclopedia of heresies and heretics /
  Leonard George.
      p.   cm.
  Includes bibliographical references.
  ISBN 1-55778-519-8
   1. Heresies, Christian—Encyclopedias.   2. Heretics, Christian—
Encyclopedias.   3. Heresies, Jewish—Encyclopedias.   4. Heretics,
Jewish—Encyclopedias.   5. Heresy—Encyclopedias.   I. Title.
BT1315.2.G46   1994
273—dc20   94-32759
                                            CIP

Manufactured in the United States of America

In Memory of my father, EARL WILLIAM GEORGE (1910–1982)

and my ancestor, GEORGE WISHART (ca. 1513–1546),
Burned at the Stake as a Heretic
at St. Andrews, Scotland

Contents

Acknowledgments

I am deeply grateful to the many people who have assisted and encouraged me during the long gestation of this book.

Richard Noll, Ph.D., of Harvard University, has been of immeasurable help in every way. He is a man of vast knowledge and kindness, and a great inspiration.

Listing the scholars who have influenced my thinking on heretical matters would double the size of this volume. I must restrict myself to acknowledging only two: the writings of Elaine Pagels, Ph.D., and Morris Berman, Ph.D., have provided the standards of rigor, grace, and creativity to which I aspire.

My agent, Bert Holtje of James Peter Associates, and my editors at Paragon House, Chris O'Connell and Nick Street, have displayed a faith in this project that helped to sustain my faith in myself.

Vivian Alie, my beloved, kept my soul alive.

From a distance, I have been encouraged by my parents, my sister, Jill Jacobson, Gaetan LaBelle, Alex Novak and Marian Buchanan. In British Columbia, many dear friends have been wonderfully supportive—thanks to the Harcos (Donna, Peter, Jeanne, and Marley), Aunt Charlotte Forsyth, Patrick DuBois, Malcolm Kennard, Beth Bosshard, Valerie Mc-Bean, Merv Gilbert and his merry band of psychologists, the CBC Gaberoids, and the Columbia Centroids.

I am indebted to countless waitresses and waiters who cheerfully stoked my caffeine level while I scribbled in Vancouver cafés.

And, of course, I pay homage to Raven Trismegistus, weird bird of my heart. Quoth the Raven, "May all beings be happy and amazed!"

Introduction:
THE VALUE OF HERESY

HERESY: SHIFTING DEFINITIONS

This is a book about choice. In particular, it concerns the most important choice a person can possibly make: the choice of reality. The collection of assumptions and beliefs we learn from the teachers of our culture shape the "real" world we perceive around us and the "real" selves we experience ourselves to be. Sane persons agree that *we believe what we see*; it is less often observed, although it is equally true, that *we tend to see what we believe*. The information that reaches our senses is sculpted by our expectations into a meaningful and familiar set of images. These images enable us to live our lives with some degree of continuity. Frameworks of belief other than the one first taught to us could be selected, however; such choices would mold other worlds and other selves.

The word "heresy" derives from a classical Greek word, *hairesis*. Originally, *hairesis* simply meant a belief chosen by an individual or sect. No negative value was attached to the term. The first century Jewish historian Josephus, for example, described the various schools of Hebrew thought prevalent at the time—the Sadduccees, Pharisees, Essenes, and Zealots—as types of *hairesis*. The early Christians even used the word to refer to themselves. In the New Testament's Book of Acts, the Christians are called "the 'hairesis' of the Nazarenes" (24:5), an interesting fact usually camouflaged by the standard English translation of this passage as "the sect of the Nazarenes."

Even at this early date, however, some Christians were beginning to condemn those who chose religious views differing from their own. In Paul's Letter to the Galatians, he includes heresy in a list of "works of the flesh," along with such items as uncleanness, murder, idolatry, hatred, and drunkenness (5:19–21). And in the Second Letter of Peter, the author proclaims that "there shall be false teachers among you, who privily shall bring in damnable heresies" (2:1). *Hairesis* or heresy was coming to mean a false choice, one that endangers the salvation of the soul.

But who can determine the correctness of a choice about the nature of reality? Only those who believe that they have already made the correct selection would presume to own the yardstick of truth. If, in addition, they have the means to persuade young children and dissenters to agree with them, these possessors of truth can establish themselves as an *orthodoxy*—a mainstream reality tradition, also frequently known as "common sense."

Reality is usually defined by those with the best weapons. Techniques of influence vary from relatively gentle peer pressure ("That's an . . . interesting idea, Laverne.") to visits to the torture chambers, which are still busily operating in most of the United Nations' member states today. Through the centuries, the following formula has been endlessly repeated: "I have the Truth. You do not. My proximity to the Truth entitles me to oppress you—to force you to say and do things in which you do not believe, to imprison and mutilate you, to take your belongings, to make you accuse others of wrong views, and even to execute you—*for your own good.*"

I offer the following definition to identify heresy in the broadest sense: A heresy is a *crime of perception*—an act of seeing something that, according to some custodian of reality, is not truly there. Heresy, therefore, is always relative to an orthodoxy. Every tradition has its heresies; from the perspective of those conventionally labeled heretics, the orthodox themselves are heretical. Martin Luther and the Pope viewed each other as heretics.

In the commonly used, narrower sense of the term, heretics are Christians who differ from orthodoxy with respect to basic points of doctrine, in particular the nature of God as a Trinity (special theology), and the nature of Christ as both fully human and fully divine (Christology). But there are also Jewish heretics, pagan heretics, scientific heretics, social and political heretics, sexual and psychological heretics. Where there is orthodoxy, there is heresy.

HERESIES WITHOUT: THE HERETICAL STRUCTURE OF CULTURE

A spotlight shines in a darkened room. Within the ring of light, objects are clearly illuminated. Surrounding that glowing circle is a domain of shadow, fading into utter blackness. This configuration of brilliant center and murky halo is also found in the structure of human societies. There is always a conventional reality tradition that crisply delineates the real and the true, the "daytime world" where ordinary people lead largely unquestioning lives. And, surrounding that tradition, is the domain of heresy. In the cultural shadows, there are individuals and groups whose world views differ in fundamental ways from "common sense."

The roots of Western culture include the mainstream reality traditions of the ancient Mediterranean world. The first Christians adopted elements of these traditions to forge their distinctive visions of reality. During the fourth century, one school of Christianity, which was especially efficient in its political organization, managed to gain control of the Roman Empire. In effect, the school "grabbed the spotlight." Since the empire was a police state, this group obtained access to the apparatus of persuasion that enabled it to establish itself as orthodox Catholic Christianity.

The details of the ancient struggles to define Christian doctrines seem remote to most of us today. The Arian controversy, for instance, was literally over an iota: whether God the Father and God the Son have the *same* nature (in Greek, *homoousios*) or a *similar* nature (*homoiousios*). But the consequences of these debates remain nearer to us than our own breath. The orthodox dogma that the Trinity subsists in three persons took centuries to define; so did the doctrine that Christ possesses complete humanity. In the process, what it means to be a "person" and a "human" was determined for Western society. If you understand yourself to be a person and a human, you are constructing yourself using conceptual tools that were honed, long ago, on an iota.

Regarding the time before the Catholic political triumph, we can speak of Christian orthodoxy and heresy based only on our present-day knowledge of the struggle's outcome. In the second century, it might have been difficult to tell which party would go on to define orthodoxy. Following that victory, though, the matter was clear. Any remaining Gnostics, Arians, Montanists, Marcionites, and pagans were the bearers of false doctrines and were treated accordingly.

Through the early Middle Ages, the orthodox world view solidified. The earth was fixed at the center of the physical universe. Surrounding it was a series of crystalline spheres, in which were embedded the planets and stars. This universe was alive, although there was debate regarding the degree of its awareness and volition. Everything in this created world had a function determined by God. If it were not for human sin and the actions of the Devil, the various parts of the universal organism would operate in harmony. Of great importance was the notion, inherited from Judaism, that the Creator and His creation were separate—God dwelled beyond the outermost sphere. Aside from a brief visit as Christ, He stayed there.

Interwoven with this physical world was the occult domain of spirits. The hidden universe was also organized into levels. There were nine choirs of angels and nine ranks of demons, or fallen angels. The love of hierarchy displayed in this world model was reflected in the social world as well. As feudal society emerged, everyone was assigned a place. Knowing one's location in the scheme—serf, noble, or royal—strictly determined what one did with one's life. Religious officials took their places on the ladder, with rural clerics at the bottom and the pope at the top. The church assumed tight control of contacts with spiritual realities.

In this period, the conventional Christian culture was in an optimistic, expansionist phase. Few survivals of the ancient competition remained, and these posed no serious threats. Conversions of pagan rulers (who usually demanded that their subjects follow them en masse) in exchange for political rewards within the newly defined world were proceeding well. The Moslems were a worry, but a distant one for most Europeans. The pagan Vikings probed southward, but were eventually converted. As the year A.D. 1000 approached, there were some squabbles over fine points of doctrine, but the Catholic monopoly on belief in Europe seemed secure.

The mood of Christian Europe shifted ominously during the later medieval period. Powerful heresies erupted, beginning in the Balkan region, where the Bogomils appeared, inspired by fragmentary survivals of ancient unorthodox doctrines. Sparks of dissent seemed to waft over the continent, igniting brush fires of heresy. In France, Italy, and Germany, the Cathars and Waldensians mounted serious challenges to Roman Catholicism. Other alternative-reality movements flared, often deriving support from the downtrodden poor and from a new class that did not have a comfortably defined place in the old map of social reality, the urban merchants. In this atmosphere, orthodox confidence in the utterly superior strength of the forces of good—that is, their own forces—began to slip. The "daytime world" began to lose its quality of inevitability in the face of the other choices now looming from the shadows. Some Catholic clerics were even experimenting with demonic evocation, wishing to tap the surging powers of darkness.

Orthodoxy developed novel methods of fighting back. The mendicant monastic orders, the Franciscans and Dominicans, were founded to beat mendicant heretics at their own game. A crusade was conducted in the heresy-infested lands of southern France, giving rise to the infamous slogan: "Kill them all, and let God sort them out." And the Holy Inquisition was launched.

But the tide of change could not be stemmed. The Renaissance saw the imagery of the ancient pagan gods return to a respected place in Western culture. Occult doctrines of dubious or forced compatibility with mainstream Christianity were being smuggled into the conventional world view. Italian philosopher Marsilio Ficino managed to teach an essentially pagan type of natural magic without attracting persecution, but many of the magicians he inspired went too far, and were not as lucky, for this was also the era of the Great Witch Hunt.

The ruling powers of society felt their world view being undermined. This age witnessed the discovery of unexpected continents, the improving position of formerly marginal social classes, and surprising insights produced by the scientific method. People in the privileged sectors of the divinely ordained hierarchy knew their certainties were crumbling and identified the threat in familiar terms, evil spirits and their human allies. For two centuries, the West condemned to death hundreds of thousands of its citizens as Satanic conspirators. All were innocent.

In the 1500s, the Protestant Reformation ruptured the Roman Catholic Church. Protestant leaders immediately defined their own orthodoxies and began persecuting Protestants who disagreed with them. They also retained the taste for burning witches. Curiously, although the Protestants damned the Catholic Inquisition as barbaric, they continued to use the inquisitors' witch-hunting manuals.

The slaughter of the witches was both the death agony of the old reality and the birth pain of the new. The Scientific Revolution and the Age of Reason that followed officially rejected the living universe with its elaborate hierarchies, an event historian Carolyn Merchant vividly labeled the "Death of Nature." The image of the world as a great inanimate machine was established in its place, its operations determined by the laws of physics. There were no witches, angels, or devils in the clockwork reality. Eventually, the emerging modern perspective would also place God and the human soul on death row.

There was, of course, resistance as the old common sense became the new absurdity. Such movements as Spiritualism and Theosophy, which attempted to give direct proof for the existence of spiritual realities, drew millions of followers during the nineteenth century. Orthodox Christians tried to use the critical tools of modern scholarship to defend their traditional certainties. Sometimes, as in the case of the Modernist movement within Roman Catholicism, the attempt backfired. The Vatican, after encouraging Catholic Modernism, was faced with increasingly uncomfortable questioning from its own best thinkers. In 1907, Modernism was pronounced a heresy.

Today, many people in the West consider themselves to be members of an organized religious denomination, but few accept the doctrines and commandments of their spiritual institution in every detail. Religious orthodoxies struggle to adapt while preserving the essence of their truths; sometimes, they still declare people heretics.

The central features of the mainstream world view today are provided by science. In a *New York Times* article (October 22, 1989), Harvard University physicist Sheldon Glashow summarized the scientific creed:

We believe that the world is knowable, that there are simple rules governing the behavior of matter and the evolution of the universe. We affirm that there are eternal, objective, extra-historical, socially neutral, external and universal truths and that the assemblage of these truths is what we call physical science. Natural laws can be discovered that are universal, invariable, inviolate, genderless and verifiable. They may be found by men or by women or by mixed collaborations of any obscene proportions. Any intelligent alien anywhere would have come upon the same logical system as we have to explain the structure of protons and the nature of supernovae. This statement I cannot prove, this statement I cannot justify. This is my faith.

Glashow's statement is refreshing because he freely admits something that is often disguised in the presentation of an orthodoxy: that it is founded on unprovable assumptions, not on absolute reality. Empirical science is a conventional reality tradition, the latest in a long series. It is indeed unique in the world it reveals, and it offers the most accurate depiction of the real world available—according to its own standards—but this is true of every orthodoxy.

As a typical conventional-reality tradition, the scientific establishment is ringed by alternative visions that it defines as heresies—that is, as false views—and that it resists. For example, astrologers are rarely welcome at astronomy conventions. And many psychologists make scornful comments about parapsychologists, usually without ever having read even one page from a parapsychology journal.

Another feature that the world view of modern science probably shares with other orthodoxies is transience. From a historical perspective, there is no reason to assume that the ever-shifting reality illuminated by the spotlight of late twentieth century science will prove to be more enduring than the sky gods of ancient times, the angelic choirs of the Middle Ages, or the broom-straddling witch of the Renaissance. R. D. Laing, in his book *The Voice of Experience*, observes: "It was all a machine yesterday. It is something like a hologram today. Who knows what intellectual rattle we shall be shaking tomorrow to calm the dread of the emptiness of our understanding of the explanations of our meaningless correlations?"

HERESIES WITHIN: THE HERETICAL STRUCTURE OF CONSCIOUSNESS

A culture is a collection of people. And the structure of central light and peripheral shadow—of orthodoxy and heresy—every culture displays is repeated in the life of every individual person. At each moment, the beam of one's attention is focused on something (in your case at this instant, the words on this page). Surrounding this foreground are potential experiences to which one can easily shift awareness (what sensations are occurring in your feet right now?). But farther from the center, it becomes less likely that the possibilities that dwell there will ever reach the illumination of everyday awareness—not without a major change in the processes that direct attention. In *The Varieties of Religious Experience*, William James notes that:

> our normal waking consciousness is but one special type of consciousness, whilst all around it, parted from it by the filmiest of screens, there lie potential forms of consciousness entirely different. We may go through life without suspecting their existence; but apply the requisite stimulus and at a touch they are there in all their completeness. No account of the universe in its totality can be final which leaves these other forms of consciousness quite disregarded.

We are not born with a "normal waking consciousness," that is, with a world view. We learn it. In most cases, parents are the first and most important source of the assumptions with which we organize sensations into meaningful experiences. And, for the most part, the beliefs of our parents derive from the conventional-reality tradition of the society in which they live. From our first breath, we receive guidance concerning what to notice and what to ignore in the world around and within us.

The territory of a human life is always richer and stranger than any possible map a culture could provide. From time to time, we encounter events that appear to violate our expectations concerning the nature of things. These occurrences can range from the trivial (noticing a set of traffic lights with the colors reversed, having a friend momentarily forget one's name) to the profound (a dream that seems to come true, an encounter with a ghost). Such events raise questions. What is happening *right here, right now*, that one's attentional habits prevent one from perceiving? And what would remain of the certainties that anchor one's daily life if these habits were altered? From the viewpoint of the "normal waking consciousness," constructed and maintained by the orthodoxy within which one is encased, such thoughts are the heresies of the mind.

Just as a conventional-reality tradition has ways to keep the heresies at bay, so does the individual embodiment of that tradition in an ordinary state of consciousness. For instance, the mind is quite capable of building *ghettos* to isolate urges, ideas, and experiences that could undermine some cherished belief. For example, a man who consorts with prostitutes on Saturday night and then preaches hellfire and damnation at his fundamentalist church the following morning, manages to keep two drastically different sets of values so insulated from each other that he can usually avoid the pain of facing the contradictions.

Consciousness also has its *inquisitions*. For example, if a woman has such confidence in the security of her marriage that she roots her self-esteem in the relationship, she might well eliminate any awareness that her spouse is keenly interested in someone else, even in the presence of rather clear evidence. Like an unfortunate Spanish peasant in the cells of Torquemada, an experience caught in the glare of her inquisitorial consciousness can be made to say anything she wants to hear.

When besieged by novelty, the individual, like the culture, sometimes mounts a *witch hunt* against the innocent. In my capacity as a clinical psychologist, I once treated a woman who was gripped by a terrible fear. Each evening before retiring, she noticed a fantasy creeping from the mental shadows; she imagined that in the middle of the night she would sleepwalk into the kitchen, pick up a butcher knife, return to the bedroom, and stab her husband. She had no history of violent behavior of any sort and no other signs of unusual conflict with her husband; in fact, many of us would probably recognize this fantasy as the kind of bizarre imaginal flotsam that often drifts meaninglessly past the mind's eye. This woman, however, feared that the fantasy would possess her and compel her to act it out. She fought the demonic thought through distraction, prayer, and self-condemnation. But the harder she fought, the more vivid it became.

As it turned out, the resolution was relatively simple: instead of attempting to destroy the fantasy, I suggested that she imagine it *deliberately* every day, and even to amplify the details to ridiculous extremes. When she did so, she found that she did not become possessed by her demonic imagination; the fantasy was just a thought, which she soon stopped having. She ended her inner "Burning Times" and discovered that there were no witches there after all.

WHY WE NEED HERESIES

On both the cultural and individual levels, perhaps it is necessary for orthodoxy to combat heresy. As the physical body requires an immune system to suppress invaders that endanger its integrity, so a body of belief might need defenses to prevent a dissolution into chaos. Anarchists would disagree. Without official belief enforcement of any sort, they feel that basic human compassion (or self-interest) would produce a free and safe society. However, there are no confirmed instances of anarchistic civilizations to show us whether such a condition is possible. In the absence of counterexamples, then, it would appear that too much heresy may be unhealthy.

But what about too little? Is there any value in heresy? An orthodox perception might hold that the energies expended in fighting false doctrines would be better spent in deepening our appreciation of the truth. Therefore, heresies are simply bad. I have come to believe otherwise. Unorthodox views fulfill several crucial roles: as resources, mirrors, and decoys.

Heresies as Resources.   At several junctures in Western history (including, perhaps, the present), old conventional-reality traditions were overthrown, and new ones took their place. In the decline of Greco-Roman paganism, the ancient visions had lost their power to bind together and to inspire people. The empire had lost its dynamism, and no one knew why. Into the gap stepped Catholic Christianity. More than one thousand years later, another tottering orthodoxy found itself too inflexible to absorb the New World, the sun-centered universe, and the confrontation with fresh ideas about the role of the church. The birth of the clockwork universe followed.

But where do new world views come from? In the case of the ancient transition, from the "hairesis" of Christianity, while during the Renaissance, they stemmed in part from the occult notions of astrology, alchemy, and ritual magic, which were being practiced by a number of the people who created the Scientific Revolution. Here is the general pattern: When venerable assumptions are strained to breaking by contact with new realities, when a segment of society perceives that the conventional view ensures its continued oppression, or when the old orthodoxy loses its capacity to serve as a vehicle for wonder, something emerges from the darkness of heresy to take its place.

The pattern recurs in the realm of the individual. When one's certainties no longer work, one may be forced to consider possibilities that one used to think were crazy. If the formerly rejected way of viewing the world brings more rewards, insight, or comfort than one's customary perspective, one may well convert to the old "madness"; one's old "common sense" is then recast as immaturity. The Soviet communist becomes a capitalist; the wealthy materialist, burning out on the treadmill lifestyle of consumerism, finds the Lord; the scandalized churchgoer, unable to forgive her child-molesting parish priest, is jolted into atheism.

Heresies form a reservoir of possibilities that float at the margins of acceptability. If dissent could be eliminated completely, cultures or individuals would have destroyed their ability to breathe fresh air into their visions. In *Coming to Our senses: Body and spirit in the hidden history of the West*, Morris Berman states: "If anomalies can be plowed back into the system . . . the system becomes stronger; if you eat your enemy, you absorb his power. If, on the other hand, you insist on purity, you become like a body without orifices, which means you die very quickly."

The dance of orthodoxy and heresy can be observed in the realm of biology. In any given species, mutations are continuously occurring. Most of these abnormalities impair the mutant's ability to survive and reproduce, and it vanishes quickly. When environmental conditions shift, however, a mutant characteristic may give the creature that possesses it an advantage over the normal members of the species. The mutant may then reproduce while the conventional model dies out. This natural selection, as it is called, is paralleled in cultural selection and individual selection. Without mutations—heresies—there is no evolution on any level.

Heresies as Mirrors.   We learn who we are through reflection. To visualize our appearance, we contemplate a polished surface. Much of our understanding of our personality comes from the feedback of others; indeed, many social researchers have argued that our concept of self is actually built out of the reactions of those around us.

Mirrors, physical or social, can reflect only what is visible. Further, objects are made visible through *contrast.* A black cat cannot be seen in a pitch-dark room, but only against a lighter background. The stars in the sky cannot be observed during the day, although they are still overhead; the brilliance of sunlight eliminates the contrast. In the case of a world view, heresies provide the contrasts that enable us to become aware of our own orthodoxies. Insofar as we lack awareness of our assumptions, we are enslaved by them, like a puppet that does not notice the strings and does not suspect the existence of the puppeteer.

In Paul's First Letter to the Corinthians, he writes: "For there must be also heresies among you, that they which are approved may be made manifest among you" (11:19). While Paul disapproved of heresy, he appreciated its value as a contrast medium; the teachings of those who agreed with Paul's version of Christianity would be made clearer by comparing them with alternatives. Indeed, these alternatives were so stimulating that they provoked the mainstream believers to explore the implications of their own beliefs. Thus was born the first orthodox work of theology, Irenaeus of Lyons's *Against Heresies*, composed as a response to the doctrines of Gnosticism. In his book *Heresies*, Harold O. J. Brown, a staunch defender of Christian orthodoxy, admits that "it is possible to say that Gnosticism is in a sense the stepmother of systematic theology and that a heresy is the stepmother of orthodoxy."

In the late twentieth century, heresies are again being offered to the Catholic Church as mirrors for self-examination. Maverick American priest Matthew Fox suggested that the church study the modern witchcraft movement in order to reflect on the need to change orthodox definitions of woman and nature. At present, all eyes in the Vatican are officially averted from this mirror. But orthodoxy *needs* heresy to enhance its self-awareness. The only other option is blindness.

Heresies as Decoys.   An institutionalized belief system, like a cornered bear, will attack if it perceives a threat to its existence. This defensive maneuver may succeed, and the danger will end; however, it may fail, and the orthodoxy will be replaced. The latter outcome is more likely if the orthodox forces fail to identify correctly the true source of the threat. If a variety of heresies exist, the defenders of outmoded world views will have more difficulty deciding which ones are the most dangerous, and will more likely fail to detect the seeds of destruction until they have already sprouted. By then, it may be too late. In this manner, an abundance of heresies helps to disarm and dispose of worn-out ideas, clearing the way for the emergence of the new.

In first century Palestine, the governing powers executed Jesus. But they were not especially interested in the new *hairesis* of the Nazarenes, which was only one of many odd faiths appearing around the Mediterranean world at the time. They were much more concerned with destroying Jewish nationalist movements, such as the Zealots. Early Christianity quietly gathered strength in the Roman Empire. During the next two centuries, Christians did suffer periodic waves of persecution, but these episodes were never sustained or thorough. If devoted first century pagans could have foreseen the future, they probably could have prevented Christianity from the start. But there was no way for them to identify the significance of this sect among the numerous decoys, such as Mithraism, Gnosticism, and Egyptian mystery religions. It would have been difficult to take seriously the idea that a little band of Jews who worshipped an executed criminal was the kernel that would blossom to choke the grand pagan world view.

Again, during the fifteenth century, Roman Catholic Europe seemed menaced from many directions. Despite the intensity of the war against heresy that had been mounted over the preceding 300 years, unorthodox movements continued to arise. Even among impeccably orthodox insiders, there was growing criticism of the church hierarchy. It was clearly Satan's work, and the Devil's human assistants were thoroughly sought and eradicated. Amidst the tumult, a few scientists, such as Copernicus and Kepler, did not attract much attention at first. By the end of the century, the magnitude of the danger posed by empirical science had been glimpsed. Giordano Bruno was burned at the stake, in part for stating that the physical world is infinite; then Galileo, who published observational evidence that the earth and other planets orbit the sun, was muzzled. But by then, the spores of scientific thinking had been released. Within fifty years of Galileo's death, victory was assured for the "new philosophy." If the Great Witch Hunt had concentrated on scientists rather than nonexistent Satanists, the Death of Nature would certainly have been postponed. The heretics, real and phantom, drew the fire of orthodoxy away from those who were constructing its replacement.

THE SCOPE AND USE OF THIS BOOK

I wrote *Crimes of Perception* in order to assemble, in a single volume, an account of the heresies and heretics that have shaped the development of the conventional world view in Western culture. I have chosen to emphasize the deepest belief structures, those that map the nature of the self and the universe. The heretical views tend to flow in three main (and often intermingled) currents: Christianity, Judaism, and the occult traditions. Although this book is mainly concerned with the West, I have included material on some heresies that were strongest in the territories of Eastern Christianity—such as Monophysitism, Nestorianism, Monotheletism, and Bogomilism—because of their importance to the evolution of Western thought.

I have excluded heresies and heretics that were primarily political, social, technological, or that involved a specific area of science. Bakunin and Marx, Tesla and Velikovsky, Rhine and Reich were all great mavericks. But a focus broad enough to include them would have expanded this text into a small library. I also did not address the very important influences of unorthodox notions arising primarily from nonWestern (Islamic, Far Eastern, African, and American First Nations) sources for the same reason.

While I have tried to include the most significant heresies (within the boundaries noted above), no single volume treatment of such a massive field can claim to be exhaustive. The amount of attention given to various topics was determined by my own sense of their interest and value, and the limitations of my knowledge. Others, no doubt, would have chosen differently. The present work is merely my own *hairesis*.

You can use this book to learn about the various ways in which unorthodox ideas have served as resources, mirrors, and decoys. Alternatively, if you desire, simply read for pleasure. The story of heresy is filled with accounts of bravery, stupidity, cruelty, ingenuity, devotion, surprise, and awe, so if you enjoy witnessing the carnival of human passions, you can find it within these pages. To find your way around the continent of heresy, I have provided a compass: in the back of the book, you will find a listing of entries organized by topic. The entries themselves are cross-referenced, enabling you to pursue themes of particular interest.

If you reflect on your own reactions as you consider the lives and thoughts of the heretics, you can harvest the greatest benefit this book offers: an enhanced awareness of the assumptions that make up your own world view. Are you fascinated by the strange cosmologies of the ancient Gnostics? Are you moved by the medieval French Cathars, many of whom offered themselves to be burned alive rather than renounce their faith? Does the Holy Inquisition repulse you, intrigue you, or both? Does some part of you cheer for the false messiahs? Why? What are the inner orthodoxies and heresies with which you define yourself and your universe?

Read on, learn, enjoy, reflect. And remember that possession of the sort of book you hold in your hands would have brought you to a fiery death at the stake in the not so distant past. From the vantage point of history, one can glean no assurance that the Burning Times will never return. Keep one eye on the door.

Leonard George
Vancouver
Summer Solstice, 1992

The
Encyclopedia

CROSS-REFERENCES ARE MENTIONED IN CAPITAL LETTERS.

Peter ABELARD   This French theologian was one of the best-known figures of the Middle Ages. He had a significant impact on the development of mainstream Christian philosophy. On two occasions, his work was condemned as heresy. He aptly entitled his autobiography *Historia Calamitatum*—"The Story of My Calamities."

Peter Abelard was born in Pallet, near Nantes, in 1079. As a young man, he studied under some of the greatest Christian thinkers of his time and quickly distinguished himself with his brilliance. He became a renowned teacher of philosophy in Paris, where he lectured to crowds of students.

A young noblewoman named Heloise was entrusted to the famous philosopher for personal instruction. They became lovers. When the scandal reached the ears of Heloise's uncle, he was so enraged that he attacked Abelard, cutting off his genitals—and effectively ending his teaching career. Heloise was sent to a convent, where she remained devoted to her beloved teacher until her death.

In disgrace, Abelard became a monk. His restless mind continued to work on philosophical problems. He was convinced that Christian truths did not need to be believed simply on the basis of the church's authority; rather, he thought they could be proven logically. His first book attempted a rational explanation of the Trinity. Many others in the church saw this approach as arrogant and disrespectful to the holy mysteries of the faith. In 1121, three years after the encounter with his lover's uncle, his book was condemned by Catholic orthodoxy. Abelard was commanded to burn the work, which he did.

Four years after this setback, he became abbot of a monastery. Over the years, Abelard continued in his philosophical investigations and contributed to the development of medieval logic. In 1136, he was able to return to Paris and resume teaching.

Abelard's provocative views eventually stirred up more trouble. He championed the importance of doubt, rather than faith, as the foundation of religious thought. Doubt, he argued, leads to questioning, which leads, ultimately, to truth. He encouraged his students to notice apparent contradictions in the Bible and to use reason in attempting to resolve them. It is important to note that Abelard did not regard his approach as heretical; he believed that his questioning technique would confirm the orthodox Christian world view.

His contemporary, Saint Bernard, was not so sure. Bernard asked Abelard to tone down his teaching, claiming that it could too easily mislead people in a time when a variety of heretical alternatives to orthodoxy were appearing in France. Abelard might have satisfied Bernard by making minor changes in his approach. However, one of Abelard's students rose to defend him. This happened to be ARNOLD OF BRESCIA, who had been driven from Italy for his attacks on the authority of the church. Abelard's association with Arnold weakened his credibility. Bernard reacted by condemning nineteen ideas from Abelard's writings as heretical. The pope agreed, and Abelard was sentenced to silent confinement in a monastery. He was reconciled to the church only shortly before his death, in 1142.

See also: ASTROLOGY.

ABRAHAM THE JEW   A legendary magician of medieval and Renaissance Europe, Abraham the Jew was the purported author of the important text of ritual magic called *SACRED MAGIC OF ABRAMELIN THE MAGE*.

Abraham ABULAFIA   A major figure in the development of the Jewish esoteric tradition known as KABBALAH, Abraham Abulafia was born into the Jewish community at Saragossa, Spain, in 1240. He was highly intelligent and studied Jewish traditions extensively, both conventional and alternative. He was especially interested in the influential philosopher Maimonides. By Abulafia's own account, he achieved a form of spiritual enlightenment at the age of thirty-one. From that time until his death, he traveled, wrote, and taught prolifically.

Abulafia was intensely charismatic and became involved in various political intrigues. One of his more bizarre projects was his plan to convert Pope Nicholas III to Judaism. After Abulafia had announced his goal and set off for Rome, reports of his intentions reached the pope, who like most good Christians of the day, was fiercely anti-Semitic. Nicholas commanded that a stake be prepared so that Abulafia could be publicly burned without delay upon his arrival. When Abulafia entered Rome, he was seized and, shortly thereafter, released. He failed to convert Pope Nicholas, but escaped with his life because the pontiff had died suddenly the night before Abulafia's arrival in Rome.

In 1290, Abulafia performed another outrageous act by proclaiming himself to be the messiah. This announcement provoked a violent response from the orthodox community, in which he was denounced in the strongest terms as a false prophet. One of his opponents, Rabbi Shlomo ben Adret, wrote of him, "There are many frauds whom I have heard and seen. One is the disgusting creature, 'may the name of the wicked rot', whose name is Abraham . . . he enticed many people with his lies." Abulafia was forced to retreat to the island of Comino, near Malta, where he is thought to have died around 1292.

Aside from his adventurism, Abulafia is remembered for his contributions to Kabbalistic thought and practice. He wrote twenty-six meditation manuals, many of which modern students of Kabbalah continue to use today. He also composed twenty-two prophetic works, only one of which still exists. The surviving books were preserved by repeated hand-copying of manuscripts over the centuries.

Abulafia's work marks the reemergence of the ancient Jewish tradition of ecstatic prophecy. Individuals who entered trance states, communed with God, and returned with divinely transmitted knowledge played an important role at various stages of Jewish history. The Old Testament contains many accounts of prophets who were told by God to call the people to remember Him. Such excursions into divine realms were suppressed in Judaism during the Second Temple period (which ended with the destruction of the Temple in A.D. 70) because prophets tended to produce political instability, which upset the occupying Romans. The pre-Kabbalistic MERKABAH tradition continued to emphasize the pursuit of personal experience of the divine, but Abulafia was the first major Kabbalist to make ecstatic trance the central concern of Kabbalah.

He determined the attainment of prophecy to be the goal of Kabbalistic practice. This feat required emptying the mind of ordinary thoughts and images. He viewed his methods as an extension of Maimonides' philosophy, which was restricted to the use of reason as a means of obtaining divine knowledge. In order to achieve the empty mind within which a direct awareness of God can arise, Abulafia constructed an elaborate set of meditation practices. These procedures included the use of special postures and repetitive recitations. Some scholars have noted the resemblance of these techniques to those of the Moslem mystical movement known as Sufism. It is known that Abulafia encountered Sufis during his travels, and he may have learned from them. His methods are also similar to the yogic practices of India. It is likely that Abulafia's teachings represent an important early entry point of Islamic and possibly Indian mystical technologies into Western culture.

A central feature of Abulafia's system was "the Way of the Names." This meditation practice involved the continuous rearranging of the Hebrew letters contained in various names of God. Just as music can affect the soul in ways that transcend a description of the note combinations, so, said Abulafia, skillful use of the letters and names of God can produce experiences far surpassing the apprehension of meaning through language: "You will whirl the letters front and back and create many melodies." His perception of the possibilities within words is allied to the understanding of language found in poetry and ritual magic. Poets and magicians do not try to eliminate all of the ambiguity and mystery from words; much of the power of poetry and of spell-casting derives from this mystery. Abulafia, too, aimed to awaken the Kabbalistic meditator to mystery, the mystery of God's presence. This feeling for the sacred power of language is very different from the sharp precision valued in scientific terminology.

Through the use of his meditations, Abulafia claimed that a practitioner could make contact with an inner spiritual guide, sometimes called the angel Metatron. In certain passages, Abulafia described the possibility of a complete merging of identity with God: "after many hard, strong, and mighty exercises . . . he and He will become one entity." This is a heretical statement. In mainstream Judaism, as in Christianity, the Creator and the created being must never be thought of as the same entity.

Abulafia was familiar with another major idea developing in Kabbalistic thinking at the time, the doctrine of the *sefiroth*, or Tree of Life. He did not promote the *sefiroth* doctrine himself but felt that it was useful for beginners, who should practice the Way of the Names as they became more advanced. Abulafia's chief student, Joseph Gikatilla, had greater reverence for the *sefiroth* teaching and attempted to unite the practice of the Names and the Tree of Life in his own teaching.

Abulafia's influence as a Kabbalist was not hindered by his outlandish antics on the political stage. His work was a major inspiration for the development of the Italian Kabbalah during the next century. Meditation on letter combinations of Hebrew God names became popular among the Palestinian Kabbalists of sixteenth century Safed, as well as the East European masters of Hasidism in the eighteenth century. In modern times, psychologist Edward Hoffman argued that Abulafia's meditations could be usefully studied by psychotherapists in order to promote healing states of awareness in their clients.

ACACIUS OF CAESAREA   An important leader in the heretical movement called ARIANISM in the fourth century, Acacius became the bishop of Caesarea (located in what is now Turkey) in A.D. 340. During the violent theological debate between the Arians and the orthodox Christians, the Arian movement splintered. The central issue was whether God the Father and the Son of God had the same divine nature. Orthodox Catholics insisted that they did, while the Arians claimed that they did not. Acacius sought to resolve the dispute; he urged the opposing sides not to consider questions regarding the nature or essence of God, and to restrict the comparison between Father and Son to more general terms. The school founded by Acacius, the HOMOEANS, held that the Father and the Son were "similar," without defining precisely the nature of this resemblance. Acacius did not live to see the orthodox victory on the issue of God's nature. He died in 366, shortly after being deposed from his position in the church.

ADAMITES   In the Book of Genesis, it is written that Adam and Eve were naked before the Fall and were not ashamed (2:25). Throughout history, groups known as Adamites have attempted to return to that primordial state of innocence by removing their clothes. They have usually been condemned as heretics.

Adamites were first mentioned by Epiphanius, a fourth century orthodox Christian who compiled an encyclopedia of heresies. Augustine also refers to them in the following century, but their number must have been quite small. In Augustine's view, practicing nudism would not redeem anyone; since Adam's fall, we all bear the burden of original sin, and only the grace of God can help us. Sacred nudism reemerged in Germany in the late thirteenth century. Pope Honorius IV ordered that those who engaged in the practice be persecuted as heretics.

In the early 1400s, a group of Adamites appeared in Bohemia. At the time, Bohemia was torn by religious strife, following the controversial execution of JAN HUS. A radical faction, the TABORITES, had gained control of a region south of Prague, which became a haven for heretics from all over Europe, including Adamites. Their belief was that after a period of strict self-denial, one could attain spiritual perfection, after which one could do anything one wanted without sinning, like Adam and Eve in the Garden. These Adamites seem to be related to the contemporary Heresy of the FREE SPIRIT. A Bohemian observer described their activities: "Wandering through the forests and hills, some of them fell into such an insanity that men and women threw off their clothes and went naked. . . . From the same madness they supposed that they were not sinning if they had intercourse with one another." These practices offended the Taborites, who were heretics of a more ascetic type. Taborite troops captured many Adamites, and burned them at the stake.

In 1925, Adamites were active in northern California. Anna Rhodes proclaimed that she was Eve; her husband, Adam; and their farm, the Garden of Eden. They hosted naked orgies, ritual dances, and animal sacrifices. The Nudist Christian Church of the Blessed Virgin Jesus was established in the United States in 1985. This group promotes public nakedness as an expression of the sacredness of God's creation, the human body.

Other contemporary religious groups have maintained the idea of holy nudity. Members of one of the sects of the DOUKHOBORS, a Russian heresy transplanted to British Columbia, periodically strip in public. Some practitioners of modern witchcraft perform their rituals in the nude or, as they say, "skyclad," in order to symbolize the equality of all before the gods, and to remove barriers to the radiation of magical power from the body.

ADOPTIONISM   This Christian heresy, also called DYNAMIC MONARCHIA-NISM, appeared early in the development of the Christian tradition and continued to surface periodically throughout history. The essential point of Adoptionism is that JESUS was not God, as orthodox doctrine holds, but was a human being who was adopted or chosen by God at some point during His life.

Orthodox Christians fought against this notion. For them, the idea that Jesus had ever been a mere human was a sacrilege against His complete divinity. In addition, they believed, if Jesus Christ had just been the adopted son of God rather than "fully God," then He could not do what only God can do, save sinners from damnation. For reasons of respect as well as of theological necessity, Catholicism rejected the Adoptionists' image of Jesus.

The origins of Adoptionism can be found in the New Testament itself. Such passages as Acts 2:32—"This Jesus has God raised up, whereof we all are witnesses"—were understood by some readers to imply that there was a time in Jesus' life before He was "raised up" by God, during which He was just a human being. *The Shepherd* of Hermas, a second century text popular among Catholic Christians of the time, also contains statements that sound Adoptionistic. Some early heretics, such as the EBIONITES, proclaimed that Jesus had been adopted by God at His baptism.

The Adoptionist heresy appeared in Rome around A.D. 190. A man who regarded himself as a strictly orthodox Catholic, THEODOTUS THE TANNER, was distressed by some of the views concerning Christ taught by GNOSTICISM. According to many Gnostics, Jesus had never been a human being at all, but a divinity who created an illusory human body while on earth. In order to emphasize Christ's human side, Theodotus proclaimed that Jesus was a man who had been adopted by God.

Theodotus the Tanner was excommunicated by VICTOR I, the bishop of Rome. Adoptionism continued to be taught by others, however, despite its rejection by the bishops. The Adoptionist heresy survived in Rome well into the third century.

Meanwhile, the bishop of Antioch (a Mediterranean city in what is now Turkey), PAUL OF SAMOSATA, devised a sophisticated version of Adoptionism. Paul was able to spread his doctrine under the protection of renegade QUEEN ZENOBIA without interference from the local allies of the Roman Catholics until the reconquest of Antioch by the Romans in 272.

Paul of Samosata's teaching that Jesus was not the "only begotten" son of God but God's adopted son was preserved by his followers, the PAULIANISTS. Shortly after the conversion of the Kingdom of Armenia to Christianity in the early fourth century, Paulianism was transmitted to Armenia, and this version of Adoptionism survived there for a few centuries.

Another form of Adoptionism, not directly related to the ancient heresies of the Roman Adoptionists and the Paulianists, appeared in Spain toward the end of the eighth century. The Moslems controlled most of the Spanish territory at the time, and the Catholic communities there were somewhat isolated from mainstream European thought. Under these circumstances, the Spanish Christians advanced the theory that there were two sons associated with Jesus Christ, the Son of God (a divine person of the Trinity) and the son of David (a human being). The son of David was adopted by the Son of God. The debate that ensued between the Spanish party and the Roman Catholics concluded with the orthodox condemnation of ELIPANDUS and FELIX, the main proponents of SPANISH ADOPTIONISM.

In modern times, many Christians have again become attracted to the notion of Jesus as a man who was chosen by God, as opposed to the traditional orthodox position that Jesus Christ *is* God. For instance, the well-known German theologian Adolf Harnack was sympathetic to Adoptionist views. Most Christians today would be surprised to learn that such an understanding of Jesus was long regarded as a poisonous heresy, threatening the possibility of salvation.

See also: AESCLYPEDOTUS, ARTEMAS, BASILIDEAN GNOSTICISM.

AESCLYPEDOTUS   A teacher of ADOPTIONISM, a Christian heresy, in Rome at the beginning of the third century A.D. Aesclypedotus was opposed by the bishop of Rome, ZEPHYRINUS, who was himself later accused of being a heretic.

AETIUS   Founder of the branch of ARIANISM called the ANOMOEANS, Aetius became influential in the Christian Church during the mid-fourth century, when the heretical emperor CONSTANTIUS ruled the Roman Empire. With the emperor's backing, Aetius was able to wield significant power in the Christian community and worked to replace orthodox Christian bishops with his own followers. Constantius was persuaded by BASIL OF ANCYRA, who belonged to a different faction of the Arian heresy, that Aetius was too extreme in his views. As a result, Aetius was banished. He died around A.D. 370.

Cornelius AGRIPPA   One of the most notorious magicians of the Renaissance, Cornelius Agrippa brought together the three main occult paths of the period: NATURAL MAGIC, DEMON MAGIC, and CABALA. He has had a lasting impact on the Western esoteric tradition and has remained a memorable figure of popular legend.

Agrippa was born in the German city of Cologne in 1486. His original name was Heinrich Cornelis; later, he latinized Cornelis to Cornelius, and added "Agrippa von Nettesheim" in imitation of the ancient Roman founder of Cologne. Agrippa attended the university in his hometown and then served in the imperial army.

By 1509, he had attained a reputation as a scholar and was lecturing at the University of Dole. His topics were unorthodox, however; a monk accused him of heresy, and he had to leave the city. Thus, a lifetime of wandering and unstable fortunes began. At times, Agrippa managed to win the favor of an aristocratic family, who would support him for awhile; at others, he was jailed for debt or for insulting a powerful personage. He died in Grenoble in 1535.

Early in his travels, Agrippa studied with ABBOT TRITHEMIUS of Sponheim. Trithemius, a renowned master of esoteric wisdom, shared his own interests in contacting the spirits of the planets with Agrippa. Shortly after his stay with Trithemius, he composed his most important work, *De Occulta Philosophia*, which has become a classic of Western occultism.

According to this three-volume text, the universe is a living being and possesses a soul as well as a body. The body is composed of the four elements, earth, air, fire, and water. Knowledge of the elemental composition of any object reveals its natural "virtues," or powers. Each object also has occult virtues, which derive from the portion of the world soul it possesses. The occult virtues of an object can be discovered by noticing its resemblance to other things; for instance, frogs' eyes can heal human blindness. Furthermore, earthly objects have occult connections with the powers of the stars and planets, again to be detected through resemblance. For instance, sunflowers contain solar powers, and an image of the constellation Sagittarius (the Horse-Man), hung around the neck of a horse, will protect the horse from harm.

Agrippa's text lists many such correspondences, which can be used to direct occult forces. These ideas resemble those of MARSILIO FICINO, and Agrippa plagiarizes passages from Ficino's works in his writings. However, Ficino states that the spiritual influences of the planets are impersonal; Agrippa writes that personal spirit beings are responsible, and discusses ways of manipulating these beings. In this way, Agrippa mingles the natural magic of Ficino with the spirit magic of Trithemius.

The wandering magician also encountered the lore of the Cabala, the Jewish mystical system that Renaissance scholars had Christianized. Agrippa continued the process of adapting the Cabala to Christian tastes. In the *De Occulta Philosophia*, he explores the magical powers of the Hebrew alphabet, an important topic in Jewish mysticism and magic. He notes, however, that the powers of the Jewish name of God, YHVH (called the *Tetragrammaton*), have been transferred to the name JESUS.

Although himself a devout Christian, Agrippa displays a great respect for other faiths: "the rites and ceremonies of religion vary with different times and places; and each religion has something good, which is directed towards God Himself the Creator." In a time of heresy hunts and witch burnings, such an attitude was rare—and not altogether safe.

Agrippa did not publish his occult masterpiece until 1531, twenty years after it was written. In the same year, he published another book, in which he seems to renounce the *De Occulta Philosophia*, along with the pursuits of reason and science, and calls on people to rely only on their Christian faith. Historians have debated Agrippa's true intentions in publishing this book. Perhaps Agrippa had a change of heart, or perhaps he felt the need to alter his public position on magic in order to avoid persecution.

Even before his death, rumors circulated that Agrippa was a black magician. These tales magnified following his death. It was said that he was always accompanied by a demon in the shape of a black dog, and that when Agrippa died, the dog threw itself into a river and drowned. A widespread story claimed that one day, a visitor, waiting for Agrippa in his library, happened to read aloud a line from one of the master's magic books. An evil spirit promptly materialized and strangled the terrified visitor. On his return, Agrippa was confronted with the problem of how to dispose of the body. He commanded the demon to animate the visitor's corpse and cause it to walk around in the marketplace before collapsing, to create the appearance of a natural death.

Such stories were fueled by the publication, shortly after Agrippa's death, of a supposed fourth volume of *De Occulta Philosophia*. This book deals mainly with various kinds of demons associated with the planets and was derived in part from the magical text called the LEMEGETON. Agrippa's closest disciple, Johannes Wierus, denounced the book as a fraud, and most historians today agree.

Agrippa's dark reputation has lived on into modern times. In European folklore, he became a bogeyman figure used to frighten unruly children into obeying their parents. An illustrated children's book of the nineteenth century depicts a fiendish Agrippa immersing his victims in a giant inkwell:

"Then great Agrippa foams with rage—
Look at him on this very page!
He seizes Arthur, seizes Ned,
Takes William by his little head;
And they may scream and kick and call,
Into the ink he dips them all;
Into the inkstand, one, two three,
Till they are black as black can be."

See also: ANGEL MAGIC, JOHN DEE.

ALBIGENSIAN CRUSADE   This attempted "final solution" to the problem of heresy in medieval southern France occurred over a twenty-year period during the early thirteenth century. The stated target of the crusade was the unorthodox movement of CATHARISM, but there was also a hidden agenda: the extension of political control by the French king into the region, which had become increasingly independent of either papal or royal influence. The resulting slaughter produced the uprooting of the Cathars (known as ALBIGENSIANS, after Albi, their northernmost stronghold), and the destruction of the proud southern French culture.

During the 1100s and early 1200s, a society unique in its time, known as Occitania, flourished in southern France. The inhabitants spoke a distinctive language (*langue d'oc*) and created a culture with the highest literacy rate in Europe. The Occitanians were quite tolerant of minorities. Jews and unorthodox Christians experienced little persecution there when the rest of western Europe was hostile toward them. The region became the center of the troubadours, wandering minstrels who defined romantic love.

This independence and tolerance was viewed with alarm from outside the region. The pope was particularly concerned that the Cathars, who regarded the orthodox church as the creation of the Devil, were not being persecuted in Occitania. In 1178, a Catholic mission went to Toulouse, the largest city in the region, to seek out and punish heretics. The mission was not very successful. It caught one well-known Cathar and punished him with fines, public humiliation, and a pilgrimage in order to discourage others from taking up the heresy. But the number of Cathars in the area continued to grow. The king of France, who lived in Paris, was also worried. He wished to consolidate his power in the region, but some of the feudal lords in Occitania seemed intent on increasing their own autonomy.

A possible answer to the problem was suggested by the invention of the Crusade. In the late eleventh century, Pope Urban II had launched the first Crusade against the Moslems. Two other major Crusades had been arranged during the twelfth century. The idea of mounting a crusade against the heretics in southern France was novel—fighting Moslems was quite different from attacking other Christians—but the Catholic and northern French powers decided that a crusade might be the only way to suppress the growing freedom in Occitania.

In 1199, the groundwork was laid. Pope Innocent III proclaimed that heretics should be treated in the same manner as traitors, that is, they should be executed.

During the following years, orthodox preaching missions in the south of France failed to stop the Cathar movement. In 1208, the pontiff called for a crusade against the "Albigensians."

Pope Innocent III proclaimed that participation in the war against the heretics would both please God and serve as a powerful act of penance for sins one may have committed. The feudal lords and knights of northern France were encouraged to take part. They would be allowed to plunder the towns they conquered and could return home rich, not only in spirit but in material wealth. A nobleman from the north named Simon de Montfort assumed command of the troops.

The violence began in 1209, with the Crusaders' assault on the Occitanian city of Beziers. The troops penetrated the city's defenses but faced a problem: how to distinguish between citizens who followed the Cathar heresy and those who were good Catholics. It is said that the pope's representative with the army solved the dilemma by uttering the famous command, "Kill them all, and let God sort them out." Egged on by the priests accompanying the army, the Crusaders murdered and plundered without restraint; contemporaneous records report that 20,000 inhabitants died.

Next, the Crusaders attacked the walled city of Carcassonne. They were unable to take the city at first, but engaged in a siege until the inhabitants ran out of water and were forced to surrender. The usual carnage followed.

The Albigensian Crusade continued, with interruptions, until 1229. The troops occupied the major population centers of Occitania, often killing indiscriminately and always searching for heretics. Minerve and Lavaur, towns known for harboring Cathars, suffered terribly. In Minerve, the first mass burning (140 people) occurred. Lavaur was the site of the largest such event; about 400 Cathars were burned at the stake, and GIRAUDE DE LAVAUR, a heretic especially revered by the townspeople for her love of God, was thrown into a pit by the soldiers of Christ and stoned to death.

The city of Toulouse, however, proved to be particularly difficult for the Crusaders to subdue. De Montfort was killed during an attack on Toulouse in 1217. His son Amalrich later became the leader of the Crusader army and terrorized the land until the Count of Toulouse, Raymond VII, finally concluded a peace treaty in 1229. He was forced to return to the Catholic Church all of its seized property, yield two-thirds of his own possessions to the king of France, promise never to resist the king's will again, and mount a vigorous campaign against the heretics.

The Albigensian Crusade only partly achieved its goals. Royal and papal authority had been imposed and Occitanian liberty crushed forever, but the population was seething with resentment, and the Cathars had not been exterminated. In 1209, de Montfort had failed in his attempt to take the Cathar stronghold of MONTSEGUR, perched atop a mountain in the Pyrenees. The heretics continued to operate covertly from this location and others, with a great deal of support from the Occitanians. It would take years of activity by the INQUISITION (established in Toulouse in 1233), and further military strikes against Montsegur and other remote sites before Catharism was driven from the region.

ALBIGENSIANS   Albigensians was the variant name for the heretical CATHARS. This unorthodox sect of Christianity became especially strong in the south of France during the late twelfth and early thirteenth centuries. The first Cathar bishop in the region was based in the town of Albi; the town's name became identified with the heresy.

ALCHEMY   The English word "alchemy" derives from an Arabic phrase, "al kimia," which referred to the mysterious art of transmuting base substances into precious ones. The Arabic term probably derives from the ancient Greek "chemeia," which refers to working with metal. Alchemy is commonly understood to be an impossible attempt by prescientific people to convert lead into gold. However, the transmutation of metals was only one of the aims of classical alchemy. The world view within which alchemy developed did not include the radical separation between humans and nature that characterizes the modern perspective; changing a material from base to precious in the premodern view could not be accomplished without the alchemist also being transmuted, on psychological and spiritual levels, from a state of dense ignorance to one of golden enlightenment. Thus, classical alchemy was simultaneously an outer and inner discipline.

Alchemy was often seen as dangerous by orthodox authorities. If alchemists could produce quantities of precious metals, they could have dire effects on an economy designed to benefit a privileged class (as all civilized economies are). Further, if alchemists could cause spiritual transformation in themselves, they would not need a hierarchy of religious officials whose reason for existence was to mediate between humanity and divinity. For these reasons, people in power frequently condemned alchemy. But the same people just as often pursued alchemy privately.

Most researchers believe that the alchemical tradition began in ancient Egypt. The earliest-known alchemist was a Hellenistic Egyptian named Bolos of Mendes, whose writings may date as far back as 250 B.C. The Greeks showed a great interest in alchemy. The theory of transmutation through undertaking the "work against nature," or OPUS CONTRA NATURAM, was based on ancient Greek physics. As early as A.D. 300, the authorities were attacking alchemy. Around that year, Roman Emperor Diocletian condemned "the old writings of the Egyptians which treat of the 'chemeia' of gold and silver."

During the first few centuries A.D., alchemy was associated with the students of mythical figure Hermes Trismegistus. Hermes was said to be an ancient sage who had mastered the three primary occult arts, ASTROLOGY, MAGIC, and alchemy. A short text attributed to Hermes, THE EMERALD TABLET, was believed to contain the secrets of alchemical practice. This tradition has persisted throughout the history of alchemy, which is sometimes called "The Hermetic Art."

Ancient alchemy established the basic map of the transmutational process. Most later alchemists retained this depiction. The work was said to progress through three or four main stages, designated by colors: black, white, yellow, and red (the yellow stage often viewed as a transition between white and red rather than as a discrete stage). These changes in color would occur in the material undergoing alchemical operations as evidence that the alchemist was on the right track; the colors have also been viewed as representations of psychological states. For instance, the black stage, called the *nigredo*, has been interpreted as signifying that spiritual development begins only when people are willing to confront the aspects of themselves that they ordinarily "keep in the dark." These are behaviors and attitudes that do not conform to one's self image, and that one would prefer not to notice in oneself. Over the centuries, elaborate bodies of symbolism became associated with the stages, as well as with the various alchemical procedures of heating, crushing, separating, and dissolving that the practitioner employed in the work.

With the rise of Christianity, alchemy and its pagan associations fell into neglect in Europe. When the Moslems conquered much of the old Roman imperial territories in the seventh century, they discovered the remnants of ancient knowledge, including alchemy. For several centuries, Moslem alchemists experimented with classical alchemical methods and devised new ones. The best known Moslem practitioner of the Hermetic Art was Jabir ibn Hayyan. His writings were so difficult to understand that his name became synonymous with meaningless scribbles, *Jabir-ish*, or gibberish.

In the twelfth century, the increased contact between western Europe and the Moslem world led to the transmission of the alchemical tradition back to Europe. During the later Middle Ages, the figure of the alchemist acquired mixed associations. On one hand, many people spent their lives unsuccessfully trying to create material wealth through alchemy; this sort of alchemist became the object of mockery, as Chaucer's description of the alchemist in *The Canterbury Tales* indicates. However, there were also tales of successful practitioners, who obtained great riches and wisdom from mysterious sources. Fourteenth century French alchemists Nicholas and Perenelle Flamel (a husband and wife team) have been revered until the present day as ones who attained the goal. They were not born into wealth, but after their deaths their will provided for the construction of fourteen hospitals, seven churches, and three chapels.

Interest in alchemy continued throughout the Renaissance and Reformation periods. Men who were noted for their roles in other unorthodox-reality traditions, such as Elizabethan magician JOHN DEE and Swiss maverick healer PARACELSUS, were enthusiastic students of alchemy.

During the seventeenth century, alchemy reached its full maturity. During that time, science was becoming established as a powerful tool for probing the nature of physical reality. The scientific approach of laboratory experimentation and careful observation of results resembles, and was partly inspired by, the methods of the alchemists. Indeed, the greatest scientist of the century (some would say of all time), Sir Isaac Newton, was himself a practicing alchemist.

Seventeenth century alchemy had become a crossroads of western occult traditions. The symbolism of the CABALA and ASTROLOGY merged with the classical alchemical images to create a rich symbolic vocabulary. Many of the most intriguing alchemy texts date from this period. Among the best known are the works of Michael Maier, Heinrich Khunrath, and Johann Daniel Mylius.

Increasingly, alchemists of this time focused exclusively on the inner aspects of the work and neglected the laboratory operations. One might say that the fate of alchemy paralleled the division of body and mind in the Western world view. The new philosophy of René Descartes depicted the mind as radically different from the body; classical alchemy, which was an integrated path of transmutation involving both material and nonmaterial aspects, split into the science of chemistry and the occult art of spiritual alchemy.

During the eighteenth and nineteenth centuries, alchemy again fell into neglect. It was perceived as an outmoded view of the world. Chemistry had replaced laboratory alchemy, and the spiritual path of the alchemists, expressed in obscure symbols, was mere "gibberish" to most people.

In the present century, interest in alchemy has again increased. Influential Swiss psychiatrist Carl Jung recognized in alchemical imagery surprising parallels with the content of his patients' dreams. When Jung conducted an intensive study of the old texts, he concluded that the alchemists had stumbled upon the basic process of psychological growth. He called this the principle of individuation. Students of Jung's psychology study alchemical symbolism to help them understand the meanings of dreams and fantasies.

Jung did not believe that alchemists could transmute metals; rather, he thought that they projected the symbolic contents of their unconscious minds onto their laboratory work. Thus, Jung was more a "spiritual" alchemist than a classical one. However, a small revival in classical alchemy during recent decades has taken place. In Europe and North America, individuals are again working in alchemical laboratories to attain the goal of physical, psychological, and spiritual trans-mutation.

ALMADEL   This text is a handbook of ritual magic. The *Almadel* instructs the reader in the methods of conjuring ANGELS and inducing the angels to perform favors. Although the book discusses angels, the orthodox viewed these practices with great suspicion, believing that the "angels" of the Almadel were in fact devilish spirits. Later occult writers often echo this view.

The age and origin of the *Almadel* is unknown. The earliest known reference to this magical book occurs in a passage written around 1500. The *Almadel* was included as Part Four of the infamous GRIMOIRE called THE LEMEGETON, which dates in its present form to the seventeenth century.

An almadel is a square of wax, upon which a magician inscribes magical symbols. This handbook reveals how almadels can be made for use in calling the angels of the four directions. During the ritual of conjuration, the almadel is supported by four candles in such a way that there is a space beneath it. An incense burner is then placed underneath it, so that the incense smoke rises through holes in the corners of the almadel. After the appropriate prayers, the text promises, the angel will material-ize in the smoky air above the inscribed symbols and will obey the magician's request as long as the request is virtuous—the *Almadel* insists that these beings are spirits of good, so asking the angels to kill someone or to provide a sexual slave would be out of bounds. The magician simply had to turn to the *Almadel*'s companion text within *The Lemegeton*, the section entitled the Goetia, to learn about demons who would happily fulfill such requests.

See also: ANGEL MAGIC.

AMALRIC OF BENA   A well-known philosopher who lived in Paris during the late twelfth century, Amalric of Bena was inspired by the teachings of the ninth century thinker JOHN SCOTUS ERIGENA. According to John, the world emanated from God and will end by returning to Him; in Amalric's teaching, God is never separate from the world, but is actually the essence of everything that exists. Neither of these views conforms to the orthodox Catholic position that God and His creation are separate entities. Amalric's idea that "God is everything" is an example of the heresy of PANTHEISM.

Amalric died in 1206. During his lifetime, his works were not condemned; perhaps they simply did not attract the attention of the guardians of orthodoxy. However, following his death, some of his disciples (known as Amalricians, or Amaurians) mixed his ideas with those of Italian visionary JOACHIM OF FIORE, and the result provoked a stern response from the Catholic Church.

Joachim taught that the history of the world is divided into three ages, correspond-ing to the Father, Son, and Holy Spirit of the Trinity. Amalric's students, who had learned from their teacher that God is not apart from the world, understood Joa-chim's theory to mean that the Persons of the Trinity actually manifest as material bodies in the three ages. During Old Testament times, the Father appeared as the Hebrew prophets; during the age of the Son, Christ was incarnated in Mary; and in the third age that was just dawning, the Holy Spirit manifested as Amalric and his students.

In 1210, the Catholic authorities in Paris burned Amalric's students for heresy, along with his writings. Amalric's influence did not end immediately. Some of the first members of the BEGUINES' movement, which arose shortly after the heretic's death, studied his work. Many Beguines were later condemned, in part for their willingness to explore such unorthodox religious ideas as those of Amalric.

AMATORY MASS   In the quest for love and sex, through the centuries people have tried just about everything, including the mass of the Roman Catholic Church. The performance of a ritual patterned after the mass, in order to use its power to seduce someone, is known as the amatory mass. When combined with practices of demonic magic or Satanism, this ceremony is classified as a form of BLACK MASS.

According to official Catholic doctrine, during the mass the substance of the bread and wine is replaced by the actual body and blood of Christ, although this change is invisible to human observers. The Bible reports that miracles happened in Christ's presence, so some Catholics concluded that Christ's attendance at the mass gave that ritual miraculous powers. In the Middle Ages, the practice of performing masses for specific goals, such as helping crops grow or repelling invaders, developed. Occasionally, a priest would conclude that he could tap the magic of the mass for his personal desires, including obtaining the love of women. Such activities were strongly condemned by orthodox councils.

With the rise of fears concerning organized witchcraft during the Renaissance and Reformation periods, the authorities became concerned that witches were perform-ing parodies of the mass during their nocturnal meetings. During this time, un-faithfulness in marriage was sometimes blamed on spells that witches cast during their gatherings. It was thought that witches helped the Devil to disrupt decent society by magically provoking forbidden passions in susceptible folk.

During the reign of Louis XIV in France, one of the king's courtiers arranged for the performance of amatory masses to make Louis fall in love with her. This ritual involved the sacrifice of two doves, baptized with the names of the king and the ambitious woman. The spell was successful for a while. (The Satanic group involved was eventually suppressed by the police.)

In modern times, the use of the Catholic mass for magical purposes has declined.

The perceived need for love spells has not decreased, however, and some magicians still use the power of Christian symbolism in their amatory rites.

See also: BERENGAR, ABBÉ GUIBOURG, LA VOISIN, RATRAMNUS.

AMISH   Now extinct in their lands of origin, the Amish have undertaken a spiritual mission to preserve their centuries-old lifestyle in the New World. They originated from a division within the MENNONITE movement toward the end of the seventeenth century. The Mennonites, a branch of the ANABAPTIST movement, disagreed with each other concerning the degree to which sins could be forgiven. One leader, JAKOB AMMANN, supported the strictest view that any deviation from tradition should be met with excommunication and shunning. The Amish, who honor Ammann's memory with their name, maintain his position.

The original Amish communities were founded in Germany, the Netherlands, and Poland. From the beginning, they resisted integration with their host cultures; they desired enough farmland to be self-sufficient and to be left alone. In the early eighteenth century, the open spaces and religious toleration of North America attracted Amish migration; over time, their numbers grew in the New World and shrank in the Old World, until the Amish movement disappeared in Europe.

The isolation of the Amish has created some problems for them. They were involved in a long disagreement with the United States government over their refusal to pay taxes for social security; such a practice implied a lack of faith in God's willingness to provide in the future, they argued—eventually they won exemption.

A more challenging difficulty has arisen from centuries of inbreeding. In a closed gene pool, the appearance of genetic defects is increased. At this point in the late twentieth century, Amish communities have become a source of fascination for genetic researchers. The elevated rates of pernicious anemia, hemophilia, muscular dystrophy, and dwarfism are not attributed to genetic factors by most Amish, however. Rather, to them, these difficulties reflect the mysterious ways of the Lord.

Jakob AMMANN   Founder of the AMISH, who take their name from him, in the late seventeenth century, Jakob Ammann was a member of the MENNONITE movement in Switzerland. He believed that other Mennonite leaders were becoming too tolerant of sinful behavior, and led his followers to form closed communities of high moral standards and extreme resistance to change.

ANABAPTISTS   This term literally means "those who baptize a second time." However, the Anabaptists did not regard themselves as *re*baptizing people; rather, they did not believe that the baptism of infants was real baptism. Only the anointing or immersion of someone who was mature enough to accept the faith consciously was a sacrament, according to the Anabaptists. When the movement appeared in the early sixteenth century, orthodox Christians, both Catholic and Protestant, viewed the Anabaptist rejection of infant baptism as heretical.

The Anabaptists can be seen as the radical wing of the Protestant Reformation. Luther, Calvin, and Zwingli, the three leading Reformation leaders, called for the discarding of much of Roman Catholic tradition, as well as a return to the Bible as the main guide to the spiritual life. Although these three men disagreed with each other concerning which beliefs and practices should be discarded, they all wished to retain infant baptism. The Anabaptists held that the mainstream Reformation did not go far enough. In addition to denouncing the baptism of babies, for which there was no precedent in the New Testament, the various Anabaptist groups called for other changes. Like mainstream Protestants, they disagreed with each other over which changes were necessary. Along with the Catholic authorities, Luther, Calvin, and Zwingli all condemned the Anabaptists and encouraged their persecution.

Some Anabaptists, such as the followers of THOMAS MÜNZER and MELCHIOR HOFFMANN, and the MÜNSTER HERETICS, supported the violent overthrow of the existing religious and social order to prepare the way for the second coming of Christ. Others, like the MENNONITES and HUTTERITES, were devoted to nonviolence (although this position did not protect them from being the targets of violence from orthodox tormentors). The rejection of private property was also common, although not universal, among Anabaptist communities.

The violent Anabaptists did not survive the sixteenth century, whereas the Hutterites, Mennonites, and the AMISH (who originated from the Mennonites) still exist today. The Baptists, perhaps the largest Protestant denomination in modern times, were influenced by Anabaptist teachings when their sect was founded in the seventeenth century, and practice the baptism of "conscious believers"—that is, of people who are old enough to understand the significance of the rite.

See also: MELCHIORITES, ZWICKAU PROPHETS.

ANASTASIUS   A priest in Constantinople during the first part of the fifth century, Anastasius preached against calling the virgin Mary by the title of *Theotokos*, which means "God bearer." Christians of the time widely used this term to honor Mary. Anastasius believed that referring to Christ's mother as the God bearer was heretical because it seemed to imply that Christ was not a real human being. According to the orthodox teachings evolving during this period, which Anastasius supported, Christ had a complete human nature in addition to being divine. Anastasius's opposition to the Theotokos was resented by many Christians, who believed that he was denying Christ's divinity. When NESTORIUS, the bishop of Constantinople, supported Anastasius in his stand against the Theotokos, a violent controversy erupted that threatened to tear the orthodox church apart. The issue was formally decided at the COUNCIL OF EPHESUS in A.D. 431, where the Theotokos was accepted as orthodox language. Nestorius and Anastasius were declared heretics.

See also: NESTORIANISM.

ANGEL MAGIC   Alongside the belief in the existence of ANGELS, attempts to establish direct contact with these benign beings have been made in every age. At almost every stage of Western culture, such activities have been discouraged or even suppressed as heretical. The tradition of angel magic, one of the main branches in the vast body of Western MAGIC, is customarily traced to the activities of the ancient Hebrew ruler, King Solomon. A Jewish legend, which may have been in circulation by the first century A.D., reported that Solomon made contact with the archangel Michael. The angel gave the king a magical ring with which he could subdue evil spirits. It is significant that, although both Jews and Christians revered Solomon for his wisdom, his reputation had an unsavory side; the Old Testament reports that he eventually strayed into the worship of "strange gods."

The perception that angel magic is spiritually dangerous continued through the centuries. Another common theme, also found for the first time in the Solomon legend, is the link between angel magic and DEMON MAGIC. Many later magical texts often imitate the old king in recruiting angelic aid to control demons.

During the early Middle Ages, the details of the Christian world view were established. A feature of this world view was the existence of a hierarchy of angels, organized into nine choirs. The higher ranks of angels were primarily concerned with praising God and rarely had anything to do with human affairs. The lower ranks, however, especially the archangels and angels, were thought to take a keen interest in the human world. The notion of guardian angels—spirits assigned to support the well-being of individuals—was also developing at this time. Against the background of such beliefs, it seemed sensible to many people to call on angels in time of need.

But orthodox officials tended to discourage contacts with angels because the practice could easily lead people into spiritual pitfalls. Praising angels and expressing gratitude to them could slip into excessive veneration, and even worship. The worship of angels, though apparently common in the earliest Christian communities, had long been regarded as heretical.

The other danger of calling on angels was that one might attract evil spirits instead. The invisible world was thought to be densely populated with DEMONS, watching for a chance to snare the unwary soul. There is evidence that all classes of society in medieval times were fond of using simple magical spells to ease their lives. Pious people might include references to angels in their incantations in order to ensure that good spirits were attracted.

For instance, one famous charm involved reciting the story of three angels who encountered a demon on Mount Sinai. In the story, the angels manage to destroy the demon's ability to inflict pain. It was thought that this charm effectively reduced pain the recipient suffered, and its content seems impeccably Christian. However, the official world view saw most magical practices as thinly disguised survivals of pagan practices; to the church, anything pagan was of the Devil. Satan could easily masquerade as an angel, and even do good works, in order to seduce the magician into trusting him.

Despite the dubious status of angel magic, some members of the clergy seemed to find the temptation irresistible. In the eighth century, a priest was overheard calling on the angels Uriel, Raguel, Tubuel, Adin, Tubuas, Sabaok, and Simiel. He was condemned by his bishops, who argued that because these angel names are not found in the Bible, they must be the titles of devils.

By the later Middle Ages, the tradition of angel magic had become more sophisticated, even though the orthodox repeatedly damned such practices. In the literature of the GRIMOIRES, textbooks of magical conjuration that began to be written at this time, angel magic and demon magic are often thoroughly mixed. The ritual magicians of the grimoire tradition continued to regard themselves as devout Christians; indeed, most of them were probably monks and clerics. They held that angels could be recruited to help the magician harness demons to do his bidding. Because the enslaved demon was busy obeying the magician's commands, it could not at the same time be carrying out the orders of the Devil; therefore, ritual magic was a good Christian act. Orthodoxy did not accept this argument and increasingly regarded ritual magic as heretical.

The best example of pure angel magic in the classic grimoires, without elements of demon magic, is a ritual in the *ALMADEL*, a division of the famous LEMEGETON or *Lesser Key of Solomon*. This ceremony reveals how to conjure the angels of the four directions into visible appearance and how to ask favors of them. Symbols and names of power, derived from the KABBALAH, are often used. The beings called by the ritual are described in thoroughly orthodox imagery. For example, the spirit of the east "appeareth in the form of an angel carrying in his hand a banner or flag having the picture of a white cross upon it, his body being wrapped round with a fair cloud, and his face very fair and bright, and a crown of rose flowers upon his head." This description is nice, but the mainstream clergy believed it was just a devil in disguise.

Angel magic became entangled in the other important division of the magical tradition, NATURAL MAGIC, during the Renaissance. Magicians at this time were anxious to define a class of spirits that were totally distinct from demons because the rise of the GREAT WITCH HUNT was making any connection with devilish topics extremely perilous. Magical theorists, like CORNELIUS AGRIPPA, were describing complex orders of natural spirits that pervaded the earth and sky and that could be influenced by magical means. Included in the lists of planetary forces, intelligences, and elemental beings in Agrippa's system are references to choirs of angels. It becomes difficult to distinguish between angels and nature spirits in these writings. One major figure, JOHANNES TRITHEMIUS, eliminated the distinction entirely when he claimed that angels are the hidden spirits underlying the natural world. The full bloom of angel magic in Western culture is expressed in two traditions that continue to the present day: ENOCHIAN MAGIC, and the practices of the SACRED MAGIC OF ABRAMELIN THE MAGE.

JOHN DEE, a renowned magician of the Elizabethan age, attempted to contact angels during rituals with EDWARD KELLY, who claimed to be clairvoyant. During their operations together, Kelly received visions while gazing into a crystal. In this way, an elaborate magical system was formulated, which included the use of the "Enochian" language and script the angels taught. Enochian magic continued to be practiced after Dee's time. Thomas Rudd, one of Dee's successors, continued to develop Enochian magic in the recently discovered TREATISE ON ANGEL MAGIC. Enochian elements heavily influenced the practices of the most important magical group in modern times, the Hermetic Order of the GOLDEN DAWN. Occultists and scholars today are still unravelling the complexities of Dee's angelic revelations.

The grimoire called the SACRED MAGIC OF ABRAMELIN THE MAGE claims to have been written in the fifteenth century, although many researchers believe it dates from the eighteenth century. The text describes a lengthy magical operation designed to conjure one's "Holy Guardian Angel," as well as a great deal of demon magic. The angelic being sought in Abramelin magic has been interpreted as the Higher Self of the magician. This suggestion makes sense, if we consider that during the eighteenth century thinkers such as EMANUEL SWEDENBORG were claiming that the angels dwell within us. Abramelin magic and the general tendency to view spiritual beings as inner, psychological forces have remained prominent in the modern occult tradition.

ANGELS   The English word "angel" derives from the Greek *angelos*, which means "messenger." During the course of Western history, beliefs concerning the nature of angels and their relationship to humans have undergone dramatic changes. Some of the heretical doctrines about these supernatural beings have had a significant impact on the conventional definition of reality.

Ancient Hebrew traditions were the most important source of notions regarding angels. It is likely that during their wanderings through Egypt and Mesopotamia, the Jews were influenced by a variety of beliefs about supernatural beings. As Hebrew culture absorbed these ideas, some of the spirits were converted into the servants of Yahweh, the Hebrew God. For instance, the Mesopotamian term *ka-ri-bu*, which refers to a winged, sword-bearing guardian of royalty, was adopted as the Hebrew *kerubim*, the class of angels guarding the gates of Eden with a flaming sword. These angels, mentioned in the Book of Genesis, in turn became the English "cherubim."

The Old Testament contains scattered references to angels and no sign of a detailed doctrine concerning them. Most of the original angel lore of the Jewish and Christian traditions derives from less than orthodox sources—namely, the PSEU-DEPIGRAPHA ("false writings," works misleadingly attributed to great Hebrew prophets) and the Apocrypha ("hidden books," texts that contained material too controversial to be included in the official collection of scriptures). From about 200 B.C. to A.D. 100, many Jews had a feeling that the end of the world was at hand. Although the pseudepigraphic and apocryphal writings were viewed with suspicion by orthodoxy, they were widely read. Their descriptions of heaven and hell, as well as angels and DEMONS, gave form to the workings of the popular imagination concerning the inhabitants of the unseen world.

The most important works in this literature are THE BOOK OF ENOCH and THE BOOK OF THE SECRETS OF ENOCH. They describe Enoch's journeys through various supernatural worlds. During his travels, he encountered and named many angelic beings. While the orthodox books mention only three angels by name, Michael, Gabriel, and Raphael, the Enoch writings and similar works identify many more. The notion of the "fallen angels" also originated in these unorthodox sources.

Christianity began at a time when there was a great interest in angels on the part of the Jewish population in Palestine. The apocryphal and pseudepigraphic Jewish works were among the favorite reading materials of the first Christian communities, and the angel beliefs derived from these sources were included in the Christian world view from the beginning. Angels are mentioned many times in the New Testament, praising God and serving as his messengers.

However, it appears that certain beliefs about angels also caused trouble for the developing Christian tradition. There are hints in the New Testament that some Christians were becoming too fond of angelic beings. In Paul's Letter to the Colossians, he warns against the "worshipping of angels" (2:18); in the Letter to the Hebrews (1:5), Paul emphasizes that Christ is infinitely superior to the angels (1:5); and in the First Letter of Peter, the author mentions that the angels themselves desire to learn the gospel of Christ (1:12).

These early discouragements apparently did not end the heretical tendency to revere angels as gods, rather than merely respecting them as God's servants. In a startling passage in the writings of Justin Martyr, an important orthodox figure of the early second century A.D., Justin states that he worships the Father, the Son, "the host of the other good angels who follow and who are made like him," and the Holy Spirit. Other early writings refer to Christ and the Holy Spirit as angels. These references indicate that a strong tradition of angel worship contradicted the orthodox idea, which was in its early stages of development at the time, that only the three Persons of the Trinity are divine.

According to some scholars the notion that Christ is an angel was at times the dominant belief in the earliest Christian communities. As the doctrine that Christ is God the Creator became more prominent, angels (because they were regarded as merely created beings themselves) were demoted. However, the followers of ARIANISM, a major heretical movement of the fourth century, proclaimed that Christ was not God the Creator. Rather, he was a created being, and they gave him the title of "angel."

Orthodox Christians objected to this "angel christology" on two grounds. First, it devalued Christ as lesser than God, which contradicted the doctrine that the Father, Son, and Holy Spirit all *are* God. Second, although the Arians regarded Christ as an angel, they continued to worship him, and the orthodox stated that worshipping a created being was blasphemous. In an attempt to resolve the Arian problem, the first council of the entire orthodox Christian Church, the FIRST COUNCIL OF NICAEA, was called in 325. At that meeting, the line between Christ and the angels was officially drawn: Christ is God, angels are creations of God.

The challenge of the Arians' angelic heresy triggered important developments in the power structure of Western Christian culture. The full ecumenical council became the accepted way to settle disputes concerning the nature of reality. Also, Arianism forced those who believed that Christ (the Son, along with the Father and the Holy Spirit) is God to clarify how the three Persons of the Trinity have a single nature. Their work on this thorny problem influenced the Western understanding of the meaning of the term "person," and so helped to mold the meaning of the individual self in Western culture.

After the defeat of the Arians, orthodox Christians could not simply erase the idea of angels from the Christian world; angels were too prominent in the Bible and in popular belief. Therefore, Christian thinkers sought ways to use angels to combat heretical thinking. In the fifth century, Dionysius the Areopagite wrote a book in which he organized the orthodox concepts concerning angels. In this text, Dionysius states that the angelic spirits were arranged in a hierarchy, consisting of nine ranks or choirs. At the top, next to God, were the seraphim and cherubim. The archangels and angels filled the lowest ranks, and were closest to the human world. Dionysius also maintains that the priestly hierarchy of the church mirrored the organization of the angelic world. The idea that the power divisions of human society are divinely ordained obviously tends to support the status quo. In such a world view, people who try to change inequalities in society are working against God. Whether or not Dionysius intended such conservative implications, his work was enthusiastically adopted by the Roman Catholic leaders and helped to justify the development of feudalism, the rigidly segregated social organization of medieval Europe.

The later Middle Ages saw the heyday of "angelology," the study of angels. Great orthodox thinkers such, as Aquinas and Bonaventure, debated the characteristics of angels and tried to determine their number (one enterprising scholar established that each of the nine choirs consisted of 6,666 legions of 6,666 spirits, and thus calculated that there are 399,920,000 angels in the universe).

During the Middle Ages and the Renaissance, some people were relating to angels in a less orthodox way. In the practices of ANGEL MAGIC, magicians attempted to make angels do their bidding. These rituals and spells were regarded by the mainstream society as dangerous to the soul because it was always possible that a demon, disguised as an angel, might appear and trick the practitioner into becoming the demon's servant. Some historical researchers believe that the attitude of these ritual magicians influenced the foundation of modern science. The magicians, like scientists, were willing to manipulate the universe (by calling up spirits) in order to discover how it works. Both magicians and scientists called their operations "experiments." It is likely that the example of the ritual magician in part inspired the experimental attitude of the early modern scientists, many of whom were involved in occult practices.

As the scientific world view became the official reality in the West, interest in angels declined. Scientists believed that the universe operated like a vast machine and according to physical laws. There was no role for angels in this image of the world. Materialists, such as Thomas Hobbes, began to argue that people who had visions of angels were hallucinating. This line of thinking produced the modern view that encounters with angels are probably a sign of mental illness.

Another point of view was held by EMANUEL SWEDENBORG, an eighteenth century scientist and mystic, who wrote that the world of angels is within us, and that our "affections" (moods and feelings) were angels. Swedenborg's writings were later studied by influential Swiss psychiatrist Carl Jung. He argued that the experience of angels was not always a sign of illness, but might represent wise aspects of a person's unconscious mind. Jung himself said that a winged figure named Philemon often appeared to him and acted as his "guru."

In the twentieth century, the mainstream view of reality holds that angels are either the hallucinations of a sick mind or psychological images of human potential. A few researchers have advanced the theory that contemporary sightings of unidentified flying objects (UFOs) and premodern stories of angels are both describing the same phenomenon, visits of craft from other worlds or spiritual beings from other dimensions.

ANOMOEANS   A branch of the heretical movement known as ARIANISM, the Anomoeans emerged during the struggle for control of the Christian Church in the middle of the fourth century. During the reign of Roman emperor CONSTANTIUS II, who supported Arianism, rifts appeared within the Arian movement. AETIUS established the Anomoean position, which held that God the Father and the Son of God were completely different (in Greek, *anomoios*) in their essential natures: the Father's nature is that of God, and the Son's nature is that of a creation of God. Catholics, by contrast, taught that the Father and Son subsisted in the same essence or nature.

At one point, the Anomoeans were politically dominant, displacing Christians who held other theological views from their positions of authority in the church. The Anomoeans and other Arians were declared to be heretical and illegal at the FIRST COUNCIL OF CONSTANTINOPLE in 381.

See also: EUDOXIUS, EUNOMIUS.

ANTI-TRINITARIANISM   During the early centuries A.D., orthodox Christians struggled to establish the mysterious idea that God is one in substance but three in

Persons. After this doctrine of the Trinity was proclaimed at the FIRST COUNCIL OF CONSTANTINOPLE in 381, it was rarely challenged until the sixteenth century. At that time, Spanish theologian MICHAEL SERVETUS taught that God was a united Person, and that Christ was a different divine being than God. In central Europe, two variants of Anti-Trinitarianism appeared. The doctrine of TRITHEISM taught that the divine Persons were separate gods; UNITARIANISM went further, discarding the triple division altogether. The latter creed became a state religion of Transylvania, as well as an important movement in Poland. From there, Unitarianism was transmitted to the Netherlands, England, and America, where it became a significant cultural force in the nineteenth century.

See also: ARIANISM, GIORGIO BLANDRATA, SIMON BUDNY, MARTIN CZECHOWIC, FERENCZ DAVID, MATTEO GRIBALDI, SOCINIANISM.

APELLES   This second century heretic was an important leader of the MAR-CIONITE movement. The teachings of Marcion had given rise to a church that competed against the Catholic Church. Apelles revised some of his master's doctrines, seemingly in an attempt to bring the Marcionites closer to the beliefs of the Catholics. Important differences remained, however, and each group continued to regard the other side as a heresy until the disappearance of the Marcionites in the early Middle Ages.

Marcion taught that there were two gods, the God of Law, described in the Old Testament, and the God of Love, who appears in the form of Christ in the New Testament. Apelles agreed with orthodox Christians that there is only one God. However, like Marcion, he rejected the relevance of the Old Testament scriptures for Christians.

Apelles also sided with the Catholics and against Marcion on the question of whether Christ had a physical body. Marcion taught the heresy of DOCETISM, which maintains that Christ's body was completely nonmaterial. Apelles argued that Christ did have a material body, but disagreed with the orthodox view that this body was made of human flesh. Instead, Christ's body was composed of material from the stars. Apelles' doctrine is perhaps the earliest example of the unorthodox belief in "heavenly flesh," which occurs again among some radical Reformation groups in the sixteenth century.

See also: GNOSTICISM, MENNONITES.

APHTHARTODOCETAE   Aphthartodocetae was a branch of the heresy known as MONOPHYSITISM, which held that Christ has a single nature, in contrast to the orthodox view that Christ has two natures. The Aphthartodocetae appeared in Egypt after A.D. 518, led by the exiled Monophysite bishop JULIAN OF HALICAR-NASSUS. They taught that Jesus did not have an ordinary human nature, which is capable of being damaged; the humanity of Christ, they stated, was indestructible (in Greek, *aphthartos*). According to their Catholic opponents, such a belief implied that Christ was not a human being, but merely appeared to be so. This is the ancient heresy of DOCETISM. Hence, the name given to them is Aphthartodocetae (roughly meaning "those who hold that Christ was an indestructible ghost"). The group's teachings differ from classical docetism, however. Docetists of the Gnostic type held that Christ's suffering during his lifetime was an illusion because his divine body was incapable of feeling pain. According to the Monophysites, Christ willed himself to suffer in order to save us from our sins, even though his nature was indestructible.

See also: GAIANUS OF ALEXANDRIA.

APOLLINARIANISM   Apollinarianism was an ancient heresy that states that the human nature of Christ was incomplete, lacking an intellect or mind. Orthodoxy condemned the idea for violating the wholeness of Christ's humanity. The heresy takes its name from its founder, APOLLINARIS OF LAODICEA.

APOLLINARIS OF LAODICEA   This teacher was active in the Christian communities of the Roman Empire during the fourth century. Apollinaris is known as the first person who attempted to work out in detail the relationship between the divine and human aspects of JESUS CHRIST. His answer to this theological question was ingenious, but it was declared heretical. The attempts of other ancient Christian thinkers to refute the doctrines of APOLLINARIANISM often led them to formulate new heresies of their own. NESTORIANISM, for example, arose in this fashion.

Apollinaris was born around A.D. 310, just three years before Christianity was legalized by the emperor, Constantine. During his earlier years, Apollinaris lived in Alexandria, the great Egyptian center of Christian studies; later, he moved to Antioch. Apollinaris was staunchly orthodox and opposed the heresy of ARIANISM, which periodically took control over much of the Christian community during this century. He became the bishop of the town of Laodicea (in what is now Turkey) in 360.

The Arians taught that Christ, the Son of God, was not God Himself, but merely one of God's creations. Apollinaris and other orthodox Christians, in their fight against Arianism, emphasized the idea that Christ was God. The orthodox position raised a difficult question: If Christ was God, then was Jesus of Nazareth in any sense a human being?

Various earlier heresies, such as DOCETISM, had concluded that the answer was no. Jesus was a deity, and his human appearance was an illusion. Others, like ADOPTIONISM, had argued that Jesus was obviously a human being, but that he had been chosen by God. If he was an adopted son, however, he obviously could not have the same divine nature as the Father who had adopted him. The orthodox view was that Christ was *both* fully God and fully human. How could this be? Apollinaris tried to explain the paradox of Christ the God-man.

According to Apollinaris, every person has both a physical component (the body) and a nonmaterial component (the soul and the intellect). In ordinary people, both components are human. In Jesus, however, the intellect was not human, but divine. In fact, the intellect of Christ was the divine Word, which has existed eternally. Although Apollinaris neatly divided Jesus Christ into a divine intellect and a human body, he emphasized that the divine and human in Christ were so thoroughly mixed that the resulting being had a single essence or nature. To teach otherwise, Apollinaris believed, was to depict Christ as split into two fragments, a most irreverent way of representing God.

The description of Christ taught by Apollinaris did not sit well with his orthodox colleagues. If Christ did not have a human intellect, they pointed out, then Christ was not really a human being, but a puppet made of flesh, being operated by God. Orthodox thinkers like Gregory of Nazianzus argued that the Christ pictured by Apollinaris could not have the power to save people from their sins. Christ had to be a human in both body and intellect in order for his sacrifice on the cross to pay for human sinfulness, because sin dwells in both body and mind.

As early as 377, Catholics in Rome officially opposed the teachings of Apollinaris, and many church leaders in the eastern part of the Roman Empire also spoke against him. Emperor Theodosius, who proclaimed Catholic Chrsitianity to be the state religion of the empire and exiled the Arians, was persuaded to ban Apollinaris and his followers in 388. Apollinaris himself died two years later.

However, Apollinaris was defended by many Christians. His description of Christ explained the paradox of the God-man better than any other suggestions at the time. Indeed, the doctrines of Apollinaris challenged orthodox thinkers to work on this theological problem, which would not be resolved until more than sixty years after his death.

NESTORIUS, a fifth century bishop of Antioch, was so opposed to Apollinaris's dehumanization of Jesus that he veered too far in the opposite direction. In order to emphasize the fact that Jesus was a man, Nestorius distinguished Christ's humanity from his divinity to such a degree that his orthodox critics accused him of falling into the trap that Apollinaris worked to avoid: splitting Christ into two fragments. This legacy of the controversy over Apollinaris's vision, known as the Nestorian heresy, survived for many centuries.

APOSTASY   In the Roman Catholic Church, an apostate is one who denies the authority of the Bible or the truth of Christianity after having become an orthodox Christian. The term is most frequently applied to lapsed priests. Roman Emperor JULIAN was dubbed "the Apostate" because he tried to revive PAGANISM after Christianity had been championed by his uncle, Emperor Constantine.

APOSTOLICI   Also known as the Apostolic Brethren and the "Pauperes Christi," this heresy appeared in Italy during the latter part of the thirteenth century. The 1200s witnessed the emergence of several groups promoting the idea that material possessions interfere with the holy life. There was also great interest in the prophecy of JOACHIM OF FIORE that a new age, governed by the Holy Spirit, would begin in 1260. The Apostolici were associated with both of these notions.

GERARD SEGARELLI founded the Brethren sometime after the fateful year 1260 had come and gone, yielding no clear indication that the new age had commenced. Joachim's prediction was not immediately dismissed as a failure. Some believed that the Holy Spirit had arrived and that indications of His presence would gradually increase. Others held that the timing of the prediction was slightly inaccurate, but that the new age would start any day now. In this atmosphere of expectation, Segarelli convinced some of the poorer citizens of Parma to follow his spiritual advice, which was based on the example of Saint Francis. From Parma, the movement spread through the towns of northern Italy.

The Apostolici preached that money and possessions corrupt the human soul, and should be avoided. They did not even own the clothing on their backs. During public gatherings, they stripped naked, threw their garments in a heap, and redistributed the clothes amongst themselves. The Brethren supported themselves by begging; if they were given more food than they could eat, they would make a spectacle of refusing to save the leftovers, preferring a life without material security.

During the early years of the movement, they received increasing support from the lay community, who tended to view them as saints. At first, the Catholic authorities paid little attention; however, the Apostolici's equation of poverty and holiness reflected poorly on the wealthy orthodox church. In 1275, a Catholic council banned the Apostolici; the ban was repeated by councils in 1285 and 1290.

Confident in their support among the citizens, the Brethren ignored the bans. The church responded with violence. In 1294, four Apostolici were burned to death in Parma; six years later, Segarelli met the same fate. The movement was forced to go underground in the towns.

The attacks by Catholic officials radicalized the Apostolici. Segarelli's successor, FRIAR DOLCINO, preached that the Holy Spirit would soon destroy the Catholic Church for its greed. He promoted the cause of the Brethren in the villages of the Italian Alps and developed a large following there.

In 1304, the Apostolici under Dolcino led a peasant uprising to throw off control by the church and the ruling classes. The usual methods of the INQUISITION for dealing with heresy were inadequate to deal with opposition of this magnitude. A crusade was called. For three years, a Catholic army fought the Apostolici, who established a fortified base in the mountains. During this period, the inhabitants experienced a reign of terror, with each side killing anyone suspected of supporting the other. When the base of the Brethren was finally conquered, the victorious Catholics tortured 140 Apostolici, including their leader, to death.

BENTIVENGA OF GUBBIO escaped the disastrous defeat. He tried to start an Apostolici group among the Franciscan friars but was quickly condemned. Few Apostolici survived, and the movement soon disappeared after one of the most successful, if short-lived, challenges to orthodox power ever organized by a medieval heresy.

ARBATEL OF MAGIC   This book, also known as *The Isagoge* or *De Magia Veterum*, is one of the most important texts in the collection of magical handbooks called GRIMOIRES. The *Arbatel of Magic* was first published in Basel, Switzerland, in 1575. Various portions of it were copied into later grimoires, and instructions in Arbatel magic still appear in textbooks of occult practices published today.

The author of the *Arbatel* is unknown. This is typical of the grimoires because the practice of ritual magic during the sixteenth century could attract the lethal attention of the INQUISITION. Although the *Arbatel* is not a work of DEMON MAGIC, it was still a forbidden text. The police of Christian orthodoxy usually did not distinguish between the categories of magic, but viewed all magical practice as demonic. The meaning of the term "arbatel" is uncertain, although it seems to be Hebrew. It has been suggested that Arbatel is the name of the spirit who taught the author the magical system described in the book.

In its present form, the *Arbatel* appears to be incomplete. The introduction claims that the published text is only one part of a nine-part work, but no one knows whether the other eight sections were ever written. The book presents a grand vision of the hidden world, reporting that we can acquire wisdom from seven sources: God, angels, embodied beings, occult connections in nature, damned souls, the rulers of Hell, and the spirits of the elements.

This scheme lays the groundwork for a comprehensive system of magic. The existing book is much more limited in scope, focusing only on the invocation of the seven Olympic spirits. These occult beings are associated with the seven planets of ASTROLOGY. Each Olympic spirit has specialized powers and rules over a vast hierarchy of lesser spirits who control the processes of the natural world.

The *Arbatel* gives the name, magical symbol, and special gifts of the spirits. For example, the solar spirit, named Och, can grant a magician a life span of 600 healthy years, a great reputation, and a big bag of gold; Phul, the Olympic spirit of the moon, provides water spirits as servants, transmutes all metals into silver, and extends the life span to 300 years.

The *Arbatel* has a pious Christian tone. The author claims that the various symbols and prayers in the book are useless without the blessing of God, and advises the magician to live a moral and religious life. Unlike many other grimoires, this book does not provide instructions on how to kill enemies, seduce women, or succeed in other sinful activities.

According to occult tradition, even holy magic, such as the rituals of the *Arbatel*, can be dangerous. Evil spirits are frequently attracted to magical ceremonies, even if they are not called, and can attack the magician if given the opportunity. A well-documented story reported by historian E. M. Butler concerns the mysterious and tragic outcome of one attempt to use the *Arbatel*. In 1715, three men spent the night in an isolated hut near Jena in Germany. They huddled inside a protective magical circle and called on Och, the Olympic spirit of the sun, to lead them to buried treasure. The three men were found in the hut the next day. Two were dead, the body of one man covered with scratches and burns. The third man was unconscious. When he revived, he could not remember what had occurred and was physically and mentally unwell for the rest of his life. The next night, three watchmen were left to guard the hut. The following morning found one guard dead and the other two unconscious. When they recovered, they reported that they had been assaulted by demons during the night. Regardless of the explanation of this report, which Butler regards as historically accurate, it serves as a caution to anyone probing the regions lying beyond consensus reality.

The *Arbatel* was the main inspiration for such later grimoires as the *Theosophica Pneumatica*, and notable nineteenth century magician Eliphas Levi referred to its practices.

See also: NATURAL MAGIC.

ARIANISM   The struggle between the devotees of Arianism and the Catholics consumed the attention of the Christian world during the fourth century A.D. At the outset of the controversy, Christianity had just been legalized after many years of violent persecution, and the orthodox Christian understanding of the nature of God had still not been fully defined. Sixty years later, Catholic Christianity had become the state religion of the Roman Empire, and the doctrine of the Trinity had become the official Christian description of God's nature. Because of its role in these decisive changes, Arianism is often described as the most important of the ancient Christian heresies.

By the fourth century, it had become clear that the descriptions of God that Christianity had inherited from its sources contained a paradox. The strong conviction in Judaism that there is only one God persisted in the Christian tradition. Nevertheless, Christian literature mentions God using various words that were not all obviously referring to the same being; the terms Father, Son, and Holy Spirit were described in sacred writings as if they were separate entities. The question "How can God be both one and three?" had been puzzling Christians for centuries and produced a range of opinions. Heresies, such as ADOPTIONISM and MODALISM, arose during the previous century in efforts to clarify the paradox. Arianism was another such attempt.

Most of the earlier debates concerning the mystery of God had focused on the relationship between God the Father and the Son. The orthodox position rejected the Modalist and Adoptionist solutions and described Father and Son as distinct Persons who were still a single God. Influential third century teacher LUCIAN OF ANTI-OCH found this position incomprehensible. Instead, he suggested (or, possibly, borrowed from DIONYSIUS OF ALEXANDRIA) the idea that the Son was not God, but was created by God before the beginning of the world. The Son, who manifested as Christ, is a great supernatural being worthy of worship, but is not the Creator of the universe. This notion that the Son is a creation of God rather than God himself became the defining characteristic of the Arian doctrine.

One of Lucian's students was a Libyan named ARIUS. After finishing his studies with Lucian in Antioch, Arius moved to the Egyptian city of Alexandria, an important center of Christianity during this period. Arius began to teach the idea that the Son of God had been created out of nothing by God. The Son had been formed at a point in time before the creation of the world, Arius stated.

He quickly attracted the disapproval of Alexander, the Catholic bishop of Alexandria. The bishop and the other representatives of orthodoxy in the ensuing debate believed that defining the Son as something less than God created problems for Christian doctrine. A tradition transmitted to Christians from Judaism held that only God should be worshipped; to worship the things that God had created, no matter how magnificent those creations might be, was an insult to the One who made them. If Christ, the Son of God, was not God but merely a creation, then the Christian practice of worshipping Christ was wrong! This conclusion was totally unacceptable to the Catholics. Arius himself continued to worship the Son; therefore, said the orthodox, either Arius's notion that the Son was merely a created being was inconsistent with his devotional activities, or Arius was offending God by worshipping a creature.

A related problem with Arius's teaching involved the relationship it implied between Christ and humanity, charged the orthodox. The Catholics taught that because Christ was God, He had the power to save sinful people from the everlasting punishment they deserved. No one *less than* God, they believed, could have the right to forgive sins *against* God. If Christ the Son was only a created being who became divine because of his moral perfection, then he could not save sinners; at best, he could serve as a moral example for humans to imitate. And yet, ancient Christian traditions clearly stated that Christ has the power of salvation. Therefore, the Catholics noted, Arius's teaching about Christ the Son must be false.

Bishop Alexander excommunicated Arius around A.D. 321. Arius replied by requesting the support of other bishops, especially in the eastern part of the empire where he had studied under Lucian and had made friends. Also, Arius attempted to recruit mass support by composing popular songs and chants featuring slogans from his theology. The Christian communities were soon split into feuding camps, and the disagreements sometimes took the form of violent conflicts.

In 313, Roman emperor Constantine had declared the practice of Christianity to be legal within the empire. Many researchers believe that Constantine took this step because he viewed the Christian communities, with their hierarchy of obedience, to be socially stabilizing influences during this period of turbulence, and hoped that legalizing Christianity would assist him in decreasing political strife. He was very unhappy when, just a few years later, the Christians became locked in a disruptive struggle over the teachings of Arius.

The emperor wrote a joint letter to Arius and Alexander, requesting that they end their dispute before Christianity destroyed itself and the empire: "Give me back my quiet days and carefree nights. Do not let me spend the rest of my days joylessly," Constantine pleaded—but to no avail. The turmoil between the Catholics and the Arians was spreading, and a settlement became an urgent priority. In 325, Constantine commanded the church leaders to meet at Nicaea to resolve the dispute.

This FIRST COUNCIL OF NICAEA, presided over by Arius's ally, EUSEBIUS OF NICOMEDIA, seemed stacked in the Arians' favor. Poor maneuvering on their part, however, allowed their opponents to convince the emperor to support the statement that the Father and the Son had the same divine nature—in other words, that the Father and the Son were both God. This formula of "consubstantiality" (meaning "same substance or nature") won the agreement of the majority at the Council. The orthodox had won this round in the controversy. Arius was banished, and his followers lost their positions of authority.

In the years following the Council of Nicaea's decision, the Arians returned to dominance. Constantine had evidently been more interested in promoting social calm than in the fine points of theology. Some senior Arians, particularly Eusebius of Nicomedia, convinced him that a gradual acceptance of Arians back into the church's authority structure would be less divisive than to leave the Arians, who were numerous, alienated from the church. The Arian bishops wielded their political influence well. By the time of Constantine's death in 337, the three most well-known supporters of the orthodox position had all been deposed and replaced by Arians.

Constantine was succeeded by his three sons, Constantine II, Constans, and CONSTANTIUS II. Constantine II died a few years after assuming power, leaving the other two brothers in charge. Constans controlled the western part of the empire, including Rome, and tended to support the Roman Catholic (orthodox) position. Constantius, based in the east, was an Arian.

In the decades that followed, the power of the Catholics and Arians in the church was largely determined by the relative power of their allied emperors. When Constantius became preoccupied with a war against the Persians, the Catholic Constans was able to extend his influence within the empire, and orthodox bishops replaced many Arians. When Constans died in 350, leaving the Arian Constantius in sole control of the empire, Arianism regained its dominance.

During the uncertainties of this time, the Arian group began to have internal disagreements and fragmented into three parties. The ANOMOEANS or RADICAL ARIANS, led by AETIUS and EUNOMIUS, steadfastly held that the nature of the Father did not resemble the nature of the Son at all. The Father was God, and the Son was not divine, but merely a created thing. The HOMOIANS or SEMI-ARIANS, on the other hand, associated with BASIL OF ANCYRA, contended that the natures of the Father and the Son were similar, but not identical as the orthodox taught. The HOMOEANS, led by ACACIUS OF CAESAREA, stated that the Father and the Son were similar in some way, but refused to say exactly what the resemblances were.

The radical Arians took advantage of the pro-Arian atmosphere following Constans's death. They secured many powerful roles in the church hierarchy and attacked the moderate Arians as well as the orthodox. Emperor Constantius attempted to end the disunity in the church, which increasingly manifested as mob violence, by calling another meeting of the church leaders and forcing them to accept the Semi-Arian position as the best compromise.

In 359, the Eastern bishops were commanded to meet in Seleucia, and the Western bishops in Rimini. The eastern leaders obeyed the emperor and upheld the idea that the Father and Son were similar in nature. The Western bishops, however, stuck to their orthodox beliefs; Father and Son had one divine nature: both are God. When representatives from the west reported the result of their meeting in Rimini to Constantius, he imprisoned them until they signed a document accepting the Semi-Arian compromise formula. The matter seemed settled.

Two years later, Constantius died, and JULIAN THE APOSTATE, the last pagan emperor, began his twenty-month reign. Julian, a non-Christian, did not support any particular party among the squabbling Christians. This imperial non-interference enabled the orthodox party to regroup. In 362 at a meeting led by Athanasius, the Catholic bishop of Alexandria, the Catholic Christians recognized that not only the Father and the Son, but also the Holy Spirit, had the same divine nature. During the next twenty years, this statement was clarified into the orthodox doctrine of the Trinity. This depiction of the three-in-one God has remained the official Christian description of God from the end of the fourth century to the present day. The three divine entities were described as different Persons who had unique relationships with each other: the Father "begets" the Son, and the Holy Spirit "proceeds from" the Father. The exact meaning of these relationships was left as a holy mystery, beyond human comprehension.

The Catholics tried to convince the moderate Arians to accept the doctrine of the Trinity. The Semi-Arians were able to affirm the unity of natures between Father and Son if this concept was interpreted in a certain way, but they could not accept the Holy Spirit as a Person equal to the Father and Son.

In 364, VALENS occupied the imperial throne in the east, while Valentinian became emperor in the west. Valens, a supporter of the radical Arians, persecuted both the moderate Arians and the orthodox Christians. Valentinian did not become involved in church politics. Under the pressure of Valens's activities, many of the moderate Arians decided that their best chance of survival lay in joining the orthodox Catholic party.

When Valentinian died, he was succeeded in 375 by Gratian. This Western emperor was a committed Catholic who moved to offset Valens's support of Arianism. When Valens died in 378, he was succeeded by Theodosius, another Catholic. With imperial power firmly in the hands of the orthodox, measures were taken to uproot Arianism from the empire forever. The crowning triumph occurred in 381 when Theodosius hosted a meeting of church leaders in Constantinople. At this

FIRST COUNCIL OF CONSTANTINOPLE, the doctrine of the Trinity—the Deity is one in nature, and three in Persons—was formally proclaimed to be the only correct belief concerning God.

Following the Catholic victory, Arianism still posed a problem. Within the empire, large pockets of popular support for the Arian doctrine existed. In order to persuade the Arians among the common people to submit to orthodox obedience, Ambrose, the bishop of Milan, promoted several characteristics of Catholic practice that would become standard procedures in the medieval church: the use of hymns praising the Trinity (a propaganda technique borrowed from Arius himself), impressively elaborate religious ceremonies, and the belief that relics (generally body parts and belongings of revered Catholic leaders) had miraculous powers.

Another difficulty for the orthodox arose from the success of ULFILAS, an Arian missionary, who had brought the heretical doctrine to the Germanic tribes in the mid-fourth century. The Gothic tribes, as well as the Vandals, had converted to the Arian version of Christianity. As these peoples infiltrated the Western Roman Empire, they were impressed by the remnants of Roman culture and often tried to imitate the old Roman lifestyle. The awesome ceremonies developed by the Roman Catholics intrigued the invaders, and eventually the Germanic Arians converted to orthodoxy.

The long-term effects of the Arian controversy on Western culture extend beyond strictly religious matters. In order to protect its doctrines from the Arian alternative, orthodox Christianity was forced to clarify the relationship between the three divine entities of Father, Son, and Holy Spirit and the unitary nature of God. In the process, it defined the concept of the "person." Although the three divine Persons shared a common nature, their differences were held to be equally real: the uniqueness of the Persons was not an illusion or an unimportant surface distinction.

This insistence on the reality of the divine Persons had implications for humans, for we, too, are persons. The importance of individual personhood, in contrast to the negation of the person in favor of the group, is a central theme in the Western world view. Recognizing the reality of the person was the first step leading to the belief in the rights of the individual that underlies modern liberal democracy. The commonly reported feeling of alienation from society—a sense that the individual person is the *only* reality—is an exaggerated version of this reality of personhood. These features of modern culture thus have ancient roots in the outcome of the battle between Arianism and orthodoxy during the fourth century.

ARIUS   Although Arius did not invent ARIANISM, the unorthodox doctrine named after him, he was certainly its best known exponent. Arius and his allies nearly overthrew the Roman Catholics within the Christian leadership during the fourth century and provoked orthodox theologians to devise the central Christian doctrine of the Trinity.

Arius was probably born in Libya in A.D. 250. At some point in his early life he moved to Egypt, where a thriving Christian community existed. The first Christian monks had appeared in Egypt during the third century, and Arius decided to join them. He is known to have associated with MELITUS OF LYCOPOLIS, a bishop who refused to obey the commands of his archbishop and formed a separate church. Perhaps the example of Melitus inspired Arius in his later willingness to defy the Catholic chain of command.

Arius also studied with LUCIAN OF ANTIOCH, who operated an academy for Christian studies. Although Lucian was reconciled with the Catholic Church shortly before his death, his teachings concerning the nature of God were actually at odds with the orthodox view. Arius was a devoted student of Lucian, from whom he learned, and later adopted, the main features of his own heretical position.

Returning to Egypt from his studies in Antioch, Arius was ordained a priest in Alexandria in 311. He devoted himself to combatting heresy and particularly loathed GNOSTICISM and MODALISM. However, he also had growing qualms about the orthodox position. The prevailing Catholic teaching held that God the Father and God the Son (Christ) were two distinct Persons although they shared one divine essence or nature. Arius found this doctrine, which at the time was not clearly formulated, difficult to comprehend (as do most people!). He worried that such a description of the deity implied the existence of two Gods, the Father and the Son, and therefore violated the basic Christian notion that there is only one God. Alternatively, Arius thought that the orthodox view might be a version of the heresy of MODALISM, which taught that the Father and the Son were merely two names for the same divine Person, a concept that violated their distinctiveness.

In response, Arius dismissed the orthodox doctrine and began to promote Lucian's depiction of the Father and the Son. The Son, taught Lucian (and Arius), was created by the Father. Since God is eternal, not created, the Son cannot be God. What, then, is the Son? According to Arius, the Son (also called the Logos or Word) acts as a bridge between God the Father and the rest of the created world. Although the Son is not God, he has become divine because of his moral purity. The Son, who became incarnated as Christ, serves as the example for all people: If we become morally pure, we, too, can become divine.

Arius's version of God and Christ was more comprehensible and appealing to many pagans than the orthodox Catholic position. The description of the Logos given by Arius resembled the teachings of the late pagan philosophy of Neoplatonism, which might have been one of his sources for the doctrine.

However, Archbishop Alexander, the guardian of Christian orthodoxy in Alexandria, became alarmed at Arius's message. Unable either to convince Arius of his error or to silence him, Alexander excommunicated Arius in 321.

When Arius was forced to leave the city, his rejection by the archbishop seemed to energize him. He had influential friends in the Christian community, especially in the eastern part of the Empire and mounted a letter-writing campaign in support of his cause. Arius attempted to woo less sophisticated Christians by composing popular songs and chants containing slogans from his theology. This ingenious propaganda was quite successful; vast numbers of artisans, soldiers and sailors became followers of Arius.

Emperor Constantine had just legalized Christianity in 312, hoping that this religion with its hierarchy of priests who required obedience of their followers would help to stabilize the Roman Empire. Instead, the church itself ruptured. The followers of Arius accused the orthodox Christians of being modalists or *bitheists* (believers in two Gods), and orthodoxy attacked the Arians as those who defiled Christ the Son by saying He was merely a created thing.

Having recruited significant support from powerful colleagues as well as the general public, Arius returned to Alexandria and continued to teach, in defiance of

Alexander. The situation deteriorated into mob rioting over the fine points of theology as the supporters of the two sides took their disagreement to the streets. In an attempt to settle the dispute, the FIRST COUNCIL OF NICAEA was held in 325. The Arian party was outmaneuvered and lost the debate. Arius's doctrines were labeled heretical, and he was driven into exile.

Arius has the historic distinction of being the first person to be censored by a state government on behalf of the Catholics. Constantine issued a proclamation:

> If any treatise composed by Arius is discovered, let it be consigned to the flames . . . in order that no memorial whatever of him be left . . . if anyone shall be caught concealing a book by Arius, and does not instantly bring it out and burn it, the penalty shall be death.

At this point, it seemed that Arius and his followers had been decisively defeated. However, over the years following the Council of Nicaea, Arian lobbyists persuaded the emperor to relent. Arians then began to replace orthodox clergy in positions of power within the church. Eventually, the tide turned against the orthodox party, and Arianism became politically dominant.

In this atmosphere of Arian victory, Arius was recalled from exile in 334. Plans were made to bring Arius back as a great leader of the church. Arius never lived to see such recognition. While walking the streets in Constantinople one day in 336, the aged founder of Arianism, more than 86 years old, collapsed and died. His movement survived his death, however, and it would take another forty years before orthodox Catholics triumphed within the empire. Arius's heretical legacy persisted for centuries among the Germanic tribes.

See also: ANGELS, ASTERIUS.

ARMENIAN CHRISTIANS   Armenians are proud of their Christian heritage because Armenia was the first nation on earth to convert to Christianity around A.D. 300; in the Roman Empire, Christianity was illegal until A.D. 313. At the beginning of the sixth century, the Armenians were involved in political strife with the Byzantines, who were orthodox Christians. As a means of emphasizing Armenia's independence from Byzantine control, the Armenian Church rejected the orthodox definitions of Christ's nature and adopted the view called MONOPHYSITISM. This, however, had been defined as heretical by orthodox authorities. The Monophysite teachings have been preserved by some in the Armenian Church to the present day, although Armenian Christian practices closely resemble those of the Eastern Orthodox Church.

ARMINIANISM   The Arminian movement emerged as a reaction to certain beliefs taught by the Dutch Reformed Church. The movement's founder, theologian JACOBUS ARMINIUS, objected to the Church's insistence that God had predestined some people for salvation and that Christ's death was only for the benefit of these chosen ones. Instead, Arminius said, Christ died to provide everyone with a chance for salvation. A year after Arminius's death in 1609, his disciples drew up a declaration, which stated that predestination was unBiblical and therefore false. At the Synod of Dort in 1618–1619, Reformed Church leaders condemned Arminianism. Arminians then either left the Netherlands or suffered persecution. Their views were finally accepted as legitimate in 1795.

Jacobus ARMINIUS   A theologian in the Dutch Reformed Church at the end of the sixteenth century, Jacobus Arminius's teachings provoked a division within the church. The Reformed Church taught the doctrine of predestination: God determined which people would be saved, even before they are born. As such, Christ died not for the benefit of all humanity, but only for those predestined for salvation. Arminius objected to these ideas. He felt that human moral choices made during one's lifetime affect whether one is saved. He also believed that Christ's crucifixion was intended to aid every Christian. After his death in 1609, his disciples, known as ARMINIANS, continued to promote his ideas in the face of persecution.

Henri ARNAUD   Henri Arnaud was leader of the WALDENSIAN heretics during the seventeenth century, when persecution by Catholic forces was especially severe. In 1686, King Louis XVI of France ordered Arnaud and the Waldensians to convert to Roman Catholicism. This command was used as a pretext to drive thousands of Waldensians from their lands in the Savoy region of the Western Alps. The Waldensians were imprisoned in Turin, in northern Italy. Four years later, a small group of the heretics managed to return to their homeland from Italy, led by Arnaud, who became a symbol of Waldensian endurance.

ARNOLDISTS   Followers of the heretical preacher ARNOLD OF BRESCIA, Arnoldists drove the pope from Rome during the early twelfth century. Arnold was executed in 1155, but the Arnoldists continued to promote his ideal of a church without wealth or political involvement for decades afterward. The orthodox Council of Verona condemned the Arnoldists in 1184.

ARNOLD OF BRESCIA   One of the most important heretics of the twelfth century, Arnold of Brescia managed to gather more popular support than any heretic before him during the Middle Ages. He even succeeded in driving the pope out of Rome. Arnold's activities sent a strong message to orthodoxy regarding the danger of lenience toward alternative beliefs and helped provoke the hard-line approach that came to characterize the Catholic response to heresy.

Arnold was born in A.D. 1100. During his early years, he studied in Paris under the controversial theologian PETER ABELARD. His talents led to his promotion as prior of Brescia in Italy. Catholic authorities soon learned of Arnold's preaching. He called for the church to renounce its wealth and political power, and to return to the state of poverty and purity he believed to be the lifestyle of the apostles in the New Testament. But the Catholic Church was not likely to do this. The papacy had spent the preceding fifty years struggling to free itself from control by secular politicians, amplify its powers over the bishops and priests throughout Europe, increase its wealth through shrewd business deals, and even exercise its military power by organizing the Crusades.

During this period, there were several uprisings of the poorer townspeople against bishops who resisted the strengthened papal power. At times, the mobs threatened to escape even the control of the pope, and ideas similar to those championed by Arnold had been discussed by the leaders of these movements. Arnold's call for a radical reform of the church resonated with the ideals of these popular uprisings and began to attract favorable attention from the less privileged classes. Church officials, on the other hand, correctly perceived that his ideal of a church without material wealth was in conflict with the current interests of the pontiff.

When the bishop of Brescia attempted to discipline some corrupt priests in his district, Arnold condemned both the priests and the bishop, stating that the two sides were degraded by their attachment to material objects. Arnold managed to raise an army of followers who prevented the bishop from reentering Brescia when he returned from a visit.

In 1139, Pope Innocent II condemned Arnold and drove him from Italy. Arnold returned to Paris and continued to preach his antimaterial views. After the powerful Catholic leader Bernard of Clairveaux forced Arnold to leave France, he wandered in southern Germany and Switzerland for a while, eventually returning to Italy. Arnold convinced Eugenius III, the new pope, that he had come back to orthodox obedience. But within a year, Arnold was again preaching publicly that the wealth and power of the church were signs of corruption. He taught that sacraments administered by a priest who owned property had no spiritual value. "Priests who have possessions, bishops with feudal tenures and monks with property will be damned," proclaimed the rebellious prior.

Before papal representatives could arrest him, Arnold had established a large following among the lower classes of society in Rome. He also made connections with secular politicians who wished to eliminate the church from the political arena in order to strengthen their own positions. In 1146, an uprising of Arnold's followers brought him to power. Pope Eugenius was chased from the city.

The heretic and his allies repulsed Eugenius when he returned with an army in 1149 and ruled Rome for five more years. One of Eugenius's successors, Pope Hadrian IV, enlisted the aid of powerful German emperor Frederick I Barbarossa and finally took back the city.

Arnold of Brescia was convicted of rebellion. In 1155, he was hanged and burned, and his ashes scattered in the River Tiber. His followers, the ARNOLDISTS, did not immediately disband. They continued to cause trouble for decades afterward. Meanwhile, the number of heretical CATHARS in Italy was increasing. The Cathars drew their followers from the same social levels as Arnold, and their doctrines concerning the orthodox church were similar. It is likely that the passionate message of Arnold helped lay the foundation for the blooming of the Cathar challenge to orthodoxy in the years after his death.

See also: APOSTOLICI.

ARRAS HERETICS   During the first part of the eleventh century, unorthodox beliefs had begun to surface in the north of France. The most notable example of this phenomenon was the heresy trial in Arras, which took place in 1025. Bishop Gerard of Cambrai had heard about the Arras heretics, a group of artisans who held views at odds with those of the Catholic Church. His investigations led to a show trial, intended to serve as a warning to anyone who would disobey the church.

The artisans of Arras confessed that they did not believe that the sacraments of the church had any value as means of salvation. Rather, they advocated a simple lifestyle based on the New Testament descriptions of the apostles: "to abandon the world, to restrain the appetites of the flesh, to do injury to nobody, to extend charity to everybody of our own faith." Their position was not based on a complex theology, but rather on a disgust with the greed and lack of interest in people's spiritual welfare displayed by many priests of the time.

Similar sentiments had been expressed a few years before by the ORLEANS HERETICS, and would appear again a few years later among the MONTEFORTE HERETICS. Bishop Gerard publicly presented elaborate philosophical arguments against the simple views of the artisans in an attempt to stem the tide of the heresy. However, Gerard's appeal to the intellect likely impressed his fellow priests more than the common people, who tended to sympathize with the heretics. The artisans were probably tortured and forced to proclaim a confession of orthodox faith. The contemporary dissatisfaction with the Catholic Church that we glimpse in the Arras affair did not disappear, however; by the following century, nurtured by the same concerns as those of the Arras artisans, the heresy of the CATHARS would rise to challenge orthodox Christianity in France, Italy, and Germany.

See also: LEUTHARD.

ARTEMAS   Artemas was a teacher of ADOPTIONISM, a Christian heresy, in Rome during the third century A.D. According to Catholic Church historian Eusebius, Artemas was the last Adoptionist heretic to preach in Rome.

ASSYRIAN CHRISTIANS   The name of the Assyrian Christians, a Christian sect originating in the Middle East, derives from a legendary connection to the ancient Mesopotamian culture of Assyria, but such a link is historically unlikely. The origins of the sect are obscure. It is probable that these Christians are the remnant of the heretical followers of NESTORIANISM in Persia, who retreated into the mountains of Kurdistan to escape persecution in the thirteenth century. Continued difficulties in Kurdistan during the early twentieth century led to their dispersal around the world. Today, small communities of Assyrian Christians exist in Iraq, Syria, Lebanon, and the United States of America. The head of the sect resides in San Francisco. Although Assyrian Christians deny that they follow the Nestorian doctrine now, they continue to honor the heresy's founder, fifth century bishop NESTORIUS.

ASTERIUS   Also known as "the Sophist," Asterius was an early ally of fourth century heretic ARIUS. While Arius concentrated on promoting his unorthodox views regarding the nature of God by writing letters and propaganda songs, Asterius attempted to compose a systematic description of the doctrines of ARIANISM. Fragments of his work, the *Syntagmation*, were preserved in quotations by his Catholic opponents, and portions of his other writings have also survived. He died sometime after A.D. 341.

ASTROLOGY   The belief in an intimate relationship between the movements of the heavenly bodies and the affairs of human life is one of the most ancient ideas of our species. Astrology is an attempt to use this supposed relationship to predict the future, or to uncover hidden aspects of the present. Through the centuries, orthodox thinkers have periodically condemned, as well as embraced, astrology.

Astrology had its beginnings in ancient Mesopotamia. The Babylonians noted that the planets, including the sun and moon, traveled along the same path in the sky with respect to the background stars. They divided this path into twelve segments, the signs of the zodiac. At first, the Babylonians were most interested in the links between planetary positions and major events in the life of a ruler or the history of a region. Later, as astrology spread eastward to India and westward around the Mediterranean Sea, the idea of studying the configurations of the planets at the moment of ordinary people's birth to learn about their characteristics and fate became popular.

Astrology was further developed in Egypt and Greece. The widespread notion that the universe was a gigantic organism, within which everything was harmoniously linked, made sense of astrology. If the brain and the liver can affect each other in a person's body, then it seemed reasonable that the moon and a human life could be connected within the body of the cosmic animal. By the time of the Roman Empire, casting horoscopes had become such a common activity that the great oracles of the ancient world, such as the one at Delphi, were in decline because of the competition of astrology. But not everyone in the Roman world accepted astrology. Some of the great Roman writers, such as Pliny the Elder, rejected the claim that astrologers knew enough about the stars and planets to predict the future.

Orthodox Christianity took more than three centuries to establish an official position about astrology. Many early Christians viewed it as a pagan practice, unsuitable for the followers of Christ. For example, third century church father Quintas Septimius Florens TERTULLIAN stated that astrology had been acceptable before the birth of Jesus; thereafter, astrologers and all other kinds of magicians were damned as enemies of the faith. The condemnation of astrology was formally adopted by the church at the Council of Laodicea, in A.D. 364 or 367. A few years later, the PRISCILLIANIST heretics of Spain were accused of promoting astrology.

Influential fifth century theologian Augustine of Hippo was interested in astrology as a young man, but completely rejected "those imposters called astrologers" in his later years. He argued that if the stars influence human lives, then their influence must either depend on God's will or not. Augustine rejected the idea that the stars could act independently of God, regarding it as a kind of atheism. He also rejected the divine dependence of stellar effects because astrologers say stars can cause evil events, and God does not will the occurrence of evil. Therefore, belief in astrology is false and contrary to Christianity.

In the early Middle Ages, astrology seemed destined to disappear in the face of orthodox disapproval. Texts from which one could learn the details of the art were nearly impossible to find in Europe. Much of the ancient astrological knowledge was rediscovered by the Moslems, however. During the increased contacts with Moslems in the twelfth century, an interest in the teachings of old Greece and Rome, including astrology, was awakened among Europeans. By then, the pagan terminology of astrology seemed less threatening to the Catholic Church, which was more worried about Christian heresy than PAGANISM.

Through the later medieval period, astrology was a topic of controversy. Many of the best-known Catholic philosophers, such as Thomas Aquinas and PETER ABELARD, saw no conflict between the influence of the heavenly bodies and Christianity, as long as God and human free will were not said to be under their control. Indeed, Abelard was so enthusiastic about the art that he named his son Astrolabe after an instrument for measuring the positions of the stars.

Other church officials feared that belief in the power of the planets competed with faith in God. Bishop Tempier of Paris issued a condemnation of astrology in 1277.

Nonetheless, actual persecution of astrologers appears to have been uncommon. An exceptional case involved Italian astrologer CECCO D'ASCOLI, burned at the stake in 1327 for attempting to calculate Christ's horoscope.

During the Renaissance, astrology became an accepted feature of the orthodox world view. Even popes had personal astrologers. Italian occultist MARSILIO FICINO promoted the idea that spiritual influences from the planets should be attracted and harmonized in one's life in order to be healthy; he tried to avoid the suspicion that his celestial spirits were actually DEMONS. Another Florentine philosopher, GIOVANNI PICO DELLA MIRANDOLA, retained the belief in astral influences, but he rejected the idea that one can foretell the future from the stars. In the sixteenth century, unorthodox healer PARACELSUS insisted that knowledge of astrology was essential for medical practitioners, so that the appropriate celestial effects could be added to medicines.

With the rise of science, the movements of the planets were explained via the physical laws of motion. The new world view of the universe as a great machine rather than as a living being, did not recognize the existence of any links between earth and the heavens except for gravity and light; astrology was increasingly seen as a pseudoscience. The discovery of two planets, Uranus in 1781 and Neptune in 1846, was not predicted by astrology. This further reduced the credibility of the ancient art. Strangely, many of the founders of modern science, such as GALILEO and Kepler, were themselves practicing astrologers.

Astrology's decline began to reverse in the later nineteenth century. A general interest in the occult, represented by such movements as SPIRITUALISM and THEOSOPHY, reflected a growing sense that the mainstream scientific perspective was too limited to grasp all of reality. In this atmosphere, astrology was resurrected, particularly by ritual magicians, who included the art of the stars in their grand synthesis of Western esoteric traditions. The return of astrology was further spurred in the 1930s when daily horoscopes proved to be incredibly popular features in mass-circulation newspapers. Although orthodox science refuses to credit astrology a shred of validity, the intuition of a deep connection between daily life and the heavens persists.

AUTO-DA-FE   The trial and public torment of heretics, known as the "Act of Faith," was a notorious activity of the SPANISH INQUISITION. After trials, the convicted heretics would be forced to parade through the streets, often forming long processions, to receive the abuse of the crowds. During the *Auto-da-fe*, the heretics were made to wear a special costume, the *san benito*, which consisted of a yellow robe that was decorated front and back with a red cross, and a tall yellow hat. Heretics who had refused to repent had hideous demons embroidered on their clothes, and received special attention from the mob. The victims of the inquisition had to be executed, by being burned at the stake, within five days of their conviction. *Autos-da-fe* were conducted in the colonies of Mexico, Colombia, and Peru, as well as in the Spanish homeland, into the late eighteenth century.

BABAI THE GREAT   An important theologian of the Christian heresy called NESTORIANISM, Babai the Great was the patriarch of the Nestorian community in Kaskar, Persia, during the seventh century. He wrote a comprehensive summary of Nestorian doctrines, attempting to clarify the points of difference among the

Nestorians, the orthodox church, and other heretical groups. According to Babai, the Nestorians agree with orthodoxy in believing that Christ has both a divine and a human nature, and is a single Person. Babai taught that Christ has two *hypostases*, a Greek word that the orthodox used as a synonym for "person." According to Babai, *hypostasis* is a characteristic of a person, but is not identical with a person. Nestorians and Catholics were unable to agree on this point. Babai died around A.D. 628.

BARSUMAS (1)   An early leader of the heresy called MONOPHYSITISM, which emerged during the mid-fifth century. Barsumas, an ally of EUTYCHES, the first Monophysite, played a role at the ROBBER COUNCIL of A.D. 449, where the Monophysites declared the Catholic belief in Christ's two natures to be a heresy. Barsumas, along with the other Monophysites, was himself labeled a heretic at the COUNCIL OF CHALCEDON in 451. He died seven years later.

BARSUMAS (2)   An early leader of the heresy called NESTORIANISM, which taught that Christ was composed of two distinct Persons. Barsumas was born around A.D. 420, eleven years before the Nestorian doctrine was declared heretical. Unwelcome within the Catholic-controlled Roman Empire, many Nestorians moved beyond its borders. Barsumas became the Nestorian bishop of the town of Nisibis in Mesopotamia. Under his guidance, Nisibis became a major haven for Nestorians. He died around 490.

BASILIDEAN GNOSTICISM   One of the earliest known teachers in the spiritual movement of GNOSTICISM, which swept the Mediterranean regions during the first few centuries A.D., was BASILIDES. He inaugurated an important school of Christian Gnosticism. Basilidean Gnosticism proved to be a major influence on other Gnostic schools and was regarded with alarm by the Catholic Church, which attacked it—first in writing, declaring it to be a heresy, and later by consigning the books of the Basilideans to the flames.

The approach of the Basilidean school shares certain features with many other Gnostic groups. For instance, the orthodox critics describe a complicated Basilidean myth recounting how the cosmos was created and showing the path to salvation. The two primary witnesses to the Basilidean tradition, the orthodox church fathers Hippolytus and Irenaeus, report differing versions of the myth. It is likely that several versions were in circulation, and that Hippolytus preserved an early account whereas Irenaeus reported a later version.

According to Hippolytus, the Basilideans believed that in the beginning there was absolutely nothing. This nothing was neither substance nor non-substance; in fact, it cannot be described in terms of any of the categories of human thought and as such is completely beyond comprehension. Within this inconceivable nothingness was an inconceivable, nonexistent God who proceeded to create a nonexistent universe, in the manner of a spider spinning a web.

Within this bizarre realm was a tiny seed that contained the entire existent cosmos. Inside the seed was a spiritual element of three parts called the Sonship. Two parts of the Sonship journeyed to meet the nonexistent God, but the third part did not. Somehow, these actions began the process of creating the world of existence.

The Holy Spirit formed a boundary in the sky, separating the cosmos from the realm beyond. A great being, called an archon, hatched from the seed material into the cosmos. He created another archon as his son, and this archon in turn created another. The first archon is known as the Demiurge. The archons proceeded to fashion the world we know, including human beings.

However, the archons did not know about the nonexistent god or the triple Sonship and believed that they themselves were the supreme beings. In addition, the part of the Sonship that had not gone to the nonexistent god was hidden within the cosmos shaped by the archons, dwelling as the spiritual element within a small group of people who themselves were not aware of it.

The world described in this myth was thought to be out of balance because the world above (the Sonship) and the world below are mixed together. This state of affairs creates suffering. The Sonship hidden in the cosmos has to be restored, with its other two parts, to the domain of the nonexistent god. In order to accomplish the restoration, an entity named the Gospel entered the cosmos.

First, the Gospel taught the archons the truth about their place in the universe. This being then descended to earth. The first person touched by the Gospel was Jesus, who was "illuminated and set on fire by the light which shone upon him." (This doctrine regarding Jesus' relationship to the divine appears to be a very early example of the heresy of ADOPTIONISM.) After teaching the Gospel message to others, Jesus ascended to the realm beyond the sky.

Those humans who contain a spiritual element (the Sonship) are called on to awaken to their true nature as beings who belong in the world beyond. This self-knowledge is called GNOSIS, and the simple recognition of one's spiritual self is sufficient to liberate the person.

When all spiritual beings have passed beyond, the worlds will be disentangled, and the restoration of balance will be complete. At this time, a "Great Ignorance" will come upon the archons and their fellow creatures. They will forget everything about the spiritual realm above them, so they will not yearn to go to there and will not be dissatisfied with their own nonspiritual world.

The alternative version of the great Basilidean myth, preserved by Irenaeus, more closely resembles other Gnostic systems, such as that of VALENTINIAN GNOSTICISM. According to this account, the original being was the unborn Father who projects from himself an entity called Mind. Thus begins a series of emanations: Mind projects Word, who projects Understanding, who projects Sophia and Power. These last two beings create a realm of angels who continue the sequence of emanations until 365 heavens populated by divine beings have been created.

The chief of the last and lowest heaven is the being known on earth as the God of the Jews, regarded in the Old Testament as the creator. In reality, said the Basilideans, this God fashioned only the visible world, not the vast spiritual realms above Him.

Power struggles between this low-level creator and other beings in the heavens are said to cause the pain and imperfection of human life. The unborn Father took pity on humanity and sent Mind to teach the means of escape. Mind appeared on earth as Jesus Christ and imparted the secret way to travel back to the Father.

Because He was purely spiritual, Jesus did not have a physical body (the heresy of DOCETISM.) Irenaeus recounts an amazing story of how Jesus tricked the Romans into crucifying another man instead of himself by magically switching appearanceswith the innocent man, Simon of Cyrene. Jesus, in the guise of Simon, stood nearby during the crucifixion, laughing at the illusion He had created.

The intricate and weird myths of the Basilideans seem distant from the realities of everyday life. The orthodox critics of the Basilideans ridiculed the stories as useless figments of imagination. However, like other Gnostic tales, the Basilidean myths were not meant to be taken only as accounts of creation, but as guides to spiritual life. For instance, the version of Hippolytus, which emphasizes that recognition (gnosis) of one's true spiritual nature produces salvation, encouraged people to engage in meditation practices designed to increase self-awareness.

The Basilidean vision presented by Irenaeus highlights the tremendous distance and myriad obstacles (365 heavens full of supernatural beings!) one must climb in order to reach the unborn Father. This Gnostic tradition taught that knowledge of the heavenly inhabitants' names, when employed in magical chants and inscribed on amulets, ensured a safe passage upward through the divine layers. Rituals involving the visualization of the spiritual journey were probably practiced. The notion of these Egyptian Gnostics that name magic could be used to travel safely in the other world is very similar to the beliefs connected with *The Egyptian Book of the Dead* and might be derived from them.

Although none of the original writings of the Basilidean teachers have survived, physical traces of this school remain. Charms of stone or gems, carved with the magical images and names of the Basilidean universe, are preserved in many museum collections today. Some of these relics depict a powerful deity named Abraxas or Abrasax, a rooster-headed being with snakes for legs, brandishing a whip. The famous magic word "abracadabra" is thought to derive from his name.

BASILIDES   This Egyptian heretic was the first great teacher within the tradition of Christian GNOSTICISM. Basilides was known, by admirer and detractor alike, as a person of immense knowledge and creativity. He promoted a version of Christianity that included mystical themes from unorthodox Jewish and pagan sources.

Little is known about the life of Basilides. He was probably born in Alexandria, the intellectual center of the Roman Empire at the time, during the late first century A.D., and remained there his whole life. Christianity was in an early, formative period, and there was no recognized authority to decide which ideas about Christ should be called orthodox and which should be condemned as heresy. As a result, there was a tremendous diversity of Christian teaching.

Basilides stated that he studied under a man named GLAUCAS, who claimed to have been taught by Peter, the chief apostle of Jesus. Glaucas reported that Christ had given secret teachings to his closest followers that were not shared with the public. Basilides was privileged to learn these hidden doctrines himself.

In the liberal atmosphere of second century Alexandria, Basilides was able to teach his ideas openly, and he soon attracted many students. His doctrine that some people could attain salvation through developing a special insight called GNOSIS stirred controversy. Many of the priests and bishops of the young Christian Church were teaching that only they preserved the message given by Christ to the apostles, and that the cultivation of gnosis was not part of the Lord's authentic doctrine. Rather, they preached, Christians should be encouraged to learn from and obey the church authorities and thereby attain heaven.

Basilides and other Gnostics presented a powerful and threatening alternative to the Christianity of this priestly group. Basilides died around 140, and students continued to propound his thought as BASILIDEAN GNOSTICISM. But eloquent critics representing the non-Gnostic party, such as Irenaeus and Hippolytus, published written attacks in which they declared that Basilides was a heretic. Ultimately their arguments and political power prevailed. The works of Basilides were destroyed, and today we must attempt to reconstruct the main features of his system from the descriptions his enemies recorded.

BASIL OF ANCYRA   This teacher of the Christian heresy called ARIANISM played a significant role in the battle for control of the church (and the church's attempt to control the Roman Empire) in the fourth century. Around A.D. 356, Basil of Ancyra founded the Arian group known as the HOMOIOUSIANS who claimed, against both the orthodox believers and the more RADICAL ARIANS, that God the Father and the Son had similar natures. Basil influenced Emperor CONSTANTIUS to banish many of the radical Arian leaders, including their founder, AETIUS. The political winds of the time shifted quickly, however; a few years later, in 360, Basil lost favor and was himself exiled.

BASIL THE BOGOMIL   Basil the Bogomil was an important leader of the heretical BOGOMILS during the early 1100s. During the century and a half since their founding, the Bogomils had organized themselves into a church with a structure parallel to that of the orthodox church in Byzantium. Basil was the Bogomil bishop of Constantinople. He was summoned by Byzantine Emperor Alexius, who pretended an interest in Bogomil doctrines in order to entrap him. While Basil earnestly explained his beliefs to Alexius, a scribe hidden behind a curtain noted everything the heretical bishop said. The emperor confronted Basil with this record of his unorthodoxy and demanded that he renounce Bogomilism. When Basil refused, he was imprisoned. It is said that Alexius visited Basil several times during his confinement, pleading with him to give up his heresy, to no avail. Finally, the emperor, following the advice of his orthodox advisers, ordered the Bogomil bishop to be burned at the stake.

One of the most important surviving sources of information concerning Bogomil doctrines is the *Dogmatic Panoply* of Euthymius Zigabenus. This book is supposed to be based on the notes taken by the hidden scribe during Basil's discussion with Emperor Alexius.

BEGHARDS   The BEGUINES' movement, which became prominent across Europe during the thirteenth and fourteenth centuries, was composed primarily of women. However, some men did become involved. In northern Europe, the male Beguines were known as Beghards. Some Beghards lived in a fixed abode, making a living by producing crafts; many others chose the wandering life, sustaining themselves through begging. The Beghards suffered a great deal of persecution. The wanderers were resented because they were fit enough to work for a living but chose to beg instead. They were also suspected of holding unorthodox views, such as the Heresy of the FREE SPIRIT. Under pressure from the INQUISITION, many Beghards decided to submit to papal authority and were allowed to continue as a Catholic movement in France. They were wiped out during the French Revolution.

BEGUINES   The late medieval Beguine movement marked the first time in Christian history that women had assumed a dominant role in a spiritual organization. In the early thirteenth century, lifestyle options for European women were quite limited: marriage or entering a nunnery were the only socially acceptable choices. However, there were more women than men in the towns, and the capacity of the nunneries was limited. The Beguines arose in part to provide an alternative. The new movement soon became a breeding ground for heresy.

Shortly before 1200, women began to band together in small communities in the towns along the Rhine River in northern France, Germany, and Holland. They viewed themselves as members of religious groups, taking vows of chastity; unlike nuns, however, they did not retreat from the world. Instead, they established communal houses in the midst of the urban bustle and participated in town life by producing crafts and caring for the sick. No one knows who started the movement. There was little organization at first; the Beguine communities emerged as a spontaneous experiment, driven by the restricted choices for women.

There was a strong response to the idea. And within a few years, houses of Beguines had appeared in cities and towns throughout western and central Europe. The name "Beguine" comes from the word "Albigensian," which is a name for the CATHAR heretics. How the name became attached to the new communities is unclear because they certainly did not hold Cathar beliefs. Although the movement primarily attracted women, some men also became involved. In southern Europe, both males and females were called Beguines; north of the Alps, women were designated Beguines, while men were known as BEGHARDS.

The Catholic Church was uneasy about the Beguines from the beginning because the movement had come into existence without its permission and tended to operate without orthodox supervision. Catholic officials suspected that heretical ideas were being discussed within the Beguine houses. Their suspicions were heightened by the admiration many Beguines displayed for the members of another dubious group, the SPIRITUAL FRANCISCANS. Both the Beguines and the Spirituals were potentially dangerous to orthodoxy; they had frequent contact with the populace, and their humble, pious lifestyles highlighted the difference between the lives of the wealthy church officials and those of the apostles in the New Testament.

In an attempt to keep the Beguines from straying into heresy, Pope Gregory IX officially recognized the movement in 1233. For several decades, the Beguines maintained their acceptability; in 1264, King Louis IX founded a house of Beguines in Paris. However, marginal and outright heretical groups were challenging the authority of the church across Europe, and the tolerance of orthodoxy toward the relatively independent Beguines began to wane.

Some Beguines were exploring unorthodox views. The teachings of the Spiritual Franciscan PIERRE OLIVI, which emphasized the decadent moral state of the Catholic Church, were popular, and some of the works of the heretic AMALRIC OF BENA, whose writings the church burned in 1210, were preserved and studied by Beguines. Mysticism, the experience of union with God, was cultivated. Mystics were on the edge of orthodoxy, and many crossed the boundary into heresy. Mechtild of Magdeburg was a Beguine who managed to remain on the orthodox side of the line; she was the author of the renowned text *The Flowing Light of the Godhead* and was one of the greatest Catholic mystics of the thirteenth century. The notion that women were discussing theology at all, much less entertaining heretical ideas, was quite irritating to many men within the church and was later used as an excuse to condemn them.

In 1274, the orthodox Council of Lyons banned the movement in France, but there was little reaction. The Spirituals, aided by the Beguines and other citizens, were becoming a popular opposition to the orthodox in southern France. In 1299, a council at Beziers repeated the call for the Beguines to disband.

In 1313, an uprising in the southern French centers of Beziers and Narbonne chased away the Franciscans favored by orthodoxy and installed Spirituals in their place. When Pope John XXII came to power three years later, he targeted the Beguines as a way to undermine the support system of the rebellious Spirituals. John issued a condemnation of the movement: "It has been repeatedly and reliably reported to us that some of them, as if possessed with madness, dispute and preach about the highest Trinity and the divine essence; therefore, we must prohibit forever their status and abolish them completely from the church of God."

The INQUISITION went into action. Many Beguines were forced to submit to the authority of the pope; some refused and were burned at the stake. As usual, the persecution radicalized some members who began to preach that Pope John and the Catholic Church were beyond redemption. The Inquisitors operated efficiently in the south of France, and there was little opposition to them after 1325.

Meanwhile, in the Rhineland, the Beguine movement had given birth to a new heresy, the Brothers and Sisters of the FREE SPIRIT. These heretics wandered from town to town, claiming that they had been perfected by the Holy Spirit and were now above all laws. The Free Spirit heretics were condemned by the Council of Vienne in 1311, and they kept the inquisitors busy for well over a century.

The Beguines endured this dark period and managed to make peace with the church. A few small communities of Beguines survive to the present day in Belgium and the Netherlands, bearing witness to the first sustained attempt at women's liberation, 800 years ago.

See also: MEISTER ECKHART.

BENTIVENGA OF GUBBIO   This friar was a member of the Italian heresy known as the APOSTOLICI. In 1304, these heretics organized a peasant uprising in northern Italy; Catholic Crusaders crushed it three years later, and the Apostolici were slaughtered. Bentivenga of Gubbio escaped and joined the Catholic order of Franciscan friars. From among the friars he put together a group called the Sect of the Spirit of Freedom. Bentivenga taught that anyone who received the Holy Spirit into their hearts was free from having to obey any kind of law or moral rule. The Franciscans did not tolerate such unorthodoxy and confined Bentivenga to a monastery for the rest of his life.

See also: HERESY OF THE FREE SPIRIT.

BERENGAR   This eleventh century theologian revived the controversy regarding the nature of Christ's presence at the Mass, which had stirred the Roman Catholic Church 200 years earlier. Berengar received condemnations for heresy from the orthodox authorities, despite the eloquence of his arguments, and the documents of papal approval he seems to have forged in his defense.

Born around A.D. 1010 in France, Berengar served in several roles within the church during his lifetime, including archdeacon and treasurer of a cathedral. His notoriety began when he wrote a book criticizing the theory of the Mass invented by ninth century theologian Radbertus. Radbertus taught that when the bread and wine are consecrated during the Mass, they are miraculously and invisibly transformed into flesh and blood from Jesus' body. This view had become the dominant understanding in the Catholic Church.

Berengar felt it was obvious that the bread and wine consumed at the Mass was not physically transformed into anything else. As a devout Catholic, he believed that Christ was actually present in the sacramental materials, but that this holy presence did not require a literal change in the substances themselves; the transformation occurs on the level of spirit, not substance. Berengar's theory became known as impanation.

The impanation theory was immediately misunderstood. Many of Berengar's contemporaries thought that Christ's *real* presence in the sacraments required His *bodily* presence. They could not grasp Berengar's idea of a *real spiritual* presence that was not substantial. Berengar was understood to mean that the holy presence was merely symbolic. Some took this notion to be heresy.

In 1050, two church councils condemned Berengar's teaching. With the protection of some powerful friends within the church, Berengar continued to proclaim his views. On three occasions, in 1059, 1079, and 1080, he was summoned to Rome, where he was forced to sign statements in favor of the doctrine of the bodily presence. Each time, Berengar reverted to his original view on the matter upon his return to France.

In addition to this doctrinal flexibility, Berengar appears to have employed another talent in his defense, forgery. Once, when confronted by a Catholic official regarding his teaching, he produced a letter supporting his orthodoxy from Pope Alexander, but the pontiff had not written the letter. On another occasion, a papal proclamation was circulated that condemned anyone who called Berengar a heretic. Again, the true author is uncertain, but it was not the pope.

The resourceful theologian died around 1088, having managed to avoid punishment for his unconventional ideas during his lifetime. The orthodox rejection of the impanation theory strengthened the position of those Christians who supported Radbertus's ideas. In 1215, the doctrine of the bodily presence (known by then as "transubstantiation") was proclaimed a dogma of the Roman Catholic Church. Thereafter, anyone who denied it was labeled a heretic, subject to automatic excommunication and bound for hell.

See also: AMATORY MASS, BLACK MASS, RATRAMNUS.

Johannes BINGGELI   Johannes Binggeli was founder of the FOREST BROTHERHOOD, an unorthodox spiritual group that flourished in Switzerland during the latter part of the nineteenth century. Born in 1834, Binggeli was a tailor; however, he was subject to visions and out-of-body experiences, during which he traveled to spiritual worlds. Around 1870, he published a book of his experiences; shortly afterward, he organized the Forest Brotherhood.

Bingelli's cult centered around divine powers attributed to his genitals. His penis was known as the "box of Christ," and his urine was thought to have miraculous properties. Using a special sexual technique, he conducted exorcisms of women believed to be possessed. In 1896, he exorcised his own daughter, who became pregnant. Binggelli was packed off to a mental asylum. His disciples lobbied for his release; five years later, this was granted on the condition that he not maintain contact with the Brotherhood. Gradually his support waned, but his book continued to sell steadily for many years.

BLACK MASS   This term has been used to refer to a variety of practices, some of them quite orthodox, and others quite the opposite. While accusations of conducting the black mass figure prominently in the history of persecuting heretics and witches, the actual performance of such rituals has been rare.

Within the tradition of Roman Catholicism, "black mass" is simply another name for the Requiem Mass, or Mass for the Dead. This ceremony, performed by a priest in order to speed the transition of the departed soul from purgatory to heaven, required the use of black candles and was known as the black mass for that reason.

In medieval Europe, the body and blood of Christ was believed miraculously to replace the substance of the bread and wine during the Catholic Mass. This is known as the doctrine of transubstantiation. Many people, including priests, maintained that this presence of Christ gave the performance of the Mass special powers. The Mass began to be viewed as a sort of magical battery, a source of miraculous influence that could be directed to whatever end the priest wished. Sometimes, the ceremony of the Mass was held for such acceptable purposes as blessing fleets of boats in order to increase the fishermen's catch. But some priests were trying to use the magic of Christ's presence to make money, attract women, or even to kill.

In the seventh century, a church council in Toledo, Spain, condemned priests who were conducting the Requiem Mass using the names of living persons in attempts to hasten their deaths. References to the cursing mass appear periodically in later medieval literature. Perhaps the most extreme case was reported in 1500 in northern France. An entire congregation gathered in the cathedral at Cambrai to participate in a mass to kill their bishop, with whom they had a disagreement.

A well-known version of the murderous mass is the Mass of Saint Secaire. This ritual was described in a nineteenth century collection of folklore from southwestern France and is thought by some to date back to the Middle Ages. Secaire is unknown to any biographer of saints. Historian H. T. F. Rhodes suggested that his name derives from the term *sekha*, which in the Basque language refers to a fat man becoming thin. This explanation is plausible because the object of this Mass was to cause the victim to waste away in a slow death. Secaire's Mass was supposed to be performed in a ruined church at night by a priest and his mistress. The ritual involved reciting prayers backward and filling the chalice with water that had been used to drown a child. These details clearly indicate that the Mass of Saint Secaire deviates dramatically from the form, as well as the intent, of the orthodox Mass.

Whether or not anyone was actually performing such distorted ceremonies as Saint Secaire's Mass, by late medieval times the authorities were beginning to worry that heretics were practicing deliberate perversions of sacred rites. Such groups as the CATHARS, WALDENSIANS, and BOGOMILS were accused of trampling on the cross and ingesting excrement in obscene inversions of the Mass. In the case of the Bogomils, the cross trampling seems possible; this sect hated the cross as the instrument of Christ's torture and condemned the orthodox for using it as a holy symbol. Generally, though, these accusations were part of the persecutors' campaign of lies to frame the heretics as devotees of SATANISM.

The notion that people met in secret to perform blasphemous ceremonies patterned on the Catholic Mass became part of the standard accusation against witches during the GREAT WITCH HUNT of the fifteenth through seventeenth centuries. The consecrated bread and wine, stolen from a church, were said to be cursed and crushed underfoot by the assembled witches as part of their Satanic practices. Urine and a rotten turnip or an old black boot were reportedly used in place of the wine and bread. The idea of the witches' mass was part of the general belief that witches were devil worshippers. Since Satan was the reverse of God, many people thought that Satanists would invert or parody orthodox practices in order to please their horned master. These Satanic masses existed mainly in the imaginations of the Inquisitors, who tortured their victims into verifying every detail of the official fantasy.

It is not until the late seventeenth century, with the confirmed appearance of Satanism in France, that we find the first evidence for the actual performance of a Satanic mass, the "black mass" in the commonly understood modern sense of the term. During the reign of Louis XIV, a decadent attitude became prevalent among the upper classes of French society. Bored rich people sought bizarre thrills, and experimentation with the occult became common. In this atmosphere, a group formed and began to practice a ritual combining the pseudo-orthodox cursing mass with elements from the imaginary Satanic masses that heretics and witches were accused of performing. A member of this circle named Madame de Montespan decided to employ magic in order to seduce the king. An AMATORY MASS was conducted three times, of which one ceremony involved the sacrifice of doves by tearing out their hearts. This enterprising woman got her wish and became King Louis's mistress.

But sometime later, she began to fear that the king's attention was wandering to other women. Madame de Montespan arranged for a more powerful form of unorthodox mass to be performed, with explicitly Satanic elements. During this ritual, presided over by the corrupt priest ABBÉ GUIBOURG, a naked woman wearing a mask lay on the altar while a priest inserted a holy wafer into her vagina. Then a child was killed. Its blood was drained into a cup while prayers were said to DEMONS Asmodeus and Ashtaroth, asking these evil spirits to draw the king's love to Madame de Montespan.

Eventually, King Louis seemed to grow bored with his Satanic lover, and the decision was made to murder the king through magical means. A cursing mass was performed. During the ceremony, a weird concoction of semen, menstrual blood, powdered bats, wine, and flour was prepared. The group planned to introduce this delicacy into the monarch's food in order to direct to him the deadly force of the black mass. Before this task was accomplished, the police discovered the Satanists' activities and ended them.

It is possible that the French interest in the black mass continued after the breakup of this Satanic circle. In the mid-nineteenth century, the heretical CHURCH OF CARMEL appeared in northern France, headed by EUGENE VINTRAS. Vintras conducted a strange version of the mass that he called the "Provictimal Sacrifice of Mary." During this ritual, Vintras wore an inverted crucifix, a Satanic trademark. While the content of these deviant masses was not overtly evil, people who attended them reported some very strange experiences. Some witnesses claimed to see blood oozing from the consecrated bread; others perceived a fat pigeon perched on the priest's shoulder, representing the Holy Spirit. Vintras might also have performed secret rituals with his closest disciples that were closer to the black masses of Madame de Montespan and her cohorts. Some former followers of Vintras claimed that they had attended ceremonies that he organized, and that featured nudity and masturbation.

Whatever Vintras had been up to, there is no doubt concerning his successor as the leader of the Church of Carmel, Abbé BOULLAN. This priest founded an order called the SOCIETY FOR THE REPARATION OF SOULS, which specialized in exorcising demons from possessed women. His special technique involved feeding the victims a mixture of sacramental bread and feces. Boullan's willingness to combine the sacred and profane in such a manner certainly indicates a personality that would not hesitate to tamper with the Holy Mass of Catholicism. And, indeed, in private Boullan and his lover were conducting black masses, probably inspired by the rituals of Abbé Guibourg. At one of these rites, they allegedly sacrificed their own child to Satan. Boullan became head of the Church of Carmel after Vintras's death and continued to practice Satanic masses involving strange sexual acts and blood sacrifices.

One of Boullan's associates was a writer named J. K. Huysmans. In a novel called *Là-Bas* (Down There), Huysmans describes the performance of a black mass. While he always refused to say whether he had ever attended such a ceremony, some researchers believe that the novelistic account is essentially an eyewitness description. Huysmans's black mass included many of the standard elements, such as reversals of orthodox Christian prayers and symbols, group sex, and the defilement of consecrated wafers. The novel has been a major influence on more recent portrayals of the black mass in books, movies, and the popular imagination.

Another nineteenth century French writer was Jules Michelet. He published a book about the Great Witch Hunt, in which he labels the ritual said to be performed by the witches the "black mass." Michelet believed that an organization of witches actually existed during the Renaissance and Reformation periods, but that it was basically a social-protest movement. According to Michelet, this organization of downtrodden peasants worshipped an image of Satan during the black mass as an act of defiance against the dominating classes. Michelet's romantic and highly inaccurate view of the factors underlying the witch hunt has been rejected by more modern scholars.

Today, very few people believe that the Catholic Mass is a reservoir of magical power that can be directed by the will of the performer. It seems unlikely that anyone still performs the cursing mass in its "orthodox" form. Regarding the Satanic mass, some occult societies perform rituals involving the inverting or defiling of Christian practices, but such groups form a tiny minority within the modern community of occult interests.

BLACK PULLET   This book is the best known of a series of magical handbooks, or GRIMOIRES, that first appeared in the late eighteenth century. As in the case of most grimoires, the author of *The Black Pullet* is unknown. According to this work, the magical secrets it contains were learned when the author, during a visit to Egypt, was taken inside a pyramid by a mysterious man. There, the author received occult instruction.

The first part of the book describes how to make magical rings that enable a magician to evoke the spirits of fire known as salamanders. These spirits give the magician many useful powers, such as invisibility, immunity from fierce animals, and good luck in lotteries. The second section of *The Black Pullet* instructs how to create a magical chicken. This creature, it is claimed, will lead the seeker to buried gold.

The book ends with a warning that all who produce pirated versions of this grimoire will be magically punished by having their ears grow to a gigantic size. Nevertheless, *The Black Pullet* inspired several other equally odd magical texts, with such names as *Red Dragon*, *Black Screech Owl*, and even *Queen of the Hairy Flies*.

The Black Pullet and derivative works are noteworthy in the grimoire genre because much of the symbolic material they contain seems to be unrelated to the standard images of the Western magical tradition.

Giorgio BLANDRATA   An important figure in the establishment of the ANTI-TRINITARIAN heresy in central Europe during the sixteenth century, Giorgio Blandrata was born in Italy around 1515. He was attracted to the more radical versions of the Protestant Reformation; like many Italian radicals of the time, he moved to Poland, which tolerated religious differences. He became the court physician and a well-known theologian who wished to reject all the elaborate dogmas that Christian orthodoxy had been accumulating since ancient times.

Blandrata spent much time preaching in Transylvania. There, he taught the heresy of TRITHEISM—that the Father, Son and Holy Spirit of the Christian Trinity are separate divine beings, made of distinct substances. Blandrata eventually rejected the notion of a Trinity altogether and claimed that everyone should adopt the UNITARIAN perspective of a single, unified God. He predicted that the Second Coming of Christ would occur in 1570. Blandrata died, presumably disappointed, around 1588.

See also: FERENC DAVID, FRANCESCO STANCARI.

BLASPHEMY   This term derives from the Greek word *blasphemia*, which means "offensive speech concerning matters of religion." The ancient Greeks took blasphemy seriously. Socrates was condemned to death for his unconventional philosophical discussions, which were thought to offend the gods. Philosopher Anaxagoras and sculptor Phidias were jailed for blasphemy, and philosophers Protagoras and Aristotle were exiled. Plato viewed the classical Greek myths, which portrayed the gods behaving irrationally, as blasphemous. In *The Republic*, he calls for such stories to be banned; in *The Laws*, he recommends the death penalty for blasphemy.

The Old Testament agrees with Plato on this matter. Leviticus (24:16) states, "And he that blasphemeth the name of the Lord, he shall surely be put to death, and all the congregation shall certainly stone him: as well the stranger, as he that is born in the land, when he blasphemeth the name of the Lord, shall be put to death."

The early Christians seem to have been somewhat more relaxed than the Jews concerning blasphemy. In the Gospel of Mark (3:28–29), Christ proclaims, "All sins shall be forgiven unto the sons of men, and blasphemies wherewith soever they shall blaspheme: But he that shall blaspheme against the Holy Spirit hath never forgiveness, but is in danger of eternal damnation." Exactly what blaspheming "against the Holy Spirit" means has been a subject of debate through the centuries.

In the period in which orthodox Christianity defined Western reality, the notion of blasphemy was extended from offensive words about God to the disrespectful use of religious symbols. Witches were accused of trampling crosses and defiling the wafer of the Eucharist during their initiation ceremonies. Traditional SATANISM is based on blasphemous inversions of standard Christian symbols, such as worshipping the Devil instead of God, displaying the cross upside down, and reciting the Lord's Prayer backward. Throughout the later Middle Ages and the Renaissance, such behaviors, when suspected by the authorities, often resulted in swift execution.

Blasphemy laws remain on the books in many Western countries today, although they are seldom used. In 1968, for example, Maryland magistrate Charles Simpson dusted off the state's 1723 blasphemy statute. In its original form the statute calls for boring through the blasphemer's tongue with a hot iron for the first offense, branding a "B" on the forehead for a second offense, and death for a third offense. Simpson encouraged state troopers to charge speeders with the crime if they uttered "God damn" when receiving their tickets. The state Court of Special Appeals overturned Simpson's convictions. But the U.S. Supreme Court has never declared a blasphemy law unconstitutional.

Madame Helena Petrovna BLAVATSKY

One of the most influential figures in the history of modern occultism, Madame Helena Petrovna Blavatsky transmitted her vision of reality to many millions through her organization, the Theosophical Society, and her major writings, *Isis Unveiled* and *The Secret Doctrine*. The world view of Blavatsky has affected or given rise to a large number of unorthodox groups in the twentieth century.

Born Helena von Hahn to an aristocratic family at Ekaterinoslav, Ukraine, in 1831, the future occultist seems to have been brilliant and rebellious during her youth. These traits characterized her throughout her life. She married Nikifor Blavatsky, a Ukrainian vice-governor, at seventeen, but the marriage lasted only briefly.

For the next few decades, Madame Blavatsky's activities are not well documented. She traveled widely, seeking adventure and wisdom. The wanderer may have had access to money from her family to finance her journeys. She often acted as a medium in the SPIRITUALIST movement that was sweeping the Western world at the time. By Blavatsky's own account, she learned esoteric secrets from many spiritual masters, especially Tibetans, during these years.

In 1873, she arrived in New York. There, she met Colonel Henry Olcott, an enthusiastic Spiritualist who quickly became a great admirer of Blavatsky and her psychic powers. By the following year, they had established an apartment that turned into a center for parties, discussions, and demonstrations of occult phenomena. It was here that Blavatsky and Olcott, along with Henry Judge, founded the Theosophical Society.

Until her death in 1891, Blavatsky was the unchallenged leader of the Society. Her writings almost had the status of gospels for the theosophists. *Isis Unveiled*, published in 1877, was an attempt to bring together various strands of mystical philosophy into a unified world view. She claimed to be in touch with a secret brotherhood that had preserved the secrets of magic since ancient times. In this work, she drew heavily on the KABBALAH, as well as Egyptian magic. Most readers have found parts of the book to be almost impossible to follow; the report that Blavatsky consumed a large quantity of hashish during the course of writing the work may be relevant here. But her lack of clarity helped to produce an impression of hinted wisdom that intrigued her devoted readers. Blavatsky was a master at creating an atmosphere of tantalizing mystery around everything she did, and many people became convinced that she had access to spiritual secrets far greater than those she shared.

In 1878, Blavatsky and Olcott went to India, where they set up the world head-quarters for the Theosophical Society in Adyar, near Madras. During the remainder of her life, the Society grew dramatically around the world. Blavatsky's teachings combined two attractive ideas: the Spiritualist promise of direct proof of the spirit world, and the notion that, behind the scenes, a society of mystic masters was working for the good of the universe. Furthermore, the masters occasionally made contact with more ordinary mortals. Blavatsky herself, of course, had many such encounters, as had some of those around her. Sometimes, letters written by a hidden master would materialize, seemingly from nowhere, to impress Blavatsky's followers. The hope—or delusion—of making contact with a master oneself was a favorite fantasy of many theosophists.

Eventually, the reports of supernatural occurrences surrounding Blavatsky, as well as allegations of fraud, attracted the attention of the newly founded Society for Psychical Research (SPR). In Blavatsky's absence, eminent psychical researcher Richard Hodgson visited Adyar and uncovered clear evidence of trickery. For in-stance, a cabinet within which letters from the hidden masters had often myste-riously appeared was found to have a false back. The SPR report concluded that the theosophical leader was "one of the most accomplished, ingenious and interesting impostors of history." Oddly, this revelation did not seriously damage Blavatsky's popularity. The Theosophical Society continued to grow. There were far fewer reports of strange phenomena, however.

Blavatsky published her masterpiece, *The Secret Doctrine*, three years before her death in 1891. This book, which is more coherent than her earlier work, presents a grand combination of ideas drawn from Eastern as well as Western sources. It thus appealed strongly to people who wanted to believe that all of the world's religions contain the same underlying truths. The universe is portrayed as a vast process of spiritual evolution. Every soul progressively reincarnates through a succession of worlds and races until enlightenment is reached. The whole process is watched over by a hierarchy of masters, from whom Blavatsky learned this doctrine.

As often happens in large movements, the death of the charismatic founder was followed by the fragmentation of the Theosophical Society. Nevertheless, many of Blavatsky's ideas continued to inspire various imitators and splinter groups. Attempts to communicate with hidden masters who live in the Himalayas, for example, have endured to the present day among some of the devotees of channeling and other esoteric practices.

See also: THEOSOPHY.

Jan BOCKELSON   Ruler over the short-lived "Kingdom of Zion," the unorthodox community set up by the MÜNSTER HERETICS in 1534, Jan Bockelson was a tailor in the Dutch town of Leiden who fell under the sway of the prophet of the ANABAPTISTS, MELCHIOR HOFFMANN. Hoffmann predicted the founding of a New Jerusalem in a European city; when Münster, in Germany, became a haven for Anabaptists, Bockelson traveled there. During the Anabaptist takeover of 1534–1535, Bockelson emerged as a leader. After besieging orthodox troops killed heretic JAN MATTHYS, Bockelson declared himself king of the city. He attracted enough support to have his enemies executed.

At God's order, Bockelson also decreed that polygamy was acceptable; he himself took sixteen wives. He allowed defenses against the siege to lapse. In June 1535, orthodox forces retook the city; King Jan was tortured to death, and his corpse displayed publicly to discourage imitators. Bockelson's excesses tainted the Anabaptist movement as a whole and triggered persecutions across Europe.

BOGOMIL   Founder of the medieval heresy that bears his name, BOGOMILISM, this Macedonian priest introduced a potent form of unorthodox Christianity to eastern Europe and the Byzantine Empire. The teachings of Bogomil, passed on and modified by his successors, formed an important bridge between the ancient doctrines of GNOSTICISM and the major heresies of the later Middle Ages in western Europe.

Although some historians question whether Bogomil ever existed, it is generally agreed that he lived during the mid-tenth century. A town in Macedonia that to this day is called Bogomila is said to be his burial place. The name "Bogomil" means "lover of God" in the Slavonic language.

Bogomil was a priest of the Eastern Orthodox Christian faith. The Kingdom of Bulgaria, which at the time included Macedonia, had officially converted to Christianity less than a century before his lifetime. Coupled with the advent of the new faith was an attempt to install a feudal social structure, in which land ownership was concentrated in the hands of an aristocratic class. People at the top of the church hierarchy tended to be drawn from the higher strata of the feudal society. The peasants, who were situated at the bottom of this structure of social privilege, harbored resentments toward the nobles and the church. Bogomil was able to give religious expression to the peasants' plight.

Bogomil's doctrines are clearly inspired by the dualistic beliefs of ancient GNOSTICISM. How he learned about them remains a mystery. He might have read accounts of the old heresies, such as MANICHAEISM, in church libraries. Contact with the MESSALIANS or the PAULICIANS, Middle Eastern sects that preserved Gnostic views, is also possible.

At some point, Bogomil abandoned his orthodox views and began to wander from village to village, spreading heretical ideas. He taught that the world was created not by a good God, but by an evil being who has opposed God since time began. Christ came to tell humanity of the heavenly world beyond and to liberate people from the clutches of the evil one. Furthermore, the Devil's servants are none other than rich priests and nobles. The preacher pointed out the discrepancy between the indulgent lifestyles of the leading churchmen and the simple ways of Jesus in the Gospels. In Bogomil's own mode of living, he demonstrated the frugality that he praised.

Bogomil's antimaterialist stance held great appeal for country folk. His message spread through the villages of Bulgaria and into the Byzantine-controlled Thracian region. The orthodox authorities perceived that this doctrine, which they regarded as a resurgence of Manichaeism, undermined their spiritual and political positions.

Violent persecution followed. A contemporary orthodox propagandist wrote that the heretic's name was actually "Bogonomil," meaning "God hater." There is no evidence that Bogomil himself ever suffered directly at the hands of the persecutors.

BOGOMILISM   The Bogomils were one of the most influential heresies of the Middle Ages. First appearing in Macedonia during the tenth century, Bogomil communities were later established both in Byzantium and throughout the Balkans. Variants of the Bogomil faith eventually became the state religions of Bosnia and Hungary. Bogomil missionaries spread their beliefs to western Europe, stimulating the rise of the medieval Catholics' most powerful foes, the CATHARS.

The heresy takes its name from its founder, BOGOMIL. He was a village priest in the mountains of Macedonia during the mid-tenth century. During this period, the Balkan region, which the Bulgars controlled, was being organized into a feudal society. The peasants, with very few rights, formed the lowest class, beneath the land-owning nobility. The Bulgars had been forced to become Christians following the conversion of their king less than a century before Bogomil appeared, and the church had quickly allied itself with the privileged classes. Bogomil was able to tap the resentment of the peasants toward the nobles and the church.

At this early stage of its development, Bogomilism was radically dualistic. In the beginning, the Bogomils taught that there were two deities: a good God who created the heavens and an evil being who made the earth. Christ was a representative of the good deity, who came to earth to show humanity how to escape the clutches of the god of matter. The orthodox church and the feudal social structure were both allied with the earthly power; the Bogomils were the bearers of salvation.

The sources of Bogomil doctrine are unclear. Their ideas share common features with several prominent ancient heresies, including GNOSTICISM and MANI-CHAEISM. The early Bogomils may have been influenced by heretics from Asia, the MESSALIANS and especially the PAULICIANS, who are suspected of preserving some of the old unorthodox teachings.

The social organization within the Bogomil movement developed in a manner strongly resembling that of the Manichaean heretics, suggesting some sort of influence. The Bogomil leaders were mainly priests and monks who had abandoned orthodox Christian beliefs and were known as the "Perfecti." They abstained from manual work, sex, and meat-eating because these activities tied one to the earth, which was the domain of evil. The Perfecti often traveled on missionary work. In order to attain this rank, one underwent a simple ceremony called the CONSOLA-MENTUM. Most Bogomils did not live as Perfecti, but married and led ordinary lives. They provided for the leaders' material needs and received their teaching in return. Often, a Bogomil supporter went through the Consolamentum when death was imminent in order to avoid the challenges of the Perfecti lifestyle and still die as one.

Bogomilism's simplicity and its antiestablishment tone led to its rapid diffusion. During the eleventh century, the Bogomils found many converts within the territories of the Byzantine Empire, including the capital, Constantinople. A Bogomil Church paralleling that of the orthodox church, complete with heretical bishops, began to form.

From the first, the mainstream church regarded the Bogomils as dangerous heretics. Violent persecutions were directed against the Bogomils, but they gradually made progress at securing some tolerance, although orthodox church opposition never wavered. A Bogomil named BASIL tried to convert Emperor Alexius, but failed and was burned to death. The Bogomils' greatest missionary success within Byzantium came during the mid-twelfth century, when a Bogomil leader established a friendship with the orthodox patriarch of Constantinople (who was, however, deposed for this lapse).

By this time, Bogomil doctrine had become less radically dualistic and more elaborate. The world had not been created by an originally evil being, but by Satanael, Christ's older brother. Satanael rebelled against God and trapped some ANGELS within material bodies. We are those captured angels, and Christ came to earth to defeat his brother and save us. The Word of God entered Mary's right ear, took on flesh, and was born as Jesus through the same orifice. He succeeded in restraining the evil one, as well as in removing the last three letters of his brother's name (leaving "Satan" as the result). Satan escaped his bondage, however, and returned to rule the earth through his servants, the nobility and the priests. Satan also arranged for Christ to be crucified. Hence, the Bogomils detested the symbol of the cross, viewing it as the Devil's instrument. Important Bogomil groups, such as the "Church of Dragovitsa," continued to promote radical dualism, but the majority appear to have embraced the moderate dualist position.

By the twelfth century, Bogomil missionaries had reached western Europe. They had encountered social conditions that did not differ much from those that had nurtured the rise of Bogomilism in the Kingdom of Bulgaria: a resentful peasantry, trapped at the bottom of a feudal hierarchy, and an ostentatiously wealthy Catholic Church. The Bogomils spread heresy throughout Italy and France. Crusaders returning from expeditions to Byzantium might have been another avenue by which Bogomil notions arrived in Roman Catholic lands.

Whether Bogomils were responsible for starting the Cathar movement is unclear. What is certain is that the early Cathars revered the Bogomils as their mentors. The twofold structure of the religious community, the Consolamentum, and details of the dualistic doctrine, were adopted by the Cathars from Bogomil missionaries. Of particular significance was the Cathar council held in France in 1167. This meeting, at which the Cathars developed an international church organization, was presided over by NICETAS, a radical dualist Bogomil bishop from Constantinople.

Byzantium had conquered Bulgaria in 1018. The Bulgarian Bogomils turned this to their advantage by identifying the Byzantine state with Satan, who was said to dwell in the Hagia Sophia, the main church of Constantinople. As a result, Bogomilism became a nationalistic rallying point for the Bulgarian people. When the Kingdom of Bulgaria regained its independence in 1185, the Bogomils were poised to become the state religion. However, the new rulers turned to the Pope for advice on combatting the influence of Byzantine Christianity, and the pontiff urged the Bulgarian authorities to suppress Bogomilism.

The political instability and violence throughout the Balkan region during the twelfth and thirteenth centuries made it easy for Bogomil missionaries to point out the evil of the world, as well as to promote the dream of an otherworldly escape. Bogomilism grew in strength in Bosnia, Serbia, and Hungary.

In Bosnia, the Bogomils succeeded in dominating the national religious scene in the form of the BOSNIAN CHURCH. The Bosnian Bogomils had extensive contact with Roman Catholics from Italy, as the nearby city of Dubrovnik on the Dalmatian coast was controlled by Venice. Numerous INQUISITIONS and a small crusade against the Bogomils in Bosnia were repelled. The Bosnian nobility supported the Bogomils because mass conversion to the Roman Catholic faith would have reduced Bosnian resistance to an invasion by the Venetians. When Moslem invaders swept through the Balkans at the end of the fourteenth century, Bogomilism vanished there; it is thought that many Bogomils embraced Islam.

In Hungary, in the uncertain atmosphere created by attacks from the Tartars, Bogomilism became popular. In fact, it attained the status of a national religion for a time. By 1450, Hungary had been officially established as a Roman Catholic state, and the Bogomils had disappeared.

See also: BLACK MASS.

BOHEMIAN BRETHREN   Bohemian Brethren is a variant name for the unorthodox Bohemian sect, the UNITAS FRATRUM.

BONIFACE VIII   In one of history's ironies, Pope Boniface VIII was a staunch defender of Catholic orthodoxy during his lifetime. Indeed, he believed that the Roman Catholic Church should rule the world. But after his death, he was charged with devil worship. Although the accusation was false, it fanned the church's fear of ritual magic and contributed to the decision to unleash the INQUISITION against magicians.

Boniface held the papal office between 1294 and his death in 1303. King Philip the Fair ruled France during this time. Both Philip and Boniface were interested in increasing their political power, and a collision was inevitable. The king, who required vast amounts of money to support his military activities, insisted on his right to tax Catholic priests. The pope objected. Philip then prevented churches in France to supply gold and other valuables to Rome, forcing a temporary compromise.

In 1302, Boniface again irritated the powerful monarch by issuing a proclamation stating that the pope is the spiritual leader of the world and, therefore, rules over all beings—including kings. Philip decided that his papal opponent had to be eliminated.

The king then struck a deal with aristocrats in Italy who envied the pontiff's power. In 1303, a small army, organized by the French and Italian enemies of Boniface, captured him. He was held prisoner for three days, during which time he was terrorized. Although supporters freed him, he died from the trauma within a month.

King Philip soon arranged for Clement V, a more cooperative man than Boniface, to assume the papacy. However, the memory of the preceding pope's opposition remained a blot on the reputation of the monarch and his assistant, Guillaume de Nogaret. In order to discredit the dead pontiff and to pressure Clement into revoking Boniface's pronouncements against the French throne, Philip instigated a postmortem slander campaign.

Witnesses who swore that Pope Boniface had engaged in a variety of astonishing crimes were produced. Boniface, they reported, had murdered his predecessor, Celestine V. He had also mocked the Christian faith and displayed a taste for sodomy. Most important, the witnesses claimed that the pope had made a pact with the devil.

They also said that Boniface was served by three DEMONS, as well as a spirit that lived in a ring on his finger. One man testified that he had watched while the pope drew a magic circle, sacrificed a chicken, and offered it to a devil. Others noted that Boniface often locked himself, alone, in a room; soon, the earth would shake, and the voices of demonic creatures would be heard coming from the room, conversing with him. The pontiff was also observed worshipping an image of Satan, which was concealed behind a silk curtain.

If Boniface had been convicted of the crimes of heresy, denying the Christian faith, and conspiring with devils, his body would have to be dug up and punished. (This had actually happened to the corpse of FORMOSUS, a ninth century pope). Such an incident would have harmed the credibility of Boniface's successor, Clement. The living pope was thus forced to retract all of the proclamations that the dead one had made against French royal power. In return, the absurd charges made against Boniface were quietly dropped.

However, the stories about Boniface added to the church's worries about the spread of DEMON MAGIC. Clement's successor, Pope John XXII, defined any deliberate contact with demons to be heresy; this meant that the INQUISITION was now permitted to persecute ritual magicians. In time, the notion of the magician's pact with the spirits would mingle with the idea of witchcraft in the minds of inquisitors. This fantasy provoked the fears that led to the GREAT WITCH HUNT.

THE BOOK OF ELKESAI   The sacred text of the ELKESAITES, a heretical Christian group that lived in the Near East during the second century A.D., *The Book of Elkesai* was said to contain revelations imparted by a gigantic ANGEL.

THE BOOK OF ENOCH   One of the most important texts in the ancient collection called the PSEUDEPIGRAPHA, this book was written during the last two centuries B.C. The author claims to be the mysterious Old Testament figure Enoch. The true author of this and the other Pseudepigraphic texts is unknown.

The Book of Genesis briefly mentions Enoch as the father of Methuselah. Enoch lived for 365 years, "walked with God," and was believed to have journeyed to heaven in his physical body (5:19–24). *The Book of Enoch* reports his experiences in heaven and hell, along with various revelations he received from God. The descriptions of ANGELS and DEMONS inspired magicians in their quests to contact and utilize these spirits.

Although orthodox Christianity eventually rejected the Pseudepigrapha, early Christians were impressed by the visions contained in *The Book*. The New Testament Letter of Jude, written around A.D. 90, actually quotes *The Book of Enoch*:

> And Enoch also, the seventh from Adam, prophesied of these, saying,
> Behold, the Lord cometh with ten thousands of the saints,
> To execute judgment upon all. . . ." (1:14–15)

THE BOOK OF MORMON   The central sacred text of the MORMONS, this work was dictated by JOSEPH SMITH, the founder of the movement, and published in 1830. Smith claimed that seven years earlier he was visited by an angelic being named Moroni, who appeared by his bed. Moroni said he was the son of a man called Mormon, who had composed a divinely inspired book that he wrote on gold plates and buried near Smith's home in New York State many centuries earlier. In 1827, Smith received another revelation that indicated the exact location of the plates. His followers believe that he excavated at the spot and uncovered the text published as *The Book of Mormon*.

The book was written in "Reformed Egyptian." Translating the text should have been challenging because Egyptologists have no record that such a language ever existed. However, along with the plates, Smith found a special pair of spectacles that enabled him to understand the mysterious inscriptions. When the translation was completed, Smith reported, he gave the plates and spectacles to Moroni, who whisked them into the spirit world.

The writing style of *The Book of Mormon* is reminiscent of the King James translation of the Bible. In fact, the text contains many passages identical to the King James version (including translation errors), as well as many paraphrases from that work. Critics cite these passages as evidence of plagiarism; Mormons hold that the resemblances demonstrate that the same divine source inspired both the King James and Mormon translators.

But much of the content of *The Book of Mormon* resembles no other known work. It tells the story of two ancient civilizations of the New World. The first, called the Jaredites, migrated to Central America from the Middle East before 2000 B.C. and were destroyed by God for their sins. In 600 B.C., a group of Jews traveled from Jerusalem to the Americas. In time, they divided into two hostile cultures, the Nephites and the Lamanites.

Christ visited the virtuous Nephites after His resurrection. However, in the fourth century A.D., the Nephites were destroyed in a battle with the Lamanites. God punished the Lamanites by turning their skins dark. Native Americans, Smith taught, are the descendants of these cursed people. Mormon was a Nephite. He buried his historical record at the site of the battle, near Palmyra, New York, where Smith was led to recover them. The stories in *The Book of Mormon* have not been supported by the findings of archaeologists and physical anthropologists.

On the basis of his revelation, Smith preached that the New Jerusalem would one day be established by Christ in America. The central importance given to America by *The Book of Mormon* helps to explain the special appeal and rapid growth of Mormonism in the United States during the nineteenth century.

THE BOOK OF THE SECRETS OF ENOCH   This influential work is part of literary collection known as the PSEUDEPIGRAPHA. A Jew in Egypt wrote *The Book of the Secrets of Enoch* during the first century A.D., but there are claims that it was written by Enoch, the Old Testament figure who "walked with God" (Genesis 5:24). This book describes in detail Enoch's visit to the various departments of heaven and hell, along with revelations concerning the creation of the world. Later magicians attempted to conjure the ANGELS and DEMONS mentioned in the text. The notion of the earliest Christians that demons are actually fallen angels likely came from this book.

See also: BOOK OF ENOCH.

BORBORITES   Borborites is an uncomplimentary name (derived from the Greek term for filth) applied by Christian orthodoxy to the heretical MESSALIANS. The

Borborites lived in communities from Armenia to Egypt between the fourth and seventh centuries.

BOSNIAN CHURCH   By the late twelfth century, the heresy of BOGOMILISM had spread from its origin in Macedonia throughout the Balkan region. The remote land of Bosnia, which had not been effectively penetrated by either the Roman Catholics to the west or the Eastern Orthodox to the southeast, proved receptive to Bogomil preachers, who established the Bosnian Church.

Bogomilism in Bosnia was the final developmental phase of this belief system. The Bogomils had begun as radical dualists, rejecting church hierarchies and material wealth as devices of the evil deity who created the world. Over time, the group modified its radicalism as the need arose for an enduring social structure to preserve and transmit the doctrine. Free from the persecution they suffered everywhere else, in Bosnia the Bogomils were able to establish monasteries and develop their own hierarchy of religious officials.

A significant factor in the flourishing of Bogomilism in Bosnia was the support of the Bosnian nobles. Outside Bosnia, the Bogomils' antimaterialistic views appealed mainly to the oppressed peasantry. Bosnian aristocrats welcomed the Bogomils, however, viewing them as a way to reduce the influence of the Roman Catholics. Catholic powers, such as Venice, were eyeing Bosnia as a potential conquest, and a Catholic base of popularity within the country would work to a Catholic invader's advantage. Under aristocratic patronage, the Bogomil monasteries became centers of trade, and some became quite wealthy.

Periodically, the Catholic Church, from its stronghold in Dubrovnik on the Dalmatian coast, would attempt to mount INQUISITIONS to vanquish the Bosnian heretics. In 1235, an anti-Bogomil crusade was organized. These efforts produced few results.

By the early fourteenth century, another tactic against the Bosnian heretics had been adopted. Posses from Dubrovnik raided Bosnian settlements and kidnapped the inhabitants. Dubrovnik became a slave market, where rich Catholics from as far away as France purchased Bosnians for their pleasure. Contemporary accounts reveal that young women and children were especially sought after. Because the slaves were regarded as heretics, the Roman Catholic Church raised no objection to this practice.

By the end of the fourteenth century, the Bosnian Church had disappeared under the onslaught of the Moslem invasion. The Bogomils left behind mute testimony to their once-thriving church—tens of thousands of tombstones carved with mysterious figures and symbols, the meanings of which scholars are still debating.

Abbé BOULLAN   A notorious SATANIST, Abbé Boullan was one of the most peculiar and influential members of the heretical scene in nineteenth century Europe. He was responsible for resurrecting the performance of the BLACK MASS, first conducted by ABBÉ GUIBOURG almost 200 years earlier.

Boullan was born in 1824. As a young man, he became a Catholic priest and quickly acquired a reputation as an expert in the subjects of mystical experience and demonic possession. When he was thirty, Adele Chevalier, a young nun, was brought to him for examination because she had been hearing mysterious voices. Boullan was asked to determine whether the experiences were divine or diabolical in origin. His final opinion on this matter was not recorded, but during the course of their time together, the priest and the nun became lovers. Eventually, Boullan and Chevalier had two or three children.

Three years after they met, the couple, with the blessing of the Bishop of Versailles, founded the SOCIETY FOR THE REPARATION OF SOULS. This organization specialized in conducting exorcisms, which is an orthodox practice. Boullan developed techniques that were far from orthodox, however; these included encouraging the victims of possession to drink his urine and eat consecrated bread mixed with excrement.

By 1860, Abbé Boullan was a practicing Satanist. He and his lover conducted a black mass that year, during which they allegedly sacrificed one of their own children to the Devil. Despite repeated investigations by church officials, Boullan was not removed from the priesthood for another fifteen years. At one point, the courts sentenced him to three years in jail for fraud; at another, he was imprisoned by the church and forced to write a confession of faith. Boullan could be eloquent and persuasive; while he publicly proclaimed his orthodoxy, he privately developed a radically heretical belief system.

Boullan was finally banned from the Catholic priesthood in 1875. During that year, he befriended EUGENE VINTRAS, a visionary leader of a sect called the CHURCH OF CARMEL. Under Vintras, this church had been accused of being a front for Satanic activities. Vintras died the year he met Boullan, who decided to declare himself the new leader of the Church of Carmel. Some of the members followed Boullan, and there is no doubt that Satanic practices occurred under him.

By this time, Boullan had evolved a novel theory of salvation. He taught that because sex had led to the fall of Adam and Eve, sex could also lead to humanity's redemption. Human beings who had sexual intercourse with ANGELS would be raised to a higher plane of spirituality, and sex with animals and lower spirits would help such creatures to evolve into human beings. It should be noted that, according to orthodoxy, the "angels" Boullan mentioned must in reality have been DEMONS because real angels do not possess material bodies with which a person could have intercourse. Boullan's sexual magic techniques included visualization while masturbating, imagining a human sex partner to be an angel, and copulation with animals.

Boullan's circle of followers was infiltrated by a group of occultists, who then denounced him. He came to believe that this group was attempting to murder him by using magic. Some evidence suggests that Boullan's fears may not have been completely unfounded, although they were denied by the individuals concerned. After a series of experiences that Boullan interpreted as magical attacks by his enemies, he died of heart failure in 1893.

BROTHER TWELVE   One of the strangest characters in the history of unorthodox groups in Canada, Edward Wilson was born in England in 1878 and later became Brother Twelve. He spent many years as a sailor, during which he studied occult practices around the world. Wilson evidently learned the teachings of THEOSOPHY, which some of his own doctrines resemble. In 1924, while visiting southern France, Wilson had a vision of the "Twelfth Master," one of a group of Secret Chiefs whom many occultists believe are using magical powers to bring about the dawn of the Aquarian Age. Wilson became convinced that he had been chosen to bring about the New Age; in honor of his Master, he called himself Brother Twelve.

Wilson toured England and Canada, teaching a combination of eastern and western esoteric ideas along the lines of the Theosophical Society, with the additional notion that he was a messiah. By the time he reached the Canadian west coast in 1927, he had attracted hundreds of followers, some of whom were quite wealthy. He was able to purchase land on DeCourcy, Valdes, and Vancouver Islands off the coast of British Columbia and established the Aquarian Foundation, a colony of his students. At the height of his popularity, Brother Twelve had about 200 students living at the colony and another 2,000 worldwide.

Between 1928 and 1932, this Aquarian project failed. Brother Twelve lobbied in support of Alabama Senator James T. Heplin, who ran as an independent candidate in the 1928 American presidential election. Heplin had close ties with the racist group the Ku Klux Klan, and Brother Twelve's connection with this man offended some of his followers. Brother Twelve began to act more and more like a dictator, ordering students at the colony to engage in exhausting physical labor, while he chose sexual partners from among the women. Charges that he had misused funds donated to him began to surface.

Brother Twelve became increasingly paranoid. He ordered the construction of a stone fortress, with armed guards on one of his islands. People passing the island in boats complained that they were being shot at. The British Columbia government then dissolved the Aquarian Foundation. In 1932, Brother Twelve suddenly left Canada, likely taking with him a large amount of money. No one knows exactly what became of him. One account claims that he died in Switzerland two years later. However, sightings of Brother Twelve continued to be reported for the next twenty years.

Giordano BRUNO   This Italian philosopher of the sixteenth century taught many ideas that would become commonplace by the twentieth; these included the notions that the earth moves around the sun, and that the stars are distant suns that may have planets orbiting them. Unfortunately, the Catholic Church of Bruno's time was struggling against the menace of Protestantism and had little tolerance for new ideas. As a result, Bruno met a flaming death at the hands of the INQUISITION.

Bruno was born near Naples in 1548. At seventeen, he entered a Dominican monastery in Naples. He was attracted to the art of debate but failed to recognize that certain subjects—the basic doctrines of the church, for instance—were out of bounds. Soon, Bruno's willingness to question these doctrines got him in so much trouble that he was forced to flee.

For the rest of his life, Bruno wandered through Europe and supported himself through teaching and writing. (During his fifty-two years, he published sixty-one books.) He had mastered the science of mnemonics, or memory improvement, to such an extent that he was frequently invited to teach his memory methods. Before his falling out with the church, even Pope Pius V had summoned him to discuss mnemonics. At this time, the study of memory was often linked to occult topics. Bruno's interest in memory may have led him to discover other unorthodox ideas.

In 1579, Bruno arrived at the Protestant city of Geneva. He so annoyed a respected local scholar with his criticisms that he had to leave town quickly. Bruno proceeded to Paris, and then to London. He remained in the tolerant English environment for some time and developed his ideas further.

Bruno published two important books in 1584, in which he described his vision of the universe. He championed the heliocentric theory of Copernicus, which held that the earth revolves around the sun rather than vice versa. But Bruno expanded Copernicus's notion by suggesting that every star in the sky was a distant sun, each with orbiting planets. Bruno believed that the universe is infinite. This idea was quite different from the conventional world view of the time, which recognized a stationary earth at the center of a finite universe.

One of the problems with Bruno's infinite universe was that it left nowhere outside of the universe for God to dwell. Christian orthodoxy insists that the Creator is distinct from His Creation. In contrast, Bruno claimed that God pervades the universe; he thus committed the heresy of PANTHEISM.

Other heretical views magnified Bruno's unorthodox status. He rejected the doctrine of the Trinity. He also advocated contacting the spirits of the dead through NECROMANCY, and evil spirits through the rites of DEMON MAGIC. Furthermore, he held that humans could become so spiritually pure that they could achieve total union with God, again violating the separateness of Creator and creature.

For six years beginning in 1585, Bruno was again on the move in continental Europe. In 1591 an aristocrat invited him to Venice to teach mnemonics. The INQUISITION, which had been anxious to silence this wandering subversive, may have been behind the invitation because Bruno's host turned him over to the inquisitors.

Despite years of imprisonment in the inquisitorial dungeons of Rome, Bruno refused to abandon his strange views. He was branded "an impenitent and pertinacious heretic." In 1600, the man who dared to imagine an infinite universe was publicly burned at the stake in Rome. Cardinal Robert Bellarmino, who had overseen the trial and punishment of Bruno, was declared a saint by the Catholic Church in 1930.

The connection Bruno had made between the heliocentric theory and his religious heresies alerted the Catholic authorities to the dangers of the sun-centered view, which had hitherto been generally regarded as a harmless oddity. Ten years after Bruno's death, Italian astronomer GALILEO announced that the discoveries he had made with the telescope supported heliocentrism. Sensitized by the Bruno affair, the church paid careful attention to Galileo and eventually condemned his works as heretical.

Simon BUDNY   A preacher of the ANTI-TRINITARIAN heresy during the sixteenth century, Simon Budny was born into the Polish aristocracy in 1533. As a young man, he became renowned for his original thinking about matters of faith; fortunately for him, Poland at the time was one of the few centers of religious tolerance in Europe. The ruler of Lithuania invited Budny to teach for a time, but he had to return to Poland when a Catholic who banned unorthodox views came into power. Controversy flared around Budny in 1574 when he published an edition of the New Testament; he had eliminated passages that supported the orthodox doctrine of the Trinity: God is three Persons subsisting in a single substance. Budny claimed that heretics had added the Trinitarian passages to the Bible long after its original composition. The orthodox, both Catholic and Protestant, viewed Budny as the heretic. He died in 1584.

CABALA   This term was originally the medieval Latin spelling of the word *KAB-BALAH*, referring to the Jewish mystical tradition. Cabala has acquired a slightly different meaning; it usually denotes the kabbalistic ideas Christian occultists adopted from the Jewish Kabbalah and modified to suit their own spiritual perspective. The Cabala came to possess such a mysterious reputation that it inspired a new word in the English language, "cabal," which means a secret group of plotters.

The earliest Cabalistic works were written in Spain, between the thirteenth and fifteenth centuries. They were composed by Jewish converts to Christianity who were familiar with Kabbalah through their Jewish background. These converts interpreted the Kabbalah in Christian terms in order to encourage other Jewish kabbalists to become Christians. But their efforts were unsuccessful and attracted little attention.

Much more important than the work of the Spanish converts was the interest the great scholar of the Italian Renaissance, GIOVANNI PICO DELLA MIRANDOLA showed in the Kabbalah. Pico believed that the various occult and philosophical traditions of ancient times all taught the same basic message, which supported the Christian religion. He thought that the Kabbalah, in particular, could be used to prove such doctrines as the divinity of Christ and the Trinity. But Catholic officials condemned Pico's ideas. However, his Latin translations of important Kabbalistic texts laid the foundation for the development of the Cabala.

During the sixteenth century, many European thinkers contributed to this fusion of Jewish mysticism and Christianity. They often claimed that the purpose of the Cabala was simply to entice Jews to convert to the "true faith" of Roman Catholicism, but this claim was largely a ruse to avoid orthodox persecution. In fact, the Cabalists believed they had discovered a key to the hidden wisdom of Christ Himself.

The two most eminent Cabalists at this time were JOHANNES REUCHLIN, a student of Pico's, and CORNELIUS AGRIPPA. Reuchlin devised a theory of revelation based on the names of God, a favorite topic of the Kabbalah. He taught that, in earliest times, God revealed himself to humanity through the name "Shaddai," which contains three letters in Hebrew; the Old Testament God expressed himself to Moses through the four-letter name "YHVH"; and finally, God's sacred name for our time is the five-letter name JESUS. Agrippa mingled the Cabala with the practices of ritual magic, indicating how the powers of the divine names can be used to control spirits.

During this time, a new direction in the Kabbalah was being opened by Palestinian mystic Isaac LURIA. The Christian Cabalists were generally unaware of Luria's revolutionary perspective until the following century, when CHRISTIAN KNORR VON ROSENROTH published Latin translations of some Lurianic texts.

The Cabala enriched other Western occult traditions. During the seventeenth century, Cabalistic notions and symbols began to appear in the textbooks of AL-CHEMY. Following Agrippa, Cabalistic materials continued to influence magicians. By the mid-nineteenth century, a unique magical tradition based on the Cabala had arisen. This tradition is generally labeled the QABALAH.

CADAVER COUNCIL   At this meeting of high church officials in A.D. 897, Pope Stephen VII accused his predecessor, Pope FORMOSUS, of illegally occupying the papal throne. Formosus had died nine months earlier, so he had to be removed from his grave and propped up during his trial. Remarkably, he was convicted during the Cadaver Council.

CAINITES   This remarkable sect belonged to the religious movement called GNOSTICISM and existed during the second century A.D. The Cainites are mentioned, in horrified tones, by several early orthodox Christian writers. All of the Cainites' own scriptures and artifacts were destroyed long ago, so we must rely for our information concerning them on the testimony of their enemies.

Like many other Gnostic groups, the Cainites apparently taught that the Creator God described in the Old Testament is actually evil, and hostile to humanity. It follows from this belief that all of the symbols and myths of the Jewish tradition should be inverted—a move that was undertaken most consistently, among all the Gnostic groups sharing this belief, by the Cainites. For example, they despised the memory of such Old Testament heroes as Moses, viewing the Creator's friends as traitors to humankind, and revered Old Testament villains. They were especially fond of Cain, the murderer of Abel, and acquired their name because of this affection.

The Cainites had two conflicting schools of thought regarding Christian doctrine. One group argued that JESUS, like His Old Testament predecessors, was an agent of the evil Creator. They praised Judas for his role in ending Jesus' life. The other school of Cainite thought held that, in fact, Jesus came to save humanity from suffering. In order to do so, He had to suffer and die Himself. The forces allied to the evil Creator had conspired to prevent Jesus from suffering, thereby preventing His work of salvation. By arranging Jesus' capture by the authorities, Judas becomes the hero in this version, too. One of the sacred texts of the Cainites was known as the *Gospel of Judas*.

One of the orthodox commentators, Irenaeus of Lyons, noted with disgust that members of the Cainite school attempted to gain salvation by "passing through all things"—that is, by seeking every possible kind of experience, even to excess, in order to wear out their attachments to the delights of the material world. In veiled terms, Irenaeus described a Cainite ritual, probably of a sexual nature, during which the practitioners prayed to draw into themselves the strength of an ANGEL.

CALIXTINES   Calixtines is a variant name for the branch of the HUSSITES called the UTRAQUISTS. In opposition to Roman Catholic practice, this group taught that the congregation should drink the wine from the cup (*calix* in Latin) as well as receive the bread during the Mass.

CAMISARDS   The name of this eighteenth century radical French group derives from the term *camisa*, which means "shirt" in a dialect of southern France. The Camisards wore white shirts over their ordinary clothing during their nighttime activities. The shirts symbolized purity and made useful decoys; when pursued, the heretics left their highly visible garments dangling from branches while they vanished into the darkness.

For several decades during the 1500s, French citizens who embraced the Protestant faith were targeted for abuse by the Catholic majority. This internal strife weakened the country; in 1598, the government issued the Edict of Nantes, granting toleration to the French Protestants, or Huguenots. However, many Catholics objected. Louis XIV, the Sun King who firmly believed he could do as he pleased, decided to revoke the Edict in 1685. Protestantism was again illegal. Its churches were closed, and its spiritual leaders were dismissed. The Huguenots were left without any civil rights.

Religious extremists began to appear among the desperate Protestant population. These preachers interpreted the Bible to prophesy that God would soon arrange for the Catholics to be overthrown. In southeastern France, a group of young children began traveling from village to village, proclaiming that Christ would soon appear to destroy the Catholic Antichrist. The Little Prophets, led by a girl of luminous beauty, "the fair Isabel," stirred up great excitement. Crowds followed the children, weeping, shaking uncontrollably, and falling into trances.

Catholic authorities perceived the region of the Cevennes Mountains to be the area of greatest Protestant unrest and stationed troops there. The locals were forced to lodge and feed the soldiers, and became quite resentful toward all representatives of governmental power. The oppression of the Cevennes Protestants increased following the English Revolution of 1688. From then on, the presence of the Protestant community in France was seen as a direct threat to the state. A reign of terror was inflicted on the inhabitants of the Cevennes, who were able to hold religious meetings only at night, outdoors, in remote locations.

In 1702, groups of armed men, wearing the distinctive white shirts, began to take action. Their first act was to free some captured Protestants from a Catholic torture chamber. They then embarked on a campaign of nocturnal raids, torching Catholic churches, murdering priests, and assaulting villages that had supported the oppression of Protestants.

Although few Camisards had military training, they knew the wild terrain of their homeland intimately and frequently managed to evade or trap their pursuers. At times during the course of the rebellion, as many as 60,000 Catholic troops were in the region, unable to defeat a force of perhaps 4,000 roving Camisards.

The Protestant fighters were inspired by increasingly weird spiritual phenomena. They would be sent off on a raiding expedition by groups of trembling, shrieking women and children who had become possessed by the Holy Spirit. Many Camisards saw visions and heard voices that encouraged them to fight for the Lord. At night, lights in the sky guided the Camisards on their way. They came to believe that bullets their enemies fired at them would turn to water.

Frustrated in their attempts to engage the Camisards, the government troops adopted a policy of mass destruction. Entire villages of Protestants were slaughtered and the buildings razed. After two years, the warring sides signed a peace treaty. In return for an end to their raiding, the Camisards were promised that the Protestants could retain their beliefs and hold religious services, provided these were conducted beyond the walls of the towns. But they were forbidden to have their own churches; this condition caused some Camisards to reject the treaty. Orthodoxy had gained the upper hand, and there was little trouble thereafter. In 1715, King Louis issued medals commemorating the extermination of the Camisards.

In 1706, some Camisards had traveled to England as refugees where they continued their unorthodox practices until 1713. English observers were amazed at the spectacle of groups of Camisards, convulsing and falling to the ground as they uttered the prophecies of the Holy Spirit. Some of the English learned the Cam-isards' ways and went on to establish the sect known as the SHAKERS.

See also: FLAGELLANTS, MARCIONISM.

Tommasso CAMPANELLA   A prominent Italian magician and unorthodox thinker, Tommasso Campanella was born in 1568. He joined the Dominican order and quickly became known for his belief that European society, including the Catholic Church, required massive reforms. Such a position was easy to interpret as support for Protestantism and rendered him suspect. His interest in magic and ASTROLOGY and the rumor that he was involved in plotting revolutionary uprisings made matters worse.

In 1599, Campanella was arrested for inciting a revolt in southern Italy. The goal of this uprising was to establish a utopian society that would prepare for the end of the world. His disobedience earned him some sessions with a torturer, and he was sentenced to perpetual imprisonment for heresy. Despite his restricted life thereafter, Campanella maintained contact with thinkers throughout Europe, and wrote and published a great deal. He was a supporter of magician-scientist GIORDANO BRUNO, who was burned at the stake in 1600. He also wrote a well-known defense of another contemporary heretic, GALILEO.

Campanella's most famous work was *Citta del Sole*, or City of the Sun, which he composed in prison in 1602. This book contains a description of an ideal soci ety, somewhat similar to that portrayed by Plato in *The Republic*. In Campanella's text, the city is a model of the solar system. Situated on a hill, it takes the form of seven concentric rings that represent the seven planets. In the middle is a round temple, symbolizing the sun. The chief priest and ruler is named Metaphysic, indicating that he is a sort of philosopher-king. Magical images placed around the city attract positive spiritual forces from the planets. This idea shows Campanella's familiarity with the magic of such Renaissance thinkers as MARSILIO FICINO.

Campanella tried to convince political and religious leaders that the sun was moving closer to the earth and heating it up. In response, he said, humanity should band together, construct the City of the Sun, and await the return of Christ. He never succeeded in gaining support for his project.

The utopian kept himself in some favor with the Catholic Church—indeed, he may have saved himself from execution—by writing missionary propaganda. In 1628, Pope Urban VIII requested Campanella's services because the pope believed in ASTROLOGY. Political opponents had recruited astrologers to predict his imminent demise in the hope of frightening him to death. Terrified, the pontiff remembered Campanella's reputation as an astrological expert and called for his aid in mounting a defense against the toxic influences of the heavens.

Campanella arranged for the construction of a special room, in which seven lights representing the planets were hung. The heretic and the pope met in this room to perform ceremonies in which they would surround themselves with symbols and substances to attract positive astral forces. Pope Urban believed that this unorthodox NATURAL MAGIC successfully protected him. He even outlived his heretical ally: Campanella died in 1639; Urban, in 1644.

CARPOCRATES   Carpocrates was an important teacher of Gnostic doctrines during the second century. Unfortunately, very little is known of Carpocrates' life. He is thought to have been active during the reign of Roman Emperor Hadrian (A.D. 117–138). After his death, his doctrines continued to be proclaimed and developed by his followers, including his son, EPIPHANES.

See also: CARPOCRATIAN GNOSTICISM.

CARPOCRATIAN GNOSTICISM   The Carpocratian School was part of the religious movement called GNOSTICISM, which swept through the Mediterranean during the first few centuries A.D. This school was founded by CARPOCRATES, who lived during the first half of the second century. The radical teachings of the Carpocratians were cited by the orthodox opponents of Gnosticism in an attempt to discredit all of the Gnostic schools. The Carpocratians have the distinction of being the first known group in Western history to call for a completely communistic society.

Our knowledge of the Carpocratian teachings derives from two surviving sources: a description by orthodox Christian writer Irenaeus of Lyons, and a letter written by EPIPHANES, Carpocrates' son. With such sparse information, it is hard to estimate how popular the Carpocratian teachings were. They must have had a significant following during the second century, however, because they were active in Rome as well as in Gaul.

Like many other Gnostic groups, the Carpocratians taught that the world was not created by the greatest God, but by inferior ANGELS. Humans are imprisoned in the physical world and long to escape to the realm of the "unbegotten Father." JESUS did not begin his life as an incarnation of God, as the orthodox claimed; in fact, he was conceived in the usual fashion through the impregnation of Mary by her husband, Joseph. Jesus became the Christ and was able to depart from the prison of life to the domain of the Father through "despising" the enslaving laws of His society. Jesus discovered that our inhibitions are the chains that bind us to the jail of the body.

According to the Carpocratians, the path to salvation for all of us is to do as Jesus did: deliberately to seek out every possible human experience and to break through every limitation society imposes on behavior. Otherwise, when we die we will be forced to be reborn into another body. The endless chain of REINCARNATION will continue as long as "something is still lacking" in our freedom—that is, until we have ended the tyranny of inhibitions the world imposes on us. It is easy to understand how orthodox Christians, with their insistence on obeying the rules of the church, recoiled at a teaching that recommended, in the words of Irenaeus, tasting all forms of "godless, unlawful and unspeakable things."

The Carpocratians preached a communal lifestyle in which fixed social rank and private property did not exist. In a sense, they went further than Karl Marx did many centuries later; they even called for the abolition of sexual property. Epiphanes wrote that righteousness means "a universal sharing along with equality." He also argued that God must have been joking when He gave the commandment against coveting one's neighbor's wife since God was the one who instilled in humans the natural desire for multiple sexual partners.

With the exception of Epiphanes' letter, all of the Carpocratians' writings have been destroyed. After the second century, this Gnostic school disappeared from history. The story of their fate remains a mystery.

John CASSIAN   This fifth century Christian monk is best known for his role in organizing monasticism in western Europe. John Cassian founded two monasteries near Marseilles and composed influential guidelines for the monastic lifestyle. In the history of heresy, however, he is known as the probable author of the unorthodox doctrine called SEMI-PELAGIANISM.

Cassian lived during an intense controversy between those who believed that people have complete free will to make moral choices (the heresy of PELAGIA-NISM), and those who held that human willpower is too weak to resist sinning (the orthodox doctrine taught by Augustine of Hippo). The Pelagians concluded that perfectly virtuous people are able to earn their way into heaven; the orthodox stated that salvation was granted by God only and could never be merited. Cassian formulated an intermediate position: people cannot achieve salvation without God's grace, but they must choose to live virtuously before God will grant His mercy. Thus, both willpower and divine grace are involved in salvation. Cassian's ideas were taken up by others and continued to be debated long after his death in 435. It was only ninety-four years later, at the Council of Orange, that the Catholic Church decisively rejected Semi-Pelagianism.

CATHARS   The increase in Western European heresies during the twelfth century culminated in the appearance of the Cathars, the most powerful unorthodox movement of the Middle Ages. Mainstream Catholic culture recognized the dire threat and reacted accordingly. By the time the Cathars were crushed, the course of Western history had been changed: a crusade of Christian against Christian had destroyed the culture of southern France, the order of Dominican friars had been formed, and the INQUISITION had been unleashed.

The Cathars first appeared on the historical stage in Cologne, Germany, in the mid-twelfth century. In 1143, two groups of heretics came to the notice of the authorities because of a quarrel they were having among themselves. One group seems to belong to the movement that came to be known as the Cathars. Both heretical groups were condemned. Within the next four years, the Cathar heresy turned up at several locations throughout France. By the early 1160s, Cathar groups were firmly established in the towns of southern France and northern Italy. In 1166, thirty Cathar missionaries arrived in England to spread the faith. They were quickly captured by the authorities, branded on the forehead, flogged, stripped, and sent into the winter fields, where "they died miserably", according to a contemporary account.

The beliefs of the early Cathars seem to have existed in two versions. The doctrine of moderate dualism held that God had originally created all spiritual beings. One of these, named Satanael, rebelled and was thrown from heaven. The rebel proceeded to create the material world and to imprison angels in physical bodies. The bodies of humans and other animals are thus the jails of divine beings who crave to be released. Christ was sent by God, in a body made of light, to teach humans the way of liberation. If people fail to achieve spiritual perfection during their lifetimes, they continue to be reincarnated until they do. The other variant of Cathar belief, extreme dualism, was similar to the moderate version with one exception: the evil creator of the world was thought to be God's eternal enemy rather than a rebellious creation

A practical consequence of Cathar beliefs was the rejection of material wealth and worldly pleasures as snares set by Satanael to keep humans locked in their bodies. The medieval Catholic Church, with its growing interest in money and power, was thought to serve the evil one, not the true God. The true Christian Church, the Cathars taught, should not accumulate wealth. This position appealed to the lower classes, who resented paying taxes and tithes to support the luxuries of the Catholic bishops. In the eyes of many, the strict lifestyle of the Cathar leaders put the Catholics to shame. The nobles and merchants of the towns were also attracted to the Cathars, in part because they wished both for independence from control by the Catholic hierarchy and for possession of the church's vast properties.

The views of the Cathars closely resembled those of the Balkan heresy called BOGOMILISM. Some scholars believe that the Cathar movement was actually founded by Bogomil missionaries; others think that Catharism began independently, arising from Western European dissatisfaction with the Roman Catholics. There is no doubt that western heretics active in the early twelfth century, such as HENRY OF LAUSANNE, TANCHELM OF FLANDERS, and the PETROBRUSCIANS, introduced many people to unorthodox ideas and laid the groundwork for the later popularity of the Cathars. It is also clear that the Cathars' contacts with Bogomils were occurring in the early years of the movement.

Furthermore, there is no doubt that Catharism adopted its organizational structure from Bogomil sources. The most spiritually advanced Cathars were known as "perfecti," the perfect ones. Both men and women were allowed this exalted rank. They ate no meat and abstained from sexual activity. Many perfecti lived in communal houses in the towns. They worked at crafts to support themselves, but did not accumulate wealth; their energies went into preaching missions and caring for the sick. Historian Morris Berman suggested that the perfecti may have engaged in chanting and postural practices to induce trance, in which they experienced soul travel to heavenly realms. The less advanced Cathars were the "credentes" or believers, who were not required to adopt the strict lifestyle of the perfecti. The credentes revered the perfecti and received spiritual guidance from them. In order to join the ranks of the perfected ones, a believer had to undergo the ritual of the CONSOLAMENTUM. Many credentes chose to receive this initiation on their deathbed, so they could die with the highest spiritual rank while avoiding the duties of the perfecti during their lifetime.

By the mid-1160s, the heretics were being called "Cathars." The term derives from the Greek word *Katharoi*, which means "the pure ones." They had succeeded in setting up an international church organization. By this time, the regions in which the Cathars were growing stronger were under the administration of a Cathar bishop.

In 1167, a grand council of French perfecti was held. NICETAS, a Bogomil leader visiting from Constantinople, encouraged the assembly to hold the radical dualistic view and oversaw further improvements in Cathar organization. An alternative church, the first serious competition Roman Catholicism had faced in many centuries, was born. From this time, the radical dualists, or Albaneses, dominated French Catharism. In Italy, the Albaneses coexisted, not always peaceably, with moderate dualist Cathar groups known as Concorezzanes or Garatenses.

Catholic authorities became alarmed at the rapid spread of the heresy. The anti-heretical propaganda that had developed during the past two centuries was applied to the Cathars: they were accused of devil worship, orgies, and murdering children. It was said that the Bogomils had taught the Cathars to practice sodomy as a method of birth control. (Because the Bogomils came from Bulgaria, both groups were referred to as *bougres*, which is French for Bulgars, from which was derived the English word *bugger*.) Particularly odd was the rumor that the word "Cathar" arose from the Latin *cattus*, for cat, because the Cathars were said to worship Satan in the shape of a cat. As orthodox commentator Guillaume d'Auvergne wrote, "Lucifer is permitted to appear to his worshippers and adorers in the form of a black cat or a toad and to demand kisses from them; whether as a cat, abominably, under the tail; or as a toad, horribly, on the mouth."

The vocal disapproval of the orthodox did little to dampen the popularity of the heresy. In 1184, Pope Lucius III initiated another approach. He commanded Catholic bishops to organize INQUISITIONS to seek out heretics. This early phase of the Inquisition was not very effective. It had to rely on local governments to carry out the punishments of convicted heretics. But these governments were often reluctant to do so because they feared the increasing power of the Catholic Church more than the Cathars, who did not aspire to political domination. In 1199, Pope Innocent III took direct control of the Inquisition and lobbied secular governments to improve their cooperation with the heresy hunters.

Around 1206, another new strategy against the Cathars was employed. A man named Dominic, along with Bishop Diego d'Osma, adopted the simple lifestyle of the Cathar leaders; they wandered throughout southern France, debating with and preaching against the Cathars. Their efforts were unsuccessful at first. However, the approach sufficiently intrigued the pope, so he permitted Dominic to found an order, the Dominicans, with its headquarters in the heart of French Cathar territory, for the purpose of combatting the heretics. Although Dominic himself used no violence against the Cathars, Dominicans were put in charge of the Inquisition by Pope Gregory IX in 1233 and converted it into an effective weapon of terror.

During the early thirteenth century, the situation in southern France had become a crisis for the Catholics. The Cathars were so well accepted that they operated openly in many towns, and the Catholic priests were powerless to stop them. The nobles of the region were increasingly free of control by either the church or the French state, and presided over the flowering of the most literate and tolerant society in Europe. The pope and the French king conspired to organize an invasion, aiming to crush the heresy-infected culture and to reestablish orthodox control. The campaign, known as the ALBIGENSIAN CRUSADE, involved the slaughter of many thousands, both Cathars and non-Cathars. The region was devastated and never recovered from this nightmarish time.

Under the repeated blows of Dominican preachers, inquisitors, and crusaders, the French Cathars were gradually driven into remote areas of the Pyrenees. The resistance to the Catholic forces was effectively broken with the conquest of MONTSEGUR in 1244; Queribus, the last stronghold of the heretics, fell in 1255.

Catharism survived in Italy throughout the thirteenth century. It was protected by the upper classes in the Italian cities, not because of religious enthusiasm on the part of the rich, but as a counterbalance to the power of the orthodox church. In 1213, the pope threatened to unleash a crusade against Milan if the city continued to shelter heretics. Catholic inquisitors often met violent resistance as they attempted to carry out their bloody duties. The Cathars were eventually uprooted from Italy. Some

French and Italian Cathars fled into isolated Alpine valleys, where they were still being pursued by inquisitors during the 1300s. These heresy hunts in the Alps gave birth to the GREAT WITCH HUNT.

Since their demise, the Cathars have become the focus of many legends and speculations. They became linked to the Holy Grail, which was supposedly in their safekeeping. Just as the medieval Catholics projected their fantasies about Satanists onto the Cathars, so in modern times these heretics have been viewed in a variety of ways unrelated to historical evidence. In the nineteenth century, a "Cathar Church" said to be the emergence from hiding of the Cathars of the Middle Ages, appeared in France. Today, several Gnostic schools claim to preserve the secret teachings of the Cathars. The Society for the Remembrance and Study of Catharism promotes a rather romanticized image of the sect. Other groups claim that their members are all reincarnated Cathars who recall their previous lives. For many, the saga of the Cathars has become a nostalgic symbol of the vanished glory of southern French culture during the Middle Ages.

See also: ENDURA, GIRAUDE DE LAVAUR, NOVATIANISM, VOYNICH MANUSCRIPT.

CECCO D'ASCOLI   A lecturer at the University of Bologna in Italy during the early fourteenth century, Cecco D'Ascoli found himself in trouble with the INQUISITION for his unorthodox use of ASTROLOGY. At the time, astrology was generally tolerated, but with restrictions. For example, it was heretical to claim that the stars could affect the will of God or completely negate human free will. Cecco employed horoscopes to explain the timing of Christ's birth and death. He also attempted to predict the appearance of the Antichrist and the end of the world using astrological calculations. In 1324, an inquisitor in Bologna decided that such practices implied the belief that God's actions were subject to astrological influence and banned Cecco from teaching astrology. He persisted, however. As a result he was burned at the stake for heresy three years later, and his writings were condemned.

CELESTIUS   One of the central figures in the fifth century heretical movement called PELAGIANISM, Celestius had a significant influence upon the man from whom that heresy takes it name, PELAGIUS. Celestius and Pelagius were both born in Britain during the latter part of the fourth century and later moved to Rome, where they met. Celestius became a lawyer. Like a growing number of Romans, he was a Christian, devoting himself to the faith that was rapidly increasing in influence since its proclamation as the imperial state religion in 381. Celestius became concerned that the doctrine of original sin, which was becoming popular through the writings of Augustine of Hippo, was leading to loose morals within the church community.

According to Augustine, all of humanity had been punished for the sin of Adam. In response to Adam's disobedience to his Creator, God weakened the ability of the human will to control the impulses of desire. As a result, we all fall prey to sin. No one can be morally perfect enough to earn salvation and, therefore, must rely on God's grace to be saved. Celestius noticed that such a belief could be used to make excuses for immoral behavior: If people cannot behave morally, why should they even try? He worried that the doctrine of original sin might encourage the leaders of the church to take unethical advantage of their recently acquired wealth and power. The church leaders themselves tended to dismiss such fears.

Pelagius shared Celestius's concerns regarding the moral health of the church. During the first decade of the fifth century, they publicly condemned the temptations of privilege and called for a greater sense of moral responsibility within the Christian community. In doing so, they made both friends and enemies.

Shortly before Rome was invaded by the Goths in 410 Celestius and Pelagius left the city for North Africa. Their new home, however, was Augustine's power base. Not long after their arrival, a church council in Carthage accused them of heresy, and they left for Palestine. Augustine and his allies appealed for support against the Pelagians to Pope Innocent I, who excommunicated Celestius.

He remained active for many years afterward, continuing to preach against the notion of original sin and favoring human freedom and responsibility. At the COUNCIL OF EPHESUS in 431, Celestius was again condemned by representatives of the entire Catholic Church. The details of his death are unknown.

CELSUS   A pagan writer during the late second century A.D., Celsus was one of the first critics of Christianity to learn about the beliefs of his opponents. Although his works have not survived intact, quotations from them are preserved in the writings of the Christian theologian ORIGEN. Celsus did not define one school of Christianity as orthodox and the others as heretical, and it is likely that many second century Christians did not make the distinction either. Celsus's writings are significant because the surviving fragments contain valuable information concerning the heresy of GNOSTICISM.

CERINTHUS   This spiritual teacher of the first century A.D. was one of the earliest known representatives of the tradition called GNOSTICISM. Cerinthus is mentioned in the writings of Irenaeus of Lyons, an orthodox Christian opponent of the Gnostics. According to Irenaeus, the Gospel of John in the New Testament was written by the apostle John in his old age in an attempt to correct the heretical misconceptions about Christ being spread by Cerinthus.

All that is known of Cerinthus's life is that he was born in the Greek city of Ephesus in Asia Minor. His doctrines resemble those of many later Gnostic schools. Cerinthus taught that the world was not created by God, but rather by a lower being called the Demiurge, or perhaps by ANGELS. Christ was not sent by this world Creator, but by a higher divine power.

Cerinthus also held that JESUS had been a mere human being until His baptism, when the divine Christ descended and began to act through Him. This description of the relationship between the divine and human aspects of Jesus Christ is a version of the heretical doctrine of ADOPTIONISM. According to Cerinthus, Christ departed from Jesus before the crucifixion, leaving the man to die on the cross. The famous passage in the Gospel of John insisting that "the Word was made flesh, and dwelt among us" (1:14) might have been aimed at Cerinthus's notion that the Word, or Christ, merely adopted Jesus' flesh temporarily.

CHALDEAN ORACLES   The sacred text of THEURGY, the last major spiritual system of the ancient pagans, *The Chaldean Oracles* were composed by JULIANUS

THE CHALDEAN in the late second century A.D. When the Christians came to power in the late Roman Empire, they destroyed all copies of the text; they regarded theurgy to be DEMON MAGIC.

CHRYSOCHEIR   Chrysocheir was the last leader of the PAULICIANS during their brief period of independence in the ninth century. Persecuted by the orthodox Christian Byzantines for their heretical views, the Paulicians founded their own state. Chrysocheir became their chief in A.D. 863 and during the next decade led many successful military expeditions against the Byzantines. His troops were overwhelmed during a battle in 872. The victorious soldiers decapitated Chrysocheir, and his head was presented to the Byzantine emperor. Following Chrysocheir's death, the Byzantines erased the Paulician state.

CHURCH OF CARMEL   This heretical Christian group thrived in the Normandy region of France during the mid-nineteenth century. The Church of Carmel was also known as the WAY OF MERCY and VINTRASIANISM. The church was founded in 1839 when EUGENE VINTRAS, the foreman of a cardboard-box factory, believed that he received a visitation from archangel Michael. Vintras was an inspired preacher who was able to convert people throughout northeastern France.

The Church of Carmel celebrated an odd form of mass, called the Provictimal Sacrifice of Mary. During the ritual's performance, members of the congregation often reported seeing apparently supernatural manifestations. Especially common was the sight of blood seeping from the wafers of consecrated bread. On one occasion, a committee of medical doctors examined the tinted wafers and concluded that the substance was indeed blood that had originated from an unseen source. Some researchers believe that the basis for this phenomenon was the presence of a type of mold in the bread, which produces a reddish color as it grows. Whatever the correct explanation, the "miracles" caused a growing number of people to consider seriously the doctrines of this new religious movement.

The Church of Carmel under Vintras believed that the world was about to undergo a major change. It taught that history was divided into three great ages, corresponding to the three persons of the Trinity (Father, Son, and Holy Spirit). The Age of the Son, which began with the lifetime of Jesus, was now ending, and the next age, that of the Holy Spirit was at hand. This doctrine resembles the teachings of twelfth century visionary JOACHIM OF FIORE.

According to the Vintrasians, the Virgin Mary was to be the focus of prayer at this time in history because she can intercede to forgive humanity its sins and ease the sufferings that occur at the transition between ages. Vintras predicted the destruction of London and Paris as part of this process.

The Church of Carmel was condemned, first by the Bishop of Bayeux in 1841, and then by the pope himself in 1848. Reports that the Church was a front for SATANISM began to circulate. Vintras relocated the headquarters of his movement to the city of Lyons in southeastern France and remained there until his death in 1875.

In that year, Abbé BOULLAN, an acquaintance of Vintras, gained control of a splinter group of the Church of Carmel. Under Boullan's direction, his closest disciples began to practice mystical techniques involving sexual intercourse with animals as well as humans, and masturbating while visualizing sex with angels. This group believed that such activities would accelerate spiritual evolution. The Church of Carmel is thought to have dissolved at the Abbé's death in 1893. Its peculiar doctrines and rituals provided inspiration for decadent French painters of the late nineteenth century.

See also: BLACK MASS.

CHURCH OF JESUS CHRIST OF LATTER-DAY SAINTS   This is the official name for the largest branch of the MORMON faith, with headquarters in Salt Lake City, Utah. Mormonism was given the lengthy name of the Church of Jesus Christ of Latter-Day Saints by its founder, Joseph SMITH, in 1837.

CHURCH OF THE NEW JERUSALEM   The Church of the New Jerusalem is the official name for the SWEDENBORGIAN movement; it follows the teachings of eighteenth century visionary EMANUEL SWEDENBORG.

CLEMENTIUS OF BUCY   The case of Clementius of Bucy, who was tried for heresy in 1114, provides an important glimpse into the medieval mind. The writings of Guibert of Nogent, his Inquisitor, reflect the development of a fantasy that would become prevalent among the educated classes of Europe, distorting their view of religious dissenters and leading to the GREAT WITCH HUNT.

Clementius and his friend Everard lived near the town of Soissons in France. They were brought before Guibert and charged with heresy by the bishop of Soissons. The accusation was based on the reports of neighbors, who had claimed that the two men performed religious ceremonies when not in church. Guibert found the first interrogation frustrating; the suspects seemed poorly educated and did not seem to understand theology well enough to hold the unorthodox views Guibert suspected them of. The inquisitor knew, however, that heretics could simulate ignorance to deceive the unwary and concluded that his suspects were attempting to dupe him.

Guibert was familiar with the propaganda the Catholic fathers of ancient times wrote about the heretical followers of MANICHAEISM; he also knew of the slanders against the ORLEANS HERETICS who had been convicted in the eleventh century, and he may have had access to writings containing the fantasies of orthodox Christian leaders regarding the PAULICIAN heresy of Armenia. He used such accounts to "reconstruct" the heretical beliefs that Clementius and Everard were unwilling to confess to him—their unwillingness arising almost certainly from their innocence of the charges. At worst, they might have held that the church was in need of moral improvement, a rather common observation at the time.

In Guibert's eyes, Clementius and Everard were Manichaeans. They hated the world, engaged in the unnatural practice of vegetarianism, and rejected every Catholic sacrament. Guibert believed his suspects to be guilty of even worse crimes; like the heretics of Orleans and the Paulicians, they attended nocturnal gatherings of heretics at which wild orgies occurred, he assumed. In Guibert's view, baby-killing was also a component of these meetings: a baby was passed from hand to hand among the heretics and was finally tossed onto a fire. The ashes were mixed with dough and made into bread, which was consumed by the heretics as an evil sacrament.

Because of their reluctance to admit to these dark secrets, Clementius and Everard were taken to the "judgment of exorcised water." In this ordeal, a person was thrown into a vat of blessed water. If the individual was guilty of the charge, it was believed, the water would reject the person, who would float; otherwise, the person would sink. Clementius went first. Guibert reported that he "floated like a stick." A terrified Everard then admitted to his heresy. When the news of the trial's outcome circulated, a mob took the heretics from jail and burned them to death.

Guibert's written account of his discoveries helped to give form to the fears of orthodox Christians regarding heretics in late medieval times. Members of later unorthodox movements, such as the CATHARS and WALDENSIANS, were automatically accused of behaving in a manner that resembled Guibert's description of Clementius and Everard, with just as little foundation. By the mid-fifteenth century, the notions of the nocturnal meeting, the orgy, the murder of infants, and cannibalism had become woven into the grand fantasy of the witches' sabbath. The witch hunters discovered that most people, when tortured, would verify the reality of Guibert's account—or of anything else they were asked.

CLEOMENES   A heretical teacher active in Rome during the early third century A.D., Cleomenes was a follower of PRAXEAS, the founder of the unorthodox doctrine called MODALISM.

COMPENDIUM MALEFICARUM   The Latin title of this book means "collection on witches." *Compendium Maleficarum* was written by Francesco Maria Guazzo, a member of the Roman Catholic Order of Saint Ambrose near Milan. It was composed at the request of the archbishop of Milan and was first published in 1608. As commentator Montague Summers noted, "The Compendium Maleficarum was at once accepted as supremely authoritative by all contemporaries, and later demonologists have not been slow to commend, apprize, and make final appeal to this most salutary and excellent treatise." The book was extensively used by lawyers and church authorities in making arguments and rendering judgments in witchcraft trials throughout the seventeenth century.

Guazzo was an experienced judge at witch trials. He was a firm believer in the reality of witchcraft, but he was also aware that every report could not be taken at face value. "Any man who maintained that all the effects of magic were true, or who believed that they were all illusions, would be rather a radish than a man," he wrote. Guazzo knew that the purpose of the witchcraft trials was to distinguish truth from falsehood, and he wrote his book to help others make such determinations.

Compendium Maleficarum is essentially an extension and updating of Kramer and Sprenger's classic, MALLEUS MALEFICARUM, published in 1486. During the following century, European beliefs in witchcraft as an international conspiracy of devil worshippers became more detailed. The new details were derived primarily from records of the ravings of people being tortured to extract confessions. *Compendium Maleficarum* drew heavily on two earlier works based largely on confessional material, *Demonolatreiae* of Nicolas Remy and *Disquisitionium Magicarum* by Martin Del Rio. It is noteworthy that the title of *The Compendium*, like the earlier *Malleus*, uses the word "maleficarum." This is the feminine form of the Latin term for witches and reflects the enduring belief that women were mainly responsible for witchcraft.

The imprint of Guazzo's legalistic mind is evident in the organization of his *Compendium*. The book is divided into chapters, each of which consists of an "argument" and "examples." In the argument, he discusses the topic of the chapter with respect to its reality and unique features. In the examples, he provides instances of the topic, drawing from classical sources, as well as trial records and current rumors.

The *Compendium* details many of the activities that filled the popular imagination concerning witchcraft. Such pursuits as raising storms, creating disease, causing impotence, starting fires, and producing infestations of "imperfect animals" (worms and bugs) are described. Guazzo does, however, reveal some skepticism about witchcraft stories, although the form of his skepticism may strike the modern reader as bizarre. He ridicules the belief that witches can turn into animals, but he states that the Devil can assume an animal form and impersonate a witch. He also admits that some women who reported going to the nocturnal witches' meetings were known to have slept in their beds all night. But he claims that witches can magically attend these meetings in their dreams. In addition, he notes that the Devil can create a "false body" to lie in the witch's bed, so she can secretly attend the meetings. In the face of such logic, gathering evidence to prove someone's innocence was nearly impossible.

The fact that a well-known religious and legal figure documented such matters in an impressive book fanned the fire of belief in the witchcraft conspiracy. When someone complained to the authorities that a neighbor was to blame for some misfortune, Guazzo's work could be consulted to decide if such a thing was possible. If it was decided that witchcraft caused the event, the suspects could be arrested and tortured until they admitted to the crimes.

Although Guazzo never raises questions about the validity of evidence collected using torture, he does discuss why some witches must undergo prolonged torment before they will confess. The *Compendium* describes how a demon can enter a witch's throat and prevent her from speaking. It also reports that a demon can hide in a witch's hair, or enter the torture cell in the form of a fly and whisper encouragement to the witch so she will resist her Inquisitors' requests. In these passages, the *Compendium* gives comfort to torturers when they encounter an unusually strong or stubborn victim.

The book is illustrated throughout with beautiful woodcuts. These images, which show the various dark activities of witches, convey the fears and fantasies of the time much more powerfully than the rather dry text. The woodcuts have appeared in most illustrated books on witchcraft to this day.

See also: DEMONS, PACT.

CONSOLAMENTUM   This religious ritual was central to two prominent medieval heresies, the BOGOMILS and the CATHARS. In both cases, the consolamentum initiated the applicant into the highest rank of the religion. In the Bogomil version, someone who already belonged to the rank of perfectus would place a copy of the Gospel of John on the head of the applicant, who had to live a strictly moral life forever afterward. The Cathar ritual was derived from that of the Bogomils. The Cathar initiator would place a hand on the applicant's head, transferring spiritual power and the accompanying moral obligations. Because a person was not allowed to eat meat or have sex ever again after receiving the consolamentum, it was often administered shortly before death to decrease the likelihood of the individual's succumbing to temptation.

See also: ENDURA.

CONSTANS II   This ruler of the Byzantine Empire (the remnant of the eastern Roman Empire by the seventh century) is a hated figure in the annals of Catholic Christianity because he championed a heresy and brutalized a pope. When Constans II came to power in 641, the church was paralyzed by a ferocious debate concerning fine points of theology. Arguments raged over the number of natures, actions, and wills in Christ. As a consequence, Christianity had divided, rather than united, the people of the empire. Moslem armies had surged forth from Arabia earlier in the century and took full advantage of the empire's weakness by conquering much of the Middle East in just a few years.

Constans perceived the dire need to unite the peoples of his empire against the Moslem threat. He felt that divisive theological debates were a luxury that could not be permitted during a crisis, so he simply forbade them. He proclaimed the doctrine called MONOTHELETISM, which taught that Christ has a single will, to be the undeniable truth.

In 647, six years into Constans's reign, Martin became the pope. He believed that Monotheletism was heresy and in 649 publicly denounced the doctrine, throwing off the emperor's muzzle on theological debate. The Moslem threat continued to press, and Constans was unwilling to tolerate disobedience from anyone. He ordered Martin's arrest and transportation from Rome to Constantinople.

The pope was convicted of high treason. He was publicly stripped, chained, and dragged over rough stones to the place of execution. His death sentence was commuted at the last moment to exile. Martin was sent, badly injured and ill-equipped, into the untamed border country of the Crimea. He died of cold and hunger in 655.

Constans, having thus attempted to quell the continued turmoil within the church, engaged in a series of unsuccessful sea battles against the Arabs and eventually lost control of the eastern Mediterranean Sea. He then tried to reconquer Italy by fighting the occupying Lombard tribe. Instead, he was killed by his own troops in 668, who mutinied in reaction to his military incompetence. Constantine IV, his son and successor, rejected Constans's heavy-handed approach to the church, and sided with the Catholics. At the THIRD COUNCIL OF CONSTANTINOPLE in 681, Monotheletism was condemned as a heresy.

CONSTANTINE V   The emperor of the Byzantine Empire from A.D. 720 to 775, Constantine V was the most ferocious supporter of the heresy called ICONO-CLASM, the opposition to the religious use of images. He convened a meeting of Christian officials in 754 and ensured that the council condemn the use of images as heretical. During the latter part of his reign, Constantine unleashed a terror campaign against the supporters of the images; killing, blinding, or exiling them. He ordered the decapitation of the patriarch of Constantinople and put the head on public display as a warning to anyone who might disobey him. After Constantine's death, Empress Irene, his son's wife, arranged for the removal of the iconoclasts from power within the Byzantine Church.

CONSTANTINE OF ARMENIA   The earliest known leader of the PAULI-CIANS, a heretical group that succeeded in founding a short-lived independent state during the ninth century. Constantine of Armenia lived during the mid-seventh century. His teaching that the world was created and governed by an evil god so enraged the orthodox Christians of the eastern Byzantine Empire that they burned him at the stake in 682.

CONSTANTIUS II   Constantius II was the ruler of the eastern portion of the Roman Empire from A.D. 337 to 350, and sole monarch of the empire from 350 to 360. He was a supporter of the heretical Christian movement called ARIANISM against the orthodox Christians, who were backed by Constantius's western counterpart, Emperor Constans, until 350. Under Constantius's sponsorship after Constans's death, Arianism overran the church, and Catholic leaders were exiled. Constantius wavered in his support between two factions of the Arians, the ANOMOEANS and the SEMI-ARIANS. In 359, he tried unsuccessfully to impose the Semi-Arian doctrine on all Christians.

COPTIC CHRISTIANS   Christianity in Egypt has a long and eventful history, beginning with the visit of JESUS himself. Great figures of orthodoxy, such as Athanasius and Cyril, as well as important heretics like VALENTINUS and APOLLINARIS, thrived in Egypt. During the fifth century controversy regarding the nature of Christ, Bishop DIOSCURUS of Alexandria sided with the Monophysites. After the COUNCIL OF CHALCEDON in A.D. 451, when orthodox Christianity declared MONOPHYSITISM to be a heresy, Egypt became alienated from the mainstream of Christian belief. The Monophysites took over the Christian Church in Egypt, founding the Coptic Church, and spread their doctrine southward to Ethiopia. Since the Moslem conquest of the seventh century, the population of Coptic Christians in Egypt has declined, but some still exist today, preserving their Monophysite heritage.

See also: APHTHARTODOCETAE, GAIANUS OF ALEXANDRIA, JULIAN OF HALICARNASSUS.

Wilhelm CORNELIUS   A Dutch heretic, active around the mid-thirteenth century, Wilhelm Cornelius taught that poverty is virtue: poor people were blessed and could do what they wished without sinning, but the rich were damned and should be avoided. He gathered a following in the city of Antwerp, where poverty was rife. This unorthodox circle was not discovered until four years after its leader's death. Catholic officials then ordered that Cornelius's body be dug up and burned as punishment for his heresy.

CORPUS HERMETICUM   This body of texts is the largest surviving sample of the ancient literary genre known as the HERMETICA. *Corpus Hermeticum* consists of fifteen short books that claim to preserve the wisdom of a mythical figure, Hermes Trismegistus. The works were likely composed in Egypt around the beginning of the third century A.D. They were preserved in Constantinople until the fall of that city to the Moslems in 1453. Manuscripts containing most of the *Corpus* were taken to Florence, where they provided the source for many of the occult doctrines of the Renaissance.

The most influential text in the collection is the first, called *Poimandres*. It describes a vision Hermes received when he was in a trance. He was visited by "a being of vast and boundless magnitude" named Poimandres, "the Mind of absolute power" who offered to answer all his questions. The text claims that Hermes learned the origin and spiritual fate of humanity from the mysterious visitor. Humans originally come from the Light, who is also Mind and God. As people descended into the material world, they became intimately connected with the seven spheres of the planets and contain these planets within them. Humans have fallen under the rule of the seven Governors (the planets), and have forgotten their true nature as Light. Their spiritual task, accomplished through knowledge, is to rise through and throw off the influences of the planetary spheres, and finally "to become God."

Florentine scholars, such as MARSILIO FICINO, believed that *Poimandres* and other Hermetic writings were divine revelations. Ficino developed an important system of NATURAL MAGIC in order to harmonize the inner planets and thus produce health. The possibility that DEMONS might be involved in such hermetic magic caused many orthodox Christian officials to be concerned about the influence of *Corpus Hermeticum*. The goal of "becoming God" also seems to contradict the orthodox dogma that the Creator and His creatures (including humans) are distinct and can never be identified as one. Many students of the *Corpus* during the Renaissance were suspected of or charged with heresy.

COUNCIL OF CHALCEDON   The meeting of church leaders at Chalcedon in A.D. 451 marked the complete establishment of orthodox Christian doctrine. The doctrines proclaimed at Chalcedon, along with those affirmed at the FIRST COUNCIL OF NICAEA in 325, provide the definitions of God and Christ (and, therefore, of humans, too) for orthodox Christianity to the present day.

The Council of Chalcedon was the culmination of several decades of violent controversies regarding the nature of Christ. The First Council of Nicaea had defined Christ, the Son of God, as fully divine in His nature. In 381, belief in this view was proclaimed as part of the official religion of the Roman Empire. The definition of Christ as divine raised a question concerning His humanity: Was the human appearance of JESUS of Nazareth an illusion, or did He possess a human nature in addition to His divine nature?

Various answers to this question were proposed. APOLLINARIS stated that Christ had a complete divine nature but only a partial human nature, and lacked a human intellect. The orthodox position developed in response to Apollinaris held that Christ had to have a complete human nature; otherwise, His death on the cross could not earn forgiveness for the sins of human nature. This conclusion raised another question: If Christ has two natures, is He, therefore, two distinct persons who inhabited a single body?

NESTORIUS replied that Christ was a single person with two natures, but he highlighted the differences between the natures to such a degree that many critics accused him of teaching that Christ was split into two. He was condemned as a heretic by orthodox authorities, who became convinced that a Christ who was fragmented into two persons (the doctrine of NESTORIANISM) could not function as a Savior. The notion of the fragmented Christ produced such loathing in the orthodox community that it provoked some Christians, notably EUTYCHES, to reject all versions of the two-natures doctrine. Eutyches' view, which became known as MONOPHYSITISM, held that Christ was a single person with a single divine nature.

Orthodoxy had already rejected the idea that Christ lacked a human nature when

Apollinaris was condemned. Through clever political maneuvering, however, the Monophysites managed to have their doctrine declared orthodox at the council held in Ephesus in 449. This ROBBER COUNCIL, as it has come to be known, labeled the supporters of the two-natures doctrine, including the pope, heretics.

The Robber Council's assault on orthodoxy called for a decisive response, the Council of Chalcedon. This meeting was called to overturn the proclamations of the Robber Council and to end the destructive debate on Christ's natures within the orthodox church. The council was carefully controlled by the dominant powers in the church, namely the bishops of Constantinople and Rome, to ensure their victory. The church leaders who had been deposed by the Monophysites were reinstated, and the Monophysites themselves were condemned. Regarding the theological issue of Christ's natures, it was proclaimed that Christ has two complete natures, divine and human; however, He is a single Person. Forever afterward, according to the orthodox view, anyone who disagreed with this formulation would not attain salvation.

The Council of Chalcedon unified orthodox Christianity. It did not eliminate dissent, however, but merely excluded the dissenters from recognition as orthodox. Both Nestorians and Monophysites were numerous, especially in the Middle East, and the decrees of Chalcedon did not cause them to abandon their views or to disappear. Indeed, the citizens of Alexandria rioted when, following the decision at Chalcedon the orthodox authorities replaced their Monophysite bishop, DIOSCURUS, with Proterius, who accepted the doctrine of the two natures. A few years later, Proterius was captured by a mob and torn apart.

After Chalcedon, Christian communities in Syria, Palestine, and Egypt remained largely committed to unorthodox beliefs. The alienation of these regions from the orthodox centers of Rome and Constantinople contributed to the ease with which Moslems spread their faith during the seventh century.

In addition to the theological and political legacies of Chalcedon, the Western sense of human identity itself was decisively affected. The council officially established that Christ's unique existence as a person is not a mere appearance masking the deeper reality of His double nature; Christ's personhood is real in its own right. Like Christ, each human being is an individual person; also like Christ, our existence as persons is not an illusion to be discarded, but a reality to be valued, according to orthodox Christianity. This emphasis on the reality and value of the individual person was built into the foundations of the Western world view at Chalcedon and has been a central theme in Western culture ever since. Many aspects of modern society, from the importance we place on personal human rights to our admiration of outstanding individuals, are based on the outcome of the church's confrontation with heresy in A.D. 451.

COUNCIL OF CONSTANTINOPLE (First)   In A.D. 381, Theodosius, the ruler of the Roman Empire, called a meeting of church leaders at Constantinople, the imperial capital. The purpose of the council was to end the decades-long struggle between the Catholics and the followers of ARIANISM over determining the official Christian view about the nature of God. The First Council of Constantinople marked both the end of the Arian heresy as a dominant force in the Christian world and the establishment of Catholicism as the state religion of the Roman Empire.

The statement produced by the leaders at Constantinople is known today as the

Niceno-Constantinopolitan Creed. (Some scholars believe that the current version of the creed was composed sometime after the council ended but accurately summarizes the council's decisions.) The creed accepts the doctrine proclaimed at the earlier FIRST COUNCIL OF NICAEA that defines the terms Father and Son, found in Christian scriptures, as beings who have the same divine nature. In short, both are God. In 381, the council went further, announcing that the Holy Spirit also shares the nature of God. The Father, Son, and Holy Spirit are defined as having the same divine nature, but also as being three distinct Persons. This formulation of the Trinity is the orthodox description of God and has remained so to this day. The Arians, who insisted that the Son has a different nature from God the Father, were condemned as heretics.

The Catholic victory over the Arians at Constantinople occurred largely because Emperor Theodosius was a devout Catholic. When he came to power, replacing VALENS, who had supported Arianism, the Catholics moved quickly to consolidate their dominance in the Christian world. Theodosius declared that all non-Catholic opinions regarding Christian beliefs were illegal. This move put the military and police powers of the Roman state at the disposal of the Catholics, who did not wait long to use them.

Before Theodosius's proclamation, Catholics could not legally kill those who disagreed with them; five years after the First Council of Constantinople, PRISCILLIAN, a Spanish priest, became the first man to be executed for heresy by the Catholics. Catholic mobs could now destroy Jewish synagogues and pagan temples without fear of legal consequences. A long and dark chapter in the history of heresy had begun.

COUNCIL OF CONSTANTINOPLE (Second)   In A.D. 553, Emperor Justinian called a meeting of Christianity's leaders in order to promote unity within the church. At issue was the movement called MONOPHYSITISM, which claimed that Christ had a single divine nature. The orthodox doctrine had been established a century earlier at the COUNCIL OF CHALCEDON. Then, the doctrine that Christ has two natures, one divine and one human, was established, and disagreement on this point was defined as heresy. Many Monophysites, particularly in Syria and Egypt where they were quite numerous, had refused to accept the decision of Chalcedon. The orthodox Catholic authorities, for their part, were not eager to excommunicate entire populations and sought ways to reconcile the Monophysites with the mainstream church.

Justinian knew that THEODORE OF MOPSUESTIA, THEODORET, and IBAS—three Christian teachers of the previous century—were regarded as heretics by the Monophysites. These three men had written about the two natures of Christ in such a way that Christ almost seemed to be divided into two disconnected parts. In an attempt to entice the Monophysites back into the Catholic Christian community, Justinian called the leaders of the church to Constantinople and commanded them to condemn the writings of Theodore, Theodoret, and Ibas.

The emperor effectively controlled the Eastern bishops, but the Christian community in the western part of the old Roman Empire had resisted compromise with the Monophysites. Pope Vigilius, their leader, had been especially unresponsive to Justinian's previous attempts to dictate church doctrine. Justinian tried to solve this problem by kidnapping the pope and imprisoning him in Constantinople, where he could be forced to obey the emperor's "suggestions." On occasion, he was tortured.

Even under these circumstances, Vigilius was less than cooperative, so he remained captive. By the time of the Second Council of Constantinople in 553, the pope had been trapped there for eight years.

The bishops attending the council dutifully supported Justinian and condemned the writings, which were known as the "Three Chapters." Incredibly, Vigilius had refused to attend the council despite his totally vulnerable situation as a prisoner. The emperor required the pope's support for the council's decisions to be universally recognized as legitimate. The captive pontiff's stubbornness was finally worn down, and the following year he accepted the condemnation of the three chapters. Vigilius was released from prison, but, broken from his harsh treatment, he died while returning to Rome.

Another source of disturbance within the church at the time was the movement called ORIGENISM. The Origenists based their beliefs on the works of the third century church father ORIGEN, but they developed his ideas in directions that seemed to go far beyond the orthodox doctrines of the sixth century. Justinian arranged for the bishops who had assembled for the Second Council to condemn the works of Origen in order to undermine the Origenists.

It is important to note that the damning of Origen was not an official act of the council, but occurred before the formal commencement of the council's proceedings. Also, there is no evidence that Pope Vigilius ever accepted the rejection of Origen. It is often assumed that Origen's condemnation at the Second Council of Constantinople was officially adopted into the Roman Catholic tradition. Given the circumstances under which it took place, the legality of the act is questionable.

COUNCIL OF CONSTANTINOPLE (Third)   The Third Council of Constantinople met in A.D. 680–681. It was called to end the violent discussions concerning the nature of God and of Christ that dominated the church in ancient times, frequently threatening to tear it apart. The council was convened by Emperor Constantine IV, whose father, CONSTANS II, had tortured and exiled Pope Martin for disagreeing with him. Constantine feared that continued doctrinal squabbling within the church would lead to the collapse of the empire. The West had already been largely lost to Germanic invaders, and the eastern empire had shrunk drastically during the preceding decades under the onslaught of the Moslems. Lack of religious unity produced social unrest, making the remaining empire vulnerable to conquest.

This council reaffirmed the decisions of the earlier church councils, proclaiming that Christ has two natures, one divine and one human, and that these natures are united in a single Person. In addition, the Third Council established that Christ has two wills and two "actions" or effects, corresponding to the two natures. This statement defines the doctrines of MONOTHELETISM (one will) and MONENERGISM (one "action") as heretical. HONORIUS, a pope during the early seventh century, had supported Monotheletism, so he was denounced as a heretic.

Following the Third Council, the Monothelete heresy was effectively eliminated from territory the orthodox Christian leaders controlled. Monotheletism was preserved by the MARONITES, a Christian community in Arab-occupied Lebanon, for another 500 years.

See also: COUNCIL OF CHALCEDON.

COUNCIL OF EPHESUS   Several times during the history of Christianity, the leading figures in the church have been called together to deal with serious threats to the faith. The Council of Ephesus, which took place in A.D. 431, was the third such meeting. (This council should not be confused with another gathering, held in Ephesus in 449, which is generally known as the ROBBER COUNCIL.)

The occasion for the Council of Ephesus was the controversy among Christian thinkers regarding the nature of Christ. Two bishops, Cyril of Alexandria and NESTORIUS of Constantinople, were locked in a violent disagreement. Nestorius had expressed concerns about a popular title for the Virgin Mary, the Greek term *Theotokos*, which means "God-bearer." Nestorius emphasized that Christ has both a divine and a human nature, and worried that calling Mary "God-bearer" implied that Christ was not human. Cyril attacked Nestorius, claiming that the rejection of Theotokos degraded Christ's divine nature. Cyril also accused Nestorius of teaching that Christ not only had two natures, but also was split into two different persons. Nestorius denied the charges and challenged Cyril's description of the manner in which Christ's two natures were united.

Political motivations can be discerned underneath the surface of the theological debate. At this time, the most important Christian centers, Alexandria, Rome, and Constantinople were maneuvering to increase their power over each other. Establishing that the bishop of a competing city was a heretic was an effective strategy in weakening that city's influence in the Christian Roman Empire.

Emperor Theodosius II relied on church unity to help keep his empire together in the face of mounting pressure from invading Germanic tribes. He called the council in order to lay to rest the controversy surrounding the position of Nestorius, known as NESTORIANISM. The political pressures caused the events of the council to play out in a confused and farcical manner. Upon Cyril's arrival, he insisted that the council begin immediately, even though the delegations from Rome and Antioch had not yet arrived. At this first meeting, under Cyril's influence, Nestorius was declared to be a heretic and deposed. When Bishop John of Antioch arrived, another meeting was held. Since John was an ally of Nestorius, the bishop of Constantinople was redeemed and Cyril was condemned. The delegation from Rome then arrived, and another meeting was held, concluding in support for Cyril and in defeat for Nestorius.

Following the Council of Ephesus, Nestorius made a strategic error: he retreated to a monastery, leaving the field open for Cyril to continue recruiting support. Cyril and Bishop John reached an agreement opposing Nestorius. Cyril already had the support of the pope and of the emperor's wife. Nestorius was finally driven into exile, five years after his condemnation at the council. The Nestorian doctrines continued to spread, however, and survived for many centuries.

Alexandria's political victory at the Council of Ephesus was undone by DIOSCURUS, Cyril's successor as bishop of Alexandria. Attempting to enlarge upon Cyril's success, Dioscurus forced the Robber Council of 449 to condemn the bishops of Rome and Constantinople. This act elicited a reaction that forever alienated Egypt from the Christian mainstream.

COUNCIL OF NICAEA (First)   During much of the fourth century, the Christian world was split into warring camps. On one side was a group that believed that

Christ, the Son of God, had the same divine nature as God the Father and, therefore, had the power to save humanity from its sins. On the other side were the disciples of ARIANISM, a belief system that held that the Son of God did not have God's divine nature, but rather was a creation of God. The First Council of Nicaea took place in A.D. 325 in that town, which is near the city of Byzantium (now Istanbul, Turkey). This gathering was the first major attempt Christian leaders made to resolve the conflict. Emperor Constantine organized the council; he wished for a speedy end to the divisions within the church because they were contributing to the social instability of the Roman Empire.

The First Council was in favor of the orthodox party: Father and Son were said to have the same essential nature, and the Father did not create the Son at some point in time. The doctrines of Arianism were rejected. The leading Arians, including ARIUS, the founder of the movement, were exiled.

Although the decision made at Nicaea supported the orthodox Catholic view concerning the nature of God, Arianism continued to challenge the orthodox for control of the church for several decades. The authority of the First Council of Nicaea proved to be an obstacle for the Arians, even at the height of their power when most of the orthodox leaders had been deposed. Eventually, the orthodox view, first established at Nicaea, became the official Christian perspective on God, and everyone who disagreed was persecuted as a heretic.

See also: EUSEBIUS OF NICOMEDIA, MARCELLUS OF ANCYRA.

COUNCIL OF NICAEA (Second)   This meeting, which took place in A.D. 787, marked the last time that representatives of the entire Christian Church gathered to defeat heresy. For centuries beforehand, the eastern part of the Catholic Church, centered in Constantinople, and the western part, based in Rome, had gradually been developing in different directions. During the period following the Second Council of Nicaea, the disagreements, particularly those involving the Romans' insistence on the supremacy of the pope over the entire church, turned into differences that have not yet been resolved.

The Second Council of Nicaea was convened by Byzantine Empress Irene in an attempt to resolve the controversy surrounding the movement called ICONO-CLASM. The iconoclasts opposed the use of icons, or depictions of Christ, Mary, and the saints, in the Christian faith, believing that icons were no better than idols. Many orthodox Christian leaders, including the pope, held that religious images were valuable as aids to piety and supported their continued use. The council condemned iconoclasm as heresy.

Thomas CRANMER   One of the most significant figures of sixteenth century English history, Thomas Cranmer played diverse roles during his fateful life: papally approved archbishop of Canterbury, leader of the Protestant Reformation, and, at the end, condemned heretic. Cranmer was born in 1489, the son of a farmer. He studied at Cambridge and was ordained a priest around 1523. Henry VIII occupied the English throne at this time. During the next several years, the king attempted, unsuccessfully, to pressure the pope to annul his marriage to Catherine of Aragon so that he could marry Anne Boleyn. Cranmer suggested to Henry that he stop involving the pope and instead obtain permission for the divorce from the theologians at the

English universities. This maneuver would save face for both king and pope. Cranmer's clever suggestion gained him powerful allies. In 1532, Archbishop Warham died. Cranmer, supported by the king and the pontiff, became the new archbishop of Canterbury.

The independence-minded king arranged for the Church of England to break away from papal control two years later and appointed himself the head of the church. Cranmer believed that a country should follow the religion of its ruler, so he went along with Henry. Until Henry's death in 1547, the archbishop generally supported his policies and managed to retain the erratic king's trust.

During the six-year reign of Edward VI, Henry's son and successor, Cranmer led the Church of England in the direction of the Protestantism emerging in continental Europe. He was the primary author of *The Book of Common Prayer*, a text that defined the ceremonies and language of the new church.

After the sickly young king died at the age of fifteen, Mary Tudor assumed the English throne. Mary was a staunch Catholic. In addition, the English rejection of papal control had rendered her technically an illegitimate child: she was the daughter of Henry VIII and Catherine of Aragon, whose marriage the pope had upheld, but Henry's sympathizers, including Cranmer declared it "incestuous and unlawful." The new queen earned her nickname, "Bloody Mary," by the violent way in which the Protestant reforms were suppressed and Roman Catholicism promoted. The most prominent victim was Cranmer, who was charged with heresy.

Cranmer's belief that one should follow the faith of one's ruler put him in a difficult position; to be consistent with this principle, he should have returned to being a loyal Catholic when a Catholic assumed the throne. At first, Cranmer followed this track and signed several declarations rejecting his Protestant views. However, his conscience stirred, and he took back his recantations.

He was burned to death before a large crowd on March 21, 1556. As the flames approached, he thrust the hand that had signed the recantations into the fire, to signal his regret at having denied his true Protestant convictions.

See also: JOHN HOOPER, HUGH LATIMER, NICHOLAS RIDLEY.

Nicholas CRELL   A chancellor in sixteenth century Germany, Nicholas Crell's death at the stake resulted not from heresy on his part, but from his support for the wrong kind of orthodoxy. Crell actively promoted the Calvinist variety of Protestantism during the five-year rule of Prince Christian I, who supported him. The prince's successor was a Lutheran.

At this time, Lutheranism was attempting to solidify its position as the unchallenged religion of the area. Crell, as the best-known local Calvinist, was targeted to be an example. He was convicted of heresy and burned to death in 1601. While the Lutherans and Calvinists strongly disagreed on many points, they were both conventional branches of the Protestant Reformation and had a great deal in common. It was extremely unusual for members of one mainstream Protestant denomination to execute a member of the other for heresy.

Aleister CROWLEY   The most influential magician of the modern era. Aleister Crowley founded a religion, Crowleyanity, featuring himself as the central figure of redemption. Crowley was born in 1875 into an English family that had made a fortune in the brewery business. His parents belonged to a strict Christian sect called the Plymouth Brethren. As a boy, Crowley was strongly encouraged to adopt such beliefs himself. Instead, the opposite occurred. He was so rebellious that his mother called him "The Great Beast" after the monster described in the Book of Revelation. Crowley identified strongly with the name, and he was known by this title throughout his life.

The Beast dedicated his life to exploring every kind of human experience. He sought out the full range of sexual possibilities, took every drug available, climbed mountains, read widely, had several different names and identities, and was not above any outrageous act. He also was not shy about publicity. In fact, when his exploits attracted the attention of the press, he seemed to enjoy his notoriety.

By his early twenties, Crowley's explorations brought him into contact with the traditions of ritual magic. In 1898, he joined the Hermetic Order of the GOLDEN DAWN. This organization had developed a rich synthesis of Western occult traditions. Crowley proved to be such a keen student that he quickly advanced up the ladder of secret initiations, which gave him access to some of the higher teachings of the Order. In particular, he was intrigued by the ritual described in the text entitled SACRED MAGIC OF ABRAMELIN THE MAGE, which had been translated into English by one of the Order's founders, S. L. M. Mathers. Through his magical experiments, Crowley was convinced of the reality and power of spirit beings.

Before long, Crowley became involved in the conflicts flaring among the leaders of the Golden Dawn. When Crowley applied for initiation into a higher rank within the Order, the officials in England refused. Poet W. B. Yeats, one of these officials, explained, "We did not admit him because we did not think a mystical society was intended to be a reformatory." Crowley traveled to Paris, where Mathers was then living. Mathers and the leadership in England were not on the best of terms. Crowley received the initiation from Mathers and returned to England, demanding the magical teachings to which his new rank entitled him. As a result of the ensuing conflict, Crowley left the Golden Dawn; the Order itself began to disintegrate. This event is but one example of Crowley's disruptive influence, which characterized his entire career.

The Golden Dawn claimed to derive its teachings and its authority from contact with the "Secret Chiefs," powerful spiritual beings of great wisdom. After departing from the Order, Crowley decided that he had to establish direct contact with the Chiefs. He traveled the world, honing his ritual magic skills and learning occult lore.

In 1904, during a visit to Cairo, Crowley received a revelation. A mysterious voice claiming to be Aiwass, "a messenger from the forces ruling this earth at present"— that is, the Secret Chiefs—dictated to him a short work called *The Book of the Law*. On the basis of his revelation, Crowley came to believe that human history could be viewed in three phases: in the Aeon of Isis, the goddess ruled, and government was matriarchal; after 500 B.C., the Aeon of Osiris dawned, marked by male deities and patriarchy; and in 1904, his own experience in Cairo marked the advent of the third age, the Aeon of Horus. All previous spiritual systems were now outmoded. The new religion, called Crowleyanity, or *Thelema* (the Greek word for "will"), was based on this principle: "Do what thou Wilt shall be the whole of the Law." The Will was not the obsessions and compulsions that motivate the average person, but the unified, consciously focused intention of the trained magician.

Crowley spent the rest of his life promoting his vision of the Aeon of Horus, with little success. In the process, however, he brought together diverse aspects of occult practice and encouraged many students to conduct experiments in magic. Three years after the Cairo revelation, he founded his own society, the Argenteum Astrum ("Silver Star") and published several volumes of magic instruction (in addition to poems and novels, some of which were pornographic). Crowley combined the magical methods of ritual magic he learned in the Golden Dawn with Asian yoga practices, thereby developing a system designed to promote the attainment of free and effective Will—a magic version of enlightenment.

The Great Beast was also keen on including sexual activity in his magical system. In 1912, Crowley was contacted by a German magical society, the ORDO TEMPLI ORIENTIS (OTO), which had been practicing sex magic. In light of his mastery, he was invited to become head of an English chapter of the OTO; in 1922, he assumed the leadership of the entire society.

Between this time and his death in 1947, Crowley lived and taught in France, England, the United States, and Italy. His most ambitious attempt to spread the gospel of Crowleyanity occurred in 1920, when he established the Abbey of Thelema in Sicily. The abbey functioned for three years. Crowley hoped that it would become a world center for esoteric studies, but it attracted few students. Rumors of bizarre ceremonies, including group sex and animal sacrifices, reached such a pitch that the Mussolini regime ran him out of the country.

Unfortunately, during his experiments with drugs, Crowley's Will could not protect him from becoming addicted to heroin. The final years of his life were devoted mainly to writing and to feeding his habit. He died of heart failure at the age of seventy-two. Crowley's last words were "I am perplexed," a statement that does not raise one's confidence in the spiritual achievements of the Great Beast. Nevertheless, his powerfully stimulating magic techniques have continued to inspire many ritual magicians to the present day.

See also: ENOCHIAN MAGIC, SATANISM.

CRYPTO-SABELLIANISM   A major challenge to orthodox Christianity during the third century was SABELLIANISM, a form of the heresy of MODALISM. In the 300s, during the power struggle between the orthodox Christians and the followers of the heretic ARIUS, the Arians frequently charged the orthodox with being Sabellians in disguise, or "Crypto-Sabellians." The orthodox supporter MARCELLUS OF AN-CYRA was often called a Crypto-Sabellian; in his case, the charge is close to the truth.

Martin CZECHOWIC   A leading Polish ANTI-TRINITARIAN heretic, Martin Czechowic was born in 1532. At the time, Poland was a land of religious tolerance, and many unorthodox believers from across Europe went there. These immigrants influenced Czechowic to develop deviant doctrines himself. With his colleague SIMON BUDNY, Czechowic was invited to Lithuania by its ruler, where he taught the heresy of TRITHEISM: the three Persons of the Christian Trinity are, in fact, three separate gods. In 1565, a Catholic came to power in Lithuania, and such views were banned. Czechowic's fate is unknown.

Sir Francis DASHWOOD   An eighteenth century British aristocrat and leader of the sacrilegious group called the MEDMENHAM MONKS, Sir Francis Dashwood as a young man, became alienated from Christianity and lived the life of a thrill-seeking playboy. In 1750, he purchased the ruined Medmenham Abbey, which became the setting for the antics of his monks. Later in life, Dashwood seemed to return to the orthodox fold. He was even involved in revising *The Book of Common Prayer*, which the Church of England used. Whether his orthodoxy was sincere or intended as a joke is uncertain.

Ferenc DAVID   Ferenc David was a prominent preacher of unorthodox Christianity in sixteenth century Transylvania. During the middle of the century, Transylvania tolerated both orthodox Catholics and Protestants, but ANTI-TRINITARIANS—those who rejected the orthodox notion of the Trinity—were not officially welcome. Nonetheless, Ferenc David, originally a Calvinist who accepted the Trinity, adopted the Anti-Trinitarian cause, probably under the influence of visiting Polish heretics. He allied himself with Italian radical GIORGIO BLANDRATA. Together, they preached the TRITHEISTIC heresy: the three Persons of the Trinity were not one God, but three distinct divine beings. David eventually rejected the Trinity dogma altogether and embraced the UNITARIAN view that the Deity is a single Person. He convinced King John II Sigismund to extend religious toleration to Unitarianism, thereby laying the foundation for Transylvania's adoption of this doctrine as a state religion in 1568.

DAVID OF DINANT   A philosopher of the twelfth century, David of Dinant was born in Belgium and probably taught in Paris; few other details concerning his life have survived. Aristotle's writings regarding the natural world strongly affected him. David came to believe that God is an essence that pervades everything in nature. Catholics viewed this idea as heresy (PANTHEISM) because they believe that the Creator and His creation are separate entities. In 1210, the church ordered that David's writings be burned. This heretic's interest in Aristotle tainted the ancient philosopher in the eyes of the orthodox: the study of Aristotle's metaphysical writings was banned in Paris.

John DEE   During his busy life in the Elizabethan period, John Dee played many roles: astrologer, magician, alchemist, author (of seventy-nine books), communist, dupe, and spy. Dee is an important figure in the history of ANGEL MAGIC. He was born in London, of Welsh parentage, in 1527. Even in childhood, he displayed a thirst for knowledge. His intense desire to learn led him to begin his studies at Cambridge University when he was only fifteen. Still in his teens, he traveled to continental Europe to continue his research and encountered occult teachings. Dee was especially interested in the works of CORNELIUS AGRIPPA, the German theorist of magic, with their detailed discussions of the various kinds of spiritual beings.

Returning to England as a young man, Dee began a lifelong series of experiments in ALCHEMY. He also started to acquire a reputation as an expert astrologer. Queen Mary requested the occultist to cast her horoscope, and Dee's personal star certainly seemed on the rise during this phase of his life. Mary's sister and eventual successor, Elizabeth, also consulted Dee, reportedly asking him to predict the date of Mary's death. When word of this reached the Queen, she ordered that Dee be arrested and thrown in jail. He was accused of being, in Dee's words, "a companion of hellhounds and a caller and conjurer of wicked and damned spirits." He was acquitted and released, but for the rest of his life had to contend with an unfounded reputation as a black magician. At one point, a mob broke into his home when he was abroad and destroyed much of his collection of rare books, in the belief that the texts were manuals of DEMON MAGIC.

With the ascension of Elizabeth to the English throne in 1558, Dee's fortune improved again. He became a confidante of the new queen and even chose the date of her coronation ceremony based on his astrological calculations. Later, during Dee's foreign travels, he was probably working as a spy for his monarch.

Dee's continued interest in the world of spirits led him to attempt communication with them. He believed in the existence of both angels and devils, but he was keen to avoid the latter, the "goblins damn'd." Dee prepared himself by praying and then meditated on a mirror or crystal ball, seeking visions of divine beings. He recorded his first success in his diary in 1581.

In the following months, Dee practiced regularly in order to sharpen his visionary skills. The climax of his personal experiences occurred the following year. While he prayed one day, a brilliant light blazed through his window. The source of the radiance was a human figure, which proclaimed that it was archangel Uriel. The angel gave Dee a crystal and instructed him to use it as a meditation object for spirit visions. Uriel's gift has been preserved and today resides in the British Museum.

Despite such high-level assistance, Dee encountered a major obstacle to his investigations of the spirit world. Although he could at times receive visions and converse with angels, he complained that he could never remember afterward what the conversations had been about. To solve this dilemma, Dee began to look for an assistant who could have the visions, so that Dee could sit nearby and record the information relayed from the angels by the visionary. Why Dee did not continue to pursue the visions himself and simply hire a secretary to record his own experiences, is not clear; perhaps his continued nervousness about the possibility of accidentally stumbling across a demon motivated him to seek the less exposed role for himself.

After some unsuccessful experiments with his first assistant, Dee met EDWARD KELLY, who was to be his collaborator for the next seven years. Most historians believe that Kelly was a con artist who simply manipulated Dee's burning desire for angelic knowledge in order to achieve his own more worldly ends of money, sex, and power. It is known that Kelly always wore a tight, black skullcap to conceal the fact that his ears had been cut off as a punishment for forgery before meeting Dee. Regardless of Kelly's motivations, however, Dee and Kelly's work produced an extraordinary series of occult revelations. The angel conjuration practices devised by Dee and Kelly are still being studied today under the name of ENOCHIAN MAGIC.

It has often been rumored that Dee and Kelly visited an English graveyard at night to dig up a newly buried corpse for the purpose of NECROMANCY. In fact, the sensitive Dee would never have participated in such an escapade because the beliefs of the time associated necromantic rites with the demons he so dreaded. Kelly, however, likely did attempt divination using a dead body, aided by Paul Waring, a shady friend. Kelly and Waring's dark ceremonies have become somewhat confused over time with the angelic vision work of Dee and Kelly, to the detriment of Dee's already blackened reputation.

Dee made no secret of his interest in angelic visions, and his fame in this regard spread throughout Europe. A visiting Polish nobleman, Count Albert Laski, was so intrigued by Dee and Kelly's experiments that he transported the pair and their families back to Poland with him. There, they continued exploring the angelic realm; they also spent large amounts of their host's money trying to create the alchemical Philosopher's Stone, without apparent success. Kelly kept Laski enthralled by reporting that the angels had selected the count to be a great world leader (to be guided by Kelly, no doubt).

When it became evident that neither their alchemical nor their political goals were likely to be attained, Dee and Kelly journeyed to Prague, where they met Emperor Rudolph. They had to leave in a hurry a few months later because Pope Sixtus V had issued orders for their arrest on a charge of heresy. Back in Poland, Kelly insisted that the angels now required the two men to share everything they possessed—including their wives, as Kelly had had his eye on Dee's attractive spouse for some time. There is evidence that the angelic commandment was followed, despite the squeamishness of Dee's wife. This unorthodox arrangement strained the magicians' partnership to the breaking point. Shortly after this episode, Dee and Kelly parted forever, and the Dee family returned to England.

Dee lived the rest of his life quietly. He earned a living casting horoscopes and continued his angel communication work with other mediums. He never found another assistant who could match Kelly in providing such rich details of angelic conversations. At the end of his life, Dee believed he had made contact, through a visionary assistant, with archangel Raphael. Dee was suffering from spontaneous bleeding from the skin, and the angel promised him a full recovery from his ailment. Shortly afterward, Dee passed away, in 1608.

The most detailed account of Dee's angel magic experiments is found in his notes, edited and published after his death by Meric Casaubon in a book entitled *A True and Faithful Relation of what passed between Dr. John Dee and some Spirits; tending, had it succeeded, to a General Alteration of most States and Kingdoms in the World.*

DEMON MAGIC   Wherever the belief in DEMONS has existed, individuals have attempted to harness these malignant beings for their own benefit. Such efforts have always been viewed as risky: a demon, by definition, will try to harm a person if it gets the opportunity. Orthodox authorities have usually regarded demon magic with disfavor, if not hostility.

Demon magic in Judeo-Christian culture goes back at least as far as the first century A.D. The Jewish legend of King Solomon, who was said to be able to control evil spirits using the names of God, inspired ancient Hebrew magicians to do likewise. An early conjuration manual, known as *The Testament of Solomon*, was popular in ancient times.

Conventional Christians have always regarded deliberate contact with demons as loathsome: one should avoid evil, not associate with it. However, in the later Middle Ages, a number of people felt that the powers of evil could be utilized for the enhancement of good. These magicians, most of whom are thought to have been such religious professionals as monks and priests, began to compose the texts of ritual magic known as the GRIMOIRES. They argued that because they were forcing demons to do their bidding, thus preventing the evil spirits from following the directions of Satan, their magic was good Christian work. Orthodox officials did not accept this argument. The sorts of things the magicians were compelling the demons to do—murdering enemies and providing women for sexual purposes were two of the more popular aims—did not strike the authorities as particularly holy. The official Catholic position on the matter was that the demons were tricking the magicians into signing away their souls in the demonic PACT. Orthodoxy condemned the magical ceremonies of demonic evocation.

The rituals of the medieval demonologists were based on a variety of sources. The Catholic Church possessed two powerful rituals that probably were well known to most clerics, the Mass and exorcism. The doctrine of transubstantiation, which stated that the bread and wine of the Eucharist was changed into the actual flesh and blood of Christ, was proclaimed dogma in 1215. As the stories about JESUS in the New Testament demonstrate, Christ was able to command demons. Therefore, it was thought that including phrases from the Mass in demon magic rites would endow the magician with some of Christ's authority over spirits. The church's exorcism ceremony could force devils out of people's bodies, so perhaps the holy names used in exorcism could be employed to enslave demons for other purposes. Elements of ancient Jewish demon magic also contributed to the lore of medieval demonology.

It is impossible to estimate the extent of such practices in the Middle Ages, or to identify the magicians. Because of the threat of persecution, the authors of demon magic texts did not sign their works. Catholic authorities of the time, challenged by a range of heresies, did not tolerate such activities within their own ranks. In 1320, Pope John XXII gave permission to the INQUISITION to pursue anyone who had concluded a pact with an evil spirit. Given the methods of the inquisitors, who usually tortured people until they would confess to anything their tormentors suggested, it is difficult to estimate how many actual magicians were among the innocent victims. By the fifteenth century, the methods of demon magic had been included in the definition of witchcraft; the persecution of magicians was absorbed into the centuries-long disaster called the GREAT WITCH HUNT.

With the exclusion of demons from the official Western world view since the 1700s, the practice of demon magic has become less credible—and less threatening—to orthodoxy. However, within the esoteric community of the last two centuries, some individuals have continued to try to call up and control embodiments of evil. ALEISTER CROWLEY, the most important magician of the modern period, is known to have practiced demon magic; indeed, some occultists believe that he became permanently possessed by a demon when a magical ceremony he was conducting went awry.

DEMONS   Throughout most of Western history, belief in evil spirits has not been unorthodox. In fact, during certain periods *disbelief* in the existence of demonic powers was viewed as heretical. At virtually all times since the end of the ancient world, deliberate attempts to communicate with demons were regarded as highly sinful and were often punishable by death. Despite the harshness with which orthodoxy treated the skeptics and the occultists, both of these unorthodox camps endured through the centuries. Western definitions of reality have always been strongly colored by the various conceptions of demons.

In the cradle of Western civilization, the ancient Mediterranean and the Near East, abundant evidence for the widespread belief in harmful spirits exists. In

Mesopotamia, for example, diseases and bad weather were associated with invisible beings. These entities could also take possession of a person's body, and exorcists were called upon to drive them out.

It is important to remember that the malign spirits of ancient pagan cultures were not regarded as "evil" in the same sense as the demons of Christian society. The idea of evil as the complete opposite or absence of good developed in Jewish culture possibly under Persian influence, and did not exist in most other early societies. Non-Jewish ancient cultures might have understood harmful spirits much like most people view such creatures as sharks and crocodiles today: dangerous and perhaps hostile, but not intrinsically evil.

The ancient Greeks also conceived that the world was populated with spirits, which they called *daemons* or *daemonia*. The English word "demon" obviously derives from the Greek term. In Greek culture, *daemons* were not always thought to be harmful. The best known example of a helpful *daemon* was the spirit Socrates mentioned. He claimed that his *daemon* would warn him if he was about to do something wrong. According to later classical belief, *daemons* were the spiritual powers that operated the oracles, such as the famous prophetic centers at Delphi and Dodona.

The Hebrews came into contact with many other cultures during their wanderings and occupations. These pagan societies all believed in harmful spirits, as well as in a number of gods (POLYTHEISM). The Jews absorbed some of the beliefs in bad spirits into their own world view. Because they were staunch believers in one God, they tended to regard their neighbors' multiple deities as mere evil spirits masquerading as gods. Traces of this Hebrew strategy of demonization can be seen in later Western demon lore. For instance, an often-mentioned demon named Beelzebub is thought to have been the Phoenician deity Baal. Ashtaroth, another prominent demon, may derive from Astarte, a Canaanite goddess, or from the Babylonian Ishtar.

As the concept of evil developed in Jewish culture and became personified as Satan, the various harmful spirits and pagan gods began to be seen as enemies of God, who were under the command of God's opponent, the Devil. During the last two centuries B.C., many stories were told about the origins and activities of the demons.

Some of these legends were recorded in the unorthodox literary works known as the PSEUDEPIGRAPHA. Although these texts were not recognized as scriptures, their detailed picture of the world of demons profoundly affected the earliest Christian thinking about evil spirits. For example, the legend that demons originated from fallen angels, found in the New Testament Book of Revelation, was likely inspired by tales in The BOOK OF ENOCH and The BOOK OF THE SECRETS OF ENOCH. These stories were an attempt to reconcile the growing belief in evil spirits with the idea that God, who created everything, is good. In order to avoid the contradiction of a benign God making evil spirits, the Enochian writers explain that originally there were only ANGELS, but some angels succumbed to the temptations of pride and lust. The fallen angels produced demonic offspring or became demons themselves.

According to the traditions of Enoch, these angels acted as culture heroes after their fall, teaching humans many of the arts and sciences of civilization. Penemuel taught the art of writing, Kokabel conveyed knowledge of the constellations, and Gadreel instructed in the manufacture of tools and weapons. The idea that dark spirits possess valuable knowledge heightens the allure of trying to consult them. The notion of tapping into demonic knowledge returned in the ritual magic practices of the later Middle Ages.

Another powerful idea found in the unorthodox writings composed between the Old and New Testaments is the concept of the demonic conspiracy. According to this belief, noted in the Pseudepigrapha and the Dead Sea Scrolls, humans can be divided into two classes, those allied with the forces of God, and those in league with the demons. Some people have drawn the conclusion that the conspirators of evil should be detected and destroyed. This idea periodically resurfaces throughout the history of the West, and has produced vast suffering.

Early Christianity inherited the belief in demons from the Jews, and began the tradition of viewing anything and anyone that stood in the way of Christianity's spread as demonic. The first Christians also utilized the Hebrew strategy of demonizing the deities of non-Christians, and their refusal to recognize the genius of the Roman emperor as a god was often used as a reason for their persecution.

Certain groups within the early unorthodox movement known as GNOSTICISM took the demonizing strategy to an extreme. Many Gnostics proclaimed that the god of the Jews themselves, the creator of the world, was actually a demonic entity known as the Demiurge. Christ was seen as the emissary of another god who came to save some humans from the prison of the material world.

During the first several centuries of the Christian era, most Christians, while believing in the existence of demons, also thought that their Christian faith generally protected them against the influences of evil spirits. Third century theologian ORIGEN taught that every time a Christian resisted temptation, another demon lost its power, so that the forces of evil were continually growing weaker. In light of this optimistic assessment, most Christians of the time felt that deliberately becoming involved with demons would be senseless.

During the fifth century, the Syrian author who wrote under the pseudonym of Dionysius the Areopagite presented the idea that because they were fallen angels, the demons were organized into the same social structure as the angels. Dionysius envisioned an angelic hierarchy of nine choirs or ranks, and a corresponding society of nine choirs of demons. This system became the orthodox map of divine and infernal reality.

Through the Middle Ages, a gradual change of mood concerning demons occurred. The confident optimism of earlier times was replaced by an ominous feeling that perhaps the tide had turned in the unseen world, and that the demonic hordes were now gathering in strength. This shift reflected a mounting sense of threat that pervaded European culture. Moslem invaders had pressed up through Spain into southern France; Christ did not return to the earth in the year 1000, confounding the predictions of many prophets; and, perhaps worst of all, powerful heretical groups, such as the CATHARS and WALDENSIANS, were steadily gaining in popularity within Catholic culture itself.

Within this anxious context, demons seemed to become a more dangerous reality. The increased sense of demonic presence manifested itself in several ways. One such expression was the heightened fear of demonic activity in daily life. Evil spirits were no longer easily kept at bay by a daily prayer, but pressed in from all sides, seeking every opportunity to attack the unwary. German abbot Richalmus claimed that he could clairvoyantly perceive demons, and reported that:

It is untrue what some people say, that each human being is pursued by only one demon, for several demons pursue each human being. Just as a man who plunges into the sea is wholly surrounded by water, above and below, so demons too flow around a man from all sides.

Indeed, Richalmus said, there are times when evil beings "surround a man like a thick vault, so that there is no air-hole between them."

It is easy to understand how people would interpret everything strange or unfamiliar as demonic in such a paranoid environment. Certainly the heresies of the day were quickly condemned as inspired by devils and were viciously persecuted. According to historian Norman Cohn, even the thoughts and feelings of ordinary people became subject to demonization at this time—"demons have come to represent desires which individual Christians have, but which they dare not acknowledge as belonging to themselves." Increasingly, the universe within and without seemed to be passing beyond the control of the orthodox authorities. The ensuing sense of desperation set the psychological stage for the madness of the GREAT WITCH HUNT.

Another reaction to an encounter with a powerful hostile force is to attempt to harness that force for one's own benefit. Some individuals in the later Middle Ages tried to control the demons directly, using the methods of DEMON MAGIC. During the witch-hunting activities of the Renaissance and Reformation periods, the interest in demons reached its height. "Demonologists," specialists in the study of demonic lore, published lists of various devils and their functions. Many demonological tracts were intended for use by the priests and judges who questioned the victims of the witch hunt regarding their supposed interactions with evil spirits. The ritual magicians, although subject to persecution, continued their practices in secret. With the advent of the printing press, the most important of the grimoires managed to find their way into print.

Martin Luther, who started the Reformation in the sixteenth century, stated that disbelief in the Devil was unchristian, for without the Evil One to tempt humans into damnation, there was no need for Christ to save them. During the dark days of the Great Witch Hunt (between the fifteenth and seventeenth centuries), people who were skeptical about the idea that a conspiracy of witches met regularly with demons were frequently attacked on the grounds of atheism or even witchcraft. Nonetheless, throughout this period such brave individuals as Johan Weyer and Reginald Scot publicly proclaimed that the apparatus of the witch hunt was based on a delusion. Weyer believed in the reality of demons but thought that only ritual magicians, and not the masses of common people murdered during the hunt, were in deliberate contact with them. Scot even doubted the existence of demons, stating that "spiritualistic manifestations were artful impostures or illusions due to mental disturbance in the observers."

Since the rise of the scientific world view, Scot's attitude has prevailed, and *belief* in demons has become a violation of the officially defined reality. The image of the universe as a giant machine, running according to the laws of physics, leaves little room for the notion of evil spirits. Even so, belief in demons endures: survey research by sociologists has revealed that a large segment of modern Western society still thinks that evil spirits exist. And the ancient habit of regarding sources of threat as demonic persists. Indeed, contemporary political commentators like Noam Chomsky argue that modern Western governments have deliberately used the strategy of demonization to create mass support for their war plans. Popular wisdom holds that society has matured in its attitudes toward demons since the time of the witch hunts. It may be, however, that only the forms of belief have shifted; the underlying impulse to paint a devil's face on something frightening and unknown seems to continue unchanged.

DIGGERS   This radical English group had a brief but notable existence, lasting only a few years after its founding in 1649. Led by GERRARD WINSTANLEY, the Diggers received their name from their practice of appearing suddenly on former common land that had been claimed by landlords, digging furrows, and sowing seeds. This behavior stemmed from their belief that private land ownership was opposed to the will of God. But the only results of their labors were convictions and fines for trespassing. The Diggers were closely associated with another English movement that combined religious convictions with calls for social transformation, the LEVELLERS.

DIONYSIUS OF ALEXANDRIA   As the bishop of Alexandria during the third century, a period crucial to the formation of orthodox Christian political and doctrinal structures, Dionysius played a significant role in the development of Western society. During his lifetime, he was frequently controversial and probably embraced heretical views. After his death, however, he was portrayed as a hero of orthodoxy.

Dionysius assumed his position as bishop in 247 and held the office until his death in 264. Three years after he became the leader of the Catholic community in Alexandria, Roman Emperor Decius unleashed a ferocious persecution of Christians throughout the empire. While Dionysius had to flee the city, his teacher, the great theologian ORIGEN, was captured in Palestine, tortured, and eventually died as a result of his mistreatment.

After the violence subsided, Dionysius returned to Alexandria. Valerian, the next emperor, started the persecution again, and Dionysius found himself banished. Yet once again, he returned to lead his flock after Valerian's campaign ended. Dionysius's persistence in his commitment as a church leader accounts in part for the posthumous admiration accorded him.

Both in Rome and Alexandria during that time, the heresy of MODALISM was threatening the Catholic authorities' attempt to exert a monopoly over Christian belief. The modalists claimed that the elements of the Trinity, Father, Son, and Holy Spirit are just different names and roles of one divine Person. Dionysius and other Catholic leaders opposed this doctrine because it seemed to imply that Christ the Son was not a human being, but God the Father masquerading as a man. Orthodoxy taught that the Father, Son, and Holy Spirit are distinct Persons, not mere names.

In his opposition to modalism, however, Dionysius overreacted theologically, and ended up veering into a different position that was equally heretical. Origen, his mentor, had distinguished the Father and the Son by noting that the Son is portrayed in some New Testament passages as being "subordinate" to the Father. If one is subordinate to another, the two clearly cannot be identical, for how can one be subordinate to oneself? Dionysius took up this theme, but he exaggerated it to the point that the unity of God seemed to be questioned. Dionysius claimed that "the

Son of God is a creature and something made, not his own by nature, but alien in essence from the Father."

The orthodox Catholic position regarding the Trinity holds that the three Persons, while distinct, all share the same essence or nature. The Son is not a mere creation of the Father. Some members of the Alexandrian Catholic community objected to Dionysius's formulation and appealed to the bishop of Rome for a comment.

During the third century, the primacy of the Roman bishop over the entire Catholic Church was not firmly established. The controversy surrounding Dionysius's doctrine was a golden opportunity for Rome to demonstrate its authority in matters of belief. The bishop of Rome, also named Dionysius, condemned his Egyptian namesake's claim that the Son was created. Under pressure, Dionysius of Alexandria was forced to "clarify" his views by publicly accepting the doctrine set forth by Rome. This political victory demonstrated and strengthened the power of the papacy.

Dionysius is also remembered for his refusal to accept the authenticity of the Book of Revelation. His arguments were eventually dismissed, but they delayed the inclusion of the book in the New Testament. The teachings of Dionysius of Alexandria are similar to those of ARIANISM, a major heresy that was about to break out in the Christian community. Some observers suspected that Dionysius was actually the father of the Arian heresy. Bishop Athanasius, his impeccably orthodox successor, argued successfully to clear Dionysius's name. Fourth century Christian historian Eusebius awarded Dionysius the title "the Great," by which this controversial figure is still known today.

DIOSCURUS   The successor to the renowned Saint Cyril as bishop of Alexandria in Egypt, Dioscurus played an important role in the controversies involving the nature of Christ, which disturbed the Christian Church during the fifth century. Dioscurus attempted to impose the heresy of MONOPHYSITISM on the church. As a result, he was excommunicated, and the community of Christians in Egypt, remaining loyal to Dioscurus, began to distance itself from orthodoxy.

When Cyril died in A.D. 444, Christians were hotly debating the relationship between Christ's human nature and His divine nature. Traditionally, Christian leaders in Alexandria had tended to emphasize Christ's divine nature, while those in Antioch and Constantinople highlighted Christ's humanity. Gradually a consensus that Christ had both natures within a single person began to form. One of Cyril's achievements had been to lead the attack against NESTORIANISM, a view that seemed to separate Christ not just into two natures, but two persons.

Discussions concerning the fine points of theology were complicated by political intrigue. The major Christian centers were jockeying for control over the entire church, which since 381 had been the state religion of the Roman Empire. Charging that competing bishops were heretics could be an effective political weapon in the struggle for dominance. Dioscurus was very ambitious and searched for ways to promote the power of Alexandria.

He saw his opportunity in 448. A monk in Constantinople named EUTYCHES had accused the bishop of Constantinople of being a Nestorian and had promptly been excommunicated. Dioscurus thought that if Eutyches could be declared correct, then Constantinople's position as a reliable center of orthodox belief would be undermined. He proclaimed that Alexandria supported Eutyches.

The following year, a meeting of the major Christian leaders was called in Ephesus. Dioscurus assumed control of the proceedings because Pope Leo, bishop of Rome, did not attend. As a result, the condemnation of Eutyches was reversed, and both the pope and the bishop of Constantinople were labeled heretics. This council was later declared illegal and is known today as the ROBBER COUNCIL.

Dioscurus and Eutyches promoted the view that Christ has only one divine nature; the human nature was absorbed into the divinity when Jesus was conceived. This doctrine went against the generally held idea that Christ needed both divine and human natures in order to be the savior of humanity. By affirming the heresy of one nature in Christ (Monophysitism) and by attacking the two most powerful men in the Christian world, Dioscurus had overextended himself. Another meeting, the COUNCIL OF CHALCEDON, was convened in order to overturn the decisions of the Robber Council. The gathering at Chalcedon was carefully controlled to ensure an orthodox victory. Dioscurus pleaded that he was a strictly orthodox follower of the revered Saint Cyril, but to no avail. He was excommunicated for his behavior at the Robber Council and sent into exile.

The fate of their bishop offended many Christians in Alexandria. In the years following the Council of Chalcedon, support for the Monophysite doctrine grew and eventually overwhelmed the Catholics in Egypt.

DOCETISM   This term derives from the Greek verb *dokeo*, "I seem." The ancient doctrine known as docetism holds that Christ's body only *seemed* to be a human body, made of the same matter as any other person's. In fact, the docetists taught, the Lord's flesh was composed of some heavenly substance, or perhaps was not even material but ghostly. In many cases, docetism arose from the notion that ordinary matter is evil and, therefore, unfit for the embodiment of a divine being.

As orthodox doctrines about Christ became clarified during the first few centuries A.D., docetism was rejected as heresy. Orthodoxy came to emphasize that JESUS had been a complete human being, as well as completely divine. Someone without a human body, they thought, could hardly be considered fully human. Several ancient heresies, most notably the GNOSTICS, held docetist beliefs. During the Protestant Reformation many centuries later, some of the ANABAPTIST heretics promoted docetic views.

DONATISM   The Donatist movement was a major Christian heresy. It marked the first time in history that a large group broke away from the Roman Catholic Church, causing a SCHISM. Donatism flourished in the Punic regions of North Africa in the early fourth century and persisted until the mid-seventh century when it was crushed by Moslem invaders. It takes its name from DONATUS, an early leader and heretical bishop of Carthage. At its height, the Donatist Church had more than 500 bishops, numerous basilicas (including one of the largest cathedrals ever constructed in Africa), and its own army, the "circumcellions."

The rise of Donatism can be understood only against the backdrop of the racial, economic, and historical conditions of the times. During the years before the appearance of this heresy, the Christian Church in North Africa had been subjected to repeated episodes of violent suppression at the hands of the pagan Roman forces. During these persecutions, the only way for captured Christians to escape execution was to deny their faith and turn over Christian books to the authorities. In the aftermath of these events, priests who had rejected Christianity under threat of death and later returned to the fold became the topic of heated controversy.

Some groups, especially those from less urban settings and more native racial stock, argued that the sinfulness of the wayward priests forever barred them from effectively administering the holy sacraments. In the presence of the mortal sin of APOSTASY (denying Christ), they argued, God's grace could not be transmitted through baptism and the Eucharist.

Against this position, other parties—mainly those more identified with the existing church hierarchy, the Roman Empire, and the rich classes—maintained a more forgiving stance. They argued that God's grace was utterly free of human control, and, therefore, the gift of grace through the sacraments could not be blocked by moments of straying in the lives of individual priests. These more lenient groups in the debate were interested in making the Catholic Church as appealing as possible to the rich and powerful classes within the Roman Empire (who were not known for their attraction to morally unforgiving doctrines). At the same time, they wished to ensure the continued supremacy of the existing Catholic hierarchy in the functioning of the universal church.

The less forgiving groups felt that such efforts to increase the acceptability of the faith in the Roman Empire were an intolerable compromise of Christian morality. Since these groups tended to be excluded from the benefits of life in the Empire, they were much less invested in the preservation of its structure. In short, the stage was set for a classic collision of the haves and the have-nots, expressed in terms of religious disagreement.

In 311, the Catholics appointed the orthodox Caecilian as bishop of Carthage. A group of regional bishops refused to recognize the appointment because Caecilian had betrayed the church during a period of persecution. The dissenters instead declared MAJORINUS, who had not committed this sin, to be the new bishop. The Catholic authorities in turn would not recognize Majorinus. When Majorinus died, Donatus succeeded him. In the following years, breakaway Donatist clergy established themselves across North Africa, refusing to obey the injunctions of the Catholic leaders. Groups of men armed with large clubs (which they called "Israels"), organized under Donatist guidance, often dislodged orthodox institutions by force.

The Donatist movement combined Punic nationalist feelings, the anger of the less privileged classes, and hostility toward the Romans. Such a volatile mix of ideas and emotions alarmed the recent alliance of the Catholic Church and the Roman police state under Emperor Constantine. Orthodox leader Augustine of Hippo, who became known as the "Hammer of Donatists," expressed a particular revulsion for the heretics' friendliness toward slaves: "What master is there who was not compelled to live in dread of his own slave, if the slave had put himself under the protection of the Donatists?" This revealing passage indicates the extent to which the interests of the social and economic status quo had become identified with those of the Catholic power structure, even at this early date in the evolution of Western culture.

The Donatists took the position of the less forgiving groups in the debate over priestly sin. They agreed that the power of the sacraments depends on the moral purity of the administering priest (which became known as the doctrine of *ex opere operantis*). They also argued that the true Catholic Church comprised only the community of morally perfect Christians; therefore, the compromised Church of

Rome, having endorsed corrupt clergy and married itself to the great oppressor (Constantine), could not be the true church. Donatism proclaimed itself to be the only Catholic Church. In this way, it isolated itself from the rest of the Christian world. The Donatists' archenemy, Augustine, mocked them: "The clouds roll with thunder, that the House of the Lord shall be built throughout the earth; and these frogs sit in their marsh and croak—'We are the only Christians!'" Augustine's teaching that the Donatist movement was heretical became official Roman Catholic doctrine at the orthodox Conference of Carthage in 411.

The Donatist threat provoked reactions from the Catholics that were to prove important in the shaping of mainstream Western beliefs concerning reality. Augustine, one of the prime architects of the conventional Christian world, developed his own theory about the power of the sacraments in opposition to the Donatist position. Augustine's theory, known as the doctrine of *ex opere operato*, said that the mere performance of the sacramental act in a technically correct manner would effectively transmit God's grace, regardless of the moral purity of the priest.

Augustine's view of the vehicles of grace was connected with his influential doctrine of predestination. This doctrine states that God grants grace to individuals who were chosen for salvation before the world was created. Those who were predestined to be saved could not lose their salvation, regardless of their acts.

The doctrine of *ex opere operato*, combined with the idea of predestination, supported the orthodox lenience toward priestly wrongdoing opposed by the Donatists. These beliefs may not have helped future generations of Catholic priests to resist temptation very well. If they strayed, their effectiveness in transmitting grace was not impaired. If they were predestined to be saved, their straying did not permanently harm their souls. Such attitudes likely contributed to the excesses of clerical corruption that eventually triggered the rupture of the Roman Catholic Church during the Protestant Reformation.

Another outcome of the Donatist controversy was more sinister. In his struggles with the Donatists, Augustine became convinced that acts of organized violence, including torture, were legitimate tools for orthodoxy to use against its opponents. He developed his ideas to provide a comprehensive theological excuse for the violent suppression of heresy. Augustine's great stature in the Roman Catholic community ensured that his position on this issue would become a lethal legacy to religious dissenters in the West for the next 1,300 years.

See also: PELAGIANISM, INQUISITION.

DONATUS   During the political and religious turbulence of the fourth century, the unity of the Catholic Church was frequently threatened. Donatus was the leader of a Christian group in North Africa that broke away from mainstream Christianity, posing a significant challenge to the survival of Roman Catholicism in that region. This schismatic movement, known as DONATISM, was named after him.

Little is known about Donatus's early life, except that he was likely born in the North African town of Casae Nigrae toward the end of the third century. The Donatist movement began in A.D. 311, when a group of regional bishops refused to accept a new bishop of Carthage appointed by the Roman Catholic authorities, and elected MAJORINUS instead. Donatus was the successor to Majorinus as the schismatics' bishop of Carthage.

Donatus proved to be a skillful organizer. Under his leadership, the movement grew rapidly, spreading to the far corners of the North African area. Optatus, a Catholic bishop, described Donatus as a man obsessed with increasing his political power: "When people visited him from any part of Africa, he did not ask the usual questions about the weather, peace and war, and the harvest, but always: 'How goes my party in your part of the world?' " Ironically, the accusation of political greed was also leveled by Donatus at the Catholics. According to Donatus, the orthodox church had sacrificed its moral integrity by uniting itself with the imperial government after centuries of persecution.

After Donatus's death sometime in the middle of the fourth century, the movement bearing his name faced increasing persecution at the hands of Roman Catholic loyalists, but managed to survive for more than 300 years.

Friar DOLCINO   During the late thirteenth century, the heresy of the APOS-TOLICI was thriving in northern Italy. The Catholic Church mounted a violent persecution and burned to death the movement's founder, Gerard SEGARELLI, in 1300. Leadership of the Apostolici was assumed by Friar Dolcino, who was himself killed by Catholic powers seven years later.

Dolcino was a priest's illegitimate son from Novara near the Italian Alps. In his early years, he studied with the SPIRITUAL FRANCISCANS, who taught that poverty was holy. This belief was also fundamental to the Apostolici, which Dolcino joined.

He developed a theory of history resembling that of JOACHIM OF FIORE, the Italian prophet. According to Friar Dolcino, there had been three historical ages. The first age corresponded to Old Testament times and came to an end when the Jewish priesthood became corrupted by greed. Christ appeared, and inaugurated the second age. During this era, the early Christian community was poor but loved by God. The rise of the Catholic hierarchy of bishops and priests marked the third age. The Catholic Church was now degraded by its power and money. A fourth age had commenced with the founding of the Apostolici and would culminate in the destruction of Catholicism by the Holy Spirit.

In 1300, Dolcino predicted that the end of the orthodox church would occur in 1303; when nothing happened, he revised the date for the destruction to 1306. Catholic Inquisitors were making life unpleasant for the Apostolici in the towns, so the friar departed for the countryside; there, he mounted a successful recruitment drive in the villages of the Alpine valleys and foothills. In 1304, Dolcino led an uprising of the peasants in the region to overthrow the domination of the church and the governing classes. He was supported by rich townspeople who wished to undermine the power of the pope.

For the next three years, pitched battles were fought between the Apostolici and an army of Catholic Crusaders who had responded to the crisis. Dolcino told his supporters that they were permitted to do anything they wanted to those who sided with the Catholics because God was on their own side. As a result, entire towns were burned for having Catholic sympathies, and no one was safe from robbery and murder.

Dolcino's headquarters was a well-fortified camp. The Crusaders eventually surrounded it, cutting off the militant heretics inside from food supplies. In 1307, the camp fell. The victorious Catholics then tortured to death about 150 Apostolici supporters, including Friar Dolcino.

See also: BENTIVENGA OF GUBBIO.

DOUKHOBORS   A sect of unorthodox Christians originating in eastern Europe, the Doukhobors have survived persecution, migration, and internal strife for more than 200 years. Their name derives from the Russian terms *doukha*, meaning "spirit," and *borets*, referring to a fighter or wrestler. The Doukhobors were called "spirit wrestlers" by their orthodox opponents, who claimed that they struggled against the Holy Spirit. The sect adopted the insulting label, but changed its meaning; to them, a Doukhobor was one who fought *on the side of* the Holy Spirit.

The first Doukhobor leader was a preacher named SYLVAN KOLESNIKOV. He appeared among the peasants of the Ukraine in 1769 and was likely related to the SKOPTSY movement. There seems to have been a Doukhobor sect in the region before his arrival, but little is known of its origins. Kolesnikov gave the sect some ritual and theological structure. A simple sacramental rite involving salt, water, and bread was established. Like the ICONOCLASTS many centuries earlier, the Doukhobors rejected the orthodox veneration of holy images, as well as the doctrine of the Trinity. They believed that the Holy Spirit dwelled within every member, so they practiced bowing to each other. Their leader was revered almost as a god. When he died in 1775, they were accustomed to being led and expected the Lord to send them another guide.

A wool merchant named Pobhirokin soon took control of the movement by claiming that he was Christ. He established a dynasty of dictatorial leaders who governed the Doukhobors throughout most of the nineteenth century. The leader was surrounded by twelve chosen apostles, as well as twelve "angels of death" who murdered any dissenters within the sect. The average Doukhobor was expected to obey the leader without question, while the leader and his associates indulged themselves in luxury. The tradition of divine leadership was so strong that opposition was uncommon.

The Doukhobors attracted the attention of Russian authorities when the ruling family began to issue decrees that opposed the authority of the tsar, the Russian ruler. Doukhobor leaders proclaimed that military service, commercial activity, and education were to be avoided because they were activities of the Devil. These antisocial policies, as well as the murderous ways of the "angels of death," provoked the Russian government to exile the Doukhobors to the Caucasus region. Unmolested in their isolation, the Doukhobor community grew and prospered there.

But in 1886, the sect suffered a split. The leader of the smaller group took a moderate stance regarding the Russian government and swore not to break any civil laws. The larger group, led by PETER VERIGIN, acknowledged no law but that of God, as interpreted by Verigin. As a result, the government saw to it that the minority group took possession of the Doukhobors' communal wealth.

Eight years later, Verigin commanded his followers to resist conscription into military service. Doukhobor conscripts built bonfires of military uniforms and equipment, thus beginning the notorious Doukhobor tradition of fire-setting. Government cossacks responded with ferocious attacks on Doukhobor settlements.

The persecution of the Doukhobors came to the attention of Leo Tolstoy, the renowned writer. Tolstoy was not fully informed regarding the nature of the sect. He believed that the simple ways of the Doukhobors represented a return to a basic Christian lifestyle, something that he himself advocated, and mounted a campaign to protect them. He reported in the western press that more than 400 Doukhobors had been slaughtered. International opinion put pressure on the Russian government to allow the Doukhobors to emigrate; the tsar, no doubt glad to be rid of the trouble-makers, agreed.

At the time, Canada was well known for its acceptance of religious refugees; groups of HUTTERITES and MENNONITES had escaped persecution in Europe by moving there. The Canadian government welcomed the prospect of industrious Russian settlers for its sparsely populated western regions. In 1899, about 7,500 Doukhobors, followers of Verigin, settled in the province of Saskatchewan.

Verigin was serving a fifteen-year sentence of exile in Siberia and was unable to emigrate until 1902. In the meantime, he sent commands to his flock in Canada. Their leader ordered that the Doukhobors had to own everything in common; in addition, they were forbidden to possess money and could not have farm animals. Confusion erupted as many Doukhobors, having been provided by their host government with resources to help them settle, tried to return their money to Canadian-immigration authorities, and released hundreds of cattle, sheep, and horses to wander freely.

When Verigin finally arrived in Canada, he quickly decided that the prairie was not the "Promised Land" of Doukhobor freedom. He purchased land in the fertile valleys in the interior of British Columbia. Within a few years, a prosperous Doukhobor community was established, centered on the immense success of the B. C. Jam Factory.

Success is often followed by compromise of one's earlier ideals, and such was the case with the B. C. Doukhobors. Many members had their own property, possessed farm animals, and led a comfortable life; Verigin was still the leader for most people in the community, but he revised his doctrines to suit the more prosperous conditions. A radical splinter group, called the Sons of Freedom, began to demand a return to the old ways. They took to destroying other Doukhobors' property by setting it on fire and parading in the nude to demonstrate their purity.

Turmoil has continued through most of the century between the Sons of Freedom, other Doukhobors, and the Canadian government. In 1924, Verigin, who rejected the radicals, was killed by a bomb, possibly planted by the Sons of Freedom. Throughout the 1950s and 1960s, the Doukhobor region was the scene of numerous arsons, explosions, and naked marches. A fireproof prison had to be constructed to contain the perpetrators, who never recognized the authority of any worldly government. Although most Doukhobors have now joined the moderate mainstream of Canadian life, occasional outbreaks of strife continue. As recently as 1992, two female Sons of Freedom were convicted of setting another Doukhobor's house on fire. They refused to wear clothing in the courtroom and had to be covered with blankets; during sentencing, one of them set a small fire in the prisoner's dock.

See also: ADAMITES.

DYNAMIC MONARCHIANISM
Dynamic Monarchianism is a variant name for the ancient Christian heresy of ADOPTIONISM.

See also: MONARCHIANISM.

EBEDJESUS   The leading thinker among the NESTORIAN heretics during the fourteenth century, Ebedjesus lived in Mesopotamia. He wrote *The Book of the Pearl*, a summary of Christian beliefs that is regarded as the classic presentation of Nestorian doctrine.

EBION   According to orthodox Christian critics during the first centuries A.D., Ebion was the founder of the Jewish Christian sect called the EBIONITES. Actually, however, Ebion never existed. The sect's name derives from a Hebrew word meaning "poor" and refers to the Ebionites' disdain for the accumulation of material wealth.

EBIONITES   Within a few decades of JESUS' death, the Christian movement split into two factions: the followers of Paul, who believed that Christianity was a new religion completely separate from Judaism; and the Jewish Christians, who held that Christians should continue to adhere to the traditional religious practices of the Jews. The Pauline party developed into orthodox Catholicism. A group of Jewish Christians, who became known as Ebionites, survived as a heresy.

There were two schools of thought within the Ebionite movement. One group, known as the NAZARENES, claimed that Jesus was the Messiah, born of a virgin. The other group held that Jesus had been conceived and born in the normal fashion, and had been an ordinary man until his baptism. At that time, an archangel called Christ had descended and turned Jesus into a mighty prophet, like Moses and the other prophetic heroes of Hebrew history.

The doctrinal position of the Ebionites overlapped the beliefs of Jews and orthodox Christians, and caused them to be condemned by both. In turn, the Ebionites regarded the Jews as unenlightened and damned Paul as the first Christian heretic. The sect proclaimed that most of the scriptures the Catholics revered were not authentic. The Ebionites had their own sacred text, THE GOSPEL OF THE EBIONITES, of which fragments survive in quotations by their orthodox opponents. This book appears to be based on the Gospels of Matthew and Luke, but contains interesting twists. For example, Jesus is portrayed as a vegetarian, declining meat offered to him at the Last Supper. Ebionite communities existed in Syria and Egypt. This sect survived into the fourth century.

See also: EBION.

Meister ECKHART (von Hocheim)   Eckhart von Hocheim, a late medieval German friar, was, in the words of Walter T. Stace, "the most profoundly philosophical, original, and independent of all Christian mystics." Such qualities were a mixed blessing within an orthodoxy that believes that it already possesses the truth and, therefore, values preservation above exploration. Eckhart's brilliance brought him admiration (hence the title of respect, "Meister," or master). It also brought him trouble: Pope John XXII condemned his ideas as heresy.

Eckhart was born in the German town of Erfurt in 1260. He joined the Dominican order of friars as a young man and quickly rose through the ranks, eventually becoming the head of the Dominicans in the regions of Saxony and Bohemia. He studied at the University of Paris, receiving a master's degree at the age of forty-two.

The Meister was a prolific writer and a spellbinding speaker. Much of his written work has not survived to the present. The most thoroughly studied materials are his sermons, which he composed in German; more than sixty still exist. When he was not busy with administrative duties, Eckhart went on preaching tours, especially in the Rhineland.

It is said that women were especially drawn to hear his words. During this period, the predominantly female spiritual movement of the BEGUINES was strong in the Rhine region, and Eckhart became a significant influence on them. Some historians believe that the Beguines, who were themselves adventurous thinkers and mystics, had at least as strong an influence on Eckhart.

The Meister taught a way to know God directly. In Eckhart's view, all people contain a spark of divine light within their souls. And by entering into a deep meditative state in which the mind is emptied of all perceptions, thoughts, and feelings people can experience this spark in their very core. Eckhart referred to this experience as "the birth of Christ in the soul."

The friar was not recommending a withdrawal from the world into some sort of permanent trance state; indeed, he remarked that such a retreat would be impossible because the concentration required to reach the soul's depths cannot be maintained for more than short periods. Instead, he favored a life of compassionate activity, illuminated by the certainty of God's presence, which is provided by Christ's birth in the soul. Eckhart suggested that human beings should stop struggling with the concerns of daily life and let God shape events; an even more challenging suggestion was for people to let go of their efforts to define themselves, thereby allowing God to mold them. This path leads to harmony with God.

The Meister's troubles began in 1326. The archbishop of Cologne, a city Eckhart often resided in, charged him with heresy. Eckhart complained that the accusation was motivated by envy rather than by a desire for truth, but he was forced to defend his orthodoxy. At this point, his originality proved to be a serious problem. Many of his poetic and paradoxical expressions could easily be interpreted as conveying the heresy of PANTHEISM; this is the idea that God the Creator is not separate from the objects (including people) He created. Consider, for instance, one of Eckhart's most famous phrases: "The eye by which I see God is the same as the eye by which God sees me." The preacher could be understood to be saying that he is God. In another sermon, Eckhart wrote: "I am (God's) only begotten Son." Is Eckhart claiming to be Christ?

In other texts, Eckhart clearly makes the distinction between the Creator and His creation: "time and space are fragments, whereas God is One! . . . God is neither this nor that, as are these manifold things (of the world)." These passages were not enough to lift suspicion from the kind of statements noted above. The German Church at the time was battling the heretics of the FREE SPIRIT, who claimed to be equal to God and, therefore, free to do whatever they wished. The Meister's writings seemed too similar to the Free Spirit doctrine for the comfort of the orthodox.

Eckhart appealed the heresy charge in the presence of the pope. The friar traveled to Avignon, headquarters of the papacy, and submitted his work for examination. The whole affair must have been very stressful, and it took its toll on his health. Meister Eckhart died at the age of sixty-eight, still awaiting the verdict.

In 1329, Pope John XXII issued a proclamation condemning twenty-eight of Eckhart's propositions as either heretical or expressed in a dangerously misleading way. The Meister's personal orthodoxy was not questioned, so Catholics were permitted to study the parts of his writings that were not condemned. Eckhart's views stimulated important Catholic thinkers and mystics for the next two centuries. John Tauler, Henry Suso, Nicholas of Cusa, and Protestant leader Martin Luther were inspired by his work.

Eckhart's ideas were neglected after the fifteenth century. Interest finally returned in the 1900s. Today many Christians, such as Catholic gadfly MATTHEW FOX, are reclaiming the Meister's vision as a way to revitalize their faith. Even non-Christians are impressed: some of the leading thinkers of modern Buddhism, such as D.T. Suzuki and Keiji Nishitani, have noted the affinity between Meister Eckhart's teaching and their own.

ELIPANDUS   Archbishop of Toledo in Spain during the late eighth century, Elipandus founded the heresy known as SPANISH ADOPTIONISM. Roman Catholic authorities repeatedly condemned him, but he countered by accusing the pope of heresy. Elipandus died unrepentant.

The archbishop was born around A.D. 718. That year, Moslem armies from North Africa completed their conquest of Spain and would rule the region throughout Elipandus's life. The Moslem conquest freed the Spanish Church from easy control by the Roman Catholic community in Europe, and the Moslems themselves did not interfere with the affairs of the church in the territory they governed.

Pope Hadrian attempted to exert some influence on the Spanish Church by sending his representatives to give theological instructions to the Spanish bishops. The papal envoys met with resistance from the Spanish Christian leaders, who were led by Elipandus. In 784, the archbishop published a statement of faith that differed significantly from the Roman Catholic doctrine concerning the relationship between Christ's divine and human natures. He taught that Jesus was God's son by adoption only—a mere human, not a divine being himself.

Elipandus and his adoptionist beliefs were condemned at several papally controlled church councils, including the Council of Frankfurt in 794. Elipandus had strong support from many Spanish bishops. Under the protective rule of the Moslems, the heretical archbishop could not be overthrown by force on the part of the Roman Catholic loyalists. As a result, Elipandus was able to preach his views freely from Toledo, in opposition to papal authority, until his death in 802. His adoptionist doctrine was popular in Spain more for political than for theological reasons. The Spanish Church did not adhere to it following his demise.

ELKESAITES   A Jewish Christian sect whose existence was first recorded around A.D. 100 in the region east of the River Jordan. This group taught that Christians had to follow all of the rules of behavior that govern orthodox Jews. This position was opposed to that of Saint Paul, whose writings the Elkesaites rejected. They had their own scripture, THE BOOK OF ELKESAI, which contains the sacred teachings of an angel who was said to be ninety-six miles tall.

The Elkesaites did not believe that Jesus had been a human being or possessed a human body. Rather, they subscribed to the doctrine of DOCETISM, which maintained that the appearance of Christ's body had been an illusion projected by a divine being during his sojourn on earth. This school resembles, and might have been related to, that of the EBIONITES.

EMERALD TABLET   This short work is often referred to by its Latin name, Tabula Smaragdina. *The Emerald Tablet* is the most important text in ALCHEMY and is said to describe the entire alchemical process whereby the base elements of nature can be transmuted into their fully evolved, golden forms. The *Tablet* comes from a body of literature called the HERMETICA, which originated in Egypt during the first centuries A.D. These books were said to be revelations from divine sage Hermes Trismegistus. Medieval and Renaissance alchemists believed that the *Tablet's* text was inscribed on an emerald slab and was found in Hermes' tomb—by Alexander the Great according to some, and by Sarah, Abraham's wife, according to others.

In fact, though, the earliest known version of the *Tablet* is written in Arabic and dates from the eighth century. This text was likely translated into Arabic from a source written in Syriac, which in turn was translated from an ancient original in Greek. The text of *The Emerald Tablet*, according to a standard translation (by R. Steele and D. W. Singer), is as follows:

True it is, without falsehood, certain and most true. That which is above is like that which is below, and that which is below is like that which is above, to accomplish the miracles of One Thing.

And as all things were by the contemplation of one, so all things arose from this One Thing by a single act of adaptation. The father thereof is the Sun, the mother the Moon. The Wind carried it in its womb, the Earth is the nurse thereof.

It is the father of all works of wonder throughout the whole world.

The power thereof is perfect.

If it be cast on to Earth, it will separate the element of Earth from that of Fire, the subtle from the gross.

With great sagacity it doth ascend gently from Earth to Heaven.

Again it doth descend to Earth, and uniteth in itself the force from things superior and things inferior.

Thus thou wilt possess the glory of the brightness of the whole world, and all obscurity will fly from thee.

This thing is the strong fortitude of all strength, for it overcometh every subtle thing and doth penetrate every solid substance.

Thus was this world created.

Hence will there be marvellous adaptations achieved, of which the manner is this.

For this reason I am called Hermes Trismegistus, because I hold three parts of the wisdom of the whole world.

That which I had to say about the operation of the Sun is completed.

Many of the phrases in the *Tablet* became central alchemical themes. The similarity of above and below, for example, suggested the relevance of ASTROLOGY to the alchemical quest. The images of separating, circulating, and the union of opposites (sun and moon) all inspired various procedures in attempts to create the "One Thing," thought to be the Philosopher's Stone, the mysterious object that possesses the power of transmutation. The ambiguity of the text's meaning ensured that occultists of every century have remained fascinated with it and unable to exhaust its meanings.

ENDURA   Endura is a name for ritual suicide, said to be practiced by medieval heretics known as the CATHARS. When members of the highest spiritual rank, the perfecti, decided that the time was appropriate to die, they would stop eating and "fast unto death." A controversial theory holds that the Endura sometimes involved groups of heretics slitting their veins while immersed in a tub of water; this gory practice might be illustrated in the mysterious VOYNICH MANUSCRIPT.

ENOCHIAN MAGIC   This complex system of ANGEL MAGIC originated with experiments in communication with spirits, conducted by Elizabethan magicians JOHN DEE and EDWARD KELLY. Enochian magic should not be confused with the traditions derived from the ancient Jewish texts known as THE BOOK OF ENOCH and THE BOOK OF THE SECRETS OF ENOCH.

In the magicians' practices, Kelly would contemplate a crystal or mirror until he began to report visions of angelic beings. Dee would then write down Kelly's descriptions of his conversations with the angels. During these sessions, Kelly transmitted a mass of unique material that Dee believed to be "Enochian," the language of the angels.

This language consists of an alphabet of twenty-one letters, and has a consistent grammar and syntax. The angels taught that the letters were related to numerical values, elements, and planetary forces. These symbols were arranged into square patterns, which contained up to 2,401 letters. Kelly used the squares in receiving messages from the angels. The spirits, seen only by Kelly, would spell out their words by pointing at the letters. Kelly would call out the letters, and Dee would record them.

Using the Enochian system, Dee and Kelly were taught a system of nineteen Calls, or Keys. The Keys consisted of poems or chants that could be recited to invoke spiritual forces. The first eighteen Keys are related to the forces of the elements. The nineteenth Key gives access to thirty *aethyrs*, or *aires*, which have come to be understood as spirit worlds or domains of consciousness.

Some of the angelic communications Dee and Kelly reported are powerful works of prose. For example, toward the end of their career together, they received the following message:

> I am the daughter of Fortitude and ravished every hour from my youth. For behold, I am Understanding, and science dwelleth in me; and the heavens oppress me. They cover and desire me with infinite appetite; for none that are earthly have embraced me, for I am shadowed with the Circle of Stars, and covered with the morning clouds. My feet are swifter than the winds, and my hands are sweeter than the morning dew. My garments are from the beginning, and my dwelling place is in myself.

Some of these Enochian messages seem reminiscent of writings of the ancient GNOSTIC heretics. It is almost certain that Dee and Kelly knew little or nothing about the Gnostics.

It is important to realize that how the Enochian material was composed is not actually known. Kelly was a con artist and might have simply pretended to be seeing angels in order to extract payment for his "psychic" services from Dee. Alternately, Kelly might have been able to produce visionary states in himself or Dee might have recorded meaningless ramblings from Kelly and unconsciously rearranged the material until it was meaningful in his enthusiasm for angelic contact. Of course, it is possible that all of these factors were involved in the origin of Enochian magic.

After Dee and Kelly, a small group of English magicians continued working with the Enochian system. One of Dee's sons continued his father's alchemical work and might also have carried on with the angel magic. The circle of Dr. Rudd, active in the middle of the seventeenth century, studied Enochian magic. Rudd's system of Enochian practice is described in THE TREATISE ON ANGEL MAGIC.

Enochian magic seems to have fallen into disuse among occultists after the early eighteenth century. In 1887, the Hermetic Order of the GOLDEN DAWN was formed. This magical society brought together the major elements of the western esoteric tradition into a grand synthesis. The Golden Dawn magicians rediscovered the Enochian Keys and made them an important aspect of Golden Dawn magic.

The best-known magician in modern times, ALEISTER CROWLEY, was familiar with Enochian practices and regarded them as potent means of contact with spirits. He wrote that "Anyone with the smallest capacity for Magick (Crowley's preferred spelling of the word 'magic') find that they work." Today, many magical groups continue in the Enochian tradition. Gerard Schueler has written the most original recent books on Enochian magic. He has attempted to combine the Enochian materials with Hindu tantric beliefs and speculations based on modern physics.

EON   Eon is a variant name of EUDES DE L'ETOILE.

EPIGONUS   A heretical teacher active in Rome during the early third century, Epigonus belonged to the school of PRAXEAS, who taught the heresy of MODAL-ISM.

EPIPHANES   Epiphanes was the son of infamous second century Gnostic teacher CARPOCRATES. One of Epiphanes' letters has survived to the present. In it, he claims that when God commanded men not to steal or to desire their neighbors' wives in the Old Testament, He was joking. After all, God created sexual desire and the many delightful objects in the world, and must have intended people to share everything. The tradition of Carpocrates and Epiphanes, known as CARPOCRA-TIAN GNOSTICISM, horrified orthodox Christians and even many other Gnostics with its communistic teachings.

EPISCOPI VAGANTES   Episcopi vagantes is the Latin variant name for WAN-DERING BISHOPS. (The singular form is "episcopus vagans.")

EUCHITES   Euchites is a variant name for the heretical sect of the MESSALIANS.

EUDES DE L'ÉTOILE   A heretic who was active in Brittany, northern France, during the mid-twelfth century, Eudes received a revelation telling him that he was the Judge of the World and commanding him to change his name to Eon. He managed to convince some of his fellow Bretons that this was true. Eudes was worshipped as a god, while his followers attacked churches and monasteries in the region. The movement collapsed in 1148 when Eudes and his supporters were caught and tried at a council Pope Eugenius III presided over. The pope was in no mood for clemency because the supporters of the heretical preacher, ARNOLD OF BRESCIA, had chased Eugenius out of Rome. Eudes was judged to be mad and sentenced to life in prison, where he died shortly afterward. His followers were burned at the stake.

EUDOXIUS   Eudoxius was a leader of the heretical school called the ANOMOE-ANS, a branch of the heresy known as ARIANISM. He became the bishop of

Constantinople in 360 A.D., during the period when the Anomoeans had taken control of the orthodox Christian Church. He died in 370.

EUNOMIUS   During the fourth century, Eunomius was a leader of the heretical ANOMOEANS, a division of ARIANISM. He was a student of the Anomoean founder, AETIUS. During the short period of Anomoean power within the church, Eunomius became a bishop but resigned after a few months. He wrote a book detailing his heretical views concerning God, which stimulated the early theologians of the Eastern Orthodox tradition to clarify their own thinking on the matters he raised. With the political triumph of orthodoxy, Eunomius was exiled and died around 394.

EUSEBIUS OF NICOMEDIA   Along with ARIUS himself, Eusebius was the leader of the heretical movement called ARIANISM, which rocked the Christian Church during the fourth century. Eusebius's influence kept the Arian movement alive during periods when its opponents were politically strong. However, his stumble at the opening of the FIRST COUNCIL OF NICAEA, called in A.D. 325 to resolve the divisions within the church, ultimately led to the victory of orthodox Catholic Christianity over the Arian heresy.

Eusebius met Arius, after whom the Arian heresy was named, while they were studying at the Christian academy LUCIAN OF ANTIOCH ran in the late third century. Both men were persuaded by Lucian's argument that because the Son of God had been created by God the Father, the Son could not be God. Many years later, when Arius fell afoul of the archbishop of Alexandria for teaching this doctrine, Arius appealed to Eusebius for help.

After completing his studies with Lucian, Eusebius had risen to a position of prominence within the church hierarchy. He had the ear of Emperor Constantine, who had legalized Christianity within the Roman Empire in 313. Eusebius proved to be a powerful ally of Arius. He wrote many letters recruiting other church leaders to accept the Arian position, which was directly opposed to the orthodox view that the Son had not been created but was eternal.

Unable to persuade the warring factions of the church to resolve their differences, Constantine called the church leaders together in Nicaea in 325. The Arians, led by Eusebius, outnumbered the orthodox representatives and were confident of victory. But this confidence led to their downfall. At the First Council's opening, Eusebius presented a summary of the Arian position, which bluntly stated that Christ is not God. This uncompromising language alienated the uncommitted representatives, who rejected it. This event caused the emperor to propose a description of the relationship between God the Father and His Son that was much more favorable to the orthodox position. The emperor's suggestion was adopted by the council, and Arianism seemed defeated. However, Eusebius was still in favor with Constantine. Over the following years, he was able to persuade the emperor to replace many orthodox bishops with Arians and to send Athanasius, the strongest supporter of the orthodox doctrine, into exile.

When Constantine became fatally ill in 336, he asked to be baptized by Eusebius. Constantine's successor in the eastern part of the empire, CONSTANTIUS II, fell under the influence of Eusebius and became a committed supporter of the Arian movement. Eusebius himself died in 342, but his powerful admirer Constantius continued to promote the Arian cause until the ruler's death in 361.

Eusebius' most enduring legacy, however, was his defeat at the First Council of Nicaea. The council's decision in favor of orthodoxy gave support to the Catholic party during the dark times that followed. By the end of the fourth century, the orthodox version of Christianity had triumphed within the empire.

EUTYCHES   This fifth century heretic founded the important unorthodox movement called MONOPHYSITISM. In order to meet the challenge of Eutyches' arguments concerning the nature of Christ, the orthodox church was forced to clarify its own views on this matter. As a result, the COUNCIL OF CHALCEDON, regarded as one of the most important meetings in the history of Christianity, was held in order to condemn Eutyches and to define an official description of JESUS CHRIST.

Eutyches was born around A.D. 378, just three years before Catholic Christianity was declared the state religion of the Roman Empire. He was an ardent follower of the new official faith and eventually became the head of a monastery in Constantinople. Because of his piety and intelligence, he was an influential figure at the court of the emperor.

During the first half of the fifth century, heated debates concerning the nature of Christ threatened to tear the church apart. Most orthodox theologians held that Christ had both a human nature and a divine nature. His divinity was required to explain how He could have the power to forgive sins, and His humanity was necessary to explain how His death on the cross could merit the salvation of human beings. There was strong disagreement concerning the relationship between Christ's two natures.

Eutyches was opposed to the view called NESTORIANISM, which had been declared heretical at a council in 431. The Nestorians were accused of highlighting the differences between Christ's two natures so much that they effectively split Christ into two Persons. Eutyches reacted to Nestorianism by stating that although Christ's divine and human natures had been distinct before Jesus' life on earth, afterward there was only one, divine nature. Eutyches claimed that Christ's single nature was clearly not the same sort of nature as that shared by ordinary human beings.

Unfortunately for Eutyches, his doctrine defined as heretics not only the Nestorians, but also the orthodox Catholics. According to orthodoxy, the death of a Christ without a human nature could not save people from their sins. Flavian, the archbishop of Constantinople, did not take kindly to being called a heretic; he deposed Eutyches in 448. However, Eutyches had a powerful ally in DIOSCURUS, the bishop of Alexandria. At the time, the three major Christian centers of Alexandria, Constantinople, and Rome were maneuvering for control of the church. Dioscurus saw the controversy surrounding the heretical monk as an opportunity to embarrass his competitors and declared his support for Eutyches.

The following year, Emperor Theodosius II called a council of church leaders to meet in Ephesus in an attempt to resolve the dispute. Dioscurus was asked to oversee the meeting, and he ensured that his views were upheld. As a result, Eutyches' condemnation was reversed, and the bishops of both Constantinople and Rome were declared to be heretics.

Eutyches' victory was short-lived. The outcome of the council in 449, known to history as the ROBBER COUNCIL, outraged too many powerful people within the church. Two years later, the leading authorities of the church met in Chalcedon. This time, the cards were stacked against Eutyches. The monk was again condemned and exiled to a remote corner of the empire, where he died around 454. To ensure that Eutyches' beliefs would never again be proclaimed as orthodox, the council decreed that Christ has both divine and human natures although He is only a single Person. This statement remains the official view of orthodox Christianity to the present day.

Eutyches' legacy has endured long after his final condemnation. Following the Council of Chalcedon, Christians who agreed that Christ has only one nature organized themselves into the MONOPHYSITE movement, which has survived to this day in Africa and Armenia.

FAUSTUS OF RIEZ   During the latter part of the fifth century, Faustus of Riez was a prominent teacher of the unorthodox Christian doctrine called SEMI-PELAGIANISM in Gaul.

FELIX   The bishop of the Spanish town of Urgel at the end of the eighth century, Felix played a major role in the controversy surrounding the heresy of SPANISH ADOPTIONISM. A group of bishops in Spain led by Archbishop ELIPANDUS declared their refusal to accept doctrinal guidance from representatives of Pope Hadrian. After the falling out between Spain and Rome over the issue in 784, Elipandus recruited Felix as an ally.

Felix was renowned for his devotion to his faith, so his willingness to support the Spanish Adoptionists was a blow to the papal cause. Early on in the controversy, the bishop was summoned to the court of Charlemagne in Regensburg and was persuaded to reject the heretical expressions of Elipandus. Visiting Rome on the way back to Spain, Felix was subjected to humiliating treatment by Pope Hadrian, which might have weakened his commitment to abide by the Roman doctrine once he was safely back in Spain.

After returning to Urgel, Felix reverted to his support for Spanish Adoptionism. Alcuin, Charlemagne's court theologian, wrote to Felix, urging him to conform to Catholic doctrine. This time, Felix refused. In 798, a church council in Rome led by Pope Leo III condemned the "heresies and blasphemies" of the bishop of Urgel.

In 800, Felix was once again called to Charlemagne's court in an attempt to remove him from the heretics' camp. And Felix, once again, was persuaded to return to orthodoxy. In light of his previous behavior, however, it was decided that he could not return to Spain. Instead, he was forced to remain in Lyons under "supervision" by its archbishop until his death in 818.

In Spain, the Adoptionist heresy did not long outlive its leader Elipandus, who died in 802. Felix's captivity in Lyons kept interest in Adoptionism alive among European theologians, who felt moved to compose theological refutations. Felix's challenging presence persisted even after his death: Archbishop Agobard of Lyons, sorting through Felix's papers, found evidence that the Spaniard was still an Adoptionist when he died, and produced a further series of attacks on Adoptionist thought. Adoptionism, thus introduced into medieval European thought, refused to disappear. Another resurgence of the heresy arose in France during the twelfth century.

François FENELON   François Fenelon was the seventeenth century Catholic archbishop of the French city of Cambrai and teacher of QUIETISM. Born in 1651, he rose to prominence, not only within the church, but also within the state; he became the tutor of King Louis XIV's grandson, the heir apparent to the French throne. In 1688, Fenelon met MADAME GUYON, who taught unorthodox mystical doctrines that had led to her brief imprisonment the preceding year. Guyon's teachings impressed the archbishop. When the church later condemned her views, he defended her. Fenelon developed his own version of the Quietist doctrine, which he presented in his book *Maxims of the Saints*.

Fenelon's ideas were recognized as being related to those of Guyon, and he was attacked by Bishop Bossuet of Meaux as unchristian. At first, the pope, Innocent XII, sympathized with Fenelon in the argument, but Bossuet persuaded King Louis to side with him and to pressure the pontiff to condemn Fenelon. In 1699, the pope caved in and declared Fenelon's doctrines heretical. Fenelon was quick to repent and to return to the Catholic party line, which tends to view mystical doctrines with suspicion. He died in 1715.

Jules FERRETTE   An important WANDERING BISHOP in the late nineteenth century, Jules Ferrette was ordained a Roman Catholic priest in 1855 but left the church within a few months. Eleven years later, he claimed to have been consecrated a bishop by a patriarch of the JACOBITES, although evidence confirming this event is lacking. Ferrette was free to consecrate anyone he chose to be a bishop because he was outside the control of orthodox authorities. By the time of his death in 1904, he had created many independent bishops around the world. Today, at least ten religious bodies, from the Ancient British Church to the Indian Orthodox Church, claim a valid apostolic succession through Ferrette.

FIFTH MONARCHY MEN   Fifth Monarchy Men was a mid-seventeenth century English sect that believed, on the basis of prophecies in the Book of Daniel, that Christ was about to return to earth. In his writings, Daniel describes the first four monarchies, traditionally interpreted as the empires of Assyria, Persia, Greece, and Rome, and awaits a fifth divine kingdom that will last 1,000 years. The Fifth Monarchy Men interpreted the downfall of King Charles I of England in 1645 as a signal that Christ was due shortly. After a while, some believers became impatient and tried to help the Lord along by provoking riots in London. After the second such incident in 1661, their leaders were beheaded.

Marsilio FICINO   The leading philosopher of the fifteenth century Italian Renaissance, Marsilio Ficino played a central role in the evolution of Western ceremonial magic. Modern scholars debate whether his teachings were a type of NATURAL MAGIC or DEMON MAGIC; he claimed they were the former, but most of his disciples developed his ideas in demonic directions.

Ficino was born in 1433. When he was six, a historic event occurred in Florence. A council of the church brought together representatives of both the Roman Catholic and Eastern Orthodox branches in an (unsuccessful) attempt to reconcile their differences. Cosimo de Medici, the leading figure in Florence at the time, was an avid collector of rare manuscripts. His contact with Byzantine scholars at the council elicited a strong interest in the writings of the ancient Greeks and Romans, some of which had been preserved in the East.

Ficino's father was a physician and kindled medical interests in his son. The younger Ficino was keenly interested in classical literature and developed a translator's mastery of Greek and Latin. These two interests, healing and ancient knowledge, combined to determine Ficino's direction in life. De Medici, eager to support Florentine scholars who could help him in bringing about a rebirth ("Renaissance") of the old wisdom, sponsored Ficino to translate Greek manuscripts.

De Medici then introduced the young scholar to the writings of Plato. Ficino learned that Plato was not merely a healer of the flesh, but also a "physician of the soul" who addressed the deepest mysteries of human life. His encounter with Plato so profoundly affected Ficino that he came to call De Medici his "second father" in gratitude. He devoted the rest of his life to reconstructing what he believed to be the ancient secrets for living a healthy life.

De Medici then gave Ficino the assignment of translating the writings of Plato into Latin. In 1460, this important work was interrupted when De Medici received a copy of an ancient collection of writings called the HERMETICA from a traveling Byzantine monk. The collector insisted that Ficino devote himself to translating the Hermetic texts, which he thought contained a great deal of ancient wisdom.

Ficino became convinced that the Hermetica were the source of Plato's knowledge (not until the 1600s was the Hermetic collection dated at around A.D. 200, several centuries *after* Plato). From these texts, the young scholar learned that all human beings contain a connection with the seven planets of classical ASTROLOGY. He also discovered that people can establish harmony among these inner planets by attracting the influences of the outer planets using images. This notion became the basis for his system of magic.

Inspired by Plato's works, the Hermetica, and other classical writings he had translated, Ficino spent several years, from 1482 to 1489, composing his masterwork, *De Vita Triplici*, or "Three Books About Life." These three volumes provide a comprehensive guide to health of the body and soul; in effect, they constitute a work of holistic medicine. The first two books focus primarily on physical health and summarize much of conventional Renaissance medicine. In the third book, *De Vita Coelitus Comparanda*, or "How Life Should Be Arranged According to the Heavens," Ficino describes his controversial methods for harmonizing the inner planets.

According to Ficino, the continual, harmonious flowing of planetary influences within an individual produces a healthy life. Often, however, these influences become unbalanced or fixated. For example, scholars, such as Ficino himself, become prone to depression because they spend so much time engaged in solitary study, an activity associated with the planet Saturn. The antidote for this Saturnian overload is to stimulate the activity of other planets, such as Venus, Jupiter, and the Sun.

Planetary influences can be stimulated by drawing into oneself the "spirits" of the planets; these affect one's own spirit, which transmits the influence to one's soul. Ficino learned from his occult studies that people can sensitize themselves to planetary spirits through the use of sounds, sights, smells, and tastes associated with the appropriate planets. For example, one of Ficino's pupils, Diacceto, described the following ritual to increase one's solar spirits:

> If for example he wishes to acquire solarian gifts, first he sees that the sun is ascending in Leo or Aries, on the day and in the hour of the sun. Then, robed in a solarian mantle of a

solarian colour, such as gold, and crowned with a mitre of laurel, on the altar, itself made of solarian material, he burns myrrh and frankincense, the sun's own fumigations, having strewn the ground with heliotrope and suchlike flowers. Also, he has an image of the sun in gold or chrysolite or carbuncle, that is, of the kind they think corresponds to each of the sun's gifts. . . . Then, anointed with unguents made, under the same celestial aspect, from saffron, balsam, yellow honey and anything else of that kind, and not forgetting the cock and the goat, he sings the sun's own hymn, such as Orpheus thought should be sung.

In his writings, Ficino emphasizes that his magic was fully compatible with orthodox Christianity. At the time, people convicted of dealing with demons were often executed. Ficino insists that his practices were not intended to call demons, but rather to utilize the forces of the planets, which were natural, impersonal powers. However, certain passages in his works are unclear on this point. Some historians have suspected that Ficino actually believed that spiritual creatures conveyed the planetary influences, but that it was too dangerous for him to admit this belief publicly. There is evidence that these suspicions were held even during Ficino's lifetime, but because of his written disclaimers and his political connections, he was never persecuted.

Ficino's influence on the later course of the Western tradition was extensive. He established an academy in Florence, where he taught his magical world view to many of Europe's brightest minds. He was also the private tutor of Cosimo De Medici's grandson and successor, Lorenzo the Magnificent. GIOVANNI PICO DELLA MIRANDOLA, who set forth the central Renaissance axiom that "Man is the measure of all things," was Ficino's student as well. Painter Allessandro Botticelli followed Ficino's doctrines, and many art historians believe that Botticelli's famous painting, *Primavera*, was a magical image designed to attract the spiritual influence of Venus. Long after Ficino's death in 1499, many prominent occultists, including GIORDANO BRUNO, JOHANNES TRITHEMIUS, PARACELSUS, and CORNELIUS AGRIPPA, were indebted to Ficino for their views concerning the workings of the magical universe. To this day, many ritual magicians employ Ficino's planetary correspondences in their ceremonies.

Danila FILIPPOV   Danila Filippov was the founder of the Russian heretical movement, the KHLYSTY. Following the SCHISM of the Russian Orthodox Church in the seventeenth century, many sects arose. Danila Filippov, a Russian peasant, came to believe that he was the equal of Christ and began to teach; he soon attracted followers in this environment of religious ferment. He taught that people could invite the Holy Spirit into their souls by participating in a ritual dance, during which they were whipped. Filippov encouraged vegetarianism and avoidance of alcohol. Some of his disciples soon began to claim that they, too, had achieved Christhood and, therefore, could do anything they pleased. Filippov was unable to control the scandalous behavior of these "Christs," and the Khlysty movement fell into disrepute.

FLAGELLANTS   The practice of whipping or beating to induce moral or spiritual progress has a lengthy history in Western culture. Christian monks and nuns have been fond of such activities since ancient times. The Rule of Saint Benedict, the model for monastic behavior, advises "the punishment of the rod" for repeated violations of discipline. Flagellation has long played a respected role in education (to discourage distractions and laziness) and medicine (to drive out demons or poisons) also. The practice has been associated with several heresies.

In the mid-thirteenth century, there was widespread fear in Christian Europe that the world was about to undergo a radical change. Italian prophet JOACHIM OF FIORE had predicted that a new Age of the Holy Spirit would dawn in 1260. As the fateful year approached, some people became concerned that the orthodox methods of repenting for their sins would not be effective enough to purify them for the advent of the Holy Spirit. In Italy, groups of men formed processions through the streets, flogging themselves and each other to atone for the sins of the world. Church authorities condemned these *flagellantes* for their lack of confidence in the usual channels of repentance, but many others were impressed by the spectacles.

After the Holy Spirit failed to manifest noticeably in 1260, the flagellants' movement died down. It resurged in the mid 1300s. The plague had begun to ravage Europe, eventually killing a third of the population. Many felt that the Second Coming of Christ was imminent and that purification was essential to avoid damnation. In central Italy, the Flagellant Brethren formed. Members wore a distinctive costume, a cloak and hood, with a red cross marked on front and back. They would wander from town to town, engaging twice a day in a public ceremony of flagellation. Stripping to the waist, men, women, and children would strike themselves with chains, rods, and leather thongs, sometimes embedded with iron spikes, until they were covered in blood. The flagellants viewed the opening of their own flesh as a powerful kind of baptism that could appease God's wrath at the degraded state of Christianity.

Such activities met with disapproval from Catholic officials. However, in the desperate atmosphere of the plague, thousands of people joined the Flagellant Brethren, which spread quickly throughout continental Western Europe. The uneducated classes, disenchanted with the powerlessness of the bishops to stop the plague, revered the flagellants as saints and obeyed their every command. Many of the Brethren believed that the world had to be "purified" of Jews in preparation for the Lord's arrival. As a result, mass murders of Jews occurred in many locations.

In Germany and the Netherlands, some flagellants organized into heretical sects. They proclaimed that the orthodox sacraments had lost their spiritual benefits because of the corruption of the church. Only flagellation was pleasing to God.

The flagellation craze eventually declined in most of Europe. In remote pockets of Spain, however, the practice endured and can still be seen occasionally to this day in connection with religious festivals. Flagellants traveled to the New World with the Spanish conquistadors; their successors, LOS HERMANOS PENITENTES, still maintain the tradition in New Mexico and Colorado.

Another outbreak of flagellation occurred in Russia in the seventeenth century. The Russian Orthodox Church underwent a SCHISM, producing a variety of sects. One of these, the KHLYSTY, encouraged ritual whipping. The activities of the Khlysty were too permissive for another group, the SKOPTSY, who added amputation of body parts to their religious practices. Finally, some members of the twentieth century Roman Catholic order called "Opus Dei" practice flagellation as an act of spiritual purification.

FOREST BROTHERHOOD   A late nineteenth century religious group, the Forest Brotherhood was notorious for worshipping the genitals of its founder, JOHANNES BINGGELI.

FORMOSUS   This pope of the ninth century has become notorious in history. Formosus was associated with a period of rampant corruption at the highest levels of the Catholic Church. He was the pontiff for only five years, from 891 to his death in 896. Nine months later, his successor, Pope Stephen VII, accused him of lying and illegally occupying the papal throne. Formosus was exhumed and propped up during the ensuing trial, known as the CADAVER COUNCIL. Since he could not deny the charges, he was convicted. The corpse was punished by having the three fingers used for blessing chopped off. Formosus's body was then thrown into the Tiber River.

The period following the disposal of Formosus was a wild one as the papacy became mired in the skullduggery of Roman politics. During the next forty years, four popes were murdered. Pope Sergius III had a close relationship with a fifteen-year-old girl, who became pregnant (in this case, a Virgin birth was thought to be highly unlikely). The resulting child became Pope John XI.

Matthew FOX   This late twentieth century American theologian is a well-known source of controversy within the Roman Catholic Church. A priest of the Dominican Order, Fox refuses to abandon his church, but he insists on raising issues that bring him into conflict with the guardians of the orthodox faith. For example, in several books, Fox calls for modern Christians to adopt a view he calls "creation centered spirituality." This perspective emphasizes the holy delights of the body and the world, and downplays the traditional focus on the idea that everyone is born with a burden of original sin. He promotes the elevation of women to positions of power and honor within the church; he even states that Roman Catholicism could learn from the modern witchcraft movement, which recognizes the sacred value of women.

Fox acknowledges that some of his inspiration derives from characters of dubious orthodoxy in Catholic history, such as MEISTER ECKHART and the BEGUINES. Not surprisingly, in 1988 the Vatican prohibited Fox from writing or teaching his ideas for one year. Since the ban has expired, Fox has continued to agitate for revolutionary changes in official Catholic attitudes.

See also: HANS KUNG.

FRANCISCANS   After the death of Saint Francis in 1226, his followers debated the best direction for the Franciscan movement to take. One group, the Conventuals, argued that the order should be allowed to own property and wealth; another faction, the SPIRITUAL FRANCISCANS, believed that they should continue to obey Francis's rule of absolute poverty. The Spirituals were eventually declared heretical.

Jacob FRANK   This Jewish "false Messiah" emerged from the heretical underground in Poland during the mid-eighteenth century. The mainstream Jewish community viewed Jacob Frank as a dangerous figure, not only because he taught unorthodox ideas, but also because he sided with anti-Semitic Christians on the question of whether or not orthodox Jews used the blood of Christians in their religious rites. He established a movement that persisted, despite persecution by the orthodox, for more than a century.

Frank was born in 1726 in Korolevo, Poland, into a family of merchants. He took up the mercantile trade himself, traveling as a young man to the Balkans to trade in cloth. Either in Poland or in the Balkan region, he encountered the heretical SHABBATEAN movement. The Shabbateans taught that the seventeenth century figure SHABBATAI ZEVI had been the Messiah. Frank became convinced that he was the reincarnation of Zevi.

Upon Frank's return to Poland, he developed his connections with the Shabbateans there, who existed secretly within the Jewish community. Soon, he rose to a position of leadership. As a divine authority, Frank believed he and his followers were permitted to transcend the ordinary moral rules. His circle experimented with rituals of a sexual nature. When these practices came to the attention of Jewish officials in 1756, Frank was excommunicated.

The Shabbatean leader escaped to Turkey, where he lived for three years. During that period, he publicly converted to Islam, probably for safety's sake, while maintaining contacts with his disciples in Poland. Meanwhile, Jewish orthodoxy had unleashed a campaign of persecution against the Frankists. Frank's followers sought protection in an unlikely direction, the Roman Catholic Church. They argued that they rejected the authority of the collection of orthodox Jewish law, the Talmud; therefore, they more closely resembled Christianity than orthodox Judaism did and therefore deserved support, not destruction. Church officials, sensing the possibility of converting the Frankists to Christianity, ordered a public religious debate between the Frankists and the orthodox Jews.

The outcome of the debate, which took place in 1757, was a foregone conclusion. Bishop Dembowski declared the Frankists the victors and ordered the public burning of all copies of the Talmud. Before this assault on Jewish orthodoxy was fully organized, however, the bishop suddenly died. The orthodox Jewish community, taking Dembowski's death as a sign from God, renewed their attacks on Frank's followers.

Frank returned to Poland in 1759. By this time, he had evolved a peculiar theology, centered around a holy Trinity of the Good God, the Big Brother, and She. Frank proclaimed that the world was currently controlled by a corresponding Trinity of evil forces. The Big Brother sent Frank to bring salvation to humanity.

Later that year, another debate between orthodox Jews and Frankists took place in Lvov Cathedral, by order of the Catholic Church. While Frank himself did not take part in the debate, he was certainly involved in organizing it, along with the Catholics. This time, the Frankists tried not only to prove their theological superiority, but also attempted to demonstrate that the Talmud calls for the use of Christian blood in orthodox devotions. Even though the Catholic judges were biased in their favor, the Frankist arguments were so weak that the debate ended inconclusively. There is little doubt that if Frank's side had won the debate, a massacre of Jews would have followed.

Two months after this event, Frank, along with hundreds of his followers, were baptized as Catholics. But this conversion was not genuine. In fact, the Frankists were merely maneuvering for political purposes. Following the Shabbatean tradition of public orthodoxy and private heresy, they continued to regard Frank as their divine leader.

When word of the Frankists' secret practices was leaked to Catholic officials,

Frank was arrested. He remained imprisoned for the next thirteen years, but he was jailed under such relaxed conditions that he continued to direct the activities of the movement. Invading Russian troops freed Frank in 1772. Until his death in 1791, he retained a large following and lived an almost royal lifestyle. Some Frankists were external Catholics; others maintained the appearance of Jews. But all submitted to Frank's authority.

After Frank's death, generations of Frankist families revered his memory. His more extreme ideas and practices, such as the blood libel against the Jews and orgiastic activities, were forgotten. In the nineteenth century, Frankists were among the more important commercial and cultural figures of Poland and Bohemia. A small group even emigrated to New York. Gradually, the disciples of Jacob Frank were absorbed back into the Jewish and Christian mainstreams.

FRATICELLI   Originally, this term was applied to all members of medieval Christian groups that renounced the ownership of property. Following the condemnation for heresy of one such organization, the SPIRITUAL FRANCISCANS, by Pope John XXII in 1317, "Fraticelli" tended to refer specifically to them.

The pope disapproved of the Fraticelli's claim that material power and wealth were obstacles to spiritual purity. He was busy accumulating such "obstacles" himself, and the preaching of the Fraticelli put his activities in a poor light. After the papal condemnation, the Fraticelli became a target of the INQUISITION. The killing began in 1318 when four Fraticelli were burned at the stake in Marseilles. In the ensuing years, many more died.

Rather than renouncing their beliefs, the Fraticelli countered by claiming that they were the true Christians, and that the pope and his bishops were the actual heretics. Their views won support from many poor people, who objected to the heavy tax burden imposed by the church. The Fraticelli were also protected by some members of the upper classes, who were opposed to the increasing interest shown by the pope in political domination. Even Holy Roman Emperor LOUIS OF BAVARIA sheltered Fraticelli who were fleeing the wrath of the pope. Such sympathies enabled the Fraticelli to continue their activities secretly in many European towns.

Some of the heretics fled beyond the reach of the Catholic powers into isolated Alpine valleys where they could preach openly. Others went to Greece, which was controlled by the Eastern Orthodox Church, and set up monasteries.

Eventually, under the pressure of relentless persecution, the Fraticelli movement shrank. The last major trial of Fraticelli occurred in Rome in 1466. At an annual festival in honor of Saint Francis, the founder of the Franciscan order, police rounded up suspected Fraticelli members. They were imprisoned and tortured into confessing their heresies. In addition to admitting to a belief in the virtue of poverty and the corruption of the Catholic Church, some of the victims also confessed to monstrous activities. After celebrating Mass at night, the Fraticelli stated that they conducted an orgy. Also, a child was passed from heretic to heretic around a blazing fire until it was dead, "quite dried up"; the body was then reduced to powder, to be added to a sacramental drink. This strange scene was certainly a fantasy of the Inquisitors, which they forced their victims to confirm. The tale was adopted from slanders made against earlier heretics, the PAULICIANS and CLEMENTIUS OF BUCY. The belief that the Fraticelli were ritual murderers has tainted their memory to this day.

Heresy of the FREE SPIRIT   In the New Testament letter to Titus, Saint Paul wrote, "Unto the pure, all things are pure" (1:15). In the towns along the Rhine River toward the end of the thirteenth century, some people believed they had understood the true meaning of Paul's statement: that those who attained spiritual perfection by living a life without material possessions were above all laws and free to do as they pleased. These radicals became known as the Brothers and Sisters of the Free Spirit.

Most of the Free Spirit heretics belonged to the movement known as the BE-GUINES and BEGHARDS. This movement was originally based in settled communities within the towns, but soon wanderers appeared, living by begging and the support of the Beguine houses. Orthodox authorities suspected both the settled members and the wanderers, but especially the latter, of spreading heretical views. In some cases, their suspicions proved true.

During the thirteenth century, several groups in Europe advocated poverty as a spiritual path. The Catholic Church was ambivalent or hostile toward all of them, primarily because of its own interest in accumulating vast wealth. The Free Spirit heretics went further than the rest, claiming that their practice of detachment from material objects had caused the Holy Spirit to take up permanent residence within them. As the equals of Christ, they said, their desires were pure, and their every action was above criticism. For them, the sacraments of the church were worthless and obedience to the priests unnecessary. They preached that everyone would be saved and that hell was unreal.

The doctrine was obviously open to abuse and even to delusions of grandeur. Most Free Spirit advocates appear to have conducted themselves in a moral manner, even if they argued that in theory nothing they chose to do would be sinful. John Hartmann, for instance, claimed that he *could* have sex with a woman lying on a church altar without offending God, although he had never done so. However, some members of the heresy justified theft and prostitution by claiming they were above ordinary morality. Others seem to have taken their identification with Christ to extremes. For example, Hermann Kuchener reported that he was able to walk across the surface of the Rhine without getting his feet wet. Of course, the heretics of the Free Spirit were accused of all sorts of immorality, including orgies and sacrilege, but the majority of scholars agree that most of the charges were exaggerated.

There were historical precedents for the Free Spirit sect. In ancient times, the heresy of MONTANISM had encouraged people to become mediums for the Holy Spirit. Earlier medieval heretics, such as AMALRIC OF BENA and BENTIVENGA OF GUBBIO, taught similar ideas without generating large followings. The heresy of the Free Spirit proved broadly popular, but never developed into an organized movement; rather, individuals and small groups maintained loose contact through visits and the exchange of writings.

Those possessed by the Free Spirit became so numerous in Germany that a council condemned the movement in 1311. The preceding year in Paris, MAR-GUERITE PORETE, a Free Spirit advocate, had been executed. The first major trial occurred in Strasbourg in 1317; as a result, several Beghards were killed by fire, and others were driven from the town. Because of their roaming lifestyle, the heretics were difficult targets for the INQUISITION. Nevertheless, trials and executions continued to take place in Germany, Holland, Switzerland, Austria, and Bohemia.

Persecution continued past the middle of the fifteenth century when the GREAT WITCH HUNT dominated the Inquisitors interest.

MEISTER ECKHART von Hocheim, the great German mystic, was suspected of involvement with the Free Spirits. Some even accused him of starting the movement, although this is unlikely. Certainly, some of his notions were similar. He believed that "if a man is rightly disposed he should not regret having committed a thousand mortal sins"; the heretics would have approved this statement. It was not, however, approved by the orthodox; the decision to condemn Eckhart's ideas in 1326 was probably influenced by their resemblance to the Free Spirit teachings.

Historian Wilhelm Fraenger suggested that the sixteenth century Dutch artist Hieronymus Bosch was secretly a member of the Free Spirit heresy. According to Fraenger, Bosch's famous painting, *The Garden of Earthly Delights*, which depicts numbers of frolicking, naked people, portrays an orgiastic ritual of the heretics. Other scholars have dismissed this idea, noting both a lack of evidence and Bosch's well-documented close ties with Catholic leaders.

GAIANUS OF ALEXANDRIA   Gaianus of Alexandria was a leader of the Monophysite heretics known as the APHTHARTODOCETAE, who flourished in Egypt during the sixth century. Gaianus followed the movement's founder, JULIAN OF HALICARNASSUS.

GALILEO Galilei   During the early seventeenth century, the authority of the Roman Catholic Church was increasingly challenged by new possibilities. Protestants had become entrenched in much of Europe, offering a viable alternative to the papal faith, and Catholic thinkers were presenting observations and ideas that seemed to contradict the cherished knowledge of the church leaders. Even the reality of witches was being questioned. Galileo Galilei proclaimed his vision at a time when the religious establishment felt it could not tolerate another major challenge. As a result, he was branded a heretic.

Galileo was born in the Italian city of Pisa in 1564. His family was wealthy and privileged, which gave the young man access to the best educational opportunities. His brilliance (and flair for self-promotion) was recognized early; by the age of twenty-eight, he obtained the prestigious chair of mathematics at the University of Pisa.

Galileo believed that the universe could be understood through numbers; "The Book of Nature is written in mathematics," he proclaimed. In order to apply his mathematical approach to the empirical world, he had to quantify the distances and intervals in that world. Galileo was a pioneer in this regard. He was the first person to devise a clock that was accurate enough to use in experiments. His research into the nature of motion laid the foundation for the physical science of dynamics.

Galileo's early work made him famous, but it was not perceived at first as a problem for the Catholic Church. This attitude changed in 1610, when he announced the discoveries he had made using a new device, the telescope. When Galileo pointed this instrument at objects in the sky, he saw things that, according to orthodoxy, were impossible. The official world view of the time held that the earth was the center of the universe. Also, the heavens consisted of crystalline spheres, within which the planets and stars were embedded; a complex theory of "epicycles" had been developed to explain their movements. In addition, because the sky is closer to God than the earth is, celestial objects were thought to be "perfect"—that is, to be perfectly circular and to move in circular paths.

The findings of Galileo's scientific predecessors, Nicolaus Copernicus and Johannes Kepler, promoted an alternative image of the universe; the heliocentric theory, which placed the sun at the center. Until Galileo, few took this notion seriously because it seemed to contradict common sense, which established that the earth did not move. Furthermore, it went against Biblical passages that implied that the sun orbited the earth. With his telescope, however, Galileo discovered mountains on the moon and spots on the sun, findings that blemished the supposed perfection of the heavens. In addition, he reported that Venus displayed phases as if it were traveling around the sun, not the earth. He also found that Jupiter had moons of its own; therefore, since Jupiter was able to move through space and not leave its satellites behind, perhaps the earth could as well.

Galileo's observations were dangerous to orthodoxy. If scientific findings could be used to interpret the scriptural passages referring to the sun's movement, then in the future science might be to used to challenge other doctrines that act as the foundation of the church's authority. In such uncertain times, this could not be permitted. In 1616, Copernicus's work was condemned and his writings included in the INDEX OF PROHIBITED BOOKS. Three years later, Kepler's work was also banned. Galileo understood the implicit message. He published a work in which he mentioned "the movement attributed to the earth, which I as a pious person and a Catholic consider entirely false and nil." Among his friends, however, he almost certainly continued to endorse the heliocentric theory.

Another unorthodox idea was circulating among scientific thinkers at the time, the atomic theory of matter. If, as Galileo's discoveries with the telescope suggest, the objects in the sky were made of material essentially similar to that of objects on earth, the question as to the nature of this universal matter arises. Scientists were coming to believe that matter consists of extremely tiny particles that combine to form observable things. The visible properties of objects arise from the characteristics of the atoms they are composed of.

The atomic theory worried the defenders of the Catholic faith, particularly the Jesuits. The Catholic doctrine of the eucharist stated that the sacramental bread is transformed into the actual physical body of Christ. Since the Middle Ages, this doctrine was usually understood in terms of Aristotle's theory of matter. According to Aristotle, the perceived features of a material object do not arise from its substance, but from another aspect of matter known as its "accidents." Substance and accidents are usually intimately linked. However, under certain circumstances, they can be detached. When the bread is transformed into Christ's flesh during the Mass, the accidents of the bread remain—an observer still sees and tastes bread—but the sacred flesh has replaced the substance of the bread. The atomic theory does not allow for the separation of matter's substance from its appearance and, therefore, calls into question the Catholic explanation of the Eucharistic "transubstantiation." To the Jesuits, who were combatting the Protestants' skepticism concerning transubstantiation, the implications of the atomic theory were dangerous.

In 1632, Galileo published *The Dialogue*, which took the form of a debate between followers of Aristotle, Ptolemy, and Copernicus. In this work, he dares to attack Aristotelian physics and argues the idea that the earth is in motion. The Inquisition took action. Galileo's writings were condemned, and he was sentenced to public silence for the rest of his life.

Galileo died near Florence in 1642. The world view he promoted could not be suppressed. Gradually it spread; by the end of the century, every important astronomer had embraced the heliocentric theory. By the late 1700s, belief in the earth-centered model was unusual anywhere in the Western world. Only in 1992 did the Vatican admit its error in charging Galileo with heresy.

See also: ASTROLOGY, GIORDANO BRUNO.

GEORGE OF PODEBRADY   The only king of Bohemia to belong to the unorthodox HUSSITE movement, George of Podebrady was affiliated with the moderate wing of the Hussites, the UTRAQUISTS. He distinguished himself in military campaigns, taking the stronghold of the TABORITE heretics in 1452. George reigned as king from 1458 to 1471 and was known for promoting religious tolerance and peace. Catholics in western Europe referred to him as the "King of the Heretics." After his death, Bohemia fell under the sway of Polish rulers.

GIRAUDE DE LAVAUR   Lavaur was a center of CATHAR activity in southern France, and Giraude de Lavaur was a noblewoman who had a reputation for intense devotion to God and became a well-known follower of the thirteenth century heresy. In 1211, when northern French troops terrorized the region during the ALBIGENSIAN CRUSADE, Giraude was accused of heresy. The crusaders threw her into a pit and stoned her to death. Even the authors of *Chansons de la Croisade*, an account of the time that was hostile to the Cathars, were repelled by the brutality. Giraude's murder came to symbolize the atrocities the southern French people suffered at the hands of the Catholic Crusaders.

GLAUCAS   Second century Gnostic teacher BASILIDES reported that he had been taught by Glaucas, who claimed to have received the secret teachings of Jesus from the apostle Peter. Basilides stated that the doctrines Glaucas transmitted to him formed the basis for his spiritual system, which was known as BASILIDEAN GNOSTICISM.

GNOSIS   This word is a Greek term that can be literally translated as "knowledge." The concept of gnosis never referred to information concerning ordinary objects, such as chairs and trees, nor to conceptual knowledge, such as mathematics and physics. Rather, gnosis is a form of understanding that produces or supports spiritual salvation. Discussions of gnosis were prominent in encounters between heretics and orthodox Christians during the first few centuries A.D.

Some early Catholic Christians, such as Clement of Alexandria, defined gnosis simply as knowledge of God and regarded all mature Christians as "Gnostics," or possessors of gnosis. After Clement, however, it is rare to find orthodox Christians endorsing the concept of gnosis because it had become identified with a heretical understanding of Christ's teaching. Gnosis became much more closely associated with the unorthodox movement called GNOSTICISM, which thrived in the Mediterranean region during the infancy of Christianity.

Historian R. M. Grant noted in his study of the Valentinian school of Gnosticism that the term gnosis was defined by the Gnostics in two interrelated ways. First, gnosis is self-knowledge: "who we were and what we have become; where we were or where we had been made to fall; whither we are hastening, whence we are being redeemed; what birth is and what rebirth is." Second, gnosis is the "redemption of the inner spiritual man." According to the Gnostics, then, self-knowledge leads directly to redemption or salvation. Defined this way, gnosis was a heretical belief, according to orthodox Christianity. The orthodox doctrine specified that faith in God and not just knowledge justified salvation.

What, according to Gnosticism, is this liberating self-knowledge? The various Gnostic systems describe the content of gnosis in differing ways, but all of the descriptions have one feature in common: the direct discovery that oneself is divine. As historian Elaine Pagels stated, gnosis is "self-knowledge as knowledge of God." Orthodox Christians declared that this idea, too, was heretical; the individual self is part of God's creation and, therefore, cannot be identified with the Creator Himself.

Furthermore, in the words of THE GOSPEL OF PHILIP, a Gnostic scripture, one who realizes gnosis is "no longer a Christian, but a Christ." This statement violates the orthodox teaching that Christ is unique and cannot be duplicated. Gnosis also implicitly undermined the efforts of Catholicism to unify the Christian Church under the authority of the bishops. Whereas a Christian would be expected to be obedient to the leaders of the church, the bishops and priests, no such requirement applies to one who is a Christ.

This gnosis from which Gnosticism takes its name is not merely the abstract *idea* that oneself is divine, but a powerful insight, experienced directly. The Gnostic schools taught many practices, involving meditation and ritual, in order to bring on the experience of gnosis. Although the idea that self-knowledge alone can lead to spiritual liberation is heretical to mainstream Christianity, it is central to Buddhism. The root of suffering, according to Buddhists, is ignorance concerning the true nature of the self. When this ignorance is dispelled through direct insight, one becomes freed from the frustrations of endless greed and hatred. Some researchers have suggested that the idea of gnosis was brought to the West from Buddhist sources in India, perhaps by Buddhist travelers to Egypt in the first century A.D. However, there is no direct historical evidence for such a transmission.

Gnosis, although firmly opposed by the orthodox, has continued to be a fascinating subject through the centuries. Many esoteric belief systems have emphasized that the true nature of the self is divine. Catholic mystics frequently found that their experiences of union with God seemed to be located within themselves, and had to be careful not to sound like Gnostics in describing their mystical adventures.

The increased fascination with the nature of the self during the twentieth century has produced a major upsurge of interest in gnosis. Influential psychiatrist Carl Jung, the founder of analytical psychology, was greatly inspired by his research into gnosis, and thought that the achievement of gnosis was the proper goal of psychology. Another sign of the modern significance of this old heretical idea is the title chosen for an important American periodical dealing with esoteric matters, *Gnosis: A Journal of the Western Inner Traditions*.

GNOSTICISM   The Gnostic movement was one of the most powerful influences on spirituality in world history. Gnostic beliefs decisively molded the doctrines of conventional Christianity. The Gnostics were the first people the developing orthodox church labeled as heretics during the early centuries of the Christian era.

The origins of Gnosticism are obscure. There are traces of Gnostic activity in Egypt and Palestine in the first century A.D. During the following centuries, the motifs of Gnostic thought spread throughout the Roman Empire and into neighboring Persia. Eventually, the Gnostic school called MANICHAEISM had followers over a vast area, ranging from Spain to China. Some scholars argue that orthodox Christianity itself adopted attitudes and ideas from the Gnostics and carried these influences around the world.

Gnosticism was never a unified movement, but rather a series of schools and teachers whose ideas had some common features. An examination of these aspects suggests that Gnostic thinking first arose as a combination of trends found in earlier Jewish, Greek, and Egyptian belief systems. The communication channels of the Hellenistic Empire created by Alexander the Great, and the Roman Empire that followed it, enabled ideas to flow freely among the cultures of the Mediterranean region for the first time. The result was the appearance of hybrid religions and philosophies. Early Gnosticism was one of them.

Most members of the Gnostic groups were Christians, claiming that Jesus Christ was the savior and that their doctrines were taught by him. Some Gnostics, however, such as the followers of SIMON MAGUS, were independent of Christian influence. Non-Christian Gnostics might have competed with the first Christians for public attention. The Manichaeans, on the other hand, were Gnostics who recognized the divinity of Christ but who believed that his message had been superseded by the more recent teachings of the prophet MANI.

While Gnostic Christians and Catholics both viewed themselves as followers of Christ, their beliefs diverged on several important points. The Catholics taught that Christ was a real human being, with a real physical body, who once lived on earth. After his resurrection, Christ ascended to heaven, having entrusted his doctrine of salvation to his apostles. Many Gnostics rejected the notion that Christ had ever had a physical body. How could a divine being have the same body of flesh as an ordinary human, they asked? Instead, the Gnostics held that Christ had appeared on earth in a nonmaterial, ghostly form, which is the heresy of DOCETISM. Either someone other than Christ had been crucified, or Christ's suffering on the cross was an illusion.

Furthermore, the Gnostics did not believe that Christ had left the earth to reside in some inaccessible heaven until the Second Coming. According to Gnosticism, Christ has never stopped appearing to his disciples. Any Gnostic can receive divine teachings in a vision.

If the teachings of Christ were only "once delivered" to the apostles as the New Testament Book of Jude reported, then the official successors of the apostles—the bishops and priests of the Catholic Church—were the sole guardians of the holy truths given by Christ. Faith and obedience to the clergy would naturally be expected of the Christian community. On the other hand, if revelations were directly available from Christ, as the Gnostics claimed, then the importance of faith in the doctrinal interpretations of other people (including church officials) would obviously be lessened.

The orthodox emphasis on faith and obedience also contrasts with another fundamental Gnostic tenet. In addition to visionary revelations of Christ or other divine beings, the Gnostics highlighted the importance of self-knowledge. In essence, the Gnostics claimed, human beings are themselves divine, so self-knowledge is the liberating realization that oneself is God. This realization is called GNOSIS. The Catholics' rigidly held distinction between the Creator and the created beings, including humans, is heretically blurred in the notion of gnosis.

Catholic Christians and Gnostics had drastically different views concerning the nature of the world and of suffering. According to Catholicism, God created the world. As the creation of a benevolent God, the world was thought to be basically a good place. Humans must endure suffering in this world because they have chosen to turn away from God toward sin. For the Gnostics, the world they live in was not created by the highest God. Rather, a lower being formed the world, trapping sparks of divine light in the process. These sparks comprise the self, experienced in gnosis. Suffering arises from human entrapment in the created world, governed by a deranged or evil being impersonating God. In complete opposition to the view of orthodox Christians, many Gnostics identified this impostor as the God of the Old Testament. They taught that Christ was not sent by the creator of the world, but by the highest God.

While orthodox Christianity, at least initially, maintained that the material world was basically good, Gnosticism seemed to have held a range of attitudes toward matter. At one extreme were the Manichaeans, who simply viewed matter as the domain of evil. Other Gnostic groups stressed that salvation involved a change in awareness rather than an escape from matter. In this view, the material world *as people ordinarily experience it* through the filter of their ignorance concerning their luminous nature, is indeed evil. In the light of Gnostic realization, however, the world is seen to be the Kingdom of God itself, no longer under the domination of the deranged being who created it. This distinction between variants of the Gnostic attitude toward matter has often been neglected by the orthodox enemies of Gnosticism, who frequently portray all Gnostics as "world-hating."

The distinctive world views of the orthodox Christians and the Gnostics were reflected in their approaches to the idea of sacred scripture. Institutional Christianity claimed that it was preserving the message Christ imparted to the apostles. Consequently, only texts believed to contain Christ's original teachings during his time on earth were recognized as holy scriptures. Scripture was viewed as finite. The Gnostics, who believed in ongoing personal revelations, had a constantly growing body of sacred writings. Irenaeus of Lyons, the foremost orthodox opponent of Gnosticism during the second century, complained that the Gnostics had a new truth every day, based only on their personal imaginings.

The doctrinal differences between Gnosticism and orthodox Christianity were reflected in the sphere of social and political activity. Orthodox Christians, during the periods of Roman persecution, believed that they should follow Christ and accept martyrdom rather than deny their Christian faith, in imitation of Christ's own suffering and death. Many Gnostics, with their docetist convictions, did not regard martyrdom as following Christ at all, and so were more flexible when it came to answering questions the Roman authorities posed.

The emphasis on faith and obedience to the church helped the orthodox party to develop a nondemocratic, hierarchical power structure within the Christian community. Elaine Pagels has noted that the books chosen by orthodox bishops for inclusion in the New Testament were selected as much for their support of this power structure as for their supposed historical authenticity. The social control the Catholic Church exercised over its members was so effective that Catholicism was eventually adopted by the Roman state itself, to improve social order within the empire. With the exception of Manichaeism, Gnostic beliefs did not lend themselves to such organizations of social control. Gnostic communities tended to be less hierarchical. The anarchistic tendencies within Gnosticism may have contributed to both its inability to acquire political power and its eventual demise in Europe. Manichaeism was very-well organized from its beginnings in third century Persia, with an established order of church officials and a doctrine of obedience to the organization. As a result, the Manichaean religion survived in Asia until the seventeenth century.

The relationship between orthodox Christianity and Gnosticism has deeply affected the world view of Western culture. Under pressure from the complex theological ideas and poetic writings of the Gnostics, the orthodox church was forced to respond by clarifying its own positions. Modern orthodox Christian writer Harold Brown writes, "it is possible to say that Gnosticism is in a sense the stepmother of systematic theology and that a heresy is the stepmother of orthodoxy." The famous modern scholar Adolf von Harnack held that the absorption of ideas from Greek philosophy into orthodox Christianity during the first two centuries A.D. was an attempt to become more sophisticated in response to the Gnostic challenge. Some scholars believe that the New Testament Gospel of John was written in an attempt to disarm the Gnostic competition to the Catholic school by reinterpreting some of the Gnostics' own concepts. Irenaeus' response to Gnosticism, *Against Heresies*, a book written in A.D. 180, is the first comprehensive attempt to construct an orthodox Christian theology.

Gnostic thought might also have seeped directly into Catholic ideas. Although the orthodox teaching held that the material world is good, mainstream Christian history offers many examples of teachings and practices that seem rather "world hating," the charge the orthodox leveled against the Gnostics. Some researchers trace this trend in orthodoxy back to Augustine of Hippo, the influential church father and former Manichaean. Augustine mistrusted his body, viewing it as corrupted by original sin. He probably acquired this attitude during his years as a follower of Manichaeism and reworked it into Christian language.

The orthodox encounter with Gnosticism may not have ended with the decline of the ancient Gnostic schools in the West. Several important heretical movements that appeared in Europe during the Middle Ages, such as the BOGOMILS and CATHARS, might have been influenced by survivals of Gnostic teaching. Even today, Gnosticism is not dead. The Gnostic emphases on self-knowledge and respect for the imagination were an important inspiration for twentieth century psychiatrist Carl Jung, the founder of the school of psychology known as analytical psychology. Within conventional Christianity, some commentators have argued that a contemporary resurgence of thinly disguised Gnostic ideas has occurred in the teachings of such well-known figures as Paul Tillich and Teilhard de Chardin. Recent years have even seen the appearance of Gnostic religious organizations, such as the *Ecclesia Gnostica Mysteriorum* in California.

See also: BASILIDEAN GNOSTICISM, BASILIDES, CAINITES, CARPOCRA-
TES, CARPOCRATIAN GNOSTICISM, CERINTHUS, GLAUCAS, GOSPEL
OF PHILIP, GOSPEL OF THOMAS, GOSPEL OF TRUTH, MARCELLINA,
NAG HAMMADI LIBRARY, OPHITES, SETHIAN GNOSTICISM, SIMONIAN
GNOSTICISM, VALENTINIAN GNOSTICISM, VALENTINUS.

Hermetic Order of the GOLDEN DAWN   This organization was the most
important group of ritual magicians in modern times. The Hermetic Order of the
Golden Dawn was founded in London, England, in 1887, and later established
branches in Scotland and France. Its membership included some of the greatest
contemporary occultists, such as ALEISTER CROWLEY, and significant cultural
figures; W. B. Yeats, Arthur Machen, and Algernon Blackwood are three well-known
examples.

The three founding members, S. L. M. Mathers, Wynn Westcott, and William
Woodman, claimed that the teachings of the Order came from beings known as the
"Secret Chiefs," a group of wise and powerful magical masters who worked in secret
for the benefit of the world. The idea of such hidden masters was also popular among
the followers of THEOSOPHY, which was quite influential during the late nineteenth century. At first, the contacts with the Secret Chiefs were maintained through
the mail via a woman in Germany serving as the liaison. Later, Mathers reported that
his wife received information from the masters through her clairvoyant powers.
While in Paris, he was to claim that he actually met three of the Chiefs in the flesh.

It seems likely that the leaders of the Order were in contact with an occult group in
Germany. But much of the Golden Dawn material was the result of a brilliant effort
on the part of the English magicians themselves to combine the various threads of the
Western occult tradition into a coherent system. Elements from such sources as
the GRIMOIRES (Mathers had been the first person to translate such classics as
THE KEY OF SOLOMON and THE SACRED MAGIC OF ABRAMELIN THE
MAGE into English), the CABALA, ENOCHIAN MAGIC, the HERMETICA,
ALCHEMY, and ASTROLOGY were arranged into a series of lessons. As each
set of materials was mastered, the magician could apply to undergo an initiation ceremony, after which access was granted to the next level of teaching. There were
eleven grades of initiation in the Golden Dawn's hierarchy.

The aims of Golden Dawn magic were twofold. The most important goal was to
promote spiritual evolution, the "higher magic" of mystical union with the divine. The
series of initiations were intended to function like steps on a ladder, marking and
assisting the magician's increasing purity and wisdom. A secondary goal was twofold:
the development of occult abilities, such as astral projection and clairvoyance, and
the effective practice of ANGEL MAGIC and NATURAL MAGIC.

In 1891, Woodman died. Six years later, Westcott resigned, leaving Mathers in
charge of the Golden Dawn. Mathers, who was living in Paris by this time, became
increasingly grandiose and dictatorial, alienating many of the members in Britain. In
1900, the English branch split with Mathers. During the following decade, the Order
continued to fragment. Mathers died in 1917.

Although the original Hermetic Order no longer exists, the Golden Dawn's presentation of the Western magical tradition as a spiritual path has had a major influence
on ritual magicians in this century. The system of initiatory ranks established by the

Golden Dawn has been adopted, with some modifications, by a great number of contemporary occult groups. In 1937, Israel Regardie, a former member of the Order, began to publish the theories and practices the Golden Dawn magicians devised, which are now familiar to all serious students of esoteric thought in the West.

GOSLAR HERETICS   A strange incident at Goslar (northern Germany) in A.D. 1052 led to the first executions for heresy in medieval Germany. The charge arose when a group of men refused to kill a chicken. Their reasons were not recorded, but apparently suspicion fell on them that they were vegetarians, a practice associated in the popular mind with the heresy of MANICHAEISM. The fate of the chicken in question is unknown, but the men who spared it were burned at the stake by order of Henry III, the Holy Roman Emperor.

THE GOSPEL OF PHILIP   The doctrines presented in this book are associated with the school of unorthodox Christianity called VALENTINIAN GNOSTICISM. *The Gospel of Philip* was written by an unknown author (and named after the apostle Philip) sometime during the late third century. The text contains important descriptions of some of the central teachings of GNOSTICISM.

According to *The Gospel of Philip*, all problems in human life arise from the separation of Eve from Adam's body. As such, Christ came to earth in order to unify Adam and Eve again. This strange teaching seems to require a psychological interpretation. Perhaps it refers to the idea that each human being's personality contains both male and female aspects, and that conflict between these aspects produces suffering. If the opposed parts of the personality could be reconciled, inner peace would then be achieved.

The *Gospel* repeatedly speaks of this reconciliation as happening like a combination of the sexes in a "bridal chamber." Some researchers believe that this reference hints at an actual Gnostic ceremony, which might have been a sacrament in the Valentinian Church. This image of a "mystical marriage" within the soul often recurs during the history of alternative-reality traditions in the West, especially in ALCHEMY.

Although orthodox critics have often charged that Gnosticism encourages the hatred and rejection of the physical body, *The Gospel of Philip* does not seem to support such a view. The author recommends, "Fear not the flesh nor love it. If you fear it, it will gain mastery over you. If you love it, it will swallow and paralyze you." Obsession with the body, not the body itself, is rejected.

Like other Gnostic works, *The Gospel of Philip* emphasizes the importance of the special knowledge called GNOSIS. In order to achieve the two spiritual goals mentioned above—the unification of male and female parts within the fragmented personality and the detached relationship to the body—gnosis is required. The text vividly states that human beings' enslavement to compulsions, and the possibility of their freedom from such behaviors, do not come from outside, but from within:

> As for ourselves, let each one of us dig down after the root of evil which is within one, and let one pluck it out of one's heart from the root. It will be plucked out if we recognize it. But if we are ignorant of it, it takes root in us and produces its fruit in our heart. It masters us. We are its slaves. It takes us captive, to make us do what we do not want; and what we do want we do not do. It is powerful because we have not recognized it. . . . Ignorance is the mother of all evil.

This confidence that self-awareness, rather than faith in doctrines or obedience to the church, is all people need to be saved is typical of Gnostic teaching. Catholic Christian leaders regarded it as heretical; they insisted that only the teachings and sacraments of their priests could help people achieve salvation.

THE GOSPEL OF THOMAS   This document might be the oldest surviving text representing the spiritual movement called GNOSTICISM. Some scholars also suspect that *The Gospel of Thomas* contains some of the first writings in the history of Christianity itself, predating the gospels of the New Testament. If this suspicion is true, it would reinforce the claim of the Christian Gnostics that their teachings derive from the message delivered by JESUS himself.

French researchers first reported the existence of *The Gospel of Thomas* in modern times at the end of the nineteenth century. They discovered fragments of the ancient text written in Greek. In 1945, a complete copy of the *Gospel* in the Coptic language was found among the manuscripts of the NAG HAMMADI LIBRARY, a collection of Gnostic books that had been hidden in Egypt since the fourth century.

Scholars believe that the Coptic version was a translation from the older Greek text. Various dates have been suggested for the composition of the original *Gospel*. The researchers who first published the text in modern translation, in 1959, suggested a date of around A.D. 140. Biblical scholar Helmut Koester, of Harvard University, has noted that the contents of *The Gospel of Thomas* closely resemble those of a book, lost long ago, that was believed to have been a source for some of the material in the New Testament Gospels of Matthew and Luke. According to Koester's theory, at least some of the material in *The Gospel of Thomas* may, therefore, date to a time before A.D. 60—within thirty years of Jesus' death.

Unlike the New Testament gospel books, *The Gospel of Thomas* is not organized into the story of Christ's life and death. Rather, it is a collection of Jesus' sayings and stories. The style is reminiscent of a set of notes recorded at a lecture. The first sentence reports that these are Jesus' "secret sayings" written down by Judas Thomas, Jesus' twin brother. (Another work in the Nag Hammadi collection, *The Book of Thomas the Contender*, also identifies Thomas as the twin of Jesus). If Christ had a twin and Christ was "born of a virgin," then the twin must also have had a Virgin birth. Such a difficulty was surely one of the reasons why orthodox Christians shunned this text; they held to the uniqueness of Jesus with respect to His miraculous mode of birth.

A central theme of the text, which identifies it as belonging to the Gnostic stream of thought, is that salvation is attained through self-knowledge (GNOSIS). Jesus is quoted as saying, "When you come to know yourselves, then you will become known, and you will realize that it is you who are the sons of the living Father."

In orthodox Christianity, people are called to follow Christ. In some Gnostic sources, including *The Gospel of Thomas*, humans are called to become Christ's equal, even to become identical with Christ. In the text, Jesus asks His disciples whom He resembles. After Peter compares Him to an angel, and Matthew compares Him to a philosopher, Thomas says that Jesus cannot be compared to anyone. Jesus responds to Thomas: "I am not your master. Because you have drunk, you have become intoxicated from the bubbling spring which I have measured out." Then Jesus takes Thomas aside for a secret conversation. This passage implies that Thomas has attained a state of consciousness very different from the ordinary one by imbibing Jesus' teaching. As a result, Thomas has achieved Jesus' state of awareness and is a Christ himself; he is no longer a mere follower.

The *Gospel* hints at the means by which humans can attain this exalted state of self-knowledge. Jesus advises, "Recognize what is in your sight, and that which is hidden from you will become plain to you." At another point, in response to His disciples' request for a statement of what they should believe, Jesus criticizes them because they "do not know how to read this moment." The tone of these passages resembles that of the basic instruction in meditation found in many traditions, western and eastern alike. In many meditation techniques, the attention is simply focused on what is present. Effort is not expended in trying to solve problems, manufacture belief systems, or attain great revelations. The result, report the meditators, is often a deepened awareness of the habits that prevent oneself from acting freely and compassionately. Several other passages in the *Gospel* suggest that the message of this text was associated with meditation practices.

Another dominant theme in *The Gospel of Thomas* is that salvation involves the integration of opposites: "When you make the two one, and when you make the inside like the outside and the outside like the inside, and the above like the below, and when you make the male and the female one and the same, . . . then will you enter the Kingdom." The notion of uniting the opposites is found in unorthodox teachings through the ages, from VALENTINIAN GNOSTICISM in the second century, through medieval and Renaissance ALCHEMY, to contemporary depth psychology.

According to the ancient teaching of orthodox Christianity, the Kingdom of Heaven will arrive on earth at some point in the future, with the Second Coming of Christ. In the meantime, good Christians should wait within the church community, obeying the instructions of those who preserved Christ's teachings, the priests and bishops. Jesus, as portrayed in *The Gospel of Thomas*, proclaims instead that the Kingdom of Heaven has already arrived: "It will not come by waiting for it. . . . Rather, the Kingdom of the Father is spread out upon the earth, and men do not see it." The text implies that the Kingdom is a state of awareness, not a future change in the state of the world.

As the well-known religious scholar Elaine Pagels has pointed out, the teachings of *The Gospel of Thomas* concerning the Kingdom, if taken seriously, tend to undermine the necessity for a hierarchy of church officials. Personal awareness, not conformity to church rules, becomes the means of salvation. This subversive implication is undoubtedly another reason why the orthodox church, struggling for existence against a hostile pagan society during its first few centuries, suppressed *The Gospel of Thomas*.

THE GOSPEL OF TRUTH   This text is one of the most important sources of information concerning the ancient heretical movement known as GNOSTICISM. *The Gospel of Truth* was written around the middle of the second century A.D. Many scholars believe that its author was VALENTINUS, one of the foremost Gnostic thinkers. *The Gospel of Truth* was mentioned by Irenaeus of Lyons, an orthodox opponent of Gnosticism, but the text itself was lost for 1,800 years. A copy was preserved in the ancient NAG HAMMADI LIBRARY, which had been hidden during the fourth century and rediscovered in 1945.

According to this work, the ultimate god of joy and truth is called the Father. The world of ordinary experience was not created by the Father but by a lesser being referred to as Error. In a state of confusion and fear, Error forgot about the existence of the Father and generated a world of terror that human beings are trapped in. Escape from the domain of Error is possible, however. The Father placed a "living book" of liberating knowledge (GNOSIS) within the heart, and appeared as JESUS to illuminate the way back to the Father.

The Gospel of Truth emphasizes that humans' ordinary type of awareness hides the path to happiness from them. Normal consciousness is described as a "drunkenness" from which people can recover, or as a nightmarish state of sleep, from which they can awaken. At the end of the night of ignorance, filled with "shadows and phantoms," the "knowledge of the Father" comes as the dawn.

Many orthodox critics have attacked Gnostic doctrines for apparently rejecting the material world as evil. Reading *The Gospel of Truth* suggests that these criticisms might be based on a misunderstanding of Gnostic teaching, or at least does not apply to all Gnostic schools. The text of the *Gospel* does not condemn the *material* world itself, but rather the world of people's ordinary, confused experience—their *psychological* world. Pain and evil are caused by a state of ignorance, and are defeated by the knowledge called gnosis. According to the author of the *Gospel*, salvation does not involve literally escaping from the physical world, but changing one's awareness of this world in a way that leads to happiness rather than suffering.

GOTTSCHALK   A Christian heretic of the ninth century, Gottschalk was a charismatic troublemaker throughout his life. His unconventional views brought him floggings, condemnation for heresy, and repeated imprisonment. Gottschalk was born around 804, the son of the Count of Saxony, and placed in a monastery as a child. He rebelled against the monastic lifestyle during his adolescence and was released from the monastery. A continued interest in matters of faith led him to become ordained as a priest.

Gottschalk studied the writings of famous fifth century theologian Augustine of Hippo and made a surprising discovery. Augustine's doctrine of grace, which stated that no one could be saved without God's assistance, was well known and accepted in the church. Lesser known at the time was Augustine's doctrine of double predestination. According to Augustine, God determined who would be saved and who would be damned even before they were created. Predestination could be understood to mean that some people have been created in order to go to hell, which sounds unjust. This notion had been downplayed by church leaders. Gottschalk rediscovered Augustine's teachings on predestination and publicized them, creating an uproar.

The controversial priest traveled around Europe, teaching people about predestination. Gottschalk even visited the pagan Bulgars, who were being courted by both the Roman and the Byzantine Christians. He seems to have had a knack for impressing many of his listeners, while alarming church leaders with his lack of respect for their authority. When Gottschalk returned to Germany following his European tour, he was summoned by Hincmar, archbishop of Mainz, to explain his teachings. Hincmar concluded that Gottschalk's interpretation of Augustine was unorthodox and punished him by scourging and confinement in the monastery at Orbais.

Within a short time, Gottschalk managed to convince many of the monks of Orbais that he, not Hincmar, held the orthodox view. When word of this reached the archbishop, he again summoned Gottschalk. This time, the monk was ordered publicly to cast his own writings into a fire. Gottschalk refused and was brutally flogged until he finally obeyed the archbishop to save his life.

Imprisoned at the monastery of Hautvillers, Gottschalk once more impressed his monastic colleagues with his teaching. Hincmar, meanwhile, decided to write a refutation of Gottschalk's ideas. The archbishop strayed so far from Augustine's position, however, that now *he* attracted severe criticism from other church leaders. The question of predestination remained controversial for centuries.

Gottschalk created another stir when he used the term "trine deity" in his writings to refer to God. Hincmar objected to this phrase, claiming that Gottschalk was violating God's unified nature by splitting Him into three—the heresy of TRITHE-ISM. Gottschalk, in response, stated that the word "deity" refers not to God's nature, but to His Personhood, and orthodox doctrine holds that God subsists in three Persons, Father, Son, and Holy Spirit. Hincmar, in turn, was accused by Gottschalk of believing in the ancient heresy called MODALISM, which denied the three Persons of the Trinity. Although Gottschalk had some eminent supporters in this debate (including Frankish monk RATRAMNUS), the phrase "trine deity" was eventually rejected by the orthodox authorities as misleading.

Gottschalk died in A.D. 869. He was begged to reject his unorthodox views on his deathbed to save his soul. Independent to the end, he refused.

GRAND GRIMOIRE

This book is a notorious manual of DEMON MAGIC. Occult scholar A. E. Waite stated that *Grand Grimoire* is "one of the most atrocious of its class" because it directs the magician to perform acts that would be possible "only to a dangerous maniac or an irreclaimable criminal." The text, written in French, is believed to have been composed sometime in the mid-eighteenth century. It contains a unique ceremony of demonic conjuration that many later magicians copied, as well as a ritual for securing a demonic PACT.

The book instructs the person who wishes to evoke a demon to complete a series of preparations. First, a magic wand is made from a hazel branch that was cut from the tree with a blood-smeared knife at the moment of sunrise. A magic circle is outlined on the floor, using the skin of a sacrificed goat, and tacked down with nails from a child's coffin. Before the conjuration, the magician must undergo various kinds of purification ceremonies.

A demon called Lucifuge Rofocale is then called, using various incantations of the standard type found in most GRIMOIRES. The words of power found in *Grand Grimoire* are likely derived from the most important magical text, *THE KEY OF SOLOMON*. The spirit supposedly feels agonizing pain whenever the magician holds the wand over a flame, so this technique is recommended for compelling Lucifuge to lead the magician to the nearest hidden treasure.

In the second part of the book, a ceremony for making a pact with Lucifuge is described. This part of *Grand Grimoire* also points out that such an arrangement should be undertaken only if the magician, for some reason, is unable to perform the ritual described above, which forces the demon's obedience without the need for a pact. The pact as given in *Grand Grimoire* is worded in such a way that the demon is tricked into thinking that the magician has promised his or her soul in exchange for twenty years of diabolical services. Actually, the magician has guaranteed only that Lucifuge will receive some sort of "reward," which could be anything the magician chooses to offer.

Grand Grimoire is an important text in the demon magic tradition. The notion that magicians who deal with demons are selling their souls was invented by the orthodox opponents of the magicians, not by the practitioners themselves. In the Middle Ages, magicians attempted to enslave demons, whom they regarded as powerless against the magical force of the words of power uttered during the evocations. By the eighteenth century, when *Grand Grimoire* was written, it seems that some of the magicians had begun to believe the propaganda of their enemies. The increased willingness to reward demons, seen in *Grand Grimoire* and other contemporary black magic texts, such as GRIMORIUM VERUM, set the stage for the rise of SATAN-ISM in the European occult underground.

GREAT WITCH HUNT   Between 1450 and 1750, at least 100,000 women and men were executed in Europe and North America for the heresy of witchcraft. Historian R. H. Robbins described this slaughter as "the shocking nightmare, the foulest crime and deepest shame of western civilization." The horror is compounded when one realizes that every victim was likely innocent of the crimes with which they were charged.

Anthropologists use the term "witchcraft" to describe a type of supernatural evildoer known in many cultures around the world. In the context of the West's Great Witch Hunt, this word acquired a more specific meaning. The classic definition witch hunter Jean Bodin offered in 1580 defines a witch as "one who knowing God's law tries to bring about some act through an agreement with the devil." The fully developed witch image of the Renaissance period included the idea that this agreement involved acts of devil worship offered at periodic group meetings called sabbaths. For the European witch hunters, then, witchcraft was a type of SATANISM and, therefore, a heresy, punishable by death.

The equation of witchcraft with heresy was an invention of the witch-hunting period. Ironically, before this time *belief* in the reality of witchcraft was an official Christian heresy. An influential document called *Canon Episcopi*, composed sometime before the tenth century, states that people who thought they flew through the air at night or had sorcerous abilities were deluded. Such beliefs were viewed as pagan, not Christian.

During the eleventh and twelfth centuries, the rise of heresies challenged the Catholic near-monopoly on European religious belief (excluding Jews, who were usually tolerated). The CATHARS, in particular, mounted serious competition with orthodoxy in some regions. In response, as more moderate forms of persuasion failed to stem the heretical tide, the mainstream church invented the INQUISITION. Social institutions that have fulfilled their original function tend to search for new reasons to justify their continued existence; following its suppression of heretics in southern France, the Inquisition followed this pattern.

As early as 1258, some inquisitors sought (and failed to receive) permission from the pope to pursue practitioners of sorcery and divination. In 1320, Pope John XXII granted the Inquisition powers to prosecute sorcerors if they were also Satanists. In

1451, Pope Nicholas V unleashed the Inquisitors on all forms of sorcery, which became heretical by definition. It took nearly 200 years of lobbying for the Inquisitors, whose task was to root out heresy, to expand the definition of heresy to the point where almost no one could be certain of exclusion.

In order to pursue the heretical witches, Inquisitors first had to deal with an inconvenience: the revered *Canon Episcopi*, which defined belief in witches as heresy. The usual strategy supporters of the witch hunt used was to argue that the witch cult they were attacking was different from the witchcraft delusions mentioned in the *Canon*. Just because people in the past held these false beliefs does not mean that no real witches exist in the present. Indeed, by 1486 belief in witchcraft had become central to the orthodox world view. MALLEUS MALEFICARUM, published in that year, stated that *dis*belief in the existence of witches was heretical.

By the beginning of the fifteenth century, the image of the witch heretic was fully developed. The elements of this image included devil worship, the PACT or agreement, evil magic, the ability to transform into an animal, and nocturnal flight to attend the sabbath. The Great Witch Hunt was based on the idea that an international conspiracy of such beings was working to overthrow decent Christian civilization.

A great deal of research into the origins of this witch image has been done, and scholarly debate continues. This image appears to have crystallized first in the minds of Inquisitors in the western Alps, in what is today eastern France and western Switzerland, where the Great Witch Hunt began. Inquisitors were searching for Cathar and WALDENSIAN heretics who inhabited isolated corners of the region. It was widely believed at the time that all heretical groups were murderous devil worshippers. Alpine heresy hunters seem to have combined this idea with elements of folklore and possible survivals of pagan religious practices that they encountered in the area. Historian Carlo Ginzburg reported evidence for the survival in Renaissance Europe of two traditions dating from pre-Christian times. One of these traditions involved groups of men who entered trances, during which they believed that they transformed themselves into animals in order to combat evil magicians. In the other tradition, groups of women induced out-of-body experiences, enabling them to fly through the night sky with a goddess. If Inquisitors in pursuit of Satanic heretics stumbled across such practices in remote Alpine communities, they might well have interpreted these activities as newly discovered features of the witch cult. Henceforth, witches were believed not only to worship Satan and make pacts with him to perform harmful magic, but also to turn into animals and fly through the air at night.

During the ensuing decades, the belief in the reality of this witch image, and the accompanying witch-hunting activity, radiated from the image's western Alpine origin throughout western Europe. The 1486 publication of the *Malleus*, which encouraged both secular authorities and religious officials to seek out witches, triggered the full fury of the Great Witch Hunt. Germany, France, Italy, and Scotland saw the most intense witchcraft persecutions, although several other countries experienced significant episodes also.

Once the hunt was in full swing, three factors tended to sustain its momentum. First, the Inquisitorial procedure virtually guaranteed a fresh supply of victims and very few acquittals. Suspects could be arrested on the basis of anonymous accusations and then tortured until they confessed and named other suspects who were subject to the same procedures. Second, economic motivations sustained the hunt. The possessions of convicted witches were often seized and awarded to the witch hunters and supportive members of the ruling classes.

The third reason for the sustained momentum: manuals of witch hunting, based on new "information" about the nonexistent witch cult derived from the confessions of the victims, continued to be published, thereby supporting the credibility of the delusion. An influential example was COMPENDIUM MALEFICARUM, written in the early seventeenth century by an experienced witch-trial judge. As a result of these factors, the persecutions intensified to the point where the witch hunters largely depopulated some areas. In Germany, where the most ferocious witch persecutions occurred, entire villages were exterminated.

The Great Witch Hunt peaked and declined at different times in various regions; by the end of the seventeenth century, official persecution of witches had virtually ended in England, yet the most significant flare-up of witch hunting in America—the infamous trials of Salem—took place in 1692. By 1750, the hunt was in decline everywhere.

The conclusion of the witch persecutions occurred for several reasons, not the least of which was mounting disgust and exhaustion at the immense toll the West had inflicted upon itself. The rise of the scientific world view, which did not have a place for supernatural powers, also played a part. The economic incentives had also shifted; the increasingly powerful capitalist class required social stability to do profitable business. The depletion of the labor pool and disruption of lines of inheritance caused by the witch hunt affected that stability.

By the end of the eighteenth century, few educated people believed that a conspiracy of witches had ever existed. In 1862, however, Jules Michelet proposed the theory that a devil-worshipping organization had actually formed during the period of the Great Witch Hunt. He thought that the witches were an underground form of protest at the oppression of the lower classes by the privileged officials of orthodox Christian culture. Margaret Murray published an influential book in 1921, in which she claims that witchcraft was actually the survival of a pre-Christian fertility religion. No serious scholar today places credence in the research of Michelet or Murray. There may have been isolated survivals of pagan rituals, and there were certainly magicians and folk healers, but it is highly unlikely that an international witchcraft organization of any sort existed during the witch hunt.

In the present century, a movement known as modern witchcraft has appeared in Europe and North America. This movement might have existed for a few decades before its public emergence in England in the 1950s, but it does not have any direct link to the events of the Great Witch Hunt. Modern witches are not Satanists. Most are magicians and believe that humans are part of a sacred, living natural world. They worship the divinity of nature, often as personified by pagan deities. Unfortunately, many people still confuse contemporary witches with the old witch image of the "Burning Times," and these harmless neopagans are subject to occasional persecution by ignorant law-enforcement officials and others.

See also: BLACK MASS, BLASPHEMY, CLEMENTIUS OF BUCY, ORLEANS HERETICS.

Matteo GRIBALDI   Sixteenth century ANTI-TRINITARIAN heretic, Matteo Gribaldi was born in 1506. With the outbreak of the Protestant Reformation, he was attracted to Calvinism at first. However, the burning of Anti-trinitarian MICHAEL SERVETUS by Calvin's allies horrified him; before the execution, Gribaldi visited Servetus in prison, a gesture that could easily have cost him his life. Gribaldi developed the notion that the three Persons of the Trinity were three distinct gods, with God the Father as the senior member. This view was a version of the heresy of TRITHEISM. Gribaldi was dismissed from his teaching post and was persecuted in other ways before his death in 1562.

GRIMOIRE OF HONORIUS   This text is a classic work on DEMON MAGIC. According to esoteric scholar Idries Shah, *Grimoire of Honorius* "is the black book generally considered among writers on the occult, both modern and ancient, to be the most diabolical work of black magic which has appeared in written form, at any time." Although all of the GRIMOIRES, or ritual-magic handbooks, were condemned by orthodox Christians during the Middle Ages and the Renaissance, *Grimoire of Honorius* was especially loathed because the book falsely claims to have been written by a thirteenth century pontiff, Pope Honorius III, for use by priests. Its true composer is unknown.

The origin of *Grimoire of Honorius* is unclear. A manuscript preserved today, dating from the fourteenth century, is thought to be an ancestor of the *Grimoire*. Entitled *The Sworn Book of Honorius*, it describes how a convention of magicians elected a man named Honorius to write down the essence of the magical arts. Honorius's text was to be carefully guarded and passed to the next generation of practitioners with great care and secrecy. Fourteenth century Inquisitor Nicholas Eymericus recorded that he confiscated and burned a book called *The Treasury of Necromancy*, by Honorius. This text might have been *The Sworn Book* or an early version of *Grimoire of Honorius*.

The existence of the *Grimoire* as it reads today was first noted in 1629. It was published in Rome in 1670. By this time, the legendary magician of *The Sworn Book* had become confused with the medieval pope of the same name. The anonymous author of the *Grimoire* wrote an introduction in the form of a papal announcement, or Bull. In it, "Pope Honorius" proclaims that Roman Catholic priests have been granted permission to evoke demons. The text argues that priests should be able to defend themselves against attacks by demons, using the methods contained in the *Grimoire*. As discussed below, however, the contents of the *Grimoire* concern attracting demons and extracting favors from them, not repelling them.

According to *Grimoire of Honorius*, an elaborate preparation is required before attempting to call a demon. As befits a work supposedly written by a pope, the saying of prayers and masses is encouraged. The requirement of sacrificing a black rooster and removing its eyes, tongue, and heart is less orthodox. A lamb must be killed also. The skin of the lamb is sprinkled with powder made from the rooster parts and then made into parchment. Using the parchment, a "Book of Spirits" is constructed. When a demon is conjured, the magician induces it to write its personal symbol in the book. The magician can then use this symbol to control the spirit.

The *Grimoire* describes a ritual for calling the spirits. The pattern of this ceremony is similar to those in many other grimoires. A magic circle is drawn, pentacles or medallions covered in symbols are displayed, and long conjurations are recited. The conjurations contain many names of God and other words of power from the Hebrew tradition, but they also refer to Christian elements. The magician commands the spirit to appear by the power of the objects of Christian faith, including JESUS, all of the saints, "every part of the body of the Virgin," the angels and archangels, the head of John the Baptist, and even the milk of Saint Catherine. The *Grimoire* describes how to evoke the demons of the four directions, and of the days of the week. The spirits are supposed to answer any question or obey any command if the ritual has been properly conducted.

Some scholars believe that *The Grimoire of Honorius* marks an important point in the early development of SATANISM, the actual worship of the Devil. The text notes that Lucifer, the demon of Monday, requires that a mouse be sacrificed to him. Although the general aim of *Grimoire of Honorius* is to master the demons, the act of sacrificing animals to them could lead to greater acts of reverence from the magician. Certainly by the late seventeenth century, some black magicians in France are known to have adopted the sacrifice of children to Satan into their practices.

GRIMOIRES   This term is derived from a medieval French word that means "grammary," or textbook. The grimoires were manuals of ritual magic. They began to appear around the twelfth century and continued to be produced into the nineteenth century. These mysterious works, whose authorship is generally unknown, feature prominently in the history of both ANGEL MAGIC and DEMON MAGIC.

Although the official powers repeatedly attempted to suppress them, many grimoires survived through the centuries. In the Middle Ages, new editions were made by hand-copying old manuscripts, a laborious process. The anonymous scribes involved in this mode of transmission took a great risk: the authorities were prone to burn not only seized grimoires, but also their possessors. After the invention of the printing press, some grimoires were published and circulated in secret.

It is widely believed that the medieval grimoires were largely inspired by magical handbooks of the ancient Jews. First century Jewish historian Josephus mentioned a book King Solomon wrote, which reveals how to conjure spirits. He may have been referring to an early version of *The Testament of Solomon*, which was probably composed during the third century A.D. The most important grimoires of Christian Europe were also attributed to Solomon, although he certainly did not write them. Ancient legends tell of Solomon's power over spirits, so listing him as the author of a grimoire was an attempt to give the book an impressive credential.

Another ancient tradition regarded as a root of the grimoires is pagan Hellenistic magic. The Egyptian Magical Papyri from the first few centuries A.D. describe the magical use of words of power, including the names of deities, to command spirits. The grimoires also rely heavily on this practice, generally utilizing Hebrew and Christian names of God and the angels instead of pagan god names.

The New Testament indicates that magical textbooks existed—and were suppressed—in the earliest Christian communities. In the Book of Acts it is written that the apostle Paul impressed the locals with his powers as an exorcist during a visit to Ephesus. In response, the Ephesians "which used curious arts [magic] brought their books together, and burned them before all men: and they counted the price of them, and found it fifty thousand pieces of silver" (19:19).

There was only fragmentary evidence for the existence of an underground written tradition of ritual magic from the first thousand years of Christian culture. During the later Middle Ages, the picture changed. The rising anxiety about the power of DEMONS in orthodox culture was apparently mirrored by an increased interest in attempting to harness devilish forces for personal gain among a group of rather entrepreneurial monks and priests.

Glimpses of the first grimoires are present in the writings of the orthodox persecutors. In 1277, the archbishop of Paris issued a condemnation of "books, rolls or booklets containing necromancy or experiments of sorcery, invocations of demons, or conjurations of demons, or conjurations hazardous for souls." Several decades later, Nicholas Eymericus, the famous Inquisitor, wrote that he had confiscated and burned wicked books, *The Table of Solomon* and *The Treasury of Necromancy*—but not before he read them himself. The Inquisitor describes an elaborate magical system, which includes a hierarchy of demons and how to command them, the use of words of power, blood sacrifices to attract spirits, and the demonic PACT. These features are prominent in many of the grimoires preserved today.

The most notorious story involving the possession of a grimoire in the Middle Ages centered on Pope Benedict XIII. The pope was accused of calling up demons using a grimoire called *The Death of the Soul*. He was condemned for sorcery after his death.

The medieval grimoires rely extensively on long proclamations the magician utters, which are intended to intimidate the demons and force them to obey. These statements are quite similar to the content of the Roman Catholic exorcism rituals in use at the time, but they differ in one critical way. Their purpose is reversed: they are intended to attract, rather than drive away, evil spirits. This prompted historian Richard Kieckhefer to conclude that the authors and users of the medieval grimoires were probably church officials familiar with exorcism rituals who altered elements of the orthodox ceremonies to their own purposes.

Another prominent feature of the grimoires is their emphasis on the influences of the stars and planets. Instructions are given concerning the appropriate timing of rituals, based on simple astrological calculations, and various substances used in the ceremonies are discussed according to the planetary influence they represent. This material derives from the branch of NATURAL MAGIC known as astral magic. The astral-magic tradition of the Moslems was introduced to Europe in the later Middle Ages via the Moslem conquest of Spain and the Crusades to Palestine; it seems to have deeply impressed the grimoire composers.

The contents of the grimoires are varied. Occult scholar A. E. Waite organized the grimoires into three groups. The first group instructs the practitioner in the invocation of good spirits and avoids demons altogether. The orthodox claimed that these practices were merely traps set by the demons, so that the magicians could be tempted into sinful deeds and thereby forfeit their souls. Waite includes the ARBATEL OF MAGIC, *The Enchiridion* of Pope Leo and *The Theosophica Pneumatica* under this heading.

Another group of grimoires describes the ritual technology for the conjuration of evil spirits. These works generally include the symbols and special powers of the demonic hosts, details concerning the pact and shortchanging the demon (an important detail, since the object of negotiation is the magician's soul), and advice on constructing a magic circle to protect the conjurer from the demon's otherwise fatal presence. Waite includes GRIMORIUM VERUM, GRIMOIRE OF HONORIUS (a work good Catholics particularly hate because it falsely claims to have been composed by a pope), and GRAND GRIMOIRE under this heading.

Waite also describes a category of composite grimoires that include both angelic and demonic materials. The most famous grimoire, The KEY OF SOLOMON, falls under this heading. Other significant composite texts include THE LEMEGETON and THE SACRED MAGIC OF ABRAMELIN THE MAGE.

The most important surviving grimoire manuscripts from the Middle Ages and the Renaissance are preserved today in the Arsenal Library in Paris and in the British Museum. The importance of this body of unorthodox literature in the development of Western reality is currently a topic of debate among scholars. Within the occult traditions themselves, the grimoires are doubtless of central importance. They integrated and preserved esoteric practices from the ancient world, Moslem astral magic, Catholic exorcism, and later Hebrew magic based on the KABBALAH. The ritual patterns the grimoires established were adopted by nineteenth century magical revivalists, such as Eliphas Levi and the magicians of the Hermetic Order of the GOLDEN DAWN, who passed them down to the occultists of today.

Some students of the grimoires believe that the rituals can be used as a sort of Western yoga practice for producing spiritual enlightenment. In this interpretation, the spirits brought under the magician's control are actually aspects of the conjurer's own personality, and the various intended outcomes of the rituals symbolize the rewards of spiritual development.

The grimoires influenced the events of the GREAT WITCH HUNT of the Renaissance and Reformation periods. The notion of the pact with the Devil became associated with the image of the witch in popular imagination. Accused witches were supposed to have made such an agreement in order to acquire harmful powers.

Researchers have discussed the possibility that the magical tradition embodied in the grimoires might have contributed to the birth of modern science. The word "experiment" was originally used in the Middle Ages to refer to the practice of evoking a spirit, and it is used in this sense in the grimoires themselves. The medieval ritual magician was interested in controlling the world of spirits by manipulating it. The magician's orthodox contemporaries took the more passive approach toward learning about the universe through the use of reason and discussion. The first modern scientists adopted the active stance of controlling nature through manipulation and called their operations "experiments." Perhaps the independent and imaginative attitude of the grimoire users influenced the founders of modern science, many of whom were occultists themselves.

See also: ALMADEL, BLACK PULLET.

GRIMORIUM VERUM   This book, also known as *True Grimoire*, is an infamous textbook of DEMON MAGIC. *Grimorium Verum* is a complete course in how to conjure demons and make them do one's bidding. As Idries Shah, a modern student of the magical literature, reports, orthodoxy considers *Grimorium Verum* to be "a book by the Devil."

The author and precise origin of the text are unknown. This obscurity is not surprising because even possessing such a diabolical book would have been enough to justify being burned at the stake during the centuries of the INQUISITION and the GREAT WITCH HUNT. Although the text itself indicates that it was published in 1517, experts believe that it actually appeared around 1750.

Grimorium Verum presents an overview of the demonic world for the novice magician. The demons Lucifer, Beelzebuth, and Astaroth are identified as chiefs, and the other demons are organized in a hierarchy beneath them. The various powers and magical symbols for all of the major devils are listed. Some of these spirits have very strange abilities. Clisthert, for example, "allows you to have day or night, whichever you wish, when you desire either." Humot instantly provides the magician with any book on request. An awesome demon called Frucissière can even bring the dead back to life. Much of this material is very similar to the demon lists in another famous grimoire, THE LEMEGETON.

Most of the classical books of demon magic explain that the spirits can be forced to obey the magician through the use of powerful threats and commands. In contrast, *Grimorium Verum* generally takes a more respectful tone. The spirits will perform favors, it declares, but only if they are rewarded, "for this sort of creature does not give anything for nothing." The sacrifice of a goat, whose head should be lopped off with a single blow, is recommended. The conjurations to be recited by the magician include names of God and other magical words to encourage the demon's attendance, but they do not contain the terrible threats and insults found in the other magical handbooks of the time.

Another unique feature of this text is its instructions for the preparation of certain charms, to be prepared according to whether the magician is a man or a woman. This passage implies that members of both genders engaged in ritual magic practices at the time the book was written. In the Middle Ages, most researchers assume that Catholic priests (all men, presumably) comprised the vast majority of the ritual magicians. It appears that an interesting change in the social composition of the magical community had begun to take place by the eighteenth century.

Grimorium Verum details both the purification practices to be undertaken before the conjuration and an elaborate ceremony for evoking the demons. Much of this material was probably derived from an influential grimoire called THE KEY OF SOLOMON. The text contains a collection of spells for various purposes, which have often been copied by other magical works. One famous spell gives the magician the power of invisibility. The first step is to insert black beans into the ears, eyes, and mouth of a severed human head, and then to inscribe a demonic symbol on the forehead. The third step involves burying the head. Each morning for the next seven days, the magician must water the head with "excellent brandy." On the eighth day, a spirit will appear. The magician gives the brandy bottle to the spirit, who will water the head himself. The next morning, the magician will find the beans germinating. The beans are dug up and placed in the magician's own mouth; the magician will then become invisible.

Because *Grimorium Verum* is a complete magical system, promising everything the novice black magician needs to know to acquire all sorts of powers, it became increasingly popular among such people. By the nineteenth century, it was the most widely used work on demon magic in Europe. Its unusual tone of respect for the demons and its willingness to offer them sacrifices may reflect the existence of a community of magicians who were moving toward SATANISM—the actual worship of the powers of darkness. It may not be a coincidence that, a few years after the presumed publication of *Grimorium Verum*, one of the earliest known groups of devil worshippers was exposed in France.

Abbé GUIBOURG   This notorious French priest was a leading figure in the ring of SATANISTS that operated in Paris during the reign of Louis XIV. Abbé Guibourg was born around 1611; he was the illegitimate child of a church employee in Paris. Little is known about his early life, although it is thought that as a young man he was a devout Roman Catholic and became a priest.

Over time, Guiborg's faith shifted; the viciousness of the GREAT WITCH HUNT continued during his lifetime, and the cruelty of the orthodox Inquisitors might have affected his loyalty to the supposed God of compassion. At some point, he began to sell love potions and to conduct Catholic Masses in order to create magical effects, such as attracting money.

In Paris during Louis's reign a thriving community of fortune-tellers and spell-casters existed, some of whom also engaged in abortions and poisonings. Many people in the upper classes used their services. Guibourg became part of this sinister group, offering to perform the BLACK MASS for a substantial fee.

The evil Abbé had no qualms about including human sacrifices and prayers to demons in his black magical ceremonies. An eyewitness described one of Guibourg's masses:

> He had bought a child to sacrifice at the mass, said on behalf of a great lady. He had cut the child's throat with a knife, and drawing its blood, had poured it into the chalice; after which he had the body taken away into another place, so that later he could use the heart and entrails for another mass.

One of Guibourg's clients was Madame de Montespan, a mistress of the king. She employed the Abbé to perform black masses in the hope of retaining King Louis's affections. She was successful for a time, but a younger woman eventually occupied the lusty monarch's bed, and Guibourg was asked to perform a Satanic ceremony to bring about the king's death. The police uncovered the existence of this occult underground and arrested Guibourg shortly after the performance of the cursing mass, which included the preparation of substances to be secretly introduced into King Louis's food. The description of the Abbé written by the officer presiding over the investigation is noteworthy:

> He is a libertine who has travelled a great deal . . . and is at present attached to the Church of Saint Marcel. For twenty years he has engaged continually in the practice of poison, sacrilege and every evil business. He has cut the throats and sacrificed un-counted numbers of children on his infernal altar. He has a mistress . . . by whom he has had several children, one or two of whom he has sacrificed . . . It is no ordinary man who thinks it a natural thing to sacrifice infants by slitting their throats and to say Mass upon the bodies of naked women.

Abbé Guibourg was executed for his crimes, but his legacy outlasted his lifetime. As a result of the activities of Guibourg and his fellow Satanists, which involved the highest-ranking nobles of the French court and even touched the intimate life of the king, Louis XIV was moved to issue an important edict in 1682. This document prescribed dire punishments for magical practices involving sacrilege; at the same time, it dismissed belief in witchcraft as a superstition. Louis's skeptical attitude toward the reality of an organized witch cult marked the beginning of the end of the witch trials in France.

Guibourg's influence persisted in another, less savory manner. In the nineteenth century, Satanists again were discovered in France performing blasphemous rites. It seems likely that the black masses performed by infamous Abbé BOULLAN were modeled to some extent on the rites of Abbé Guibourg. In isolated instances, it is possible that versions of the Guibourg Mass have been celebrated in our own century.

George GURDJIEFF   An influential mystical teacher in the early twentieth century, George Gurdjieff was born in southern Russia around 1877. As a child, he developed an urge to understand the mysteries of the world, not through faith, but on the basis of direct experience. This desire took him on extensive travels, during which he sought out every sort of spiritual guide. (An account of these journeys, of questionable historical accuracy, is contained in his book, *Meetings with Remarkable Men*, which was made into a movie.) Gurdjieff traveled throughout the Middle East; he might also have visited India, Tibet, and Siberia around this time.

By 1915, Gurdjieff was teaching his occult doctrine in St. Petersburg. The sources of this doctrine have been the subject of great speculation. The esoteric teachings of Eastern Orthodox Christianity and the Islamic mystical tradition called Sufism appear to be major influences; Tibetan Buddhism and Siberian shamanism may also have inspired some ideas. But the result of Gurdjieff's studies was a unique system of spiritual development that many have found specially suited to the modern mind.

Gurdjieff taught that most people spend their entire lives "asleep," in the sense that they are completely governed by mental and physical habits they are completely unaware of. As such, the first step toward realizing the possibilities of human life must be to wake up to one's enslaved condition; one can then strengthen one's will to achieve what one truly desires. Gurdjieff offered a range of methods to promote this awakening. Best known among these are his movement exercises, executed in groups (which can be viewed, performed by Gurdjieff students, in the film mentioned above).

The Russian mystic provided a complex world view to buttress his awakening techniques. His famous diagram called the enneagram, a circle containing a nine-pointed symbol, was used to illustrate the laws that govern the universe; by understanding these laws, a person can use them rather than be blindly subjected to them. Gurdjieff taught that ordinary people do not survive death. Only those who have awakened and used their will to construct an immortal body distinct from the familiar physical one do so.

From 1915 until his death in 1949, Gurdjieff based himself in various locations in western Europe and the United States, teaching and writing. Gurdjieff's thought has affected many spiritual seekers, including architect Frank Lloyd Wright, physiologist Moshe Feldenkrais, writers Rudyard Kipling and J. B. Priestley, and painter Georgia O'Keefe. Gurdjieff study groups have traditionally kept a very low profile, but in recent years some of these groups have been publicly promoting their views.

Madame GUYON   In 1675, Spanish Catholic writer Miguel de MOLINOS published a book of spiritual advice. This work, which discusses the mystical practices known as QUIETISM, intrigued French noblewoman Madame Guyon. She went on to become the foremost proponent of Quietism in her country.

Born in 1648, she was named Jeanne Marie Bouvier de la Mothe. Early in life, she showed interest in mysticism, the direct experience of divinity. When she was a young woman, her husband was not sympathetic to her spiritual curiosity, but he died when she was just twenty-eight years old. Madame Guyon then discovered Molinos's writings. She was excited by his belief that one should totally eliminate one's personal will in order to be controlled by the will of God, and began a preaching tour of France to promote the idea.

The Quietist doctrine implies that individuals who are completely united with God's will cannot be guilty of sinning, regardless of what they do. The temptations of such a view are evident. In 1687, Molinos was condemned as a heretic; the same year, Catholic authorities arrested Guyon and her traveling companion, a friar, on suspicion of heresy and sexual misconduct.

Guyon spent a short time in prison, but powerful friends arranged her release. She continued her teaching and became quite popular among the highest ranks of society for a time. During this period, she became an influence on ARCHBISHOP FENELON. Other Catholic officials continued to raise suspicions regarding her orthodoxy, however. In order to clear the air, Guyon demanded that a commission of the Catholic Church examine her views. To her surprise, the commission concluded that she was indeed presenting heretical ideas. In 1695, her teachings were officially condemned, and she was forbidden to teach again. Guyon died in 1717.

Patrick HAMILTON   The first Protestant Reformer to be executed for heresy in Scotland, Patrick Hamilton was a member of the aristocracy and had the opportunity to study in France and Germany as a young man. There, he became intrigued by the ideas of Luther. After Hamilton's return to Scotland, he was invited to present his religious views at the University of St. Andrews. However, the Catholic authorities would not tolerate dissent in spiritual matters. Hamilton was burned at the stake at St. Andrews in 1528.

See also: GEORGE WISHART.

HEATHENISM   According to the Roman Catholic Church, a heathen is someone who does not belong to any of the great monotheistic religions of Christianity, Judaism, and Islam. Orthodox Christians often felt a duty to attempt to convert heathens in order to save their souls. Some have interpreted the following verse from the Gospel of Luke as permitting the use of force to encourage conversion: "And the lord said unto the servant, Go out into the highways and hedges, and *compel* them to come in, that my house may be filled" (14:23).

HELL-FIRE CLUB   One of the names given to the MEDMENHAM MONKS, the Hell-fire Club was a band of eighteenth century British aristocrats who enjoyed performing sacrilegious ceremonies and acquired a reputation as SATANISTS.

HENRY OF LAUSANNE   The preaching career of Henry of Lausanne (also known as Henry of Le Mans) spanned forty years and ranged from northern France to Italy. He was one of the most successful heretics of the twelfth century. His impact was so great that Bernard of Clairvaux, the most powerful defender of the orthodox faith during the later medieval era, felt compelled to mount a preaching mission to combat the heretic's influence.

Henry's heretical career began in the northern French town of Le Mans in 1116. An unknown lay preacher at the time, he asked Bishop Hildebert for permission to speak publicly in the town. After the bishop granted this request, he set off for a meeting in Rome. Upon Hildebert's return several weeks later, he was shocked when the townspeople greeted his blessing by shouting, "It is of no value to us to accept your blessings—go bless the filth!" During his absence, Henry had quickly won the support of the people and taken over Le Mans.

The teachings of Henry of Lausanne are similar to those of his contemporary heretics, PIERRE DE BRUYS and TANCHELM OF FLANDERS. Henry proclaimed that greed had corrupted the Catholic Church and invalidated its sacraments. He maintained that priests who refused to acknowledge this fact should be run out of town, and the mistresses of priests should be forced to marry. This call for a nonmaterialistic, morally purified church was well received by the poorer classes, who resented the gap between their living conditions and those of the church officials they were forced to support through tithes. Just as significant as the content of Henry's teachings was his personal charisma. It was said that Henry used his influence to feed a large sexual appetite for women and boys, but most historians view this claim as Catholic propaganda.

Hildebert enlisted the help of the town's upper classes, whose privileges were threatened by Henry's popular movement, and drove the heretic from Le Mans. In the words of a contemporary chronicler, Henry "fled to disturb other regions and infect them with his poisonous breath." He proceeded to the south of France and northern Italy where he wandered for many years, spreading his views. He encountered other heretics, including the PETROBRUSCIANS, whose doctrines he considered identical to his own. Henry also tangled with orthodox authorities. In 1135, he was captured by the archbishop of Arles and ordered confined to a monastery, but he escaped.

During the early 1140s, Henry's preaching was especially successful in the southern French city of Toulouse. This site was soon to become a hotbed of activity involving the heretical CATHARS, and it is likely that the anti-orthodox message of Henry prepared their way. By 1145, Henry's popularity had risen so far that Bernard of Clairveaux engaged in a preaching mission to fight the heresy. Reports of miracles were circulated in order to establish that God was on Bernard's side. Bernard arranged that supporters of Henry would not be protected by the legal system. Eventually, the heretic was captured by the bishop of Toulouse. Henry disappeared from history at this point; some historians believe he died in prison, while others suspect that he escaped and joined the emergent Cathar movement.

George HENSLEY   Founder of the American sect of SNAKE HANDLERS, a believer in the literal truth of the Bible, George Hensley thought that passages in the New Testament called on the faithful to handle poisonous snakes and to drink poison, and that God would protect them from harm. In 1909, he introduced the practice to rural churches in Tennessee and Kentucky. Hensley died from a snakebite in 1955.

Los HERMANOS PENITENTES   The practice of flogging oneself for spiritual purification was brought to the New World by the conquistadores from Spain, where the unorthodox FLAGELLANTS' movement was popular. This activity has endured to the present day among the sect called "Los Hermanos Penitentes," which exists in remote areas of New Mexico and Colorado. They use whips, sometimes made of cactus strips. The week before Easter is the most popular time for flagellation, when many flog themselves into unconsciousness. Other forms of self-torture, including being tied to a cross in imitation of Christ, have been reported. Initiation into the sect entails being whipped by other members.

HERMETICA   The word "hermetic" has become closely associated with many unorthodox-reality traditions in Western culture. ALCHEMY is known as the "Hermetic Art"; the most important magical society in modern times was the Hermetic Order of the GOLDEN DAWN. *The Hermetica* are the ancient texts that stimulated much occult thinking at various phases of Western history.

During the first centuries A.D., writings said to be authored by "Hermes Trismegistus" began to circulate in the Egyptian city of Alexandria. The name, meaning "Thrice Greatest Hermes," referred not to an ordinary human author, but to a mythical figure who was a fusion of the Greek deity Hermes and the Egyptian god Thoth. Both beings represented wisdom and magic in their pantheons and were merged into a single figure by the Hellenistic Greek colonists of Egypt. He was "thrice greatest" because he was the lord of the three major occult disciplines: alchemy, ASTROLOGY, and MAGIC.

The content of these ancient writings is derived from the variety of magical and mystical systems popular in the Roman Empire at the time. Ideas borrowed from GNOSTICISM figure prominently, as do those from the followers of Plato and Pythagoras. There was probably never an organized cult of Hermes Trismegistus; rather, the literature connected with his name circulated among intellectuals and occultists who tried to understand the mysterious writings and added texts of their own composition under Hermes' name.

Ancient commentators varied in their accounts of the size of the Hermetic literature. Iamblichus, a devotee of THEURGY, estimated that 20,000 titles existed; church father Clement of Alexandria reported only forty-two. Because of the accidents of time and the hostility of orthodox Christianity toward pagan texts, few of these works have survived. The most important texts include *The Asclepius*, THE EMERALD TABLET, and a collection of 15 works known as CORPUS HERMETICUM.

During the later medieval period, western Europe recovered many classical Greek and Roman writings that the Arabs had preserved. *The Emerald Tablet* was probably one such document. It became the most revered text among European alchemists, who scrutinized it for hints concerning the successful attainment of transmutation.

In 1453, Constantinople fell to Moslem armies, marking the end of the ancient Byzantine Empire. In the process, many of its treasures were dispersed. Seven years later, a monk from the fallen city appeared in Florence. He presented a set of Hermetic texts to Cosimo de Medici, who was renowned for his interest in rare manuscripts. Cosimo immediately ordered his translator, MARSILIO FICINO, to decipher the writings and convert them into Latin.

Cosimo and Ficino were convinced that *The Hermetica* documented the earliest religious revelations of humanity, predating even Plato and Moses. This belief enabled them to appreciate *The Hermetica* as pre-Christian writings that predict and support the Christian revelation, rather than as a pagan literature that offer an alternative to Christianity.

The ideas in *The Hermetica* largely defined the world view of the Italian Renaissance. From *Poimandres*, the best-known book of *Corpus Hermeticum*, Ficino learned that every person contains inner planets, corresponding to the celestial ones. A passage in *The Asclepius* suggested to him a method of NATURAL MAGIC, in which the planetary spiritual influences could be made available for promoting well-being. Another section of *The Asclepius* inspired GIOVANNI PICO DELLA MIRANDOLA to frame the central notion of the Renaissance—that "man is the measure of all things." The Hermetic documents remained popular among the magicians of the Renaissance who attempted to develop a synthesis of classical, Christian, and occult interests, often with heretical results. Because of its association with unorthodox doctrines, the name of Hermes Trismegistus fell into disrepute.

In 1614, the careful scholarship of Meric Casaubon demonstrated that *The Hermetica* were written around the beginning of the third century A.D. Clearly, then, they were not pre-Christian but clearly pagan and, thus, could not be taken to be a legitimate revelation by the orthodox. By then, the name of Hermes had acquired such a strong association with magical power and mysterious revelations that the occult traditions had become generally known as "hermetic" doctrines. During the return of European interest in magic in the nineteenth century, and again in the late twentieth century, the writings of Hermes have attracted much attention for their historical importance and poetic power.

Melchior HOFFMANN

One of the early leaders of the sixteenth century ANABAPTISTS, Melchior Hoffmann was born around 1498 in southern Germany. He became a furrier and traveled widely in western and central Europe. Sensing the cultural turmoil about to erupt into the Protestant Reformation, Hoffmann became convinced that the end of history as he knew it was imminent. In fact, he began to preach that the heavenly city of Jerusalem would soon appear on earth.

Hoffmann's message was well suited to the prevailing atmosphere of uncertainty, and he acquired a following during his travels. He contacted Reformation leaders Huldrych Zwingli and Martin Luther, but they shunned contact with him. In 1529, Hoffmann became aligned with the Anabaptist movement, which believed that the mainstream of the Reformation was too mild in its reforms.

In addition to rejecting the validity of infant baptism, Hoffmann developed other unorthodox themes. He could not accept the view Catholics and Lutherans shared: that JESUS had a body composed of the same material flesh as other humans; instead, Christ must have been made of supernatural flesh. Orthodox theory holds that Christ had to be incarnated in a real human body, so that His death on the cross could merit salvation for humanity. Mainstream Christianity, therefore, could not tolerate Hoffmann's view.

Hoffmann's ideas concerning his own role in history were also provocative. He compared himself with the prophet Elijah, warning the godless world to repent before Christ returned in judgment over humanity. Hoffmann predicted that the Lord would return in clouds of glory in 1533. Hoffmann himself would be at Christ's right hand on Judgment Day, after which the New Jerusalem would be set up in the city of Strasbourg.

The prophet was indeed in Strasbourg in 1533. Having arrived to await the coming of the Lord, he had continued his preaching. However, the authorities were hostile to Anabaptists and had him locked up. Hoffmann was imprisoned for the remaining ten years of his life and died around 1543.

Hoffmann had established communities of disciples, called MELCHIORITES, in several locations; they kept the faith despite their leader's incarceration. Shortly after his imprisonment began, some of his followers played a leading role in the attempt by the MÜNSTER HERETICS to establish the New Jerusalem in that town. Following that disaster, which fragmented the Anabaptist movement, MENNO SIMONS, another of Hoffmann's students, managed to regroup many Anabaptists into the MENNONITE movement. This group retained some of Hoffmann's teachings, such as the doctrine of the heavenly flesh.

HOMOEANS   A branch of the heresy called ARIANISM, which struggled against the Catholics for control of the church during the fourth century, the Homoean movement was founded by ACACIUS, bishop of Caesarea, in an attempt to settle the dispute between the orthodox and the Arians concerning the basic nature of God. The Homoeans taught that certain questions, such as whether God the Father and the Son of God had the same or different natures, were beyond human comprehension and should not be discussed. They claimed that the Father and Son were similar (in Greek, *homoios*), but did not specify whether this similarity entailed a resemblance in their basic natures. By the time of the orthodox victory in 381, the Homoeans had either been deposed or had converted to the orthodox position that the Father and the Son had the same divine nature.

HOMOIOUSIANS   The Homoiousians were a branch of the ARIAN heresy, which contended with the Catholics for dominance in the Christian Church during the fourth century. While the orthodox claimed that God the Father and the Son of God have the same divine essence, and the RADICAL ARIANS declared that the Father and the Son have completely different natures, the Homoiousian position attempted a compromise. The Homoiousians held that the natures of the Father and the Son were similar (in Greek, *homoi* means "similar," and *ousios* means "nature" or "essence"). Although Arian emperor CONSTANTIUS II attempted to force the entire church to accept the Homoiousian compromise formula, the Catholic party firmly refused. Its members claimed that the idea of two similar divine natures, rather than one, fragmented the unity of God, and was not really monotheism.

At a meeting in A.D. 362, Catholics officially adopted the position that the Father, the Son, and the Holy Spirit have the same divine nature. By that time, many Homoiousians were willing to accept the statement that the Father and the Son had the same nature, by defining "nature" in a rather loose manner. But the inclusion of the Holy Spirit was unacceptable to a number of Homoiousians, and they remained separate from the orthodox party. In 381, the orthodox view had triumphed, and the Homoiousian school was declared heretical and illegal.

See also: BASIL OF ANCYRA.

HONORIUS   The pope from A.D. 625 to 638, Honorius has the dubious distinction of being the only bishop of Rome to be officially condemned as a heretic by a full council of the church. During the sixth and seventh centuries, the Byzantine emperors had sponsored attempts to entice the heretical followers of MONOPHYSITISM back into the orthodox church. Various doctrines that compromised aspects of orthodox belief in a Monophysite direction were proclaimed without attracting many Monophysite converts. Honorius advanced the notion that Christ had a single will (MONOTHELETISM), hoping that it would form a basis for common agreement between orthodoxy and Monophysitism. While the Monophysites, who believed that Christ has a single nature, had no trouble accepting the idea, the orthodox community itself threatened to divide. Many Catholics believed that Christ must have two wills, one divine and one human, because He has both a divine and a human nature.

Honorius died in 638, and the popes who succeeded him denounced Monotheletism. He was damned as a heretic at the THIRD COUNCIL OF CONSTANTINOPLE in 680. Many scholars have argued that the case of Honorius poses a challenge for the doctrine of papal infallibility, proclaimed in 1870.

John HOOPER   In 1552, during the period when the Church of England was being formed, John Hooper became bishop of Worcester. He was an enthusiastic supporter of Protestant reform, but his timing was terrible. The following year, Mary Tudor came to power and began a revival of Catholic power by executing Protestant leaders for heresy. Hooper was burned at the stake in 1555.

See also: THOMAS CRANMER, HUGH LATIMER, NICHOLAS RIDLEY.

HOREBITES   The Horebites were one of the radical groups of HUSSITES who caused a reign of terror in Bohemia during the early fifteenth century. Like their more famous contemporaries, the TABORITES, the Horebites opposed the institutions of conventional society, particularly the Roman Catholic Church. From their fortified headquarters at Horeb, the radicals roamed the country, destroying property and killing priests and nobles. The Horebites were destroyed by the forces of the Catholics and moderate Hussites.

HUGH DE PAYENS   A French nobleman, Hugh Payens founded the KNIGHTS TEMPLAR, a medieval order that was charged with heresy in the early fourteenth century. In 1118, Hugh de Payens, along with several companions, formed the Templars for the purpose of defending Christian pilgrims traveling from Europe to the Holy Land. He was a friend of Saint Bernard, the most influential man in Europe, who secured the support of the pope for the new order, and modeled the knights' conduct on the rule of Bernard's own Cistercian Order.

HUMILIATI   This Italian Christian group has the distinction of being one of the only religious movements to be excommunicated from the Catholic Church and then promptly readmitted. The brief period when the Humiliati were defined as heretics occurred around the beginning of the thirteenth century. The Humiliati were founded by Hugo SPERONI, a citizen of Piacenza in northern Italy, around 1165. Speroni preached that the sacraments of the orthodox church, such as baptism and the Mass, could not lead one to God. Luxuries, he taught, were distractions to spiritual progress. Only a lifestyle of simple labor and prayer, modeled on that of the New Testament apostles, would please the Lord. Those who responded to this message, the Humiliati, or humble people, were often poor artisans, such as weavers. They formed cooperative settlements in towns throughout northern Italy.

The Humiliati, unlike such contemporary heresies as the CATHARS and WALDENSIANS, were well integrated into the life of the Italian towns. They continued to marry and to work. Catholic officials perceived them as a threat, however, because they also preached. The Humiliati emphasis of a simple lifestyle reminded the orthodox of similar views held by the heretical groups mentioned above. Their leader's rejection of the orthodox sacraments, and their refusal to acknowledge the authority of priests with respect to preaching, led to the excommunication of the Humiliati, along with the Waldensians and Cathars, by Pope Lucius III in 1184.

Even though the Humiliati were declared unorthodox, they did not suffer intense persecution, perhaps because of their obvious harmlessness. Innocent III, Pope Lucius's successor, witnessed the rising threat of the more dynamic Cathar and Waldensian heresies. Innocent showed no mercy in his assault on these groups, but he decided to attempt a reconciliation with the Humiliati. In 1200, the pontiff revoked the excommunication of the Humiliati and granted them permission to preach to their own communities, provided they submitted themselves to the authority of the Catholic Church. Many Humiliati thus rejoined orthodoxy; some chose to band together with the Waldensians instead.

During the following centuries, the Humiliati communities prospered. They became important producers of textiles and fed the growing mercantile activities of the Italians. Eventually, the Humiliati declined, and they were officially disbanded in 1571.

Jan HUS   At the beginning of the fifteenth century, the Protestant Reformation was still more than 100 years in the future. But demands for church reform were already being made by men like Jan Hus. For his willingness to criticize the Catholic Church, he was betrayed and murdered. The movement that took its name from him, the HUSSITES, played an important role in central European history, and Hus himself has become the preeminent cultural hero of the Czech people.

Hus was born in Bohemia around 1373. His father died when he was young, and he was raised by his mother. Earlier in the century, Prague had become a major center of learning with the founding of a university. Hus studied philosophy and theology there. He was exposed to the writings of English heretic JOHN WYCLIFFE, and was impressed by the Englishman's denunciation of corruption within the Catholic Church.

Although apparently only an average student, Hus had a persuasive personality; by his early thirties, he was a lecturer at the university and an ordained priest. Hus rather quickly rose to become the dean of philosophy, and the rector of the University of Prague. The Queen of Bohemia chose Hus as her personal confessor.

At the same time, Bohemian nationalism was on the rise. Hus preached eloquently in Czech, the language of the people, as well as in Latin, and won wide favor. He spoke against the selfishness of many Catholic leaders, who seemed more interested in a comfortable lifestyle or in the pursuit of political power than in discharging their religious duties. While he was less radical than Wycliffe, who called the pope the Antichrist, Hus did not hesitate to criticize the papacy: far from being infallible, he observed, many popes had been heretics.

Hus's preaching was well received by the lower classes and by many aristocrats, but it was less appreciated by Catholic officials. The tension mounted when a power struggle between conservative German theologians and Czech followers of Wycliffe broke out at the university. King Vaclav and Hus, backed by nationalistic feeling, supported the Czechs. The Germans were forced to leave. Alarmed at this attack on orthodox influence, the archbishop of Prague demanded that Hus stop preaching; when he refused, he was excommunicated.

To make matters worse, Hus managed to alienate his most powerful supporters by condemning the Catholic tradition of selling indulgences, the practice of giving money to the church in return for forgiveness of one's sins. Vaclav objected to Hus's position because the king received a percentage of the indulgence money; the theological faculty at the University of Prague felt that Hus was becoming too radical.

Hus had to leave Prague, but he continued to preach in the Bohemian countryside, where he was enthusiastically welcomed. This state of affairs concerned the Holy Roman Emperor Sigismund. The emperor wished to heal the growing rifts in the Catholic Church and suggested that Hus meet with the orthodox Council of Constance in Switzerland to resolve his disagreements with the Catholic leadership. Sigismund guaranteed Hus's safety. In 1414, Hus traveled to debate the council.

Upon Hus's arrival in Constance, he was immediately imprisoned. He was charged with supporting the doctrines of the infamous heretic Wycliffe, as well as teaching his own erroneous views. The preacher was asked to reject his heresy; he replied that he was not a heretic. Hus refused to recant, even after several miserable months in jail. So, he met the fate of many heretics of the period: on July 6, 1415, Hus was burned at the stake in Constance. As the flames reached toward him, he repeated the words of Christ on the cross: "Lord, into Thy hands I commend my spirit."

Hus's execution provoked outrage in Bohemia. Even many of his former opponents united with his followers to condemn the actions at Constance. Nationalistic feelings erupted. For the next nineteen years, Bohemia was torn by war as Catholics and various kinds of Hussites fought each other.

Over the centuries that followed, Hus became a central symbol of Czech nationhood. His most famous proclamation, "Truth prevails," has been used as a slogan in every popular Czech revolution since his lifetime. Today, the massive Jan Hus Memorial, in the center of Prague's Great Square, bears witness to the continuing reverence that modern Czechs feel for this pioneering reformer.

Martin HUSKA   Martin Huska was the leader of the PIKARTS, an unorthodox Christian group that settled in Bohemia during the early fifteenth century. The Pikart doctrine, which included the idea that spiritually perfect individuals are above all laws, so annoyed another heretical group, the TABORITES, that the Pikarts came under attack. Huska was captured by the Taborites, tortured, and burned at the stake.

HUSSITES   In 1415, Czech religious reformer JAN HUS was burned at the stake for heresy. Before his death, Hus had lost favor among the inhabitants of Prague, although he was broadly supported by rural people. His execution so outraged the Czech people that most of them temporarily united under his followers, the HUSSITES.

The major church reform the Hussites brought about was to allow the congregation to partake of both bread and wine during the Mass. The Catholic practice was to reserve the wine for the priests. Four years after Hus's death, Vaclav, the Bohemian king, permitted Catholic priests to return to their parishes, where they refused to continue the Hussite practice. Violence broke out, culminating in an incident known as the "First Defenestration." Several Catholic officials were tossed out of a window in Prague to their deaths. Such mob actions so terrified Vaclav that he died of a heart attack.

Following the Defenestration, the pope declared a Crusade against the Hussites. For the next fifteen years, Catholic Crusaders from across Europe trooped to Bohemia to battle the heretics. The Hussites fought well, but began to split into factions. The moderate wing was known as the UTRAQUISTS; the more radical Hussites were called the TABORITES and HOREBITES.

In 1433, the Utraquists struck a deal with the Catholics; the communion of both bread and wine would be permitted, provided that Catholic authority was recognized. The radicals rejected this compromise. They were intent on sweeping away the status quo. In the following year, the radicals' army was destroyed, ending the Crusade.

Eventually, Catholic domination was restored in Bohemia. The Utraquists joined the Protestant camp during the Reformation. Another group, the UNITAS FRATRUM, which included former Utraquists and Taborites, became an important influence on the Moravian Church.

Anne HUTCHINSON   Seventeenth century religious radical in the American colonies, Anne Hutchinson in her youth was a pious Puritan, living comfortably in the strict religious atmosphere of Massachusetts. She became convinced, however, that individuals can discover the Holy Spirit within themselves, without needing to follow religious authorities to do so. Such talk could not be permitted, especially from a woman.

In 1639, Hutchinson and her followers were forced to leave the Puritan lands, so they headed for Rhode Island. Three years earlier, ROGER WILLIAMS had founded Providence, Rhode Island, as a haven for religious refugees. Wishing to distance themselves even more from their persecutors in Massachusetts, they journeyed into the wilderness of Long Island. Unfortunately, the group encountered natives who mistook them for hostile Dutch settlers. Anne Hutchinson, who opposed violence against natives, died at their hands in 1643.

See also: THOMAS MORTON.

Jacob HUTTER   Jacob Hutter was leader of the HUTTERITES in the early sixteenth century. The sect derives its name from him. He organized a community of ANABAPTISTS in the Tyrolean Alps and attracted persecution from orthodox forces, who condemned their rejection of infant baptism. He and his followers moved to the more tolerant region of Moravia (in what is now the Czech Republic). There, they joined other Anabaptist refugees and established a group that shared all property; they also held to pacifism, even when under attack. As the political currents changed, religious toleration ended, and Hutter was expelled from Moravia. Returning to his homeland, he was captured, tortured, and burned to death as a heretic in 1536.

HUTTERITES   A branch of the ANABAPTISTS, Protestant extremists who appeared in the early 1500s, the Hutterites have survived into the twentieth century;

indeed, they have thrived. The movement began in the Moravian region of what is now the Czech Republic, where many Anabaptists had fled to escape religious persecution in western Europe. Under JACOB HUTTER (from whom the sect derives its name), a community formed that practiced communism and pacifism. They were so devoted to their ideals that when a friendly local lord used weapons to defend them against attack, they left his properties in disgust.

Hutterites were scattered through central Europe when religious toleration ended in Moravia. Small groups often found protection on the lands of sympathetic nobles, for whom they would make crafts. But the Catholic Church eventually convinced the civil authorities that the Hutterites were dangerous heretics who should be forced to convert to orthodox practices. Again, they fled, this time to Russia and the Ukraine, where Catherine the Great did not impose religious conformity on minorities.

The Hutterites lived peacefully there until the 1870s. The Russian government then announced a policy of compulsory military service, which violated the Hutterites' nonviolent convictions. The entire sect, which numbered about 700, relocated to South Dakota. During World War I, however, German-speaking pacifists were not popular in the United States, and attempts were made to ban their lifestyle. Another migration resulted, this time to the tolerant atmosphere of Canada. The vast majority of Hutterite settlements remain there today.

The Hutterite communities have resisted absorption into modern culture more successfully than most latter-day heretical groups. They permit the use of modern technology, as long as it is used for work, not pleasure. Their disciplined, common use of their land has led to great efficiency. Hutterites are renowned for establishing productive agricultural enterprises on marginally arable land.

See also: PETER RIEDEMANN.

THE HYMN OF THE PEARL   The literary masterpiece of the Gnostic religion called MANICHAEISM, which challenged Christianity in ancient times, *The Hymn of the Pearl* describes the adventures of a prince who is sent forth from his home into the world. His task is to retrieve a pearl that is guarded by a serpent. During his stay in the world, he is tricked into forgetting his identity. His parents send him the call to awaken, and he regains self-knowledge by reading a message written in his heart. The prince then proceeds to overcome the serpent using magical language, to take the pearl, and to return in triumph to his heavenly home.

The prince is taken to represent the true nature of the Manichaean self. Trapped and confused in the material world, human beings are advised to realize their identity as sparks of divine light through the act of GNOSIS. The pearl symbolizes the liberation from suffering that follows this enlightenment.

HYPATIA   In the decades following A.D. 381 when Christianity was proclaimed the official religion of the Roman Empire, PAGANISM began to decline in the face of Christian persecution. Hypatia was one of the most notable victims of Catholic violence directed against pagans, and perhaps the first woman Christians killed for stepping beyond the bounds of the female roles dictated by the orthodox church.

Hypatia was born in the Egyptian city of Alexandria during the late fourth century. She was the daughter of Theon, a noted mathematician. Alexandria had been the intellectual center of the Roman Empire during its pagan glory days, and retained its importance as a focus of Christian activity after Emperor Theodosius's proclamation in 381. Throughout the fourth century, the city was often in turmoil. The government of the city frequently resisted the bishop's attempts to control it, and Christian factions were struggling for dominance within the church. Both conflicts often took the form of violent mob action.

As a girl, Hypatia left the unstable atmosphere of Alexandria for Athens, where she studied the most refined aspects of pagan culture. She specialized in philosophy and mathematics. Upon her return to Alexandria, she was invited to teach at the university. Through her teaching and writing, she quickly attained a reputation as a scholar. Students traveled from all over the empire to study with Hypatia, who became known as "The Nurse" and "The Philosopher." Her presence in Alexandria became a hopeful sign for members of the besieged pagan community, who still valued their non-Christian heritage.

Cyril, the bishop of Alexandria, was unhappy with Hypatia's activities. He believed that the study of philosophy and mathematics distracted people from the study of Christian teachings, which were much more important. Also, he objected to the notion of a woman acting as a teacher, a role not permitted to women in the Catholic Church at the time. Cyril began to preach against her.

In 415, a Catholic mob, incited by the bishop, captured Hypatia. She was then tortured, killed, and dismembered. There were no objections from Christian leaders to this act. Her death was an important milestone in the destruction of classical paganism, which survived until the closing of the Academy in Athens by Emperor Justinian in 529.

IBAS   During the first half of the fifth century, the Christian Church was strained by a conflict over the nature of Christ. Ibas, who served as the bishop of Edessa (in what is now southern Turkey), attempted to mediate between the various groups in the debate; unfortunately, he ended up pleasing no one. After his death, the Catholic Church labeled his writings heretical.

Ibas attained the rank of bishop in A.D. 435. Four years earlier, a theological controversy between Cyril of Alexandria and NESTORIUS had been resolved in Cyril's favor. The doctrines of NESTORIANISM (which emphasized the differences between Christ's divinity and humanity) had been declared heretical, but Nestorius still had many sympathizers and the atmosphere within the Christian communities was tense.

Another rift in the church threatened in 448. EUTYCHES, with the support of Bishop DIOSCURUS of Alexandria, accused the orthodox church leaders of having lapsed into Nestorian beliefs regarding the correct way to describe Christ's divine and human natures. Many Christians of the time realized that a serious rift could imperil the future of Christianity. The political situation was unstable; the Roman Empire in the West was being overrun by Germanic tribes, and the culture of the ancient world, including the church itself, seemed in danger of vanishing forever.

In the face of this threat, Ibas believed that church unity should be the highest priority. He attempted to devise a theological position that would be acceptable to both sides in the new controversy.

However, neither side was interested in compromise. Although on the surface the disagreement concerned details of theology, a political struggle for dominance within the church was also involved. If one of the bishops in the debate could be shown to be a heretic, the importance of his city as a center of Christian orthodoxy would be lessened. Total victory, not agreement with their opponents, was ruthlessly sought by both the orthodox and the supporters of Eutyches.

One of the strategies employed in the controversy was the recruitment of mobs to intimidate the supporters of the other side. To the Eutychians, Ibas's mediating efforts were seen as lack of support for their own stance, so some local citizens organized to show their displeasure. At one point, the bishop was met by an angry crowd, shouting "Ibas has corrupted the true doctrine," "To the gallows with the Iscariot," and "The Christ-hater to the arena." He narrowly escaped being torn limb from limb, a fate that befell other unlucky participants in the controversy.

Ibas attended the church council held in 449 in an attempt to settle the dispute. This meeting, known to history as the ROBBER COUNCIL, was manipulated by Dioscurus into condemning his opponents, the bishop of Constantinople, and the pope. Bishop Ibas was also deposed at this time.

Two years later, the orthodox-controlled COUNCIL OF CHALCEDON was held in order to overturn the proclamations of the Robber Council. This time, Dioscurus and Eutyches were condemned. Ibas was restored to his rank as bishop, more because of his condemnation by the Eutychians than for his doctrinal convictions.

Ibas is thought to have died peacefully around 457. Although he was regarded as orthodox at the time of his death, a letter he wrote during the Eutychian controversy was reviewed during the SECOND COUNCIL OF CONSTANTINOPLE in 553, and declared to be heretical. In the pursuit of theological truth—and in church politics—compromisers like Ibas are rarely rewarded.

ICONOCLASM   The iconoclastic controversy rocked the Byzantine Empire during the eighth and ninth centuries. The debate centered around the use of religious images called icons in the Christian religion. "Iconoclasm" literally means "image smashing." The iconoclasts opposed the depiction of Christ and the saints, although not all iconoclasts actually supported the violent smashing of icons. By the end of the debate over icons, the Eastern and Western branches of the Catholic faith had drifted apart, never again to function as a united church.

The act of paying respect to images of Christ dates back to ancient times. In western Europe, it was generally agreed that pictures of Christian figures were useful in educating the illiterate masses about Catholic beliefs, but that worshipping the images themselves should be discouraged. Nonetheless, depictions of saints, the Virgin Mary, and JESUS often provoked very reverent responses that bordered on image worship. In the east, the official policy was less clear. Many Byzantine church leaders condoned the idea that the icons were points of contact between the divine and human worlds. For example, prayers offered to Mary's picture would be transmitted directly to her, and she could convey her blessed influences to her devotees through her icons.

Byzantine Emperor LEO III is generally regarded as the first iconoclast. Scholars have debated the origins of his opposition to religious imagery. Leo seems to have believed that creating pictures of Christ out of matter, even if the matter was as precious as gold, was an insult to God, who transcends all material objects. This hostile attitude toward the physical world has suggested to some historians that Leo was influenced by the ancient heresy of MANICHAEISM, which taught that an evil spirit created matter. Others think that the emperor was simply trying to make Christianity more attractive to potential Jewish and Moslem converts, who were strongly opposed to any depictions of divinity.

In A.D. 720, three years after coming to power, Leo ordered that the image of Christ's head should no longer be stamped on Byzantine coins. From 727, the emperor forbade the use of images in the church. This policy was unacceptable to Pope Gregory II, who insisted on the educational usefulness of religious pictures and condemned iconoclasm. This rejection broke the political connection between Rome (the papal residence and ancient capital of the empire) and Constantinople (the imperial headquarters since the fourth century).

CONSTANTINE V, Leo's son and successor, intensified the iconoclastic campaign. Constantine composed a work defending iconoclasm on theological grounds. He observed that separating the divine and human natures of Christ was heretical (specifically, the heresy of NESTORIANISM), and that reducing the divine to a mere image was blasphemous. As a result, images of Christ that claimed to portray only His human nature were heretical, and those that aimed to depict His divinity were blasphemous.

During Constantine's reign, the persecution of orthodox Christians who refused to give up their use of religious images grew increasingly severe. Monasteries and churches containing icons were torched. The iconoclasts blinded or murdered their opponents and forced orthodox monks and nuns to marry or be killed. Some of this hostility, particularly that directed toward monks, grew out of the belief that the monasteries were a major drain on the Byzantine economy at a time when the empire was threatened by Moslem armies to the south and pagan invaders to the north.

After Constantine's death in 775, LEO IV, his successor, assumed a much more tolerant attitude toward the orthodox Christian view of images although he himself was an iconoclast. When Leo died in 780, Irene, his wife, took control of the government. She supported the orthodox position regarding icons and took steps to restore orthodoxy to power in the church.

Irene convened the SECOND COUNCIL OF NICAEA, which met in 787 to affirm the legitimacy of icons in Christianity. Pope Hadrian presented his views via a letter; he supported the use of icons, provided that worship was directed at the saint depicted in the image and not at the image itself. Iconoclasm was declared a heresy. This meeting was the last council to represent the united view of the entire Catholic Church, both Eastern and Western.

But iconoclasm was not dead yet. In 813, LEO V assumed the Byzantine throne and again ordered the destruction of icons. Leo proved to be unpopular, however, and was murdered. He was replaced in 820 by MICHAEL II. The new emperor reigned for nine years. During this time, Michael did not persecute Christians who revered icons, although he himself was an iconoclast.

Michael's successor was his son THEOPHILUS, who ruled from Michael's death until his own demise in 842. Theophilus's reign marked the last resurgence of iconoclasm. Once more, the images were smashed, and orthodox monks were murdered because of their devotion to icons.

When Theophilus died, power fell into the hands of his widow, Theodora. She strongly supported the orthodox view and hosted a council of the Byzantine Church in 843 that permanently restored the icons to a prominent position in religious devotion. Historians regard this council as the foundation of the faith known as Eastern Orthodox Christianity.

The damage done by the iconoclastic controversy to the relationship between Eastern and Western Christians was irreparable. The decades of Byzantine vacillating between orthodox and heretical positions regarding icons underlined the conviction in Europe that only the bishop of Rome was a reliable guardian of the Christian faith and that, therefore, the Byzantine Church should declare its subservience to the pope. Many Eastern Christians refused to do this. By the end of the ninth century, East and West had decisively split into two separate churches. In the late twentieth century, prospects for a reconciliation between the Roman Catholics and the Eastern Orthodox still seem remote.

Although the struggle over iconoclasm took place in Byzantine lands, it had a significant impact on Western thought. Roman Catholicism favored the use of images, but in order to avoid being accused of idol worship by the iconoclasts, it had to make a firm distinction between the image and the saint depicted. The image is not real, the Catholics argued, but is merely a representation of the holy person, who exists in heaven. Furthermore, the unreal pictures should not be adored, rather the saints themselves. This definition of images as mere symbols, lacking their own reality, became a deep bias in the Western mind. Many cultures do not make this separation; to them, images are not just symbols pointing to a reality outside of themselves, but actual living beings in themselves. To this day, most members of our culture tend to view the images in fantasies and dreams as "unreal," compared to the "real" external world perceived during ordinary waking consciousness.

INDEX OF PROHIBITED BOOKS   A book entitled *Index Librorum Prohibitorum* was a device the Roman Catholic Church established to shield the faithful from dangerously unorthodox publications. With the invention of the printing press in the late 1400s and the Protestant Reformation beginning in the early 1500s, Catholicism faced the possibility that ideas contrary to church dogmas could be made readily available to all literate people. In 1557, Pope Paul IV authorized the Holy Office of the INQUISITION to prepare a list of books that good Christians should avoid. If people read a work on the list, the pope warned, they could be committing a mortal sin.

The job of maintaining the *Index* proved to be large. In 1571, Pope Pius V set up a "Congregation of the Index," a committee devoted to monitoring the literary scene and continually updating the list of banned books. By the twentieth century, local bishops had largely assumed responsibility for suppressing books in the Catholic community. In 1917, the Congregation was disbanded, and the maintenance of the *Index* referred back to the Holy Office. The *Index* itself was terminated in 1966 under the influence of Pope Paul VI.

Over the centuries, the Index tried to protect Catholics from many of the landmarks of Western thought. Such works as Kant's *Critique of Pure Reason*, Locke's *Essay Concerning Human Understanding*, Berkeley's *Alciphron*, Descartes's *Meditations*, and Pascal's *Lettres*, were placed on the list.

See also: PONTIFICAL BIBLICAL COMMISSION.

INFIDEL   In Roman Catholic terminology, an infidel is a member of a religion opposed to Christianity, including Judaism and, in particular, Islam. Calls for Crusades to fight the infidels were common during the later Middle Ages.

INQUISITION   The Holy Office of the Inquisition was responsible for the deaths of more heretics than any other single institution in Western history. From its birth in the twelfth century to its restraint in the nineteenth, the Inquisitors were unleashed on popular movements, such as the CATHARS and WALDENSIANS; inspired the GREAT WITCH HUNT against imaginary enemies of Christian civilization, which led to the death of many thousands; prosecuted innovative thinkers like GALILEO and GIORDANO BRUNO; and generally brought lasting disgrace on their religion in the eyes of the rest of the world. It is important to remember that, for the most part, the Inquisitors were not mere sadists; they earnestly believed that they were defending God and truth against the forces of darkness.

As early as A.D. 430, the Christian Roman Empire passed the death penalty for heresy, but the law was rarely applied. When violence was employed against heretics over the ensuing centuries, it was usually at the hands of the secular authorities, rather than the church. By the latter part of the 1100s, unorthodox versions of Christianity seemed to be gaining significant popularity in western Europe. Pope Lucius III became alarmed and decided that a new weapon had to be devised against the spread of free religious thought. In 1188, he authorized the first Inquisition.

Local bishops were to carry out Lucius's Inquisition in regions infested with heresy, such as southern France. Anyone accused of holding a non-Catholic belief had to prove their innocence; failure to do so led to the heretics being presented to the secular government for the appropriate punishment. Torture was not yet officially used, but other forms of intimidation that left no obvious marks on the body were undoubtedly employed.

This early Inquisition was not very successful in stemming the tide of unorthodox belief. But the methods of the heresy hunt were refined during the following decades. In 1199, Pope Innocent III proclaimed that all property of convicted heretics should be seized. The proceeds were often shared with local government officials in return for their continued support of the Inquisition.

These two features—the assumption of guilt until proven innocent and the confiscation of victims' possessions—provided the Inquisitors with a steady flow of easy convictions, as well as with the continued support of the powerful classes who were being financially rewarded. In 1233, Pope Gregory IX centralized control of the Inquisition and put the Dominican friars in charge. No one, not even a bishop, was permitted to interfere with the Inquisitors' work.

Pope Innocent IV added a finishing touch in 1257; torture was authorized as a means of extracting confessions. Favorite techniques included: the application of thumbscrews, toe screws, or boots that could be tightened to crush the feet; the strappado, in which the victims' arms were tied behind their backs, and they were then hoisted by their arms into the air, dislocating the shoulders; squassation, or jerking the suspended victim in the strappado up and down, which often proved fatal; and insertion of the mouth pear, a vise-like device that could pry the jaws open to a very painful extent. Anal and vaginal pears were also devised. Many of the torture procedures still in use today are derived from the inventiveness of these defenders of Christ.

When the Inquisitors arrived in a town, their first acts were usually to preach a sermon against heresy and to call on all local heretics to come forward. If the heretics did so, they would receive penances to perform but usually were not killed. Then, a call was made for the informants to give the names of suspects to the Inquisitors. This information could be given anonymously, and everyone accused in this way would be interrogated. The tradition of handing over a convicted heretic to the nonreligious authorities for punishment continued throughout the history of the Inquisition. Its efficiency was enhanced by the device of charging any official who refused to execute a heretic with favoring heresy.

This improved papal Inquisition was much more effective than Lucius's original version. Most people, when undergoing torture or even when threatened with it, said whatever they thought their tormentors wanted to hear. The Inquisitors thus received confessions, confirming their notions that the suspects were indeed heretics; in addition, they extracted the names of other people to interrogate. The process spiraled in a reign of terror wherever the Inquisition established itself until the heresy hunters were satisfied and moved on.

Over time, the Inquisition proved so thorough that it threatened to bring about its own demise. One Inquisitor complained in 1360 that "In our days there are no more rich heretics; so that princes, not seeing much money in prospect, will not put themselves to any expense." The Inquisitors needed to expand their mandate. They began to lobby the papacy to allow them to hunt magicians, as well as heretics. At first, their requests were denied, but Pope John XXII, who believed he was under constant attack by sorcerors, granted permission in 1320. Twelve years later, the permission to pursue magicians was revoked unless heresy was also involved. Since the official view held that all magic involved demons and that deliberate association with demons was heretical, the revocation did not pose much of a restriction. In 1451, Inquisitors were granted permission to try sorcerors, even if heresy was not involved.

Torture is a poor way to get at the truth, but it can be an impressive method of verifying one's worst fears. Many Inquisitors were familiar with the slanders made against unorthodox believers in the eleventh century, such as the ORLEANS HERE-TICS, that heresy involved devil worship and child sacrifice. Their interrogations revealed these practices to be widespread. In addition, some of their victims mixed in bits of folklore with their confessions, such as stories of people being transformed into animals and flying through the air at night. These fantasies of the torture chamber eventually fused in the minds of the Inquisitors into the notion of an international conspiracy of SATANISTS—the witches.

The papal Inquisition was deeply involved in the GREAT WITCH HUNT during its first phase in the fifteenth and early sixteenth centuries. A contemporary source observed that these Inquisitors killed about 30,000 witches. Once the hunt was well under way and the economic rewards of property confiscation were made plain, bishops as well as secular governments began their own Inquisitions, adopting the methods of the pope's agents. From the early 1500s on, papal Inquisitors were rarely active in the witch hunt. They did, however, continue to provide the witch finders with guidance in the form of witch-hunting manuals. The best known of these works is MALLEUS MALEFICARUM, composed by two Dominican Inquisitors. In

Spain, Jews rather than witches became the main focus of the heresy hunters' attention.

With the outbreak of the Protestant Reformation, the papal Inquisition had a new target. The Protestants condemned the vicious acts the Inquisitors inflicted on them, of course—but then took up the witch hunt themselves, with undiminished ferocity.

With the decline of the witch hunt and the rise of the scientific world view in the eighteenth century, the activities of the Inquisitors declined. Religious bodies were no longer the gatekeepers of reality for the entire culture, with the authority to attack those who disagreed with their dogmas. The SPANISH INQUISITION, which operated independently of the pope's authority, continued its pursuit of heretics until 1834.

Within the Roman Catholic world, the Inquisition survives to this day. Since 1965, it has been known as the Congregation for the Doctrine of the Faith. The official head of the congregation is the pope. The executive chief's role is held by the secretary of the congregation, who is ordinarily an archbishop. The Congregation acts as a watchdog for the purity of the faith. Its agents scrutinize public pronouncements Catholics make about religious belief. Throughout the twentieth century, many prominent Catholic thinkers have been called before the judges of the Congregation to answer charges of heresy. Trials are conducted in private. Penalties for erroneous beliefs no longer include execution but can range from bans on writing and public speaking to excommunication.

See also: INDEX OF PROHIBITED BOOKS, PONTIFICAL BIBLICAL COMMISSION.

ISOCHRISTS   By the sixth century, the teachings of the ancient Christian ORIGEN had been developed and distorted in many ways. One Origenist group, the Isochrists, believed that at the end of the world everyone would be saved and would attain equality with Christ. The Catholic authorities condemned ORIGENISM, including the doctrines of the Isochrists, at the SECOND COUNCIL OF CONSTANTINOPLE in 553.

JACOB BARADAEUS   Jacob Baradeus was a sixth century bishop who founded a church of MONOPHYSITE heretics in Syria. These Monophysites were known as JACOBITES, in honor of their founder. Jacob Baradaeus became the bishop of Edessa (in what is today southern Turkey) in A.D. 542. He spent much of his life traveling throughout the Middle East, spreading the beliefs of Monophysitism, and died in 578.

JACOBITES   After the COUNCIL OF CHALCEDON in A.D. 451 defined the doctrine of MONOPHYSITISM as a heresy, many Christians living in the Middle East felt they could not accept the Council's decision. Monophysitism, the doctrine that Christ has a single divine nature, was popular in Syria, and JACOB BARADAEUS organized the Monophysites living there into a church in the sixth century. The church members then adopted his name, calling themselves the Jacobites. Orthodox Christians viewed the Jacobite Church as heretical. The Jacobites survive to this day as the Syrian Orthodox Church (to be distinguished from the Eastern Orthodox Church, whose members are the descendants of the victors at Chalcedon).

See also: JACOB OF EDESSA.

JACOB OF EDESSA   A leader of the Monophysite community of JACOBITES in the Middle East at the end of the seventh century, Jacob of Edessa is regarded as the person who organized the doctrines of MONOPHYSITISM into a sophisticated and coherent system of belief.

JACQUES DE MOLAY   The grand Master of the KNIGHTS TEMPLAR when they were charged with heresy in 1307, Jacques de Molay was a friend of Philip IV, the French king, but the monarch was more interested in acquiring the Templar's wealth than in preserving his friendship. In order to destroy the Knights, Philip had them arrested, including the Grand Master. Gruesome tortures were used to extract confessions of diabolical and homosexual activities; Jacques confessed without being tortured, but he certainly was in fear of it. He was jailed for seven years while the rest of the Templar order in France was being dismantled. In 1314, Jacques was paraded in public, his confession proclaimed, and a sentence of life imprisonment announced. But the Templar leader loudly announced his innocence, as well as that of his Knights. King Philip immediately ordered him burned at the stake.

Cornelius JANSEN   This seventeenth century Catholic bishop was considered to be thoroughly orthodox during his lifetime; however, when his book was published two years after his death, a controversy that threatened the unity of the church erupted. The JANSENIST movement, which carried on his teachings, was declared a heresy.

Jansen was born in 1585 in Utrecht, Holland. His uncle was a well-known bishop, so it was natural that this intelligent child would become involved in religious studies. He studied at Louvain and Paris. At thirty-two, he was appointed director of a college at Louvain.

During Jansen's research he became fascinated by the writings of the fifth century theologian Augustine of Hippo. Jansen interpreted Augustine to be saying that people can perform good deeds only with the help of God's grace. When God grants His grace, it is irresistible; human beings cannot choose not to be good. Free will, in this view, seems to play a very small role in an individual's attaining salvation. During Augustine's lifetime, he fought against the PELAGIANS, who credited human will a much greater role than Jansen did. Jansen believed that, since Augustine's day, the Pelagian heresy had again affected the theology of the Catholic Church.

Two years before his death in 1638, the church hierarchy regarded Jansen as orthodox enough to be appointed bishop of Ypres. However, the theologian wrote a book on Augustine that criticized the contemporary church's position on human will and divine grace. This work, *The Augustinus*, was published in 1640. The resulting controversy continued well into the eighteenth century.

JANSENISM   The Jansenist movement took its name from seventeenth century theologian CORNELIUS JANSEN. At issue was the relationship between the human will and divine grace in the performance of good deeds. The roots of the controversy go back to the fifth century, when Augustine of Hippo fought against PELAGIUS over this matter. In 1640, the publication of Jansen's book on Augustine, *The Augustinus*, in which he suggests that the Catholic Church abandoned Augustine's position, reignited the discussion in France.

According to the Jansenists, people are so thoroughly corrupt that they are incapable of being good without God's help. When God grants His grace, human beings cannot resist it—they are then compelled to do good. There seems to be little role for free choice. Such a pessimistic view of humanity led to very strict religious practices, as well as accusations that the mainstream Catholic Church had become soft. In particular, the Jansenists attacked the Jesuits, who had become powerful in France.

Six years after the publication of Jansen's book, Blaise Pascal, the great French thinker, encountered Jansenist teachings. He was so impressed that he composed a work supporting Jansenism and criticizing the Jesuits. This document was seen as so dangerous to orthodoxy that it was listed in THE INDEX OF PROHIBITED BOOKS.

In 1653, Pope Innocent X condemned Jansenist doctrines as heretical. The Jansenists responded that the pope's understanding of their views was inadequate, and that they were rigorously orthodox. Eventually, they were forced to accept the papal ruling, but the movement continued to gather support.

In 1713, Jansenism was again condemned. This time, persecution followed, and many Jansenists left for Holland, where there was greater toleration than there was in France. A split occurred in the Dutch Catholic community over the issue, and in 1724 a splinter church, the Dutch OLD CATHOLICS, was formed. Jansenist ideas continued to circulate in French Catholic intellectual circles into the nineteenth century.

See also: QUIETISM.

JEHOVAH'S WITNESSES   From a small American sect that predicted the return of Christ in 1878, the Jehovah's Witnesses have expanded into a highly visible worldwide organization. Their doctrines are so unusual that mainstream Christian writers debate not only their orthodoxy, but also whether sect members should even be regarded as Christians. In fact, the position of this sect in some ways resembles the view of the ancient heresy known as ARIANISM.

CHARLES RUSSELL, the movement's founder, was inspired by the MILLE-RITE predictions that the end of the world would occur in the 1840s. Russell chose 1878 as the crucial year instead and managed to attract a following. The sect has maintained its promise by revising its date for Christ's appearance following each disappointment. Since 1878, the prediction has been made for 1914, 1918, 1925, 1941, and 1975. At present, the leadership is shy about committing to another precise date, but many members expect something big to happen at the close of the millennium. Some members have seriously considered the possibility that popular singer Michael Jackson (who once was a Jehovah's Witness himself) is the Archangel Michael in (very effective) disguise, preparing to inaugurate the end of history.

The Witnesses hold that only the name "Jehovah" (a sixteenth century English attempt to translate the Hebrew YHWH) is the correct way to refer to God. They reject the orthodox tenet that Christ is God; instead, like the Arians, they consider Him to be God's first creation. The life of JESUS on earth is taken to be an example of a perfectly moral life for all people to follow, but not a supernatural event of salvation, as orthodox Christians believe. The Devil is Christ's younger brother.

Jehovah's Witnesses also teach that the soul is merely the life force of the body and cannot exist separate from it. Therefore, the soul is destroyed at death. When Christ returns, the virtuous dead will be reanimated, to live forever on a heavenly earth. Sinners will be left in the state of death. A group of 144,000 Witnesses will live as spirits in heaven; some of these people are alive today, and Christ will return before the last of them has died.

In 1951, the Witnesses published their own translation of the Bible, known as the New World Translation. The text deviates in many places from all other versions and is based, according to the sect, on the superior scholarship of their translation committee. The special features of the New World Translation give support to the Witnesses' particular doctrines.

This sect is best known for its distribution of literature in public places. This act is the central religious duty of the Witnesses, and everyone is expected to devote much of their spare time to the practice. The Witnesses run one the world's largest and most advanced publishing operations, putting out hundreds of thousands of publications each day.

The power of the Jehovah's Witness organization is centralized and unchallengeable. Any deviation from obedience is punished by "disfellowship," or excommunication. This is a terrible price to pay because it means that the offender will be left rotting in the grave when the Lord returns.

Because the Jehovah's Witnesses are in principle opposed to nationalism and warfare, owing allegiance only to Jehovah, they have frequently been in conflict with governments who view them as unsupportive. From Russia to the United States, Witnesses have spent time in jail for refusing to accept government-imposed duties, and they have often been identified as prisoners of conscience by Amnesty International.

See also: JOSEPH RUTHERFORD

JESUS   During Jesus' lifetime, His teachings were so disagreeable to the powerful and privileged members of society that they had Him killed. In one of history's greater ironies, for most of the next 2,000 years, the controlling interests in Christian society violently suppressed any challenge to their authority—in the name of Jesus. As a heretic in His own time, and as a topic of controversy between conventional and alternative believers ever since, Jesus is the most important person in the story of heresy in Western culture.

In Palestine during the first century, ultimate power lay with the occupying army of Rome. Jesus, as portrayed in the New Testament, tried not to antagonize the police forces of the occupiers. He did not call for a political revolution, disobedience of secular laws, or refusal to pay taxes: "Render unto Caesar the things that are Caesar's" (Mark 12:17).

Jesus did, however, openly attack the religious powers of the day. The Sadducees and Pharisees are two Jewish groups frequently mentioned in the New Testament writings. The Sadducees represented the priestly aristocracy. They believed only in the written rules of the faith and rejected such ideas as the existence of angels and the eventual resurrection of the body, two concepts Jesus taught. The Sadducees controlled the great Temple in Jerusalem and must have been outraged when Jesus chased out the merchants and created a chaotic scene.

The Pharisees were Jews who had decided to work with the Roman rulers in order to quell disturbances and preserve the status quo. The Pharisees were different from the Sadducees in that they accepted the oral tradition of religious law, as well as the written tradition. Both groups believed completely in the importance of conforming to the fine points of lawful behavior. Jesus, on the other hand, did not elevate conformity above the sincere love of God and neighbor, and claimed that a person should violate the prescribed behaviors if they interfere with opportunities to act lovingly: "The Sabbath was made for Man, and not Man for the Sabbath" (Mark 2:27).

Jesus' scorn for the worship of rules and His hatred of injustice put Him at odds with a society whose unjust distribution of wealth and opportunity relied on mass obedience. In the words of historian Jaroslav Pelikan, Jesus was "the one who challenged every social system and called it to account before the judgment of God." Throughout its history, Western society has had a profoundly unjust structure, so Jesus in his role as challenger of convention is "one whom the first century—or any other century of human history—was bound to reject," Pelikan suggests. According to the broadest definition of heresy—the promotion of an unconventional way to view reality—Jesus was evidently a heretic in the context of His culture's conventions.

From the beginning, there were those who did not regard Jesus as His believing followers did. The writings of these critical observers were almost completely destroyed in the book burnings the orthodox Christians ordered after they converted Emperor Constantine in the fourth century. Historian Morton Smith has reconstructed the life of Jesus as seen by nonbelievers in first century Palestine:

> The son of a soldier named Panthera and a peasant woman married to a carpenter, Jesus was brought up in Nazareth as a carpenter, but left his home town and, after unknown adventures, arrived in Egypt where he became expert in magic and was tattooed with magical symbols or spells. Returning to Galilee he made himself famous by his magical feats, miracles he did by his control of demons. He thereby persuaded the masses that he was the Jewish Messiah and/or the son of a god. Although he pretended to follow Jewish customs, he formed a small circle of intimate disciples whom he taught to despise the Jewish Law and to practice magic. These he bound together and to himself by ties of "love", meaning sexual promiscuity, and by participation in the most awful magical rites, including cannibalism—they had some sort of ritual meal in which they ate human flesh and drank blood. . . . Pilate had him crucified, but this did not put an end to the evil. His followers stole his body from the grave, claimed he had risen from the dead, and, as a secret society, perpetuated his practices.

Smith has suggested that the gospels of the New Testament were written largely in response to such stories, in an attempt to answer and discredit them. Twenty centuries later, it is difficult to disentangle the authentic details of Jesus' life from the propaganda launched by believers and nonbelievers.

Even within the earliest communities of Christian believers, there was disagreement concerning the life and work of Jesus. The group that was to become the orthodox Catholic Church argued that Jesus had lived, died, and was resurrected as a real human being with a physical body. After making a few appearances following His resurrection, He departed for heaven, leaving His message with His apostles—including a promise that He would return soon.

Other Christian groups disagreed. These parties, regarded as branches of the movement called GNOSTICISM, reported that Jesus continued to appear to them, bringing new teachings. After the resurrection, Jesus had not walked the earth in a physical body but in a purely spiritual form. Some Gnostic teachers propounded the doctrine of DOCETISM, that even during His lifetime, Jesus did not possess a material body but appeared as a sort of ghostly projection.

The orthodox version implied that only the apostles' direct successors, the priests and bishops, possessed the way to salvation because they had preserved its transmission by Jesus during His brief time on earth. Those who were not priests could be saved only by obeying the priestly doctrines. The Gnostic Jesus did not rely merely on frozen memories of His old teachings. As a result, the Gnostics did not feel they had to obey priests to obtain salvation.

The hierarchy of the orthodox church, reinforced by their image of Jesus, proved more politically effective than the loosely organized Gnostic movement. The Catholics succeeded in gaining control of the Roman imperial government. The orthodox proceeded to use their new powers to suppress those who disagreed with their views and were fairly successful right up to the beginning of the Reformation in the sixteenth century.

During the period following its political triumph, the Catholic Church struggled to hammer out the details of its doctrines concerning Jesus. These debates, which fanned passions not just among theologians but also among ordinary believers, became sharply focused in two meetings, the FIRST COUNCIL OF NICAEA (325) and the COUNCIL OF CHALCEDON (451).

The teachings of a popular figure named ARIUS partly triggered the convention at Nicaea. Arius believed that Jesus Christ was not God but rather was a creation of God—a powerful supernatural being like an angel. The Council condemned the Arian image of Jesus Christ as heretical and proclaimed the doctrine of the Trinity. God was three Persons, Father, Son, and Holy Spirit, with one essential substance.

The formula of the Trinity left the relationship between the "Son" who is fully God and the human being named Jesus unclear. There were many opinions on this relationship. The meeting at Chalcedon declared all of these views except one to be heretical.

The doctrine of ADOPTIONISM, believed by such well-known Christian teachers as PAUL OF SAMOSATA, held that Jesus began His existence as a mere human being. At some point in His life (perhaps at His baptism), Jesus was "adopted" by God, almost in the manner in which demons were believed to possess people. The Adoptionists apparently did not agree that the divine Person known as the Son (part of the Trinity) adopted Jesus; rather, God as a unity did. The notion that God possessed Jesus, as opposed to the idea that Jesus Christ is the divine Son of the Trinity, was rejected by orthodoxy as heretical.

APOLLINARIS was another Christian teacher who attempted to be orthodox (he agreed with the Council of Nicaea's doctrines), but who was condemned for his view on Jesus' human and divine aspects. Apollinaris taught that Jesus had a human body and soul, but that his mind was divine, not human. APOLLINARIANISM was banned from the Roman Empire in 388.

The doctrine proclaimed at Chalcedon argued that Jesus Christ was fully divine and fully human at the same time. If Jesus was not completely God, He would not have the divine power to save human beings from damnation. But if Jesus was not completely human, his crucifixion would not serve as a sacrifice that earned forgiveness for the sins of humanity. The creed of Chalcedon indicates that the human mind cannot solve the mystery of how one person could have these two seemingly incompatible natures; to attempt to do so surely leads to heresy.

On the basis of the formulation of Chalcedon, the orthodox authorities condemned two other understandings of Jesus. The school of MONOPHYSITISM, according to the orthodox, did not distinguish clearly enough between the divine and human natures of Christ and fell into the trap of presenting Jesus as less than fully human. The Monophysite view of Jesus continued to prevail in Armenia, Syria, Palestine, and Egypt. Some historians believe that the inability of the orthodox forces in Byzantium and Rome to become reconciled with the Monophysites so weakened Christian culture in the eastern Mediterranean region that it made possible the rapid spread of Islam throughout the area following Mohammed's death in the seventh century.

Another position was associated with the name of the prominent teacher NESTORIUS. The orthodox accused the Nestorians of separating the two natures too much, leading to a fragmentation of Christ into two distinct persons. The Nestorian Church remained strong in Persia and even established communities in India and China. Monophysites and Nestorians continue to live in the Middle East today.

Another outbreak of Adoptionism occurred in Spain during the eighth century. Unlike the adoptionist beliefs that the ancient church suppressed, SPANISH ADOPTIONISM held that the human Jesus was adopted by the Son, one of the persons of the Trinity. Therefore, this doctrine was orthodox in its version of the Trinity but heretical in its depiction of Christ's two natures.

The orthodox image of Jesus as one person with two complete natures continued as official Roman Catholic doctrine and was accepted by the major schools of the Protestant Reformation. However, the convention-challenging aspects of Jesus' life continued to appeal to unorthodox believers, who criticized conventional authorities for converting the radical Jesus into a standard of conformity.

During the later Middle Ages in Europe, the Catholic Church had grown immensely rich. Church officials often enjoyed lives of luxury and did not practice the moral life they preached. The glaring unfairness of a wealthy church functioning comfortably within an often brutal and unfair feudal system caused some people to question whether this sort of Christianity was what Jesus really had in mind.

For example, ARNOLD OF BRESCIA, a disciple of the great twelfth century theologian PETER ABELARD, concluded that the Catholic Church with all its wealth could not represent the spiritual message of Jesus, a man who owned nothing. Had Jesus not advised that "If you would be perfect, go and sell everything you have, and give to the poor" (Matthew 19:21)? Arnold succeeded in rousing the masses in Rome and forced Pope Eugene II to leave town. Hadrian IV, Eugene's successor, captured Arnold and had him beheaded for rebellion.

The medieval heretical sect called the WALDENSIANS, or the "Poor Men of Lyons," also revered the ideal of Jesus' voluntary poverty. The founder of the movement, WALDO, renounced all his possessions. Francis of Assisi, the great Catholic saint who managed not to fall afoul of the orthodox authorities, did the same. However, a group within the Franciscan order founded by Francis insisted that poverty was an ideal condition for a person because Jesus and the apostles had been poor. Obviously, the teaching of these SPIRITUAL FRANCISCANS tended to undermine the credibility of the fabulously wealthy pope as the guardian of Christ's teaching. In 1323, Pope John XXII declared the notion that Jesus and the apostles had practiced voluntary poverty heretical.

Within the Protestant Reformation, mainstream and alternative doctrines concerning Jesus quickly sprang up. In contrast to the definers of orthodox Protestantism, such as Martin Luther and John Calvin, radical teachers rejected the picture of Christ devised by the ancient church councils. Some radicals, such as MENNO SIMONS (founder of the Mennonite Church) and KASPAR SCHWENKFELD (founder of the Schwenkfelder Church), argued that Jesus was so holy that He could not have had a body made of normal human tissue. Rather than acquiring His body from His mother, they claimed that Christ's body was composed of a supernatural substance, "heavenly flesh."

Other Protestant radicals, including MICHAEL SERVETUS, an early teacher of UNITARIANISM, taught that God is a unity, not a trinity, and that, as such, Christ was not identical with God. Rather, Christ literally was the Son of God: Jesus' body was formed in heaven and later descended to earth. Calvin arranged Servetus's entrapment and public burning on account of this heretical doctrine.

With the breakup of the Catholic power monopoly in Europe, the use of ideas about Christ to support traditionally privileged groups lessened. The ancient image of Jesus as moral challenger of the status quo gained in popularity. The example of Jesus as a heretic in His own time inspired many of the social revolutionaries whose efforts led to the official abolition of slavery in the West (unofficially, it continues in various locations).

Many revered figures in recent times who have spoken out for justice on behalf of the oppressed have been motivated by the image of the nonconformist Jesus. Leo Tolstoy, Mahatma Gandhi, and Martin Luther King are well-known examples. The modern Roman Catholic movement called liberation theology, still popular today in Latin America, argues that Jesus' vision of social inequality is consistent with Karl Marx's view of society and his call for revolutionary change.

Today, few Christians know the details of the traditional orthodox picture of Jesus. Many believers, both Catholic and Protestant, now consider Jesus to be an "inspired man" or someone who was "guided by God," rather than as someone who was literally God. Such beliefs could have brought them to a flaming death at the stake for heresy just a few centuries ago.

JOACHIM OF FIORE   An Italian visionary who rose to prominence toward the end of the twelfth century, Joachim of Fiore was not considered to be a heretic during his lifetime. However, unorthodox thinkers seized his radical ideas about history during the following century and inspired heretics of various sorts into the 1800s.

Joachim was born around 1132. As a young man, he had a mystical experience that prompted him to follow the religious life. He made a pilgrimage to the Holy Land and then became a monk. In 1177, he was appointed abbot of a monastery. His exploration of mystical domains interfered with his practical duties as a monastic administrator. He soon resigned and founded a monastery of his own, in which he devoted himself to spiritual exercises and writing.

Until Joachim's time, orthodox Christians had tended to divide history into two phases that corresponded to the two main components of the Bible. In the first, the Old Testament phase, God's people were ruled by Jewish law; in the second phase, associated with the New Testament, Christ's followers obeyed the gospel message and awaited their Savior's return at the end of history. Joachim argued instead that humanity's time on earth has three ages, reflecting the structure of the Trinity. The first two ages, represented by the Father and the Son, correspond to the phases of law and gospel noted above. During the third age, the Holy Spirit would be the dominant principle.

Joachim taught that the third age was about to begin. During the reign of the Holy Spirit, he predicted, the Catholic Church would change from a wealthy institution organized in a hierarchy of power into a church of poor monks who would lead the masses into a spiritual rebirth. At the head of this renewed church would be an "angel pope." He would battle the Antichrist, who would manifest in the guise of a secular leader.

The Italian prophet's views had parallels in other unorthodox sources. Joachim's idea of a continuous spiritualization of humanity under the influence of the Holy Spirit resembled the teachings of the ancient MONTANIST heretics. Joachim's notion that an emphasis on poverty should replace the church's interest in material power and wealth was shared by the contemporary heresy of WALDENSIANISM. Unlike the Waldensians, however, Joachim did not want to eliminate the church hierarchy's leadership role, but rather to replace wealthy bishops with poor monks.

Joachim's dramatic prophecies caused great excitement. "The end of the age" would be, in a sense, "the end of the world," and those who took the prophet's visions seriously watched for signs of revolutionary change. The authorities had a mixed reaction to Joachim's work. They approved of his strictly orthodox beliefs about God and Christ and of his hostility toward the Waldensian heretics. But, they warned, his statement that the present order would soon be replaced, could inspire those who opposed the status quo to assist the new age into being by staging a revolution.

The Fourth Lateran Council met in 1215, thirteen years after Joachim's death. While the prophet himself was not declared a heretic, some of his less conventional notions were condemned as unorthodox by Catholic officials. However, the fascination with Joachim's vision of history continued. The radical branch of the Franciscan movement, the SPIRITUAL FRANCISCANS, adopted the prophet's doctrines; some of them believed that Joachim's writings comprised the sacred scripture of the new age and that the Franciscans themselves were the beginning of the Church of the Holy Spirit. Another important late medieval figure, the poet Dante, was an admirer of Joachim. Right up to the nineteenth century, when the heretical French prophet EUGENE VINTRAS announced the commencement of the third age, Joachim's ideas fascinated Christians who reflected on the meaning of history.

See also: ALEISTER CROWLEY.

JOAN OF ARC   Known by various names, including Jehanne, La Pucelle, and the Maid of Orleans, Joan of Arc is one of the best-known figures in late medieval history. Contrary to popular belief, she was not executed for witchcraft, but for heresy. Joan was born in 1412 in the village of Domremy in eastern France, the child of peasants. When she was three, the smoldering Hundred Years' War between England and

France broke out again; England's King Henry V invaded and within a few years had conquered much of northern France. In 1422, the two warring monarchs, Henry of England and Charles VI of France, died. Henry VI, the English king's infant son, was declared the ruler of France; French forces rallied around Charles's son, the Dauphin.

This political turmoil probably had little direct impact on Joan's childhood. She lived far from any military activity and seems to have led a normal early life. But everything changed for Joan in 1425 when she was thirteen. During that year, she began to have visits from mysterious beings who manifested themselves as a brilliant light and were accompanied by voices. These voices told the girl that they were Saint Catherine, Saint Gabriel, Saint Marguerite, and Saint Michael—and that she had been chosen for a great task: to lead the French people in driving the English out of France.

Joan's visions and voices were strange occurrences, but they were not symptoms of psychosis. Rather than displaying the inability to function effectively that usually occurs with severe mental disorders, Joan acted as if inspired. When the voices issued the preposterous instruction that she, a seventeen-year-old peasant girl, should go to save the city of Orleans, then under siege by English troops, she acted decisively. First, she convinced a local military commander to provide her with a horse and guard, so that she could travel to meet with Charles, the Dauphin. When Joan arrived at his court, the Dauphin donned a disguise and hid among his courtiers. She recognized him immediately although they had never met before. Joan then told him intimate details of his life, which the voices had conveyed to her. Charles was so impressed that she was granted command of an army to fight the English at Orleans.

As Joan's guiding saints predicted, the young visionary succeeded in freeing the city. The French forces under Joan pursued the retreating English troops and liberated several more towns. Later that year, when the Dauphin was crowned King Charles VII the amazing teenager was at his side, fulfilling another of the voices' prophecies.

The following year, Joan's luck turned. While attempting to free the besieged city of Compiegne, she was captured by Burgundians. Although these soldiers were allies of the English, they were willing to sell the famous visionary to the highest bidder. An offer came from the English, who felt her death would demoralize their opponents. No ransom came from the French; King Charles had become fascinated by a shepherd boy who claimed to be a prophet and abandoned Joan to her fate.

The following year, she was subjected to a series of hearings and interrogations leading up to her trial. The process was managed by the bishop of Beauvais and the Inquisitor General of France, both English sympathizers. The charges were sorcery and heresy; she was accused of being "a soothsayer, an idolater, an invoker of devils, a blasphemer against God and his saints." The trial's conclusion, prearranged for political purposes, was never in doubt.

Joan gave an impressive performance. Confronted with complicated theological questions, a wrong answer to which would have led to an immediate conviction for heresy, she responded with a sophistication that seemed incredible for an uneducated peasant. She steadfastly denied that her voices were demonic and rejected the claim that she produced them by eating the narcotic root of the mandrake. Nonetheless, she would not recognize the authority of the bishops over that of her saintly voices. She was convicted as a heretic for this insolence. The charge of sorcery was dismissed, but it was now unnecessary: the penalty for unrepentant heresy was death.

Joan briefly delayed her fate by recanting but again changed her mind and retracted her confession. On May 30, 1431, Joan was publicly burned at the stake. The authorities wished to destroy her mystique and prevent any rumors of last-minute supernatural rescue that could feed the hopes of the French cause. When her clothes had burned off, the executioner was instructed to reduce the flames to enable the spectators to view "all the secrets which can or should be in a woman." After she died, her remains were thrown in a river, so that no one could take a bone as a sacred relic.

As it happened, the French triumphed; less than twenty years after Joan's death, the English had been virtually driven from France. Joan also triumphed in a way. In 1456, at a retrial held by the victorious French, she was declared innocent. In 1920, Pope Benedict XV declared Joan of Arc a saint.

JOHN OF WESEL   John of Wesel was the subject of one of the last major heresy trials before the Protestant Reformation. Born in 1400, he became a monk of the Augustinian order. He achieved fame as a preacher in the German towns of Mainz and Worms. John came to the attention of the INQUISITION for his rejection of any religious doctrine that could not be found in the New Testament—which meant most of Roman Catholic tradition. In particular, John attacked the pope's practice of granting indulgences (forgiveness of sins), in return for money. His position was similar to that of the Bohemian reformer JAN HUS, who had been executed earlier in the century, and was probably influenced by Hus's teachings.

In 1477, John was deposed for heresy. Under interrogation, he agreed to recant his own views. John was sentenced to life in prison, and his writings were burned. He died in 1481. Thirty-six years later, John's fellow German, Martin Luther, initiated the Reformation, proclaiming ideas very similar to those for which John had been condemned.

JOHN SCOTUS ERIGENA   During the so-called "Dark Ages" between the collapse of the ancient world and the flowering of the later medieval period, higher learning was rarely seen in Europe. John Scotus Erigena, who lived during the ninth century, was one of the few great thinkers of his age. However, rational thought was not always valued in the Dark Ages: Erigena's work was repeatedly condemned during and after his lifetime.

Erigena was born in Ireland around A.D. 810 (his name means "John the Irishman"). Educated in one of the monasteries that served to keep learning alive during this relatively uncultured time, he later moved to France where he became a teacher. He was one of the most learned people in Europe, displaying fluency in Greek and Latin, as well as a familiarity with classical literature in both languages.

Erigena became the favorite philosopher of King Charles the Bald and spent a great deal of time at the king's court. With Charles's protection, the Irishman was able to enter into the great debates of the day with little fear of being physically punished by his opponents (unlike his contemporary GOTTSCHALK, for example, who was whipped and imprisoned on more than one occasion for stating unconventional ideas). Because of the unorthodoxy of his opinions, however, some leading churchmen accused him of heresy.

The brilliance of the ancient pagan philosophers inspired Erigena; he was also a devout Christian. One of his philosophical projects was to unite the notion that the universe was the creation of God (the view of mainstream Christianity) with the doctrine that the world emanates from and returns to God (a belief of pagan thinkers and the followers of GNOSTICISM). According to Erigena, reality is divided into four parts: that which creates and is not created (God as the beginning of all); that which creates and is created (the world of pure ideas); that which is created but does not create (the world of the senses); and that which is not created nor creates (God as the end of all). Thus, reality begins and ends in God. This depiction of the world was criticized because it seemed to be based more on a desire for logical neatness than on anything to be found in the Bible.

The philosopher expressed his opinions about the two major theological battles of the day: the nature of the mass and predestination. Concerning the mass, Erigena expressed the view that the bread and wine are not literally transformed into Christ's flesh and blood, but rather that the ordinary substances are related to Christ in a symbolic way. As Erigena explained, when the communion wafer of bread is consumed, Christ is eaten "mentally, not dentally." Orthodoxy rejected Erigena's view of the mass in favor of the more literal position of Radbertus.

King Charles asked Erigena to become involved in the stormy debate Gottschalk triggered regarding predestination; this centered on the idea that God had chosen who would be saved and who would be damned before they were created. Erigena rejected the idea on logical grounds and even went so far as to deny the existence of hell. He was accused of heresy, not only because he dismissed a doctrine that the revered Augustine of Hippo taught, but also because he relied on rationality rather than scripture.

After Erigena's death around 877, his writings on the mass were lost. His creationist/emanationist version of the universe was taken up in the early thirteenth century by some of the followers of AMALRIC OF BENA. Unlike Erigena, these Christians had no earthly ruler to protect them; they were burned at the stake in 1210.

See also: RATRAMNUS.

JOVINIAN   This Catholic monk, who lived at the beginning of the fifth century, claimed that married people could be as holy as those who abstained from marriage. This statement enraged some of the leading figures within the church, who favored celibacy. As a result, the pope condemned Jovinian as a heretic.

During his early years, Jovinian himself believed that indulging in the pleasures of the flesh, such as the enjoyment of food and sex, prevented a person's salvation. He practiced an austere lifestyle involving avoidance of contact with women and good food, but he did not notice any improvement in his sense of holiness. As his doubts grew, Jovinian studied the Bible and concluded that the scripture, in fact, taught that sexuality within marriage was completely acceptable to God. Furthermore, he concluded that abstaining from food was no holier than eating, if one was grateful to God for the meal.

During this period, the church was increasingly influenced by ascetic teachers, such as Ambrose, Augustine, and Jerome. According to these men, human beings are so corrupt that such pleasures as good food and sex are almost sure to lead them into sin. They argued that it was better to minimize or avoid these delights altogether whenever possible. Jerome bluntly proclaimed that "all sexual intercourse is unclean," while Augustine railed against the "diabolical excitement of the genitals." Some Christians believed that the position of the ascetics was extreme and rallied around Jovinian. Jerome said that Jovinian's teaching was "the hissing of the old serpent; by counsel such as this, the dragon drove man from Paradise." Jerome was moved to compose a work called *Against Jovinian*, which emphasized the superiority of virginity over marriage.

Jovinian's attitude toward humanity was optimistic. He believed that the human will was strong enough to enjoy decent pleasures without tumbling headlong into mortal sin. In its confident view of the will, Jovinian's doctrine resembled the contemporary heretical movement called PELAGIANISM, which held that people have the ability to live a moral life if they choose to do so. Augustine, who became the Pelagians' archenemy, believed that such votes of confidence in human willpower tended to undermine the power of the church. If the human will is strong enough to earn salvation without outside help, then people do not need to bother following the instructions of priests. Opposed to this idea, Augustine argued that the will is hopelessly corrupted by original sin. No one is strong enough to resist temptation and earn salvation on his or her own. Therefore, the spiritual aid given to Christians who obey the proclamations of the church hierarchy is crucial.

Under the influence of the ascetics, Pope Siricius excommunicated Jovinian for heresy. Jovinian died around A.D. 405. Despite his admiration for marriage, he had chosen to remain celibate throughout his life. Ambrose, Augustine, and Jerome, his chief opponents, were all proclaimed saints of the Catholic Church. The attitudes shared by these saints—hostility toward sexuality, and lack of confidence in the human will—became important features in the Christian world view of the Middle Ages and persist in some minds to the present day.

JULIAN OF ECLANUM   This fifth century Italian bishop was a leading defender of the heretical movement known as PELAGIANISM. Julian of Eclanum engaged in a written debate with the great theologian Augustine of Hippo that lasted for many years. At stake, in the words of religious scholar Elaine Pagels, was "the nature of nature." The Catholic authorities concluded that Augustine won the debate, thus permitting Augustine's understanding of nature to define the Western world view of the Middle Ages.

Julian was born around A.D. 386. He was active in the church and was appointed bishop of the Italian town of Eclanum in 416. At that time, the Pelagian controversy was raging. Theologian PELAGIUS had claimed that humans have free will and, therefore, can choose to earn their spiritual salvation through morally perfect behavior. Augustine was opposed to this position. According to Augustine, Adam's disobedience in the Garden of Eden had been punished by weakening the human will to the point that it was unable to resist sinning. Therefore, salvation cannot be earned; God in His mercy grants salvation to those He selects, even though they do not deserve it.

The new bishop of Eclanum became convinced that Augustine was wrong. When Pope Zosimus asked Julian to sign a document condemning Pelagius as a heretic, he refused. As a result, he was denounced and removed from office. Julian wrote and traveled, defending the orthodoxy of the Pelagian view for the rest of his life.

In his attacks on Augustine, Julian showed himself to be a sophisticated philosopher. He rejected the notion that all of humanity is punished for Adam's sin, doubting that God would harm everyone in response to the disobedience of one man. Rather, Adam was simply a bad example. Adam chose to do evil, but people can choose to do good.

Augustine believed that Adam's sin had corrupted not only humanity, but the entire universe. The natural world itself was now filled with suffering and evil in order to torment sinful humans throughout the course of life. In particular, death was a punishment for original sin. Julian disagreed. He believed that human choices could be good or evil, but that they do not control nature, including death. He concluded that "what is natural cannot be called evil." Julian claimed that evil behavior did not necessarily cause *physical* death, but *spiritual* death—the misery of being far from God.

Julian also objected to Augustine's opinion that sexual impulses were completely corrupt. Julian regarded sexual desire as "vital fire," a potentially life-enhancing part of human life if expressed within the boundaries of Christian marriage. Augustine mocked Julian's view that sexuality could be channeled by virtuous intentions, using the image of an uncontrollable erection: "Behold the 'vital fire' which does not obey the soul's decision, but, for the most part, rises up against the soul's desire in disorderly and ugly movements."

Although Julian's arguments in favor of the innocence of nature were not philosophically weaker than those of Augustine, the opinions of the latter prevailed. Elaine Pagels suggested that Augustine's portrayal of a human will too corrupt to save itself made more sense to the leaders of the Catholic Church, who were interested in promoting the belief that Christians needed the assistance of the bishops in order to be saved from hell. The view of Julian and other Pelagians that everyone has the power to choose good for themselves, without the aid of the church leaders, could be taken to support self-reliance rather than obedience.

Julian continued to journey widely to promote his views until his death in A.D. 454. The influence of Augustine within the church was such that he rarely found a friendly audience. Augustine's written responses to Julian's arguments fill six volumes. The darker vision of nature Augustine offered was adopted as the view of orthodox Christians, and his hostility toward nature, sex, and death became persistent themes in the history of the West.

JULIAN OF HALICARNASSUS   This bishop founded a radical branch of MONOPHYSITISM, the belief that Christ has a single nature. Orthodox Christians insisted that Christ has two natures and regarded any disagreement on this point as heresy. Julian became the bishop of Halicarnassus (a town in what is today western Turkey) during the reign of Emperor Anastasius in the early sixth century. Anastasius was a protector of Monophysites against persecution by the Catholic authorities. Justin I, Anastasius's successor, was not kindly disposed toward heretics; when he became emperor in 518, Julian was condemned and fled to Egypt. There, he started a group called the APHTHARTODOCETAE, who taught that Jesus did not have an ordinary human nature, but an indestructible one; although Christ had suffered voluntarily, it was not part of His *nature* to suffer, according to Julian.

JULIAN THE APOSTATE   The emperor of the Roman Empire from A.D. 361 to 363, Julian is known as "the Apostate" because he committed the sin of APOSTASY, or rejecting Christianity. Julian's importance lies in two areas: He was the last pagan emperor, who attempted to revive the idea of a world that tolerated all religious views; and he refused to give military support to any religious group. This policy enabled the Catholic Christians, who had lost recent political battles against the ARIAN heretics, to regroup.

Julian was the nephew of Emperor Constantine, the man who first legalized and promoted Christianity. When Julian was young, he was exposed to both pagan and Christian traditions. EUSEBIUS OF NICOMEDIA, the leading figure in the Arian movement, taught him an unorthodox version of Christianity. Julian, however, was not attracted to any Christian view; he preferred the ancient pagan understanding of the world.

Before Julian's assumption of imperial power, two co-emperors, Constans and CONSTANTIUS II had ruled the empire for a time. Constans had supported the Catholics in their battle for a monopoly on Christian thought, whereas Constantius had backed the Arians. The result was social turmoil, as well as a continually shifting balance of power among the Christian factions. At times, Christian mobs slaughtered those they declared to be heretics. Julian believed that the Roman Empire would be better served by removing imperial support for the Christians and proclaiming religious toleration throughout the empire.

When Julian became emperor, he summoned representatives of the various Christian groups to his palace. He said that everyone who had been exiled for religious reasons was now free to return home, and that the police powers of the Roman state would neither support nor tolerate violence among Christian factions. In essence, everybody was free to believe whatever they wished. Julian noted that before his reign: "Many whole communities of so-called heretics were actually butchered, as at Samosata, and Cyzicus in Paphlagonia, Bithynia and Galatia, and among many other tribes villages were sacked and destroyed; whereas in my time exile has been ended and property restored."

The Christian community's response to Julian's pronouncements was mixed. Many Christian leaders viewed Julian as a demon. They were keen to secure sole control over the definition of Christian belief, and the emperor's banning of violence from the arena of debate made this goal more difficult to achieve. Other Christians joined Julian in rejecting the church and returned to pagan practices. One bishop told Julian that he had always been a sunworshipper, but he had done so in secret because of the imperial favor the Christians formerly enjoyed.

In order to strengthen the resurgence of PAGANISM, which had been eroded during the preceding decades, Julian banned Christians from public teaching and elevated pagans to high government offices. He observed that Christianity's increasing popularity among common people was based in part on the operation of Christian charities, which provided aid to the poor and sick. Julian sponsored the development of pagan charities as a counterbalance.

Julian himself was a devotee of THEURGY, the last major school of pagan thought. Theurgy claimed to offer people the means to have direct access to the gods and their wisdom, and even to achieve union with divine beings. Julian encouraged paganism to organize itself into a hierarchy of priests in imitation of the Christian Church because he was impressed by the effectiveness of the church in spreading its views.

The pagan revival under Julian was short-lived. After his sudden death in battle, he was succeeded as emperor by Jovian, a devout Catholic. Paganism was again suppressed and remained so until the twentieth century. The Jews, many of whom had welcomed the tolerance of religious diversity under Julian, found themselves viewed as allies of the "demonic" emperor and subject to increasing persecution at the hands of Catholics.

JULIANUS THE CHALDEAN   The founder of THEURGY, the last important school of pagan spirituality, Julianus the Chaldean, little is known for certain about life. He lived in the latter part of the second century, when he composed a text called THE CHALDEAN ORACLES. Theurgy was promoted as an alternative to Christianity during the reign of JULIAN THE APOSTATE in the fourth century and was suppressed by the Catholics when they came to power.

JUMPERS   Jumpers is a variant name for the SHAKERS.

KABBALAH   This word derives from Hebrew roots meaning "that which is received," or "tradition." Kabbalah is the central tradition of Jewish mysticism. The doctrines and practices of the Kabbalah have been developed and preserved over the past 2,000 years and have constituted one of the most important esoteric systems in Western culture.

Throughout the Kabbalah's long history, it has been tolerated uneasily, if at all, by orthodox Judaism. The Kabbalists themselves have almost always held that they were orthodox; at times, they argued that they alone knew the true meaning of the orthodox tradition. Nonetheless, several features of Kabbalistic thought have provoked repeated charges of heresy. For instance, the Kabbalah claims to possess knowledge concerning the inner structure of God. Most commonly, the Kabbalists' God is conceived as manifesting in ten *sefiroth*, or stages. Some orthodox observers have accused the Kabbalists of believing in ten gods rather than one. (Similar problems arose for early Christians as they struggled to reconcile their belief in one God with their doctrine of the Trinity).

Other orthodox concerns have centered on the Kabbalistic doctrine of emanation. The sefiroth are said to manifest as emanations of God. Some kabbalists went further, claiming that the universe itself is a divine emanation. Mainstream Judaism insists on maintaining a strict separation between the Creator and His creation—a separation that seems blurred in the notion of an emanated, rather than created, universe.

A similar problem arises in the relationship between the Kabbalists and God. All Kabbalists wished to be closer to God. While most claimed that they yearned for a nearness or communion with God, some went further and spoke of actual union with the divine. The notion that a mere human could become completely identified with God is a heresy in both Judaism and Christianity.

Many orthodox thinkers, even those who did not regard the Kabbalah as heresy, feared that it could easily mislead people into dangerously inflated ideas about themselves. These fears are borne out by history. Several of the most notorious "false messiahs" in Jewish history, such as ABRAHAM ABULAFIA, SHABBATAI ZEVI, and JACOB FRANK, were Kabbalists.

The main claim of the Kabbalah is that the Jewish tradition possesses a secret knowledge concerning the nature of God. This knowledge is contained, in hidden form, within the sacred scriptures. It may also be obtained through certain esoteric practices. Many Kabbalists regarded the doctrine of the ten sefiroth, which developed over many centuries, as a description of the process by which God manifested Himself out of "infinite nothingness" into conceivable form. The sefiroth have been interpreted as aspects or qualities of the deity. The most popular depiction of the sefiroth shows them as ten circles, arranged on a diagram known as the "Tree of Life." Many other arrangements of the sefiroth are also found in the Kabbalistic literature.

After emanating His ten holy aspects, God proceeded to make the world and humanity. Because God was said to have created people in His image, Kabbalists held that the sefiroth could also be seen as a diagram of human beings.

In addition to studying the mysteries of the sefiroth, Kabbalists paid great attention to the mysteries of words and numbers. The twenty-two letters of the Hebrew alphabet and the various names of God composed of them were thought to contain divine power. Each letter corresponded to a number. By utilizing these correspondences, one could convert words and phrases in scripture to numbers; they could be replaced by other words and phrases with the same numerical equivalence, which supposedly gave the hidden meanings of the passages.

The ideas of the Kabbalah were employed in a variety of ways. Many Kabbalists were mainly interested in increasing their intellectual understanding of God and studied the texts in a speculative manner. Other Kabbalists, however, wished for a direct approach or union with the divine and invented a rich legacy of meditation practices to this end. Yet others attempted to use Kabbalistic knowledge to bring themselves worldly benefits; these people used the Kabbalistic images and words of power in their magical rituals.

The first stirrings of what would become the Kabbalah can be traced to the first centuries A.D. At that time, there was great popular interest in achieving direct contact with divine realities, rather than simply taking such matters on faith. Jewish mystical speculations and practices centered on two themes: the creation of the world, as portrayed in the Book of Genesis, and the prophet Ezekiel's vision of God's throne-chariot. Ancient Judaism banned public discussion of either theme, but groups met privately to ponder these mysteries. The tradition of MERKABAH MYSTICISM developed elaborate meditations that gave the practitioner visions of heaven. The tradition that focused on creation produced a small book called SEFER YETZIRAH. This text introduced the concept of the sefiroth, as well as the idea that the letters of the Hebrew alphabet are mystical forces.

Both of these ancient mystical traditions inspired the later Kabbalists. In addition, notions from ancient GNOSTIC and pagan sources entered the elaborate Kabbalistic descriptions regarding the structure of God. The old esoteric traditions were partially preserved in European Jewish communities. In the early twelfth century, a German group called the Hasidim utilized the ideas of ancient mysticism to analyze sacred texts for hidden meanings. It is likely that fragments of Hasidic writings comprised the first book of classical Kabbalah, *Sefer ha-Bahir*, or *Book of Brilliance*. This text, which appeared in Provence around 1175, stimulated a "golden age" of Kabbalah in southern France and Spain during the next few centuries. The sefirothic Tree of Life is first mentioned in *Bahir*, although the diagram did not reach its typical form until the fourteenth century. The most important fruit of this golden age is

ZOHAR, a massive synthesis of Kabbalistic concepts that was written in the late thirteenth century. Ever since, *Zohar* has remained the key text of the tradition.

In 1492, following the final departure from Spain of the Moslems (who had provided a tolerant environment within which Jewish culture could flourish), the victorious Christians expelled all Jews. The Spanish Kabbalists were scattered around the Mediterranean region and then settled mainly in Italy and Palestine. During the next several decades, the Palestinian town of Safed became the center of Kabbalistic creativity. In particular, ISAAC LURIA reinterpreted *Zohar* in a radically new way. Lurianic Kabbalah emphasized the importance of every single human act in contributing to the restoration of perfection to the universe. Luria's ideas produced two main effects: the gradual diffusion of Kabbalistic thought among the Jewish masses, and the raising of expectations concerning the imminent appearance of a Messiah.

The trauma inflicted on the Jewish world by the rapid rise and fall of Shabbatai Zevi in the 1600s caused many to condemn the Kabbalah as a danger to Judaism. Nevertheless, in the following century, a movement known as Hasidism (not to be confused with the Hasidism of medieval Germany) became popular in eastern Europe. The Hasidic teachings were based on Luria and conveyed simple meditations that were intended to aid the uneducated masses achieve nearness to God.

In the nineteenth century, Jewish interest in Kabbalah generally declined. The more rationalistic Jewish writers viewed the Kabbalah as a body of superstition that had oppressed Hebrew culture. In the twentieth century, a yearning for a nonrational closeness to God has again awakened the interest of many Jews in their Kabbalistic heritage.

The Kabbalah became an important stimulus to non-Jewish occult thought. In the late fifteenth century, Florentine scholar GIOVANNI PICO DELLA MIRANDOLA discovered the Kabbalah and believed that it could be used to unveil the mysteries of Christianity. This idea led to the development of a Christianized Kabbalah, generally known as CABALA, which included metaphysical, mystical, and magical applications. One of the main branches of modern occultism, usually labeled QABALAH, was inspired by the work of the Cabalists.

KARBEAS   A leader of the PAULICIAN heretics during the ninth century, Karbeas had been an officer in the Byzantine Army. During this period, Paulician communities on the border between Byzantine and Moslem-held territories were subjected to vicious persecution. Karbeas's father was executed by the Byzantines for his Paulician beliefs, and Karbeas became a bitter foe of Byzantium. He convinced the Paulicians, most of whom were traditionally pacifists, to become more militant.

Karbeas also led the Paulicians to found their own independent state. He recruited the support of the Moslems, on the understanding that Paulician troops would harass the Moslems' enemies, the Byzantines. In 844, the new nation was established, and in 856 Karbeas founded its capital, Tephrike. He led the Paulician soldiers to victory in battles with the Byzantines until his death in 863. Within a decade after his passing, Byzantine forces had devastated the state he founded.

Edward KELLY   The notorious Edward Kelly may have been a talented medium, an unscrupulous con artist, or both. He is best known for his work in ANGEL MAGIC with famous Elizabethan magician JOHN DEE. Little is known of Kelly's early life.

He was born in 1555. Before meeting Dee, Kelly had already been in trouble with the law. He had been convicted of "coining" (counterfeiting) and had been punished by having his ears cut off.

Dee, a famous astrologer and alchemist, had become interested in attempting communication with angels. He was seeking an assistant who could have visions of the angels, and who could dictate to Dee the divine knowledge he hoped the spirits would share with him. Kelly, hearing of Dee's strange experiments, offered his services. Many researchers believe that Kelly simply thought that Dee, who was a brilliant but gullible man, could be easily manipulated to Kelly's own material benefit.

Kelly had no trouble producing visions, as Dee requested, by staring into a crystal. For his services, Kelly ensured that he was well paid. After Kelly convinced Dee that he was essential to the work of communicating with the angels, Kelly would periodically threaten to leave unless he received more money. Dee always gave in. During the next seven years, Dee and Kelly produced a complex system of angel magic known today as ENOCHIAN MAGIC.

Kelly finally went too far in his abuse of the credulous Dee. The angels, Kelly reported, were requesting that Dee and Kelly engage in "the common and impartial using of matrimonial acts"—in other words, wife swapping. Despite his surprise, and his wife's reluctance, Dee is thought to have complied with this rather unangelic suggestion. The situation proved to be unworkable. Mrs. Dee and Mrs. Kelly began to have violent arguments, and the communal family was experiencing serious financial hardship. Finally, Dee and Kelly had a falling out and went their separate ways.

For the next six years, Kelly wandered around Europe, engaging in fortune-telling and seeking a wealthy patron. In 1593, he was arrested on charges of sorcery and heresy. Kelly fell from a prison wall during an escape attempt and died from his injuries.

THE KEY OF SOLOMON   This work is regarded by many as the single most important handbook of magic in the Western occult tradition. *The Key of Solomon*, along with THE LEMEGETON, another text in the class of unorthodox literature known as the GRIMOIRES, established the standard form for the activities of ritual magic. Later works dealing with both DEMON MAGIC and ANGEL MAGIC copied the details of the Solomonic approach from the *Key*. Occult scholar A. E. Waite viewed the book as a composite of both sorts of magical practice.

As in the case of so many other European magical texts, tradition has it that *The Key of Solomon* was composed by the ancient king of Israel, King Solomon himself. While this authorship is extremely unlikely, there may well be elements of ancient Jewish magic that have survived in the *Key*. First century Hebrew historian Josephus mentions the existence of a magic book written by Solomon. A text entitled *The Testament of Solomon* definitely existed by the fourth century. *The Key of Solomon* as it is known today probably derives from the same underground tradition of Jewish magical practice hinted at by these ancient references to the magic of Solomon.

Several manuscripts of *The Key of Solomon* have been preserved from medieval and Renaissance times. Over the centuries, the *Key* was recopied by hand, resulting in differences (accidental and deliberate) between copies. The earliest surviving copy, stored in the British Museum, is in Greek and may have been written in the twelfth century.

In the late Middle Ages, ritual magicians were secretly composing and circulating their handbooks. They left no account of their activities, and the enforcers of the orthodox reality were busy trying to destroy every trace of them. Despite these unfavorable conditions, one can discern traces in the historical record that suggest that *The Key of Solomon* was a well-known work of the occult underground at the time.

Around 1350, Pope Innocent VI ordered the burning of *The Book of Solomon*. At about the same time, famous Inquisitor Nicholas Eymericus torched a book he had confiscated from a sorcerer, entitled *The Table of Solomon*. Perhaps these works were versions of the *Key*. An anti-magical pamphlet of 1456 mentions *The Key of Solomon* by name. In 1559, the INQUISITION specifically condemned the *Key*, and one can be sure that the Inquisitors were referring to the text that exists today.

The world view found in *The Key of Solomon* was very similar to that held by most Europeans in premodern times. It was generally believed that an invisible world of spirits, divine and diabolical, coexisted with the visible world of nature. The two realms interacted in various ways. For example, demons were capable of appearing in the visible world to inflict harm on humans. Both magicians and ordinary folk also thought that holy symbols intimidated evil spirits, and that the names of God and the angels could restrain the spirits. Another belief both many orthodox people and magical practitioners held was the notion that the ever-changing positions of the planets and stars influenced the visible and invisible domains.

There was a crucial difference between the mentalities of the orthodox and the magician. While conventional people sought to avoid demons at all costs and used the powers of religion to keep spirits at bay, practitioners of Solomonic magic attempted to master the spirits, using the lore of ASTROLOGY and ceremonial religious practice.

Concerning the use of astrological influences, the *Key* gives a table showing which planets rule the various hours of the day and night, and the days of the week. The book recommends that every magical operation should be performed at the appropriate day and hour to ensure success. For example, the spirits affiliated with the moon were said to be specialists in the recovery of stolen property. A magic ritual for this purpose should, therefore, be performed on the moon's day (Monday) and hour (6 A.M., 1 P.M., or 8 P.M.).

The Key of Solomon also teaches that the powers of planetary spirits can be harnessed by making medallions, inscribed with magical symbols, at the correct day and hour. The designs for these talismans, which feature geometric patterns and arrangements of letters, are often quite beautiful. One of the talismans of Saturn is especially significant. It features an acrostic array of letters:

```
S   A   T   O   R
A   R   E   P   O
T   E   N   E   T
O   P   E   R   A
R   O   T   A   S
```

This charm establishes that at least some parts of the *Key* predate the Middle Ages because the same arrangement of letters found inscribed on a wall in England dates back to the time of the Roman occupation. Historian Richard Cavendish stated that the charm is likely derived from *Pater Noster*, the opening words of the Lord's Prayer in Latin. If so, the talisman of Saturn represents a trace of Christian influence in the otherwise thoroughly Jewish content of the *Key*.

The text outlines a complex magical ritual for evoking spirits. Careful preparation for the performance of the "Grand Rite" is required, including ceremonial bathing and praying, the manufacture of a costume (shoes, gown, and crown, all marked with symbols), and a set of magical tools (wand, knives, sword, sickle, and medallions, among other items).

The Key of Solomon emphasizes the importance of constructing a magic circle, within which the magicians stand during the performance of the ritual. The slightest error in the drawing of the circle would leave the practitioners open to demonic attack. A series of long conjurations was included in the ceremony. The names of God and other magic phrases they contain were believed to compel the spirits to appear and obey the magicians.

A disturbing feature of the *Key* is its suggestion that the sacrifice of animals to the spirits increases the effectiveness of the magical practices. Good spirits are said to prefer white animals, and evil spirits prefer black ones, but all spirits particularly appreciate the death of virgin creatures. The author seems to have a detailed knowledge concerning the sacrifice. If a bat is used, for example, the *Key* notes that blood can be collected from "the vein which is in the right wing." Such practices tend to justify the dark reputation of this work.

The book also contains simple magical methods for various aims. These include making oneself invisible and attracting love. One unusual spell, which might go some way toward redeeming the *Key* in the eyes of modern animal-rights activists, is intended to prevent hunters from catching their prey.

The Key of Solomon, having survived every attempt to suppress it, went on to become a significant influence among the magicians of our own time. The magical world view—with its belief in spirits, astrological influences, and the occult power of words—was preserved by the magicians of the nineteenth century, who viewed the Solomonic practices as a potent ritual technology.

S. L. MacGregor Mathers, a leading figure in the important British occult society called the Hermetic Order of the GOLDEN DAWN, published the first English translation of the *Key*. He argued that the less attractive features, such as the blood sacrifice, were not authentic parts of the text. Most scholars today disagree.

ALEISTER CROWLEY, the most influential magician of the twentieth century, experimented with the Solomonic magical rites. Crowley was much less concerned about the nasty parts than Mathers was. *The Key of Solomon* continues to be studied by pupils of the Western magical tradition to this day.

KHLYSTY   This term is derived from the Russian word *khlyst*, which means "horse-whip." The Khlysty were a Russian sect, notorious for their practices of self-inflicted pain and extramarital sex. They were also called the FLAGELLANTS, or "Men of God." The Khlysty emerged from the fragmentation of the Russian Orthodox Church in the seventeenth century. When Nikon, patriarch of the Russian Church, introduced reforms into religious ceremonies, Archpriest Avvakum led those who resented the changes out of the orthodox community. Russian Christianity continued to splinter into various sects. DANILA FILLIPOV, one of the followers of Avvakum's movement, founded the Khlysty at the end of the 1600s.

The sect believed that they could call upon themselves the gifts of the Holy Spirit. Alcohol and meat were to be strictly avoided, as well as sex with one's spouse. Curiously, sex with someone *other* than one's marital partner was acceptable and gave the Khlysty their sinister reputation among the orthodox.

The practice for which the Khlysty are best known is ritual whipping. The centerpiece of the flagellation ceremony was a jar of water heated over a fire. As the water began to boil, those who wished to acquire spiritual powers—the "Christ bearers"—engaged in a wild, whirling dance. Virgin girls dressed in white cotton robes flogged the dancers with twigs because it was believed that only virgins could give birth to Christ. The dancers fell into a trance, believing they were possessed by the Holy Spirit. When they recovered, they would claim to have unusual powers that they could use to heal the sick, cast out demons, and foretell the future. It seems likely that this ritual was based on ancient methods shamans employed to induce journeys to the spirit world, with a thin overlay of heretical Christian doctrine.

Advanced members of the sect were believed to become Christs and were then beyond the need to obey moral laws. The outrageous behavior of some Khlysty provoked a split. Some members thought that the movement had become corrupt and formed their own sect, the SKOPTSY. This group was hostile to all forms of sexuality, but approved of pain; they continued the flagellatory practices and encouraged the amputation of body parts.

The Khlysty survived into the twentieth century. The best-known member was GRIGORI RASPUTIN, the notorious Russian monk. He associated with the sect as a young man. Rasputin felt that he did not achieve the full state of Christhood, but he thought he had progressed far enough to have acquired special powers; the stories of his remarkable influence over others suggests that his belief had some merit.

KNIGHTS TEMPLAR   The heresy trial of the Knights Templar brought an end to one of the most powerful organizations of the later Middle Ages. This incident is one of the best-known landmarks in the history of heresy. Nevertheless, many questions about whether the charges against this order amounted to anything more than a politically motivated frame-up remain.

The Order of the Knights Templar was established in 1118. At that time, the efforts of the Crusaders had established a beachhead in Palestine, which Christians regarded as the Holy Land. Many pilgrims traveled from western Europe to Jerusalem. A society of knights called the Hospitallers had formed to provide medicine and money for sick and poor pilgrims in Palestine. But the journey to the Holy Land remained a dangerous one; outlaws often robbed and harmed travelers. A knight from Champagne named HUGH DE PAYENS, along with eight colleagues, founded the Templar Order for the purpose of defending Christian travelers along the pilgrimage route.

The Templars had an early ally in Saint Bernard, who won them the favor of the pope. The rules of the Order were based on those of the Cistercian monks. Each knight took a vow of celibacy and renounced all material possessions, although the Templar Order itself was allowed to own property and money. The Templars were declared an independent monastic Order, accountable only to the pope. Within the

Order, the highest officer, the Grand Master, had complete power over the rest of the knights. The image of a galloping horse, being ridden by two men, was adopted as the Templars' symbol.

Unlike the other monastic Orders, the Templars were active warriors. They quickly expanded their role from protecting travelers to doing battle against the Moslems and became admired throughout the Christian world. The Order received many gifts from pious Catholics, as well as tax exemptions.

They established a network of impregnable fortresses. This development led to their other major role as the first bankers of Europe. Templar strongholds seemed so safe from attack that the wealthy, including kings, asked to leave their money and treasures in the knights' safekeeping. Soon, the Order was able to lend money and charge interest, and to claim people's property if they defaulted on repayment.

As with so many institutions founded on ideals, the acquisition of wealth and the passage of time led to corruption. The upper classes began to resent the Templars for their arrogance and independence from common laws; the working people were annoyed by the knights' tax exemptions, which enabled the Order to undercut others' prices when they sold produce from their estates.

At the end of the thirteenth century, the experiment of the Crusades had failed, and the European Christians were chased out of Palestine. The Knights Templar were the last to leave. But once the Holy Land was closed to pilgrims, their original reason for existence disappeared. They were so well established in European society, however, that the Order was not dissolved, but continued with its economic activities.

Most historians believe that the Templars' wealth led to their downfall. King Philip IV of France had an ambition to rule Europe and engaged in many military campaigns. In order to finance his armies, he borrowed money from the Templars. Rather than repay his debts, the king decided to destroy the Order and confiscate its immense riches for himself.

Philip knew that the Templars, although resented in many quarters, would not be easy to crush. He would be able to act directly against the knights only within the borders of France, and if he did so, the Templars in other countries would probably respond violently. He needed a way to close down the Order internationally. To accomplish this end, he required the cooperation of Pope Clement V.

Clement had obtained the papacy with Philip's aid, so he was open to the king's influence; however, the Templars had always been fiercely loyal to the pope and could not easily be betrayed. Philip's ingenious solution to the problem was to arrange for the Knights to be charged with heresy. Torture would provide the necessary evidence for a conviction, and the pope would then be forced to dissolve the entire Order.

The plan was sprung on October 13, 1307. JACQUES DE MOLAY, the Grand Master, was arrested in Paris. Throughout France, the Knights Templar were captured by the king's forces, and the state took over their possessions. The masses were appeased by announcing that the Templars' misuse of their tax exemptions had nearly destroyed the French economy. The heresy charges were proclaimed, and the interrogations began.

The Templars had maintained a tradition of keeping their initiation rituals secret; this gave the king's agents free rein in concocting descriptions of unorthodox ceremonies. Witnesses reported that Templar initiates were required to spit or urinate on the cross, and to renounce Christ. Homosexuality was said to be an accepted common practice. The Templar leaders were observed worshipping an object called the *Baphomet*, variously described as a stuffed human head, a skull, and a three-headed idol, which was anointed with the fat of murdered children. At certain rites, the Devil himself would appear in the form of a black cat, and the knights would kiss him under the tail.

Historians have long debated the meaning of these odd statements. It is difficult to take them all as literally true; some scholars believe they are simply lies. The charge of homosexual permissiveness is not outrageous, however, particularly in connection with an exclusively male organization. It is also possible that during their many years of contact with Palestinian culture, the Templars adopted some Eastern spiritual practices, which might be described in a distorted way in the accusations. Hugh Schonfield, a modern researcher, believes this to be true; he reported that the mysterious term Baphomet is actually the Greek word *Sophia* (wisdom), expressed in a language code invented by Jews in first century Palestine.

During the next seven years, Inquisitors were busy collecting confessions from the French Templars, nearly all of whom complied. Their cooperation is not surprising given that the "encouragements" to state what the interrogators wished to hear included roasting the suspect's feet until the bones fell off, if necessary. Following an Inquisitorial session, one Knight appeared in court carrying a handful of his own bones. Those who refused to confess, or who retracted their confessions later, were burned at the stake. The grisly persecution concluded with the fiery execution of Grand Master de Molay in 1314, who died proclaiming the innocence of the Knights Templar.

Pope Clement tried to dissolve the Order throughout Europe. However, the Templars in Spain and Portugal were on good terms with their governments, which created new monastic Orders and permitted the banned knights to transfer to them. These successor Orders to the Templars, the Order of Montesa in Spain and the Order of Christ in Portugal, still exist today, but only as titles of honor for favored citizens.

Mainstream historians believe that the actions of King Philip effectively ended the role of the Knights Templar. Others speculate that the Knights continued in secret and played an important role in the development of esoteric traditions: the Rosicrucians and the Freemasons are just two of the groups said to have been started by the Templars. Today, many occult organizations continue to claim that they have received the secret teachings, preserved through the centuries, of the Knights Templar.

Bernt KNIPPERDOLLING

A leader of the MÜNSTER HERETICS who took over that German town in 1534, Bernt Knipperdolling, a textile merchant, met MELCHIOR HOFFMANN, the prophet of the ANABAPTISTS, in Sweden and was impressed. Knipperdolling later became mayor of Münster, an influential position that enabled him to lobby to make the city a haven for Anabaptists. An influx of Hoffmann's followers ensued; Knipperdolling supported them in becoming the dominant force in Münster, driving out all who refused to be rebaptized by Anabaptists. In 1535, an army backing the Catholic bishop captured the city. Knipperdolling was tortured to death for heresy, and his torn body displayed as a warning to anyone entertaining thoughts of disobeying authority.

Sylvan KOLESNIKOV   The first known leader of the Russian sect called the DOUKHOBORS, Sylvan Kolesnikov entered a Ukrainian village in 1769 and proclaimed that God sent him to lead the people to holiness. During the next eleven years, he taught his disciples that the Holy Spirit was not in a far-off heaven, but lived inside each person; therefore, all Doukhobors should greet each other by bowing deeply to the Spirit within the other person. Kolesnikov might have had connections with another Russian sect, the KHLYSTY. He died in 1780. His memory is still revered by Doukhobors today, who now live in Canada.

Hans KUNG   This Swiss theologian was one of the most eminent thinkers in the Roman Catholic Church until he fell afoul of papal authority. Born in 1928, Hans Kung became a professor of fundamental theology at the University of Tubingen, Germany, and wrote several influential works. In 1970, his book entitled *Infallible? An Inquiry* was published. In this volume, Kung rejects the dogma of the pope's infallibility, a notion that had been proclaimed in 1870. Kung viewed the papal position against most forms of birth control as clearly wrong; the Pope's dictum demonstrated to Kung that the dogma of infallibility was also clearly false.

In 1979, in response to Kung's independence of thought, Pope John Paul II forbade him from writing or publishing as a Catholic theologian. Following his official muzzling, Kung commented in an article with the pointed title "The Fallibility of Pope John Paul II": "I have been condemned by a pontiff who has rejected my theology without ever having read one of my books and who has always refused to see me. The truth is that Rome is not waiting for dialogue but for submission." Kung remains formally silenced.

See also: INQUISITION.

Hugh LATIMER   One of the first Protestants in England, Hugh Latimer survived several of the religious upheavals of the time but died a heretic. He was born in 1485 and was an active Protestant preacher by 1522, just five years after Martin Luther's inauguration of the Reformation in Germany. At first, Latimer was persecuted; but following Henry VIII's proclamation separating the Church of England from the Roman Catholic fold, he became a close advisor to the king. He urged more radical reforms than Henry was willing to make, however, and fell out of favor. He returned to prominence under Edward VI, Henry's Protestant successor.

When Mary Tudor became queen in 1553, she brought Catholicism back to power and viewed people like Latimer as heretics. He was punished by being burned to death, with NICHOLAS RIDLEY, in 1555. Latimer is reported to have soothed his comrade with these famous words, which have long inspired English Protestants: "Be of good comfort, Master Ridley, we shall this day light such a candle by God's grace in England as, I trust, shall never be put out."

See also: THOMAS CRANMER, JOHN HOOPER.

LATROCINIUM   When the meeting of Christian leaders at Ephesus in 449 condemned Pope Leo as a heretic and upheld the unorthodox doctrine of MONO-PHYSITISM, the pope described the gathering as a "latrocinium," or "ROBBER COUNCIL." The decisions of this council were overturned two years later at the COUNCIL OF CHALCEDON.

LA VOISIN   Catherine Monvoisin, a notorious SATANIST and poisoner in seventeenth century France, went by the name of La Voisin. She made her living by selling aphrodisiacs and ending unwanted pregnancies in Paris. La Voisin came to include among her clientele members of the royal court, including Madame de Montespan, the mistress of Louis XIV, the Sun King. La Voisin provided Montespan with various substances to slip into the king's food in order to keep him sexually interested in her. When these measures no longer produced the desired effect (in fact, it is probable that La Voisin's love potions were slowly poisoning Louis), the two women turned to Satanic magic.

ABBÉ GUIBOURG, a notorious corrupt priest who performed the BLACK MASS, was an associate of La Voisin. Indeed, it has been claimed that she obtained unwanted babies for him to sacrifice to demons in his dark rites. Guibourg was hired to conduct Satanic ceremonies to enhance the power of La Voisin's concoctions.

La Voisin, along with Guibourg and many others, was arrested shortly after performing a black mass intended to kill King Louis through DEMON MAGIC. Curiously, she was apprehended while returning home from attending Sunday Mass at the local church. Somehow, La Voisin seemed able to separate her orthodox piety from her devil-worshipping activities. She was tortured mercilessly for three days but proclaimed her innocence, calling on God and the Virgin Mary to help her. Circumstantial evidence and a mass of testimony that identified her as a ringleader of the Satanic circle in Paris led to her conviction. La Voisin was burned at the stake in 1680.

Ann LEE   Known to her followers as "Mother Spirit in Christ, an Emanation of the Eternal Mother," or more simply as Mother Ann, Ann Lee brought the religion of the SHAKERS to America. Lee was thought to be a fourth divine being, rounding out the Trinity of Father, Son, and Holy Spirit.

Lee was born in Manchester, England, in 1736, into a blacksmith's family. Earlier in the century, England had been visited by refugees from the persecuted French sect, the CAMISARDS. Their practice of serving as mediums through which the Holy Spirit could prophesy while they danced and convulsed impressed a few observers. When Lee was seven, a Shaker group began meeting in Manchester.

Throughout Lee's youth, she experienced visions of angels and heard the voices of the dead speaking to her. Her family discouraged her from pursuing these experiences, fearful that she might be accused of being a witch. Lee herself remained convinced that she was having divine revelations. During one of these episodes, she saw Adam and Eve engaged in a sinful sex act and yearned to live her life as a virgin. The Shakers' claims to be in direct contact with God suited this visionary; she joined the group when she was twenty-three.

Despite Lee's reverence for virginity, she was married four years later to please her parents. The marriage produced four children, all of whom died shortly after birth. Lee herself came close to death during the fourth delivery. This experience triggered a bleak period of soul searching, when she renounced sexual intercourse forever and begged God to forgive her sins.

When Lee recovered, she began preaching to her Shaker friends that sex was the origin of all evil and encouraged them to follow her example. Her colleagues made her the leader of the sect and confessed their sins to her. Through her suffering, Mother Ann had been purified of earthly faults and was now regarded as God.

Lee's opposition to the Biblical command, "Be fruitful and multiply," as well as her attacks on the permissiveness of the mainstream churches, brought condemnation from the authorities. She often found herself in jail. At one point, a legal representative set off from Manchester to London to request permission from King George II to execute Lee for sorcery. The representative died suddenly before reaching the king. The event was taken as a judgment of God, and the Shaker prophet was freed.

Lee began to have visions instructing her that America would be the new homeland of the Shakers. In 1774, along with eight devotees, she traveled to the New World. The group obtained land at Watervliet near Albany, New York, and established the first Shaker colony there. Their leader established the strict principles that have defined the Shaker lifestyle since that time.

Despite fires, crop failures, and the assaults of suspicious neighbors—Lee herself was repeatedly beaten by mobs accusing her of heresy and witchcraft—the community endured. During the last few years of Lee's life, she saw a rapid expansion of the Shaker colony, due largely to a religious revival that swept through New York in 1779. The founder died in 1784 at the age of forty-eight. Three years later, the Shaker Church was formally organized. One of its defining beliefs was that Mother Ann was the female aspect of God.

THE LEMEGETON   This book is also known as *The Lesser Key of Solomon. The Lemegeton* is a classic in the notorious literary tradition of the GRIMOIRES and is a principle source of DEMON MAGIC. Although the text states that it was composed by King Solomon, this is highly unlikely. The authors of ritual-magic handbooks were fond of attributing their works to such famous figures as Solomon in order to enhance the credibility of the contents.

The earliest complete manuscripts of the *Lesser Key* that survive today were written in French and date back to the seventeenth century. There is a reference to part of *The Lemegeton* from around 1500, and Johan Weyer, the famous sixteenth century writer on witchcraft and demons, includes material from *The Lemegeton* in his catalog of demons, *Pseudomonarchia Daemonum*.

The meaning of the term "Lemegeton" is unknown. The text is divided into four parts, which may originally have been four separate books. Part One, entitled "The Goetia" (which is the Greek word for sorcery), contains the most influential material. The Goetia gives a detailed list of the seventy-two most powerful demons, describing the special powers and the appearance of each when ceremonially evoked. Supposedly, King Solomon imprisoned these demons in a brass cauldron, which was then thrown into the sea. Later, the cauldron washed ashore and was opened by its finders, who thought it contained treasure. The demons were liberated, and today can be controlled only by the powerful Solomonic magic described in *The Lemegeton*.

These demons can be compelled to perform a variety of useful acts. Many of the spirits are said to grant knowledge, such as astronomy, mathematics, logic, and even ethics. This instructional skill of the demons reflects the tradition of the fallen angels who taught humankind the arts of civilization, recounted in the ancient Jewish text, THE BOOK OF ENOCH.

Other demons bring disease and death upon the magician's enemies. The seduction of women is another specialty. The author thoughtfully includes one demon, named Procel, who will even warm the magician's bathwater.

The demon lore in the Goetia preserves fragments of belief systems that predate Christianity. Examination of this material is like an archaeological investigation into the foundations of Western reality. For example, one encounters Beelzebub and Astaroth, devils who are simply demonized versions of the ancient Near Eastern deities Baal and Astarte. A demon named Amon, who can reveal the past and future and bring love, seems to be a distorted image of the ancient Egyptian sun god, also named Amon.

The Lemegeton describes a standard ritual for evoking and controlling these infernal beings. After undergoing acts of purification, the magician must stand inside a magic circle. Outside the circle, a triangle is drawn, within which the demon will appear. The demon is supposedly forced into the triangle by the power of long passages the magician reads. These conjurations are studded with magic words and names of God from the Hebrew magical tradition. For example, the opening formula of the ritual reads:

> I conjure thee, O Spirit (name), strengthened by the power of Almighty God, and I command thee by Baralamensis, Baldachiensis, Paumachie, Apolorosedes and the most powerful Princes Genio and Liachide, Ministers of the Seat of Tartarus and Chief Princes of the Throne of Apologia in the ninth region.

The text includes a series of increasingly powerful incantations in case the demon is resistant. The use of the five-pointed star, the Pentagram of Solomon, is also recommended.

The general ritual pattern presented in *The Lemegeton*—initial purification, use of the magic circle and the triangle of evocation, the various magical tools employed, and the use of words of power to command the spirits—is the classic ceremony in the Western ritual-magic tradition. Just as the demon lists of the Goetia summarize and transmit the major strands of Western demonology, the ritual pattern of *The Lemegeton* expresses the main features found in most ritual-magic practices to this day.

Part Two of *The Lemegeton* is entitled "Theurgia Goetia." This section states that a race of spirits is associated with each of the four directions. Magicians can utilize these beings, some of whom are good and some evil, for their own benefit.

"The Pauline Art" is the name of the third part of *The Lemegeton*. This section lists the angels of the hours and of the zodiac signs. If the magician prays and then contemplates a crystal, an angel can be made to appear and grant any knowledge requested by the practitioner. This text appears to be related to the experiments of ANGEL MAGIC undertaken by British magicians JOHN DEE and EDWARD KELLY during the late sixteenth century. Part Four, "The ALMADEL," is also a text of angel magic, and was almost certainly absorbed into the body of *The Lemegeton* from another source.

LEO III   Ruler of the Byzantine Empire from A.D. 717 to 741, Leo III is thought to be the founder of the heresy known as ICONOCLASM, which disrupted relations between orthodox Christian Churches in the East and West. By the early eighth century, much of the land the Byzantines formerly controlled had fallen to the Moslems. Leo believed that this fate had befallen the empire as a punishment from

God for the laxity of the Byzantines' Christian practices. In particular, he regarded the use of images of Christ and the saints in religious devotion to be idolatry and ordered their destruction ("iconoclasm" literally means "image smashing"). Pope Gregory II rejected Leo's opposition to the images as unorthodox, and the political links between Rome and Byzantium were severed.

LEO IV   Ruler of the Byzantine Empire from A.D. 775 to 780, Leo IV was a supporter of the heretical movement called ICONOCLASM. This emperor promoted the iconoclastic view relatively mildly. Although he opposed the use of religious icons, he did not order their destruction or the execution of those who revered them.

LEO V   Emperor of the Byzantine Empire from A.D. 813 to 820, Leo V revived the heresy of ICONOCLASM. During his reign, he ordered the destruction of all icons in his territory and met with much resistance from orthodox Christians. Leo was murdered by supporters of his successor, MICHAEL II, who was also an iconoclast.

LEUTHARD   This French farmer was one of the first heretical leaders of the later Middle Ages. Leuthard was active in the Champagne region of France around A.D. 1000. Although there is no record that he belonged to any sort of unorthodox organization, the nature of his beliefs has suggested to some scholars that he might have encountered the heresy of BOGOMILISM, which was spreading in eastern Europe at the time.

Leuthard himself claimed that he received his teachings directly from God one day while he was working in his field. He first came to public notice when he drove his wife from their home, claiming that marriage was sinful. He then went to a local church and smashed the religious symbols displayed there.

This is how the heretic's preaching career began. He proclaimed to the peasants that the Catholic Church was the embodiment of evil and that people should refuse to pay tithes to support it. He also criticized the Bible, observing that not everything in the scripture was true. Leuthard's views proved popular among the poorer classes, and he acquired a following. The bishop of the region soon learned of Leuthard's ideas and succeeded in winning most of the heretic's converts back to the orthodox fold. Seeing his movement dissolving, Leuthard fell into despair and killed himself by leaping into a well.

Leuthard's rejection of the orthodox church and its institution of marriage is reminiscent of Bogomilism. However, such ideas may have occurred to Leuthard independently. The Roman Catholic Church of the time often seemed more interested in maintaining its wealth and privilege than caring for the spiritual well-being of the poor, and could easily be regarded as corrupt. Perhaps because of Leuthard's activities or those of Bogomil missionaries from the east, heretical preachers with views resembling his began to appear in many western European towns within a few decades of his death.

LEVELLERS   This English dissident group appeared in London between 1647 and 1660. JOHN LILBURNE led the Levellers. According to the sect's members, the existing social hierarchy violated God's law. They opposed monarchy and believed in rule by a parliament elected by all men. They also promoted complete freedom of religion, a very unusual view for the time. In the political confusion of this period, the Levellers' call to equalize the ranks of society attracted considerable attention.

However, the Levellers did not draw enough support to prevent the enthronement of King Charles II, and they disbanded.

See also: DIGGERS, FIFTH MONARCHY MEN, RANTERS.

John LILBURNE   John Lilburne was the founder of the seventeenth century English sect, the LEVELLERS.

LOLLARDS   The term "Lollard" was first applied to the members of the BEGHARD movement in the fourteenth century. It was also used to describe the followers of English heretic JOHN WYCLIFFE by their enemies, intending to insult them; Wycliffe's people adopted the name with pride. *Lollard* probably derives from a Middle Dutch word meaning "to sing or hum," as does the word "lullaby."

Wycliffe, who was active during the second half of the fourteenth century, preached that the Catholic Church should abandon its interest in wealth and political power and throw out all religious beliefs not found in the New Testament. His views attracted many members of the poorer classes, who felt they had little in common with the rich priests and bishops. English aristocrats were also interested: they resented the pope's support of France rather than England in the Hundred Year's War, and fantasized about grabbing the church's extensive property holdings. Both poor peasants and powerful lords became part of the Lollard movement.

After Wycliffe's forced retirement and his death in 1384, JOHN PURVEY, his secretary, became the leader of the Lollards. Lollard preachers were active in several parts of England, often setting themselves up near the entrances of churches and denouncing the Catholic clergy as they passed by. The orthodox belief in the saving power of the mass was ridiculed; the way to understanding salvation lay in Bible study, according to the Lollards, and to this end the first English translations of the Bible were distributed.

Catholic officials urged the secular authorities to act against the Lollards. Purvey, for his part, lobbied King Richard II to confiscate the property of the church. At first, neither the Catholics nor the Lollards had their way. The Lollards were protected by powerful friends among the nobility. The king, although tempted by the prospect of acquiring the possessions of the church, felt it would be politically explosive to do so.

The tide shifted in favor of orthodoxy in 1399. Richard was deposed and replaced by Henry IV, who was sympathetic to the Catholic cause. Laws were passed against the Lollards, and persecution began. Against a hostile monarch, the heretics appealed to Parliament, the counterbalance to royal power in the British political structure. A Lollard presented a petition, which explained to the Parliament the financial benefits of taking over the property of the Catholic Church: the state would be able to employ 15 barons, 1,500 knights and 6,200 landowners in their service, and fund all of the refuges for the homeless, with the money currently spent on maintaining church properties and priestly lifestyles. However, their sympathizers still felt that moving against the Catholics would undermine the country's stability.

Desperate, the Lollards plotted an uprising. The royal family, the highest nobles, and the Catholic leaders, were to be murdered, and a new political structure imposed based on Lollard views. In 1414, the organizers, led by SIR JOHN OLDCASTLE, called for Lollard loyalists to assemble in London.

Estimates of the number of Lollards who gathered vary wildly, from 300 to 20,000;

the lower figure is probably closer to the truth. The plot was betrayed, and royal troops easily rounded up the heretical army as it was forming. The ringleaders were hanged and burned, a double punishment for treason and heresy. A few years later, Oldcastle himself was captured and sentenced to death.

Following this disaster, the Lollard movement went underground. The crown and Parliament were now firmly united against the heresy. Another uprising was attempted in 1431, but it fared even worse than the first. Lollard groups survived into the sixteenth century, meeting in secret to study the Bible and condemn the status quo. When representatives of Martin Luther's Reformation arrived in the early decades of the 1500s, they established their first footholds in the regions where Lollard sympathies were strongest. These English heretics, who had been promoting essentially Protestant ideas for more than 100 years, were absorbed into the new and larger Reformation movement.

LOUIS OF BAVARIA   Ruler of the Holy Roman Empire from 1314 to 1347, Louis of Bavaria offered shelter to some members of the SPIRITUAL FRANCISCANS after that group was declared a heresy in 1317. In 1324, Pope John XXII proclaimed that the emperor himself was a heretic. Louis and John traded a series of denunciations. Louis and his army then seized Rome and appointed a new pope; John, in the French town of Avignon, managed to retain his authority within the Catholic Church, and the emperor's papal candidate was forced to step down.

LUCIAN OF ANTIOCH   Lucian of Antioch operated an academy for Christian study at the beginning of the fourth century A.D. Although he died a martyr and was regarded as an orthodox Christian in good standing at the time, he played a major role in setting the stage for the outbreak of the heresy known as ARIANISM.

Little is known of Lucian's early life. As an adult, he developed a reputation for his piety and compelling teaching, and a group of students formed around him. One of his most devoted followers was ARIUS, the monk who learned from him the basic doctrines of what would come to be called the Arian heresy.

Lucian's thought regarding the nature of God was influenced by the teachings of PAUL OF SAMOSATA, who had proclaimed the heresy of ADOPTIONISM in Antioch during the late third century before he was deposed by the Catholics (with the support of Roman soldiers). Paul emphasized that Christ was different from God. Lucian adopted this idea. Unlike Paul, however, Lucian regarded Christ as a divine being resembling an angel rather than a mere man.

Lucian was also affected by the doctrines of Egyptian theologian ORIGEN. Origen emphasized the idea that God the Father and God the Son were distinct Persons by noting that the Son obeys the Father; therefore, the Son is "subordinate" to the Father and cannot be the same Person as the Father. Lucian adopted "subordinationism," but he expanded the notion into the claim that the Father and Son were completely separate beings, not only in being different Persons but also in having different essences—a position that Origen would have regarded as too extreme. Some scholars believe that this distortion of Origen's thought was transmitted to Lucian by DIONYSIUS OF ALEXANDRIA, an Egyptian bishop who had gotten in trouble with orthodox authorities because of his subordinationist views.

At Lucian's school in Antioch, he taught that the divine Son (also referred to as the Logos, or Word) was God's first and most perfect creation and was made from nothing. The Son became incarnated in a human body as JESUS Christ, but He did not have a human soul. Thus, the Son is defined as a creation of God and, therefore, not fully God; also, the Son does not have a human soul and, therefore, is not fully human either.

The orthodox position on this matter states that Christ the Son is both fully God and fully human. Origen, and orthodox Christians after him, believed that the Son was not created by the Father, but rather that God the Father and God the Son have always existed together in eternity. Lucian's worship of this created Son was at odds with the Catholic view that only God should be worshipped, not what God creates. By orthodox standards, Lucian's teachings regarding the Son of God are clearly heretical.

Lucian also considered the nature of the Holy Spirit. He believed that the Holy Spirit was a creation of God the Father "through" God the Son. Although orthodoxy's view of the Holy Spirit had not been fully worked out during Lucian's lifetime, the idea that the Holy Spirit was a mere creation of God seemed to insult the Spirit's holiness, according to many Christians. In the struggle against ARIANISM during the fourth century, orthodox theologians concluded that the Holy Spirit was fully God, not a creation, and that, therefore, Lucian had been heretical on this issue, too.

During most of Lucian's teaching career, he was not affiliated with the Catholic hierarchy in Antioch but remained independent. Maximinus Daza, the last emperor before Christianity was legalized, inaugurated a bloody persecution of Christians, causing the various Christian groups in Antioch to draw together. Lucian was accepted as an orthodox Catholic shortly before his capture and murder by Roman Inquisitors in 312.

Lucian's heroic death added to his reputation and increased the impact of his teachings on the Christian community. It would take several decades before orthodox doctrines prevailed over the ideas of Lucian's followers. Lucian's description of God, as presented by his student Arius, prompted Catholics to formulate their doctrine of the Trinity.

LUCIFERANS   Belief in the existence of a secret cult of devil worshippers was widely held during the later Middle Ages. This fantasy received a boost when a thirteenth century Inquisitor convinced the pope that Germany was in danger of being overrun by a Satanic group called the Luciferans. For centuries afterward, suspected heretics and witches were thought to belong to the Luciferan cult.

In the early 1200s, a German priest named Conrad of Marburg distinguished himself by his support for the Crusades and his enthusiasm for pursuing heretics. In 1231, Conrad was appointed Germany's first official Inquisitor by the archbishop of Mainz. Conrad Torso and Johannes, two assistants who had previous experience in persecuting heretics, joined him.

At that time, the INQUISITION had not yet developed standard rules of procedure, so the trio could proceed as they wished. During the next year and a half, western Germany was subjected to a reign of terror. Conrad and his crew claimed that they could detect heretics by their appearance. On this basis, they could convict anyone, without the slightest evidence, and order them burned at the stake. The Inquisitors were not particularly worried about making mistakes: "We would gladly burn a hundred," they proclaimed, "if just one among them were guilty."

At first, they restricted their practice to the powerless lower classes but soon became convinced that devil worshippers existed among the privileged as well. However, to attack the upper ranks, they needed the support and protection of the most powerful men of the land, the king and the highest feudal lords. They secured this cooperation by proposing to share the property of executed heretics with their protectors.

Eventually, the Inquisitors overreached themselves. They tried to persecute some of the most respected members of the church and provoked a backlash. When a council of nobles and church officials refused to permit the conviction of someone Conrad of Marburg had accused, he quickly left town in disgust without his usual armed escort. Traveling unprotected through a rural area, he was murdered by a group of knights. Shortly afterward, Conrad Torso was stabbed to death, and Johannes was hanged.

Conrad of Marburg left a terrible legacy. Through progress reports he sent to Pope Gregory IX during his Inquisitorial activities, Conrad convinced the pontiff of the existence of the Luciferan cult. In Conrad's view, these heretics believed that Lucifer, not God, was the creator of heaven. Lucifer had been cast out of heaven unfairly and would one day return to defeat God. In the meantime, the heretics maintained that Lucifer's servants should do as much evil as they could in the Devil's honor. The Luciferans were said to meet at night when their master would appear to them in various forms, such as a toad, a cat, or an ice-cold man. After kissing him (often on the behind), they would have an orgy. The pope continued to believe in this weird tale even after Conrad's downfall. In 1233, Gregory issued a proclamation containing details of the Luciferans' activities and calling for their extermination. This endorsement increased the credibility of the Satanic fantasy.

Throughout the following years, the pope's description of the Luciferans was consulted as a reliable guide to the activities and beliefs of heretics. Inquisitors accused the two great unorthodoxies of the later Middle Ages, the CATHARS and WALDENSIANS, of Luciferanism, and dealt with them without mercy. Details of the Luciferan legend were included in the idea of the witches' sabbath, which inspired the GREAT WITCH HUNT.

See also: SATANISM.

Lukas of Prague   A Bohemian preacher, Lukas of Prague organized the unorthodox UNITAS FRATRUM movement into a church. The sect achieved some popularity under his influence. He died in 1527.

Isaac LURIA   So important and daring were the teachings of this master of KABBALAH that since his lifetime in the sixteenth century, he has been known as the "Ari," the Sacred Lion. Isaac Luria is the best-known and, along with Moses de Leon (author of the *ZOHAR*), the most significant figure in the history of Jewish mysticism.

Luria was born in Jerusalem in 1534. His family had immigrated to Palestine from Germany; when he was a child, they moved again to Egypt for financial reasons. Luria lived with a rich uncle in Cairo, who provided for his education. According to legend, he demonstrated an almost miraculous grasp of the Jewish scriptures even as a young boy. This genius would later be explained by the belief that Luria was the reincarnation of Rabbi Simeon bar Yochai, the famous second century sage.

At seventeen, Luria first encountered the central Kabbalistic text, the *Zohar*. He decided that this work contained the secrets of the universe and devoted himself almost exclusively to its study. His uncle owned a small island in the Nile River; Luria is said to have spent seven years alone there in a small hut, pondering the *Zohar* and practicing meditation. Later, when a student asked him how he had managed to penetrate the mysteries of the Kabbalah more deeply than anyone before him, he denied any special abilities; rather, he said, he had simply worked harder at developing his insight than anyone else.

Following this retreat, the sage spent several more years living in Cairo. He shared ideas with other Kabbalists, but also maintained a worldly life, running a business that dealt in grains and spices.

Around the beginning of 1570, Luria felt a spiritual call to move to the Palestinian town of Safed. Located there was the most important community of Kabbalists at the time. Shortly after his arrival, Moses Cordovero, the leader of this community, died. Although Luria was not well known before he moved to Safed, he was hailed as Cordovero's successor because of his wisdom. Other leading Kabbalists, such as Chaim Vital, asked for Luria's teachings.

The Ari lived in Safed for less than three years. He died in an epidemic in 1573 at the age of thirty-nine. Luria wrote only one small book, along with a number of short essays, poems, and hymns. His doctrines were mainly preserved by his disciples. Through the works of Chaim Vital and Israel Sarug, Luria's ideas were transmitted throughout Europe.

Luria contributed radical ideas to both the theoretical and practical sides of Kabbalah. On the theoretical side, he presented a new world view, a story describing the origin and fate of the universe, combining Zoharic concepts with his own ideas. The three key concepts in this world view are *zimzum*, *qlippoth*, and *tikkun*.

Before creation, the Ari noted, God was all that existed. In order to create something outside of Himself, He had to contract His infinite being to make a space. This initial contraction of God is called *zimzum*. Within the space, ten vessels, or *sefiroth*, were created to receive the outpouring of the divine light. Through a process of emanation, the universe, including humanity, was created from this light. All acts of creation were thought to involve the interplay of two movements, pulling back (*zimzum*) and pouring forth.

In order for the vessels of creation to contain the divine light, they had to be as similar as possible to God, the source of the light. God is the perfect giver and receiver. The vessels could receive, but they were poor at giving, and in this way did not resemble God. The first three *sefiroth* managed to hold the light, but those below them were overwhelmed. A cosmic catastrophe ensued. The vessels shattered into fragments, or "husks" (*qlippoth*). The twisted wreckage of the lower vessels gave rise to evil. Sparks of the divine light became trapped in the material world, dominated by the *qlippoth*. These sparks are human souls. Luria's ideas on this topic strongly resemble those of the ancient VALENTINIAN GNOSTICS, but no researcher has been able to demonstrate a direct historical connection between the two schools of thought, which are separated by 1,300 years.

The appearance of evil was part of God's plan. In order for the created world to be perfected, it must come to resemble God, the perfect one, as closely as possible. Since God has free will, creation must also have free will, which is only possible if a choice between good and evil exists. Evil was included in the creation in order for humans to exercise their free will to choose good. More generally, the purpose of human life is for human beings to strive to resemble God. By doing so, people act to restore the created world to its intended perfection, which was disrupted by the breaking of the lower *sefiroth*. In effect, as humans redeem themselves through becoming holy, they redeem the universe. This process of restoring the world to perfection is called *tikkun*.

Every human act, even the most seemingly insignificant, either supports or impedes the cosmic process of *tikkun*. Luria's world view thus provides a vast backdrop that gives great meaning to each human life. The practical techniques he taught for spiritual development were understood as ways to promote the redemption of the cosmos.

The Ari developed simple meditations that could be performed during the activities of daily life to harness these activities for *tikkun*. He is best known for the specialized meditations called *yechudim*, or "unifications." In these practices, various Hebrew names of God are brought together in the mind and merged into a single word. Luria taught that the *yechudim* helped to integrate the aspects of the person, as well as the fragments of the shattered universe. The *yechudim* meditations were thought to be so powerful that they could seriously damage the practitioner if they were not performed perfectly. Even Chaim Vital wrote that he got into trouble after trying a *yechud* for which he was unprepared:

> I was immediately filled with emotion, and my entire body trembled. My head became heavy, my mind began to swim, and my mouth became crooked on one side. I immediately stopped meditating. . . . In the morning, my master (the Ari) saw me, and he said, "Did I not warn you? If not for the fact that you are a reincarnation of Rabbi Akiba, you would have [gone mad] like Ben Zoma. There would have been no way to help you."

The Kabbalah of Isaac Luria became the dominant system of Jewish mystical thought after his lifetime. Scholars disagree about the role Luria's ideas played in the disastrous events surrounding the career of the Jewish heretic SABBATAI ZEVI in the seventeenth century. Some historians, such as Gershom Scholem, argued that Luria's notion of *tikkun*—the movement of the universe toward perfection—aroused Messianic hopes among many Jews, who became receptive to Zevi, the self-proclaimed Messiah. Others, like Moshe Idel, feel that Luria's notions did not help Zevi's popularity; he pointed out that the Ari taught that holy actions undertaken by anyone help to restore perfection, not just those of a Messiah. Regardless of whether or not the Lurianic Kabbalah aided Zevi's initial popularity, many of Zevi's followers were quite interested in the Ari's ideas. In Jerusalem, a Jewish school devoted to the study and practice of the Lurianic system has continued into the twentieth century.

Luria's world view was brought to the attention of Christian Cabalists by seventeenth century writer CHRISTIAN KNORR VON ROSENROTH, who included Lurianic concepts in his influential book *Kabbalah Denudata*. By this route, the teachings of the Ari entered the lore of QABALAH, the modern occult tradition that is rooted in Kabbalah. For example, some Qabalistic magicians personify the *qlippoth* as DEMONS, and conduct ceremonies to dispel them or bring them into harmony with the world.

MAGIC   Attempts to use the hidden powers and connections in the universe for one's benefit have occurred in every culture. The goals of magic have ranged from the mundane, such as choosing lottery numbers, to the sublime, such as becoming a god. In the West, magical practices have often been condemned. A magician is one who desires direct access to the sources of occult power, and orthodox religions tend to reserve such access for their own officials.

Despite much persecution, magic has persisted through Western history. The practices of magic in the West can be divided into several headings: ANGEL MAGIC, the conjuration of benevolent beings; DEMON MAGIC, the conjuration of evil spirits; NATURAL MAGIC, the utilization of occult forces in the sky and the earth, which may or may not be thought of as spirit beings; and NECROMANCY, or contact with the spirits of the dead. A special division of Western magic, known as QABALAH, uses concepts borrowed from the Jewish mystical tradition of KAB-BALAH.

MAGONIA   An important strand in the history of belief in nature spirits, the legend of Magonia was first recorded in *Liber de Grandine et Tonitruis* by ninth century French priest Agobard of Lyons. He describes a notion, prevalent among "many men plunged in such great stupidity, sunk in such depths of folly," in an aerial country called Magonia that sent forth ships to sail upon the clouds. The Magonians had an arrangement with "storm wizards" who would evoke hail and wind to damage crops. The wizards would collect the resulting harvest for the cloud sailors, in return for (unspecified) "rewards."

Agobard describes a curious incident that occurred in the city of Lyons. One day, he came upon a mob preparing to stone to death three men and a woman. The mob claimed that these individuals had fallen from the sky out of Magonian cloud ships and, therefore, were evildoers who should be executed. Whereas most contemporary defenders of orthodoxy did not question the common belief in the reality of occult beings but held that all unseen entities except ANGELS were creatures of the Devil, Agobard was skeptical. He persuaded the crowd that Magonia was nonexistent and that their prisoners were innocent.

Seventeenth century writer Montfaucon de Villars gave an account of this event more in keeping with traditional esoteric beliefs. He reported that the Magonians belonged to the race of spirits known as sylphs. The magician Zedechias invited them to become visible in order to demonstrate their existence to such nonbelievers as Agobard. The sylphs readily complied, but the ignorant masses were so terrified that they presumed the Magonians must be DEMONS in league with harmful wizards. To clear their reputation, the sylphs carried off human witnesses and showed them "their beautiful women, their Republic and their manner of government." Afterward, the witnesses were returned to earth to serve as "Ambassadors of the Sylphs." The four unfortunates Agobard mentioned were just such ambassadors and, reported Montfaucon, stated as much to the frightened crowd after alighting from the cloud ship.

The Magonia stories permit a rare glimpse into the survival of belief in elementals from ancient times into the Middle Ages. Magonians, like other aerial entities in this tradition, are mortal and are not always good, thus distinguishing them from the angels of Christian orthodoxy. They may be related to the "neutral angels" of the Holy

Grail stories, a mixture of pagan and Christian beliefs that became embodied in the Grail literature of southern and central France a few centuries after the Magonian sightings. The tradition of encounters with aerial beings represented by the Magonia legend also surfaces in the reports of meetings between Elizabethan medium ED-WARD KELLY and a strange dwarf who traveled "in a little fiery cloud" (as described in the diaries of JOHN DEE). The great German hermetist PARACELSUS also reported encounters and devoted a book to discussing their nature.

In recent times, unidentified-flying-object (UFO) researcher Jacques Vallee has related the legend of Magonia to the modern phenomenon of mysterious objects in the sky. Some of these objects have reportedly abducted human beings and later returned them to earth. Vallee argues that these persistent modern reports are recent visitations by the same other-dimensional beings who assumed the garb of Magonian encounters in ninth century France.

MAJORINUS   In A.D. 311, a group of North African bishops refused to recognize the new bishop of Carthage appointed by Rome because he had once allowed Roman persecutors to destroy copies of the Bible. Instead, they elected Majorinus bishop. This event marked the formation of a rebellious Christian movement, known as DONATISM, in the region.

MALABAR CHRISTIANS   A Christian community that has existed in southwest India since ancient times. According to legend, Saint Thomas founded their movement in the first century, although most historians regard the story as highly unlikely. Much more plausible is the idea that the Malabar Christians originated from missionary activity by the heretical followers of NESTORIANISM, who came from Syria in the sixth century. The Indian Christians renounced Nestorian doctrines and joined the Roman Catholic Church in 1599. Since that time, there have been many SCHISMS and reconciliations within this community.

MALLEUS MALEFICARUM   This text, literally the "Hammer of Witches," was the most important witch hunter's manual of the Renaissance GREAT WITCH HUNT. First published in 1486, *Malleus Maleficarum* was reprinted in more than thirty editions during the next two centuries. Although other manuals appeared later in the Witch Hunt period, such as COMPENDIUM MALEFICARUM, most of these books merely elaborated on the foundation the *Malleus* laid. Even though the Protestants rejected the authority of the Catholic INQUISITION, they carried on their own witch persecutions and continued to use this book as their guide.

The authors were Heinrich Kramer and James Sprenger, two Dominican friars. Sprenger was the Dean of Cologne University and brought to the text a deep knowledge of Catholic theology. Kramer, an experienced witch hunter, had been active in the Tyrolean Alps, where he developed an effective way to secure convictions for witchcraft. First, an assistant was hidden inside an oven. Pretending to be the Devil, the assistant would call out the names of local people, whom Kramer would apprehend and torture until they confessed. The scheme provoked such an uproar that eventually the regional bishop drove Kramer out.

Pope Innocent VIII was a supporter of Kramer and his witch hunt. Outraged at the treatment received by his Inquisitor, the pontiff issued his famous bull of 1484. In this proclamation, he rejects skepticism concerning the reality of witchcraft and orders the excommunication of anyone who fails to help the witch hunters in their work. Innocent's bull was distributed throughout Europe and fanned the fires of persecution. It was included as the opening section and justification of the *Malleus*.

Kramer and Sprenger's book is divided into three sections. The first section is devoted primarily to arguing for the reality and danger of witches. The authors proclaim that disbelief in witches is a heresy. Witches renounce the Catholic Church, worship Satan, sacrifice unbaptized babies, and have sex with demons. People in league with the Devil can cause men to become infatuated, change into animals, become impotent, and even believe that they have been emasculated.

The *Malleus* notes that most witches are female. This fact is explained by presenting a host of quotations from Christianity's vast legacy of woman-hating literature. They establish the female's naturally weaker faith and morality in tones of real horror: "Their face is a burning wind, and their voice the hissing of serpents; but they also cast wicked spells on countless men and animals."

In the second section, the various spell-casting activities of witches are explored in greater detail. Three kinds of witches are discussed: those who can curse but not cure, those who can both curse and cure, and those who only cure. Thus, even utterly harmless people engaged in folk healing practices are targeted for persecution because their cures are said to be caused by demons. Some defenses against evil magic are recommended, including prayers, exorcism, charms (provided they refer to strictly orthodox beings, such as recognized saints), and even burning fish livers in order to drive away a demon.

The third section of the *Malleus* presents a complete guide to the conduct of a witch trial. Kramer and Sprenger argue that the task of hunting witches should not be left up to the Dominican Inquisitors alone; bishops and secular government officials are also responsible. This claim permitted the spread of the GREAT WITCH HUNT even into regions where there were no representatives of the Inquisition. If, through a technicality, a suspect could not be prosecuted by an Inquisitor, the non-inquisitorial agencies could take over, ensuring that almost no one accused could escape.

The *Malleus* instructs that when Inquisitors arrive in a town, they should post an announcement calling for informants. These witnesses may remain anonymous and never have to confront those whom they accuse. The interrogation process, from the initial questioning of witnesses to the torturing of the witch, is described in detail. The most important task of the interrogation is the extraction of a confession from the witch; only self-confessed witches can be punished. Regarding torture, Kramer and Sprenger note that "unless God, through a holy Angel, compels the devil to withhold his help from the witch, she will be so insensible to the pains of torture that she will sooner be torn limb from limb than confess any of the truth." Rather than concluding that torture is therefore useless, the authors proceed to argue that torture should not be neglected because "the devil sometimes of his own will permits them to confess their crimes." Such logical inconsistencies are found throughout the text.

If, following torture, the suspect has not yet confessed, she can be offered the chance to undergo an ordeal. In this trial, the person is required to carry a heated piece of iron for three paces; if the suspect can do so, this is taken as a sign from God that the individual is innocent. In the case of suspected witches, however, the offer is a trap: witches "all desire this, knowing that the devil will prevent them from being hurt; therefore a true witch is exposed in this manner . . . they are never to be allowed to undergo this ordeal by red-hot iron." The *Malleus* encourages witch hunters to trick the suspect into believing that her life will be spared if she confesses: "let the Judge come in and promise that he will be merciful, with the mental reservation that he means he will be merciful to himself or the State; for whatever is done for the safety of the State is merciful."

In the face of all the traps and twists of logic found in these proceedings, it is hardly surprising that few suspects in trials guided by the *Malleus* failed to confess. As a result, the biases of the judges were confirmed. Witches' confessions verified the existence of the supernatural conspiracy thought to be threatening Christian civilization.

Not everyone of the time was enthusiastic about the "Witches' Hammer" and its effects. The *Malleus* closes with a letter from the Faculty of Theology at the University of Cologne praising the work; curiously, it was signed by only four faculty members, suggesting that the rest had different opinions. When Sprenger died in 1495, his colleagues at the university did not give him a Requiem Mass, which was unusual. Again, misgivings regarding his bloody contribution to history may have been responsible.

MANES   Manes is a common variant name of MANI, the third century Persian founder of MANICHAEISM.

MANI   This Persian spiritual innovator founded the religion of MANICHAEISM. In the history of orthodoxy and heresy in the West, Mani's name became synonymous with some of the most menacing brands of nonconformist thinking. Orthodox Christian writers attacking Mani's teaching frequently made humorous use of the coincidence that Mani's name closely resembled the Greek word for madness, *mania*.

Mani was born near the Tigris River in Babylonia in A.D. 216. The region was part of the Persian Empire at the time. Mani traveled widely, visiting far-flung corners and borderlands of the Empire. During his journeys, he encountered a variety of spiritual systems. Among these, Buddhism, GNOSTICISM, and Zoroastrianism, the dominant faith of Persia, strongly affected the development of Mani's own world view.

None of the religions Mani studied satisfied him. He came to believe that they all contained the same basic message, but in an incomplete form. He took what he believed to be true from each one and constructed a new religion. From Zoroastrianism, he adopted the idea that the universe was the battleground of two gods who had existed since the beginning, the Lord of Light and the Lord of Darkness. From the mythologies of Gnosticism, Mani adopted the notion that divine beings create by "emanation," or producing other beings from themselves. He also agreed with the Gnostics that awakening to one's true nature—GNOSIS—led to salvation. Finally, Mani is thought to have borrowed the idea of REINCARNATION from Buddhist sources.

Mani proclaimed himself the Messiah of his new religion. He announced that he had come to complete the work of the great teachers of the other religions, such as Buddha, Zoroaster, and JESUS. During the reign of Persian ruler Shapur I, Mani saw much success in his mission. He spread his message far and wide and made converts.

Mani believed that a problem with earlier great teachers was that they had not written down their doctrines. He was a prolific writer and a visual artist, portraying his views in a series of drawings. Manichaean communities reverently preserved and studied his words and pictures for many centuries after his death. Unfortunately, the enemies of Manichaeism did a fairly thorough job of destroying this material. Today, only fragments and brief quotations from Mani's writings exist, and his illustrations have been lost.

The luck of the new Messiah began to change when Shapur was succeeded by a new ruler, Bahram I. The Magi, the priests of the Zoroastrian faith, campaigned to reform their religion. They regarded Mani as a heretic, or a competitor, and influenced the king to condemn him. There are various accounts of Mani's death. Some sources report that he was crucified. Others state that, alternatively, he was flayed alive, or that he was beheaded and that his head was mounted on a pole for public scorn. The most poetic account recorded that the imprisoned Mani ended his life by leaving his body:

> the Apostle of Light took off the warlike dress of the body and sat down in a ship of Light and received the divine garment, the diadem of Light and the beautiful garland. And in great joy he flew together with the Light-gods that are going to the right and to the left of him, with harp-sound and song of joy. . . .

Mani was both revered and reviled during his lifetime. With the spread of the Manichaean religion following his death, Mani's memory acquired the luster of divinity. In Asia, Mani was referred to as the Buddha of Light. In some writings, Mani is identified simply as God. And to Christians, competing with his followers for souls, he was "Mani the madman."

MANICHAEISM   This great religious movement takes its name from its founder, a third century Persian martyr named MANI. At the movement's peak, followers of Manichaeism existed from Spain to China. Historian Kurt Rudolph counts Manichaeism as one of the four "world religions" in history (along with Buddhism, Christianity, and Islam), and as the only one that became extinct. Manichaean beliefs provided stiff competition for Christianity in ancient times. The religion's tenets decisively affected the development of Christian doctrines, both mainstream and heretical.

Knowledge of the Manichaean faith is derived from two sources: surviving Manichaean scriptures and attacks composed by its opponents. Most of the authentic Manichaean material has been discovered in the twentieth century. In the early 1900s, a Manichaean library was found in Turfan, Western China, dating from the days of the Uighur Empire (seventh to thirteenth centuries), which adopted Manichaeism as the state religion. An even more astonishing discovery was made in 1930. A lucky browser in a used bookstore in Egypt turned up a Manichaean manuscript, 3,500 pages in length. This material, including hymns and lectures by Mani, has been dated to the fourth century.

The best-known hostile writings concerning Manichaeism are a collection of letters by Augustine of Hippo, composed around the beginning of the fifth century. Augustine knew his topic well; he had been a Manichaean himself for nine years before converting to Christianity. Another important hostile source is the work of Theodore bar Konai, a Babylonian who lived in the eighth century.

Persia, the originating point of Manichaeism, borders both Western and Eastern cultural spheres. Influences from both directions became blended in Manichaean doctrines. A major contribution came from GNOSTICISM, the spiritual movement that thrived in the Mediterranean region for the first few centuries A.D. Manichaeism is often regarded as a Persian variant of the Gnostic movement.

The Manichaean explanation of the origin of the world is as elaborate as the systems found in other Gnostic schools. A distinctively Manichaean feature is the teaching that two radically opposed forces, one luminous and good, the other material and evil, have existed since the beginning of time. This extreme dualism was adopted from Zoroastrianism, an ancient Persian religion.

According to Mani, the Kingdom of Light is ruled by the Lord of Light, who produced from himself five beings called aeons. In the Kingdom of Darkness, the Lord of Darkness generated five archons, each ruling an army of demons. The dark powers prepared to attack the Kingdom of Light. In response to the threat, the Lord of Light, in typical Gnostic fashion, set off a sequence of "emanations," or productions of divine beings. The Lord himself emanated Sophia, who in turn emanated the Mother of Life, who then emanated Ohrmuzd, the primal man.

Ohrmuzd battled the forces of darkness but was defeated and devoured by them. He even lost awareness of his own true identity. His light became fragmented and encased within the darkness of matter. This event seems to have been a ruse by the Lord of Light, however, in preparation for the ultimate defeat of his evil opponents.

The Lord of Light sent forth another emanation, called Mithra, to awaken Ohrmuzd to his identity. Ohrmuzd's realization that his nature is divine light serves as a model for all humanity. People are all essentially sparks of holy light, imprisoned by their attachments to matter. The first step toward liberation lies in recognizing this predicament. The awakening of the primal man from his forgetfulness was described with great poetic power in THE HYMN OF THE PEARL, a literary masterpiece of Manichaeism.

Because the light of Ohrmuzd was trapped within matter, additional steps had to be taken to free him. A third emanation from the world of good, named God of the Realm of Light, appeared in a sexually attractive form. This appearance aroused the archons into a frenzy. They proceeded to ejaculate and vomit, thus discharging the captured light from their bodies. The light was still mixed with particles of matter, however.

In order to prevent the departure of the light, the archons formed Adam and Eve to contain the expelled luminosity. From that day to this, fragments of light remain anchored in human bodies. Like the followers of SETHIAN GNOSTICISM, the Manichaeans revered the serpent in the Garden of Eden, even identifying it as the Christ, because it attempted to convey knowledge to the first couple. The Creator God portrayed in the Old Testament was believed to be none other than the Lord of Darkness.

The Manichaeans also believed that the ensnared light particles pass from body to body in an endless cycle of REINCARNATION, until they are freed. This process could involve rebirth in an animal form or perhaps even in the body of a plant. Consequently, Manichaeism was uncomfortable with agriculture, viewing the harvest as a sort of mass murder.

The mission of Manichaeism was to separate completely the spiritual light and the material darkness. Followers believed that when this process of separation was finished, the Kingdom of Darkness would be utterly defeated. Mani taught that a series of teachers had appeared on earth to impart the means of liberating the light within. He included Buddha, Zoroaster, and JESUS. The life and crucifixion of Christ was regarded as an illusion enacted by a nonmaterial, ghostly image sent by the Lord of Light. This portrayal of Christ, also found in some other unorthodox Christian traditions, is the heresy of DOCETISM. Mani proclaimed that he himself was the greatest teacher, the Messiah. Manichaeism was the first known system of thought to claim that both Eastern and Western religions teach the same basic message.

As particles of light are released from their material traps, they travel to the moon. (This strange doctrine recurs, with a twist, in the teachings of twentieth century mystic GEORGE GURDJIEFF). They are then drawn to the sun, home of the God of the Realm of Light, and transferred to a heavenly domain. One of the keys to achieving the liberation of one's own spiritual essence was unveering obedience to the Manichaean Church. Unlike other Gnostic schools, Manichaeism was organized into a hierarchy of community power from the beginning. The two main divisions within Manichaean society were the elect, who could attain liberation without more incarnations, and the hearers, who required additional lives before they would be purified enough to be freed (Augustine was a hearer during his stint as a Manichaean). The elect class was organized into a system of apostles, bishops, elders, and regular elect.

The hearers purified themselves, in the hope of achieving rebirth as one of the elect, through providing support for the elect, and through devotion to Mani as the savior. This devotion took the form of singing hymns, and studying and copying scriptures. The elect, for their part, led a strictly disciplined life. They abstained from sex because babies were seen as fresh prisons for the entrapped light. Their diet was strictly vegetarian, with one bizarre exception. Augustine reported that the sacrament of the Manichaeans was a combination of dough and semen. The theory justifying this culinary novelty was that the semen contained trapped light particles. These little prisoners could be released from matter if they were ingested by members of the elect, who were close to liberation themselves.

Augustine eventually rejected the Manichaean doctrines; he went on to become one of the most influential thinkers in Christian history. His Manichaean past most likely shaped some of the attitudes he retained as a Christian. Through Augustine, the flavor of the Manichaean world view entered conventional Christian thought.

Augustine the Christian dismissed the Manichaean notion of an independent and primordial evil being as inconsistent with God's supreme greatness. Evil for Augustine was simply the absence of good. He also argued against the Gnostic claim that knowledge can lead to liberation. According to Augustine, human will is too corrupted by original sin to accomplish salvation through any amount of knowledge or effort on its own. But he retained the Manichaeans' basic distrust of matter, especially with regard to sex. Augustine taught that Adam's arrogant turning away from God's will produced a state of unbalanced desire, called concupiscence. This disordered, sinful desire infects every act of sex, aside from pleasureless encounters within marriage for the sake of producing children. Augustine's attack on sexual delight, likely inspired by his Manichaeist-conditioned degradation of physical pleasures, has led untold millions of orthodox Christians to feel guilty because they had sexual feelings.

In addition to influencing orthodox beliefs directly, Manichaeism might also have inspired some of the important Christian heresies. The PAULICIANS and BO-GOMILS were significant heresies that spread into eastern Europe during the Middle Ages. These schools promoted an extreme dualism, positing the primordial existence of an evil being who created matter. Some scholars hold that these groups were direct descendants of Manichaean communities. The heresy of the CA-THARS, which challenged Catholicism in western Europe during the later medieval period, has also been linked to Manichaeism by some historians. Others believe that the Cathar movement, while superficially resembling Manichaeism, arose independently from sources in medieval society. Whatever the case, the orthodox opponents of the Paulicians, Bogomils, and Cathars freely labeled them as Manichaeans.

The staunch opposition of Catholic Christianity to the Manichaeans following Augustine's conversion led to their demise in Europe during the following centuries, as well as to the destruction of their literature. Manichaeism continued to thrive in central Asia for many hundreds of years. Portuguese travelers in China reported contact with Manichaean traditions as recently as the seventeenth century. Today, Manichaeism is a dead religion. The Mandaean faith, a belief system related to Manichaeism, is still followed by a small group in Iraq.

MARCELLINA   A teacher of the second century heresy called CARPOCRATIAN GNOSTICISM, Marcellina came to Rome and, in the words of orthodox Christian writer Irenaeus of Lyons, "led many astray." Marcellina scandalized the orthodox Christians for two reasons. First, she was a woman, and Catholic women were discouraged from religious leadership roles. Second, her school taught that people should share everything freely, including their sexuality.

MARCELLUS OF ANCYRA   This bishop of Ancyra (modern Ankara, Turkey) played an important role in the church's struggle against the heresy of ARIANISM during the early fourth century. Like many other zealous Christians through history, Marcellus of Ancyra reacted against the heresy by embracing very opposite views, which the orthodoxy declared to be heretical. The Arians, who believed that Christ was not God but rather a divine being God created, had grown powerful during Marcellus's early life. The Arian definition of Christ was opposed by theologians who argued that Christ was God. This view became the orthodox position on the matter, but the struggle with the Arians was long and bitter. Marcellus became a major spokesperson for the orthodox view.

Marcellus participated in the fateful FIRST COUNCIL OF NICAEA in A.D. 325, when the Arian doctrine was officially refuted (although it was far from defeated). He favored the definition that described the elements of the Trinity—the Father, Son, and Holy Spirit—as being "consubstantial," that is, having the same essence. During the turbulent times that followed, the Arian party deposed Marcellus from his role in the church at Ancyra.

When Marcellus retreated to Rome, he was interviewed by the pope and declared to be orthodox in his beliefs. However, it soon became evident that aspects of Marcellus's teaching were close to the heresy of MODALISM. This doctrine states that the Father and the Son are simply different names for the one divine Person, rather than being distinct Persons.

Some scholars refer to Marcellus's ideas as CRYPTO-SABELLIANISM. In their view, this belief system resembled the doctrine of the modalist SABELLIUS in a cryptic or disguised way. Marcellus stated that the Son did not exist before the conception of JESUS Christ, ceases to exist as the Son after Christ's lifetime, and does not exist at all as a Person distinct from God the Father. Furthermore, Marcellus seems to have believed that the Holy Spirit is not a Person, but rather an impersonal function of God.

These views are at variance with the fundamental Catholic doctrine that the Father, Son, and Holy Spirit, although they are consubstantial, are distinct, eternal Persons. (Arianism, although it disagreed with orthodoxy concerning consubstantiality, also held that the Persons of the Trinity are distinct.)

The orthodox Christian leaders had a dilemma: They valued Marcellus's support, but his teachings enabled the Arians to claim that the formula of consubstantiality established at Nicaea was a disguised form of the modalist heresy. The Catholics' response to this difficult position was to evade the issue of the number of distinct divine Persons when Marcellus was in attendance at a debate against the Arians, and to argue for the distinctiveness of the Persons when he was absent. In the final version of the Nicene Creed, the official Catholic statement of faith, a clause was added: "of his (Christ's) reign there will be no end." The clause was included as an explicit rejection of Marcellus's theory that the Son ceased to reign after Christ's lifetime.

MARCION   This spiritual teacher, active during the second century A.D., was seen as a menace by the early Catholic Church. Historian Harold Brown designated Marcion as "the first great heretic" in Christian history. In response to the allure of Marcion's teachings, the leaders of the orthodox Christian community were forced to codify their beliefs by composing the Apostles' Creed, and to decide which books to include in the New Testament.

Marcion was born around A.D. 85, in the town of Sinope by the Black Sea. He was a shipowner and became prosperous. His wealth gave him the opportunity to move to the heart of the empire, and so he relocated to Rome. Marcion joined the Catholic Church in Rome, but his understanding of Christianity was so unorthodox and tenacious that he was excommunicated four years later. Catholic writers of the time claimed that he was expelled from the church for an act of "immorality," probably sexual in nature. Given the antisexual nature of his teachings, this charge is almost certainly an attempt by the orthodox to discredit Marcion through slander.

Although rejected by the Catholic Church, Marcion believed that he, and not they, preserved the true Christian teachings. He devoted the rest of his life to continuous traveling and teaching throughout the empire and founded Marcionite communities in many locations. Marcion died in A.D. 160, leaving as his legacy a Marcionite "counter-church" to compete with Catholicism. The Marcionite movement continued until the end of the following century in the heart of the empire. In border regions like Armenia, Marcion's teachings were reverently preserved for several centuries. But the triumphant Catholic Church destroyed all of Marcion's writings. All that is left are fragments of his work, preserved in quotations that were included in the surviving books of his orthodox opponents.

The feature of orthodox Christian doctrine that struck Marcion as a serious error was the belief that the God of the Old Testament, the Creator, was the same deity as that presented in the New Testament as the God of Love. Marcion pointed out that the Old Testament God was war-like, wrathful, and unforgiving. This God issued a strict set of laws for humans to live by and punished disobedience. The God described by Christ, merciful and joyous, seemed radically different. The tension between the two sides of God—justice and mercy—has been a recurring theme in Catholic theology through the centuries, and was resolved in various ways by orthodox theologians. Marcion resolved it in the simplest way: by proclaiming that there is not one God, but two.

According to Marcion, the Old Testament God of the Law did create the world, including the human race. The God of the Law predicted, in the Old Testament prophecies, that that he would send a Messiah who would bring salvation to humanity. However, Marcion claimed, this promised salvation would only improve conditions on earth; it would not involve spiritual freedom because the God of the Law would still expect to be strictly obeyed. This predicted Messiah had not yet arrived.

The God of Love is completely alien to the world. He became aware of the suffering of humanity, however, and chose to appear on earth as Christ, in order to lead people to a salvation of a higher kind than that promised by the Creator God. The God of Love offers freedom from the constraining laws, as well as liberation into a nonmaterial realm of happiness.

In Marcion's view, Christ was never a human being but was the God of Love himself. This lack of distinction between the Persons of Christ and God the Father is an early echo of the heresy of MODALISM. The idea that Christ's body was not made of matter but was a ghostly spiritual image was a notion shared by Marcion and his heretical contemporaries, the Gnostics, and is known as the doctrine of DOCETISM.

During Marcion's lifetime, many writings concerning Christ's nature and message circulated among the Christian communities. The Catholic Church had not yet attempted to declare which of these works contained authentic teachings and which were spurious. In order to support his version of Christianity, Marcion stated that the books of the Old Testament were irrelevant to Christians because they pertained to the God of the Law and not the God of Love. Marcion recognized portions of the letters of Paul as authentic. Indeed, he thought that Paul was the only apostle who accurately understood JESUS' teaching. Marcion also accepted parts of the Gospel of Luke. He rejected all other Christian writings as fraudulent.

As the God of the Law created human bodies, their features and activities held no value for Marcion. He claimed that differences in gender meant nothing in the realm of spiritual activity. One of Marcion's greatest sins in the eyes of the orthodox was to allow women full equality in his church, even permitting them to become priests and bishops. The Catholic Church father (and, later in life, heretic) TERTULLIAN, one of the main opponents of the Marcionites, commented with horror: "These heretical women—how audacious they are! They have no modesty; they are bold enough to teach, to engage in argument, to enact exorcisms, to undertake cures, and, it may be, even to baptize!"

Marcion rejected the institution of marriage and taught that sex was unspiritual because it led to offspring. The reproduction of the species simply created more people who would have to suffer under the burdens the God of the Law imposed. Since the physical body is the creation and, therefore, the property of the God of the Law, Marcion did not believe that a resurrection of the body was part of the God of Love's salvation.

Although Marcion is sometimes classified as a Gnostic, his teachings differ in fundamental ways from most Gnostic schools. Whereas the Gnostics said that salvation was attained through a special knowledge, called GNOSIS, Marcion taught that only faith in Christ led to freedom. Most Gnostics taught that the world creator was somehow descended from God the Father; Marcion argued that they were unrelated.

Marcion's challenge of orthodoxy's claim to be the preservers of Christian truth drew a response, the consequences of which are still felt. Many scholars believe that Marcion's rejection of most of orthodoxy's favorite texts from his short list of authentic Christian writings provoked the Catholics to form their own collection of approved books, the New Testament. Some historians also believe that Marcion's system of two Gods spurred Catholic Christianity to underline its commitment to one God, the deity of both justice and mercy, world creator, and begetter of Christ. Historian Elaine Pagels suggested that the composers of the Apostles' Creed, the authoritative statement of basic Catholic doctrine, might have been targeting Marcionites when they wrote the first sentence: "I believe in one God, Father Almighty, Maker of heaven and earth."

MARCIONISM   One of the first Christian heresies, the Marcionite movement began during the second century. It takes its name and fundamental teachings from its founder, MARCION. Marcionism spread throughout the Roman Empire. In response to the Marcionites, who declared that almost all of the writings in existence regarding Christ were false, the orthodox church was forced to declare which texts they believed were authentic, thereby selecting the contents of the New Testament.

MARONITES   This Christian community traces its origins to Maro, a Christian hero of the fifth century. Historians believe, however, that the Maronites originally comprised a group of Lebanese Christians who adhered to the doctrine of MONO-THELETISM, a heretical belief that arose during the first part of the seventh century. The Monotheletes maintained that Christ has only one will. This idea was declared a heresy at the THIRD COUNCIL OF CONSTANTINOPLE in 680–681, which supported the orthodox notion of a Christ with two wills. The Maronites managed to retain their belief following the Council's condemnation because the Moslems had conquered Lebanon, and the orthodox Christians were unable to enforce their doctrinal monopoly there. During the twelfth century, Roman Catholic Crusaders established themselves in the region. In 1182, the Maronite community thought it wise to establish an association with the Roman Catholic Church, so they abandoned the Monothelete heresy at that time.

Arnold MATHEW   An important WANDERING BISHOP at the beginning of the twentieth century, Arnold Mathew was born in England in 1853 and ordained a Roman Catholic priest in 1877. Twelve years later, he left the church and tried a variety of other groups. In 1908, Mathew was consecrated a bishop by the OLD CATHOLIC Church in the Netherlands, but was repudiated two years later. He had led his Dutch hosts to believe that he had a congregation in England, which was not the case. Thus freed of all ecclesiastical authorities, Mathew could consecrate as a bishop anyone he chose, and frequently did so. His best-known follower was James Wedgwood, of the family famous for its manufacture of fine china; Mathew consecrated Wedgwood in 1913.

Mathew was notorious for his odd behaviors and beliefs. On one occasion, he brought a live tiger with him to the pulpit in a church. He was also an outspoken advocate of the theory that Francis Bacon was the true author of Shakespeare's plays. Mathew died in 1919. Today, at least twenty independent churches, from the Mexican Old Roman Catholic Church to the Diocese-Vicariate of Niagara Falls, trace their claims of validity to Mathew's consecration.

Jan MATTHYS   Jan Matthys was a leader of the ANABAPTISTS during the early sixteenth century. He was a baker in the Dutch city of Haarlem. He heard the prophecy of the Anabaptist preacher MELCHIOR HOFFMANN that God would soon set up the New Jerusalem, a holy city, in Europe. In 1533, when Anabaptists came to power in the German city of Münster, Matthys concluded that the New Jerusalem was at hand. He traveled to Münster, rapidly becoming one of the leaders of the governing group. As an orthodox army surrounded Münster, Matthys decreed that anyone who refused to be rebaptized according to Anabaptist rules should be expelled. This heretic met his end when he heard God's voice informing him that he was invincible; accompanied by only twenty comrades, he engaged the besieging troops in battle and was killed almost instantly.

See also: MÜNSTER HERETICS.

MAXIMILLA   One of the early leaders of the second century heretical movement called MONTANISM, Maximilla claimed to be able to receive messages from the Holy Spirit, an ability shared by MONTANUS, the heresy's founder, and PRISCA, another disciple. Maximilla's female gender, as well as her unorthodox teachings, shocked many Catholic Christians, who believed that women should not give spiritual instruction to men.

MEDMENHAM MONKS   This group of British aristocrats who used to conduct secret meetings in the ruins of Medmenham Abbey during the mid-1700s was led by SIR FRANCIS DASHWOOD. The Medmenham Monks enacted ceremonies, the nature of which is not actually known. They probably involved such mainstream Christian rites as the mass, and possibly included sexual activities and the worship of pagan deities. Their political enemies charged the Monks with SATANISM, but it seems unlikely that the group actually worshipped the Devil.

MELCHIORITES   A group of sixteenth century ANABAPTISTS who followed the teachings of MELCHIOR HOFFMANN and were particularly strong in number in the Netherlands. Such Melchiorites as JAN MATTHYS played a leading role in the violent attempt by the MÜNSTER HERETICS to establish the New Jerusalem in Germany. Following this episode, the Anabaptist movement came under terrible persecution and threatened to dissolve; MENNO SIMONS, another Melchiorite, reorganized many Anabaptists in a more moderate direction, establishing the church of the MENNONITES.

MELITUS OF LYCOPOLIS   At the beginning of the fourth century, the Catholic Church was about to succeed in its long-sought-after goals of acquiring legitimacy and ending persecution in the Roman Empire. At this time, Melitus provoked a SCHISM within the church. He was the bishop of the town of Lycopolis in Egypt. During the previous centuries, the community of Christians in Egypt and throughout the empire had been subject to waves of persecution at the hands of the Roman authorities. Some of the persecuted individuals chose to endure torture and death rather than renounce their faith; others opted to deny their Christian beliefs during the hostilities and sought readmission to the church when the persecution ended. The general policy of the Catholic Church had been to accept these "lapsed" Christians back into the fold provided they performed appropriate penances. This policy was reaffirmed in a proclamation by Peter, the bishop of Alexandria, in 306.

Some Christians, including Melitus, felt that the Catholic position was too lenient. They argued that mortal sinners, including people who had renounced the faith, could not be forgiven. Melitus was under the authority of Peter. Since they were unable to resolve their differences, Peter excommunicated Melitus. He responded, not by retiring from his position, but by stating that the mainstream church had become morally corrupt. Melitus then began to ordain priests who agreed with his uncompromising position regarding church morality, and led a community of followers out of the Catholic Church.

The Melitian Church was orthodox in its doctrine, but deviated from Catholicism in its refusal to obey commands from higher levels in the Catholic power structure. This independent-mindedness may have influenced one of Melitus's associates, a young monk named ARIUS. This man was soon to spearhead a much more dangerous threat to the Catholic Church: the heresy of ARIANISM. The church Melitus founded was never large. The movement is thought to have survived in Egypt until the eighth century.

MENANDER   A disciple of first century Gnostic SIMON MAGUS, Menander succeeded Simon as the leader of SIMONIAN GNOSTICISM, a tradition identified by the early Christians as the source of all heresies. Menander reportedly taught his followers that their belief in him would prevent them from dying.

MENNONITES   The Mennonite movement emerged from the communities of ANABAPTISTS during a period of persecution in the sixteenth century. Following the violent insurrection the Anabaptist MÜNSTER HERETICS staged in 1534 and the equally violent suppression that followed, the teachings of MENNO SIMONS provided an alternative vision for Anabaptists to follow. The Mennonites derive their name from that of their founder.

The early Mennonites shared with other Anabaptist groups the belief that the Protestant Reformation was too small a step in the right direction of returning Christianity to its roots. For example, the Mennonites rejected the baptism of infants because the practice could not be supported with references from the New Testament. From Simons, the Mennonites learned that orthodoxy (both Catholic and Protestant) was wrong in claiming that JESUS had walked the earth in a body made of ordinary matter; rather, Christ's flesh was composed of a heavenly substance. The divine flesh actually became present during the Holy Communion ceremony. Only Christians who led a pure life should be allowed to participate in this sacred presence. As a result, Mennonites who suffered serious moral lapses were quickly excommunicated and shunned forever afterward. Such strict discipline among the Mennonite congregations helped to strengthen the community bonds in the face of pressure from their orthodox persecutors.

During the 1500s, the Mennonites were most numerous in the Netherlands, the country of their founder's birth; indeed, for a time they were the largest Protestant group there. Significant Mennonite communities also existed in Germany and Switzerland. Under constant attack, the scattered communities tended to turn inward, and differences developed among Mennonite groups. Major disagreements arose concerning the strictness of shunning and the degree to which forgiveness of sins should be allowed. In the late seventeenth century, the very strict AMISH branch split off from the Mennonite mainstream.

From the eighteenth century, Mennonites have migrated all over the globe; they were drawn first to southern Russia by the promise of religious toleration granted by Catherine the Great, then to various locations in the Americas. Some groups became communistic, permitting no ownership of private property. In attempts to maintain undiluted spiritual purity, many communities actively resisted the intrusion of their host culture; in modern times, such innovations as electricity and automobiles are still forbidden in some Mennonite communities.

Recently, the Mennonite reputation of moral rigor has been tarnished in North America. In the early 1990s, a drug smuggling scheme operated by Mennonites was uncovered. Investigators found that, for many years, some Mexican Mennonites had been driving truckloads of marijuana past unsuspecting border guards for sale in the United States and Canada. It remains to be seen whether the Mennonite dream can much longer withstand the temptations of modern materialistic culture.

MERKABAH MYSTICISM   The word *Merkabah* is Hebrew for "chariot"— specifically, the chariot upon which God's throne rests, according to the vision of the Old Testament prophet Ezekiel. During the first few centuries A.D., a mystical school devoted to meditations that aimed to produce a vision of the divine chariot and throne developed in Palestine. The *Merkabah* tradition was one of the primary sources of the Jewish esoteric path known as KABBALAH.

The roots of *Merkabah* mysticism are found in the ancient Jewish literature called the PSEUDEPIGRAPHA, as well as in the ideas of GNOSTICISM. The Pseudepigraphic writers described elaborate visions of heaven. These accounts inspired some readers to attempt to induce such experiences themselves. The Gnostics claimed to possess knowledge that gave them direct contact with the divine. Some Gnostic groups, such as the BASILIDEAN GNOSTICS, practiced meditations in which they used chanting and visualizations to ascend by stages into the domain of the Father.

The practices of *Merkabah* were not viewed as heretical by most orthodox Jews, but as so powerful that only a select few could be allowed to learn about them. Any error during the meditations could lead to madness. Students had to be male, past the age of forty, knowledgeable in Jewish doctrine, ethical in their daily behavior, and possessing certain features on the hands and body.

The meditator began the visionary journey by placing his head between his knees, blocking out the sights and sounds of the outside world. He would visualize descending into his soul, traveling through seven heavenly palaces guarded by angels. In order to pass by these guardians, he would chant magical names that acted as passwords. Finally, the visionary attained the presence of God, who appeared in human form, seated on the throne of glory.

Secret circles in Palestine, Babylonia, and Europe preserved and studied the texts of the *Merkabah* mystics. A later tradition reported that the meditation would be successful only if the practitioner had first been purified with the ashes of a red heifer that had been sacrificed in the great Jewish Temple in Jerusalem. When the Temple was destroyed in A.D. 70, a small quantity of the special ashes was preserved and used sparingly. However, the supply was used up by the fifth century, and since then the *Merkabah* practices have not worked, according to this tradition. The writings of the *Merkabah* visionaries continued to circulate and inspired the Jewish mystics in twelfth century France to devise other means of approaching God, thereby establishing the practices of Kabbalah.

MESSALIANS   This name, derived from a Syrian word meaning "to pray," was applied to an unorthodox Christian sect that existed in the Middle East from the fourth to the seventh centuries. Little is known concerning the Messalians' doctrines, but it is likely that they preserved ideas of the ancient spiritual movement known as GNOSTICISM. Some historians believe that the Messalians transmitted Gnostic views to the PAULICIANS, dualistic Christians who appeared in Armenia in the seventh century, who in turn inspired the heretical European dualists of the Middle Ages, such as the BOGOMILS.

MICHAEL II   Ruler of the Byzantine Empire from A.D. 820 to 829, Michael II favored the heresy of ICONOCLASM, which opposed the use of images in Christian worship. Unlike some of his predecessors, Michael did not impose his views on his subjects through violence, but he tolerated the orthodox Christians' attachment to their holy pictures of Christ and the saints.

William MILLER   In the 1840s, America was thrown into turmoil by William Miller, a Baptist preacher who prophesied that Christ was about to return to earth. Most people today know nothing of this episode, but its legacy remains; from Miller's disciples, the MILLERITES, emerged the SEVENTH DAY ADVENTISTS, who are still strong in the late twentieth century.

Miller was born in Pittsfield, Massachusetts, in 1782, and moved with his family to upstate New York when he was a young boy. Although his mother was a devout Christian, Miller rejected her faith and became an atheist. Confronted with the horrors of violence when he fought on the losing side of the War of 1812, he was cast into a time of soul searching and converted to Christianity of the Baptist variety.

Miller's new-found fascination with religion led him to intense Bible study. Like many of his contemporaries (and some people today), he understood the scripture to contain information about the future history of the world, leading up to the second coming of Christ. This information was concealed, however; only the diligent true believer could uncover it. Miller became convinced that the mysterious prose of the Old Testament Book of Daniel indicated the date of Christ's return.

Daniel 8:14 contains the obscure phrase, "And he said unto me, Unto two thousand and three hundred days; then shall the sanctuary be cleansed." Miller thought this "cleansing" was Christ's return and that the "days" were actually years. Based on evidence elsewhere in the book, he concluded that the countdown began in 457 B.C. when Artaxerxes, the Persian King, ordered the rebuilding of Jerusalem. Simple arithmetic revealed the crucial date; the Lord would arrive in 1843. According to the Jewish calendar, the year actually ran from March 21, 1843, to March 21, 1844.

Miller kept the news to himself for a while, but eventually he began to preach. As the fateful year approached, his listeners started to react strongly. A number of Baptist ministers became convinced that he was right and helped to spread the news. The size of his following mushroomed. The mainstream churches and the secular press viewed him as a crackpot and dubbed him "Mad Miller."

On March 22, 1844, his shocked followers turned to him for an explanation. Where was the Lord? Miller announced that he had made a small error; the correct date of Christ's arrival was October 22, 1844. But once again, that day came and went and no Lord appeared. Following this second disappointment, Miller turned away from the game of theological calculation. He denounced the efforts of others to interpret the dates mystically rather than literally, and he insisted that he had simply erred in his calculations. However, Miller maintained his faith in the imminent appearance of Christ even if the precise arrival time could not be determined. And for him, perhaps, it was true: the failed arithmetical prophet died on December 20, 1849, at the age of sixty-seven.

MILLERISM   Through the 1820s and 1830s, WILLIAM MILLER preached in the northeastern United States, announcing that Christ would return to earth between March 21, 1843, and March 21, 1844. As the fateful year approached, the Millerite movement formed around him. The movement survived two failed prophecies but fragmented after a third. From the remnants of Millerism arose the SEVENTH DAY ADVENTISTS and, somewhat later, the group that became the JEHOVAH'S WITNESSES.

Miller's first important convert was Joshua V. Himes of Boston. Himes had the means to start a Millerite newspaper, *Signs of the Times*, which greatly increased the public's exposure to the prophecy. Soon afterward, other Millerite publications were founded, *The Midnight Cry* in New York and the *Philadelphia Alarm*.

Despite the expulsion of Millerites from mainstream church congregations and their ridicule in the conventional press, excitement mounted. In early 1843, a Millerite temple was dedicated in Boston, with 3,500 devotees in attendance. As March 21 loomed, the true believers prepared for the Lord to sweep them away. They put on white "ascension robes," climbed trees and haystacks, faced eastward, and waited.

And waited. March 21, 1844, came and went. The movement's leader announced that he had made a calculation error. Christ was actually coming on October 22. The initial disappointments seemed only to fuel the enthusiasm of the Millerites. An editorial in *The Midnight Cry* stated, "Let your actions preach in the clearest tones. The Lord is coming, the time is short. Prepare to meet thy God." Farmers throughout New England neglected their fields, expecting never to see another winter.

As Josiah Litch, a Philadelphia Millerite leader, put it in the October 24 issue of *The Midnight Cry*: "It is a cloudy and dark day here—the sheep are scattered—the Lord has not come yet." While Miller himself and many of his followers abandoned the attempt to predict the second coming, others were more creative. Following the disappointment of October 22, Millerite Hiram Edson received a revelation while slipping home through a cornfield to avoid the mockery of his neighbors. On the crucial date, Christ had not come to cleanse the earth but rather had emerged from His palace to begin the cleansing of heaven! Only after the Lord completed this task would He make Himself manifest on earth. Thus, the expectation of Christ's advent was enabled to persist in the face of a triple failure. From this seed grew the main Adventist movements of the twentieth century.

MODALISM   This important heresy concerns the nature of the Christian Trinity. Also known as MODALISTIC MONARCHIANISM, Modalism played a significant role in the struggle to formulate a universally accepted Christian doctrine during the third and fourth centuries A.D. Modalism has periodically resurfaced throughout Western history. A simple version of this doctrine is common among Christians today, many of whom would be shocked to learn that their understanding of the Trinity is technically heretical.

The Christian doctrine that God is a Trinity has never been easy to comprehend. Indeed, the orthodox position has been that humans cannot fully understand the mystery of the Trinity through the use of reason alone. However, during the first four centuries A.D., two important aspects of the Christian view of God became clear: that there is only one God (monotheism), and that God is a Trinity comprising the Father, Son, and Holy Spirit. How can God be both one and three? Efforts to clarify this paradox produced several responses in the ancient Christian community.

One of these responses was Modalism. According to the Modalists, God is a single divine Person. God's apparent multiplicity in the terms of the Trinity merely reflects the fact that God has taken on various roles over time. When He is in heaven, God is called the Father; when He incarnated on earth, God was the Son; and when He has affected human life since His incarnation, God is known as the Holy Spirit.

Modalism is perhaps the simplest way to untangle the Trinitarian paradox of one and many. However, the implications of Modalism clashed with several important beliefs of Catholic Christianity, and had to be rejected. For example, if the Son is just another name for God the Father, then Christ, the Son of God, was not a human being, but the Creator of the universe masquerading as a man. Catholic Christians have always insisted that Christ was a human being, who was also God (another doctrinal paradox that produced another spate of heresies, climaxing in the disagreements at the COUNCIL OF CHALCEDON).

The Modalists' idea that God the Father lived on earth produces even more difficulties, according to orthodox belief. If Christ was only God and not a man, then there is no reason to think that He had a human body made of flesh, and, therefore, He could not have been crucified (DOCETISM). If God the Father somehow did appear on earth with a human body, He would have suffered the physical agony of the crucifixion, and for most Christians the idea that the Creator could experience pain inflicted on Him by His own creation (PATRIPASSIANISM) was unthinkable.

The Modalist conviction that Father and Son are one Person fails to explain passages in the New Testament that seem to describe interactions between the Father and Son, the orthodox charged. These Biblical passages form the foundation for the Catholic description of Christ's role in salvation: Christ's suffering acted as a sacrifice to God the Father that atoned for the sins of Christians. It would make no sense for God to sacrifice Himself to Himself; therefore, Father and Son must be distinct Persons.

Modalism appeared in Rome at the end of the second century A.D. Immigrant preacher PRAXEAS convinced the bishop of Rome, VICTOR I, that Modalism should be promoted in order to combat another non-Catholic doctrine called ADOP-TIONISM. Adoptionism was a threat because it was seen as denying the divinity of Christ. This explains the appeal of Modalism for opponents of Adoptionism; Modalism emphasizes the divinity of Christ to the point of merging Him with the Creator.

Praxeas was followed in Rome by a succession of Modalist teachers; Pope Victor was succeeded by ZEPHYRINUS, who continued to support the Modalist doctrine. By the time Pope Callistus denounced SABELLIUS, the most prominent Modalist teacher of the time, around A.D. 220, the heresy had begun to spread through the Roman Empire.

By 260, Modalism proved so popular in the Egyptian city of Alexandria that Bishop Dionysius felt he had to magnify the distinction between the Father and Son in response. Many of his contemporaries thought that Dionysius went so far as to threaten the unity of God. Some scholars believe that Dionysius invented the heretical view known as ARIANISM in reaction to the theological provocation of the Modalists.

The Arian heresy taught that Father and Son are not only two distinct Persons, but that they do not even share the same nature. Christ was a divine being, but was not God. The orthodox party held that God was one in nature, but three in Persons. From the Arian perspective, orthodox Catholics and Modalists were not significantly different in their views. Both equated God and Christ at some level.

During the stormy debates that rocked the late Roman Empire over the Arian controversy, the charge of Modalism was frequently leveled at the orthodox position. The reason for this misunderstanding was largely linguistic. The Roman Catholics, writing in Latin, often used the word *persona* to refer to the idea of a divine Person. For Greek speakers, such as the Arians, however, the word *persona* was understood to mean "mask" or "role." The Arians thought that when the orthodox spoke of three "personae" in the Trinity, they meant three "masks" that God wore when performing various "roles"—in other words, Modalism. German historian Adolf von Harnack believed that the early Catholics actually *were* Modalists, and that they abandoned Modalism for what is now known as the orthodox formula later in the fight with Arianism.

MARCELLUS OF ANCYRA complicated the efforts of Catholicism to distinguish itself from Modalism. This bishop was a supporter of the orthodox position, but he derived implications from it that were very similar to Modalism. Marcellus was not officially declared to be a heretic—his support for orthodoxy was politically too useful to sacrifice—but he became an enduring source of embarrassment to the orthodox campaign for monopoly control of the Christian world view.

Orthodoxy had triumphed over both Modalism and Arianism by the end of the fourth century. Much later, in the sixteenth century, Modalistic doctrines resurfaced among some of the radical Protestants known as ANABAPTISTS. These Reformation Modalists were rejected by the mainstream Protestant leaders, who retained the orthodox formula for understanding the Trinity—God is three in Persons, one in nature. The logical next step beyond Modalism, the position that speaking of God as three Persons is meaningless, was taken by some members of the radical Protestant camp and eventually developed into a new religion, UNITARIANISM.

In the twentieth century, the orthodox doctrine of the Trinity has been downplayed in many quarters of the Christian community. Thus, the appeal of Modalism, with its fairly simple explanation of this ancient Christian mystery, has again increased.

See also: CLEOMENES, EPIGONUS, NOETUS, PHOTINUS.

MODALISTIC MONARCHIANISM   Modalistic Monarchianism is a variant term for the ancient Christian heresy called MODALISM.

See also: MONARCHIANISM.

MODERNISM   During the second half of the nineteenth century, historians began to examine the Bible using the same critical approach that they would employ to understand any other ancient documents. They discovered many inconsistencies, suggesting that the Biblical accounts of events, such as the life of JESUS, could not be considered accurate historical records. The Roman Catholic Church decided to fight back against such skepticism, using the critical tools of their enemies. Young Catholic scholars were encouraged to learn the methods of historical criticism in order to show that modern analysis could just as easily be used to support the beliefs of the church as to attack them.

This defensive attempt backfired. As a result of their critical studies, many of the brightest Catholic researchers found that they, too, were becoming skeptical about the literal truth of the New Testament accounts. The church claimed to be the final authority on matters of faith, so it was forced to take action to stem the flood of "Modernist" thinking within its own ranks. In 1893, Pope Leo XIII declared:

> All those books . . . which the church regards as sacred and canonical were written with all their parts under the inspiration of the Holy Spirit. Now, far from admitting the coexistence of error, Divine inspiration by itself excludes all error, and that also of necessity, since God, the Supreme Truth, must be incapable of teaching error.

In other words, the descriptions of events in the Bible must be literally correct, because God inspired the Bible's authors and God would not inspire falsehood. All the critical scholarship in the world amounts to nothing if this premise is accepted.

In 1903, Pope Leo created the PONTIFICAL BIBLICAL COMMISSION to monitor the orthodoxy of Catholic Biblical scholarship. Leo did not take punitive action against the Catholic Modernists, but Pius X, his successor, did. In 1907, Pius declared Modernism a heresy. Texts that examined the Bible from the standpoint of critical history were placed on THE INDEX OF PROHIBITED BOOKS. In addition, Catholic scholars who continued to hold Modernist views were excommunicated. A secret society, the Sodalitium Pianum, operated out of the Vatican, with the purpose of gathering information concerning the orthodoxy of Catholic intellectuals who might have Modernist leanings. The Sodalitium continued its operations until 1921.

See also: INQUISITION.

Solomon MOLCHO   A Spanish Jew who was forced to leave his homeland when Jews were banned from Spain in 1492, Solomon Molcho moved to Italy. Like many others, he became convinced that the mass expulsion of Spanish Jews was a sign that the long-awaited Messiah was about to appear. When DAVID REUBENI appeared in Venice in 1524 and proclaimed himself the savior, Molcho was deeply impressed. He acted as Reubeni's spokesperson for a while. Some accounts state that Molcho came to believe that he himself was the Messiah. In 1530, he ran afoul of Emperor Charles V, who had no tolerance for Jewish Messiahs. Molcho was burned at the stake in Mantua.

Miguel de MOLINOS   This Spanish mystic, who lived in the seventeenth century, founded the unorthodox spiritual system called QUIETISM. Born in 1640, Miguel de Molinos moved to Rome and rose to prominence in the Catholic hierarchy, becoming renowned for the quality of his spiritual guidance. In 1675, he published a book, *The Spiritual Guide*, in which he emphasizes Christian meditation practices.

Molinos believed that the way to God lay in completely ceasing all mental activity, especially that of the personal will. The mystic can then surrender totally to the will of God. If the mind is kept quiet, one can exist in a state of perpetual union with God. At this point, it is impossible to sin, no matter what a person does because all of one's acts must be the will of God.

Such a doctrine was open to abuse. Quietists could claim, or even believe, that they were surrendering to God's will when actually they were merely indulging their own desires. And indeed, Molinos himself seems to have succumbed to this temptation. He was accused and convicted of sexual activities with nuns who were under his supervision. Molinos was sentenced to life imprisonment. In 1687, his teachings were condemned as heresy. He died ten years later. His writings inspired MADAME GUYON to teach Quietistic views in France, provoking a hostile reaction from French Catholic officials.

MONARCHIANISM   This term is used to refer to two heresies that challenged the unity of the ancient Christian community, ADOPTIONISM and MODALISM. While these unorthodox systems differed in many respects, both arose from the belief that the mainstream Christianity of the day did not adequately emphasize the greatness and rulership of the one God. The two systems highlighted the "monarchy" of God, hence their common title, Monarchianism.

The Adoptionists felt that the notion of God's incarnation as a human being (JESUS Christ) demeaned God's greatness, so they claimed that God had merely "adopted" Christ, not incarnated as Christ. The Modalists were concerned that dividing God into distinct Persons, as in the orthodox Trinity of Father, Son, and Holy Spirit, fragmented God, and argued that the various "Persons" were actually just different names applied to one Person—God—as He performed various activities.

MONENERGISM   During the first half of the seventh century, the Christian Church struggled to end the centuries-long battle over the proper way to describe the nature and characteristics of JESUS Christ. The doctrine of Monenergism was an attempt to unite the two major factions in the debate: the orthodox (who held that Christ has both a human and a divine nature) and the adherents of MONOPHYSI-

TISM (who believed that Christ has only one nature, that of divinity). The latter group had been declared a heresy in the fifth century.

At issue in the Monenergist controversy was the number of "actions" Christ could perform at the same time. The exact meaning of the term "action" (in Greek, *energeia*) was not agreed upon by all sides, which added to the difficulty in reaching a consensus. The Monenergist ("one action") position argued that Christ's action is done by Him as a Person; because He is a single, unified Person, His action must also be single. Many Christians opposed this formulation; they believed that action arises from one's basic nature, not from one's personhood. Since Christ has two natures (human and divine), He, therefore, has two actions.

This seemingly trivial theological detail became involved in political maneuvering. The rift between the orthodox and the Monophysites had seriously weakened the church, and Catholic leaders were seeking ways to entice the Monophysites back into the orthodox fold. Some leaders felt that the Monophysites would abandon their heretical belief in Christ's single nature and rejoin the mainstream church if they were allowed to retain the doctrine of a single action in Christ. Catholic Emperor Heraclius agreed to this compromise. In 624, he proclaimed the doctrine of Monenergism as the official Christian description of Christ's action.

Monenergism did indeed attract the Monophysites, but many orthodox Christians had misgivings. They feared that the doctrine of a single action obscured the idea that Christ has two natures, a crucial part of the Catholic description of Christ established almost two centuries earlier. The debate over "energeia" continued to divide Christianity rather than unify it. In 634, POPE HONORIUS suggested that the controversy could be resolved to the satisfaction of all parties by replacing the notion of "energeia" with that of will. The pope proposed that Christ had a single will, which is the doctrine of MONOTHELETISM.

Far from pacifying the debaters, this proposal made the arguments grow even more heated. Four years later, Heraclius banned the discussion of the number of actions in Christ because it was wasting the resources of the church and the state. But the damage was already done. While Christian leaders argued over the fine points of Monenergism and Monotheletism, the Moslems had appeared in the Middle East with their simple, compelling message: "There is no God but Allah, and Mohammed is His prophet." Within two decades, Christianity had lost the entire region, from Egypt to Syria, to Islam. Monenergism was formally condemned as heretical at the THIRD COUNCIL OF CONSTANTINOPLE in 681.

MONOPHYSITISM   The Monophysite movement was the last major heresy of ancient Christianity. The name derives from two Greek terms, *mono* (one) and *physis* (nature), and refers to the central doctrine of the Monophysite school: Christ has only one nature, and that nature is divine. This view contrasts with that of orthodox Christianity, which teaches that Christ has both a divine and a human nature. The threat the Monophysites posed to orthodox control over the Christian Church led to the COUNCIL OF CHALCEDON in A.D. 451. At this meeting, the orthodox doctrine was officially defined and is still taught today.

The Monophysites traced their belief back to Cyril of Alexandria, a bishop in the early fifth century. Cyril taught that Christ had "one incarnate nature." The precise meaning of this phrase was unclear. Orthodox Christians interpreted Cyril to mean that Christ had two natures that were united but still distinct in some way. For the Monophysites, it was obvious that Cyril meant precisely what he said: Christ has a single nature.

The first undisputed Monophysite was EUTYCHES, a monk in Constantinople who declared that the Catholic leaders were heretics for teaching the doctrine of two natures. With the support of Bishop DIOSCURUS of Alexandria and others, the Monophysites succeeded in pronouncing the orthodox view heretical at the notorious ROBBER COUNCIL of A.D. 449.

Catholic theologians argued that Christ had to have two natures. He had to be divine in order to have the power to forgive sins; He also had to be human, so that His sacrifice on the cross merited the forgiveness of human sins. Monophysitism, in Catholic eyes, defined Christ in such a way that His death would not accomplish the salvation of humanity. This theological debate also had political implications. Monophysitism was associated with the Egyptian city of Alexandria; if the Monophysite doctrine triumphed, Alexandria might take over control of the church from Rome and Constantinople. Therefore, it was very important that the Monophysites be defeated.

The official Catholic victory occurred at the Council of Chalcedon, where the doctrine of two natures was established as the only correct way to regard Christ. Monophysitism had a great deal of popular support, however. It had become identified not just with a theological view, but with regional pride, especially in Egypt, where Cyril and Dioscurus were both revered as heroes.

During the century following the meeting at Chalcedon, teachers like JULIAN OF HALICARNASSUS and GAIANUS OF ALEXANDRIA promoted the Monophysite view in Egypt. The Monophysites overwhelmed the Egyptian Catholics and took control of the Egyptian Church. Ever since, the COPTIC CHRISTIANS, the dominant Christian community in Egypt, have endorsed the Monophysite view. From Egypt, Monophysitism was transmitted to Ethiopia. The Monophysite doctrine also retained its popularity among the JACOBITES of Syria, and the ARMENIAN CHRISTIANS converted to Monophysitism at the beginning of the sixth century. Many Copts, Jacobites, and Armenians keep the beliefs of the Monophysites alive to the present day.

Sixth century Emperor Justinian recognized that the religious differences between the orthodox and the Monophysites threatened the unity of the empire. Much of the western territories had already been lost to Germanic invaders. He realized that Syria, Palestine, and Egypt, with their predominantly Monophysite populations, felt increasingly alienated from the officially Catholic empire and might not mount effective resistance against invaders. Justinian attempted to entice the Monophysites back into the orthodox fold by holding the SECOND COUNCIL OF CONSTANTINOPLE in 553. He arranged for the assembled orthodox bishops to condemn some long-dead theologians whom the Monophysites had especially resented and to reduce the emphasis on Christ's human nature in their theological position. But this attempt at a compromise ended up pleasing no one.

In the ensuing discussions, however, another thorny question was raised: Does Christ have one will or two? The Monophysites supported the doctrine of one will in Christ, called MONOTHELETISM, but the orthodox were split. By the time the issue was finally resolved at the THIRD COUNCIL OF CONSTANTINOPLE in 680, Justinian's fears had been realized: the Monophysite populations of Syria,

Palestine, and Egypt, tired of the religious persecution they had suffered under Byzantine rule, had offered little resistance to the invading Moslems.

See also: APHTHARTODOCETAE, BARSUMAS (1), THEOPASCHITES.

MONOTHELETISM The Monothelete controversy marked the last chapter in the long struggle within the Christian Church to define the nature of Christ. Monotheletism is the belief that Christ has a single will (*mono*=one, *thelema*=will). The debate concerning the number of wills in Christ was sparked by an attempt to unify the Christian dominions. Instead, the result was a disaster for the church. By the conclusion of the argument, one pope had been declared a heretic, another had died in exile, and the Middle East, once the heartland of Christianity, had been lost to the new world religion of Islam.

The seventh century, during which the debate raged, found the Christian Church seriously threatened. The Roman Empire, its political power base since the early fourth century, was disintegrating. This catastrophe was occurring in part because of divisions within the church itself. Throughout the preceding 200 years, a debate had raged concerning the proper way to describe Christ. The controversy had become theologically technical, yet still stirred passions connected to regional pride and political maneuvering. As a result, there was no unity of faith within the old empire, and this disunity was reflected in a lack of political and military cooperation against external threats.

Emperor Justinian had attempted to unite the two largest Christian factions, the orthodox and the Monophysites, by imposing a compromise solution to their disagreements at the SECOND COUNCIL OF CONSTANTINOPLE in 553. Orthodoxy held that Christ has both a divine nature and a human nature; MONOPHYSITISM taught that Christ has only a divine nature. The Council supported the doctrine of two natures. The Catholic victors limited the significance of Christ's human nature before the earthly life of JESUS in the hope of avoiding a complete alienation of the Monophysites—the human nature was merely an impersonal potential, not an actual person, until it was united with the divine nature at Christ's conception. The divine nature, by contrast, was a Person even before this union: the Son, the second Person in the Trinity.

Many Monophysites did not accept that Christ had a human nature, even in the limited form Justinian promoted. During the ensuing discussions, challenging questions were raised. If, as the orthodox claim, Christ is one Person with two natures, does He have one will or two? If He has one will, is it divine or human? If He has two wills, could the wills ever be in conflict with each other?

The Monophysites themselves held that Christ is a single Person with a single nature and so had no trouble accepting the Monothelete position, that Christ has a single will. Many orthodox believers also found the notion of a Christ with two wills repugnant; the Savior of humanity could hardly be so flawed as to have disagreements with Himself! The orthodox feared that the doctrine of the double will would destroy the unity of Christ as a single Person. POPE HONORIUS himself, in a letter written around 635, had formulated Monotheletism as a truth beyond doubt.

The supporters of the two wills position noted that if Christ only had one will, then either the divine nature or the human nature lacked its own will and was, therefore, incomplete. Defining either of Christ's natures as incomplete had been declared a heresy in the fifth century. Orthodox Catholics thus remained divided on the question of the wills, which threatened to produce yet another rupture in the church.

During the reign of Emperor Heraclius in the early seventh century, the self-destructive feuding continued. Moslem armies were preparing for their lightning sweep through the Middle East. In his decree of 638, the emperor followed the lead of Pope Honorius and called for all Christians to adopt the doctrine of Christ's single will. Politically, however, it was too late. In only three years, the Monophysite populations of Syria, Palestine, and Egypt, still alienated from the orthodox Christian empire, would prove to be easy conquests for the Moslem invaders.

In the domain of theology, the Monothelete victory was short-lived. The popes who came after Honorius reversed his stand and supported the doctrine of the two wills. When Emperor CONSTANS II banned all discussion of the number of Christ's wills, Pope Martin denounced him; this pope continued to insist that Monotheletism was heretical. Constans arranged for the pope to be captured and exiled in the wild territory of the Crimea, where he died of hunger and cold.

But because of the efforts of the church leaders who continued to support the doctrine of two wills, Monotheletism was bound for defeat. At the THIRD COUNCIL OF CONSTANTINOPLE, which took place in 680, the notion that Christ has one will was officially condemned as heresy. Pope Honorius, the best-known Monothelete, was also condemned, forty-two years after his death. Monotheletism was kept alive for some time by the MARONITES, a Christian community that survived the Moslem invasion of Lebanon. The Maronite Church abandoned the Monothelete doctrine when it joined the Roman Catholic Church in the twelfth century.

See also: MONENERGISM.

MONTANISM   The Montanist movement was an important force within the Christian community during the second and third centuries A.D. Montanism takes its name from its founder, MONTANUS. In response to the challenge of this movement, the Catholic Church refined its own teachings in ways that have had a significant impact on the Christian world view.

A key feature of Montanism was its belief that the Holy Spirit was still active on earth. During their meetings, some Montanists would enter a trance state and speak as if they were possessed by the Holy Spirit. The practice of "speaking in tongues" was not unknown among Christians before the advent of Montanism; it is mentioned in the New Testament's Book of Acts. However, as the Catholic Church became more organized and increasingly emphasized faith in the doctrines priests taught rather than direct experience, such occurrences had become rare. In earlier days, Catholic Christians had argued that the episodes of divinely inspired speech in their midst, as well as the absence of these phenomena among Jews, proved that the Catholics had been chosen by God to succeed the Jews as the religious leaders of humanity. The Montanists were now pointing to the same phenomena and making the same claim for themselves against the Catholics.

The first generation of Montanists was informed by the Holy Spirit, through Montanus himself and other Montanist channelers, that Christ would return in their lifetime. A strictly moral lifestyle was encouraged, involving fasting and praying. When JESUS did not appear as announced, the doctrine was altered slightly. Montanists were now told that Christ would return very soon, but the exact date was still unknown. Rigorous moral behavior was still required, however, so that the Montanists would not be caught off guard by the Second Coming.

Montanist morality differed in three main ways from the moral requirements of the Catholic community. First, remarriage following the death of a spouse was strictly forbidden by Montanism. The Catholics forbade having more than one spouse at the same time, but allowed having more than one spouse over the course of a lifetime. Second, the Montanists emphasized the importance of fasting, which was not practiced as extensively among most Catholics. Third, Montanists did not forgive a Christian who fled from persecution to avoid martyrdom. Catholic Christianity had the deepest reverence for its martyrs, but it had not yet resolved the issue of whether to forgive those who felt compelled by their terror to avoid a painful death, yet who still wished to be part of the church.

Montanism spread throughout the Roman Empire and became particularly strong along the Mediterranean shores of Africa. Among the generations following the death of Montanus, reverence for his memory increased, apparently to the point of actually identifying him with the Holy Spirit. An inscription discovered in Africa reads, "In the name of the Father and the Son and of the Lord Muntanus. What he promised, he delivered." This deification of Montanus further distanced the Montanist movement from the orthodox mainstream.

Several quotations from Montanist sources provide evidence that Montanists organized their understanding of God into the form of a trinity. MAXIMILLA, one of Montanus's disciples, while in a trance uttered, "I am the Word and the Spirit and the Power." During the second century, the Catholic Church had not yet defined their famous doctrine of the Trinity, consisting of Father, Son, and Holy Spirit. Church father QUINTAS SEPTIMIUS FLORENS TERTULLIAN was the first person to use the term "Trinity" in Latin, and is generally regarded as the first formulator of the Catholic hierarchy of the three divine Persons. Tertullian was familiar with Montanism; indeed, he eventually became a Montanist. His exposure to the trinities of the Montanists might even have inspired Tertullian's formula of the Trinity.

The Catholic Church declared Montanism to be a heresy. Several features of the Montanist movement were perceived as a threat by orthodoxy. The Montanists' expectation of Christ's imminent return made them dismiss Catholic efforts to establish lasting church institutions, such as the priesthood. The strict morality taught by Montanism was beyond the capacity of many people. If the Catholic Church had adopted such strictness, its efforts to convert large numbers would have been hampered. The Montanists' claim of direct access to the Holy Spirit through trances undermined the role of the church: if people can receive messages directly from God, why should they listen to the teachings of a priest?

In response to the Montanist heresy, the orthodox refined their own doctrines. Hippolytus, a Catholic opponent of the Montanists, argued that no one, including the Montanists, knew when Christ would return. The church, therefore, needed to prepare itself for the possibility of a very long wait. In order to survive until the end of history, Hippolytus stated, the Christian community required discipline and strict obedience to its leadership, the Catholic bishops and priests. He also taught that John, author of the Book of Revelation in the New Testament, had been the last person to be directly inspired by the Holy Spirit. After John, the Holy Spirit would not return with new revelations. The trance behaviors of the Montanists were likely caused by DEMONS, he noted.

Thus, the orthodox Christian community's reaction to Montanism involved the continued institutionalization of the Catholic Church, and a decreased tolerance for spontaneous spiritual experiences. Historian Jaroslav Pelikan summarizes it thus:

> To validate its existence, the church looked increasingly not to the future, illumined by the Lord's return, nor to the present, illumined by the Spirit's extraordinary gifts, but to the past, illumined by the composition of the apostolic canon, the creation of the apostolic creed, and the establishment of the apostolic episcopate [hierarchy of priests].

MONTANUS   This spiritual reformer was active during the second century A.D. in the Roman Empire. Montanus claimed that the Christian Church of the time had become morally permissive. This observation prompted him to start a movement, known as MONTANISM, that the Catholic Church declared to be a heresy.

Little is known of Montanus's life story. He was born in Phrygia, a region within the modern borders of Turkey. Phrygia was known in the ancient world as the home of strange religious practices featuring ecstatic dances, orgies, and self-mutilation, all of which believers participated in to become possessed by the deity of the cult. The worship of Cybele, a goddess who required her priests to be castrated, was strong in this area. While there is no direct evidence linking Montanus with such pagan practices, scholars have speculated that his Phrygian cultural background suggested to him the central feature of his Christian practice: possession by the Holy Spirit.

At some point in the middle of or toward the end of the second century, Montanus began to claim that he was able to enter a trance and become a mouthpiece for the Holy Spirit. He recognized that PRISCA and MAXIMILLA, two of his disciples, also had this ability. Although some of the statements these mediums uttered sound like they were claiming to be divine, they seem to have viewed themselves merely as instruments, just as modern channelers do. Through Montanus, the Holy Spirit is said to have stated, "Behold, man is like a lyre, and I fly over it like a plectrum."

The messages Montanus and his fellow mediums received stated that Christ was returning to earth in the very near future. Christians should not waste their energy organizing church institutions for succeeding generations, but should focus on leading lives of strict morality. They should dissolve marriages, fast frequently, and pay close attention to the utterances of the mediums. If persecution against Christians broke out (as it often did during this period), there should be no resistance: martyrs to the faith would return with JESUS shortly.

Montanus eventually announced a date for Christ's return. His followers were told to gather near the town of Pepuza in Phrygia for the happy event. The outcome was disappointing. The teachings concerning the Last Day had to be revised into the idea of the Last Days; Christ could appear at any moment, so rigorous moral behavior must be observed.

Despite the error of Montanus's prediction, the combination of ethical discipline and Christian possession trance in his teaching continued to have wide appeal. His movement became particularly strong in the north African holdings of the Roman Empire. The Montanist movement lasted for several generations. As the memory of Montanus faded, later Montanists tended to regard him not merely as a medium, but as something close to divine himself.

MONTEFORTE HERETICS   The largest heresy trial in Europe during the eleventh century resulted from the activity of unorthodox Christians in northern Italy. A group of heretics was discovered in the castle of Monteforte near Turin in 1028. Six years earlier, a precedent had been established when the ORLEANS HERETICS had been burned at the stake. The Monteforte heretics met the same fate.

A community of about thirty people, hosted by the Duchess of Monteforte, had taken up residence in the castle. The archbishop of Milan learned of their strange beliefs and had them taken to that city for questioning. The doctrines they confessed clearly established them as heretics. A committee of Milan's leading citizens insisted that the entire group be burned at the stake. The archbishop went on record as protesting this harsh treatment. However, there is no reason to believe that the church's objection was intended seriously. As was the case later during the GREAT WITCH HUNT, religious officials were expected to offer verbal gestures of compassion, even while enthusiastically supporting the death sentence.

The unorthodox doctrines the heretics held included vegetarianism, the rejection of sexuality and marriage, disbelief that the Bible should be taken literally, and the renunciation of wealth. Some historians have seen the influence of the BOGOMIL heretics of Bulgaria in these notions. Others believe that such ideas arose independently in medieval western Europe.

Whatever its origin, the simple, spiritually focused lifestyle of heretics, such as those at Monteforte, contrasted with the flagrant greed and sexual abandon that characterized many Catholic priests of the time. Poor people and townsfolk alike were impressed by the heretics' imitation of the apostolic lifestyle. Despite the opposition of orthodoxy, heretical movements resembling the Monteforte group began to appear across northern Italy within a few years of the trial and mass burning at Milan. In less than a century, the Italian unorthodox scene would coalesce into the beginnings of an underground heretical church—the CATHARS—and eventually trigger the formation of the INQUISITION.

See also: LEUTHARD.

MONTSEGUR   During the bloody ALBIGENSIAN CRUSADE that wracked southern France in the early thirteenth century, Catholic Crusaders tried to exterminate the heretical CATHARS, who were thriving in the region. Montsegur was the stronghold of the Cathars. This castle, perched atop a remote mountain in the Pyrenees, became a symbol of resistance against the attempt by northern France and the pope to destroy the unique Occitanian culture of southern France.

Montsegur had become a center of Catharism by 1203, when it was the site of a community of female Cathars. The following year, when rumors of impending action against them reached the Cathars, the mountaintop retreat was fortified. Surrounded by steep cliffs on three sides and a difficult slope on the fourth, the walled peak was thought to be impregnable.

Indeed, it withstood its first test in 1209. A Crusader army led by Simon de Montfort attempted to take Montsegur but was forced to retreat in frustration. The Crusaders were more successful elsewhere in the region, and by 1229 had forced a peace treaty on terms favorable to the Catholic Church.

The Cathars continued to operate in secrecy throughout Occitania. They traveled at night and were sheltered during the day by a sympathetic populace, who resisted the loss of their freedom to the French king and the pope. When the INQUISITION was established in Toulouse in 1233, a reign of terror aimed at detecting and destroying the remaining Cathars and their supporters began. Montsegur became one of the few places where the heretics were safe.

In addition to serving as a refuge for Cathars, Montsegur became a haven for members of the Occitanian noble class who had refused to submit to the authority of the French king. In 1240, an uprising against the French forces had failed, causing many to flee the wrath of the victorious army. At that time, the population of Montsegur reached around 500; more than 200 of these people were Cathars of the highest rank, the perfecti.

In 1242, ten inquisitors were murdered near the town of Avignonet. This event alarmed the French Catholic forces. They resolved to break the resistance decisively by moving once more against Montsegur. In the spring of the following year, an army of French Crusaders appeared at the foot of Montsegur. Taking the castle by force proved to be impossible, so they decided simply to wait until the inhabitants ran out of supplies.

But because villagers in the area smuggled food into the stronghold at night, the siege took ten months, which was much longer than anticipated. Finally, in March 1244, the occupants of Montsegur, losing hope in the possibility of escape, sent word to the Crusaders that they were ready to surrender. Those knights and nobles within the castle who were not Cathars were spared because they swore to uphold the Roman Catholic faith. The Cathar perfecti refused to do so, knowing full well what the consequences would be. As the Cathars left their mountainous shelter, the Crusaders lit immense bonfires on the field below. More than 200 heretics walked into the flames, singing of their faith. To this day, the site of their deaths is known as the Field of the Burnings. A monument at Montsegur, erected by the Society for the Remembrance and Study of Catharism, commemorates the martyrdoms.

Those who witnessed the events within the castle during its last days told a strange story. The night before the surrender, they reported, four Cathars had escaped, lowered on ropes down the cliff, to vanish in the forest below. It was said that they took with them the "treasure" of the Cathars. No one knows what this treasure was, but many have speculated. One popular legend holds that the Cathars were the guardians of the Holy Grail, which they carried from Montsegur to an unknown hiding place, where it may still rest today.

The fall of Montsegur broke the back of Occitanian Catharism. The political resistance to French royal dominion crumbled. Other Cathar castles, tucked away in isolated corners of the untamed Pyrenees, were sought out and conquered by Catholic forces over the ensuing years. The last stronghold fell in 1255. Catharism retained a significant presence in northern Italy through the 1200s and endured in the Alps into the 1300s.

MORMONS   This movement grew from obscure beginnings in the early nineteenth century to become the most successful religion founded in the Americas. Its current worldwide membership has been estimated at more than 6 million. "Mormon" is the supposed supernatural author of a sacred text, *The* BOOK OF MORMON, revealed to the movement's founder, JOSEPH SMITH. Over the years, the Mormons have fragmented into many smaller groups with varying beliefs. More than twenty-five organizations claim to represent authentic Mormonism. By far the largest group is known as the CHURCH OF JESUS CHRIST OF LATTER-DAY SAINTS.

In 1820, Smith was a fifteen-year-old boy living near the town of Palmyra in New York State. In that year, he experienced the first of a series of visions, which informed him that all existing branches of Christianity were corrupt, and commanded him to start a new movement based on his revelations. He published the most important of these, *The Book of Mormon*, in 1830. This text combined with two other books by Smith, *The Doctrines and Covenants*, and *The Pearl of Great Price*, to form the core of the new faith.

Over the next nine years, Smith moved from state to state, frequently facing local hostility because his novel religious ideas were clearly beyond the limits of orthodoxy. He attracted new followers wherever he went, however; after passing through Ohio and Missouri, the Mormons arrived in Illinois in substantial numbers. In Illinois, the Mormons founded the community of Nauvoo (erroneously claimed by Smith to mean "beautiful plantation" in Hebrew). Nauvoo rapidly grew to be the largest city in the state. Missionaries were sent to Europe. Another significant development was Smith's introduction of the practice of polygamy. Some Mormons would not follow their leader on this issue, and dissent flared; an opposition group began publishing a paper critical of the Mormon leadership, and Smith ordered it destroyed. The polygamy issue further soured relations with the Mormons' already suspicious neighbors. In 1844, Smith was murdered by a mob.

After Smith's death, the movement splintered. The majority of Mormons supported BRIGHAM YOUNG, one of Smith's closest followers and the man who had led the first Mormon mission to Britain. He possessed considerable leadership and organizational skills, and successfully led his Mormons to Utah, where a new settlement, far from persecution, was founded. Indeed, these Mormons jealously guarded their privacy. For example when the Fancher party traveled across Mormon territory on their way to California, Young ordered an attack, resulting in the slaughter of 120 of the travellers.

The encouragement of polygamy continued to be a barrier against the Mormons' acceptance by mainstream society. In 1882, the American government passed the Edmunds-Tucker Act, which called for the imprisonment of polygamists and the confiscation of their property. Eight years later, the largest Mormon branch finally rejected the practice and threatened to excommunicate polygamists. This pronouncement produced another fragmentation of Mormonism. One branch, the Reorganized Church of Jesus Christ of Latter-Day Saints, claimed that neither Smith nor Young had ever promoted polygamy; others held that polygamy was essential to attaining the highest salvation. To this day, a sizable minority of Mormons maintain polygamous relationships.

During the present century, the Mormons have seen great success. Renouncing polygamy enhanced their appeal for a broader spectrum of the population. Intensive missionary work, significant involvement in American political and public service, and such popular cultural endeavors as the Mormon Tabernacle Choir, have made the Mormons an integral feature of American society.

The doctrines of the Mormons are much less well known than their choir. Their view of human development is summarized in the slogan, "As man now is, God once was; as God now is, man may become." In other words, humans can attain the status of gods by following the practices of the Mormons. Spreading their beliefs is viewed as an especially virtuous activity. Every Mormon is expected to devote two years to full-time missionary work. Devotion to "family values", free enterprise, and strict opposition to drugs (even including soft drinks containing caffeine) are emphasized. Participation in religious ceremonies is also important, but these are done in private, and non-members know few details.

Eventually, everyone attains immortality, but only good Mormons—and selected ancestors—become gods. No one who died before the founding of Mormonism in 1830 can reach the highest stage of spiritual perfection, unless a present-day Mormon conducts a special ritual of baptism for that person. Mormons conduct research into their own family trees in order to discover ancestors to save in this fashion.

Although Mormons accept the three Persons of the orthodox Trinity—Father, Son, and Holy Spirit—they define the nature of these beings in an unorthodox way. Mormon doctrines concerning God have shifted over the years. God the Father is believed to have a physical body that exists in space. He created all human souls by impregnating a divine wife. According to Young, God took on human form and inseminated Mary, producing JESUS in this fashion. After His resurrection, Christ came and preached in the New World. In the future, He will return to rule from a new Zion in America. The Holy Spirit can manifest in human life through visions, prophecies, and speaking in tongues.

Controversy developed around Mormonism's view of non-white races. Smith taught that native Americans are descended from Jews who arrived in the New World around 600 B.C.; their skins were darkened as a punishment for their evil deeds. African Americans fared little better in Mormon doctrine. Traditionally, they have been viewed as cursed because they descended from Cain. Until 1978, they were barred from Mormon temples.

The Mormon doctrine of blood atonement states that certain sins can only be redeemed by spilling the blood of the sinner. If someone commits such a sin, it is morally correct for another person to injure the sinner in order to redeem the sin. This unusual belief is rarely discussed openly among Mormons, but it has never been officially renounced.

Thomas MORTON   In addition to its shrinking native population, seventeenth century America was largely occupied by Europeans whose unorthodox religious beliefs had made life uncomfortable for them back home. Thomas Morton stands out as a "heretic's heretic," a nonconformist who invited the colonizers to embrace a lusty PAGANISM. He was an educated Englishman who had contacts among the more occult members of the British intellectual scene. In 1624, he moved to Massachusetts. Before long, his interest in ancient pagan mythology irritated the local Puritans. To avoid persecution, he moved into the forest, where he built a small trading post and tavern.

Morton's establishment attracted the fringe members and non-members of Puritan society: woodsmen, prostitutes, and natives. Far from cultured society, his interest in the wilder side of religion—the celebration of life's passionate juices— expanded. When he compared his marginalized friends with the Old Testament Canaanites, who were driven from their lands by the Israelites, he clearly sided with the Canaanites.

On May 1, 1627, Morton invited all the inhabitants of the region to gather at a clearing in the woods he had named "Merry Mount." He had erected a maypole that was 80 feet tall and topped with a pair of deer antlers. When Morton's guests arrived, he led a festival of unrestrained dancing, drinking, and sex in the names of the ancient gods.

The Puritans were not amused. They sent a posse that in Morton's words, threatened to "make it a woefull mount and not a merry mount." The mighty maypole was knocked down, and Morton was jailed. He managed to escape and returned to England. In 1637, he published a book promoting his religion of revelry entitled *New Canaan*, his optimistic name for the New World.

Morton returned to America, where he spent the last ten years of his life causing trouble for the orthodox. He died in 1647. Nineteenth century writer Nathaniel Hawthorne noted the historical significance of the Puritan triumph over this free-spirited pagan:

> The future complexion of New England was involved in this important quarrel. Should the grisly saints establish their jurisdiction over the gay sinners, then would their spirits darken all the clime, and make it a land of clouded visages, of hard toil, of sermon and psalm, forever. But should the banner-staff of Merry Mount be fortunate, sunshine would break upon the hills, and flowers would beautify the forest, and late posterity do homage to the May-pole!

MUGGLETONIANS   Founded by Ludowicke Muggleton in 1651, this English sect was the longest lasting of the minor unorthodox groups that appeared at the time. Muggletonians rejected the doctrine of the Trinity, perhaps under the influence of UNITARIANISM. They believed that God the Father and Christ the Son were actually one Person. Consequently, they believed that God was absent from heaven during the years Christ lived on earth; the prophet Elijah had taken God's place on the divine throne during that period. They also maintained that reason is the invention of Satan and, therefore, not to be trusted. The last known Muggletonian died in 1979.

MÜNSTER HERETICS   When members of the ANABAPTIST fringe of Protestantism took over the German town of Münster in 1534, they believed that a glorious new age was about to begin. Instead, they were encircled and attacked by an orthodox army. The Münster heretics, under siege, became more extreme and tainted the rest of the Anabaptist movement, bringing down ferocious persecution upon Anabaptists across Europe.

In the early 1530s, Münster was spiritually divided: a respected Catholic bishop resided there, but the town council was Lutheran. Two influential citizens guided public opinion away from both Catholic and Protestant orthodoxy and toward heresy. The mayor, BERNT KNIPPERDOLLING, and a chaplain, BERNT ROTHMANN, had been impressed by Anabaptist teachings and began to proclaim that Martin Luther had not gone far enough in his reforms. The orthodox practice of infant baptism was wrong; only the baptism of consenting adults was spiritually meaningful. By 1533, Münster became known as a town that welcomed Anabaptists. At this time, members of the sect were rarely appreciated elsewhere in Europe.

By January 1534, Anabaptists were streaming into the town, primarily from the neighboring Netherlands. Many disciples of heretic MELCHIOR HOFFMANN appeared in Münster. The immigrants provided Knipperdolling and Rothmann with their power base, and they proclaimed the town to be a "new Jerusalem" from which the original Christianity taught by JESUS—and rediscovered by the Anabaptists— would sweep the world.

In the following month, two more significant characters arrived, the Dutch baker and Anabaptist preacher JAN MATTHYS and wild prophet JAN BOCKELSON. Charismatic and radical, they took over the leadership within Münster. A law requiring all adult citizens of the New Jerusalem to be rebaptized was passed; anyone who refused was chased out of town. With the exception of the Bible, all books were thrown into bonfires.

The bishop left Münster in disgust, and proceeded to organize a military force to drive out the heretics. Orthodox believers remaining in Münster who refused to comply with the heretics' demands were pushed beyond the town walls. There, they were assumed to be Anabaptists and speared to death by the besieging troops.

Matthys heard God's voice telling him that the enemy could not harm him. With only twenty followers, he charged the assembled army and was promptly killed. Bockelson crowned himself ruler of the Kingdom of Zion in Münster. From his throne, he decreed the execution of anyone who opposed him. Private property was abolished. Bockelson also proclaimed that polygamy was acceptable and took sixteen young wives for himself.

Eventually, food began to run low within the town. People were forced to eat rodents, and morale dropped. Informants notified the besieging forces about the weaknesses in Münster's defenses; in June 1535, orthodox troops stormed the walls and conquered the city. Many Anabaptist defenders were slaughtered. The leaders, Knipperdolling, Rothmann, and King Jan, were tortured to death. Their bodies were put in an iron cage that was hung from the church steeple as a lesson about the outcome of heresy. The Roman Catholic faith was reestablished in Münster.

This disaster triggered persecutions of Anabaptists throughout Germany and the Netherlands, even though most Anabaptists were repelled by the extremism of the Münster heretics. Into the chaos of the Anabaptist community stepped MENNO SIMONS, who convinced many of them to adopt his more moderate version of the Anabaptist view. Thus, from the ashes of Münster, the MENNONITE movement was born.

See also: THOMAS MÜNZER.

Thomas MÜNZER   The Protestant Reformation was not the only expression of dissatisfaction with conventional society in sixteenth century Europe. Thomas Münzer called for a revolution rather than a reformation, and aimed to bring a purified Christian society into being through violence. Born around 1488 into a comfortable German family, Münzer showed intellectual promise. He became a priest and learned to read Greek, Hebrew, and Latin. Münzer's curiosity brought him in contact with unorthodox systems of thought. It is believed that he was impressed by the rejection of papal authority proclaimed by radical HUSSITES, as well as by the direct contact with the Holy Spirit claimed by the Heresy of the FREE SPIRIT.

By 1520, Münzer was preaching unusual ideas, apparently based on personal revelations, in the German town of Zwickau. He taught that spiritual evolution occurred in three stages. First, one had to experience the pains of hell. Next, one became resigned to one's personal helplessness. Finally, thus humbled, one's heart could be filled with the Holy Spirit and act in God's service. Münzer hoped to organize Christians who had passed through these experiences into a new church, the aim of which was to overthrow the existing privileged sectors in religion and society. His vision had special appeal for the lowest classes, who had nothing to lose by such a shake-up.

In 1521, the authorities ran Münzer out of town. For the next few years, he continued to preach at various locations in Germany. His rejection of Catholic orthodoxy merged with a hatred for the new orthodoxy of the Lutherans. He wrote a piece on Martin Luther entitled *Against the spiritless soft-living flesh in Wittenberg*, in which he dubs the reformer "Dr. Liar" and "The Dragon." Münzer railed that Luther was a mere compromiser, making deals in order to preserve an oppressive system that should be completely discarded.

At the time, a violent change in the social order seemed quite possible. Many Catholics advocated the suppression of the Reformation using force, and the peasant classes were restless about their downtrodden position. Münzer's rhetoric both reflected and fed the building tensions. To do away with "evils" ranging from private property to the baptism of infants, the preacher called for a peasant uprising. He signed his letters "Thomas Münzer the Hammer" and adopted as his symbol a red cross accompanied by a sharp sword. He hinted at a sacred slaughter that was about to break out: "The living God is sharpening his scythe in me, so that later I can cut down the red poppies and the blue cornflowers."

By 1524, class tensions in Germany had erupted into open conflict. Bands of peasants roamed the countryside, and many heeded Münzer's advice never to allow the blood to dry on their weapons, but to kill all representatives of the status quo. In the region of Thuringia, a heretics' army formed under Münzer. He incited them into battle, claiming that he would catch the bullets of their enemies in his sleeves.

Several princes joined forces to put down the uprising. The final confrontation occurred at Frankenhausen on May 15, 1525. Münzer's sleeves proved ineffective: the peasant army was routed. The preacher was captured later that day, hiding in a bed. A week later, he was beheaded. Although the violence he helped to unleash was quelled, the idea of overthrowing social and religious convention in favor of a divinely inspired utopia did not die. Less than a decade after Münzer's execution, the MÜNSTER HERETICS, another group of Protestant radicals, struggled to bring his vision into being and suffered much the same fate.

As for Münzer's adversary "Dr. Liar," the reformer had the last word. A collection of Münzer's letters, found in his satchel, was obtained by Luther, who published them with suitably humiliating commentary, as *A dreadful story and a Judgment of God concerning Thomas Münzer.*

See also: ANABAPTISTS, ZWICKAU PROPHETS.

NAG HAMMADI LIBRARY   The discovery of the Nag Hammadi Library in 1945 was one of the greatest archaeological finds of the century. The library, hidden beneath the sands of Egypt in a large earthenware jar since the fourth century, includes a selection of writings belonging to the spiritual movement called GNOSTI-CISM. Before this discovery, modern knowledge regarding the Gnostics was based entirely on descriptions recorded by the orthodox Christians, who were their enemies, and on a few surviving fragments of their own works.

The library was uncovered by accident. An Arab peasant digging near the town of Nag Hammadi for soil to be used as fertilizer struck the buried jar with his mattock. Opening it, he found thirteen volumes of leather-bound papyrus. He brought his find home, where his mother used much of the papyrus as kindling for her cooking fires. Fortunately, the remainder of the texts made their way into the hands of merchants and, eventually, into the possession of scientists who recognized their value. Twelve of the volumes are currently housed in the Coptic Museum in Cairo, and one is owned by the Jung Institute in Zurich, Switzerland.

The Nag Hammadi Library consists of fifty-two texts written in the Coptic language that was common in early Christian Egypt. The reason for the burial of these texts has been lost, but scholars have constructed a likely scenario. In the vicinity of Nag Hammadi is the monastery of Saint Pachomius, one of the first Christian monasteries. Historian Frederik Wisse suggested that the Nag Hammadi texts originally belonged to monks at the monastery. In 367, Athanasius, the archbishop of Alexandria, ordered the destruction of all books in Egypt that contained non-Catholic ideas. This prohibition would certainly have included the Gnostic literature found at Nag Hammadi since the Gnostics disagreed with, and even inverted, many key beliefs of the orthodox party. In response to Athanasius's decree, someone at the monastery might have stashed the collection of Gnostic writings, hoping to recover them after the end of Athanasius's reign of intolerance. Instead, the library remained hidden for 1,600 years.

See also: GOSPEL OF PHILIP, GOSPEL OF THOMAS, GOSPEL OF TRUTH.

NATHAN OF GAZA   This seventeenth century Jewish visionary was the prophet of the false Messiah SHABBATAI ZEVI. Born in Jerusalem around 1643, Nathan of Gaza was named Abraham Nathan ben Elisha Hasyyim Ashkenazi. His father was a rabbi and scholar of KABBALAH, the Jewish mystical tradition, and Nathan also took up religious studies. He was drawn to the Kabbalah of ISAAC LURIA, which promoted meditation practices to induce spiritual states. Nathan proved adept at these activities and began to experience visions and revelations.

Nathan had married and moved to the town of Gaza as a young man. He acquired a reputation for his wisdom and counseled people regarding spiritual problems. In 1665, Nathan received a visit from Shabbatai Zevi, who sought a cure for his uncontrollable mood swings and compulsive behaviors. Nathan, whose religious studies had led him to believe that the appearance of a Messiah was imminent, believed that Zevi's symptoms were not signs of illness. Rather, he thought, his visitor had been chosen to be the savior of the world.

The young prophet managed to convince Zevi that he was the Messiah. During the next year, Zevi traveled around the eastern Mediterranean, proclaiming his divine mission; Nathan remained in Palestine, writing letters and essays explaining the nature of Zevi's messiahship. Nathan was a brilliant scholar. His revision of Luria's Kabbalistic world view convinced many Jewish intellectuals that Shabbatai Zevi was who he claimed to be.

In September 1666, when his captors forced Zevi to become a Moslem, the SHABBATEAN movement threatened to end in disillusionment. Nathan, however, kept the faith, maintaining that Zevi's conversion was part of a divine plan to save the Moslem world from domination by evil. Again, Nathan's ingenious explanation convinced many Shabbateans to continue their devotion to the new messiah. The prophet of Gaza died in January 1680, three years after the death of his savior, Shabbatai Zevi. Nathan's tomb at Skopje in Macedonia remained a place of pilgrimage for Shabbateans until its destruction during World War II.

NATURAL MAGIC   The magical harnessing of the hidden forces in nature is a very ancient practice. In pagan times, caves, trees, ponds, mountaintops and skies were felt to be populated by invisible intelligences with great power and knowledge. These spirits were believed to respond to requests or offerings. When Christianity rejected PAGANISM, it did not dismiss the reality of these beings. Rather, it defined them as DEMONS and, therefore, as creatures to be avoided. For orthodox Christianity, natural magic became loathsome DEMON MAGIC.

A different view developed among the Moslems. Islamic culture inherited knowledge from ancient times that had been lost in Europe during the early Middle Ages. Part of this ancient lore was a natural-magic tradition concerning the stars and planets. According to this tradition the occult powers of the heavenly bodies could be drawn to earth and utilized. The various astral forces were attracted to objects that they resembled. For example, sunflowers and other yellow objects were connected with the powers of the sun. When the classical ideas the Moslems preserved were transmitted back to Europe in the twelfth century, European scholars began to study manuals of astral magic, such as *The Picatrix*.

In the late medieval period, lists of plants, animals, and stones that indicated the planetary forces to which these life forms and objects were attuned became popular in Europe. Catholic orthodoxy remained suspicious: who could be sure that these "planetary forces" were not demons in disguise, pretending to be helpful in order to snatch unwary souls?

Renaissance scholar MARSILIO FICINO made the most successful attempt to legitimize natural magic. He developed an elegant magical system based on the idea that every human being contains "inner planets." Disharmony among these planetary forces produces ill health; inner harmony can be promoted by attracting the appropriate astral influences. Ficino used lists of correspondences largely derived from the earlier natural-magic traditions. He argued that his version of natural magic simply involved the channeling of *impersonal* energies, but many historians suspect that Ficino privately believed that spirits delivered his planetary influences.

Certainly, many of Ficino's later disciples, including CORNELIUS AGRIPPA, believed that planetary spirits were involved in natural magic. Such a position made the practice of natural magic very dangerous during the centuries of the GREAT WITCH HUNT, when any attempt to contact spirits could be taken as virtual proof that a person was a witch.

Since the rise of the scientific world view, the dominant image of the universe has been that of a gigantic machine. The mechanistic view of nature holds that the laws of physics, not mysterious astral influences, explain the interactions between objects. Nevertheless, folk beliefs persist concerning such items as "lucky stones" and crystals as containers of psychic power, testifying to the enduring attraction of natural magic.

See also: ASTROLOGY.

James NAYLER   A seventeenth century Englishman who became convinced that he was the Messiah. Born around 1618, James Nayler became a soldier but then converted to the Quaker faith, which preached nonviolence. He became a leading figure in the Quaker movement. Around 1656, Nayler encountered the unorthodox group called the RANTERS. Members of this group recognized Nayler as Christ. An account circulated that Nayler had raised a woman from the dead. He was then expelled from the Quakers.

Nayler rode into Bristol on a donkey, imitating Christ's arrival in Jerusalem. He was arrested for this blasphemy. The English Messiah was punished by having a hole bored through his tongue and was imprisoned until shortly before his death in 1660.

NAZARENES   A branch of the EBIONITES and an ancient heresy that combined elements of the emerging Christian faith with orthodox Jewish beliefs, the Nazarenes were the Ebionite group that most closely resembled mainstream Christianity. They accepted that JESUS Christ was the Messiah, born of a virgin. They rejected Saint Paul, however, and, therefore, could never be reconciled with the Catholic Christians, who viewed them as heretics.

NECROMANCY   The practice of attempting to predict the future by communicating with the spirits of the dead has existed in virtually every culture. In the history of the West, necromancy has generally been viewed with horror. This negative attitude can be found in the Old Testament. In the Book of Deuteronomy, God commands, "There shall not be found among you . . . a necromancer. For all that do these things are an abomination unto the Lord: and because of these abominations the Lord thy God doth drive them out from before thee" (18:10–12). The First Book of Samuel (28:6–20) tells the story of how King Saul, threatened by an army of Philistines and unable to learn his fate from God, turned to necromancy. He asked a "witch" to call Samuel from the underworld. Samuel informed him that, because he had angered the Lord, he and his family would be killed the next day. In the Second Book of Kings (21:6), King Manasseh was portrayed as a necromancer; his "abominations" so infuriated God that He threatened to "wipe Jerusalem as a man wipes a dish" (21:13).

In *The Odyssey* of Homer, composed around the ninth century B.C., the hero Odysseus calls a spirit from the beyond with a blood offering; there is no sense of wrongdoing implied. However, by Plato's time (the fourth century B.C.), necromancy was viewed with revulsion. In Roman times, necromancers who reanimated decaying corpses in order to question them were well-known figures of horror fiction and folklore.

With both Hebrew and Greek traditions condemning this practice, it is not surprising that orthodox Christianity rejected necromancy. The Catholic Church has always been deeply suspicious of experiences involving contact with spirits; the souls of the departed are busy in heaven, hell, or purgatory, so a spirit responding to a magical ceremony is most likely a DEMON. Indeed, by the later Middle Ages, the term "necromancy" had become a synonym for DEMON MAGIC.

Elizabethan magicians JOHN DEE and EDWARD KELLY are probably the best-known figures in the history of necromancy. A widely reproduced engraving portrays the two men in a church graveyard at night. They have drawn a protective magic circle on the ground. One man bears a GRIMOIRE and wand, while the other, holding aloft a torch, fearfully converses with a gibbering corpse that stands at the edge of the circle. Unfortunately, this dramatic image slanders Dee, who was never involved in necromancy. Kelly, however, almost certainly was.

With the rise of science and rationalism in the eighteenth century, belief in the magical reanimation of dead bodies declined. Interest in contacting the departed never dies, however. By the mid-nineteenth century, the mediumistic communications of SPIRITUALISM had become an international sensation.

NESTORIANISM   The Christian heresy of Nestorianism takes its name from NESTORIUS, a bishop who played an important role in the controversies that disturbed the church during the fifth century. The Nestorians are prominent in the history of Christianity in Asia. In fact, it is likely that these heretics were the first Christians to penetrate the Far East, establishing communities in India and China.

Bishop Nestorius taught that Christ has two natures, divine and human. Orthodox Christians agreed. Christ must be divine in order to have the power to grant salvation, and He must be human for His sacrifice on the cross to apply to the sins of humans. Some Catholic leaders accused Nestorius of teaching not only that Christ had two natures, but also that Christ was composed of two distinct persons, thus splitting the Lord into two parts. Such a fragmentation of Christ was heretical; someone with two personalities was more like a possessed person than like a savior. Although Nestorius denied that he taught such a concept, he was deposed from his position in the Catholic Church in 431 and exiled to Egypt.

Some of Nestorius's followers formed their own church rather than submit to the opinion of the orthodox authorities. Although Nestorius himself did not teach the doctrine of two persons in Christ, it seems that the early Nestorian Church did evolve such a belief, thereby misunderstanding Nestorius's writings much the same way his orthodox critics did.

The Roman Empire was controlled by the Catholics, who defined Nestorianism as a heresy. The Nestorians were forced to leave the empire dominated territories for lands under Persian control. There they established the Nestorian Church, with its headquarters at Seleucia-Ctesiphon on the Tigris River.

The Nestorian heresy thrived as a minority faith in Persia, and the Nestorians turned to missionary work. By the sixth century, there is evidence that Nestorians had founded a community in India, the MALABAR CHRISTIANS; by the seventh century, they were also active in China. In contrast, orthodox Christianity was brought to China in 1294 and did not arrive in India until 1498. Nestorian thought continued to evolve. BABAI THE GREAT, a Nestorian leader in Mesopotamia during the early seventh century, wrote a summary of Nestorian doctrines that is as complex as any Catholic theology.

After the conquest of Persia by the Moslems in 651, the Nestorians continued to be well treated. They transferred their headquarters to Baghdad. After the Mongol conquest of the thirteenth century, however, the Nestorian Church was subject to persecution. Many Nestorians fled to the mountains of Kurdistan, where communities of Nestorians survived until the twentieth century as the ASSYRIAN CHRISTIANS.

In India, the Malabar Christians renounced Nestorius and joined the Roman Catholic Church in 1599. The Chinese Nestorians survived until the fourteenth century. They then disappeared amid the political turbulence surrounding the establishment of the Ming Dynasty.

See also: BARSUMAS (2), EBEDJESUS, SIGAN-FU STONE.

NESTORIUS   This Christian teacher was one of the most influential heretics of ancient times. Nestorius began his career as a staunch opponent of the heresy known as APOLLINARIANISM; his overreaction to this doctrine resulted in a position that was declared to be just as heretical by the orthodox authorities. As a result of Nestorius's rejection by the Catholic Church, his followers carried their brand of Christianity to distant lands, such as India and China.

As a young man, Nestorius was a monk in the city of Antioch (in what is now Turkey). During this time, the early fifth century, Christian thinkers were attempting to define the relationship between the divine and human aspects of Christ. APOL-LINARIS had claimed that Christ had a human body, but that His mind was the divine Word of God. The orthodox theologians had denounced this view; they argued that it portrayed JESUS as less than fully human because He was said to lack a human mind. Instead, they insisted, Christ was completely human—and also completely divine. Nestorius and other thinkers grappled with this seeming paradox. THEODORE OF MOPSUESTIA, a contemporary of Nestorius, taught that Christ had two complete natures, divine and human, but was a single person, a position Nestorius himself adopted.

Nestorius's opposition to the Apollinarian teaching highlighted his commitment to orthodox Christianity. He rose through the ranks of the Catholic Church, until, in 428, the emperor appointed him the bishop of Constantinople.

In his newly eminent position, Nestorius quickly began to stir up controversy. It was a common practice of the day to refer to the Virgin Mary using the term *Theotokos*, which means "God-bearer." ANASTASIUS, one of Nestorius's colleagues, preached against the use of this word, arguing that it did not refer to Christ's human aspect and, therefore, contained the Apollinarian implication that Christ was not completely human. Anastasius' attack offended many people, who believed that the rejection of Theotokos was a denial of Christ's divinity. In a fateful move, Nestorius decided to support Anastasius.

Nestorius's concerns about the Theotokos, as well as his association with the works of Theodore of Mopsuestia, provoked a reaction from other church leaders. Theodore was under suspicion of teaching that Christ was split into two persons, a divine and a human one. If Christ was divided in this way, the orthodox believed, then He could not have the power of salvation. Bishop Cyril of Alexandria and Pope Celestine I were concerned that Nestorius too was denying the unity of Christ's Person.

Unfortunately, almost all of Nestorius's own writings were destroyed by his enemies. Modern historians do not agree about the precise nature of Nestorius's actual beliefs concerning the two natures of Christ. Many now think that Nestorius was actually orthodox in his doctrine. However, in order to distinguish his view from that of Apollinaris, he highlighted the complete humanity of Christ. Some observers felt that Nestorius overemphasized Christ's human features and neglected Christ's divinity.

Evidently, however, the developing opposition to Nestorius was not based solely on theological concerns. The Christian community of Alexandria, once the most important center of Christianity in the world, had declined in significance compared to Rome and Constantinople by the fifth century. Most likely, Cyril and Celestine hoped that arranging for the bishop of Constantinople to get into doctrinal trouble would strengthen their own positions in the church's political scene.

In 430, the pope condemned Nestorius for teaching that Christ's divine and human natures were two distinct persons. Nestorius denied the charge. Christians took sides, and the possibility of violent conflict loomed. The following year, Emperor Theodosius called a meeting of church leaders at Ephesus to resolve the question of Nestorius's views.

Cyril managed to convince the majority of those present at the COUNCIL OF EPHESUS that Nestorius was a heretic, "sick with many and strange blasphemies." Cyril's task was made easier because the meeting began before Nestorius's chief supporter, Bishop John of Antioch, had arrived. When John finally appeared, another council was quickly convened; it condemned Cyril and supported Nestorius.

But Cyril's supporters eventually triumphed because of superior political connections with the emperor. Nestorius was deposed as bishop, and John of Antioch was persuaded to side with Cyril. In 436, Nestorius was exiled to a remote location in Egypt.

Just as Nestorius had reacted against the teachings of Apollinaris by emphasizing Christ's humanity, so EUTYCHES, a Christian leader in Constantinople, reacted against Nestorius's teachings by magnifying Christ's divinity. The COUNCIL OF CHALCEDON, held in 451, condemned Eutyches' teaching and proclaimed that Christ has two natures, but is only one Person. Nestorius stated that his own position was identical to that proclaimed by this council. The orthodox refused to revoke their condemnation of him, however. Perhaps they continued to misunderstand his views. Some likely felt that a reversal of Nestorius's earlier condemnation would establish a dangerous precedent, enabling future generations to challenge the conclusions reached at Chalcedon. Nestorius died in Egypt, still labeled a heretic even though he held the same beliefs as his orthodox persecutors.

Nestorius's legacy continued long after his death. His followers formed the movement known as NESTORIANISM. The Nestorians established communities as far away as India and China; these survived for many centuries. The doctrine Eutyches formulated in opposition to Nestorius developed into the heretical movement of MONOPHYSITISM, which was popular in many parts of the Middle East.

NICETAS   A leader of the BOGOMIL heretics during the latter part of the twelfth century, Nicetas was bishop of the underground Bogomil Church in Constantinople. He traveled to western Europe in order to spread the teachings of his movement. They were earnestly received by the CATHARS, an unorthodox version of Christianity that was rapidly becoming a threat to the Catholic Church in Europe.

In 1167, Nicetas presided over a council of Cathar leaders that was held in southern France. The Bogomil bishop instructed the Cathars on his dualistic views. He also helped the French and Italian heretics to develop an international organization along the lines of the Bogomil Church in Byzantium. Each of the European regions in which Cathars were concentrated was assigned a bishop to compete against the Catholic bishop in that area.

NOETUS   An unorthodox Christian teacher who was prominent in Rome during the early third century. Noetus was a follower of PRAXEAS, the founder of the heresy known as MODALISM.

NOVATIAN   This church leader of the third century A.D. caused one of the first SCHISMS of the Catholic Church. Novatian did not disagree with any of the basic Catholic doctrines; indeed, he regarded himself as more orthodox than the church leaders who opposed him. Nonetheless, he was declared to be an enemy of the faith for the crime of splitting the body of the church.

During the third century, Christian communities suffered waves of persecution. The hostilities were instigated by various Roman emperors who felt threatened by the rising popularity of the church, or who needed a scapegoat on which to blame the growing problems within the empire. In the face of such danger, some Christians refused to deny their faith (the confessors), and often paid for their firmness with their lives (the martyrs). These individuals were universally admired throughout the Catholic community.

Other Christians, when captured and faced with the possibility of martyrdom, chose instead to deny their beliefs; rich Christians sometimes bribed their way out of captivity. When each wave of persecution ended, the church was faced with the problem of what to do with these "lapsed" Christians, who often sought readmission to the Christian community.

Orthodox Catholic leaders generally showed considerable tolerance on this issue, readmitting the lapsed members after appropriate penance. Various heretical groups, such as the followers of MONTANUS, objected to the policy of readmission. Such groups did not seriously challenge the general policy of orthodoxy because they were clearly outside the community of authentic Christians, by the orthodox definition.

The case of Novatian, a well-known Catholic in Rome who had effectively preached against the spread of the heresy of MODALISM in that city, was more problematic. In Novatian, the Catholic community had a man with impeccable orthodox credentials, who began to proclaim that people who commit mortal sins (including denying the Christian faith, even under threat) could never again be acceptable Catholics.

Novatian was opposed by Cyprian, the bishop of Carthage, who argued that the church was invested by God with the power to forgive such sins. Cyprian's concern was that if the Christian community became too severe in its judgments on these matters, thereby effectively restricting church membership to a moral elite, the Christian religion would lose its growing popularity. Novatian replied that forgiveness of mortal sins was itself a corruption of the true Christian message: better a small church of true Christians than a large church full of moral weakness.

Novatian's argument was unsuccessful in swaying Catholic leaders. Around 251, he founded a network of church communities that agreed with him. The Novatian Churches were orthodox in their doctrine, but differed from orthodoxy in their unwillingness to forgive moral lapses.

The pragmatic approach of Cyprian proved more beneficial to the survival of the church. NOVATIANISM endured into the fifth century, but the Catholic church, which declared Cyprian a saint, became the state religion of the Roman Empire, and is still powerful today. Novatian's unforgiving view was a direct ancestor of the more dangerous schism known as DONATISM, which emerged during the early fourth century.

NOVATIANISM   This movement split from the Catholic Church during the middle of the third century. NOVATIAN, the movement's leader, claimed that the orthodox church had become too morally permissive. The Novatian movement was the first known group to be called CATHARS, or "Pure Ones", by their orthodox enemies. In the Later Middle Ages, the term "Cathar" would be applied by Catholic propagandists to a major heresy unrelated to Novatianism.

John Humphrey NOYES   Founder of the nineteenth century American religious experiment known as the ONEIDA COMMUNITY. John Humphrey Noyes was born in Vermont in 1811. He was educated at Dartmouth College and became a Biblical scholar. Rejecting the idea, taught by mainstream Christianity, that humans are condemned to sin, he believed that spiritual perfection was possible for everybody, provided that they renounce all desire for private possessions and exclusive relationships. Noyes attracted enough followers to found a communistic settlement at Oneida, New York, in 1848. Noyes oversaw the community until its renunciation of his doctrines in 1879. He moved to Niagara Falls, Ontario, where he died in 1886.

Sir John OLDCASTLE   An English nobleman, *Sir John Oldcastle* was a leader of the LOLLARD heretics during the early fifteenth century. He was born into the lower ranks of the nobility in 1378, just a few years before the death of JOHN WYCLIFFE, the man whose teachings inspired the Lollards. As a young man, he was successful in military ventures; an opportune marriage into a powerful family ensured his entry into the upper classes.

Oldcastle did not keep secret his Lollard views, which included the belief that the Catholic Church should have all of its property confiscated. At first, he was protected from Catholic attack by his friendship with King Henry V. However, the king decided to strengthen his ties with the church for political reasons; ending his support for his Lollard friend was the price. Oldcastle was confined in the Tower of London and given forty days to repent his heresy.

The resourceful heretic managed to escape. He then set about organizing an uprising of Lollards, which aimed to overthrow the entire political power structure of England. The royal family, the highest aristocrats, and the leaders of the church were all to be killed and replaced with Lollards. Oldcastle himself would become king.

It seems that the revolt was poorly organized from the start; many Lollards did not respond to Oldcastle's call to gather in London, most likely because they never received the message. But the authorities were tipped off and arrested the heretics as they arrived. The leaders of the aborted rebellion were executed, but Oldcastle again escaped. Three years later, he was captured; this time, he was sentenced to death and could not elude the hangman's noose.

OLD CATHOLICS   During the past 250 years, many Roman Catholics have found it impossible to accept some of the proclamations of the Vatican. A number of these dissidents, known collectively as Old Catholics, have retained most of the basic Catholic beliefs and rituals, but have developed other features that distinguish them from the mainstream Catholic church.

In 1724, the Catholic church in Holland experienced a SCHISM over the doctrines of JANSENISM, which had repeatedly been pronounced heretical by the papacy. In Utrecht, three bishops who supported Jansenist views were consecrated in defiance of the pope. This Church of Utrecht, the first Old Catholic denomination, continues today. There are also Austrian, German, and Swiss Old Catholic Churches, founded by Catholics who objected to the proclamation of papal infallibility in 1870. The bishops of these groups were consecrated by the Church of Utrecht. There are various other small groups, generally of Slavic descent, affiliated with the Old Catholics. Since 1932, the Old Catholic movement has enjoyed mutual recognition with the Anglican Church.

See also: WANDERING BISHOPS.

Pierre OLIVI   Leader of the SPIRITUAL FRANCISCANS during the second half of the thirteenth century, Pierre Olivi was strongly influenced by the prophecies of JOACHIM OF FIORE. Olivi believed that a new age, ruled by the Holy Spirit, was about to begin. According to Olivi, the Catholic Church was the "whore of Babylon" (a symbol of corruption in the Book of Revelation) because church leaders had become obsessed with wealth and power.

Olivi believed that the Spiritual Franciscans would have to undergo a time of persecution by the Antichrist, but would emerge to take over the church. Before his death in 1298, some of his ideas were criticized by Catholic authorities, but he persuaded them of his orthodoxy. The Spiritual Franciscans revered him as a great teacher. This group was denounced as a heresy in 1317; two years later, the Franciscan order repudiated Olivi; and finally, in 1326, Pope John XXII banned his writings on the Book of Revelation.

ONEIDA COMMUNITY   Nineteenth century America was a place of widespread religious experimentation. The Oneida Community was one of the best known of the unorthodox Christian groups that flourished at this time. Founded in 1848 in Oneida, New York, the Community survived for thirty-two years.

The Oneida Community's founder was JOHN HUMPHREY NOYES, an American biblical scholar who believed that the mainstream church had lost its way long ago, in the first century A.D. Since JESUS' lifetime, Christians had been waiting for his Second Coming. Noyes preached that Christ had actually returned in A.D. 70 when the Romans destroyed the Temple in Jerusalem. The scholar believed that modern Christians should adopt the lifestyle of Christians who were alive when Christ had returned. Noyes invited everyone to join with him in founding a community of faithful members who would imitate those blessed early believers visited by the Lord. He taught that perfect holiness required the sharing of all possessions.

In 1846, Noyes's followers made their first attempt to establish a community in Putney, Vermont. Their neighbors viewed them as heretics and drove them away. Two years later, in Oneida, a firmer foundation was laid; about 300 people agreed to live according to Noyes's communistic doctrines.

The Oneida Community supported itself through a range of activities, including farming, trapping, printing, and manufacturing. The quality of their silverware, known as Community Plate, became world-renowned. Community members shared all produce and income.

The most notorious feature of the Oneida Community's lifestyle was the members' rejection of sexual property. They believed that any form of "selfish love" was inappropriate, including the idea that sexual relations should be restricted to one partner. Rampant promiscuity was discouraged, but planned physical relationships between consenting adults was acceptable. Every man in the Community was regarded as being married to every woman, an arrangement known as complex marriage. In order to keep the birth rate under control, the men of Oneida trained themselves to retain their semen when they had orgasms, a skill that is difficult but not impossible to develop.

The offspring of these nonpossessive relationships were not themselves possessed by the parents, but were raised by the entire Community. The Oneida sect regarded its reproductive activities as a kind of "scientific propagation" in which the purely conceived children, raised in an enlightened environment, would easily grow into spiritual perfection. In order for such an arrangement to work, a high moral standard had to be maintained. The Community was largely successful in accomplishing this through the holding of assemblies, during which members who had fallen short of the spiritual ideal would be invited to confess their faults and to criticize themselves. The other members present would express support for the one who had lapsed, helping the individual to feel improved rather than condemned by the confession.

Indeed, during its thirty-two years of existence, there was little evidence of serious internal strife within the Community. However, the rest of the state never accepted its sexual practices, and harassment was continuous. Eventually, in 1880, enthusiasm for this experiment had diminished among the participants themselves. They abandoned their religious doctrines and converted the Community into a joint stock company, Oneida Community Ltd., which continued to manufacture their coveted silverware. Noyes, the disappointed founder, moved to Canada, where he died six years later.

OPHITES   The Ophites were an important school within the GNOSTIC movement, which posed a prominent alternative to orthodox Christianity during the first few centuries A.D. The Ophites had their own scriptures and used a complicated diagram depicting the structure of the universe in their teaching. This material was destroyed long ago. Current knowledge of this Gnostic sect is based on the writings of orthodox Christians, who attacked the Ophites as heretics, and the observations of the pagan writer CELSUS, who targeted the Ophites along with the Catholics in his anti-Christian writings.

The Ophites' world view generally resembled that of VALENTINIAN GNOSTICISM. In the beginning was the Father of All, the First Man. He emanated forth a Thought, who was the Second Man. The Holy Spirit, or First Woman, then appeared. This Trinity emanated Christ and his sister, Sophia or Wisdom. Ialdabaoth, one of Sophia's children, rebelled against her. As part of his rebellion, he created the world, including the first humans. Ialdabaoth pretended to be the highest deity and demanded worship from Adam and Eve.

The creator God of the Old Testament was identified with Ialdabaoth. The Ophites continued this inversion of Hebrew belief by portraying the serpent in the Garden of Eden as an agent of Sophia. The serpent convinced Eve and Adam to taste the fruit forbidden to them by Ialdabaoth. This fruit gave them the knowledge of the creator's relatively lowly status in the divine realm. For this deed, Ialdabaoth punished the serpent with confusion, and it became a demon. The Greek word *ophis* means serpent, and the Ophites adopted their name to signify that they were the followers of the wisdom-serpent. The Ophites taught that a reminder of the serpent's alliance with humanity can be seen within each human body, in the convoluted shape of the intestines.

Sophia also implanted "moist light" within Adam and Eve. This spiritual luminosity contained the knowledge of their distant origin in the Father of All. Ialdabaoth attempted to confuse humanity, so that people would not be aware of this inner light. Moved by pity for humanity's suffering under the tyranny of Ialdabaoth, Christ descended and combined with JESUS. Jesus Christ proclaimed that knowledge (GNOSIS) of the moist light within people leads them to freedom from the enslavement of the material creator.

The Ophites' reverence for the serpent in the Garden of Eden, who was conventionally understood to be an evil creature, caused orthodox Christians to view them as blasphemers. The serpent as a symbol of wisdom can be found in many cultures, including those of ancient Egypt and Greece. The serpentine imagery of the Ophites probably seemed much less strange to their pagan contemporaries than it does to people today.

OPUS CONTRA NATURAM   This Latin phrase means "work against nature." *Opus contra naturam* is a central doctrine in the tradition of ALCHEMY and represents some of the most important contributions of alchemy to the modern sense of reality. One of the meanings of the Latin phrase refers to the alchemists' deliberate interference with the natural composition of metals. A goal of alchemy is the creation of the Philosopher's Stone, an agent that can change base metals, such as lead, into gold. One of the theories that guided this quest was Aristotle's idea that every material object is composed of the four elements—earth, water, air, and fire—in various combinations. Through altering the proportions of these elements, anything can be changed into anything else. Lead can be changed into gold, for example, by changing the proportions of the elements in lead until they match the proportions in gold. A related theory proposed that all metals were made of two substances, sulphur and mercury, the relative amounts of which determined the kind of metal. Gold was thought to be a perfect balance of sulphur and mercury, so other metals could be converted to gold by equalizing the sulphur and mercury in their composition.

To accomplish this rearranging of proportions, the alchemist must first break down the substance into the raw material out of which the elements themselves are made. Alchemists conducted various chemical operations in their laboratories in order to generate this *prima materia*. *Opus contra naturam* is this reversal of the natural emergence of material objects from the *prima materia*. Matter was thought to arise from the *prima materia* in a circular motion, so another name for alchemy was *opus circulatorum*, which refers to the circular work of reversing the wheel of creation.

A second meaning of *opus contra naturam* pertains to ancient and medieval beliefs concerning the ripening of metals. Before the development of modern science, there was general agreement that the cosmos was alive. Everything within the cosmos, including metals, was also considered to be endowed with life. One popular theory proposed that metals were conceived when sunlight, a male energy, penetrated and fertilized Mother earth. Metals were thought to gestate in the ground like fetuses in the womb, gradually developing from base metals into gold, the most mature substance.

Another understanding of metals suggested that they grew like plants from seeds in the earth. Gold was thought to be the fruit of the germination of metals. In this context, the work of alchemy was viewed as an attempt to accelerate the gestating or germinating processes of metal development in order to make gold, the end product of that development. Here, *opus contra naturam* is a work against the naturally slow pace of the earthly processes.

A third meaning of the term refers to the alchemical work on a psychological level. The alchemists felt that they were an inseparable part of the cosmic organism. Because of this connectedness, they could not cause changes in metallic processes without changing themselves at the same time. Classic alchemy was thought to occur on both the material and psychological levels. Understood psychologically, the quest for the *prima materia* involves a journey within oneself to uncover one's basic nature. During this inner passage, one encounters many aspects of oneself that might be very painful and embarrassing for one to accept. Naturally, people tend to avoid these unpleasant insights and will resist efforts to have them pointed out. On the level of the mind, alchemy is an *opus contra naturam* in the sense that it works against people's natural resistance to painful truths about themselves. In order to reconstruct themselves into "spiritual gold", however, they must first confront and dissolve this resistance.

Two of alchemy's contributions to modern reality involve its role as an *opus contra naturam*. Many of the founding figures of modern science were involved in esoteric disciplines, including alchemy. Sir Isaac Newton, for example, was more interested in alchemy than in physics. One of the basic assumptions of science is that human knowledge is itself a kind of *opus contra naturam*. Early scientists taught that in order to learn about nature, people cannot simply contemplate it or think about it—they must *interfere* with it by conducting experiments. It seems likely that this belief was derived from alchemy and related heretical traditions because the mainstream belief of the time was opposed to this mode of understanding.

In the hands of science, however, the meaning of *opus contra naturam* changed. Unlike the alchemists, who saw themselves as part of the the living universe they were trying to change, the scientists separated themselves from nature and viewed it as a vast machine. The results of scientific experiments were thought to be independent of the mental or spiritual states of the scientist.

In the twentieth century, the second important contribution of the alchemical *opus contra naturam* emerged in the form of depth psychology. Famous Swiss psychiatrist Carl Jung believed that alchemy contained important knowledge about the workings of the mind. His branch of depth psychology, analytical psychology, viewed the process of human psychological growth as an *opus contra naturam* in the sense of working against natural resistances to insight.

ORDO TEMPLI ORIENTIS   This important twentieth century magical organization was based on the use of sexual arousal in ritual magic. According to the practitioners of sex magic, ordinary people cannot create magical effects with their sexual energy because their ability to concentrate their will is poorly developed; the trained magician, on the other hand, can direct the force of erotic arousal to cause spiritual and physical transformations.

The *Ordo Templi Orientis* (the "Order of Eastern Templars," or OTO) was founded in the early 1900s in Germany by Karl Kellner. It seems that he studied the sexual mysticism of the Hindu Tantra during his travels in India and met practitioners of a type of sex magic devised by P. B. Randolph, an American magician. During its early years, the true nature of the organization remained secret. The Order stated that it preserved the occult methods of the medieval KNIGHTS TEMPLAR, but this claim is historically unfounded. In a 1912 publication, the OTO defined its approach: "Our Order possesses the KEY which opens up all Masonic and Hermetic secrets, namely, the teaching of sexual magic, and this teaching explains, without exception, all the secrets of Nature."

In the same year, famous magician ALEISTER CROWLEY was initiated into the OTO. After Kellner's death in 1905, Theodor Reuss had assumed the Order's leadership. Reuss had understood from Crowley's published writings that Crowley knew the secrets of sex magic, and invited him to found an English branch of the OTO. In 1922, Reuss resigned the leadership of the Order, and Crowley took over. Crowley included the sexual rites of the OTO in his system of magic, which he taught for decades, until his death in 1947. Largely because of Crowley's promotion, the practice of sex magic has become a sizable branch of the contemporary ritual-magic scene. Today, active branches of the OTO are located in several countries.

See also: CHURCH OF CARMEL.

ORIGEN   The Egyptian city of Alexandria produced many of the most significant figures in ancient Christian heresy and orthodoxy. Origen played a major role in both heretical and orthodox streams. He was an architect of the orthodox doctrine of the Trinity, yet he was condemned after his death as a heretic and an instigator of the most dangerous challenges to mainstream Christian belief.

Origen was born into a Christian family around A.D. 185. Christians were still a persecuted minority within the Roman Empire at the time. When Origen was eighteen, his father was martyred, and Origen would have accompanied his father to a pious death if he had not been restrained by his mother. Because of the ferocity of their persecution, most Christians had fled from Alexandria. The Christian school there, the first such institution in the world, was severely understaffed. Origen was chosen to be the head teacher of the school during this time of trouble.

Origen's reputation as a Christian instructor spread quickly after his youthful assumption of the role at the Alexandrian school. He became ascetic in his lifestyle, insisting on owning only one cloak and sleeping on the floor. In response to an ambiguous passage in the Gospel of Matthew, "and there are eunuchs who have made themselves such for the sake of the kingdom of heaven" (19:12), he castrated himself.

While Origen studied the Christian scriptures and doctrines deeply, he was also intimately versed in the wonders of classical pagan spirituality. He is known to have attended the lectures of Ammonius Saccas, the Alexandrian who established the mystical philosophy called Neoplatonism. Origen was acquainted with VALENTINUS, the founder of an important school of Christian GNOSTICISM. The influence of Ammonius and Valentinus on Origen has been the subject of scholarly debate, but there are evident similarities between Neoplatonism and VALENTINIAN GNOSTICISM, and Origen's thinking.

In Origen's day, the details of the orthodox doctrine of the Trinity had not yet been established. The relationship between the Father and the Son contained a paradox: If the Father and the Son are both God, then They must be equal. But if the Son was begotten by the Father, then the Son presumably came into existence after the Father did and, therefore, must in some sense be inferior to the Father. A coherent portrayal of the Trinity could not be made until this puzzle was solved. Origen suggested that the relationship between Father and Son, "begetting," does not happen within time because God transcends time. This begetting, unlike the begetting of human sons by human fathers, is, therefore, eternal. The Father does not precede the Son in existence; They are *coeternal*. Furthermore, the Father and Son, although They are distinct Persons, share a single nature or substance. The Son is subordinate to the Father in that His duty is to carry out the Father's will; however, the Son is equal to the Father in His substance. Origen's solution to the paradox was adopted as the orthodox Christian position at the FIRST COUNCIL OF NICAEA in 325.

Concerning the role of the Holy Spirit, however, Origen sometimes seemed to argue that this member of the Trinity was inferior to the Father and Son. Later theologians would disagree with Origen on this issue, claiming that all three persons of the Trinity are coeternal and consubstantial; that is, they share a single substance.

Another of Origen's significant contributions to the orthodox Christian view of God concerns the nature of Christ. Early in the development of Christianity, theologians had borrowed from pagan philosophy the term "Logos," or Word, to describe Christ. In pagan systems of thought, the Logos acts as a bridge or mediator between the divine world of Being, which is unified and simple, and the world of ordinary human experience, which is filled with diversity.

Christians and pagans alike were mystified as to how a cosmic, impersonal function like the Logos could be identified with JESUS, a carpenter's son who lived in first century Palestine. For Origen, the key to this mystery was the idea that before Jesus' birth, His soul had been so pure and devoted to God that it was able to become united with the Logos. God created a perfect human body, which housed this union of Jesus' pure soul and the Logos during Christ's lifetime. Following the resurrection, the human Jesus became "divinized," or completely transformed into the divine nature. Although later orthodoxy did not fully accept the details of Origen's solution to the puzzling identity of Jesus and Logos, his brilliant attempt helped to show that the relationship between the human and divine aspects of Jesus Christ could be explored by human thought.

Origen's teachings regarding human nature were not generally accepted by orthodox Christianity. According to Origen, all human souls were created together before the material world was formed. This is the doctrine of the preexistence of the soul. Those souls that chose to turn away from God became incarnated in bodies. Through the ages, these souls undergo repeated reincarnations, the type of body inhabited during each life depending on the moral qualities of the person's behavior during previous lives.

Origen taught that the goal during this journey through lifetimes is to become so pure that souls can escape from entrapment within matter and achieve union with the Logos. When this occurs, they become divinized, just as Jesus did. In fact, Origen's descriptions of this process sound as if all saved persons become identified with the Logos. Origen was optimistic about the fate of the world. He taught that everyone would eventually be saved—even the Devil himself. In Origen's panoramic world view, after the universe is emptied of suffering souls, the whole process of soul creation, their straying from God and embodiment, their reincarnation, purification and salvation, begins again.

Origen was a staunch supporter of the Catholic hierarchy of power. He preached that laypersons should obey the commands of priests and bishops. Origen himself, however, had some difficulty following his own advice. He had frequent conflicts with Demetrius, the bishop of Alexandria. During a visit to Palestine in 230, local bishops ordained Origen a priest, without Demetrius's permission. Demetrius declared the ordination invalid on the grounds that men with mutilated genitals could not be priests, and exiled him from Alexandria.

Barred from his home, Origen spent the rest of his life in Palestine, where he continued to share his Christian insights. During a flare-up of persecution in 250, Roman interrogators captured and tortured Origen. When the persecution stopped, a result of the sudden death of the emperor, Origen was released. His death three years later probably resulted from the lingering effects of his ill treatment.

After Origen's passing, his views continued to provoke debate within the Christian community. The orthodox stream of Christianity absorbed some of his ideas but excluded others. For example, it rejected Origen's grand vision of human spiritual development within cycles of straying and redemption. Catholicism regarded the events of history, and the life of Jesus in particular, as unique and unrepeatable. The pagan understanding of time tended to view historical events as manifestations of a great cycle, just as the changing seasons manifest the cycle of the year. Origen's cyclical view of time reminded many orthodox observers of pagan views. His doctrine of the preexistence of souls was condemned when church leaders met at the SECOND COUNCIL OF CONSTANTINOPLE in 553.

The richness of Origen's teachings inspired Christian heretics for centuries after his death, often in ways that would likely have horrified Origen himself. The ARIAN heretics took Origen's teaching that the Son is dutifully subordinate to the Father and proclaimed that the Son is less divine than the Father. This clearly was not an implication Origen intended. PELAGIUS, the teacher of human perfectability whom Augustine opposed, counted himself a follower of Origen. The idea that the human aspect of Jesus was divinized appealed to the adherents of the MONO-PHYSITE heresy, who taught that Jesus Christ had a single nature. The NESTORIAN heretics, their staunch opponents, also believed that they followed Origen in their separation of the divine and human aspects of Christ into two distinct natures.

See also: ORIGENISM, REINCARNATION.

ORIGENISM   Following the death of the great Christian thinker ORIGEN in A.D. 254, his ideas sparked a movement, known as Origenism, to promote his vision of reality. Scholar Geddes MacGregor has cautioned against identifying the teachings of the Origenists with those of Origen himself; his followers creatively interpreted Origen's ideas, moving their thinking away from Origen's original thoughts.

Over the next three centuries, the status of Origenism with respect to orthodoxy varied. Origenism was frequently lumped together with such heresies as ARIA-NISM, an association many Origenists who counted themselves as strictly orthodox denied. Saint Jerome, an important figure in the fourth century Catholic community, shifted from being a vigorous supporter of Origenism to a forceful opponent of this movement.

During the reign of Emperor Justinian in the sixth century, Origenists became a major force in the Christian community. Their enemies recruited the emperor's support and issued a list of Origenist teachings, declaring them to be erroneous. The doctrine of the preexistence of souls—the belief that all souls were formed at the creation of the world—was especially targeted by the anti-Origenists.

Justinian's opposition to Origenism shook the Origenist community and caused it to split into two factions. These were the ISOCHRISTS, who believed that everyone attains equality with Christ at the end of the world, and the PROTOCTISTS, who regarded Christ as eternally excellent without equal. The death blow was delivered to Origenism at the SECOND COUNCIL OF CONSTANTINOPLE in 553, when Origen's teachings concerning the preexistence of souls was declared to be heretical. Some historians have questioned whether the condemnation of Origenism was made during an official session of the Council and, therefore, whether it should be viewed as necessarily binding on the Catholic Church.

ORLEANS HERETICS   In A.D. 1022, a sensational trial took place in the city of Orleans, France. Charges of heresy were leveled at a group of aristocrats and priests, including the confessor of French Queen Constance. For the first time in the Middle Ages, those on trial were accused of worshipping Satan. The conclusion of the trial was also unique. Fourteen people were burned at the stake, the first instance of a fiery execution for heretics in Europe north of the Alps.

The origins of the affair lay in both politics and religion. At the time, King Robert I of France was engaged in a power struggle with Count Eudo of Blois. Robert had assisted his ally Thierry to become bishop of Orleans, rather than Odalric, the candidate backed by Eudo. Shortly afterward, an associate of Eudo reported that he had infiltrated a group of Robert's allies in Orleans and discovered that their Christianity was far from orthodox. In fact, they were servants of the Devil.

The trial that resulted from this claim was undoubtedly part of the political battle between Robert and Eudo. Although the charge of SATANISM was an invention of Robert's enemies designed to embarrass him, it is clear that the group at Orleans held unorthodox beliefs. Reports at the time indicated that heretical beliefs had been brought to the town by "Italians." Some historians have suggested that the visitors from Italy may have been missionaries of the Balkan heresy known as BOGOMILISM, who had entered western Europe via Italy.

The unorthodox doctrines confessed at the trial do resemble the Bogomil heresy in some respects. The accused admitted that they did not believe the miracle stories in the New Testament, nor did they think that the sacraments of the Catholic Church, including marriage and the Mass, had any significance. They stated that the material world was evil, and that eating meat was a sin. Only those in whose hearts the Holy Spirit lives can truly understand the Christian teaching.

The political distress these revelations concerning his wife's associates caused the king was so great that he was forced to take drastic action. Robert ordered the public burning of the heretics. The Orleans heretics may also have believed in REINCARNATION; like their successors in French heretical history, the reincarnationist

CATHARS, the prospect of execution seemed to hold no fear for them, and they went laughing into the flames. Thierry, the bishop the king favored, was deposed and replaced by Odalric. Robert's actions set a dangerous precedent. The burning of heretics increased in frequency through the next century, and culminated in the mass destruction of the Cathars during the 1200s.

Several decades after the trial, Paul of Chartres wrote an account of the affair. Allied with the faction of Eudo of Blois, he not only included the false charges of Satanism in his story, but also amplified them to a lurid degree. According to Paul, the heretics of Orleans met at night by candlelight and chanted the names of demons until the Devil materialized in the form of an animal. The candles suddenly then went out, and an orgy followed. If children were born as a consequence of this diabolical festivity, they were burned and their ashes made into a magical potion. The heretics then introduced this substance into food. If someone unwittingly ate it, they fell under a spell and were compelled to join the sect.

This wild tale was not original. Similar stories had been told during the third century—not about heretics, but about Catholics. The pagan authorities of Lyons had accused the Christians in that city of orgies and infant killing, in order to whip up sentiment against them, which led to persecution. The accusations had been preserved over the centuries in Christian archives and resurfaced to be used against the heretics of the twelfth century. In this way, ancient anti-Christian imagery entered the anti-heresy propaganda of the later Middle Ages. By the fifteenth century, such stories had become part of the standard description of the witches' sabbath, which fanned the GREAT WITCH HUNT.

See also: LEUTHARD, MONTEFORTE HERETICS.

PACT   The demonic pact is an agreement made with the Devil. For almost as long as the concept of evil has existed in Western culture, the orthodox have feared that people were making secret deals with dark forces. Generally, it was thought that the pact involved the human partner receiving diabolical aid in acquiring money, sex, and power. In return, the demon expected that the human partner would undertake acts of evil, and the person's soul would become Satan's property when the pact expired. Through the centuries, many groups and individuals perceived to be strange or frightening were suspected of making pacts with demons. Eventually, some of those unorthodox groups and people began to believe it themselves.

The Dead Sea Scroll entitled *The War of the Sons of Light and the Sons of Darkness*, written around the time of Christ, describes an army of people in league with the forces of evil. This was the prototype for the demonic conspiracy. The devilish pact is not explicitly mentioned as part of this ancient legend, but it is implied.

The Bible itself does not mention the idea of demonic pacts. Later, Christians claiming that such pacts do occur felt the need to justify their belief with a Biblical passage, particularly the Protestant witch hunters with their insistence that the Bible, and not Catholic tradition, was the only reliable authority. They often quoted a passage from the Book of Isaiah: "You have said, We have made a covenant with death, and with hell are we at agreement" (28:15). Isaiah was referring to the ruling class of ancient Jerusalem, but taken out of context the passage served to support the orthodoxy of belief in the pact.

Third century orthodox theologian ORIGEN (later condemned as a heretic) was the first major Christian thinker to hint that deals with the Devil could be made. The idea of the pact underwent an important expansion at the hands of Augustine of Hippo, the influential Christian thinker of the fifth century. In his work *De Doctrina Christiana*, Augustine argues that all of the occult arts, including astrology and divination, involve "the pestiferous association of men with demons, as if formed by a pact of faithless and dishonourable friendship." If people innocently draw up a horoscope or use a simple spell without realizing that demons are involved, they have unwittingly entered into an alliance with the Devil.

Orthodox thinkers worked out the implications of Augustine's broad definition of the pact in the centuries that followed. Theologians of the Middle Ages and Renaissance explained that two kinds of demonic pact existed. The *explicit* pact involves deliberately requesting the Devil's assistance and expecting or perceiving a response. An example of the explicit pact is conducting a ritual of DEMON MAGIC, in which an evil spirit is called upon to harm an enemy. In the *tacit* pact, a person simply wishes for something that cannot happen naturally, and that is not done by God or the angels. Accordingly, carrying a lucky charm, such as a rabbit's foot, is an example of a tacit pact with Satan.

While the intellectuals within the church were refining their ideas concerning the pact, the common people were sharing stories about individuals who had made bargains with Satan. The tale of Theophilus was one well-known legend. Theophilus was a good Christian who was dismissed from his position as steward in the local church by enemies in the religious bureaucracy. Outraged, he consulted a sorceror who conjured the Devil. Theophilus signed a contract with this evil spirit in his own blood. The next day, he was reappointed as steward. But his joy was overshadowed by the memory that he had promised his body and soul to Satan. Repentant, he prayed to the Virgin Mary, who retrieved the document from hell.

The circulation of such rumors served to discourage common people from dabbling in unorthodox practices. These stories also laid the groundwork for the advent of the GREAT WITCH HUNT. Naturally, the belief, in both the educated and popular levels of society, that humans could make a pact with the Devil became part of the growing fear that civilization was under attack by a conspiracy of devil-worshipping witches. The accusation that witches made pacts implied that witches acted against Christianity. Therefore, witches were heretics and not merely criminals, and so fell within the purview of the INQUISITION.

In 1398, scholars at the University of Paris declared that witches sign pacts with Satan, establishing the belief as an accepted doctrine among scholars. As the witch hunt unfolded and spread during the ensuing decades, the reality of the witches' pact was confirmed in the confessions of many suspects who, under torture, would likely confess to anything the Inquisitors expected to hear. By the time the definitive witch hunters' manual, MALLEUS MALEFICARUM, was published in 1486, the fantasy of the witches' contract with the Devil had developed in great detail.

Occasionally, an actual contract was produced as evidence during a witch trial. The most famous such case was that of the Catholic priest Urbain Grandier. In 1634, he was accused of bewitching the nuns in a convent at Loudun, France. The prosecutors presented a pact, in which Grandier renounces Christ and vows to do "as much evil as I can." This bizarre document, which survives to the present day, bears not only Grandier's signature, but also the signatures of seven demons, including

Satan himself. Partly on the basis of this forgery, Father Grandier (who was almost certainly innocent of any wrongdoing), was burned at the stake.

Even though the rewards granted through making a pact with evil powers were said to be acquired at grave risk to one's immortal soul, some people began to think that the risk was worth taking. Firm evidence exists that actual attempts to make pacts with the Devil were being made by the seventeenth century. In 1677, a Bavarian painter named Christoph Haizmann began having panic attacks. He admitted to the police that he had written an agreement with the Devil, using his own blood, nine years earlier. Haizmann had sold his soul to Satan in return for material success, a decision he now regretted as he grew older and got closer to his hour of reckoning. After three days and nights of praying at a shrine, Haizmann saw the Virgin Mary in a vision and believed that she had nullified the pact.

The practitioners of demon magic specialized in evoking evil spirits, but during medieval and Renaissance times felt they had no need to barter their souls; they believed that they could control the spirits with the use of magic words. By the eighteenth century, the orthodox understanding of the demonic pact began to make its way into the ritual-magic literature. The famous magical manual called GRAND GRIMOIRE, written at this time, gave details of a ceremony to conjure a demon and conclude a pact. The grimoire's version of the contract includes a loophole, so the magician can easily avoid payment when it is due. Some people were actually involved in such practices. In 1785, two women in Germany were convicted of murdering a man in order to use his blood for writing pacts with Satan.

PAGANISM   According to the Roman Catholic Church, pagans are individuals who worship more than one god. And because orthodox Christianity insists on the unity of God, pagans, therefore, commit the heresy of POLYTHEISM.

Jacob PALEOLOGUS   A sixteenth century heretical author, Jacob Paleologus was born in Greece but became a religious refugee in Poland. He taught that two groups of people would receive God's salvation at the end of time, Christians and people with Jewish ancestors. Paleologus influenced prominent Polish heretic SIMON BUDNY. During a visit to Bohemia, Catholic authorities arrested Paleologus. He was sent to Rome, where he was convicted of heresy and executed in 1581.

TIBERIUS PANTERA   The rumor that JESUS' father was not God but a mortal man can be found in ancient literature questioning the divinity of Jesus. A candidate for the paternity of Jesus mentioned in Jewish texts is "Panteri" or "Pandira," who has been tentatively identified by classical scholar Morton Smith as Tiberius Pantera, a soldier of the Roman Empire.

Traditional accounts of the life of Rabbi Eliezer, a leader of the Palestinian Jewish community in the late first century, contain possible references to Jesus' Family. Eliezer was likely a child or adolescent when Jesus was crucified. One account describes the rabbi's encounter with a heretic who taught "in the name of Jesus the son of Panteri." The statement given as Jesus' teaching in this passage, "From filth they came, and to filth they shall return," is not recorded in the Gospels, but resembles the style of Jesus' orthodox sayings. The "son of Panteri" may well be the same person as the founding figure of Christianity.

In another passage, Rabbi Eliezer is quoted concerning a heretical "madman" whose mother was "Miriam the hairdresser" (or Mary). She is said to have had an illicit lover named "Pandira." (This passage also asserts, in accord with several other contemporary non-Christian accounts, that Jesus' body was covered with tattoos he received while studying magic in Egypt.)

Who was this "Panteri" or "Pandira" whose name was so scandalously linked to the names of Mary and Jesus? One plausible candidate is Tiberius Julius Abdes Pantera. He was identified from separate sources as a Sidonian archer stationed with Roman troops in Palestine at around the time of Jesus' birth; he was later transferred to the Rhineland where he died. His tombstone, found at Bingerbruck, exists to this day, and is described by Smith as possibly "our only genuine relic of the Holy Family."

It is possible that the Christian story of Jesus' virgin birth was partially a maneuver aimed at combatting persistent rumors about His dubious parentage. The stories of Jesus' adulterous origins form part of an ancient skeptical tradition regarding the Christian version of Jesus' life story. Most of the early literature reporting these stories was understandably suppressed by the Christians when they acquired the police powers of the Roman state. Today, researchers must reconstruct these accounts from fragmentary evidence. However, unorthodox versions of Jesus' life have continued to arise, and have constituted a central part of heretical interests to the twentieth century.

PANTHEISM   This doctrine states literally that God (Theos) is everything (pan). The term was first used by seventeenth century theologian John Toland. Pantheistic beliefs characterize many of the world's religions. Mystically inclined individuals from a wide range of cultures, including the West, have reported experiences in which they perceive the universe to be identified with God. The Judeo-Christian tradition disapproves of pantheistic intepretations because they contradict a basic feature of its world view: the distinction between the Creator and His creation. In this view, just as a pot cannot be identified with the potter, God cannot be identified with the world.

From the orthodox perspective, pantheism is dangerous because it can easily lead to idolatry, the worship of a created object instead of the creator. According to pantheists, the following syllogism is true: A tree is God; God should be worshipped; therefore, the tree should be worshipped. But the deification of such objects as trees, mountains, and statues is precisely what Jews and Christians have always thought to be the great error of the pagan faiths.

Throughout the Christian era, pantheism has been viewed as a heresy, often punishable by death. Orthodox Christian mystics have struggled with the challenge of reconciling their experiences, which often seem to involve a sense of nondistinction between God and the world or the self, with accepted doctrines. Those who succeed, such as Saint John of the Cross, are revered and even canonized; those who fail, like MEISTER ECKHART (von Hocheim), find their writings or themselves condemned as pantheistic.

See also: ALMALRIC OF BENA, GIORDANO BRUNO, DAVID OF DINANT.

PARACELSUS   Born Philippus Aureolus Theophrastus Bombastus von Hohenheim, this physician named himself Paracelsus, which means "beyond Celsus." Paracelsus thought that he had transcended the conventional medical knowledge of his day, symbolized by Roman writer Celsus. Paracelsus is a central figure in the history of ALCHEMY, as well as that of medicine, both mainstream and alternative.

Paracelsus was born in a village near Zurich, Switzerland, in 1493. His father was a physician and encouraged him to join the medical profession. As a youth, Paracelsus is thought to have traveled to various locations in Europe, studying under a variety of scholars before he received his doctorate from the University of Ferrara in 1516. One of these early mentors was probably occult scholar TRITHEMIUS of Sponheim. Trithemius was likely the person who taught the young student the doctrine of the "inner planets," which MARSILIO FICINO popularized during the Renaissance. According to this notion, within each person are the essences of the seven planetary forces; through understanding and balancing these forces, one maintains health. Paracelsus adopted this theme of a deep relationship between the inner world and the universe as a cornerstone of his thinking.

Following his graduation, Paracelsus continued his travels for seven more years. By this time, he had developed an unorthodox view of medical learning. He believed that humans were the pinnacle of material creation and, therefore, contained within themselves the *arcana*, or hidden essences, of all things. Knowledge of an object does not arise from reasoning about it or by simply observing it; rather, one must experience a kind of union with the object, which is made possible by awakening its arcanum within oneself. When this occurs, one will know the healing properties of the object and can use it to cure illnesses. Instead of studying medical books, Paracelsus studied the "book of Nature." He believed that by using his keen observation and intuition, he would be able to discover curative powers unknown to conventional medicine.

When Paracelsus settled in Salzburg, Austria, in 1524 to commence his medical practice, he had developed a contempt for traditional medicine: "were Jupiter to come down from his planet, he would encounter here below no inquirers but only schools of men who repeat the wisdom gathered by their forefathers from the stars. These schools of old are dead and their followers remain blind. . . ." During his career, Paracelsus expressed his sense of superiority in such offensive tones that he quickly made an enemy of almost every other physician he encountered. Referring to his medical colleagues, on one occasion he wrote, "Even in the most distant corner there will not be one of you on whom the dogs will not piss. But I will be the king and mine the kingdom."

Paracelsus achieved the height of his success during a ten-month stay in the town of Basle in 1527. When he cured an eminent citizen of a serious illness that had resisted conventional treatment, he was appointed town physician. But he proceeded to outrage the medical community. Invited to lecture at the university, Paracelsus announced that he would speak in German, not in the Latin favored by his colleagues. Furthermore, he presented his own findings, not ideas from the traditional texts. He made matters worse by publicly burning copies of the works of the great medical authorities. Finally, he managed to alienate a local judge; advised of his imminent arrest, he was forced to flee.

For most of the rest of his life, Paracelsus wandered Europe, experiencing several rises and declines in his popularity. He continued to make his life difficult by refusing to compromise on his beliefs and by expressing them bluntly. His view that all people contain within themselves the greatness of the universe caused him to be an early champion of individual human rights, as well as a critic of the privileges of the powerful classes. He had supported the peasant uprising of 1525 at serious risk to himself and was a known associate of such heretical groups as the ANABAPTISTS. On another occasion, he attacked the use of guaiac in the treatment of syphilis; however, the sale of this useless substance was very profitable for the Fuggers, a powerful German family. Paracelsus refused to censor himself, so he was chased out of town and his writings were banned.

The wandering healer wrote many volumes during his lifetime, but he rarely had the opportunity to publish his writings. Paracelsus acquired a small number of disciples; after his death, they collected his manuscripts, which were gradually published. In this way, his ideas were transmitted throughout Europe and became quite influential.

Using his methods of empirical study of "the book of Nature" and intuitive union with the objects of study, Paracelsus discovered that the entire universe, including humanity, was a living process of evolution. He rejected the traditional view that the world was basically composed of four elements, air, earth, fire, and water. Underlying these elements, he identified three principles that governed the movement of the world toward perfection. He called the principle of solidity "salt" and identified it with the body; "mercury" was the principle of change and activity, identified with the spirit; and "sulphur" was the principle of establishing patterns in the objects and activities of the universe, identified with the soul.

By altering these processes, which are closely connected to the essence of each object, Paracelsus believed that one could change any object into anything else. He applied this theory to his medical practice, trying to find ways to alter disease into health. He reported that many illnesses responded favorably when the patient was given a sample of the disease's arcanum, prepared using alchemical techniques. For example, someone with a fever could be treated by administering belladonna, which itself can produce a fever. This practice of treating like with like, rather than the traditional practice of treating something with its opposite, established Paracelsus as the father of homeopathy.

Some historians also view Paracelsus as the father of modern conventional medicine because of his refusal merely to parrot old authorities, but to learn through studying his patients. His theory of the three principles was adopted by many later alchemists, who were trying to transform the lower features of nature (such as lead) into more refined features (represented by gold). The holistic attitude found among many health practitioners today can trace its origin to Paracelsus's insistence that every person is an embodiment of the world's arcana, linked to the processes of universal transformation.

Paracelsus spent the final year of his life back in Salzburg, supported by the local bishop. In September 1541, he apparently suffered a stroke and died. Some historians have speculated that agents of the medical profession may have poisoned him.

PASTORELLES   Pastorelles is the variant name for the PASTOUREAUX.

PASTOUREAUX   During the early thirteenth century, a series of famines wracked France. As usual, the poor suffered the most. Under these adverse conditions, faithful Christians wondered if God was punishing them, and what they could do to please Him. The Pastoureaux ("Shepherds") movement formed among the peasants in the north of the country when some preachers suggested that a Crusade to the Holy Land would evoke the Lord's mercy.

There was an element of hostility toward the church and the wealthy classes in the message of these preachers. Christ had abandoned the knight-crusaders because of their love of money, they proclaimed; only the poor were pure enough to succeed against the infidel Moslems. In response, a small army of impoverished peasants began to wander southward, hoping to reach the Mediterranean ports and sail to Palestine. Most of them were children and teenagers. They had no leadership and no equipment, only hunger and faith. Contemporary estimates of the number of Pastoureaux range up to 60,000, a figure modern scholars think is greatly exaggerated.

As the journey continued, the peasants' sense of divine guidance—and divine rights—increased. Gangs of Pastoureaux took to murdering or mutilating priests and monks. They forced Jews to convert to Christianity, killing all who refused. Popular resentment against Jewish moneylenders and rich clergy provided the Pastoureaux with support. They began to act like priests themselves, preaching, blessing, and even presiding at marriages.

The goal of the Pastoureaux was as impossible as their fate was inevitable. Pope John XXII, the great persecutor of heretics, condemned them, and Catholic knights slaughtered them before they reached the Mediterranean coast.

PATARENES   Patarenes is a variant name for members of the late medieval BOSNIAN CHURCH who maintained the heretical beliefs of BOGOMILISM.

PATRIPASSIANISM   Literally, this term means "the doctrine of the suffering Father." Patripassianism refers to the belief that God the Father actually suffered during Christ's life and execution, that the Creator of the universe felt pain when Christ was flogged and experienced the death agony on the cross. This heretical doctrine violates two basic assumptions orthodox Christians made about the nature of God.

According to orthodox Christianity, a fundamental part of the definition of God is that nothing can act upon God to change Him. Since God is the Supreme Being, surely only He can change Himself. Therefore, God cannot be caused to suffer by events taking place in the world. Patripassianism clearly requires the violation of this principle.

Orthodox Christians also believe that God has a threefold structure, the Trinity. The doctrine of the Trinity states that the Father and the Son are identical in Their essential nature, but are different Persons. As Christ the Son experienced suffering as a Person while on earth, it would seem that this suffering would not be felt by the Father, a distinct Person.

Patripassianism was held by some Christians during the second and third centuries A.D. The doctrine was associated with the heresy of MODALISM. Modalists taught that there is only one divine Person, God, and that the Father, Son, and Holy Spirit are merely three different "modes" or costumes in which He presents Himself. If the "Father" and the "Son" are like different clothes worn by the same Person, then the suffering He experienced while wearing the costume of the "Son" is part of the experience of that one divine Person who also sometimes wears the costume of the "Father."

Although Catholic enemies of heresy such as QUINTAS SEPTIMIUS FLO-RENS TERTULLIAN accused Modalists of believing in the suffering Father, some Modalists tried to refine their positions in order to avoid the implication of Patripassianism. PRAXEAS, the first Modalist teacher, argued that while the Father and the Christ were modes of one being, Christ and Jesus were different. Praxeas maintained that Christ was divine and could not suffer, but Jesus was human and bore the sufferings during his life. Although Praxeas's doctrine avoids Patripassianism in this way, it seems to divide the Savior, Jesus Christ, into two disconnected parts, which most Christians found unappealing.

Historian Harold Brown argued that Martin Luther emphasized the identity of the Father and the Son so much in his teaching that he unwittingly came close to Patripassianism. Such twentieth century theologians as Thomas Altizer, who claimed that God actually died on the cross and therefore no longer exists, extended Luther's thought into an extreme version of Patripassianism, according to Brown.

PAULIANISTS   Followers of the heretical Christian teacher and bishop of Antioch, PAUL OF SAMOSATA. After the Roman Catholics defeated Paul toward the end of the third century A.D., the Paulianists were temporarily without a home base. When the king of Armenia converted to Christianity around 300, the sect carried their heresy of MODALISM there, where they continued for a few centuries.

PAULICIANS   The Paulician movement became one of the most powerful Christian heresies. By their peak in the ninth century, the Paulicians had founded an independent state, with an army strong enough to threaten the once-mighty Byzantine Empire. Although the center of Paulician activity was in Armenia, distant from western Europe, their influence on medieval European heresy was significant.

Scholarly opinion is divided concerning the source of the Paulicians' name. Some scholars believe that they revered the writings of Saint Paul, so they took his name in his honour. Others suggest that the name refers to PAUL THE ARMENIAN, a seventh century leader of the movement. A Byzantine writer of the ninth century claimed that PAUL OF SAMOSATA founded the Paulicians but this writer seems to have confused the Paulicians with the PAULIANISTS.

The origins of the Paulician movement are as obscure as the source of the group's name. Their orthodox opponents called them "Manichaeans," suggesting a link with the ancient Gnostic religion of MANICHAEISM. The Paulicians themselves, however, denied any relationship with the Manichaean faith. The Paulicians and Manichaeans both believed in the existence of an evil god who ruled the material world, but their attitude toward religious organizations was quite different. The Paulicians opted for simple spiritual communities, while the Manichaeans devised an elaborate hierarchical structure.

It seems more likely, however, that the Paulicians descended from non-Manichaean branches of GNOSTICISM and other ancient heresies. The MESSALIANS, who may have taught Gnostic doctrines, were active in Armenia by the fourth century. Followers of MARCIONISM had also migrated there. Both the Marcionites and the Paulicians rejected the Old Testament and were especially fond of Saint Paul.

The Paulicians first appear in history when a group of them settled in the eastern borderland between Armenia and the Byzantine Empire during the mid-seventh century. They might have migrated into Byzantine territory to escape persecution by the Armenian church, or to avoid the threat of the advancing Moslem army to the south. The Paulicians were not warmly welcomed by the strictly orthodox Christian Byzantines either. CONSTANTINE OF ARMENIA, the first known Paulician leader, was burned at the stake in 682.

The early Paulicians were dualists. They believed that an evil deity—the enemy of a good god who dwelled in a realm beyond matter—created and governed the world of the senses. This distant divinity sent Christ to invite humanity to his heavenly world. Christ did not have a physical body, but merely appeared to do so. This constitutes the heresy of DOCETISM, which was popular among the ancient Gnostics. The Paulicians saw themselves as continuing the work of this phantom Christ. Their identification of matter with evil led the Paulicians to oppose all the material trappings of religion. They refused to revere the cross or any other religious image, and rejected the sacraments and priestly organization of the orthodox church.

By the early eighth century, the Armenian Church, which itself followed the heresy of MONOPHYSITISM, was accusing the Paulicians of SATANISM. Armenian Church leader John of Ojun published an account of Paulician practices. He described how they met at night to commit ritual incest. If a child was born from these unholy unions, the baby was passed roughly from hand to hand among the heretics until it died. The person in whose grasp the infant expired became the leader of the sect. The victim's blood was then mixed with dough and made into sacramental bread. This account is a complete fabrication, but it had a major impact on public opinion at the time.

The border regions in which the Paulicians dwelled remained politically unstable throughout the eighth century. Battles between Byzantine and Arab armies were frequent. When the Byzantine authorities were not occupied with fighting Moslems, they organized violent persecutions of the heretics, driving them into Arab-held territory. The Moslems were traditionally tolerant toward Christian heretics, but the Paulicians came under suspicion because many of them spoke Greek, the favored language of Byzantium, and were thought to be agents of the Byzantines.

Despite these difficulties, the Paulician movement grew throughout the century. The Moslem threat had caused the Byzantine Empire to decentralize its power and to grant land to peasants in return for military service. This increased importance of rural culture found expression in a popular resentment against the rich lifestyles of the urban centers. In the eyes of many peasants, orthodox Christianity represented urban values, whereas the simple Paulician movement, which regarded the material wealth of the orthodox church as evil, was seen as teaching a faith for country people.

Another source of strength for the Paulicians arose from a controversy over the issue of ICONOCLASM, which wracked the orthodox church at this time. As the iconoclasts and their opponents fought over the proper use of images in religious practice and committed acts of barbarity against each other, the orthodox community appeared to be tearing itself apart. To a growing number of Christians, the Paulicians' straightforward theology and uncomplicated rejection of all religious symbols seemed preferable.

Eighth century Paulicians tended to shun violence themselves, believing that military activity was the work of the evil god of the material world. A more militant attitude appeared during the early ninth century. Paulicians began to join Arab troops in fighting the Byzantines, who, for their part, increased their persecution of the Paulicians. In 843, Byzantine soldiers carried out a particularly bloody slaughter of Paulician communities. This event appears to have triggered a determination by a group of Paulicians to found their own state.

In 856, with the support of the Arabs, the Paulician leader KARBEAS founded the town of Tephrike, which became the center of a buffer state between the Moslems and the Byzantines. Karbeas was an effective military leader. He mounted several expeditions against the Byzantines, who had to deal simultaneously with attacks from the Bulgars to the north. One Paulician assault pressed as far as the outskirts of Constantinople itself.

The tide turned against the Paulicians when the Byzantines defeated their army in 872. The victorious general presented the head of the Paulician leader CHRYS-OCHEIR to the Byzantine Emperor. Shortly afterward, Byzantine troops destroyed Tephrike, crushing the Paulicians' brief independence.

On several occasions between the eighth and tenth centuries, the Byzantines forced groups of Armenians, many of whom were Paulicians, to resettle on the Balkan frontier between the Byzantine Empire and territories controlled by such Slavic peoples as the Bulgars. This practice proved fateful for medieval Europe. The transplanted Paulicians inspired the Bulgarian heretics called the BOGOMILS. Some scholars believe that Bogomil missionaries wandering in western Europe ignited the largest heretical movement in medieval history, the CATHARS, who became a real threat to the Roman Catholic Church.

Although the Paulicians themselves never traveled to western Europe, the lurid descriptions of their Satanic rites by John of Ojun did. John's fantastic story of incest, elevation of the baby's murderer to leadership, and consumption of substances from the body mixed with bread, was retold in fifteenth century Italy. This time, the target of the false charges was the heretical group called the FRATICELLI. Historian Norman Cohn believes that John's writings concerning the Paulicians were the source of the later tale. Small communities of Paulicians in Armenia and the Balkans survived through the centuries. They were united with the Roman Catholic Church in the seventeenth century.

See also: SERGIO, SYMEON.

PAUL OF SAMOSATA   A bishop of the city of Antioch during the third century, Paul of Samosata is best known as an influential teacher of the heretical doctrine of ADOPTIONISM. The struggle between Paul and orthodoxy resulted in the strengthening of the Rome-based Catholic Church's leadership position over the rest of the Christian community, as well as the founding of a heretical school that persisted for centuries.

Little is known of Paul's life, and all of his writings have been destroyed, so one must reconstruct his beliefs from the accounts of his enemies. He was born around A.D. 200 and became the bishop of Antioch in his sixtieth year. Paul also served as the treasurer to ZENOBIA, Queen of Palmyra, who acted under the authority of the Roman Empire to govern the region that included Antioch.

In Paul's formulation of Adoptionism, JESUS did not begin His life as the Son of God, but as an ordinary human. Jesus was incredibly virtuous, however, and became morally perfect. At His baptism, God adopted Jesus and granted Him miraculous powers. God remained in constant union with Him for the rest of His life. This teaching was difficult to reconcile with the prevailing doctrine of the orthodox church, which held that Jesus had been the Son of God throughout his life, and that the relationship between divine and human in Jesus was much more intimate than mere adoption.

Paul of Samosata also claimed that God is a Trinity consisting of the Father; the Logos, or Word; and Sophia, or Wisdom. Of these three aspects, only the Father was regarded as a Person; Logos and Sophia were impersonal functions. The developing orthodox doctrine of the Trinity held that all three aspects of God are distinct Persons (although they share a single nature).

The Christian community in Antioch, one of the oldest and most important in the world, was split regarding their bishop's ideas. In 268, a local group allied with the church in Rome condemned Paul as a heretic. At this stage in the development of Christianity, the bishop of Rome was not recognized by all Christians as the head of the entire church, but only as one of the senior bishops—along with the bishop of Antioch. It was not universally accepted that the Roman party had the authority to condemn Paul.

Politics intervened fatefully into this theological squabble. Zenobia rebelled against the Roman Empire. Naturally, she supported her own employee as bishop during the period of her independent rule. The Roman army recaptured Antioch in 272. At that time, the Christians affiliated with Rome sued Paul and his party, claiming that Paul had "stolen" the church property in Antioch from its rightful owners. Aurelian, the emperor, was not hostile to Christianity, unlike some of his predecessors and successors. Not surprisingly, given the imperial connection with Rome and Paul's association with the rebel Zenobia, Aurelian ruled in favor of the Roman Catholics. This judgment by a pagan ruler significantly enhanced the Roman Church's preeminent position within the Christian community.

Disenfranchised, Paul died three years later. However, the PAULIANISTS, his followers, arrived in Armenia shortly after that country converted to Christianity around A.D. 300, and the school survived there for several hundred years.

Paul of Samosata is sometimes mentioned as the founder of another heretical group, the PAULICIANS, who were first noted in Armenia in the seventh century. Since the doctrines of the Paulicians do not resemble those of the Paulianists, it is unlikely that the same man started both movements. Either there were two people with the same name, or the attribution of the Paulician teachings to Paul of Samosata was a mistake. It is certain, however, that Paul of Samosata, third century bishop of Antioch, had a strong influence on another important figure in Christian history: LUCIAN OF ANTIOCH, whose teachings were likely the source of the great heresy called ARIANISM, which almost toppled orthodox Catholicism.

PAUL THE ARMENIAN   Leader of the heretical sect called the PAULICIANS from A.D. 688 to 718, Paul the Armenian did not found the movement, which might date from the fifth century. Some scholars believe that the Paulician heretics adopted their name in Paul's honor.

PELAGIANISM   During the early years of the fifth century, an important debate concerning the human will commenced in the West. The devotees of Pelagianism argued that every individual has the free will to choose to perform good or evil acts. If people always choose to behave virtuously, their moral perfection will earn them spiritual salvation. Mainstream Christians, who were led by the famous theologian Augustine of Hippo, resisted the Pelagian view concerning the will. Its supporters were condemned as heretics.

The Pelagian movement derives its name from an early leader, British-born theologian PELAGIUS. Along with CELESTIUS and RUFINUS THE SYRIAN, Pelagius objected to the portrayal of the will that was increasingly popular within the Catholic Church. According to such influential Christians as Augustine, God punished all of humanity for Adam's original sin in the Garden of Eden. This punishment took the form of a weakening of the human will, to the point that people are often unable to resist the temptation to sin. As a result, no one is good enough to deserve being saved from eternal damnation. God has chosen certain people to be saved, not because they deserve salvation, but simply because He is merciful.

According to the Pelagians, this portrayal of humanity as too weak to save itself was dangerous. People might conclude from the original-sin doctrine that they should not waste their time trying to live a holy life because no one can avoid sin, and God does not grant salvation on the basis of a person's behavior. Because the church was growing in wealth and power, and the temptations available to Christian leaders were ever more abundant, the Pelagians' fears were well-founded.

Augustine and the other church leaders themselves did not share this view. They argued that belief in free will was contrary to Christianity. If people can earn salvation through their own moral perfection, then what need was there for Christ to save humanity from its sins?

In addition to theological considerations, the realities of political power may have played a role in the Pelagian conflict. In a letter to the pope, Augustine noted that Pelagianism tended to undermine the power of the church leadership over the lives of rank-and-file Christians. The Pelagian belief in the ability of individuals to save themselves through moral effort reduced people's dependency on the spiritual instructions of priests. Conversely, the idea that human nature is helplessly corrupt supports the need to obey the rules of the church, in the hope of avoiding eternal damnation.

Orthodox Christian leaders repeatedly branded the leading Pelagian teachers as heretics in the early fifth century. The Pelagian viewpoint continued to develop, particularly in the writings of JULIAN OF ECLANUM. Julian engaged Augustine in a debate to which the latter theologian devoted the last twelve years of his life, producing a six-volume refutation of Julian's teachings.

The condemnation of Celestius at the COUNCIL OF EPHESUS in A.D. 431 marked the end of the first phase of Pelagianism. The victory of the orthodox position was not complete, however. Although the notion that people can save themselves through their own moral power without God's grace was clearly rejected, many Christians were not satisfied with the idea that the human will is completely incapable of helping itself. How can people be held responsible for their evil acts if they cannot choose to be good? Augustine replied that people are free enough to be blamed for their sins, but not free enough to choose a morally unblemished life. Despite Augustine's proposed solution, hints of the Pelagian confidence in willpower continued to surface, particularly in Britain and Gaul.

JOHN CASSIAN, an important figure in the development of the Christian

monastic tradition, founded a movement midway between Pelagianism and orthodoxy that came to be known as SEMI-PELAGIANISM. Cassian agreed with Augustine that people cannot attain salvation without God's grace, but he leaned toward
Pelagius in his view that the individual person had to choose freely the first steps
toward salvation.

The ongoing controversy surrounding free will was resolved at the Council of
Orange in 529. This assembly of church leaders decided that Augustine's lack of
confidence in the human will was to be the only acceptable view among Christians.
For the duration of the Middle Ages, the mainstream view held that human nature
was hopelessly corrupt, and that it must depend on outside agencies to help it
toward goodness. As Augustine foresaw, this attitude promoted dependency on the
authority of the church rather than self-reliance, and most likely it contributed to
the stability of feudal society. Only during the Renaissance did a more optimistic
understanding of human potential return.

PELAGIUS   This fifth century theologian was the first major heretic to hail from
Britain. Pelagius taught that humans possessed free will and were, therefore, wholly
responsible for their good and evil choices. He also claimed that death was a natural
part of human existence, rather than a divine punishment for sin. The Catholic
Church rejected his ideas in favor of the view that all people are compulsive sinners
who richly deserve to suffer and die. The defeat of Pelagius set the moral tone of the
dawning medieval world view in the West.

Pelagius was born sometime around A.D. 360. Twenty-one years later, Emperor
Theodosius declared Christianity to be the official state religion of the Roman
Empire. Throughout the fourth century, the church had been gaining legitimacy and
power and now had acquired full prestige. Some Christians observed that this rise to
power had been accompanied by significant changes in the attitudes of church
leaders. During the times when Christians were subject to persecution, the church
taught the importance of a person's *freedom* to disobey the pagan authorities. But now
that bishops had become identified with political authority themselves, orthodox
Christian leaders downplayed the freedom of individual Christians. Rather, the
leaders emphasized the weakness of the human will and the necessity to pursue
salvation through *obedience* to the external government of the (Christian) state.

Pelagius had moved to Rome by the last decade of the fourth century. He was
dismayed by the condition in which he found the Roman Church community. It
seemed to him that high-ranking Christians had become more interested in enjoying
the material delights of their newly privileged social positions than in striving to attain
moral perfection. He felt that the limited role the church gave to human willpower
served to justify the lax moral behavior of some Christians.

In order to combat this loss of ethical rigor, Pelagius began to preach that humans
have free will, and that it is the responsibility of each person to choose whether to
move toward God by cultivating a holy lifestyle, or to retreat from God through self-
indulgence. Pelagius did not originate this belief. It was popular during the first
centuries of Christianity and served to justify the brave choice the early martyrs
made: to face death rather than to renounce Christ.

However, by the fifth century, the orthodox doctrine had shifted. In particular, the
notion of original sin, as described by Augustine of Hippo, was becoming popular

among church leaders. According to Augustine, every human who ever has or ever will live was present within Adam when he sinned in the Garden of Eden. Therefore, everyone is in some sense responsible for Adam's original sin, and everyone is punished by death as a result. Furthermore, all humans are also punished for this sin by having their capacity for free will weakened to the point that they are unable to avoid committing sins. People simply cannot behave well enough to earn salvation, so they must rely on God's grace, which they do not deserve, to avoid eternal damnation.

Pelagius's position in favor of free will, and the Augustinian position of human helplessness, each attracted supporters. While Pelagius advanced his arguments in theological circles, Pelagians and their opponents struggled in street riots.

In 410, the invading Goths were about to take Rome. Pelagius and CELESTIUS, his companion, retreated to North Africa, home of Augustine, but were not well received by the Christian community there. Pelagius was condemned by the Council of Carthage in 411 for denying that Adam's sin was transmitted to his descendents. Pelagius headed for Palestine, but Augustine sent his friend Orosius there to maintain the attack. During the next few years, followers of Pelagius continued to preach in Carthage. During this time, Carthage's church council, which Augustine controlled, repeatedly issued condemnations of Pelagius and his teachings.

Augustine's campaign against Pelagius spread from North Africa to Rome. Augustine wrote to Pope Innocent I, pointing out that Pelagius's claims about the freedom of the will were undermining the power of the church hierarchy. Augustine explained his view: If Christians believed they could save themselves through correct moral choices, they would perceive no need to follow the instructions of the priests. The pope saw the light and declared Pelagius to be a heretic.

When Pope Innocent died in 417, he was succeeded by Zosimus. At first, the new pope was inclined to favor Pelagius but could not oppose the opinion of Augustine, who by now had become powerful within the church. As a result, Zosimus excommunicated Pelagius. Emperor Honorius, who had just received a bribe of eighty fine horses from a friend of Augustine, followed suit, so by imperial order, Pelagius was fined and sent into exile.

Pelagius is believed to have died around A.D. 420. Although the notion that the human will is too corrupt to save itself officially triumphed, Pelagius's ideas refused to disappear. PELAGIANISM, the movement that took his name, continued to do battle with orthodoxy. Today, many Christians would probably agree with Pelagius that people can freely choose to be good and that death is natural without realizing that they are following a notorious fifth century heretic.

PERFECTIONISM   Broadly defined, perfectionism refers to the idea that human beings can attain perfection through their own efforts. To orthodox Christians, such a notion eliminates the need for the saving grace of God and has been viewed as heretical since the defeat of the ancient doctrine of PELAGIANISM. Perfectionistic teachings reappeared in the Middle Ages, particularly among the Heretics of the FREE SPIRIT. In stricter usage, Perfectionism refers to various nineteenth century American sects that believed that people could attain spiritual perfection. The best-known of these groups was the ONEIDA COMMUNITY.

PETROBRUSCIANS   The Petrobruscans were followers of PIERRE DE BRUYS, a heretic who preached in southern France during the early twelfth century. De Bruys was hostile toward the Catholic Church, and the Petrobruscians expressed this enmity by destroying church buildings, terrorizing monasteries, and burning crosses. The abbot of Cluny called for their violent suppression. The destructiveness of the Petrobruscians caused many who held unorthodox Christian views to shift their support to the more peaceful CATHARS.

PHOTINUS   A notable heretic active during the fourth century, Photinus was a pupil of MARCELLUS OF ANCYRA and extended his teacher's dubiously orthodox views into clearly heretical territory. At first, Photinus was accepted as an orthodox Catholic, and he even became the bishop of Sirmium in 344. However, his teachings were so alarming that a church council in Milan twice condemned his views, in 345 and 347. Photinus was removed from his post and exiled in 351. All of his writings were destroyed, but accounts of his enemies suggest that he taught a version of the heresy of MODALISM: that the Father, Son, and Holy Spirit are not distinct Persons, but merely different names for the one divine Person of God.

Giovanni PICO DELLA MIRANDOLA   A leading figure of the Italian Renaissance, Giovanni Pico Della Mirandola promoted several radical ideas: the possibility that humans could become divine; the validity of magic; and the notion that Christianity and ancient pagan belief systems contained the same spiritual message. As a result, elements of his work were judged heretical.

Pico was born in 1463 to an aristocratic family that claimed descent from the Roman Emperor Constantine. During his youth, the writings of classical Greece and Rome were being read again in western Europe for the first time since the end of the ancient world. Pico thrived in this intellectual atmosphere. At fourteen, he began attending the University of Bologna and learned to read Greek, Latin, Hebrew, and Arabic. Pico broadened his knowledge through extensive traveling.

By the age of twenty-three, Pico had come to believe that the diverse philosophies of ancient times, including Greek thought, Judaism, and Christianity, all expressed the same underlying truth. In order to spread his theory, young Pico issued an invitation. He called on the scholars of Europe to meet in order to debate 900 ideas he had compiled from his readings of world literature. He even offered to pay the travel expenses for scholars coming from remote regions.

For the occasion of this conference, Pico composed his best known work, *The Oration on the Dignity of Man*. The *Oration* was the manifesto of the Renaissance world view; it contains the famous statement, "Man is the measure of all things." Pico also suggests that God created humans without a predetermined form, unlike all other creatures. As such, people were granted the ability to shape themselves in whatever manner they choose: "You shall be able to descend among the lower forms of being, which are brute beasts; you shall be able to be reborn out of the judgment of your own soul into the higher beings, which are divine."

In Pico's vision, both humanity and God are creators. What, then, is the difference between people and God? Pico explains, "There is this difference between God and man, that God contains in himself all things because he is their source, and man contains all things because he is their centre." Such an optimistic depiction of humanity—unburdened by original sin, able to raise itself to divinity, the very heart of the world—had not been heard in orthodox Christian thought for 1,000 years.

Indeed, Pico's inspiration for his positive view of human potential was not a

Christian source, but the HERMETICA, a collection of pagan mystical writings that had been rediscovered by western Europe shortly before his birth. Pico quoted a passage from the Hermetic texts in the *Oration*.

Pico's scholarly conference never took place. Pope Innocent VIII decided that 13 of Pico's 900 propositions were heretical and forbade any meeting to discuss them. Roman Catholicism has always been strict about making a clear distinction between God the Creator of the world, and the creatures (including humans) He created. Pico did not draw the boundary between God and humanity clearly enough.

Although shamed by the pope's decision, Pico was supported by other great Renaissance scholars, such as MARSILIO FICINO, and continued his studies. The mysteries of the Jewish tradition intrigued him—a most unusual interest for a Christian of the time since mainstream culture tended to be anti-Semitic. Pico was one of the first Christians to take a serious interest in the Hebrew mystical system called KABBALAH. Of his 900 theses, 119 referred to Kabbalistic themes. For example, Pico claimed that "no science can better convince us of the divinity of Jesus Christ than magic and the Kabbalah." Pico inspired a fellow scholar, JOHANN REUCHLIN, to study the Kabbalah. As a result, Reuchlin devised an influential synthesis of Christian thought and Hebrew Kabbalah, the Christian CABALA.

As the humanistic values of the Renaissance permeated Italian society, Pico continued to rise in prominence. Six years after Pope Innocent condemned his theses, a new pontiff, Alexander VI, cleared Pico of any suspicions of heresy. In the early 1490s, Pico fell under the influence of charismatic preacher GIROLAMO SAVONAROLA. This friar called passionately for a purification of the church and was opposed to the pagan aspects of the Renaissance. Under Savonarola's sway, Pico wrote a book condemning ASTROLOGY; whether he also rejected his earlier Hermetic inspiration at this time is unknown. In 1494, the year that Savonarola took control of Florence, Pico died of fever. He was only 31.

PIERRE DE BRUYS   Pierre de Bruys was one of the most important heretics of the twelfth century. He wandered through southern France proclaiming that good Christians did not need the Catholic Church, thereby preparing the way for the rise of the powerful CATHAR heresy. The danger Pierre and his followers represented provoked the church into a more militant stance with respect to heretics, ensuring that the forthcoming confrontation with the Cathars would be violent.

Details concerning the early life of Pierre are unclear, but it is thought that he was born in the village of Bruys in the French Alps at the beginning of the century. Around 1119, he descended to the valleys and plains of southern France. Pierre wandered through the towns of the region, where his bare feet, uncut hair, and simple robe elicited comment. For twenty years, he preached his unorthodox message and gathered a large following.

In the eyes of Pierre, all good Christians have direct access to God. Priests, sacraments, and churches simply are not necessary. The Catholic Church, and the symbol of the cross it reveres, are hoaxes. At this time, the church was increasing its political, financial, and military power. Priestly corruption and neglect of parishioners were rampant. Pierre's teaching found a ready audience, especially among the lower classes, who had to pay tithes out of their meager earnings to support the extravagances of the church.

Some historians believe that Pierre was influenced by missionaries from Bulgaria who taught the heresy of BOGOMILISM. Both Pierre and the Bogomils rejected the cross and the other trappings of the orthodox church. However, his ideas may also have arisen directly from local concerns about the changing role of the church. These concerns were also being expressed by other heretical leaders of the period, including TANCHELM and HENRY OF LAUSANNE.

Pierre's followers, known as PETROBRUSCIANS, became more violent over time. They began burning churches and forcing monks to marry. The followers expressed their disdain for orthodox symbols by holding festivals where they made bonfires of crosses, roasting meat over the flames.

On Good Friday, 1139, one of these events led to Pierre's death. On a visit to the town of St. Gilles, he denounced the local church, as was his usual practice. Pierre and the Petrobruscians then retired to the forest nearby, where they built their bonfire. Some citizens of St. Gilles, angry at Pierre's actions, threw him into the fire and burned him to death.

Catholic officials did not believe that the Petrobruscian menace had ended with Pierre's demise. Peter the Venerable, the powerful abbot of Cluny, sent letters to the bishops in the areas where Pierre had been active, calling for the violent suppression of the movement. Peter wanted to nip heresy in the bud, but it was too late. Within a few years, the Cathars had established themselves in southern France as a much greater danger to the Catholic spiritual monopoly than the Petrobruscians had ever been.

PIKARTS   A late medieval heretical movement originating in the French region of Picardy, the Pikarts taught that people could achieve spiritual perfection through discipline. Once they achieved perfection, the enlightened souls could do anything they pleased without sinning. The doctrine is closely related to the Heresy of the FREE SPIRIT. In the early fifteenth century, a number of Pikarts traveled to Bohemia to escape Catholic persecution. At the time, the TABORITES, a heretical group, controlled part of Bohemia. But the Taborites themselves viewed the Pikarts as heretics and began to persecute them. The Pikarts, under MARTIN HUSKA, their leader, initially protected themselves in a castle on an island, but they were eventually conquered and dispersed.

POLYTHEISM   The traditions of Judaism, Christianity, and Islam agree that there is only one God. Belief in a plurality of deities constitutes the heresy of polytheism. Orthodox Christianity in particular has had to struggle with this heresy because of its doctrine of the Trinity, which states that God is three divine Persons subsisting in a single nature. Heretics have often taught versions of the Trinity that orthodoxy has condemned as polytheistic—specifically, the heresy of belief in three gods, or TRITHEISM. The ANTI-TRINITARIANS simply rejected the Trinity altogether, claiming that all versions of the doctrine, including the orthodox one, fall into the category of polytheism.

PONTIFICAL BIBLICAL COMMISSION   In 1903, Pope Leo XIII established the Pontifical Biblical Commission for the purpose of overseeing the orthodoxy of Catholic Biblical scholarship. The commission decreed that "at all times the [Biblical] interpreter must cherish a spirit of ready obedience to the Church's teaching authority." During Leo's tenure, a growing number of Catholic researchers were casting doubt on the literal accuracy of the stories in the New Testament, based on their historical analyses. This MODERNIST attitude, declared a heresy in 1907, has continued to arise within the church throughout the century, challenging the views of the Catholic leadership. The Pontifical Biblical Commission has close ties with the current version of the INQUISITION, the Congregation for the Doctrine of the Faith.

POOR LOMBARDS   The Italian branch of the late medieval heresy called WALDENSIANISM, the Poor Lombards emphasized community organization and productive work. This enabled the movement to survive centuries of ferocious persecution.

POOR MEN OF LYONS   The Poor Men of Lyons were the French manifestation of the WALDENSIANS, a late medieval unorthodox movement. The heresy began in the French city of Lyons, home of the founder, PETER WALDO.

Marguerite PORETE   An early leader of the Heresy of the FREE SPIRIT, Marguerite Porete taught that people could attain a state of perfect freedom by concentrating their soul on God until the difference between the self and God disappeared. After this attainment, people could do anything they wished without sinning; therefore, they no longer had to obey the commandments of any church. Porete's writings were condemned in 1308, but she continued to proclaim her doctrine. Two years later, she was consigned to the flames in Paris by Catholic authorities.

PRAXEAS   This Christian teacher and confessor was the first major proponent of the heresy known as MODALISM. All of his own writings were destroyed long ago, so one must rely on the works of his opponents for information concerning his life and teachings. The main surviving source is QUINTAS SEPTIMIUS FLORENS TERTULLIAN's famous work entitled *Against Praxeas*. The extent to which Tertullian presents an accurate depiction of Praxeas's doctrines and the degree to which he distorts them for purposes of ridicule are open to debate.

Praxeas was born in Asia Minor (part of what is now Turkey) sometime in the latter second century A.D. He was a vocal Christian there at a time when the Roman authorities persecuted the Christian community. He won respect among the Christians for his refusal to retract his beliefs when the persecutors questioned him. For reasons still unknown, the authorities did not execute him.

Praxeas moved to Rome around 190. At that time, Catholic Christianity, under the sway of the bishop of Rome, faced competition from other Christian groups that understood Christ's message differently. The MONTANISTS proclaimed that they received messages from the Holy Spirit warning that the end of the world was soon to come, and argued that there was no need to develop long-lasting church institutions. The ADOPTIONISTS taught that Christ was not God, but was only a man whom God adopted. Praxeas regarded himself as a member of the Catholic Church and opposed the teachings of both the Montanists and the Adoptionists.

Praxeas's status as a confessor (a person who had refused to deny the faith, even when threatened with death) lent him prestige among the Roman Christians, and he is thought to have had some influence on VICTOR I and ZEPHYRINUS, bishops of Rome. Praxeas may have been responsible for convincing Zephyrinus to condemn the Montanists. For his own part, Praxeas was especially outspoken against the teachings of ADOPTIONISM. The notion that JESUS was merely a man, albeit a special one, was taken by many orthodox Christians as an insult to the divinity of Christ. Praxeas taught the extreme opposite position: that Christ was not a man, but God; and not just God the Son, but God the Father. The only difference between the divine Father and divine Son, claimed Praxeas, was a difference in modes, or roles. When God is in heaven, He acts as the Father. During His time on earth, God acted the role of the Son. In contrast, the orthodox Catholic position, still developing during Praxeas's lifetime, holds that the Father and the Son are distinct Persons, not just modes of a single divine Person.

Tertullian, Praxeas' great opponent, claimed to find logical flaws in the Modalist's argument. He asked how a God who died on the cross could be the God who can resurrect Christ: "He who raised up Christ and is also to raise up our mortal bodies will be as it were another raiser-up than the Father who died and the Father who was raised up, if it is the case that Christ who died is the Father."

Despite the attack of Tertullian, Praxeas was not opposed by either of the bishops (Victor or Zephyrinus) who led the Catholic community during his lifetime in Rome. Others took up the Modalist position after Praxeas's death, and orthodox Christianity did not decisively reject Modalism until well into the third century.

See also: EPIGONUS, CLEOMENES, MODALISM, NOETUS, SABELLIUS.

PRISCA   One of the early leaders of the heresy called MONTANISM, which flourished during the second century A.D., Prisca claimed that she had the ability to receive messages from the Holy Spirit. Many orthodox Christians were opposed to Prisca and her colleague MAXIMILLA, not only because of their heretical claims, but also because of their gender. It was a common belief among Christians that women should not offer spiritual instruction to men.

PRISCILLIAN   A leader of the Christian community in Spain during the second half of the fourth century, Priscillian founded a heretical movement, PRISCILLIA-NISM, that persisted until the sixth century. Priscillian has the distinction of being the first Christian heretic to be legally executed for his beliefs.

Little is known of Priscillian's early life. Indeed, even the details of his teachings are unclear, although they seem to have been related to the heresy of MANICHAE-ISM. According to Priscillian, the Devil is the embodiment of evil and has always been the archenemy of God. The orthodox view states that the Devil was originally an angel of God whose pride led to his fall from grace. According to Catholicism, the notion that the Devil has always been independent of God denies God's supremacy as the Creator of the universe and, therefore, is a heretical belief.

Records indicate that the orthodox authorities first expressed concern regarding the religion of Priscillian's followers in the Spanish city of Saragossa in 380. Their worries were not serious enough to prevent Priscillian from becoming the bishop of Avila shortly afterward. But in 381, Emperor Theodosius proclaimed Catholic Christianity to be the official religion of the Roman Empire. This statement strengthened the power of the Catholics, and Priscillian was driven into exile.

Through political maneuvering, however, Priscillian was able to arrange his return to Spain. He resumed teaching his heretical doctrines and won a large following. By this time, however, the Catholics, with the support of the Roman state, often used violence against their competitors for control of people's religious beliefs. The temples of pagans, Jews, and any Christians who did not express their faith according to the official formulas were no longer safe. In 386, the violence went beyond the destruction of property: Priscillian was seized, convicted of "sorcery," and killed.

Some church leaders, most notably Saint Martin of Tours, protested the barbarity of the act. Priscillian's execution was merely the beginning, however. Within a few decades, the influential Augustine of Hippo—a former Manichaean himself— endorsed the use of torture and murder against unorthodox Christians. Since that time, untold numbers of Christians have joined Priscillian in his fate.

Priscillian's death did not end his influence; indeed, it seems to have increased his following by casting him as a martyr. Priscillianist doctrines continued to develop, absorbing elements of several other heretical belief systems, until Priscillianism was finally eradicated almost 200 years after the execution of the movement's founder.

PRISCILLIANISM   The Priscillian heresy combined elements of several heretical belief systems of fourth century Spain. Priscillianism took its name from its founder, Bishop PRISCILLIAN, who was executed by the Catholic authorities of Spain in 386. The world view of Priscillianism seems to have been derived from the religion of MANICHAEISM, a serious competitor of Christianity in some regions of the Roman Empire at the time. The Priscillians, like the Manichaeans, believed that the universe was divided into two domains. The material world was created by the Devil, who enslaved human souls by trapping them within physical bodies. The souls themselves were the creations of God, who wished to free them from the Devil's trap.

According to Priscillianism, Christ was God Himself, appearing as a human being. God the Father and Christ the Son were not regarded as distinct Persons by the Priscillians, but rather as different roles played by one divine Person. This belief is the heresy of MODALISM, which mainstream Christians had rejected during the preceding century.

Fourteen years after Priscillian's death, a Catholic council deposed all Spanish bishops who were Priscillians. This action indicates that the movement must have had a significant following. References to Priscillianist doctrines continue in church literature as late as 563, when a council at Braga issued the following statement:

> Whoever denies that the Devil was originally a good angel created by God, contending instead that he arose from the chaos and the darkness and has no Creator but is himself the principle and the substance of evil . . . let him be anathema (excommunicated).

PROFANITY   Many religious traditions divide the world into two regions, the sacred and the profane. Orthodox faiths generally try to keep these worlds separate by restricting the use of sacred symbols to those who have set themselves apart from the domain of everyday activities (by donning or removing clothing or footwear; taking purifying baths; and making a ritual gesture, such as the sign of the cross). But humans, even devout ones, sometimes slip. The most common type of profanity— that is, a violation of the boundary between sacred and ordinary—is the utterance of a holy name at a moment of frustration. Profanities of this kind are generally not taken too seriously. Some heretics have deliberately profaned a sacred symbol, which is a much graver action. Intentional or serious acts of profanity usually provoke a defensive response from orthodox authorities and are usually referred to as BLAS-PHEMY.

PROTOCTISTS   A group of ORIGENIST Christians during the sixth century, the Protoctists stated that Christ was God's greatest creation. According to orthodox belief, Christ was not created by God, but *is* God, and has always coexisted with God the Father and the Holy Spirit. The Protoctist position is similar to the notorious heresy of ARIANISM. Along with the other school of Origenism, the ISOCHRISTS, the Protoctists were condemned at the SECOND COUNCIL OF CONSTAN-TINOPLE in 553.

PSEUDEPIGRAPHA   This term, which means "false writings," refers to a body of texts written during the period between the composition of the Old and New Testaments of the Bible—roughly, between the third century B.C. and the end of the first century A.D. This collection of writings derives its name from the authors' practice of stating that the books were composed by famous figures of Jewish spiritual history, such as Solomon, Isaiah, and Enoch. Neither orthodox Judaism nor orthodox Christianity recognized these works as divinely inspired. However, the Pseudepigrapha were a source of concepts and images that greatly enriched the development of both orthodox and unorthodox traditions at the root of Western culture.

The Pseudepigrapha were written in Palestine and Egypt. The true identities of their authors are lost. During this time, the Jewish communities were embedded within the Hellenistic and Roman Empires and were exposed to many ideas from other cultures. The content of the texts reflects the influence of Greek and Mesopotamian thought, as well as the development of notions within Judaism itself.

Many of the most influential Pseudepigraphic texts provide detailed descriptions of the spirit world. The most important of these books are THE BOOK OF ENOCH and THE BOOK OF THE SECRETS OF ENOCH. These works claim to be the prophet Enoch's eyewitness account of his travels through heaven. "Enoch" was not modest regarding the thoroughness of his records:

> I know all things and have written them into books concerning the heavens and their end, their plenitude, their armies, and their marching. I have measured and described the stars, their great and countless multitude. What man has seen their revolutions and entrances? Not even the angels see their number, yet I have recorded all their names . . . I recorded the height from earth to the seventh heaven and down to the very lowest Hell, the judgment place, the great, open, and weeping Hell.

Enoch's immense vision, in which he details the layers of heaven and hell and names their inhabitants, gripped the imagination of magicians who wished to make contact with spiritual beings. Both ANGEL MAGIC and DEMON MAGIC are indebted to the authors of the Enoch texts for the information they provided about these creatures.

The Jewish esoteric path called KABBALAH is also rooted in the Pseudepigrapha. The traditions of MERKABAH and Hekhalot mysticism, in which meditators induced visions of God's throne and palaces, emerged from ancient groups that studied the Pseudepigrapha. These traditions also formed the foundation of classical Kabbalah.

The early Christians, perhaps including JESUS himself, were students of the Pseudepigrapha. The term "Son of Man" as a title for the Messiah, used in the Gospels to refer to Christ, made earlier appearances in Pseudepigraphic sources. Also, the New Testament writers borrowed the idea that DEMONS are fallen angels from the "false writings."

PTOLEMAEUS   An important teacher of the heretical Christian doctrine known as VALENTINIAN GNOSTICISM, Ptolemaeus was a student of the founder of the movement, VALENTINUS, and succeeded him as the leader of the Italian school of Valentinianism during the latter part of the second century A.D. Few other details of Ptolemaeus's life are known today.

Ptolemaeus is best known as the person who developed Valentinian thought into a detailed system of belief. His teachings were the most sophisticated formulation of Christian doctrine at the time and attracted a number of converts to the Gnostic view of life. In response, Ptolemaeus's opponents within the Christian community were forced to formulate their own doctrines. As a result, the first works of orthodox Christian theology were composed. In the late second century, Irenaeus of Lyons composed attacks on Gnostic teaching, particularly the Valentinian ideas of Ptolemaeus.

Modern knowledge of Ptolemaeus's system comes from the descriptions his enemies, such as Irenaeus and Hippolytus, provided. Most of the Gnostics' own works were destroyed by orthodox Christian forces when they came to power in the Roman Empire during the fourth century. The only confirmed writing of Ptolemaeus to have survived is *Letter to Flora*, a short work directed to a woman (who seems to represent a non-Gnostic Christian group) that attempts to persuade her of the truth of Gnosticism.

John PURVEY   John Purvey became leader of the LOLLARD heretics following the death of JOHN WYCLIFFE, the man on whose teachings the movement was based. During Wycliffe's lifetime, Purvey served as his secretary. He participated in translating the Bible into English—an important project for the Lollards, who regarded the Bible, not the church, as the only religious authority. As the Lollard leader, he petitioned the English Parliament to "purify" the Roman Catholic Church by confiscating its property. Purvey died around 1428, having witnessed the Lollards' disastrous attempted uprising against the government.

QABALAH   This term usually refers to the modern magical tradition that grew out of the Jewish and Christian mystical schools known respectively as KABBALAH and CABALA. The Jewish tradition, the Kabbalah, is the oldest, with roots extending back 2,000 years; the Christian Cabala arose in the late fifteenth century; and the magical Qabalah gradually developed since that time, reaching a mature form in the later nineteenth century.

A basic premise all three traditions share is the existence of secret methods that enable humans to acquire divine knowledge and, perhaps, divine power also. Knowledge and power are two traditional goals of magic, so it was natural for magicians to tap the mystical lore of the Jews and Christians. Even in the GRIMOIRES, the magical handbooks of the Middle Ages, the names of God were used to command spirits. By the sixteenth century, such practitioners as CORNELIUS AGRIPPA had adopted Kabbalistic methods to the same end.

After a century of relative neglect, there was an upsurge of interest in occultism in nineteenth century Europe. By this time, the lore of the Cabala was easily available to anyone who wished to study it. Eliphas Levi, an early leader of the occult revival, used Cabalistic notions to construct a map of the unseen world that magicians were attempting to contact. By the end of the century, the two most important influences in modern ritual magic, the Hermetic Order of the GOLDEN DAWN and Aleister CROWLEY, had adopted the Qabalah as the core of the contemporary magical world view.

Qabalists have been especially interested in the ancient doctrine of the ten *sefiroth*. In Jewish tradition, the *sefiroth* were understood to be aspects or qualities of God; the typical diagram of the *sefiroth*, the Tree of Life, was taken to represent the structure of God. In the hands of the Qabalists, the Tree became a chart of the spiritual domain. The magician, following the paths of the Tree, could rise through the *sefiroth*, acquiring the powers associated with each stage; by traveling the entire Tree and absorbing all of the divine aspects, Qabalists believed that they could actually attain godhood, or spiritual enlightenment.

In order to journey in the Tree, Qabalistic magicians practice meditations in which they visualize an astral or spiritual body, into which they project their consciousness. This astral form is able to move along the paths. The *sefiroth* and the paths connecting them are used as a system of pigeonholes to organize the mass of symbols and ideas from the various occult traditions. For example, the *sefirah* called Geburah is associated with the number five, the image of a warrior in a chariot, the planet Mars, the color red, the Hebrew God-name Elohim Gibor, the archangel Khamael, the Egyptian deity Horus, etc. By visualizing or contemplating these elements, the astral body is directed toward Geburah. The Qabalah teaches that mastery of this sefirah enables the magician to comprehend the hidden workings of Cosmic Law, as well as to attract "gold, books, women and the like," according to Crowley. This odd combination of the loftiest and most profane aims characterizes much of the Western ritual-magic tradition.

QUARTODECIMANISM   Quartodecimanism is the practice of celebrating Easter on the date of the Jewish Passover, rather than on the following Sunday. Choosing Passover for the Easter observance dates back at least as far as the early second century in Asia Minor (modern Turkey). Although the Church of Rome observed Easter on Sunday, it was not very concerned about the variant timing in Eastern churches until the beginning of the third century. VICTOR I, bishop of Rome, threatened the Quartodecimans with excommunication if they continued the Passover Easter. The Quartodecimans responded by forming their own church, which survived into the fifth century.

QUIETISM   The Quietist heresy disturbed the Catholic Church in western Europe during the seventeenth century. Quietism derives its name from the movement's central practice: the stilling of all mental activity, especially the will, in order to achieve union with God. The Protestant Reformation of the preceding century had arisen from a feeling, held by many, that the Catholic Church had drifted away from true Christianity. In response, Catholicism examined its own traditions. One of the elements some people considered missing from the orthodox Catholic path was a way to experience God's presence directly. A Spanish Catholic named MIGUEL DE

MOLINOS proclaimed that the practice of Quietism could provide such an experience, and possibly even lead to continuous union with God. If the personal will was stilled, he taught, the will of God could control the person instead.

Quietism proved popular in some Catholic circles, particularly among the higher classes in France. But church authorities tended to view it with alarm. The concept of union with God's will blurred the difference between God the Creator and the human being He created; the mainstream Jewish and Christian traditions have always emphasized the importance of distinguishing the two. Also, the Quietists believed that people who were united with the will of God were incapable of sinning, no matter what they did, because obviously God does not sin. This notion opened the door for the Quietist to follow every impulse, including immoral ones, without being inhibited by the fear of sinning.

Because of these concerns, the Catholic Church suppressed the Quietists. Molinos was sentenced to life imprisonment in 1687; the teachings of MADAME GUYON and ARCHBISHOP FENELON, the two leading French Catholics associated with Quietism, were condemned in 1696 and 1699, respectively.

See also: HERESY OF THE FREE SPIRIT.

RADICAL ARIANISM   Radical Arianism is a variant term for the ANOMOEANS, an important movement within the fourth century Christian heresy of ARIANISM.

RANTERS   These English radicals challenged the limits of social acceptibility in seventeenth century England. During the political chaos of the time, various groups arose that promoted alternative world views. The Ranters taught that the only authority that one should obey is the experience of Christ within oneself. This mystical doctrine implied that religious organizations and scriptures were unnecessary.

The more extreme Ranters felt free to violate every type of restriction in order to express the freedom granted by the Christ within. They preferred taverns to churches and were known for their smoking, drinking, swearing and outrageous preaching. These Ranters were accused of holding orgies; the charge does not seem farfetched. Ranters would greet each other by proclaiming "Rejoice, fellow creature—all is ours!"

Ranters were reported in the American colonies, where they greatly annoyed the Puritans. Some might have migrated voluntarily, seeking religious toleration; others were probably exiled criminals.

See also: LEVELLERS, DIGGERS, FIFTH MONARCHY MEN, MUGGLETONIANS.

Grigori Efimovich RASPUTIN   Grigori Efimovich Rasputin was known as the "Mad Monk" and the "Holy Devil," although he was neither a monk nor a SATANIST. Rasputin was a roaming holy man who wandered onto the stage of Russian history in 1905 when he befriended the royal family. His involvement with the rulers of Russia is thought to have been a factor that contributed to the triumph of communism in that country.

Rasputin was born in Pokrovskoe, Siberia, in 1871. At the age of twelve, he was playing with his brother in a river; his brother drowned, and Rasputin, puzzling over why his brother had died while he had not, concluded that he must have a special mission in life. Over the years, he became convinced that his mission was religious in nature. He consulted hermits, went on pilgrimages, and had a vision of the Virgin Mary.

In his twenties, Rasputin encountered the unorthodox sect called the KHLYSTY. This group practiced ceremonies involving frenzied dancing and flagellation, during which the dancers would supposedly become spiritually purified and acquire powers of prophecy and healing. Rasputin is thought to have studied with the Khlysty. From then on, he seems to have had an unusual ability to influence the people around him. Possibly, he learned hypnotic techniques from this sect.

Gripped with a sense of divine purpose, Rasputin wandered from town to town, preaching and healing. He attracted the attention of some bishops of the Russian Orthodox Church. After meeting Rasputin, they were impressed by his spiritual intensity and religious knowledge. Eventually, in 1905, word of the Siberian wonder-worker reached the highest levels of court society in St. Petersburg.

Nicholas and Alexandra, the tsar and tsarina, were attracted to Rasputin upon meeting him. He became a frequent guest in their palace. Alexis, the ruler's son and heir to the throne, had hemophilia, a disease in which scratches or cuts bleed continuously. Physicians were helpless to control this condition and predicted a short life for Alexis. Rasputin, however, seemed to have the ability to stop the child's bleeding. This apparently supernatural feat convinced Alexandra that Rasputin was a true holy man—the answer to her prayers.

In many ways, Rasputin was a rather unlikely saint. All accounts comment on his penetrating gaze, which seemed more commanding than compassionate. He never shaved and often wore strong cologne rather than bathing. Next to religion, his greatest passions included sex and vodka, both of which he indulged in as often as possible. His charisma and ability to care for Alexis cancelled these inconsistencies in the eyes of the tsarina, who fell strongly under his influence.

Through his association with Alexandra, Rasputin became a powerful force in the Russian government. He arranged for his friends to be promoted to rewarding positions, and he attempted to influence Nicholas's policy decisions. The tsar, however, came to distrust the strange Siberian peasant, despite his healing powers. When Rasputin urged Nicholas not to drag Russia into World War I, the tsar rejected his advice. Nicholas periodically dismissed Rasputin from court circles, but at the insistence of Alexandra, he was always allowed to return.

Rumors began to circulate that Rasputin was having an affair with the tsarina (which was untrue). Some people suspected that the Holy Devil was actually a German agent, whose bad advice to the tsar was impairing the Russian war effort. For others, the presence of Rasputin in the highest levels of state power indicated that Nicholas was unfit to govern and they began to plot the tsar's overthrow. In this charged political atmosphere, plans to murder Rasputin were made.

Rasputin's death was as remarkable as his life had been. In 1916, Prince Felix Yusupov decided to rid Russia of the "Mad Monk." One night, Prince Yusupov invited Rasputin to his palace for a private party. Rasputin was served cakes laced with cyanide and poisoned wine, but, to the astonishment of his host, he was unaffected, and suggested that they go and invite some gypsies to the party. Yusupov then shot Rasputin in the neck, who collapsed. When the Prince returned a minute later with assistants to carry the body away, Rasputin was running around the palace, trying to find an unlocked door through which to escape. After being shot several more times, Rasputin broke through a locked door and ran from the palace. It took another shot to bring him down. He was tied up and then dropped into a frozen river through a hole in the ice. Later, when the body was recovered, it was discovered that Rasputin had still been alive when he was dropped in the river; he had managed to free one hand and had frozen while making the sign of the cross.

Tsarina Alexandra had a special chapel built to house the body of Rasputin. As the shadows of Russian discontent grew, she spent many hours there in meditation. The memory of the Siberian healer could not defend her against the Bolsheviks, who killed the entire royal family in 1918 (their bodies were recovered in 1992).

RATRAMNUS   The monastery of Corbie in northern France was an important center of Christian learning during the ninth century. Ratramnus, a monk at Corbie, played an important role in the debate concerning the nature of the Catholic Mass. The outcome of the debate, which Ratramnus lost, affected more than just Catholic theology. Many historians regard the controversy over the Mass as a turning point in Christian history, leading eventually to the Protestant Reformation.

The Mass had been the central ritual of Christianity since ancient times. Believers had always held that Christ was present at the performance of the Mass, but few had attempted to define exactly what "Christ's presence" actually meant. Most were content to believe that they somehow communed with their Savior when they ate the holy wafer. Radbertus, abbot of Corbie during the mid-ninth century, felt the need to understand the nature of Christ's presence at the Mass more precisely.

Radbertus decided that the traditional reference to the communion bread and wine as Christ's "body and blood" was not merely symbolic: participants in the Mass were actually consuming the human flesh and blood of JESUS. The communion bread and wine did not change in *appearance*, Radbertus observed, but the *substance* of the bread and wine was miraculously transformed into material from the body of Mary's son. Christians received the spiritual benefits of partaking in the Mass if they had faith that the invisible transformation had taken place during the ceremony.

When Radbertus published his cannibalistic theory of the Mass, an uproar ensued among European theologians. The notion that Christians were literally nibbling on pieces of Jesus' corpse struck many as bizarre and unsettling. King Charles the Bald asked Ratramnus, a monk, to examine Radbertus's doctrine and to comment on it.

Ratramnus rejected his abbot's ideas on the Mass. Like all Christians of the time, he had no quarrel with the notion that Christ was present at the Mass. Ratramnus, however, believed the manner of this presence to be a divine mystery that could not be reduced to a literal transformation of the bread and wine. Furthermore, Ratramnus argued, the body in which Christ is present at the Mass is His divine body, not the embodiment of flesh that was born in Bethlehem many centuries before. The faith required during the ritual entails confidence in Christ's promise of salvation, not belief in a miraculous alteration of wine and bread. Despite the strangeness of Radbertus's ideas, his version of the Mass became the accepted understanding within the Roman Catholic Church. The vague "mystery" presence of Christ Ratramnus taught was harder for most people to comprehend than the amazing but straightforward idea that Christ's presence means His bodily presence.

Ratramnus was not declared a heretic during his lifetime. Indeed, he was a respected participant in several other significant theological controversies before his death in A.D. 868. However, when heated debate regarding the Mass broke out again in the eleventh century, many Christian thinkers turned to the doctrine of Radbertus as the orthodox position. Since Ratramnus's writings were an attack on Radbertus's view, they were condemned as heretical and burned at the Council of Vercelli in 1050. Curiously, by that time, Ratramnus's authorship of the banned work had been forgotten: church officials at the council mistakenly thought that it had been written by Ratramnus' famous contemporary, JOHN SCOTUS ERIGENA.

During the sixteenth century, some Protestant Reformers came to view Ratramnus as a forerunner of their own views. As a result, one of his books was included in the INDEX OF PROHIBITED BOOKS by the Roman Catholics in 1599 (it was removed from the *Index* only in 1900). Some historians believe that the Protestants were correct; the triumph of Radbertus's doctrine of the Mass shifted the focus of Catholic attention from faith in Christ's promise of salvation to faith in the miraculous transformation at the Mass. The Reformers tried to shift the emphasis back to what they took to be the "original" understanding of Christianity, as represented by Ratramnus' teaching.

Another result of Ratramnus's defeat was that the Catholic Mass, with its miraculous component as defined by Radbertus, began to seem less like a ritual of communion with God and more like a magical ceremony. Priests were encouraged to celebrate the Mass every day; even if no one else was present, the mere performance of the rite would have a positive effect on the world. This sense of magical power suggested to some priests that the effect of the Mass could be utilized for various ends, such as healing people—or cursing them, as in the BLACK MASS. Others came to believe that components of the Mass could be used magically to call up spirits and control them. Thus, in the ritual-MAGIC tradition of the Middle Ages, one finds many ceremonies and spells based on the Mass.

REINCARNATION   The belief that people have lived before and will live again is usually associated with Eastern religions. Belief in reincarnation can be found in almost every culture, however, including the West. In Judaism, the doctrine of reincarnation has had a long career. According to ancient Jewish historian Josephus, the sect of the Pharisees spread the doctrine. Whereas Eastern systems taught that spiritually advanced people could escape from the tedious cycle of rebirths, the Pharisees said that righteous people continued to reincarnate but that evildoers were cast into "eternal punishment." The Karaites, a Jewish sect that began in Iraq in the eighth century, endorsed the reincarnation doctrine.

The KABBALAH, the great Jewish mystical system, frequently discusses rebirth in its texts. The most important Kabbalistic work, the *ZOHAR*, observes that:

> The souls must re-enter the absolute substance whence they have emerged. But to accomplish this end they must develop all the perfections, the germ of which is planted in them; and if they have not fulfilled this condition during one life, they must commence another, a third, and so forth, until they have acquired the condition which fits them for reunion with God.

Another book, the *Kitzur Sh'lu*, notes that only a person who observes all 613 moral rules can escape reincarnation—and that not even Moses had managed to keep every rule perfectly. A third text, the *Yalkut Reubeni*, states that a man who is very selfish will be punished by being reborn as a woman. Kabbalists even taught that, under certain conditions, two souls could be born within one body.

The CABALA, the Christian version of Jewish Kabbalism, continued the belief in rebirth. The prominent seventeenth century Cabalist CHRISTIAN KNORR VON ROSENROTH wrote a book on reincarnation called *Rashith ha Gilgalim*, the "revolutions of souls." In the early Christian community, belief in reincarnation was popular. In the New Testament Gospel of Matthew, JESUS states that John the Baptist is the Old Testament prophet Elijah (Matthew 17:9–13). Some Christians understood this passage to mean that John was the reincarnation of Elijah, although the defender of orthodoxy (and later heretic) QUINTAS SEPTIMIUS FLORENS TERTULLIAN condemned this interpretation.

The most famous of the early Catholic leaders who believed in reincarnation was ORIGEN. He taught that the world is periodically destroyed and then re-created, each time better than the last. Human souls reincarnate continually, even surviving the cosmic destructions, until they attain perfection. Throughout most of Christian history, Origen's doctrine of the preexistence of souls, the foundation of his reincarnation theory, was thought to have been formally condemned as a Catholic heresy at the SECOND COUNCIL OF CONSTANTINOPLE in 553. Origen's condemnation may not have taken place during an official meeting of the council, however. Therefore, belief in reincarnation may not *technically* be a heresy for Catholics, even though it has been regarded as such for centuries.

The books of GNOSTICISM, the first serious competition to Catholicism regarding the definition of the Christian message, speak of the preexistence and the rebirth of souls. A Gnostic text called *Pistis Sophia* discusses how Jesus arranged for the souls of John the Baptist and the disciples to be reborn. It also describes the kinds of rebirths to be experienced by various kinds of sinners and virtuous persons, the result of their actions in this lifetime. During medieval times, the late Gnostic heresies of the CATHARS and the BOGOMILS taught the doctrine of reincarnation. A belief in rebirth provides a possible explanation for the willingness of 205 Cathars to march into the bonfires of the Crusaders rather than to renounce their faith after the siege of MONTSEGUR in 1244.

The mainstream world view of ancient and medieval times held that the soul and the body were different. From this perspective, reincarnation, therefore, was possible. Why, then, was there such resistance to the idea? One reason for orthodoxy's rejection of reincarnation was that the rebirth doctrine seemed inconsistent with some Church dogmas. For example, the orthodox believed that the righteous would be resurrected in their physical bodies at the end of time. If, however, people pass through many lives, which body will resurrect? As noted earlier, many rejected the preexistence of souls before the present life as heresy, so the possibility of future births was also ruled out. The idea that people's actions in past lives affects their present situation goes beyond the Catholic dogma of original sin. Augustine of Hippo explained, original sin is inherited from Adam and Eve, and the other sins are evil actions in the present life; there is no third category for sins from previous lives. The Catholic doctrine of grace—the idea that God's help is always needed to attain salvation—is also threatened by the notion that people's fate after death is controlled by their present behavior. If perfectly good behavior in this life can free people from the pains of rebirth, what need do they have for God's grace to help them attain this salvation?

Another reason for reincarnation's dismissal as a heretical belief is its tendency to undermine the power structure in Western society. In Eastern cultures, belief in reincarnation was used to support the social structure. For example, in India the caste system was justified by explaining that birth into a low caste was caused by bad actions in a previous life. In the West, however, the possibility of rebirth threatened the established division of authority. The Old Testament gives humans dominion over the animals. This teaching has justified the use of animals as slaves without rights. If animals are reborn as people, and people as animals, the right of humans to abuse animals seems questionable.

Another social practice that the rebirth idea threatened was the control of women by men. Traditional teachings of Roman Catholicism and Protestantism state that wives should obey their husbands. Throughout history many men have understood this teaching to mean that their wives were their property. If men could be reborn as women, and women as men, the oppression of women would be much less appealing to men. Saint Jerome wrote that the worst part of Origen's heresy was that "we may have to fear that we who are now men may afterwards be born women."

In early modern times, many scientists believed that the soul and the body were separate. In this dualistic world view, reincarnation is not ruled out as impossible, and some famous scientists did believe in rebirth. Benjamin Franklin and Thomas Huxley are two well-known examples.

Many modern scientists have tried to solve the problems of dualism by denying the existence of the soul or by proclaiming that the mind is just an experience of the body. In this view, the soul or mind ends at death; therefore, reincarnation is impossible. Some open-minded researchers have tried to use scientific methods to discover if reincarnation occurs. These scientists have examined the stories of hypnotized people and children who recalled previous lives. They have also studied reports of people who spoke languages they allegedly learned in a past existence. So far, most researchers have concluded that no firm evidence exists for the reality of reincarnation.

David REUBENI   One of the more successful "false Messiahs" in Jewish history, David Reubeni was probably born in Ethiopia sometime in the early sixteenth century. Following the expulsion of the Jews from Spain in 1492, many European Jews felt that the appearance of a savior must be imminent. As a result, when Reubeni, a charismatic figure, showed up in Venice in 1524 and proclaimed himself to be the Messiah, he received a sympathetic response from the Jewish community.

Reubeni announced that one of the lost tribes of Israel was hiding in Asia, awaiting his signal to attack the Moslem occupiers of Palestine. He was so convincing that even Pope Clement VII and Portuguese King Joao III met with him. The king offered Reubeni weapons and ships for a military campaign to free the Holy Land. But this "Messiah" lost favor among both Jews and gentiles before he could depart and spent the rest of his life in a Spanish jail.

See also: SOLOMON MOLCHO.

Johannes REUCHLIN   An important figure in the evolution of the CABALA, the Christian version of the Hebrew mystical tradition known as the KABBALAH. Johannes Reuchlin was born in Germany in 1455. Inspired by Italian scholar GIOVANNI PICO DELLA MIRANDOLA, he was convinced that the Jewish mystical writings could be used to understand the secrets of Christianity. Many of his contemporaries disagreed, however. In the dominant Catholic view, Judaism was an outmoded religion with nothing to contribute to the Christian revelation. When the Dominican order in Cologne began to destroy Hebrew writings, Reuchlin opposed the action. His orthodoxy was questioned, but he managed to avoid persecution. This Christian Hebrew scholar died in 1522. Because of Reuchlin's defense of the value of Cabalistic study, succeeding generations of Christians were able to continue his work in synthesizing esoteric Jewish and Christian thought.

Nicholas RIDLEY   One of the best-known victims of Queen "Bloody Mary" Tudor, Nicholas Ridley became bishop of London in 1550, during the early heyday of the Church of England. He worked with THOMAS CRANMER to compose the work that defined the practices of the new church, *The Book of Common Prayer*. In 1553, Mary came to power and prepared the way for England's return to Roman Catholicism by killing Protestant leaders. Ridley was convicted of heresy and burned at the stake, along with HUGH LATIMER, at Oxford in 1555.

See also: JOHN HOOPER.

Peter RIEDEMANN   After the execution of JACOB HUTTER, leader of the HUTTERITE heretics, in 1536, Peter Riedemann took over the movement. While in prison, he wrote *Confession of Faith*, which summarizes Hutterite beliefs, including pacifism, communism, and opposition to infant baptism. Riedemann's text remains the definitive statement of the Hutterite faith to this day.

ROBBER COUNCIL   In A.D. 381, orthodox Christianity became the state religion of the Roman Empire. During the next sixty years, the Christian community was in turmoil over who would control the now-powerful institution of the church. The political struggles were intertwined with the efforts of theologians to determine exactly the beliefs of orthodoxy. The meeting of Christian leaders held in Ephesus in A.D. 449 was the last, short-lived victory of heresy within the orthodox church in ancient times. The Robber Council, as Pope Leo later labeled it, was the only major church council to be declared heretical.

The theological issue that led to the Robber Council was a war of words between DIOSCURUS, bishop of Alexandria, and Flavian, bishop of Constantinople. A monk named EUTYCHES had accused Flavian of following the NESTORIAN heresy, which separated Christ into two persons. Dioscurus supported Eutyches. Flavian noted that Eutyches taught that Christ had only a single divine nature, whereas the orthodox view stated that Christ had two natures, one divine and one human.

The political side of this controversy involved the power struggle between Alexandria and other Christian centers for dominance within the church. Dioscurus knew that if he could establish that the other influential Christian leaders, Flavian of Constantinople and Bishop Leo of Rome, had unorthodox beliefs, Alexandria would be recognized as the center of orthodox Christianity.

The Roman Empire at this time faced severe pressures from the Germanic tribes who were overrunning the western part of the imperial territory. Emperor Theodosius II wished for unity within the church in the hope that a united church would strengthen the empire. He called for church leaders to gather at Ephesus in 449 in order to end the strife over Eutyches' views. Pope Leo did not travel to Ephesus, but he sent a delegation and a letter outlining his views. According to Leo, the teaching of a single divine nature in Christ was heresy. Christ needed a human nature as well, so that his sacrifice on the cross would earn humanity forgiveness for its sins.

Dioscurus managed to pack the council with his supporters. They refused to read the pope's letter. Instead, Eutyches was proclaimed orthodox, and both Flavian and Leo were declared to be heretics. This condemnation of the two most powerful men in the church provoked a strong reaction. Two years later, another church council, the COUNCIL OF CHALCEDON, was held. The Catholic parties of Constantinople and Rome carefully controlled this meeting. The decisions of the 449 council were overturned, Eutyches and his followers were pronounced heretics, and Dioscurus was stripped of his rank in the church for disobedience.

See also: IBAS, MONOPHYSITISM.

ROSICRUCIANS   In the second decade of the seventeenth century, a series of strange documents were published in Germany. These writings reported the existence of a secret group, which had been founded in the fifteenth century by a man named Christian Rosencreuz. The Rosicrucians, as they came to be called, possessed great magical and spiritual knowledge and worked secretly for the benefit of the world. No one knows for sure who wrote the Rosicrucian texts, but the probable author of at least one of them was a Protestant minister named Johann Valentin Andreae.

While Andreae and his friends may well have formed some sort of secret society, Rosencreuz himself was a fictional character, and the Rosicrucian society as described in the manifestoes did not exist. Nevertheless, great excitement swept through Europe. Leading figures in the occult community publicly called on the Rosicrucians to make contact with them; others began to claim that they were already in touch with these mysterious sages.

Since that time, the legend of the Rosicrucians has continued to fascinate Western occultists. The fantasy of the Hidden Masters or Secret Chiefs became prominent during the nineteenth century in such movements as THEOSOPHY and the Hermetic Order of the GOLDEN DAWN, which reported that they received their esoteric knowledge from these Masters. The Golden Dawn used the symbolism of the Rose and Cross and the life story of Rosencreuz in their initiation ceremonies. To this day, many occult societies call themselves Rosicrucians or report that they possess the secret teachings of Christian Rosencreuz.

Bernt ROTHMANN   This German preacher was partly responsible for the notorious episode of the MÜNSTER HERETICS, which led to the mass persecution of the Protestant ANABAPTISTS during the sixteenth century. Bernt Rothmann was teaching Protestant doctrines in the German town of Münster by the late 1520s. His influence was such that the town council became supporters of the Lutheran cause. However, Rothmann's own beliefs, affected by contact with Anabaptists, became more radical. When he started preaching against the baptism of infants, the Lutherans turned against him; however, he defeated them in a public theological debate. As a result, his influence increased to the point that Münster became known as a haven for Anabaptists. By 1534, Rothmann and his colleagues effectively controlled the town, prompting an armed response from orthodox authorities. When the siege ended the following year with an Anabaptist defeat, Rothmann was tortured to death and his body put on public display. The takeover of Münster by the heretics so offended mainstream Protestants that Anabaptist communities became targets of intense persecution.

RUFINUS THE SYRIAN   An early leader of the heresy known as PELAGIANISM. Rufinus the Syrian was a friend of the well-known Pelagian leader CELESTIUS, and is thought to have been responsible for convincing Celestius to oppose Augustine's doctrine of original sin. According to Augustine, Adam's disobedience to God led to the inability of anyone to resist sin. Rufinus and the Pelagians, on the other hand, maintained that like Adam, everyone is free to choose good or evil.

Charles RUSSELL   In mid-nineteenth century America, great interest arose in the idea that Christ would shortly return to earth. Charles Russell founded the most successful of the unorthodox sects based on this notion. His followers, known as RUSSELLITES, evolved into the JEHOVAH'S WITNESSES.

Born in 1852, Russell became a businessperson in Pennsylvania. He was restless concerning religion, trying out a variety of mainstream Christian congregations. A philosophical argument with an atheist—which the atheist won—prompted him to begin intensive Bible studies in order to strengthen his ability to defend his faith.

In the course of his research, Russell came across the work of WILLIAM MILLER. This preacher had caused a stir in the 1840s with his Bible-based predictions that Christ would return to earth in 1843 or 1844. Russell was inspired to do his own calculations and concluded, in 1875, that the Lord had indeed come back the year before, but as an invisible "presence in the upper air." Christ would manifest visibly in 1878, he deduced.

The businessperson-turned-prophet used his wealth to communicate his spiritual insights and gathered a following. When Christ did not appear as predicted in 1878, Russell indicated that the dead had been resurrected in heaven instead during that year. He then chose 1914 as the year for Christ's earthly appearance.

Russell had a keen appreciation for the power of the written word. He developed an efficient system of publishing and distributing his materials, such as *The Watch Tower* and *Awake!*, through his corporation, Zion's Watch Tower Tract Society, founded in 1884. Russell also tried to bolster the movement's funds in creative ways. One scheme involved the sale of expensive "Miracle Wheat," which would supposedly grow five times greater than the ordinary item. When the *Brooklyn Daily Eagle* newspaper denounced the operation as a fraud, Russell sued. Government officials conducted tests, revealing nothing miraculous about the wheat. The prophet lost his lawsuit.

The year 1914 came and went, and World War I began, but there was no sign of Christ. This disappointment caused membership in Russell's movement to dwindle. But the leader's faith was unshaken, and he continued his work, certain that the return of the Lord was at hand. Two years later, on board a train during a preaching tour in Texas, Russell fell suddenly ill. One of his disciples invited the porter to "come and see how a man of God dies." It is reported that he passed on serenely. Although it would have seemed unlikely at the time, in the face of the failed predictions, the disruption of its creative financing scheme, and the death of its leader, the movement Russell started has since grown manyfold.

See also: JOSEPH RUTHERFORD.

RUSSELLITES   The Russellites were members of an unorthodox movement, founded in 1870 by CHARLES RUSSELL, on the premise that Christ was about to appear on the earth. JOSEPH RUTHERFORD, Russell's successor, transformed this sect into the JEHOVAH'S WITNESSES.

Joseph RUTHERFORD   Leader of the RUSSELLITES between 1916 and 1943, a period when the movement's name was changed to the JEHOVAH'S WITNESSES. Under Joseph Rutherford, membership mushroomed because of his efficiency in organizing the distribution of the sect's publications, as well as his enticing slogan: "Millions Now Living Will Never Die!" He discarded many of the teachings of the founder, CHARLES RUSSELL, and advanced his own speeches and writings as authoritative. During Rutherford's leadership, the return of Christ to the earth was predicted for 1918, 1920, 1925, and 1941. No confirmed sightings were made during these years.

SABELLIANISM   The version of MODALISM founded by the heretic SABELLIUS, who lived in the early third century in Rome. Later, the term Sabellianism became a synonym for all teachings claiming that the elements of the Christian Trinity are just different names for one Person, rather than three distinct Persons.

SABELLIUS   This Christian teacher flourished in Rome during the early third century. Sabellius was an important proponent of the heresy known as MODALISM. He became so closely associated with the Modalist heresy that successive generations of orthodox Christians referred to Modalism as SABELLIANISM.

Little is known today concerning Sabellius's personal history; his orthodox opponents did not preserve much biographical information about this hated figure. Indeed, even his ideas are currently available only as quoted in the works of his enemies. Sabellius is believed to have come from Libya, and was active among the Christians of Rome during the reign of POPE ZEPHYRINUS (198–217) and Pope Callistus (217–222). According to ancient Catholic historian Hippolytus, Zephyrinus was actually a supporter of Sabellius, thereby tarnishing himself with the brush of heresy. While Callistus supposedly rejected Sabellius's teaching, the influence of Modalism was still quite apparent in Callistus's theological language.

Shortly before Sabellius appeared in Rome, the heretic PRAXEAS had introduced a type of Modalism in opposition to another popular heresy, ADOPTIONISM. The teachings of Praxeas undoubtedly inspired Sabellius and he devised his own more sophisticated version of the Modalist doctrine. At issue among the quarrelling theological parties in Rome was how to make sense of the various descriptions of God in sacred Christian texts. Some works clearly refer to God as a single being, without any basic division (the Judeo-Christian tradition of monotheism). However, the New Testament contains many passages in which the Father, Son, and Holy Spirit each seem to be referred to as God. According to Sabellius, the basic question for

Christians seeking to understand God is "Do we have one God or three?" Sabellius felt that preserving the unity of God was of primary importance. This emphasis is not surprising since he lived in Rome when the city was still primarily POLYTHEISTIC in its religious commitments. Also, many Christians viewed the Adoptionist heresy as a threat to the majesty of the divine Christ by claiming that JESUS was a mere man "adopted" by God.

Sabellius explained the apparent threefold portrayal of God as implied by the language of Father, Son, and Holy Spirit. He claimed that these three terms were merely three different names for one divine Person. When God is in heaven, He is the Father; when He lived with humanity on earth, He was the Son; and His more recent manifestations are His acts as the Holy Spirit. God took on these different modes one after the other; the Father, Son, and Holy Spirit do not all exist at the same time, but in sequence.

In order to emphasize the unity of God's Person, despite the diversity of names and modes in the New Testament, Sabellius referred to God as the "SonFather." He also represented God by the image of the sun. Sabellius argued that just as the sun's light, warmth, and astrological influence cannot be separated because they are all one entity, so it is with the Father, Son, and Holy Spirit.

Sabellius's understanding of God violated several orthodox beliefs concerning the Trinity, which were still developing during his lifetime. The Catholic view held that God is one in His essence or basic nature, but three in Persons. To reduce the Father, Son, and Holy Spirit to mere names or modes is to blur their distinctiveness, and to leave unexplained the Bible passages in which the divine Persons are described as interacting.

Another problem with Sabellius's position, according to orthodoxy, is its implications concerning Christ. If the Son was just a name for God in His entirety, then Jesus Christ, the "Son of God," was not a human being, but God. Both implications of this idea are heretical. Either this nonhuman Jesus did not have a real human body and, therefore, could not have died on the cross—the heresy of DOCETISM—or He did have a human body, so God the Father was made to suffer the pains of a dying body during the crucifixion—the heresy of PATRIPASSIANISM.

The teachings of Sabellius are significant in Christian history for several reasons. First, the support this heretic garnered from Pope Zephyrinus raises questions for the proponents of papal infallibility. Second, Sabellius's inclusion of the Holy Spirit as one of the modes of God highlighted its theological importance at a time when most orthodox thought was focusing exclusively on the Father and Son. Some historians have suggested that the Sabellian accent on the Holy Spirit actually caused orthodoxy to include it as the third member of the Trinity. Third, Sabellius's sophisticated portrayal of Modalism fueled the enduring popularity of this heresy, which has persisted and resurfaced throughout the history of Western culture.

SACRED MAGIC OF ABRAMELIN THE MAGE   This magical manual is regarded by scholars and practitioners of MAGIC as one of the most important works among the European texts known as GRIMOIRES. ALEISTER CROWLEY, the most famous magician of the twentieth century, said that *Sacred Magic of Abramelin the Mage* was the "best and most dangerous book ever written." Another prominent modern magician, Dion Fortune, claimed that the Abramelin magical system is "the most potent and complete that we possess."

The book was supposedly composed by ABRAHAM THE JEW, a legendary magician of the fifteenth century. During his travels, Abraham reports, he met a man named Abramelin, who taught him the esoteric matters contained in this work. The oldest copy we have today, written in French, is stored in the Arsenal Library in Paris and is believed to be no older than the eighteenth century. It was first translated into English by S. L. MacGregor Mathers, co-founder of the Hermetic Order of the GOLDEN DAWN.

According to the magical theory of Abramelin, the universe is populated by invisible DEMONS. These demons are controlled by ANGELS, who put them to work maintaining the universe. Occasionally, a demon manages to escape from this enslavement and then does its best to cause trouble. Apparently, quite a few demons evade captivity because the text teaches that every human is pestered by a Malevolent Demon. Fortunately, each person has a Holy Guardian Angel, too.

Abramelin reports that people can gain control over the demons and force these creatures to do their bidding. This is a common statement in the grimoires, but *Sacred Magic* approaches the claim in a unique manner. The text is filled with magic squares, consisting of arrangements of letters that read the same (or almost the same) when scanned in different directions. For example, the following square causes the demons to reveal knowledge of all things past, present, and future:

```
M  I  L  O  N
I  R  A  G  O
L  A  M  A  L
O  G  A  R  I
N  O  L  I  M
```

Through the proper use of the squares, Abramelin promises that the magician can attain such powers as invisibility, flight through the air, irresistible sexual attractiveness, wealth, magical healing, and even the ability to revive a corpse to life.

The book is careful not to reveal exactly how to use the squares, however. Magicians must first make contact with their Holy Guardian Angel which is no easy task. *Sacred Magic* recommends a preparation of six months. During this period, a magician is to lead a life of strict purity. The practitioner must withdraw from the world, pray intensely, burn a special incense, and read holy books for two hours daily. At the end of this spiritual marathon, the magician is told to recruit a child, who is supposed to receive visions from the angel by contemplating a silver plate. Only after this is done will the angel appear to the magician and grant instruction on the use of the magic squares.

The lengthy ritual preparation and the angelic instruction seem to make the magician supremely powerful over the demons, or at least very confident. In the *Sacred Magic* there is no mention of the magic circle, a protection device against demonic attack described in most other magical manuals.

Occultists have warned against attempting to employ Abramelin magic without completing the preparation. The squares are regarded as batteries charged with magical energy, which can harm the unwary user. The esoteric literature provides instances of the dangers of casual use. For example, a friend of Crowley who was reading *Sacred Magic* inserted a bill from a local butcher's shop as a bookmark. Shortly afterward, the butcher accidentally hacked himself to death—an event Crowley believed to be caused by the unintended linking of the butcher with the evil forces bottled within the squares. Mathers reported many sinister events during his translation of the text. Another magical practitioner wrote in *Occult Review* that, after dabbling in the Abramelin system, she underwent a series of nightmarish experiences, culminating in the terrifying vision of a great red obelisk that crashed through the wall of her room, shattering all the windows.

The importance of *Sacred Magic* for the Western magical tradition lies in its emphasis on establishing contact with Holy Guardian Angels. Modern magicians often equate the Angel with one's higher Self. In this view, the preparatory practices are a parallel to Eastern meditative traditions, which aim to produce a state of enlightenment. The promises of personal power through mastery of the demons seem more appealing to a worldly person, rather than someone interested in high spiritual development. Perhaps the promised magic powers were included as bait to motivate a selfish individual to undertake the rigors of the purification practice. After receiving the Angel's teaching, the magician might no longer be controlled by the Malevolent Demon of greed. Similar teachings can be found in the tantric Buddhist traditions of Asia. There is no evidence of direct contact between Buddhists and the author of *Sacred Magic*.

The spiritual aspect of the Abramelin system and the discussion of potent magical techniques have greatly influenced the modern magical scene. Nineteenth century French magician Eliphas Levi studied the text. Elements of Abramelin entered the Golden Dawn practices through Mathers. Much of Crowley's magical career was devoted to communicating with his Holy Guardian Angel. Occult groups continue to explore the methods of Abramelin the Mage to the present day.

SATANISM   Traditionally, the term "Satanism" has referred to a body of practices and beliefs that invert the values of orthodox Christianity. Satanists were thought to worship the Devil instead of God; defile Christian symbols, such as the cross; and conduct parodies of holy rituals, such as the Mass. In this traditional sense, Satanism was a conspiracy opposed to the values of conventional society, plotting to corrupt and overthrow them. Satanism has been feared through the centuries, and yet it has rarely been practiced; it has existed primarily in the imaginations of people encountering the unexpected or unknown.

The idea of a secret group worshipping an evil principle and working against the ideals of mainstream society is ancient. One of the Dead Sea Scrolls, written in the first century B.C. or first century A.D., contains a reference to a conspiracy of the "Sons of Darkness," also known as the "army of Belial" (a prominent demon in Hebrew folk belief). The "Sons of Light," meaning members of decent Jewish society, are called on to fight against the allies of the demons.

Ironically, the early orthodox Christians themselves were often accused of revering an evil deity. From one direction, the followers of GNOSTICISM (regarded as heretical by the Christian group that developed into the Roman Catholic Church) charged that the creator of the universe was actually a demon. According to these Gnostics, anyone who worshipped the creator, including orthodox Christians, were, therefore, unwitting Satanists.

Pagan Roman authorities accused Christians of deliberately devoting themselves to evil. Because of the threat of persecution, early Christian communities in the Roman Empire met and conducted their acts of worship in private. Rumors began to circulate that the Christians practiced human sacrifice and cannibalism. These notions were likely misunderstandings of the Christian rite of consuming the "body and blood of the Lord" in the form of bread and wine during the Mass. Under the pretext that Christians were engaged in such antisocial acts, the Romans periodically targeted them for suppression.

Later, when the Christians themselves came to power in the fourth century, the tables were turned. The old pagan deities were then thought to be demons, so anyone who followed pagan religious practices was viewed as a devil-worshipper. This belief motivated Christian authorities to order both the banning of pagan religions and the destruction of pagan temples (or their conversion into churches).

Christian concerns regarding Satanism did not end with the defeat of PAGANISM. During the Middle Ages, suspicions of devil worship were aroused by three groups in European culture: magicians, heretics, and women. Medieval practitioners of DEMON MAGIC held ceremonies in which they attempted to harness the powers of evil to serve them. Such activities, often performed in secret by monks or priests, alarmed orthodox authorities. The officials of the church expressed concern that the magical rites might involve making sacrifices to the devils. Actually, medieval demon magic generally dealt with demons in a rather imperious manner, threatening them with terrible consequences if they disobeyed the magician, rather than treating the demons with reverence. Nonetheless, the Satanistic portrayal of magicians presented in the orthodox propaganda aroused widespread fear and hostility toward them. As a result, ritual magicians of the time were compelled to remain underground.

Groups that disagreed with orthodoxy on points of Christian doctrine were also labeled Satanists. Heretical groups, such as the CATHARS and WALDENSIANS, became popular in some regions of France and Italy, and posed a serious threat to Catholic control over spiritual views. According to orthodox belief, the Devil was behind anything that stood in the way of the official church. Therefore, heretics must be in league with Satan. The old charges of cannibalism, ritual murder, and forbidden sexual acts were flung at heretical groups, and fueled the persecutions inflicted on them.

An example of such an "anti-Satanism" campaign in the Middle Ages was the Inquisition operated by Conrad of Marburg in the early thirteenth century. For more than a year, Conrad and his assistants roamed the Mainz region of Germany, seeking out members of a cult called the LUCIFERANS. The cultists supposedly engaged in the usual Satanic activities (mentioned above); in addition, they were said to worship a giant toad by kissing its anus. Conrad's campaign had the support of the pope. A large number of people were burned to death on this basis before an angry mob cornered and killed Conrad on an isolated country road. Today it is agreed that the Luciferans never existed. The victims of the persecution were innocent orthodox believers, and perhaps a few Waldensians, who thought of themselves as pious Christians.

The third group of Satanic suspects in medieval culture were women. A tenth-century list of beliefs to be abolished from Catholic communities includes the following:

One mustn't be silent about certain wicked women who become followers of Satan . . . seduced by the fantastic illusion of the demons, and insist that they ride at night on certain beasts together with Diana, goddess of the pagans, and a great multitude of women; that they cover great distances in the silence of the deepest night; that they obey the orders of the goddess as though she were their mistress; that on particular nights they are called to wait on her.

Occasionally, priests would encounter women in their parish who held to this belief of night flying with a goddess. Such a notion might be a fragmentary tradition from pagan times, perhaps manifesting as a dream or vision, but it certainly was not an act of devil worship. Nevertheless, orthodox authorities viewed the experience as inspired by Satan because its content was clearly unorthodox. Since the women were thought to be tricked by the Devil, the authorities usually did not harm them but assigned penitential practices to the women to cleanse themselves of the sin.

With the dawn of the Renaissance, the assumptions of the medieval Christian world view were increasingly questioned. At the time, it was difficult for people to understand the source of these complex changes. In this atmosphere of anxious uncertainty, a growing number of orthodox believers began to worry that a conspiracy of Satan's servants had infiltrated Christian society and was using magic in an attempt to overthrow it. The elements of this fear were drawn from a variety of sources and congealed in the belief in witchcraft.

From the fifteenth to the seventeenth centuries, many thousands were executed in the GREAT WITCH HUNT after being charged with the practice of Satanic witchcraft. As in the earlier accusations against heretics, magicians, and goddess-worshipping women, it is doubtful that any of the victims were actually Satanists. Toward the end of the witch-hunt period, the first evidence for real Satanists appears in the historical record. A Satanic group, that included members of the court of Louis XIV, the "Sun King," was uncovered in France in the late seventeenth century. This organization, which included the sorceress LA VOISIN and a defrocked priest named ABBÉ GUIBOURG, conducted a ceremony resembling the Catholic Mass. Here, however, a naked woman lay on the altar, a child was sacrificed, and demons were called upon. This AMATORY MASS was one of the prototypes for the more recent Satanic practice of the BLACK MASS.

As mentioned earlier, the magicians of the Middle Ages and the Renaissance were falsely accused of worshipping Satan. Some of the magical manuals called GRI-MOIRES composed during the seventeenth century, probably in France, begin to move closer to revering demons rather than merely commanding them. Both GRI-MOIRE OF HONORIUS and GRAND GRIMOIRE, for example, encourage the magician to sacrifice animals to evil spirits. It seems that some French occultists were so impressed by the church's fear of Satan that they tried to strike an alliance with this powerful being. During the eighteenth century there are few traces of actual Satanic activities in Europe. The MEDMENHAM MONKS, a society of wealthy Englishmen, were suspected of devil worship. However, it is more likely that they performed ceremonies in honor of the pagan goddess Venus and did not worship an embodiment of evil.

Confirmed Satanic activity reappeared in France in the nineteenth century. The heretical CHURCH OF CARMEL was founded in 1839 and was condemned by the pope in 1848. This movement became popular for a time in some areas of northern France, and most of its followers probably viewed themselves as good Christians. EUGENE VINTRAS, the founder, and his closest disciples may have secretly taught Satanic beliefs. A photograph still in existence today shows Vintras wearing an inverted crucifix, which is a standard Satanic symbol, while conducting a mass.

Vintras's successor as the leader of the Church of Carmel, ABBÉ BOULLAN, was undoubtedly a Satanist. Boullan is reported to have sacrificed a child, conducted black masses, and encouraged his congregation to engage in orgies. These sometimes included performing sex acts with animals. Boullan's onetime friend, J. K. Huysmans, wrote a detailed description of Satanic rites in the guise of fiction (Huysmans later renounced his dark past as a time of "dwelling in privies" and converted to Roman Catholicism).

A more recent figure linked to Satanic practices is ALEISTER CROWLEY. Crowley vigorously explored almost every nook and cranny of the Western occult tradition, and inevitably he experimented with BLASPHEMY. On one occasion, he baptized a toad in the name of Christ and crucified it. In the larger context of his life's work, however, Crowley cannot accurately be described as a Satanist. His religion was "Crowleyanity," featuring himself as the Savior. Crowley named his dog "Satan"—an unlikely choice for a real follower of the Devil.

Does Satanism exist in the twentieth century? The current status of Satanism is a complex question because today the term has at least five different meanings, which must be carefully distinguished to avoid confusion. First, a number of young people are involved in the "heavy-metal" subculture. This phenomenon centers around certain popular musicians who often employ Satanic imagery, such as inverted crosses and pentagrams, skulls, and depictions of grotesque demons. Although some commentators refer to heavy-metal devotees as "Satanists," the adolescent need to demonstrate one's independence from parental values is the central motivation among this group, not the serious worship of evil.

Second, mentally disturbed murderers have occasionally mentioned to the police that their crimes were guided by the Devil or that they worshipped Satan. There is no reason to take these statements as evidence for the existence of an organized Satanic cult.

Third, a few modern magicians continue to perform ceremonies of demonic conjuration using traditional methods, such as animal sacrifice. The activities of these black magicians might border on devil worship, but they operate in isolation or in very small groups, and are not linked together in an organized fashion.

Fourth, since the 1960s some "Satanic" groups, originating in California, have sought public attention. These organizations, such as the Church of Satan and the Temple of Set, deny that they simply reverse Christian values and images. Rather, they claim to revive a supposedly pre-Christian value system involving the guilt-free pursuit of pleasure and power. Some of these groups utilize traditional Satanic symbols to represent their freedom from conventional morality, but they are not Satanists in the traditional sense of revering the Christian god's enemy. Furthermore, they do not practice human sacrifice.

Finally, in recent years a number of people have reported that they have been forced to witness or participate in Satanic rituals. The sacrifice of animals and humans, group sexual acts, and the veneration of the Devil are common components of these stories. Often, the witnesses claim that they were so traumatized that they repressed their memory of these events for many years, retrieving them only with the aid of a therapist. Self-help groups for "ritual-abuse survivors" exist. Some observers have concluded that the experiences reported by the "survivors" point to the existence of an international organization of murderous devil worshippers.

Concerning this claim, it is noteworthy that repeated police investigations of the survivors' accounts have never yielded any physical evidence in support of their assertions. No one has ever been convicted of criminal activities as the result of such investigations. Some historians, such as Richard Noll, have pointed out that the descriptions of Satanic practices given by the survivors resemble the witchcraft stories reported by the Renaissance witch hunters, the smear campaign against medieval heretics by the Inquisitors, the attacks on pagans by the early Christians, and the rumors the Romans spread about the first Christian communities. All of these previous accusations were unfounded fantasies. In the face of any evidence to the contrary, there is no reason to take the current stories about a Satanic conspiracy as true either.

Noll suggests that these reports do not indicate the presence of a mass Satanic conspiracy, but rather a "mass psychological phenomenon." Perhaps, like the previous outbreaks of Satanism stories, the present cases reflect an individual or mass anxiety over the inability of traditional assumptions to explain the rapidly changing experiences of the post-modern world. As the saying goes, "Better the Devil you know than the Devil you don't."

Girolamo SAVONAROLA   Perhaps the best known heretic of the Renaissance, Girolamo Savonarola embodied the increasing popular resentment of the corruption that gripped the Catholic Church. "The Black Friar," as he was known, called for a radical purging of church and society; he was answered by the pope's Inquisitors, who had him burned at the stake. Savonarola's invitation to reform proved to be the last chance for Roman Catholic Europe; nineteen years after his death, Martin Luther set off the Protestant Reformation and the still unresolved rupture of western Christianity.

Born in the Italian city of Ferrara in 1452, Savonarola was a sensitive and studious child. While quite young, he became disgusted at the materialism and corruption of the church. He was no admirer of the new reverence for pagan cultural ideals, such as the appreciation of the naked body in art, which characterized the Renaissance. After an early disappointment in love, he joined the Dominican order. For many years, he concentrated on study, teaching, and spiritual devotions.

In 1481, Savonarola joined a monastery in Florence, the center of the Italian Renaissance. For ten years, he attracted little attention. When the Black Friar began his preaching tours, however, he proved very popular. His sermons gave voice to the anxieties of the people, who had witnessed rapid social and political change. Savonarola's eloquent warnings of impending doom and calls for repentance filled the churches to overflowing.

Among the preacher's audience was the brilliant young scholar GIOVANNI PICO DELLA MIRANDOLA. Pico was deeply impressed. He influenced his patron, Lorenzo de Medici, to arrange for Savonarola to become the prior of the Dominicans in Florence. With surging popularity, Savonarola grew more extreme. He attacked the innovative art of the city as obscene, even charging Botticelli and Leonardo da Vinci with sodomy. On Good Friday, 1492, the Friar terrified his congregation with his description of the looming destruction of Florence by God. Lightning would rain from the sky, and an army of barbers, armed with gigantic razors, would slaughter the faithless inhabitants.

By 1494, the ruling Medici family had lost their popularity, while Savonarola's support had continued to grow. Florence was then occupied by French troops. The Friar impressed the French, who came to him for advice. When both the Medicis and the French army withdrew, many Florentines believed that Savonarola was responsible for liberating the city. A republican government was established, but Savonarola was now so popular that he effectively ruled Florence.

Savonarola called on the city, the Catholic Church, and the world to purify themselves by giving up their interest in wealth and frivolous entertainment. Many Florentines responded. Rich men gave their belongings to the poor and joined monasteries, and proud noblewomen, accustomed to dressing in finery, walked the streets clothed in gray. But some of the richer citizens did not wish to renounce their advantages and complained of the friar's actions to Pope Alexander VI. The pontiff, himself no stranger to luxury and no admirer of independent activities by underlings, ordered Savonarola to stop preaching.

For several months, Savonarola obeyed the papal edict. Privately, he encouraged the penitential activities of the Florentines to continue. Reassured that the friar was not a rebel against his authority, the pope released his order of silence the next year. However, Savonarola's renewed preaching continued to include calls for church reform. Pope Alexander arranged for the Dominican monastery in Florence to come under Rome's direct control. This time, Savonarola openly defied the pontiff's command. Furious, Alexander excommunicated him. The friar questioned the pope's spiritual authority to carry out the act since the church was possessed by the spirits of greed and lust.

In 1498, Savonarola sponsored the famous "Bonfire of the Vanities." Florentines were urged to cleanse the city of its "boils and sores"—its indecent works of art, musical instruments, literature (aside from the Bible and Savonarola's own writings), beautiful clothing, cosmetics, and games. These items were piled high in the marketplace. To the sound of cheers and hymn singing, the Black Friar stepped forth and ignited the heap. Most of Botticelli's paintings, and many other priceless treasures, went up in smoke.

The pope's language then became more threatening. He ordered the government of Florence to restrain the friar or to send him to Rome to go on trial as a heretic. A Franciscan monk, loyal to the pope, publicly accused Savonarola of heresy and challenged him to the medieval test of God's will, the ordeal by fire. Savonarola declined the test, and the masses began to turn against him.

The Florentine government arrested the Black Friar and his two closest followers. They were turned over to the INQUISITION, who tortured them to confess to heresy. On May 23, 1498, the three were hanged and their bodies burned in the great central square in Florence. A few years later, the Medici family returned to power. Savonarola's radical mission had failed. In the following years, his sincere faith and eloquence were remembered more than his excesses, and he was revered as a hero of Florence.

SCHISM   In Roman Catholic terminology, a schismatic is one who promotes division within the government of the church, but who does not embrace unorthodox doctrines. Schismatics might form a group that fails to recognize the authority of the bishops, for instance, but they would still accept the basic beliefs concerning the Trinity and the nature of Christ. The two best-known schisms are: the rupture between the Eastern Orthodox and Roman Catholic Churches in 1054; and the "Great Schism" period of the fourteenth and fifteenth centuries, when the Roman Catholic Church had two or three popes simultaneously contending for power.

SCHWENKFELDER CHURCH   An unorthodox Protestant movement that takes its name and doctrines from its founder, CASPAR VON SCHWENKFELD, Schwenkfelder Church communities persisted in parts of Germany following the leader's death in 1561. The Jesuits tried to dissolve the Schwenkfelder movement in 1720. Some members of this church fled to the tolerant atmosphere of Freistatt, Pennsylvania, where their descendants have survived to the present day.

SEFER YETZIRAH   This text, the Hebrew title of which means "Book of Creation," was a key influence on the Jewish mystical tradition called KABBALAH. *Sefer Yetzirah* is a short work—less than 2,000 words long—that was composed in Palestine, most likely in the second or third centuries A.D. Its author is unknown.

The book describes the formation and structure of the universe. The ideas contained in the work represent a convergence of several esoteric schools of thought prevalent in the ancient world, including both Jewish and pagan Greek notions. A link with VALENTINIAN GNOSTICISM is suggested: a certain magical syllable appears in the creation accounts of *Sefer Yetzirah* and in the works of the Valentinian PTOLEMAEUS.

According to *Sefer Yetzirah*, the central elements in God's acts of creation are the ten *sefiroth* and the twenty-two letters of the Hebrew alphabet, known collectively as the "32 secret paths of wisdom." The word *sefirah* is related to a Hebrew term meaning "to count." The *sefiroth* are the numbers from one to ten, but are also the servants of God and the dimensions of existence. The idea that the world was created out of living numbers indicates a relationship between the world view of *Sefer Yetzirah* and that of the followers of Pythagoras, who believed in the mystical powers of numbers.

The first *sefirah* is the spirit of God. Out of this spirit, the next three *sefiroth* condense, representing air, water, and fire; out of these three elements, the twenty-two letters and earth and heaven are carved. The six lower *sefiroth* form the dimensions of space. The text indicates that, in some mysterious way, the ten *sefiroth* exist within each other.

In another section of the *Sefer Yetzirah*, the letters are described as the materials out of which the universe is created. Three letters produce the three elements of air, water and fire, the three primary divisions of the year, and the three main segments of the human body. Another seven letters give rise to the seven planets, heavens, days of the week, and openings in the body. The remaining twelve letters generate the signs of the zodiac, the months, and the major limbs of the body.

These two, somewhat contradictory, versions of creation might indicate that two different traditions were joined in *Sefer Yetzirah*. Alternatively, the stories have been interpreted as suggesting two levels of reality. The level of the sefiroth is the world of perfect forms, without substance, beyond time, that underlies the domain of ordinary experience. The level of the letters is the dynamic world of substantial bodies within which we live. The idea that the world we experience is constructed with language has also been suggested by some modern anthropologists—the "Whorfian hypothesis" states that the concepts in one's language determine which features of the world one can perceive.

Because *Sefer Yetzirah* is rich in suggestion but rather vague in details, readers over the centuries have found many different ideas in it, and put it to various uses. Some Kabbalists interested in a philosophical understanding of reality took it as a work of metaphysics, describing the nature of God and the universe. Others, more interested in MAGIC, reasoned that if language was used to create the world, one could learn to use magic words to affect the world for one's own benefit. Yet others believed that it was possible to travel on the "secret paths of wisdom," finally attaining mystical contact with God. All three types of Kabbalistic activity, metaphysical, magical, and ecstatic were stimulated by the mysteries of the Book of Creation.

Gerard SEGARELLI   Founder of the Italian heresy known as the APOSTOLICI, Gerard Segarelli was inspired by the life of Saint Francis to reject all material possessions. In 1260, Segarelli started a small group in the city of Parma, dedicated to living the life of spiritual beggars. The idea proved popular among those who were poor already because Segarelli associated their poverty with holiness. The movement spread, and alarmed the Catholic Church into repeated condemnations. Segarelli was supported by many people in the northern Italian towns and ignored the calls of the bishops for him to disband the Apostolici. In 1294, the church escalated its tactics—four of Segarelli's followers were burned at the stake, and the leader himself was imprisoned. Even then, the movement continued to operate underground. Segarelli was burned to death in 1300, but the Apostolici persisted for another seven years.

Kondrati SELIVANOV   Founder of the notorious Russian sect called the SKOPTSY, Kondrati Selivanov was born in 1730. Around this time, the KHLYSTY movement was becoming popular in Russia. The Khlysty believed that people could stimulate spiritual progress by engaging in ritual dancing while being whipped. Selivanov became a Khlyst, but he was disappointed when he learned that the Khlysty condoned sexual relations (as long as the participants were *not* married to each other). At the age of twenty-six, Selivanov began to preach that sex was the root of all evil, and that a truly spiritual person would totally abstain from it. To underline his commitment to his beliefs, he had himself castrated.

Selivanov's followers were called *Skoptsy*, or "eunuchs"; many of the men were voluntarily castrated, and the women had their breasts cut off. Although the orthodox church opposed Selivanov, many were impressed by his spirituality. His enemies triumphed, but only temporarily. He was declared insane and sent into exile in Siberia. He managed to return, however, and was honored by a visit from a curious Tsar Alexander I in St. Petersburg. After being recognized by the tsar, Selivanov's opponents could not touch him. He died in a monastery in 1832. The movement he founded has endured into the twentieth century.

SEMI-ARIANISM   Semi-Arianism is a variant term for the HOMOIOUSIANS, a moderate group within the fourth century Christian heresy called ARIANISM.

SEMI-PELAGIANISM   In the fifth century, a debate raged concerning human nature. On one hand, the heresy known as PELAGIANISM maintained that everyone has free will. According to the Pelagians, it is possible always to do good, thereby earning one's way into heaven. On the other hand, orthodox Catholics, led by Augustine of Hippo, held that human willpower is so weak that people cannot resist sinning. The orthodox argued that no one can be good enough to merit salvation, but God in His mercy has chosen an undeserving few for eternal life. The movement that historians label Semi-Pelagianism appeared as a compromise between the extreme positions of the Pelagians and the followers of Augustine.

It is thought that JOHN CASSIAN, who was one of the first active Christian monks in fifth century Gaul (later France), founded Semi-Pelagianism. He sided with Augustine in his view that no one can earn salvation without the grace of God. Like the Pelagians, Cassian believed that the human will has an important role to play in attaining heaven: each person must freely choose to live in obedience to God before the Lord will grant His grace.

The roles of the human will and divine grace in achieving salvation was debated among Roman Catholics well into the sixth century. Finally, at the Council of Orange in 529, church leaders condemned the Semi-Pelagian view and upheld Augustine's belief in the inadequacy of the human will. The Augustinian position on the will was the official view during the Middle Ages. However, many people still believed that their personal efforts had some bearing on their spiritual lives. Indeed, by the time of the Protestant Reformation in the sixteenth century, the belief that one could earn redemption by performing good works was so widely accepted by Catholics that the Reformers denounced Roman Catholicism for having abandoned Augustine.

See also: FAUSTUS OF RIEZ.

SERGIO   Leader of the PAULICIAN heretics during the first part of the ninth century, Sergio was born into an orthodox Christian family that lived in the border region between the Byzantine Empire and Armenia. He converted to the heresy when a Paulician friend convinced him to read the Bible for himself; among the orthodox, Bible reading was reserved for priests. During his tenure as leader of the sect, violent oppression by the Byzantines was increasing. Paulicians, traditional pacifists, were joining the army of the Arabs to the south in order to fight Byzantium. Sergio argued against this change in direction; he believed that Paulicians should stay apart from such worldly activities as fighting because the world itself is evil. But he was unable to stop the increasing militarism of his fellow heretics. Sergio died in 834.

SERGIUS   Patriarch of Constantinople during the seventh century, Sergius was associated with various views concerning the nature of Christ that were later declared heretical. He wished to reconcile the heretical followers of MONOPHYSITISM with the orthodox church. To achieve this end, he devised the notion of MONENERG-ISM: Christ has two natures (divine and human), but a single *energeia*, or mode of activity. In consultation with POPE HONORIUS, Sergius changed the idea to MONOTHELETISM: Christ has two natures but only one will. The THIRD COUN-CIL OF CONSTANTINOPLE in 681 condemned both of Sergius's doctrines.

Michael SERVETUS   Although he lived to be only forty-two, Michael Servetus made significant contributions to Western culture. As an early medical researcher, he discovered the phenomenon of blood exchange between the heart and lungs. As a heretic, he is regarded as the founder of UNITARIANISM, although this term was not used until several decades after his death.

Servetus was born in 1511 in the Navarre region of northern Spain. He became fascinated with the nature of God early in life and devoted himself to theological studies. During this time, the Protestant Reformation was challenging the authority of Roman Catholic tradition. At the center of this tradition was the ancient description of God as a Trinity subsisting in Father, Son, and Holy Spirit. Until Servetus turned his attention to the doctrine, it had rarely been questioned since its firm establishment in the fourth century.

In 1531, he wrote a work called *On the Errors of the Trinity*. In the text, Servetus concludes that the Father and Son do not share the same divine substance, a key component of trinitarian belief. Instead, Servetus argues, the Son, although divine, was a separate being in his substance and his personhood. This idea echoed the ancient heresy of ARIANISM, which orthodoxy had fought to extinguish for centuries.

The theologian's friends were so shocked at his idea that they persuaded him to leave the field of theology and take up the less controversial career of medicine. Servetus went to Paris, where he studied to become a physician. Eventually, he became the physician of the archbishop of Vienne in France, a post he held for twelve years. As noted earlier, he was as innovative in his medical research as in his theological work.

Servetus's interest in religious thought would not be stifled, however. He wrote to Protestant leader John Calvin, attempting to persuade him to reject the doctrine of the Trinity as part of his reforms. Instead, Calvin came to loathe Servetus, vowing that the Spaniard would be treated without mercy if he ever set foot in Geneva, Calvin's base.

In 1553, Servetus published another text, *Christianity Restored*. In it, he again denounced the Trinity as a false view without foundation in scripture. He also took aim at other venerable Catholic beliefs, such as the notion that God has predestined some people for salvation, and the spiritual validity of infant baptism. Although Servetus did not sign his work because he was aware of the dangers of heresy, an agent of Calvin discovered his identity and informed the INQUISITION. The famous doctor was suddenly thrown into prison.

The resourceful heretic managed to escape a short time later, only to make a fatal error. To flee the Catholic Inquisitors, Servetus went to Protestant-controlled Geneva, in the belief that he would be safe there. Upon his arrival, he began to preach his provocative doctrine. Calvin arranged for Servetus's arrest, and he stood trial for heresy.

Acquittal would have been a blow to Calvin's prestige and power in Geneva, so he used his influence to ensure a guilty verdict. The punishment was death by fire. Calvin softened somewhat toward his adversary at this point: he requested that Servetus be granted the more humane method of execution by strangulation. However, the town council, perhaps annoyed at Calvin's earlier manipulations, denied the request. On October 27, 1553, the heretic was burned at the stake. With his dying breath, he called out to the divine being he had been convicted of offending: "O Jesus, thou Son of the eternal God, have pity on me."

This spectacle intimidated all opposition to Calvin in Geneva. Following Servetus's death, there was little resistance to the imposition of Calvin's strict moral rules on the citizens of the Genevan republic, and any deviation, such as dancing or playing games, met with swift consequences.

Servetus's challenge to the centerpiece of orthodox theology was not forgotten, however. His writings affected some radical Protestant thinkers, such as FAUSTUS SOCINUS, and they spread the anti-Trinitarian view that came to be called *Unitarianism*. Servetus's fiery death has also left its mark. Many historians consider Calvin's participation in the murder of Servetus to be one of the most shameful blots on the story of Protestantism.

SETHIAN GNOSTICISM   The Sethians were a Christian school within the GNOSTIC movement, which competed with the Catholic Church during the first centuries A.D. The Sethians' own writings were destroyed by the Catholics, so one must rely on the descriptions of the Sethians given by their orthodox opponents. The Sethians themselves seem to have vanished by the fourth century.

The Sethians believed that the world was created not by God, but by lower supernatural beings they called ANGELS. Sethian Gnosticism maintained that the world is composed of three elements: light, darkness, and spirit. These forces are represented by Abel, Cain, and Seth, the three sons of Adam in the Old Testament. Abel and Cain symbolize two groups of angels who are struggling for supremacy, and thereby bring suffering to the world. Seth was chosen by the divine Mother to be the bearer of purity and salvation. The task of salvation is to free the spiritual element from being trapped within the world the angels created.

The Sethians viewed human history as the turbulence created by the warring angels, the Mother's attempts to destroy those under their control (the descendants of Cain and Abel), and the angels' evasions of the Mother. JESUS was thought to be the descendant of Seth, or Seth himself, returned to bring knowledge of salvation. The Sethians rejected the orthodox doctrine that Jesus was resurrected in His physical body following the crucifixion. They claimed that most of the disciples had mistakenly taken the ghostly body in which the risen Christ appeared to be material. The wise few, to whom Jesus revealed His true resurrected nature as a spirit, were the Sethians.

SEVENTH DAY ADVENTISTS   The Seventh Day Adventist movement was born out of the anxieties and disappointments of America in the 1840s. Prophet William MILLER had announced Christ's return for three successive dates in 1843 and 1844; after the third failed prediction, his followers scattered. But three groups of MILLERITES revised their faith enough to keep it and formally established the Seventh Day Adventist Church in 1860.

The Lord had not appeared on schedule, Millerite Hiram Edson discovered through revelation, because Christ was busy cleansing heaven in preparation for the momentous occasion. Other revelations, as well as clever interpretations of obscure Bible passages, followed. It was reported, for example, that before His establishment of the heavenly kingdom on earth, Christ must assess all human beings in terms of their sinfulness and decide their fate. This takes time. When the Lord has completed His research, He will come.

Another reason proposed to explain the delay was that Christians on earth neglected certain laws of the Old Testament, particularly the prohibition on eating pork and the tradition of keeping the sabbath on Saturday. Hence, the movement's name: "Seventh Day" refers to their respect for Saturday, the seventh day of the week, and "Adventist" to their expectation of Christ's advent on earth.

Other curious beliefs of the Adventists include the notion that dead people are merely in a deep sleep. When Christ returns, the corpses of the righteous will reawaken. This interest in the physical body produced an emphasis on the maintenance of health. The consumption of alcohol and tobacco has always been forbidden in the movement, and healthy nutrition is urged. Perhaps as a result, the Seventh Day Adventists bear the distinction of having the longest life expectancy of any group in the United States.

See also: ELLEN G. WHITE.

SEVERUS   At the COUNCIL OF CHALCEDON in A.D. 451, orthodox Christianity defined its official position on the nature of Christ and condemned the alternative belief called MONOPHYSITISM. Severus was the first major leader to arise among the Monophysites following the council. He was born in Antioch, around 465. He was an eloquent defender of the Monophysite position that Christ had a single nature rather than the two natures specified by the Catholics. He must have been an impressive speaker, for he managed to convince Emperor Anastasius to protect a group of Monophysite monks who were being persecuted by the orthodox Christian powers, even though their beliefs were clearly heretical.

Severus was granted the influential position of bishop of Antioch by the emperor in 512. He became the leader of a "moderate" version of Monophysitism. Severus claimed that the orthodox teaching of two natures, divine and human, in Christ was wrong. He emphasized, however, that Christ was neither a mere human nor a nonhuman God, but was both human and God combined in a single nature.

Monophysites like Severus could maintain their positions within the church only with the support of the emperor because their beliefs went against the state religion of Catholic Christianity. When Anastasius was succeeded as emperor by Justin I in 518, Severus lost his imperial protection and was deposed as a heretic. He died in 538. Although orthodox authorities attempted to destroy his writings, many have survived to the present day—a surprising fact given that the penalty set for copying Severus's works was amputation of the hand.

SHABBATEANS   The unorthodox movement founded by SHABBATAI ZEVI and NATHAN OF GAZA, which recognized Zevi as the Messiah was established in 1665 and survived its leader's forced conversion to Islam the following year. The world view of the movement is derived from the Jewish mystical tradition of KABBALAH, as interpreted by Nathan. Many Shabbateans pretended to be orthodox Jews or Moslems and practiced their heretical devotions in secret to avoid persecution. In the mid-eighteenth century, JACOB FRANK led a Shabbatean group to convert superficially to Roman Catholicism while privately worshipping him as Zevi's reincarnation. Shabbatean communities have persisted into the twentieth century.

SHAKERS   This sect acquired its name from its practice of holding mass meetings during which members would become possessed by spiritual forces and tremble "like clouds agitated by a mighty wind," as one observer put it. Alternatively, they have been called JUMPERS and SHIVERERS. Although they suffered persecution in England and America and banned all sexual activity, the Shakers have managed to survive for almost 250 years.

The inspiration for Shakerism came from a French movement of the early eighteenth century, the CAMISARDS. When Camisard refugees, fleeing persecution in France, arrived in England in 1706, they attracted much comment because of their dramatic public rituals. During these performances, they would be seized by divine powers and fall into convulsions. Although most viewers ridiculed the practice, some people were impressed. During the first part of the century, Camisard missionaries traveled throughout Britain. By the 1740s, English groups had formed to practice the shaking trances.

The most important of these groups operated in Manchester. In 1758, a young Manchester woman named ANN LEE joined the movement and quickly became the leader. Guided by a vision, she led a Shaker mission to America in 1774. The first community was established in Watervliet, near Albany, New York. During the following decades, several more colonies were established in the northeastern United States.

In England, Shakerism declined rapidly following Lee's departure, but the nineteenth century saw the movement thrive in the New World. The Shakers reached their greatest popularity in the 1850s. It has been estimated that 6,000 members were active in America at that time. By 1900, their numbers had declined to about 1,000. Two small communities of Shakers still exist, in Canterbury, New Hampshire, and Sabbathday Lake, Maine.

The best-known doctrine of the Shakers is the notion that sex is the root of all evil. The serpent in the Garden of Eden awakened lust in Adam and Eve, which led to their fall. In order for people to lead a holy life, they must completely avoid sexual relations. Not only did Shakers abstain from intercourse, but a man and a woman were forbidden to be alone together, the viewing of mating animals was banned, and even playing with cats or dogs was considered too sensuous to be permitted. In a Shaker community around 1793, three girls who were caught staring at a pair of copulating flies were ordered to strip naked, whip each other, and then jump into a cold stream to purify themselves.

Under such conditions, there were obviously no Shaker babies. The movement maintained itself by inviting adoptions, and it became a home for many unwanted children who were then brought up in the Shaker faith. Although the Shakers did not preach to the general public, many adults wishing to escape from the pressures of conventional life (or, in some cases, from the law) joined as well.

The Shakers' rejection of sexual interest freed them from the battle of the sexes. Males and females were viewed as completely equal, a very rare perspective during the eighteenth and nineteenth centuries. God was regarded as both female and male. The Trinity of the Father, Son, and Holy Spirit was expanded by adding Mother Ann Lee as the female equivalent of Christ.

The Shakers saw themselves as returning to the lifestyle of the first apostles. They owned no private property and performed no activity for personal benefit. As a result, their communes were efficiently run and became well known for their orderliness and productivity. Other unorthodox communal movements of the nineteenth century, such as the ONEIDA COMMUNITY, based their social organizations on the Shaker model.

The religious rites of the Shakers more closely resembled those of ancient heresies, such as the MONTANISTS, than those of early orthodox communities. The Shakers would dance and clap, the men forming a ring around the women, and imagine that they were trampling the Devil underfoot. Often, members would become possessed by angels and speak in tongues; sometimes, animal spirits would intrude, and the members would find themselves barking like dogs, mewing like cats, or screeching like squirrels.

The Shakers also believed in communication with the dead. Visions were reported, as well as possession by spirits of the departed. All Shakers were thought to have invisible spirit guides to assist them throughout their lives and to welcome them into the world beyond at death. Today, almost all of the Shakers have passed into that world. Perhaps their best-known legacy is their wooden furniture, which is renowned for its simple elegance and is much sought after by collectors.

SHIVERERS   Shiverers is a variant name for SHAKERS.

SIGAN-FU STONE   A monument erected in A.D. 781 in China by missionaries spreading the heretical doctrines of NESTORIANISM. They likely arrived from Persia sometime in the preceding century and founded a Christian community in China that survived until the fourteenth century. The Sigan-Fu Stone is the earliest trace of the Christian faith in the Far East, proving that heretical Christianity preceded orthodox Christianity there by about 600 years.

SIMONIAN GNOSTICISM   This school was founded by the legendary figure of SIMON MAGUS. Scholars believe that there may have been more than one teacher named Simon active in first century Palestine, but it is impossible to sort them out today. The importance of the Simonians lies in the fact that their doctrines are the earliest known example of the influential spiritual movement called GNOSTICISM, which flourished in the Mediterranean regions during the first few centuries of the Christian era.

In the eyes of the early orthodox Christian community, the Simonians were the first heretics and the source of all other heresies. This assertion is certainly false. It is unlikely that the Simonians were even Christians, but rather were in direct competition with Christianity. One orthodox writer, Irenaeus of Lyons, noted the rumor that Simon Magus "suffered in Judaea, but he did not suffer." This passage seems to indicate that the legend of Christ's suffering had become confused with the story of Simon by the late second century. The cause for Christian concern is clear if the public was having trouble distinguishing Simon Magus from the Christians' own candidate for Messiah.

The doctrines of the Simonians included the typical Gnostic claim that the world had been created by a female power who had then become lost in her own creation. The deity from whom she had originated came to earth, in the form of Simon. His mission was to save her and to redeem all who believed in him.

According to their opponents' accounts, the Simonians conjured demons, made love potions, and encouraged unrestricted sex. It is unclear to what degree these descriptions are merely attempts to slander the Simonian school.

Simonian Gnosticism survived alongside the expanding community of Christians in the Roman Empire for more than 150 years. The first Simon was active around the middle of the first century. Church father ORIGEN, in his writings against paganism in the early third century, reported that there were fewer than thirty Simonians left by that time. In between, little is known about the history of the Simonians beyond the name of MENANDER, Simon's successor as leader of the movement.

SIMON MAGUS   The name of Simon Magus is one of the most notorious in the history of heresy. Second century orthodox Christian bishop Irenaeus of Lyons wrote that Simon was the man "from whom all the heresies take their origin," and throughout Christian history Simon has been a symbol of arrogance and pride. Simon and his followers are mentioned by several early Christian writers, and he appears briefly in the New Testament itself (Acts 8:9–25). Modern scholars believe that these sources might not all refer to the same individual. In addition to the Simon whom Peter the apostle encountered, there was likely another teacher, or possibly even two other teachers, named Simon who were active about a generation later. It is difficult to distinguish the identities of the various Simons, but they all seem to be early teachers of the spiritual movement known as GNOSTICISM.

In the Book of Acts, Simon is portrayed as a wandering magician who was converted to Christianity. He observed Peter transmitting the Holy Spirit into people through the practice of laying on of hands. Simon wished to acquire this ability himself and offered money to Peter in exchange for the secret. Simon responded to the inevitable rebuke by asking Peter to pray for him. From this story comes the word "simony," referring to the practice of buying positions of power within the church.

In later legend, the encounter between Simon Magus and Peter was elaborated. A popular story recounted how Simon challenged Peter to a contest of magical powers. Simon called on demons to carry him through the air and dared Peter to duplicate this feat. In response, Peter used the power of his prayer to dispel the demons, sending Simon crashing fatally to earth in another victory for Christian compassion. These tales are clearly orthodox propaganda and reveal nothing about the popular teacher or teachers named Simon Magus. The writings of Simon's school were burned long ago, but his opponents' accounts given of his teachings aid in reconstructing the general outline.

Simon's account of the world's creation is typically Gnostic. The cosmos was not created directly by God, but by a female emanation from him named "Ennoia," or "Thought." After she created the angels, they rebelled against her. Their assault was so ferocious that Ennoia became confused and forgot who she was. She wandered through successive reincarnations, becoming more confused, until she ended up as a prostitute named Helena in the Phoenician city of Tyre. (This strange notion of a prostitute as a divine being might be related to the ancient Phoenician custom of "sacred prostitution." In this practice, women representing the fertility goddess engaged in sex with men who gave financial offerings to maintain the goddess's temple.)

During Ennoia's amnesic wanderings, the angels tried to govern the world but fell to fighting among themselves over which angel was the greatest. As a result, the world became full of suffering, which was not the creator's intention. God, desiring to rescue Ennoia and to provide humanity with a means of salvation, decided to appear on earth. The role of the saving God on earth was filled by Simon himself. His girlfriend, the former prostitute Helena, was presented as the creator Ennoia, who had regained her memory thanks to Simon.

Simon taught that anyone who recognized him as God was saved. As a saved person, an individual no longer needed to obey the rules of conventional morality because the angels created such restrictions to keep people enslaved. Two of the orthodox sources, Irenaeus and Hippolytus, reported that Simon's followers engaged in unrestricted sexual activity. Such behavior would not be surprising among people who worshipped a prostitute as the creator of the world.

See also: SIMONIAN GNOSTICISM.

Menno SIMONS   This Dutch preacher was the most important leader in the unorthodox ANABAPTIST movement of the sixteenth century. Menno Simons saved the movement from extinction following the crushing of the MÜNSTER HERETICS in 1535 and established the most enduring Anabaptist group, the MENNONITES. Simons was born in the Low Countries in 1496. Drawn early to religion, he became acquainted with Christian writings in both Latin and Greek and was ordained a Catholic priest in 1524. By that time, the Protestant Reformation had begun. In the prevailing mood of questioning existing dogmas, Simons examined current beliefs and did not like what he found.

Regarding the Catholic position, Simons doubted the orthodox understanding of the Mass. Orthodoxy held that Christ possessed a body made of ordinary human flesh; it also insisted that Christ's body was physically present every time a Mass was celebrated. How could this be? Simons concluded that Anabaptist prophet MELCHIOR HOFFMANN was correct in teaching that Christ's body was not composed of earthly matter, but of a divine substance.

Simons also found fault with mainstream Protestantism, especially in its conviction that the baptism of infants was valid. Simons concluded from his Bible studies that the baptism of only consenting adults was acceptable to God. Thus, he found himself in closer agreement with the Anabaptists than with orthodoxy.

In 1536, Simons publicly renounced his role as a Catholic priest and was rebaptized as an Anabaptist preacher. This was a brave move; the bloody events of Münster the preceding year had tainted the image of Anabaptists, and Simons immediately became a target for orthodox persecution.

For the next seven years, Simons wandered in the Netherlands and Germany, risking his life to spread the Anabaptist word. He eventually found a safe haven in Denmark but continued on preaching missions through dangerous territories until his death in 1561. He encouraged Anabaptists to give up the violent approach to establishing God's kingdom taken by the Münsterites. Simons focused attention on the importance of the Mass; rejecting the idea that mere earthly flesh was present, he believed that Christ's heavenly body was involved. Communion with this body was held to be so sacred that only pure Christians should have access to it. As a result, Simons insisted on the highest level of moral discipline among his followers and enforced swift excommunication for any deviation.

Simons's moderate doctrines and strict morality appealed to Anabaptists who wished to disown the excesses of Münster. Communities of Simons's followers survived the period of persecutions, especially in the Netherlands, despite the violence orthodox Christians inflicted on them.

SKOPTSY   An eastern European sect that originated in eighteenth century Russia, the Skoptsy were notorious for acts of religious self-mutilation. Their name means "the castrated ones" in the Russian tongue. During the mid-1700s, the Russian Orthodox Church split into two branches. The more traditional branch, known as the Old Believers, continued to fragment into sects and generated some heresies. One such group was the KHLYSTY, from which the Skoptsy emerged. The Khlysty combined ancient shamanic rituals with Christian ideas and celebrated a ritual in which some of the participants danced and received whippings until they passed into a state of possession by the Holy Spirit. They also condoned extramarital sex; for the leaders of the movement, no moral restrictions existed.

A peasant named KONDRATI SELIVANOV rejected the sexual freedoms of other Khlysty heretics. Instead, he preached that the spiritual path required the complete suppression of sexuality. To demonstrate his seriousness, he announced that he would undergo a "baptism of fire," and had himself castrated.

Selivanov attracted many followers, who could not doubt his sincerity (although the authorities did question his sanity), and the Skoptsy movement was born. Skoptsy men were permitted to father a few children before undergoing their own bloody baptism; many Skoptsy women cut off their breasts. Flagellation was also encouraged to suppress worldly desires.

Such extremes put the Skoptsy movement far beyond the bounds of orthodoxy. Although third century theologian ORIGEN had castrated himself as a religious act, such feats of mutilation had been forbidden by the FIRST COUNCIL OF NICAEA in 325.

While church officials disapproved of the sect, the radical spiritual commitment and work ethic of the Skoptsy evoked awe and reverence from many others; Tsar Alexander I himself paid a visit to Selivanov. The movement spread throughout central Russia. In the face of persecution, some Skoptsy fled to remote regions of Siberia and to the islands of the Danube River Delta in Romania.

The sect survived into the present century. A Soviet source indicated that in 1929, about 2,000 Skoptsy lived in the Soviet Union. During World War II, many Skoptsy were killed, along with millions of other Russians. After the war, an outbreak of breast amputations among mourning Skoptsy women was reported. The last known castration among the sect was recorded in 1951. There may still be a few adherents of this unique belief system in Romania, Moldova, or Russia today.

See also: FLAGELLANTS.

Joseph SMITH   The founder of the MORMONS, Joseph Smith was born in 1805 in Sharon, Vermont. During his childhood, he moved to Palmyra in western New York with his parents. At the time, various Protestant denominations competed for converts in the area. Joseph and his father were more concerned with attempting to find buried treasure; they tried various occult methods to detect the location of pirate hordes, and the vicinity of their home was pocked with their excavations. As Joseph entered his mid-teens, however, religious questions became more important to him.

In 1820, Smith later recounted, he was praying alone in the woods, asking for divine guidance about which version of Christianity was correct. God the Father and Christ appeared in a vision. They informed him that every type of Christianity had become corrupt. This experience marked the beginning of a series of revelations over the next ten years that would form the basis of the Mormon faith.

Smith published the text of a mysterious document in 1830. He supposedly unearthed THE BOOK OF MORMON, as he called it, near Palmyra by following directions given to Smith by an angel. Smith announced that he had been called to establish the true faith and promoted his book as an important revelation. In the atmosphere of spiritual questing that characterized the period, Smith's claim quickly attracted attention. Some hailed him as a prophet, although many others thought he was a charlatan and a heretic.

Smith's declaration that all beliefs except his own were false provoked persecution. In 1831, Smith moved to Ohio with a band of his followers and constructed the first Mormon temple. He continued to receive divine messages, which he collected in another text Mormons revered, *The Doctrines and Covenants*. Here, Smith gave his movement the name by which its major branch is still known today, the CHURCH OF JESUS CHRIST OF LATTER-DAY SAINTS.

Soon, Smith had made enemies in the region. On one occasion, a mob tarred and feathered him. In 1838, he led his disciples into Missouri. He received no welcome there; the state governor viewed him as a troublemaker, and Smith was briefly jailed. The Mormon prophet and his followers were ordered to leave Missouri before the end of the year. They then moved to Illinois. Smith decided to establish a Mormon community there; in 1839, he founded the settlement of Nauvoo. Mormon missionary activities were showing some success, and converts were flocking to Smith. Nauvoo expanded quickly, becoming the largest city in the state.

Smith believed that the ancient Egyptians were connected with his revelations; he had translated *The Book of Mormon* from a language called "Reformed Egyptian." He acquired an ancient Egyptian mummy and published a text supposedly based on inscriptions found on the mummy. Mormons accept this work, entitled *The Pearl of Great Price*, as divine revelation. In the 1970s, Smith's mummy, long thought to be lost, was rediscovered and studied by non-Mormon experts. The inscriptions on the mummy were found to have no relation to the contents of *The Pearl of Great Price*.

During the Nauvoo period, the prophet introduced his most controversial practice: the taking of multiple wives. Smith set an example; no precise count of his spouses is available, but estimates range from twenty-seven to eighty-four. The prophet's new message and behavior prompted a split in the movement. Sidney Rigdon, one of the most senior Mormons, left after accusing Smith of attempting to seduce his daughter. When a dissident group started to publish a newspaper attacking polygamy, Smith ordered the paper destroyed.

Smith's promotion of polygamy and his use of violence to suppress opposition were beyond the tolerance of many non-Mormons in Illinois. In 1844, the Mormon leader and his brother, Hyrum, were arrested and jailed in Carthage, Illinois. A group of the prophet's enemies broke into the jail and murdered them both. Within a few years, Nauvoo was abandoned. Controversy over whom should succeed Smith as leader fractured Mormonism into several branches, but it has continued to thrive to the present day.

Mormons still revere Smith as the most important figure in the movement's history. The main group of Mormons renounced the practice of polygamy, which cost Smith the unity of his following and his life, in 1890 under pressure from the United States government. His written revelations continue to form the core of Mormon belief.

SNAKE HANDLERS   The practice of handling live poisonous snakes in religious rituals can be found in Asia, Africa, Europe, and North America. Its best-known manifestation occurs in a Christian sect that has congregations in isolated rural settings scattered across the eastern United States. Although some researchers have speculated that this sect was inspired by snake cults among Native Americans, most agree that its basis is the New Testament. The Gospel of Mark (16:17–18) states, "And these signs shall follow them that believe; In my name shall they cast out devils; they shall speak with new tongues; They shall take up serpents; and if they drink any deadly thing, it shall not hurt them; they shall lay hands on the sick, and they shall recover." This passage summarizes the main practices of the American snake-handling sect.

In 1909, fundamentalist GEORGE HENSLEY introduced snake handling to congregations in Tennessee and Kentucky. In the years that followed, the practice spread from Ohio to Florida, and even to California. Some states tried to ban religious snake-handling, but such efforts failed to stop an activity its practitioners believed to be ordained by God.

The touching of snakes usually occurs during the climax of lengthy church services that last several hours. Sermons are preached, hymns are chanted, and rhythmic clapping is performed. Many church members become possessed by the Holy Spirit; they babble in unknown tongues and shake uncontrollably. When a signal is given, a box is opened at the front of the church, revealing a writhing mass of venomous creatures. Copperheads, rattlesnakes, and water moccasins are preferred. Anyone who wishes to demonstrate faith in God may then pick them up. Participants drape the snakes on their bodies, kiss them, and tread on them.

The snakes react predictably to such treatment. Snake handlers have been bitten, and many, including the movement's founder, have died as a result. Medical treatment is refused; if the bitten person dies, it is believed that the individual has passed the test of faith and has gone straight to the Lord. Even children are encouraged to take such risks; as one snake-handling father said, "I'd rather lose a child now and have it go to heaven than keep it 100 years and have it go to hell."

Multiple bites do not seem to discourage devotees. The champion in this regard may be Dewey Chapin, bitten ninety-one times during his snake-handling career. One observer described a woman who, during a service, passionately kissed a snake along the length of its body, despite being repeatedly struck.

In addition to touching snakes, many members of this sect drink strychnine during church services. Again, fatalities have resulted. Exposing one's flesh to fire is another way to demonstrate trust in God.

Such practices flourish in poor communities that have limited access to the benefits of modern culture. Snake-handling demonstrates to them that they are spiritually superior to the mainstream, even though they are materially deprived. As modern communication technology reduces the isolation of the snake-handling communities, the frequency of these hazardous performances can be expected to decline.

SOCIETY FOR THE REPARATION OF SOULS   A religious organization founded in France in the late nineteenth century by Abbé BOULLAN and his assistant, the Society for the Reparation of Souls was a front for unorthodox practices, including, most likely, human sacrifice.

SOCINIANISM   Socinianism is an unorthodox religious movement founded in the late sixteenth century by FAUSTUS SOCINUS, after whom it is named. The Socinians, who discarded the doctrine of the Trinity held by orthodox Catholics and Protestants, founded churches and schools in Poland, Lithuania, Hungary, and Transylvania during the 1500s and 1600s. In 1658, a Catholic resurgence forced the Socinians to flee to Transylvania and the Netherlands. Their teachings reached England, promoting ANTI-TRINITARIAN thought there. Socinianism is regarded as an early variant of UNITARIANISM.

Faustus SOCINUS   Despite their conflicts during the sixteenth century Reformation and Counter-Reformation, Catholics and mainstream Protestants remained in agreement concerning the doctrine of the Trinity. This central feature of orthodoxy, that God subsists in the three Persons of Father, Son, and Holy Spirit, was challenged by MICHAEL SERVETUS; his ANTI-TRINITARIAN position inspired Faustus Socinus to establish a new unorthodox church. This organization, called the SOCINIANS after its founder, developed into UNITARIANISM.

Socinus was born in the Italian city of Siena in 1539, three years after Servetus wrote his first attack on Trinitarian doctrine. Laelius, Socinus's uncle, tended toward Protestant beliefs of an unorthodox sort; he protested the execution of Servetus, which had been arranged by Protestant leader John Calvin, and had serious disagreements with mainstream Protestant theologians. Laelius had a strong influence on Socinus's thinking.

During Socinus's young adulthood, he conformed outwardly to Catholicism while he nurtured radical Protestant thoughts. He worked for many years as a court secretary in Florence, but he eventually departed for the Swiss town of Basel; he hoped to find a more tolerant atmosphere where he could openly express his beliefs. From there, he moved to the relatively permissive land of Transylvania, and then to Poland, where he lived from 1579 until his death in 1604.

Socinus agreed with Servetus that Christ was not the same as God the Father and that, therefore, the Trinitarian doctrine was false. Socinus went further than Servetus in his heresy. Servetus still believed that Christ was a divine being; Socinus taught that JESUS had been a mere man, although an extraordinary one. Socinus also disagreed with the orthodox notion that Christ's death was a sacrifice to atone for humanity's sins. Instead, Christ was a role model: if people follow His example and live a spiritual life, they will be granted eternal life.

The Italian heretic made a major impact in Poland, which at the time was the most tolerant country in Europe. There was already a group of Anti-Trinitarians in Poland when Socinus arrived, but they were of the TRITHEISTIC variety; they held that the three Persons of the Trinity were separate, divine beings, all of whom should be worshipped. Socinus, however, refused to worship Christ. Eventually, many Polish Anti-Trinitarians converted to Socinus's view. The movement Socinus founded thrived in Poland until the Jesuits suppressed it in 1658. His ideas were also well received in Lithuania and Transylvania. From these central European Socinian groups, the views of Socinus were eventually transmitted to England, where they played a part in establishing Unitarian doctrines in the English-speaking world.

SPANISH ADOPTIONISM   The ancient Christian heresy of ADOPTIONISM stated that JESUS was merely a human being adopted by God, rather than a divine being by nature. The view that Jesus was fully divine as well as fully human was fixed as orthodox doctrine by the mid-fifth century, and Adoptionism was almost forgotten. Toward the end of the eighth century, however, a new version of the old heresy resurfaced in Spain, with important consequences for the development of medieval religion and politics.

During the early eighth century, Moslem armies had overrun Spain and had even occupied southern France for a short time. Under Moslem rule, the Spanish Church was tolerated, but it was cut off from the mainstream of European Christian culture. In its relative isolation and beyond the influence of the pope, Spanish Christianity began to deviate from orthodox Catholic beliefs.

Pope Hadrian tried to return the Spanish Church to papal control, even though he could not use force to do so because of the Moslem presence. His representatives in Toledo, the seat of the Spanish archbishop, insisted on doctrinal reforms in accordance with the wishes of Rome. In response, Archbishop ELIPANDUS accused the Roman Catholics of teaching heresies and presented his own statement of faith. This document no longer exists. The descriptions of Elipandus's statement by his enemies indicates that it contained the basic doctrines that came to be called Spanish Adoptionism.

At issue was the relationship between the divine and human natures of Christ. Elipandus and the Romans accepted that Christ had both natures. Elipandus held that the human nature had been adopted by the Son of God, who was one of the divine Persons of the Holy Trinity. The Spanish position implied that Jesus Christ was a "son" in two different ways: Jesus was the *adopted son* of God, and Christ was the *divine Son*, God Himself. This emphasis on Jesus' humanity may have been an attempt to make Christianity more attractive to the followers of Islam. Moslems could not accept the orthodox Christian claim that the man who had been crucified was a fully divine being.

According to the pope, Elipandus's doctrine of "double sonship" was heretical. It resembled the despised heresy called NESTORIANISM, which emphasized the difference between Christ's divine and human natures to such a degree that Christ was virtually split into two unrelated parts. Elipandus took exception to this interpretation and, in response, accused the Romans of MONOPHYSITISM, a heresy that denied that Christ had a full human nature.

The Spanish archbishop recruited support for his cause among regional bishops, and convinced Bishop FELIX of Urgel to become his ally. Meanwhile, Frankish ruler Charlemagne had become interested in the debate. He had plans to conquer Spain and believed that strengthening the Roman Catholic influence in the area might help him to do so.

Elipandus ignored the condemnations and calls for theological correctness that the Roman Catholics issued, and he continued to do so until his death. Felix was invited to the court of Charlemagne twice to discuss matters with leading theologians; on his way back to Spain from the second visit, he was detained at Lyons in

Frankish territory. He remained there for the rest of his life under the supervision of papal authorities.

Spanish Adoptionism was declared a heresy in a series of European church councils. Historically, the most important of these meetings was the Council of Frankfurt, which Charlemagne called in 794. For the first time, a pope had arranged a major meeting of Catholic leaders without involving either the Byzantine emperor or the Eastern branch of the Catholic Church. This event signaled the independence of the West from Byzantine domination in both the political and spiritual domains.

The memory of Elipandus's heretical dismissal of the pope produced a lasting mistrust of Spanish Christianity on the part of Roman Catholic authorities. As European forces gradually drove the Moslems from Spain, "liberated" Spanish Christians were accused of harboring all sorts of unorthodox ideas, and purges were frequent. This hostile legacy continued for centuries afterward; from the later Middle Ages to the mid-nineteenth century, the rigorously orthodox SPANISH INQUISITION was notorious for its ferocious and thorough heresy hunts.

The challenge of Spanish Adoptionism provided a stimulus to the development of medieval theology. Unable immediately to suppress the heresy through force, European thinkers were left to devise ingenious theological attacks. Indeed, some of the great medieval thinkers embraced Adoptionism. In the eleventh century, Adoptionist arguments appeared again, championed by theologian PETER ABELARD, among others.

SPANISH INQUISITION   The Inquisition in Spain had a different character than the INQUISITION taking place throughout the rest of Europe. The Spanish Catholic Church traditionally resisted tight control by the pope. The Spanish Inquisition was more closely tied to the Spanish government than to the international Catholic community. For this reason, the GREAT WITCH HUNT, which papal Inquisitors promoted in the rest of Europe largely bypassed Spain.

The Inquisition was established in Spain in 1479 by Ferdinand and Isabella, whose marriage united the regions of Castile and Aragon to form the Spanish nation. Spain contained many Jews, Moslems, and Christians, but the non-Christians had been forced to convert to Christianity. The depth of commitment to Christ held by these involuntary converts was questionable. The first task of the Spanish Inquisitors was to investigate claims that Jews and Moslems had retained their old beliefs and practices.

The name of the first Grand Inquisitor in Spain became the most notorious one in the history of the Inquisition. Tomas de Torquemada was a Dominican friar who enthusiastically pursued his suspicions regarding unorthodox views. He favored the liberal use of torture to gather evidence and did not hesitate to execute convicted heretics. Torquemada is thought to have burned more than 2,000 people during his tenure.

In addition to Jewish and Moslem individuals suspected of relapsing, the Spanish Inquisition pursued astrologers and other fortune-tellers, possessors of GRIMOIRES, and even keepers of lucky charms. The Spanish authorities were divided during the 1500s as to whether magic and fortune-telling were heretical, and whether the Inquisition or the secular courts should deal with these matters. In 1600, the Inquisition was officially given the duty to persecute magicians and diviners.

The sixteenth century saw witch trials in great numbers outside Spain. The Spanish Inquisition burned relatively few witches during this period. The fantasies that fueled the witch hunt, concerning a widespread Satanic cult with supernatural abilities, were not taken seriously by most of the Spanish Inquisitors. There were some outbreaks of witch hunting in the region during the 1600s, but there were fewer executions for witchcraft in Spain than elsewhere in Europe.

Spain's isolation from mainstream European opinion had its drawbacks. By the eighteenth century, most of Europe had officially abandoned belief in the powers of witches and magicians, but the Spanish Inquisition continued to persecute accused individuals. The last execution by burning at the stake occurred at Seville in 1781. The Inquisition in Spain persisted in imprisoning people for BLASPHEMY and making a PACT with the Devil until it was finally abolished in 1834.

See also: AUTO-DA-FE.

Hugo SPERONI   Hugo Speroni was the founder of the HUMILIATI, an Italian movement that was briefly declared heretical during the late twelfth century. Between 1164 and 1171, Speroni preached in northern Italy. He declared that the sacraments and wealth of the Catholic Church were of no help in living a spiritual life, and encouraged his listeners to adopt a simple lifestyle of work and prayer. In 1184, the members of the movement he founded were excommunicated. They were readmitted into the Catholic community in 1200, when they agreed to submit to the authority of the Church.

SPIRITUAL FRANCISCANS   The life of Saint Francis of Assisi, which lasted from 1181 to 1226, had a huge impact on the later Middle Ages. Francis founded an important order of friars, the Franciscans, which tried to carry on his work following his death. Like most such attempts, the Franciscans were soon quarreling among themselves about how best to preserve their founder's vision. The Spirituals, one branch of the new order, became involved with unorthodox ideas and eventually veered into heresy.

Saint Francis insisted that his followers give up all of their property and take a vow of poverty. During the first decades of the Franciscan order, tension arose concerning this point. One group, the Conventuals, argued that the Franciscan order needed wealth and property in order to survive and to continue preaching. The Spirituals, on the other hand, insisted on absolute poverty. Christ and the apostles had owned nothing, they observed, and the Franciscans should follow their example.

The Catholic Church found the poverty of the Franciscans useful. The most dangerous heresies of the time, the CATHARS and WALDENSIANS, impressed the poor by attacking the materialism of the orthodox church; the Franciscans could compete against these heretics without themselves having to face accusations of worldly corruption. However, the Catholics could not permit placing too much emphasis on the value of poverty: the popes considered accumulating treasure and power for themselves a priority. As a result, the Conventuals, not the Spirituals, tended to receive papal support. In 1279, Pope Nicholas III proclaimed that the Franciscan order could have property and wealth, although technically the pope would still own it.

By the mid-1200s, some Spirituals had become intrigued by the prophecies of JOACHIM OF FIORE. This contemporary of Saint Francis proclaimed the imminent dawning of a new age, when monks who owned nothing would govern the church. Was this a prediction that the Spirituals would inherit the church? By the end of the century, some prominent Spiritual Franciscans, such as PIERRE OLIVI, described the present church as the "whore of Babylon." He taught that following a time of persecution, the Spirituals would form the basis for a renewed church of the Holy Spirit.

The debate over the correctness of poverty threatened to tear the Franciscan order apart. Pope John XXII intervened on the side of the Conventuals. In 1317, he denounced the Spirituals as heretics; in 1323, he proclaimed that anyone who believed that JESUS and the apostles had been poor was guilty of heresy. The Spirituals now faced terrible persecution, including torture and death at the stake. Some of the condemned friars received protection from Holy Roman Emperor LOUIS OF BAVARIA, whom the pope excommunicated for sheltering heretics.

Following their official dissolution, the Spiritual Franciscans carried on in secret or retreated to remote regions beyond the reach of the Inquisitors. During the fourteenth and fifteenth centuries, they were best known as the FRATICELLI. Under constant pressure from the orthodox authorities, their numbers gradually declined. The last major trial of the Fraticelli took place in Rome in 1466.

SPIRITUALISM   This influential movement arose in the mid-1800s and continues to have a significant following today. Spiritualism is rooted in one of the fundamental human concerns: whether any aspect of a person survives death. The reality traditions of most cultures include the notion of survival. Many societies also believe in the possibility of communicating with the dead. In Western culture, the practices of NECROMANCY were generally discredited with the triumph of scientific thinking in the 1700s. Hopes regarding an afterlife continued, however, and blazed forth again among the Spiritualists during the next century.

In the early 1800s, several influences converged to lay the groundwork for the rise of Spiritualism. The scientific attitude, which requires empirical evidence rather than faith as a basis for belief, became dominant among the educated classes. At the same time, people continued to have experiences that failed to fit neatly into the scientific view of the world; sightings of ghosts and apparent instances of clairvoyance were still being reported. Such experiences suggested that there might be more to the human personality than a mere mechanism.

A third factor was the writings of EMANUEL SWEDENBORG. A respected inventor and scientist, Swedenborg claimed to have established contact with heaven and described it in terms that were more appealing to his contemporaries than earlier versions. According to Swedenborg, the afterworld is not a static place of eternal harp-playing or hellfire; rather, it is a continuation of life's activities. In heaven, people have bodies and meet deceased relatives; most important, people continue to undergo spiritual development, digesting the lessons of life and encountering new challenges. As the Industrial Revolution got underway, driven by the dream of never-ending progress on earth, Swedenborg's vision of a progressive heaven made sense. Although relatively few people actually joined the SWEDENBORGIAN Church, its founder's ideas enjoyed wide circulation.

The cultural atmosphere was ripe for a movement that could offer scientific evidence for the existence of a progressive afterlife. The spark that triggered this movement occurred in 1848 in the village of Hydesville, New York. The Fox family, which included three young daughters, were annoyed by mysterious rapping sounds until the girls discovered that the rappings responded to questions. The daughters established a code and found that the raps claimed to be manifestations of departed spirits. Journalists circulated the story; eventually, the Fox sisters went on performing tours. Many years later, one of the sisters confessed that the sounds had been made by the girls themselves, by cracking their joints. By then, however, Spiritualism had become the passion of millions.

Before the Fox phenomenon was exposed as a hoax, it inspired others to attempt communication with the dead. Within a few years, specialists in this art, known as mediums, traveled throughout North America and Europe and attracted large audiences. It appeared as if anyone who cared to hold a seance or visit a medium could obtain proof of an afterlife. As early as the mid-1850s, it has been estimated that between 2 and 4 million people had become involved in Spiritualism.

Spiritualists tended to resist the development of any universal dogma or centralized authority. As a result, the beliefs of Spiritualist organizations evolved in different directions. Many Spiritualists were Christians. These people believed that the messages of the spirits confirmed the teachings of Christ: There is an afterlife where goodness is rewarded. Others held that Spiritualism pointed to universal truths underlying all the major religions. Still others viewed the movement as a new religion, rendering all beliefs based on mere faith obsolete. In England and the United States, where Spiritualism was strongest, the Swedenborgian model of heaven dominated. An alternative version of Spiritualism, which emphasized the doctrine of REINCARNATION, thrived in South America.

Spiritualism developed or absorbed a wide array of methods for communicating with the dead. These approaches are usually grouped into two categories: physical mediumship and mental mediumship. Physical mediums called on the spirits to manifest themselves through rappings, movements of objects, writing messages on slates, mysterious voices, and even materializations. Mental mediums allegedly used psychic abilities to hear or see the departed ones and then conveyed their messages to the living. Alternately, these mediums invited the spirits to take possession of their own bodies and to speak using their vocal cords. Some mediums used both physical and mental approaches.

While many Spiritualists believed that their activities were "scientific," most people who were actually trained in science were more cautious. The possibilities for fraud in darkened seance rooms were numerous, and the human capacity for wishful thinking was well known. A few scientists did not dismiss out of hand the possibility that some of the reported phenomena were genuine, however. Serious research into accounts of paranormal occurrences began in 1882 with the founding of the Society for Psychical Research in London, England, largely in response to the curiosity Spiritualist claims aroused.

Scientific investigation of mediumistic phenomena has uncovered many instances of fraud and self-delusion. But not all cases have been easily explained in such terms. Some of the early researchers became converts to Spiritualism. Even today, a number of scientists are willing to consider the possibility that a factor unaccounted for in the materialistic world view might be involved in some of the Spiritualists' reports.

In the twentieth century, interest in Spiritualism peaked between the World Wars.

Its appeal has waned since that time, and today most Spiritualist organizations are largely composed of elderly people. (Mental mediumship experienced a massive revival among a younger generation in the 1980s, under the name of "channeling." Most channelers claim to be in contact with extraterrestrial intelligences rather than spirits of the dead.) Many religious organizations, such as the Roman Catholic Church and the JEHOVAH'S WITNESSES, remain convinced that the spirits contacted by mediums are actually DEMONS; other groups, such as the Church of England, have been somewhat more sympathetic.

Francesco STANCARI   One of the first Protestant heretics, Francesco Stancari was born in Italy in 1501. After the rise of the Protestant Reformers Martin Luther and John Calvin, he joined the Protestant movement and was compelled to leave Catholic Italy. He sought refuge in Poland, which did not persecute Protestants. Stancari promptly caused a furor by proclaiming that every Christian in Poland, except himself, was a heretic. Specifically, he accused the Polish nation of ARIANISM, an ancient heresy that argued that Christ was not God, but rather a divine being created by God. Stancari's claim that he was the only true Christian in Poland provoked the countercharge that his beliefs amounted to MODALISM, a detested heresy that did not recognize the Father, Son, and Holy Spirit as distinct Persons in the Trinity.

Stancari was so annoying that on one occasion, Polish Protestant leader John Laski was moved to throw a Bible at him during a meeting. Stancari eventually left Poland for Transylvania, where he continued to promote controversial views. He died in 1574.

Emanuel SWEDENBORG   One of the great scientists of the European Enlightenment period (seventeenth and eighteenth centuries), Emanuel Swedenborg founded the science of crystallography and was the first to express the view that the planets were formed through the congealing of clouds in space. He is best known, however, for his teachings concerning spiritual, not material, reality. The SWEDENBORGIAN movement preserves his unorthodox religious views to the present day.

Swedenborg was born into an aristocratic family in Uppsala, Sweden, in 1688. Early in life, he displayed an aptitude for learning, as well as a special interest in science and engineering. When he was twenty-eight, King Charles XII appointed him to be an assessor for the Royal College of Mines. Swedenborg wrote many books filled with new and startling ideas, which gained him an international reputation. His work included designs for a submarine, an airplane, and a system for transporting ships overland.

By 1736, this successful man of the world began to show an interest in the unseen realms. In that year, he published a book in which he reports that the universe is a living being rather than an inanimate mechanism, and notes that behind the realm of the senses lies a spiritual domain. Around this time, Swedenborg had begun to have visions of a mysterious light.

In the following years, his interest in the spiritual world grew. He believed that he had the ability to be aware of nonphysical beings and to have conversations with them. Eventually, Swedenborg thought that he was in frequent contact with angels, such long-dead people as Saint Paul and Martin Luther, and God Himself.

By 1745, Swedenborg had come to believe that God had chosen him to convey a new revelation to humanity, a fulfillment of the New Testament in the same manner that the New Testament fulfilled the Old Testament. He realized that his claim would be difficult for others to accept, despite his imposing reputation as a thinker:

> I am well aware that many persons will insist that it is impossible for anyone to converse with spirits and with angels during his lifetime in the body; many will say that such intercourse must be mere fancy; some, that I have invented such relations in order to gain credit; whilst others will make other objections. For all these, however, I care not, since I have seen, heard and felt.

The visionary resigned his government job in 1747, accepting a pension of half pay in order to devote himself to recording his insights into the invisible world. Two years later, he published *Arcana Coelestia*, the first book of an eight-volume work. He issued many more books on spiritual topics until his death in 1772.

Swedenborg's beliefs were Christian but were heretical in nature. He rejected the orthodox doctrine of the Trinity, which claims that God is three Persons: Father, Son, and Holy Spirit, subsisting in a single nature. Swedenborg thought this view to be the heresy of TRITHEISM, the belief in three gods. Instead, he taught that God was a single Person who was both Father and Son; Swedenborg denied that the Holy Spirit was a person.

Swedenborg claimed to have learned, through conversations with spiritual beings, that only some parts of the Bible should be taken to be divine truths. He rejected the truthfulness of everything in the New Testament except for the four Gospels and Revelation. Much of Swedenborg's later writings is devoted to uncovering spiritual knowledge hidden in Bible passages.

One of the most influential teachings of the Swedish seer concerned the relationship between the worlds of the spirit, mind, and matter. His contemporaries had to admit that he had a masterful understanding of the material realm; Swedenborg himself claimed to have penetrated the mysteries of all three worlds. He taught that spiritual forces were as real as matter, and that patterns in the spirit world gave rise to the structures of matter. Swedenborg located the spiritual domain in the interior realm of the human mind: "It can in no sense be said that heaven is outside of anyone: it is within . . . and a man also, so far as he receives heaven, is a recipient, a heaven, and an angel." This acknowledgment that the contents of the inner world were real rather than "mere" imagination, affected the views of important later figures. Both English artist and poet William Blake and Swiss psychiatrist Carl Jung were indebted to Swedenborg for their views concerning the reality of the mind.

Swedenborg did not wish to found a new religion. Rather, he held that members of existing Christian denominations could deepen their spiritual understanding by studying his works. Few orthodox Christians agreed, however, and branded him a heretic. After Swedenborg's death, in violation of his wishes, some of his followers established the religious movement that still bears his name.

See also: SPIRITUALISM.

SWEDENBORGIANISM   The movement that preserves the teachings of Swedish visionary EMANUEL SWEDENBORG is also known as the CHURCH OF THE NEW JERUSALEM. Swedenborg himself did not favor the formation of a separate religious group to transmit his doctrines; he wanted his followers to remain within orthodox Christian denominations. This proved impossible, however, because his views were hardly orthodox. Clearly, then, in order to support each other in their spiritual quest, the Swedenborgians needed their own organization.

The Swedenborgian Church was founded in 1787, fifteen years after the death of Swedenborg, by a small group of former Methodist ministers in Lancashire, England. Swedenborg's disciples established the first Swedenborgian Church in the New World in Baltimore, Maryland, in 1792. Since that time, the church has spread around the world. Membership has remained relatively small, and the church has a tendency to attract primarily intellectuals. At present, there are approximately 60,000 Swedenborgians, about two-thirds of whom live in South Africa.

From time to time, episodes of disagreement have occurred within the movement; in 1890, the Pennsylvania branch of the American Swedenborgian Church split off because its members felt that Swedenborg's writings should be revered as sacred scripture. All Swedenborgians place great emphasis on the study of the founder's books. They follow the Swedish visionary's methods of decoding esoteric meanings in the Bible, which they believe to be the contents of God's mind. Swedenborgians understand that spiritual progress does not end at death, with souls going directly to a static heaven or hell forever. Rather, they believe in further learning and development beyond the grave. This notion of the afterworld as an educational opportunity, derived from Swedenborg's conversations with spirit beings, has become widespread in the nineteenth and twentieth centuries, influencing such movements as SPIRITUALISM and THEOSOPHY.

SYMEON   A leader of the heretical PAULICIANS, Symeon lived in Armenia and the eastern Byzantine Empire. Symeon took over the sect when orthodox Christian authorities burned CONSTANTINE OF ARMENIA, his predecessor, at the stake in 682; Symeon himself met the same fate six years later.

TABORITES   In 1415, Bohemian reformer JAN HUS was burned at the stake for teaching unorthodox ideas. His execution caused an uproar in Bohemia and set off decades of strife. The Taborites were the most extreme group of HUSSITES active during this chaotic period in Bohemia. They called for the overthrow of not only the Catholic Church, but also of Western civilization itself.

The Taborites adopted Hus's belief that the Bible, not the pope, should be consulted to define Christian life. However, they went further than Hus by rejecting every Christian dogma and practice that is not described in the New Testament. Such a position amounted to a complete rejection of the Roman Catholic Church. Because the Taborites endorsed the use of violence in spreading their views ("Think not that I am come to send peace on earth: I came not to send peace, but a sword," Matthew 10:34), they launched a war against Catholicism in Bohemia.

These militant heretics also interpreted the New Testament to mean that human society on earth should display perfect equality, "as it is in heaven"; therefore, they rejected the class system, sexual discrimination, and private ownership of property. The slogan of the Taborite community was "Nothing is mine, nothing is yours, everything is common to all."

In a rural area south of Prague, the radicals constructed an armed camp with a vast network of underground passages where they could hide. The place became known as Tabor (which means "fortified camp" in Czech), and its occupants as Taborites. From Tabor, the heretic army streamed forth, destroying churches and slaughtering anyone who refused to join them. This activity deeply alarmed Catholic authorities, as well as members of the privileged classes who had everything to lose if the Taborites triumphed. The Taborites themselves were mostly rural peasants and poor people from the towns.

News of the Taborite uprising spread through Europe. Soon, heretics from as far away as France appeared in Tabor, attracted by the promise of escape from the harassment of mainstream society. Some of these groups, such as the PIKARTS and the ADAMITES, were so bizarre that the Taborites themselves took to persecuting them.

Catholic Europe resolved to stamp out the Hussite menace and declared a Crusade against them. Knights from thirty nations marched into Bohemia, battling both the Taborites and the more moderate Hussites, the UTRAQUISTS. Amazingly, the Taborites won a string of military victories under their blind but brilliant general, JAN ZIZKA. Bohemia itself was divided in its loyalties among the Catholics, Utraquists, and Taborites, which gave the rebels an advantage. Attempts to reconcile the two Hussite groups were made, but the Taborites continued their ferocious ways, which the Utraquists could not condone.

In 1433, the moderate Hussites came to an agreement with the Catholics. The social status quo would be preserved, and some changes in church ceremony would be allowed. The Taborites condemned this arrangement. With Bohemia united against them, the radicals could not survive for long. The following year, their army was crushed at the Battle of Lipany. Tabor itself endured as a center of heresy until 1452, when George, the Utraquist king, took the town by force.

TANCHELM OF FLANDERS   During the twelfth century, the sparks of heresy that had appeared in Europe during the preceding hundred years ignited into mass movements. One of the first of these was centered on Tanchelm of Flanders, whose three-year preaching career started a lasting disturbance in the region. As a young man, Tanchelm worked as a diplomat for the Duke of Flanders, traveling on one occasion to Rome on a political mission. There is no record that Tanchelm was ever consecrated as a priest. However, around A.D. 1112, he became involved in the internal power struggles of the church.

During this period, the papacy was attempting to gain greater control over the Catholic priests and bishops of Europe, many of whom lived rather independent and irresponsible lives. Their actions made the church an easy target for heretics, who could point out many obvious abuses of the trust communities placed in their clergy. As part of a reform, the pope issued a decree stating that sacraments—including baptisms and marriages—administered by married priests were not valid.

The decree caused an uproar. Married priests had conducted many baptisms and marriages, and suddenly, because of a papal policy shift, the legitimacy of these acts was in doubt. Around 1112, Tanchelm started wandering through Flanders, preaching that not only married priests but the entire church was corrupt and worthless. He advised people to stop paying tithes. His message was well received by those whose faith the papal decree had undermined, and particularly by the poor, who resented supporting the bishops' wealthy lifestyles.

As Tanchelm's popularity increased, he proclaimed that he had been specially blessed and was the equal of God. Reports that he could work miracles circulated. He received an excited welcome whenever he entered a town. Tanchelm dressed in sumptuous robes, and it was said that he had sex with his female disciples in the belief that his holiness placed him above conventional morality. His more devoted followers eagerly drank his bath water.

On one occasion, Tanchelm and his mob chased a priest from a church and rededicated it for the preaching of Tanchelm's doctrines. It was said that on another occasion, Tanchelm married himself to a wooden statue of the Virgin Mary and then commanded his followers to place offerings of silver and jewelry in the buckets he had suspended from the statue's arms. The local nobility did not interfere with his activities, viewing him as a useful counterbalance to the power of the Catholic Church. The archbishop of Utrecht was less pleased, however, and had Tanchelm imprisoned for a time, but his popularity continued to surge.

In 1115, a Catholic priest murdered Tanchelm. Nevertheless, his followers continued to believe in his divinity and to reject the authority of the church. During the following decades, reports of the activities of his devotees appear in records from Flanders and Germany. One such report, dated 1144, noted that Tanchelm's followers were proclaiming MANICHAEAN doctrines, a term usually employed at the time to refer to groups that developed into the CATHAR heresy. Tanchelm himself did not teach Cathar ideas. His attacks on the authority of the orthodox church helped to lay the groundwork for the rise of the Cathars, who likely absorbed the movement he started.

See also: HENRY OF LAUSANNE, PIERRE DE BRUYS.

TEMPLARS   *See* KNIGHTS TEMPLAR.

Quintas Septimius Florens TERTULLIAN   This citizen of the second century Roman Empire was one of the most important figures in the development of Christian thought. Quintus Septimius Florens Tertullian was a paradox. He was a profound intellectual who laid the major foundations of Christian theology, yet he forcefully rejected the idea that the intellect could lead one to salvation. He was an advocate of obedience to the orthodox church and a ferocious opponent of heretics, who ended his life belonging to a heretical movement.

Tertullian was born in the North African city of Carthage around A.D. 160. He was probably a lawyer by profession. A pagan in his youth, he enjoyed attending the gladiatorial games, the gory mass entertainment of the time. One day, some Christians who had refused to swear an oath to the pagan gods were led into the arena and slaughtered. Deeply moved by this martyrdom, Tertullian decided to investigate the notorious cult of Christianity and ended up joining the faith.

Tertullian became known as a defender of orthodox Christianity from its enemies, both within and without. He repudiated rumors circulating among the pagans that Christians engaged in antisocial acts, and he counterattacked PAGANISM for its reverence of idols and its supposed moral weakness. He also wrote treatises criticizing three important heretical movements of the time: GNOSTICISM, MARCIONISM, and MODALISM.

According to Tertullian, only the Catholic Church preserved the teachings Christ gave to the apostles. Everyone who wished to be saved had to believe in the contents of the Bible and to obey the traditions the priests preserved. He noted that people who relied on their personal experience or on reasoning alone would reject the claims of orthodox Christianity, such as the resurrection of JESUS' dead body. The orthodox doctrines must, therefore, be taken on sheer faith, "because they are absurd." And once the Christian vision is embraced, there is no need for further analysis: "We want no curious disputation after possessing Christ Jesus, no inquiring after enjoying the gospel! With our faith, we desire no further belief."

This seemingly anti-intellectual position contrasts with Tertullian's precise development of concepts regarding Christ and God. Orthodox Christian thought has come to be practically defined by two propositions: that Jesus Christ is fully God and fully human, and that God has a single nature yet is three Persons (Father, Son, and Holy Spirit). Tertullian transmitted the first proposition from his predecessor, Irenaeus of Lyons, to future generations of Christian thinkers. Concerning the threefold Personhood of God, Tertullian was the first to express this belief in a clear way.

Many scholars believe that Tertullian's contact with the heresy of MONTANISM influenced his basic definition of the Trinity as the structure of God. In his earlier writings, Tertullian, like other orthodox Christians, emphasized the Father and the Son, but rarely mentioned the Holy Spirit. The Montanist movement, by contrast, focused on the Holy Spirit, even claiming that this Spirit was still on earth speaking through entranced mediums. Furthermore, Montanists were experimenting with the idea that God had three names or possessed a structure of three divisions. During a time when Tertullian is known to have been studying Montanism, he began to emphasize the divinity of the Holy Spirit, and included it, with the Father and Son, in his description of the Trinity. It is likely that Montanist ideas inspired these innovations.

In his later years, Tertullian felt that the Catholic Church had morally lapsed. He became increasingly sympathetic to Montanism and finally joined the movement. Tertullian, the architect of Catholic theology, died a heretic in A.D. 225.

THEODAS   The teacher of the great second century Gnostic teacher VALENTINUS, Theodas claimed to have been a student of one of JESUS' own disciples and to have learned Christ's secret teachings. Valentinus said that he elaborated the doctrine he received from Theodas with material he received in visions, and in this way developed the ideas of VALENTINIAN GNOSTICISM.

THEODORE OF MOPSUESTIA   This Christian theologian of the early fifth century was one of the first thinkers to attempt to describe the relationship between the divine and human aspects of JESUS Christ. Although most Christians viewed Theodore of Mopsuestia as orthodox during his lifetime, he was condemned as a heretic after his death because the notorious heretic NESTORIUS had adopted his ideas.

Theodore was born around A.D. 350. At this time, the Christian community in the Roman Empire was in an uproar over whether the church would be controlled by the orthodox party, who claimed that Christ is God, or the heretical followers of ARIANISM, who taught that Christ, although a morally perfect being, was not God. In 392, eleven years after the triumph of the orthodox doctrine and the banning of the Arian view, Theodore became the bishop of Mopsuestia, a town in what is now Turkey.

The orthodox view of Christ, which all Christians were now supposed to believe, maintained that he was both God and man. He had to be God in order to have the power to save sinners, and he had to be human so that his death on the cross would atone for human sins. Theologians had only begun the struggle to understand the paradox of the God-man. A first attempt by APOLLINARIS was declared to be heretical because he argued that Christ did not have a human mind. Critics pointed out that a person without a human mind can hardly be called a human being. Theodore tried to devise a more acceptable description of Christ—one that preserved Christ's complete humanity, as well as His complete divinity.

Theodore was careful to state that Jesus' human nature included a human body and a human mind, and, therefore, consisted of the same components as other humans. Christ's divine nature was the Logos or Word of God, also called the Son, the second Person of the Trinity. The two natures, human and divine, had been united since the moment of Jesus' conception.

The orthodox notion of Christ's two natures could be understood to mean that Christ was composed of two different persons. Such a fragmented being would seem more like someone possessed by a demon (or, in modern language, like someone suffering from a multiple personality disorder) than like a Savior. Theodore tried to dispel this idea by emphasizing that although Christ has two *natures*, he is only a single *Person*—the Son of God.

Unfortunately, when discussing the person of Christ, he used the Greek word *prosopon*. This term has two meanings: "person", the meaning Theodore intended, and "face" or "appearance." Some orthodox critics, confused by the dual meaning, understood Theodore to be saying that the two natures only appeared to be united in Christ, but that they were actually separate. Such a division of Christ was seen as heretical.

Theodore died in 428. Theologians continued to wrestle with the thorny problem of Christ's natures. At the COUNCIL OF EPHESUS, a meeting of church leaders held three years after Theodore's death, his work was condemned on the basis of his supposed fragmentation of Christ. As noted earlier, Theodore did not hold such a view, but his writings were not clear enough to fend off the charge, and he was no longer able to clarify the point. Emperor Justinian again branded Theodore a heretic in his edict of 543; the pope accepted this condemnation at the SECOND COUNCIL OF CONSTANTINOPLE in 553.

See also: COUNCIL OF CHALCEDON, NESTORIANISM.

THEODORET   During the first half of the fifth century, this Syrian bishop played a significant role in the debate concerning the nature of Christ. In the controversy between Cyril of Alexandria and NESTORIUS, patriarch of Constantinople, Theodoret tended to side with Nestorius. The Nestorian position was labelled a heresy. After his death, Theodoret's writings were also condemned as heretical.

Theodoret was born around A.D. 393. He was appointed bishop of Cyrrhus in Syria in 423. At the time, Christian thinkers were struggling to formulate a description of the relationship between the divine and human aspects of Christ. It was generally agreed that Christ was a complete human being and also was God. Nestorius emphasized the distinction between the divine and human natures in Christ, prompting Cyril to accuse him of teaching that there were two Christs inhabiting a single body. Cyril claimed instead that Christ's two natures were united in "one incarnate nature."

Bishop Theodoret was concerned that Cyril's view tended to neglect Christ's human nature. Cyril's phrase, "one incarnate nature," had also been used by APOLLINARIS, an Egyptian heretic who had been condemned for teaching that Christ did not have a human mind. Theodoret wrote a letter in which he accused Cyril of mixing Christ's two natures to form a single divine nature. This union would violate the completeness of Christ's human nature.

In 431 at the COUNCIL OF EPHESUS, a meeting of church leaders during which they tried to resolve the controversy, Cyril arranged Nestorius's condemnation as a heretic. Six years later, Cyril called for Nestorius's teachers, including theologian THEODORE OF MOPSUESTIA, to be condemned as well, even though Theodore had died many years before. Theodoret wrote in defense of Nestorius and Theodore.

After Cyril's death in 444, he was succeeded by DIOSCURUS, who attacked Theodoret as a heretic who taught that Christ was not divine. Dioscurus's charge is false, but the theological debates raging then were so complex and politically charged that many of the participants routinely misunderstood and misrepresented each other's positions.

At the ROBBER COUNCIL of 449, a meeting that Dioscurus controlled, Theodoret was deposed from his office and forced into exile. Two years later, the COUNCIL OF CHALCEDON was held to correct the effects of the Robber Council, which the Church declared illegal. In Chalcedon, Theodoret was given the opportunity to redeem himself: he would be permitted to resume his role as an orthodox bishop if he publicly condemned Nestorius as a heretic. It must have been difficult for Theodoret to damn Nestorius, who had become a close friend, but he did so and spent the rest of his life without controversy. He died around 466.

The Council of Chalcedon established the orthodox position on the two natures of Christ. In the decades following the council, the role of Cyril in the controversy was increasingly admired by the orthodox leaders even though his position was actually farther from the orthodox doctrine than that of Nestorius. This peculiar stand was probably motivated in part by orthodox fears that Egypt, Cyril's homeland, was being taken over by the heretical followers of MONOPHYSITISM. In order to gather support for orthodoxy in Egypt, the orthodox leaders declared the Egyptian hero Cyril to be a saint. By the middle of the sixth century, any criticism of Saint Cyril was regarded as heretical. At the SECOND COUNCIL OF CONSTANTINOPLE in 553, Theodoret's stand against Cyril was labeled heresy: "If anyone defends the remembered writings of Theodoret and does not condemn them, let him be anathema [condemned]."

THEODOTUS THE COBBLER   Also known as THEODOTUS THE TANNER, Theodotus the Cobbler is thought to be the founder of the Christian heresy called ADOPTIONISM. This movement began in Rome toward the end of the second century A.D. VICTOR I, the bishop of Rome, excommunicated Theodotus.

THEODOTUS THE MONEY CHANGER   A follower of THEODOTUS THE COBBLER and a teacher of the heresy of ADOPTIONISM in early third century Rome, Theodotus the money changer was excommunicated by the bishop of Rome, ZEPHYRINUS.

THEODOTUS THE TANNER   Theodotus the Tanner is a variant name of THE-ODOTUS THE COBBLER, the founder of the ADOPTIONIST heresy.

THEOPASCHITES   By the sixth century, the belief that Christ had two natures (divine and human) but was a single Person, had been adopted as the official doctrine of Christianity. Attempts to work out the implications of this mysterious notion led to many controversies, including the Theopaschite debate. Orthodox Christians believed that Christ suffered while dying on the cross; otherwise, his life and death would not have been a real sacrifice and, therefore, could not have earned the forgiveness of human sins. The Theopaschites, who appeared in Constantinople in A.D. 519, drew a controversial conclusion from this belief. They argued that because Christ was the Son (one of the divine Persons in the Trinity), it was logical to say that the God of the Trinity experienced the suffering on the cross.

The problem for orthodoxy was that by definition God was said to be incapable of suffering. After much discussion, both the pope and the patriarch of Constantinople declared that although Christ suffered, it was wrong to say that the God of the Trinity suffered. Although Catholics rejected the Theopaschite doctrine, it appealed to the followers of MONOPHYSITISM—the heresy that Christ has only one divine nature—because it emphasized Christ's identity with God.

Emperor Justinian wanted to heal the division between the orthodox and the Monophysites. He thought that if orthodoxy adopted the Theopaschite doctrine, the Monophysites might return to the orthodox church. Overriding the orthodox theologians' objections to Theopaschitism, he insisted that the doctrine be declared correct at the SECOND COUNCIL OF CONSTANTINOPLE in 553. Neither this gesture nor other compromises that Justinian engineered succeeded in reconciling the Monophysites and the orthodox Christians.

See also: PATRIPASSIANISM.

THEOPHILUS   Ruler of the Byzantine Empire from A.D. 829 to 842, Theophilus was the last emperor to support the heresy of ICONOCLASM. He instigated the violent persecution of the supporters of icons, particularly the monks, whom he viewed as parasites on the state economy. Theodora, his wife, assumed power upon his death and restored control of the Byzantine Church to the orthodox Christians.

THEOSOPHY   This term literally means "wisdom of God." In 1875, a group of occultists in New York, led by MADAME BLAVATSKY, chose the word as the best description of their spiritual goal and founded the Theosophical Society. This organization was dedicated to developing "the nucleus of a universal brotherhood of humanity" and the "investigation of powers latent in man." The group quickly became one of the most important influences in modern Western occultism.

From the Society's founding until 1891, the year of Blavatsky's death, she was the unquestioned leader. During these years, the Society established its headquarters in Adyar, India, and spread around the world. By this time, interest in SPIRITUALISM, the other major unorthodox movement of the century, had begun to level off. Many people had been impressed by the strange experiences of the seance room, which seemed to provide evidence for the existence of a spirit world. The Spiritualists, however, did not offer a rich philosophical system or a detailed path of spiritual development. The new Theosophical Society provided precisely these elements, and membership swelled.

Early Theosophical beliefs were derived from Blavatsky's two books, *Isis Unveiled* and *The Secret Doctrine*. In these works, she proclaims the existence of "Mahatmas," or hidden masters, beings of great wisdom and mystical power. These masters actively work for the evolution of humanity, but few people ever knowingly encounter them. Blavatsky did, of course, and shares their grand vision of the universe in her writings. The development of psychic abilities, as well as meditation upon the occult notions Theosophy teaches, are said to mark and to assist spiritual progress. But an investigation revealed that Blavatsky had been producing seemingly miraculous materializations of letters from the masters by fraudulent means. The enthusiasm of most Theosophists was not dampened by this embarrassment, though—a clear indication of the widespread appeal of Blavatsky's personality and teachings.

As it turned out, allegiance to Blavatsky had been holding the Theosophical Society together. Following her death, a squabble broke out between two of the Society's founders over who should succeed Blavatsky as leader. The two men, William Judge and Colonel Henry Olcott, each reported that they had received letters from the masters designating themselves to be the chosen one. A schism resulted. Many American Theosophists followed Judge, while the rest of the Theosophical world recognized Olcott.

When Judge died in 1896, leadership of his branch passed to a well-known medium, Katherine Tingley, also known as the "Purple Mother." Tingley emphasized compassionate social action more than mystical contemplation. She founded a Theosophical community in San Diego. Tingley died in 1929, but her community continued until 1942. This branch of Theosophy survives today in the form of a small American organization, known simply as the Theosophical Society.

Meanwhile, Olcott's branch had come under the influence of Annie Besant, who succeeded Olcott as leader upon his death in 1907. Olcott and Besant emphasized the Indian aspects of Blavatsky's teachings. They encouraged the development of clairvoyance and astral travel. Deserving Theosophists were said to be able to commune with the Mahatmas while traveling out of their physical bodies. Although Besant's Theosophical organization was scandalized by the sexual interest her close colleague, Charles Leadbeater, showed in young boys, this branch of the movement remained dominant.

The decade of the 1920s saw two important developments in Theosophy. First, Theosophical writers associated with Besant's branch, Alice Bailey and Leadbeater, elaborated the notion of the hidden masters into an elaborate pantheon. At the top is the Solar Logos, an intelligence that dwells in the sun and oversees the spiritual evolution of the solar system. Sanat Kumara, who lives in the Gobi Desert, is the earth's spiritual director. From the realm of the higher masters emanate seven rays, which beneficially influence various spheres of earthly activity. Each ray is guided by a master. Theosophists can tune in to the rays to absorb their virtues and perhaps make direct contact with the masters themselves.

The other major event of the 1920s was the rise and departure of Krishnamurti. Besant and Leadbeater had decided that a child they met at Adyar was the Messiah. Throughout his youth they groomed the boy, Krishnamurti, for his glorious role. Their enthusiasm for this project excited some Theosophists but alienated others. In 1929,

Krishnamurti announced that he wanted nothing more to do with the Theosophists' Messianic fantasies; for the rest of his life, he encouraged people to develop their own wisdom, and not to rely on others.

Since that time, the Theosophical movement has seen further divisions, but no major scandals. The lineage of Olcott and Besant continues to be the most popular kind of Theosophy; in the United States, this branch is represented by the Theosophical Society in America. It publishes a popular journal, *The Quest*, and books on spiritual topics, not necessarily of a specifically Theosophical viewpoint. The current organization serves more as a forum for discussion of ideas concerning spiritual development than as a vehicle for promoting the notions of Blavatsky and her successors.

The Theosophical Society and its derivatives have greatly stimulated the esoteric world. Many people have studied the thoughts of Krishnamurti, who may be better known today than Theosophy itself. Bailey left the Society to found her own group, which continues to study her revelations. Rudolf Steiner renounced the leadership of the Theosophical Society's German division and established the Anthroposophical Society, best known for its Waldorf Schools. Dozens of other occult groups continue to seek the "wisdom of God" through contact with the hidden masters.

THEURGY   During the gradual decline of PAGANISM and the rise of Christianity during the first four centuries A.D., both pagan and Christian practices underwent significant changes. Theurgy was the last major manifestation of pagan spirituality. The world view of the Theurgists brought together the main aspects of the ancient world's magical traditions and served as a foundation for the magical tradition in later European culture.

The earliest Theurgist was JULIANUS THE CHALDEAN, who lived during the latter part of the second century. Little is known of Julianus's life. His book, *The CHALDEAN ORACLES*, became the basis of Theurgical practice. Unfortunately, the work was destroyed long ago.

At first, it seems that Theurgy attracted little attention. During the third century, however, Theurgy merged with the pagan philosophical system called Neoplatonism. The Neoplatonists taught that the entire universe is linked together by a dense network of invisible connections; clever people could use these links to create magical effects. Important figures of Neoplatonism, such as Porphyry and Iamblichus, noted that Theurgy taught ways to apply the theory of hidden connections to achieve spiritual goals. Unlike lower forms of magic that aimed at such mundane effects as attracting money and fame, Theurgy claimed that its purpose was to promote divine knowledge in the magician.

The Theurgic tradition borrowed magical practices from Egyptian and Greek sources. In one Theurgical technique for gaining divine knowledge that was derived from ancient Egyptian religion, the Theurgist chanted magic words to cause a god or spirit to inhabit a statue. The statue could then be asked questions, and the Theurgist, presumably in a trance, would perceive the statue giving an answer. Classical scholar Georg Luck suggested that Theurgists may have taken drugs to enhance such experiences.

The ancient Greeks believed that some people could allow themselves to be possessed by gods; in the grip of the deity, they would have divine wisdom and could function as an oracle. Theurgy took over this practice. Theurgists tried to induce trance states in young children (chosen for their purity and innocence) in the hope that the children would be able to communicate directly with the gods.

In the most advanced type of Theurgical practice, the Theurgists themselves took on the identity of a god, so that they could acquire the knowledge and power of that deity. The ritual required the Theurgist to imitate the god by wearing the clothing and symbols associated with it, and to visualize wielding divine powers. Iamblichus describes the process:

> The theurgist, by virtue of mysterious signs, controls the powers of nature. Not as a mere human being, or as one who possesses a human soul, but as one of a higher rank of gods, he gives orders that are not appropriate to the condition of man. He does not really expect to perform all these amazing things, but by using such words he shows what kind of power he has and how great he is, and that because of his knowledge of these mysterious symbols he is obviously in touch with the gods.

Theurgy became popular among some members of the Roman aristocratic class, but it was not able to compete with Christianity in appealing to the masses. Although both Theurgy and Christianity offered contact with the divine, Theurgy required the development of complex psychological skills, including the induction of trance states, whereas the church required only simple morality and obedience to priests.

JULIAN THE APOSTATE, the last pagan emperor, tried to revive paganism after several decades of state support for Christianity. Julian was initiated into Theurgy and appointed Theurgists to high government posts. After Julian's short (twenty-month) reign, a Christian emperor came to power. From the Christian perspective, Theurgy was nothing more than a way to communicate with DEMONS. The Theurgists were removed from office and became subject to persecution by Christians.

The last great pagan thinker was Proclus, who lived in Athens during the fifth century. He taught Theurgy at the Academy, which had been founded by Plato himself. Theurgy was finally banned, along with all other pagan practices, by Emperor Justinian in 529. The influence of this pagan school continued, however. The practice of magical identification with a god in order to gain the god's wisdom and abilities became a feature of the high magical tradition in Western culture, and is still important in ritual magic today.

TREATISE ON ANGEL MAGIC   This English manuscript is a summary of occult traditions dating from the early seventeenth century. *The Treatise on Angel Magic* was probably written by Thomas Rudd, a scholar and magician who is thought to have studied esoteric doctrines with the son of famous Elizabethan occultist JOHN DEE. The version of the Treatise that exists today is a copy made in the early eighteenth century and preserved in the British Library. In the opinion of Adam McLean, its rediscoverer, this text is "an important link in the chain of the transmission of esoteric traditions."

The treatise gathers many threads of Western occultism to weave a detailed picture of the hidden world. Rudd brings together material from such varied sources as the Jewish KABBALAH; the ritual magic of GRIMOIRES, such as THE LEMEGETON and THE ARBATEL OF MAGIC; Dee's ENOCHIAN MAGIC; the NATURAL MAGIC of AGRIPPA and TRITHEMIUS; the writings of PARACELSUS on elemental spirits; and the depictions of witchcraft found in the MALLEUS MALE-FICARUM.

The *Treatise* encourages an attitude of curiosity about the cosmos: "There is a light in man which is above the light of Nature. This light causeth him to search and learn and experiment supernatural things." The use of experiments to probe the world is a feature of the modern scientific approach, which was taking form during the period when the *Treatise* was written (probably within a few years of 1660, when England's first scientific institution, the Royal Society, was founded). Some historians argue that this similarity between the magical and scientific attitudes of the age was no coincidence. Many key figures in the Scientific Revolution were intimately involved in occult studies themselves and may have adopted the experimental approach from the magical tradition.

Rudd's experiments were not scientific but magical. In the *Treatise*, he describes a method of conjuring angels from the nine hierarchies of heaven to appear in a crystal or mirror, where they can be asked to grant favors and reveal secret knowledge. The world of angels described in the book corresponds to the orthodox Christian view, combined with Kabbalistic elements. Instructions for conjuring "olympic spirits"—helpful beings associated with the planets—and for making talismans are given, along with a collection of astrological and numerological lore.

The author also examines the darker corners of the occult realm. Rudd describes ways to unmask and banish demons that might attempt to answer the magician's conjurations disguised as angels. Nature spirits, such as hobgoblins and Robin Goodfellows, are said to wish for the destruction of humanity. Rudd appears to be an uncritical believer in the existence of a Satanic conspiracy of witches, as described by the witch hunters.

During this period of turmoil in Europe, when a new way of thinking and discoveries were undermining the assumptions supporting the old world view, a culture-wide anxiety existed. It was often expressed as fear of witches and demons. The *Treatise*, in its great concern for avoiding contact with evil spirits, displays an attitude typical of the age.

TRITHEISM   Orthodox Christianity inherited the belief that there is only one God from the Jews; early Christian theologians noted that God appears in the New Testament as three Persons: Father, Son, and Holy Spirit. The FIRST COUNCIL OF CONSTANTINOPLE in A.D. 381 established the doctrine of the Trinity as a way to reconcile these apparently contradictory images of God. The orthodox view states that the three divine Persons share (technically, "subsist in") a single nature and, therefore, are a single Deity. Those who have disagreed with or misunderstood the orthodox description by believing that the Persons of the Trinity are three gods, not one, are called Tritheists. Such people have always been seen as heretics, guilty of dividing the one and only God into fragments.

After the establishment of the Trinity doctrine in the fourth century, many years passed without much disagreement. In the tenth century, troublesome monk GOT-TSCHALK was accused of being Tritheistic because of his use of the term "trine Deity" to refer to God. Gottschalk himself denied the charge, however, and swore allegiance to the orthodox Trinity.

In the sixteenth century, a serious outbreak of the Tritheistic heresy occurred.

Some radical Protestants, on the fringe of the Reformation, called for the abandonment of the orthodox Trinity as a relic of Catholicism. A number of these ANTI-TRINITARIANS were Tritheists who worshipped Father, Son, and Holy Spirit as distinct divine beings. They were chased out of Italy and the Swiss lands to Poland, where they formed a splinter church. By the end of the century, most had converted to UNITARIANISM, which eliminated the Trinity concept completely.

See also: POLYTHEISM.

TRITHEMIUS of Sponheim   An influential occult scholar of the sixteenth century, Trithemius of Sponheim was born in 1462 in the German village of Trittheim, from which he took his name. His father died when he was quite young. His mother remarried and showed no affection for her son, treating him like a servant. Under these less-than-promising circumstances, the boy began to have visions, which he believed were spiritual revelations. He also showed a keen interest in learning but had little opportunity to do so. Trithemius escaped from his unhappy home when he obtained his portion of an inheritance from his father. He went to study at the University of Treves.

At twenty, Trithemius already had a reputation as a scholar. He wished to share the news of his academic success with his mother. Journeying from Treves to Trittheim, he encountered a snowstorm and was forced to shelter at the Benedictine monastery of Sponheim. He was so attracted to the place that he remained there for twenty-one years. Within two years of arriving, Trithemius had been elected abbot.

The abbot of Sponheim devoted much of his energy to accumulating a library, which became known as one of the greatest collections of classical and magical knowledge in Europe. He also composed works of his own. One of these, *Steganographia*, became controversial. Although it was not published until 1606, many years after its author's death, it was circulated in manuscript. The main topic of this text is cryptography, or the writing of secret codes. In the first two sections of the work, Trithemius describes methods of encoding and deciphering messages. He refers to these coding techniques as "angels" and "spirits." When critics charged him with writing a GRIMOIRE, a textbook about conjuring spirits, the abbot replied that the references to spirit beings was merely a literary device to prevent uneducated readers from learning the secrets of cryptography.

Many commentators since Trithemius's time have accepted his explanation. However, the third section of *Steganographia* describes an operation that seems to be pure ANGEL MAGIC. The author outlines a method of sending a message by reciting it over a picture of an angel at the astrologically appropriate moment. The book seems to be about both codes and angels, presented in a deliberately confusing fashion in order to avoid the attention of the INQUISITION.

From Trithemius's other, lesser-known writings, it is clear that he had a keen interest in the spirits of the planets. He studied the doctrines of MARSILIO FICINO, who taught the use of planetary images for healing. Trithemius shared his interests with other important figures in occult history: CORNELIUS AGRIPPA and PARACELSUS visited him, and *Steganographia* inspired JOHN DEE to continue his researches into communication with spirits.

A letter of Trithemius, written in 1507, contains the earliest-known reference to the figure of Dr. Faustus. The abbot describes him as a well-known charlatan and blasphemer. In time, the story of this obscure magician mingled with other legends and became immortalized in literature as Faust by such writers as Christopher Marlowe and Goethe.

Eventually, Trithemius lost the support of the Sponheim monks and was replaced as abbot. He later became the abbot of a monastery in Wurzburg, where he died in 1516.

ULFILAS   During the mid-fourth century, Ulfilas converted the Germanic tribe alled the Goths to a heretical form of Christianity. Ulfilas had been born and raised as a Goth, but he somehow became a slave in Constantinople, the capital of the late Roman Empire. Arian bishop EUSEBIUS OF NICOMEDIA converted him to the heresy of ARIANISM. Ulfilas eventually returned to his people and successfully preached his faith. He translated the Bible into the Gothic language, which increased his influence. As a result, by the time the Germanic tribes had overrun the western part of the Roman Empire, many of them were Arians. It took centuries of missionary work by the Roman Catholics to convert them to orthodox belief.

UNITARIANISM   The Unitarian faith developed from the ANTI-TRINITARIAN heresies of the Protestant Reformation. The term "Unitarianism" was first used by the government of Transylvania in 1600 to designate its state religion, which rejected the orthodox Christian Trinity. American minister William Ellery Channing adopted the Unitarian label for the anti-Trinitarian movement in the United States, and it is known by this name today.

In 1536, Spanish theologian MICHAEL SERVETUS was burned at the stake for rejecting the doctrine of the Trinity. He taught that Christ, although a divine being, was not the same as God. His writings circulated after his death and impressed some Protestant thinkers in northern Italy and Switzerland. These early anti-Trinitarians did not deny the existence of the three Persons of the Trinity—Father, Son, and Holy Spirit—but rejected the idea that these three entities were a single God. Driven from their homelands for this heresy of TRITHEISM, the anti-Trinitarians migrated to more tolerant lands, particularly Poland.

An Italian refugee in Poland named FAUSTUS SOCINUS convinced the anti-Trinitarians there that they should abandon the idea of a divine Trinity of Persons. In his view, Christ was an inspired man, not a God, and the Holy Spirit is a sacred power, not a Person. God, Socinus taught, is a single, unified being. This belief, known as SOCINIANISM, was the essence of early Unitarianism.

In Transylvania, preachers like GIORGIO BLANDRATA and FERENC DAVID had great success spreading Unitarian views. From 1568, Unitarianism was a state religion. When a Catholic ruler banned anti-Trinitarian views in Poland in 1658, many SOCINIANS found refuge in Transylvania.

Socinian refugees also settled in the Netherlands and broadcast their radical ideas throughout western Europe. Unitarianism found its most fertile new audience in England where various Christian groups were attacking each other's doctrines, and there was a growing respect for the role of reason, rather than dogma, in arriving at truth. The doctrine of the Trinity had always been difficult to understand, and even its supporters agreed that it was a divine mystery, beyond the reach of rationality. Rationalists who were not emotionally committed to the Trinitarian position argued that the doctrine was a dogma that should be abandoned.

Unitarianism developed a solid following in England, appealing mainly to intellectuals and the upper classes. One of the most famous members was scientist Joseph Priestley, the discoverer of oxygen. In 1774, the Unitarians formally split from the Church of England, establishing their own denomination; but the anti-Trinitarian view remained illegal in England until 1813. From England, Unitarianism was transmitted to the American colonies, where its strength grew in relatively free-thinking areas. In 1785, King's Chapel of Boston, the oldest Anglican Church in America, formally rejected the doctrine of the Trinity.

The nineteenth century saw the height of Unitarian influence in the United States. As mainstream Protestant congregations embraced Unitarianism, legal battles broke out over who should keep the church buildings, the orthodox church, or the "heretics" who had now claimed them. Unitarians were always a minority in American religious life. They exerted a far greater influence than their numbers would suggest, however, because they usually belonged to the most wealthy and educated levels of society. Ralph Waldo Emerson, one of the most important figures of American culture in the 1800s, was profoundly affected by Unitarianism.

In the present century, the Unitarian faith persists, although its influence has declined. Rejection of the Trinity is no longer the crucial rallying point it once was because most mainstream Christians do not pay much attention to the Trinity any more. Reverence for the power of reason has increased among Unitarians to the point that many do not regard themselves as Christians, and some are even atheists. The movement that began during the Reformation as an abandonment of belief in the Trinity seems, for some, to have led to the abandonment of belief in any sort of personal God, just as the Inquisitors of old feared it would.

UNITAS FRATRUM   Also known as the BOHEMIAN BRETHREN, this group, whose Latin name means "Society of Brothers," arose in Bohemia in 1467. *Unitas Fratrum* was composed at first of members of other movements that opposed Roman Catholicism, including the UTRAQUISTS, TABORITES, and WALDENSIANS. *Unitas Fratrum* emphasized living apart from the activities of the materialistic mainstream culture and turning exclusively to the New Testament for guidance.

Members became organized as a church under LUKAS OF PRAGUE in the early sixteenth century. They were persecuted, and some members moved to other countries. *Unitas Fratrum* influenced the formation of the Moravian Church and the group's members contributed to Czech culture by translating the Bible into that language.

Anton UNTERNAHRER   During the early 1800s, this shepherd founded a cult that attracted a sizable though short-lived following in Switzerland. Anton Unternahrer preached that everything in the Bible actually refers to various sacred sexual practices. He regarded the snake in the Garden of Eden as the true savior of humanity; he also taught that feelings of guilt and shame connected with sex were the work of the Devil. Unternahrer attracted the attention of the law because of his proclamation that incest was a holy act. At his trial, he tried to prove his claim that he had been selected by God to be a prophet by pointing out that he had three testicles.

See also: OPHITES.

UTRAQUISTS   The Utraquists were a branch of the fifteenth century Bohemian movement, the HUSSITES. The name of the Utraquists derives from the Latin phrase *sub utraque specie*, which means "in both kinds." The name refers to the Utraquists' practice of allowing the congregation to receive both bread and wine during the Mass. Roman Catholic tradition permitted only priests to partake of the wine. From 1419 to 1433, the Utraquists and other Hussites were the target of a Catholic Crusade. In 1433, the Catholics and Utraquists concluded an agreement. Receiving communion in both species was recognized as valid, in return for the Utraquists' submission to Roman Catholic authority. The following year, Utraquist and Catholic troops defeated the army of the radical Hussites.

But the pope then refused to recognize the agreement with the Utraquists. Nevertheless, they enjoyed a brief period of political dominance in Bohemia. GEORGE OF PODEBRADY, an Utraquist king, ruled Bohemia from 1458 to 1471. After his death, a Polish dynasty ruled Bohemia in absentia; Catholics then regained control. Utraquist nobles later merged with the Protestant Reformation.

VALDESI   Valdesi is a variant name for the POOR LOMBARDS, the Italian branch of the WALDENSIAN heresy.

VALENS   Ruler of the eastern portion of the Roman Empire from A.D. 364 to 379. Valens was a staunch supporter of the heretical Christian movement called ARIANISM. During the first part of his reign, his counterpart in the Western Empire, Emperor Valentinian, did not interfere in the workings of the church; this gave Valens a free hand in backing the Arians against the orthodox believers. As a result, the more extreme Arians persecuted both orthodox Catholics and even the moderate SEMI-ARIANS. After Valentinian's death, Catholic ruler Gratian came to power in the West and provided some protection for the Catholic party. After Valens's death in 379, Theodosius, his successor, proclaimed Catholic Christianity as the state religion of the Roman Empire and outlawed Arianism.

VALENTINIAN GNOSTICISM   By the second century A.D., schools of spiritual teaching known collectively as GNOSTICISM had appeared in various locations within the Roman Empire. Gnostic doctrines drew variously from Jewish, Christian, and pagan sources to fashion unique systems of belief. Within the Western branch of the Gnostic movement, centered in Egypt and Syria, a tradition of Christian Gnosticism founded by VALENTINUS began.

After Valentinus's death, his teaching was refined and spread by his chief followers, PTOLEMAEUS and MARCUS. Valentinian Gnosticism became a serious rival to the developing Catholic Church, which was forced to clarify its beliefs in response to the growing popularity of the Gnostics. Many of the Valentinians were intellectuals. They produced a spiritual literature of great sophistication, most of which orthodox Catholics destroyed following the conversion of Emperor Constantine in the fourth century. Valentinian works surviving today include THE GOSPEL OF TRUTH, possibly composed by Valentinus himself, and THE GOSPEL OF PHILIP. The influence of Valentinian Gnosticism is often evident in the writings of the other Gnostic groups.

The Valentinian school taught that it was possible to receive direct revelations from Christ through visions. As a result, many differing versions of Gnostic doctrines were produced. Indeed, Irenaeus of Lyons, the orthodox critic of Gnosticism, regarded this diversity as an obvious weakness. The Valentinians themselves, however, may not have been troubled by the variations in doctrines. New spiritual experiences and new interpretations of them were thought to be as valuable as the preservation of old teachings from the past. This attitude was completely alien to orthodox thought.

The Valentinians taught a complex mythology that explained the origin of the world, the source of human suffering, and the way to salvation. The best-known version of this world view is the one Ptolemaeus developed. Little of Ptolemaeus's writing has survived to the present, but his mythology can be reconstructed from descriptions of it in the works of his opponents, Irenaeus and Hippolytus.

In the beginning, Ptolemaeus said, was the unborn Father, called Depth. Depth planted a seed in his partner, Silence, who produced a being called Mind. A partner for Mind, named Truth, was created. Mind and Truth together produced Word and Life. This chain reaction of emanations continued, until there were thirty beings, referred to as the thirty Aeons. Together, the Aeons existed in the realm of light, the Pleroma.

The last of the thirty Aeons to be emanated was Sophia, or Wisdom. Sophia felt a yearning to have direct knowledge of her father, Depth. However, only Mind was able to know the Father directly. Sophia, in frustration and confusion, became filled with emotional turbulence. Eventually, when she realized the impossibility of her desire, the passionate disturbance split off from Sophia, as an "abortion," and had an independent existence.

This free-floating mass of emotions formed a being called Achamoth. This creature was so disruptive that she threatened the Pleroma itself, so she was exiled outside the realm of light. Achamoth's emotional states crystallized into material substances: her grief became air, her fear became water, her confusion became earth, and all three combined to produce fire.

Meanwhile, in the Pleroma, Depth emanated two more Aeons, Christ and Holy Spirit, to teach the Aeons about the Father, and to calm the disturbances Achamoth caused. Then, in an expression of gratitude, all the Aeons emanated another Aeon, JESUS, and surrounded Him with attendant ANGELS.

Christ paid a visit to Achamoth, which left her pining for the light of the Pleroma. Out of these feelings the psychic or mental element of the universe was made. Jesus felt pity for the suffering Achamoth and went forth to visit her in order to give her a glimpse of the radiant Pleroma. Her encounter with Jesus gave her great joy. Achamoth's joy took form as the element of pure spirit.

Achamoth then fashioned a creature out of the material and psychic elements, called the Demiurge. This being proceeded to form the heavens, the earth, and living creatures from his own substance. The nature of the Demiurge is ignorance; he is not even aware that Achamoth, his mother, exists, much less the magnificent Pleroma. In fact, the Demiurge labors under the delusion that he has created the world himself, from nothing.

Secretly, Achamoth inserted the spiritual element within the Demiurge, so that some of his creations would contain small amounts of spirit. The Demiurge himself is strictly a psychic and material being, however. The Valentinian myth, like those of other Gnostic schools, identifies the Demiurge with the God of the Jews, the Creator in the Old Testament.

And so, in this convoluted way, the world came to be. The Valentinians taught that some people, "hylics," are composed entirely of matter, without psychic or spiritual aspects at all; others, "psychics," are made of the material and psychic elements; and a few, "pneumatics," contain, in addition to matter and psyche, the spiritual element.

In the Valentinian account, the Savior came to earth to remind the pneumatics and psychics of their true nature. They can attain freedom from suffering if they can detach themselves from an obsessive involvement with material objects and turn their awareness toward the distant realm of the Pleroma. The hylics, who are essentially machines without soul or spirit, cannot be redeemed.

When the liberating awareness is complete, the universe will come into a harmonious state. Achamoth and the pneumatics will enter and perfect the Pleroma; Achamoth will unite with Jesus; and the pneumatics will unite with the angels, thereby completing each other. The Demiurge will rise to the realm beyond his created world vacated by Achamoth, and will rule benignly over a heaven for the psychics. The merely material world will be destroyed.

What is the purpose of this intricate and peculiar story? To understand the function of Valentinian cosmology, it is important to keep in mind that Achamoth and Demiurge, the divine Aeons, were not meant to be taken only literally, as beings outside of oneself, but also as aspects of the inner world. The Gospel of Philip states, "God created humanity and humanity created God. So is it in the world. People make gods and they worship their creations. It would be appropriate for the gods to worship people!" Each person has Achamoth and Demiurge within, or emotional obsessions and ignorance. Because of these elements within them, people experience the everyday world as an unsatisfying and painful place. There is also, within some, a yearning, like a vague memory, for a realm of light and peace, the Pleroma.

If one views the Valentinian myths as psychological as well as literal, it becomes clearer how salvation is brought about through the special knowledge called GNOSIS. Ignorance and emotional turmoil can be eliminated only by becoming aware of them. This awareness is sufficient to dispel the "fog of terror" that veils the truth about humanity and the world.

The Valentinians illustrated the meaning of gnosis using the metaphor of a tree. If people want to kill a tree, they might try cutting off the branches. If the root is left intact, however, the tree will simply grow more branches. Human beings' ordinary lives are filled with anxieties and frustrations. These states are like the branches of the tree: people struggle to cut off each one, but the root of the problem (ignorance, and the associated emotional turmoil) is unaffected. But if people dig up this root, by recognizing it (the act of gnosis), the tree of confusion will no longer grow.

The Valentinian school taught methods to awaken the liberating insight of gnosis. The study of sacred texts, both those recognized by the orthodox as well as esoteric works by Gnostics, was emphasized. Ceremonies were also conducted, many of which resembled the rituals of Catholic orthodoxy, such as baptism and the Mass. In addition, Valentinians performed two rituals, referred to as the "bridal chamber" and "redemption," the nature of which have been lost. Valentinians, like other Gnostic groups, accepted the validity of personal revelations in the form of visions. It seems likely that awareness practices, such as meditation, played a role in the cultivation of gnosis.

By the end of the third century, the Valentinian school and other Gnostic schools of the Western branch were declining, whereas Catholic orthodoxy was growing stronger. The emphasis on individual salvation through gnosis was not conducive to the formation of tight-knit communities. The Catholic doctrine of salvation through the mediation of priests, however, supported such groups, organized into a strict hierarchy of authority. The Catholic Church proved to be quite effective politically and eventually gained control of the Roman police state during the early fourth century. The orthodox then destroyed the remnants of the Valentinian teaching by force.

VALENTINUS   This man was a preeminent teacher in the movement known as GNOSTICISM, which swept through the Mediterranean world during the first few centuries after Christ. His doctrines were so sophisticated and appealing that they provoked Irenaeus, the bishop of Lyons, to write the first work of orthodox Christian theology, declaring Valentinus and his beliefs to be heretical.

Valentinus was born in Carthage, in northern Africa, around A.D. 100. He moved to the Egyptian city of Alexandria and was educated there. At that time, Alexandria, on the delta of the Nile River, was a center of intellectual and spiritual activity. As part of the Roman Empire, the city was a crossroads of ideas from every corner of the Roman world, and beyond: even Buddhists from India visited Alexandria. In this tolerant environment, where every weird cult and fad were welcomed, Valentinus encountered the strange new religion of Christianity.

At that time, the Christian community and its doctrines were not well established. Christian books were relatively few; some scholars believe that the New Testament Gospel of John had not been written by the time Valentinus was born. Many Christian teachers claimed to know JESUS' true message, and they contradicted each other to a significant degree. There was no recognized central authority to declare which of the ideas being taught in the name of Christ were authentic.

Valentinus studied the various versions of the developing Christian doctrines. He was especially impressed by the teaching of a man named THEODAS, who said that he had studied under one of Christ's own disciples and had learned the secrets that Jesus did not share with the public at large. Exactly what Theodas passed on to Valentinus is not known. However, the teachings of Valentinus himself are certainly at variance with the Catholic version, which denies the transmission of a secret doctrine.

Valentinus also received guidance from visions. According to one account, the glowing form of a newborn baby visited him. When he asked the visitor who he was, the infant replied, "I am the Word" and imparted to Valentinus the mysteries of Gnosticism.

By the year 135, Valentinus had moved to Rome, the hub of political power. He was active in the Christian community there. Indeed, this Gnostic teacher became so prominent that he came close to becoming the bishop of Rome. Valentinus spent many years in Rome, where he actively promoted his beliefs and founded the Valentinian school of Gnosticism. Valentinus knew the church father ORIGEN, and it is thought that he greatly influenced Origen (although Origen did not become a Gnostic himself). Valentinus moved to Cyprus toward the end of his life, and died around A.D. 180. Valentinus's two main disciples, PTOLEMAEUS and MARCUS, continued to teach and develop Valentinian doctrines after the founder's death.

Valentinus's teachings cannot be completely distinguished from those found in some other early Christian writings that are now regarded as orthodox. The works of such orthodox heroes as Justin Martyr and Clement of Alexandria (who actually uses the term GNOSIS, the central Gnostic concept) resemble Valentinian thought to a certain extent. There is no firm evidence that Valentinus experienced any serious rejection from the Christian community during his lifetime. These facts establish that the boundary between Christian "orthodoxy" and "heresy," as they were defined later, had not yet become clear.

However, shortly following Valentinus's death, the anti-Valentinian books of Irenaeus appeared. In these works, the distinctions between the "truth" of orthodoxy and the "falsehood" of the Gnostics were set forth. While Valentinus held that a person could learn about salvation from several sources—the public teachings of Jesus that the priests preserved, Jesus' secret doctrines passed down in private, and personal visions—Irenaeus argued that only the teachings of the priests were valid. Irenaeus's position implies that obedience to the church hierarchy is the duty of all good Christians, while that of Valentinus suggests that salvation can be attained without the involvement of priests. Obviously, Irenaeus's stance supported the power of those in positions of authority within the church. Not surprisingly, then, church authorities generally accepted his version as orthodox, rather than Valentinus's.

Most of the information on VALENTINIAN GNOSTICISM available today has survived in the writings of its orthodox enemies and in the works of Valentinus's disciples. Many researchers believe that Valentinus himself may have written one of the books in the fourth century Gnostic library of NAG HAMMADI, recovered from the Egyptian sands in 1945. This work, called THE GOSPEL OF TRUTH, is joyful and poetic. The writer (Valentinus?) presents the Gnostic theme that the world was not created by the ultimate God, but by a lower being named Error. The true God, called the Father, sent Christ to remind people that they can be liberated from enslavement to the world. The key to liberation is a change in awareness, described in *The Gospel of Truth* as discovering a "living book" placed in their hearts by the Father. One can only wonder what directions orthodox Christianity might have taken if Valentinus, a man of the inner "living book" rather than the unchanging doctrines of the past, had succeeded in becoming pope.

VAUDOIS   Vaudois is a variant name for the POOR MEN OF LYONS, the French branch of the WALDENSIAN heresy.

Peter VERIGIN   Leader of the Russian DOUKHOBOR sect, who oversaw the migration of the Doukhobors to Canada at the beginning of the twentieth century, Peter Verigin assumed the leadership of the sect's radical branch and refused to abide by Russia's laws in 1886. He was exiled to Siberia but maintained control of the movement. The Russian government gladly rid themselves of Verigin's Doukhobors when Canada agreed to accept them as religious refugees. In 1902, Verigin moved to Canada. He oversaw the establishment of a prosperous Doukhobor community in British Columbia.

Verigin came to modify his extreme rejection of modern life, but he was opposed by the Sons of Freedom, a radical group within his sect. In 1924, Verigin was murdered when a railcar he was traveling in was bombed. Some observers blamed the Sons of Freedom; others suspected Peter's own son, also called Peter, who wished to take control of the Doukhobors. The case has never been solved.

VICTOR I   Bishop of Rome from A.D. 189 to his death in 198, Victor I is known for his role in the histories of three unorthodox Christian belief systems. During his tenure, the heresy of ADOPTIONISM, which taught that Jesus was not God but rather was a mere man "adopted" by God, was gaining strength in Rome. Victor strongly opposed this belief and excommunicated its proponent, THEODOTUS THE COBBLER.

Victor's objection to Adoptionism, which was based on the degradation of Christ's divinity, made him vulnerable to another heresy, MODALISM. During his reign, the heretic PRAXEAS arrived in Rome and proclaimed that God the Father and God the Son were one divine Person, who functioned in different "modes" called "Father" and "Son." This teaching certainly seemed to emphasize the divinity of Christ the Son, but it also implied that Christ was purely a deity, not a human being. According to the orthodox view, Christ is both divine and human, and Father and Son are distinct Persons. Victor supported Praxeas and his Modalism to counteract the influence of Adoptionism. This flirtation with heresy on the part of a pope has been raised as a challenge to the adherents of the belief in papal infallibility.

Victor also became involved in the debate over the appropriate day on which to celebrate Easter. The orthodox position, which Victor vigorously defended, held that Easter should be observed on the Sunday following the Jewish Passover. An alternative view, known as QUARTODECIMANISM, stated that Easter occurs on the day of Passover. Victor was more severe than his predecessors in combating the Quartodeciman position, even threatening Quartodeciman bishops with excommunication. It is unknown whether he acted on his threats.

Joseph VILATTE   One of the most active WANDERING BISHOPS of the past century, Joseph Vilatte was born into a French Catholic family in 1854. He was consecrated a bishop in 1892; accounts differ concerning who actually consecrated him. Having broken away from the Roman Catholic Church, he felt free to exercise his authority as a valid bishop to consecrate a large number of other people as bishops. Vilatte died in 1929, but his legacy survives. Today, at least twenty-seven independent religious bodies around the world, from the African Orthodox Church to the Autonomous British Eastern Church (Orthodox-Catholic Province of our Lady of England, Devon and Cornwall), claim legitimacy because they received a valid consecration from him.

Eugene VINTRAS   This Frenchman switched his career from foreman of a cardboard-box factory to founder of a heretical sect. The movement he founded, variously known as the WORK OF MERCY, CHURCH OF CARMEL, or VINTRASIANISM, became popular in northern France during the mid-nineteenth century.

Vintras was born in 1807 in Normandy and led a completely undistinguished early life. But everything changed one evening during his thirty-second year. Answering a tapping at his door, he found an old beggar. Vintras let the stranger in and gave him some money. After a chat, the beggar disappeared, leaving the money behind, along with a letter. The contents of the note convinced Vintras that he had just been visited by none other than the archangel Michael.

Soon, Vintras was conversing with Michael again, along with Saint Joseph and the Virgin Mary, who visited him in visions. They informed Vintras that he was a reincarnation of the prophet Elijah, and that his task was to prepare the world for the beginning of a "Third Age" (following those of the Father and the Son), that of the Holy Spirit. This doctrine closely parallels, and was no doubt inspired by, the teachings of twelfth century mystic JOACHIM OF FIORE (Joachim, however, identified 1260 as the year the Third Age would dawn).

The factory-foreman-turned-prophet set about his task, and the simple sincerity of his preaching soon won him converts. Starting in his hometown of Tilly, Vintrasian groups spread through Normandy. Although Vintras declared himself to be an orthodox Catholic, certain details of his practices struck the Catholic authorities as suspicious. In particular, Vintras's habit of wearing an upside-down crucifix while conducting a mass of his own invention (the "Provictimal Sacrifice of Mary") appeared rather Satanic. Vintras explained that the inversion of the cross merely symbolized the passing of the Age of the Son, but he did not convince the growing number within the Catholic Church who opposed him.

While his movement spread and orthodox fears mounted, Vintras continued to experience visions and to utter prophecies. He predicted that a "terrible explosion" sent from hell would soon flatten Paris and London, and that Vintrasian ceremonies would help to purify the sins of the world before the Holy Spirit's arrival. Reports of miracles circulated, including the appearance of blood from the communion wafers at Vintras's masses.

The orthodox authorities could no longer tolerate the situation. In 1841, the bishop of Bayeux declared that Vintras's teachings were contrary to Catholicism. In the following year, Vintras was convicted of fraud and spent a short time in prison. The prophet continued his work, however. He visited England, and then moved his base of operations to the city of Lyons in southeastern France. In 1848, the pope condemned the movement and excommunicated Vintras. A few years later, some former followers began to claim that the eccentric visionary was in fact a worshipper of Satan, who conducted secret rituals featuring nudity and sex. Whether there is any foundation to these charges or whether they were part of a campaign by Catholics to discredit Vintras, remains unclear. The founder of the Church of Carmel continued to proclaim the advent of the Third Age, to a small but devoted audience, until his death in 1875.

See also: ABBEÉ BOULLAN, SATANISM.

VINTRASIANISM   The nineteenth century religious movement originated by French visionary EUGENE VINTRAS, Vintrasianism was declared heretical by the Roman Catholic Church in 1848.

Christian Knorr VON ROSENROTH   An important figure in the development of the Jewish-Christian occult tradition called the CABALA during the seventeenth century, Christian Knorr Von Rosenroth was a German political adviser and well-known poet. He developed an interest in the *Cabala*, as well as its sources within the Jewish KABBALAH. He was apparently the first Cabalist to encounter the Kabbalistic work of ISAAC LURIA. Von Rosenroth's masterpiece was a two-volume summary of Cabalistic ideas entitled *Kabbalah Denudata*, or "Kabbalah Unveiled," which was published in 1684. This work introduced the Lurianic Kabbalah to Christian Cabalists and had a great effect on the development of the modern magical QABALAH. Von Rosenroth died in 1689.

Caspar VON SCHWENKFELD   A leader in the Protestant radical fringe during the sixteenth century, Caspar von Schwenkfeld, born in 1490, came from the German region of Silesia. When Martin Luther inaugurated the Reformation, von Schwenkfeld became a Lutheran. However, he gradually departed from Lutheran orthodoxy in his beliefs. For example, he held that Christ was too pure ever to have had a body made of ordinary flesh; He must have been embodied in some heavenly material instead. This idea violated the orthodox understanding of Christ as a complete human being, with a real human body. Schwenkfeld also emphasized making contact with the inner light of Christ within one's own heart, a teaching that seemed to Catholics and mainstream Protestants alike to neglect the importance of such external authorities as the Bible. Suffering persecution, Schwenkfeld spent most of his later years wandering in Europe. The SCHWENKFELDER CHURCH, which he founded, has long outlasted him; his death came in 1561.

The VOYNICH MANUSCRIPT   This text has been called "the most mysterious manuscript in the world" by historian Robert Brumbaugh and "one of the great mysteries of twentieth century scholarship" by anthropologist Terence McKenna. The book contains script and illustrations, is seven by ten inches in dimension, and nearly 170 pages in length. The manuscript made its first confirmed historical appearance in 1586 when Rudolph II of Bavaria purchased it from an unknown source. Rudolph was a Protestant ruler known for his fascination with Western esoteric traditions. Accompanying the manuscript at the time of purchase was a letter identifying the text's author as medieval occultist and proto-scientist Roger Bacon.

After Rudolph's death, the work eventually came into the possession of Athanasius Kircher, the renowned seventeenth century hermetist. Despite his great knowledge in esoteric matters, Kircher was unable to make any sense of the book. When Kircher took a vow of poverty and gave away his library, *The Voynich Manuscript* was sent to a Jesuit seminary in Italy. It lay there forgotten until it was discovered and acquired by New York book merchant Alfred Voynich in 1912. The text currently resides in the Benicke Rare Book Room at Yale University.

The mystery of the manuscript lies in the fact that its written characters do not resemble those of any other known script. Also, the style and content of the illustrations seem to be unrelated to any tradition. As a result, most modern attempts at translation have left scholars as puzzled as Rudolph and Kircher must have been. Shortly after the modern rediscovery of the text, medievalist William Newbold reported a successful translation. He stated that the book concerned historical events during the life of Roger Bacon, but other scholars were unable to duplicate Newbold's translation. In 1978, Robert Brumbaugh claimed that the manuscript described the combination of various solid and liquid substances. Perhaps this was a previously unknown chemical tradition, completely unrelated to Western ALCHEMY. Again, other researchers have failed to duplicate Brumbaugh's translation. Anthropologist Terence McKenna has speculated, without much evidence, that the manuscript was penned by JOHN DEE, the court astrologer and magician of Elizabethan England. The challenge of this text proved irresistible to the American intelligence community, which, utilizing the most advanced code-breaking technologies, has also been unable to come up with a translation.

The mystery of *The Voynich Manuscript* is deepened by the peculiar accompanying art, which depicts unknown botanical specimens, vaguely astrological symbols, and rows of naked women seemingly encased in chambers within elaborate systems of plumbing. The most recent translation claim, by Leo Levitov, attempts to explain the meaning of the text *and* the illustrations. Levitov's effort (yet to be verified by other scholars) states that the manuscript is a handbook for conducting ritual group euthanasia—the rite of ENDURA, reportedly practiced by the medieval heretics of southern France known as the CATHARS. The women in the illustrations are bleeding to death in tubs of warm water, and the "botanical specimens," according to Levitov, are actually religious emblems of the Cathars.

The most controversial aspect of Levitov's translation may be his report that the text portrays Catharism as a cult devoted to the worship of the Egyptian goddess Isis. Although nineteenth century occult authority A. E. Waite and 1980s writer David Wood have reported links between the Cathars and the cult of Isis, mainstream researchers have not uncovered any evidence for such a connection in the historical record. Since current knowledge regarding the doctrines of Catharism is based almost entirely on the accounts of its persecutors, confirmation of Levitov's work would revolutionize the current understanding of Western heretical traditions.

WALDENSIANS   One of the most enduring Christian heresies, the Waldensians have survived for more than 800 years. They took their name in honor of their founder, twelfth century preacher PETER WALDO. The irritation that the sect's existence caused the orthodox powers helped to provoke the creation of the INQUISITION. In addition, the fantasies that gave rise to the GREAT WITCH HUNT first crystallized during the course of Waldensian persecutions in the fourteenth and fifteenth centuries.

Following a conversion experience in 1176, Waldo wandered through southern France and northern Italy, preaching his message. He taught that people should renounce the desire for wealth and power and study the New Testament to learn the way to salvation. His message proved very popular among the lower classes. It alarmed the Catholic authorities, however: at the time, the pope was bent on increasing the very items Waldo claimed were obstacles to the spiritual life. The Waldensians' refusal to obey orthodox officials led to the excommunication of the movement by Pope Lucius III in 1184.

The Waldensians valued missionary work and carried their message throughout western Europe. During the first centuries of their existence, Waldo's original preaching territories in France and Italy remained the area of greatest Waldensian concentration. The French Waldensians, known as the POOR MEN OF LYONS, tended at first to reject manual labor, marriage, and living in a fixed location as inappropriate for religious people. The Italian branch, the POOR LOMBARDS, were more practical. They accepted these activities as part of life, and emphasized the importance of developing leadership within their communities to ensure their survival. For a time, the two Waldensian groups could not resolve their differences.

Following Waldo's death around 1205, many Waldensians rejoined the orthodox fold. In 1215, the great Catholic council known as the Fourth Lateran called for the extermination of the sect. Thousands of Waldensians took refuge in the foothills and isolated valleys of the Western Alps.

Up until the Fourth Lateran Council, both Catholics and Waldensians continued to believe that reconciliation might be possible. However, under the pressure of violent persecution, Waldensianism became more radical. At a secret Waldensian council held in 1218, the French branch adopted the more pragmatic attitudes of the Italians; both sides agreed that the materialism of the Catholic Church called for its total rejection by good Christians (meaning themselves).

In the eyes of Catholic officials, the menace to church unity posed by the Waldensians and the other main unorthodox group of the time, the CATHARS, called for drastic action. In 1233, the Inquisition was unleashed against the heretics. Inquisitorial posses prowled the Western Alpine region, and Waldensian missionaries caught anywhere in Catholic Europe were given no mercy.

The assault on the Waldensians continued for centuries, alternately sponsored by the pope, the king of France, and the duke of Savoy (the mountainous region in which many Waldensians settled). During this time, other heretics sought refuge in the Alpine vastness and shared their views with the Waldensians. It is likely that many combinations of unorthodox doctrines, infused with elements of folklore, arose in the region. The Inquisitors, for their part, rarely bothered to discriminate among the different kinds of heretics they caught. They tended to label any heretic from the Alps a "Waldensian."

Confronted with such variety, it is not surprising that the Inquisitors used their own preconceptions to make sense of the unorthodox beliefs they encountered. Consulting the results of earlier heresy trials, such as that of the eleventh century ORLEANS HERETICS, they read that heretics worshipped the Devil and engaged in all sorts of evil activities. By torturing captured Waldensians to extract confessions, they found evidence to confirm their false views. For example, trials of Waldensians in the Italian Alps around 1380 produced a confession that the heretics had celebrated a nocturnal orgy. Before the orgy, the witness said, participants were made to drink a revolting liquid, made from the feces of a giant toad that one of the heretics kept under her bed. Once individuals consumed the toady brew, they were unable to leave the sect.

Such fantasies, superimposing the Inquisitors' stereotypes onto Waldensian and folkloric beliefs, were the seeds that the mass persecutions of the Great Witch Hunt grew out of. Just before 1400, a book called *Errores haereticorum Waldensium* ("Errors of the Waldensian Heresy") was published. The text described Waldensianism as entailing the worship of Lucifer, ritual sex, and child sacrifice. Within a few decades, the term "Waldensian" had become synonymous with "witch." Another contemporary manuscript attacking the heretics was adorned with pictures of Waldensian women flying through the air on broomsticks.

But by the fourteenth century, groups of Waldensians were established throughout Germany, Austria, and Bohemia, as well as southern France and the Alps. They became the targets of wave after wave of Inquisition over the next 150 years. Sometimes, entire villages were assaulted, the women and elderly were burned alive, the young men were taken as slaves, and the property was grabbed by local barons.

Even during the height of the persecution, some Waldensian communities managed to preserve their medieval doctrines. Messages sent between Waldensian groups were often in disguised or coded form in order to avoid the attention of the Inquisitors; it has been suggested that the mysterious symbolism of the Tarot cards might have been invented by Italian Waldensians to conceal their spiritual teachings.

With the advent of the Protestant Reformation in the sixteenth century, the Waldensians found allies at last. Like the Protestants, they rejected the authority of Catholic tradition and recognized scripture as the sole source of religious truth. The Alpine groups made contact with Swiss Calvinists and became defined as a Protestant sect.

Catholic hostilities toward the Waldensians continued throughout the seventeenth century. At one point, a Catholic army rounded up thousands of Waldensians and marched them into imprisonment in Italy. Four years later, a few were released and returned to their mountainous home. HENRI ARNAUD, a revered Waldensian hero, led them. The plight of the Waldensians evoked the sympathy of leading Protestants. John Milton, the English poet, wrote a sonnet about a famous slaughter of Waldensians in 1655, entitled "On the late Massacre in the Piedmont." During the following century, as the Great Witch Hunt wound down, the violence directed against the heretics also declined. The Waldensians were finally granted religious freedom under the law in 1848.

Waldensianism is thriving today. Waldensians are most numerous in Italy, where about 50,000 live. The largest Protestant Church in Italy, located in Rome, is operated by the Waldensians. Congregations of these hardy heretics exist in several European countries, as well as South America and the United States.

Peter WALDO   This French preacher established an important heresy of the later Middle Ages, the WALDENSIANS. During his lifetime, he was known as Waldo; the name Peter became associated with him long after his death. Waldo's teachings resemble those of many later Christians, from Saint Francis of Assisi to the Protestants. Unlike Saint Francis, Waldo was condemned as a heretic. The teachings of Waldo were preserved by the movement he founded, which joined the Protestant side during the Reformation.

In the earlier part of his life, Waldo's main interest was making money. He became a wealthy merchant in the city of Lyons, which was a trade center during the twelfth century. Waldo had not been much involved in religious matters, but this disinterest changed one day. Some reports stated that the sudden death of a friend shocked him into a spiritual insight; others said that he had been moved by the story of Saint Alexis, who had abruptly given up the life of the world and devoted himself to religion.

Whatever the cause, Waldo's sudden change in behavior was startling. After arranging for the security of his wife and two daughters and commissioning a translation of the New Testament into the Provençal language so he could read it, this successful businessperson gave his fortune to the poor. Around 1176, Waldo began to wander around Lyons and the nearby towns, dressed in a simple robe. He preached that obsession with money and power leads to the death of the spirit.

Instead, he taught, people should concentrate on studying the Bible and living the simple life of the apostles.

Waldo quickly won a following among the poor people. Resentment against the Catholic Church, with the splendid lifestyles of the bishops paid for by the tithes of the peasants, was widely felt. Waldo embodied a Christian ideal that did not demand massive material support and that allowed the poor to study the sacred scriptures. Waldo's literate followers could read the New Testament in Latin or Provençal; illiterates were encouraged to hear and memorize the scriptures, as Waldo himself had done.

Although Waldo never criticized the church directly and taught no unorthodox doctrines, his activities raised an alarm among the Catholic priests and bishops. He was not a priest, he had not received permission to preach, and his ideas cast the financial and political ambitions of the pope in an unfavorable light. Two years after Waldo started his preaching career, the archbishop of Lyons forbade him to continue. Waldo then took his case to Pope Alexander III, who would not give him permission to preach without the support of his archbishop. But Waldo refused to desist, claiming that he was called to follow the will of God, not that of men.

In 1182, Catholic authorities drove Waldo and his followers out of Lyons. At the Council of Verona two years later, Lucius III, the new pope, excommunicated Waldo. However, these disruptions seemed only to inspire fervent missionary activity on the preacher's part. Even before his condemnation, Waldo's beliefs had spread into northern Italy. Despite orthodox hostility, over the next twenty years his following swelled in southern France and even extended northward toward Germany. Waldo was revered by the underprivileged classes wherever he went.

Before the end of his life, Waldo saw the community of his followers begin to divide. He and his French disciples rejected marriage and manual labor and focused on travel and teaching. The Italian Waldensians continued to marry and to work. Also, the Italian communities became more organized, favoring the appointment of leaders for each group—a policy Waldo opposed. Occasionally, the founder used his influence to exclude certain groups from the Waldensian fold, but his authority was increasingly challenged.

When Waldo died around 1205, the future of his movement was in doubt because of internal discord. However, under the pressure of persecution at the hands of a common enemy, the Catholic authorities, the Waldensians drew together. The movement Waldo started has survived into the twentieth century, and followers continue to revere his memory.

WANDERING BISHOPS   The apostles of Christ were wanderers, moving from town to town to spread their doctrines. In the earliest days of Christianity, bishops who did not reside in a particular region were common. But as the Catholic Church became firmly established, Christian lands were organized into dioceses, and rootless *orthodox* bishops became rare. Wandering preachers were more likely to be adherents of some heresy, such as MONTANISM or ARIANISM, driven from their home territory by Catholic officials. During the Middle Ages, traveling religious teachers were the main vehicles for the spread of such unorthodox movements as the PE-TROBRUSCIANS, CATHARS, and WALDENSIANS. So successful was this method of transmitting ideas that the Catholic Church was forced to create its own order of wanderers, the Dominicans, in response.

Aside from heretics or mendicant friars, other religious dignitaries could be met on the road in medieval times. If a bishop was dismissed from his post because of misconduct, or if a congregation refused to accept a newly appointed bishop, he might be forced to wander, seeking a diocese that would accept him. According to a theory expressed by Augustine, known as the Augustinian doctrine of holy orders, these homeless bishops retained the religious powers associated with their priestly rank. These powers include the ability to invest other people as bishops as long as the intentions of the bishop and the candidate are pure. The Augustinian doctrine is still held by many Catholic officials to this day.

The Augustinian doctrine creates an interesting possibility: wandering bishops could consecrate others as bishops, who could then consecrate others, producing an increasing number of validly initiated, but not necessarily orthodox, bishops. In the past two centuries, this is exactly what has occurred. Renegade bishops, many of whom received their consecrations from such marginally orthodox groups as the OLD CATHOLICS and the Indian churches descended from the MALABAR CHRISTIANS, have appeared in Europe and North America. Some of these men have offered valid consecrations in exchange for a sum of money—and have become financially comfortable in the process.

Most wandering bishops today trace their legitimacy to one of three men who were active during the late nineteenth and early twentieth centuries, JULES FERRETTE, JOSEPH VILLATTE, and ARNOLD MATHEW. Dozens of independent "apostolic" churches, from the Orthodox-Keltic Church to the Diocese-Vicariate of Niagara Falls, derive from successions these irregular bishops established.

While most wandering bishops have gone about their business quietly, even secretly, some have become notorious. Perhaps the best known was His Grace Mar Joannes (Harold Nicholson, former head waiter at the St. James Hotel in London, England), who died in 1968. During his heyday, Mar Joannes lived in luxury and traveled in style, paying high-profile "state visits" to many countries. The bishop was funded by donations (estimated at 100,000 British pounds per year) from wealthy sponsors, usually elderly women whom he had charmed. In 1956, he reestablished the Roman Empire by crowning a young man emperor (His Imperial Majesty Marziano II); in return, the new ruler bestowed many honorary titles on the bishop.

In addition to the churches derived from the three wanderers mentioned above, other organizations claim to represent lines of apostolic succession that have always existed outside the Roman Catholic Church. Perhaps the most intriguing of these are the groups, found mainly in France and California, whose leaders report that their consecration has been transmitted through the centuries, without interruption, from Mary Magdalene. Some Magdalenian bishops also claim to possess secret teachings given by Christ to Mary. These doctrines are generally forms of GNOSTICISM.

Ellen G. WHITE   Ellen G. White was the first spiritual leader of the SEVENTH DAY ADVENTISTS. In 1840, at seventeen, White joined the MILLERITE movement that was sweeping the northeastern United States. She was convinced that Christ would return to earth in 1843. When this prophecy, and two subsequent ones, proved inaccurate, the movement broke up.

White had a vision, however, showing her that people who held to the belief that the Lord was about to return would be saved from Hell. She also learned that God had deliberately misled those who had calculated the dates of the return in order to glorify those who could still keep the faith after the disappointment. Along with other Millerites, White founded the Seventh Day Adventists in 1860. The record of her revelations, known as *The Spirit of Prophecy*, is revered among Adventists to this day. Belief in the divine inspiration of White's visions is not required in order to be an Adventist, however.

Roger WILLIAMS   Roger Williams pioneered the advocacy of religious toleration in the New World. During the seventeenth century, most regions in Europe tried to enforce religious conformity on their inhabitants, and this habit had been exported to the colonies in America. Williams established the colony of Rhode Island as a haven of spiritual freedom.

Born in England around 1604, Williams was educated at Cambridge University. When he was twenty-six, his restless spirit brought him to the colony of Massachusetts. He believed that America was a place where differences of belief were respected. He was wrong. Five years after his arrival, the Puritans forced this idealist out of the colony because of his attempts to start an alternative church.

For a while, Williams traveled through the wilderness among the Native Americans, who had no trouble respecting the varieties of belief. In 1636, he founded a settlement at a remote spot and named it "Providence." In his famous work, *The bloody tenent of persecution for the cause of conscience discussed*, Williams proclaims that:

> the form of government established in Providence Plantations is DEMOCRATICAL, that is to say, a government held by the free and voluntary consent of all, or the greater part, of the free inhabitants. . . . And otherwise than (conformity to secular laws), all men may walk as their consciences persuade them, every one in the name of his God.

Thus, the Providence colony became the first political entity in Western history to be based on full religious freedom. Its example deeply affected the evolution in America of the principle of the separation of church and state.

This beacon of freedom attracted heretics of many kinds from the other New World colonies. Williams's commitment to his principles was tested by the arrival of the Quakers, a sect whose views he rejected. He expressed his disagreement, but left them in peace. In his later years the founder's behavior was less consistent with his noble purpose. When some groups protested various political decisions Williams made, he targeted them for persecution by passing laws against "loose living" and "immorality." He died in 1683.

See also: ANNE HUTCHINSON, THOMAS MORTON.

Gerrard WINSTANLEY   Gerrard Winstanley was the founder of the DIGGERS, a seventeenth century English sect.

George WISHART   An early Protestant preacher in Scotland, executed for heresy. George Wishart was born in Pitarrow, Scotland, around 1513. As a young man, he was a teacher of Greek but found Martin Luther's calls for religious reform intriguing.

Wishart was accused of heresy since the ruling forces of Scotland were staunchly Roman Catholic. He moved to England in 1538. There, he associated with HUGH LATIMER, another Protestant leader. The following year, Wishart preached the Reformation in Bristol, where he was again accused of heresy. After traveling across continental Europe and returning briefly to England, Wishart went to Scotland to resume his preaching there.

In Scotland, Catholic authorities were intent on persecuting dissenters. Wishart agreed to enter the "protective custody" of the Earl of Bothwell, on the condition that he would not be turned over to Cardinal Beaton, the mastermind of the persecutions. The earl, however, was a supporter of the Catholic cause and promptly violated the agreement. Wishart was brought before the cardinal, who condemned him. He was burned at the stake in St. Andrews on March 1, 1546. There was a public outcry at this horror. Three weeks later, Cardinal Beaton was murdered in his castle. Fourteen years later, Scotland officially became a Protestant country, due in large part to the efforts of John Knox, one of Wishart's students.

See also: PATRICK HAMILTON.

WORK OF MERCY   Work of Mercy is a variant name for the unorthodox religious movement of VINTRASIANISM, which flourished in nineteenth century France.

See also: ABBÉ BOULLAN, EUGENE VINTRAS.

John WYCLIFFE   This English philosopher inspired the only significant heresy to appear in Britain during the Middle Ages, the LOLLARDS. The challenge he mounted against the Roman Catholic Church prepared the way for the arrival on English soil of the Protestant Reformation 200 years later.

Wycliffe was born around 1330. As a young man he studied philosophy and divinity at Oxford; at the age of thirty, he was appointed master of a college there. Wycliffe's early interest lay primarily in philosophy. He became intrigued by philosophical problems concerning the relationship between God's nature and that of the individual beings He created. In the course of Wycliffe's thinking about this abstract issue, he began to pay attention to the current condition of God's official representation on earth, the Catholic Church.

The philosopher did not like what he saw. He believed that the church was meant to follow the example of Christ and the apostles as described in the New Testament. Christ had shown no interest in accumulating wealth or political power; the priests and bishops Wycliffe knew were quite different. Wycliffe also found that the Bible makes no mention of the Catholic doctrine of transubstantiation, which is the notion that the bread and wine of the Mass actually turns into Christ's flesh and blood and is then consumed by believers. This doctrine evolved much later in Christian history, becoming official dogma only in the thirteenth century. Wycliffe rejected it.

Wycliffe began to preach his views at a politically sensitive time. England and France were locked in the Hundred Years' War. The Pope sided with France. There was widespread resentment toward the bishops, many of whom lived in high style off the tithes they collected, and neglected their spiritual duties. The English knights, as well as royalty, were aware of the church's wealth, and of the benefits they would receive if they could find a reason to take over the Church's property.

Wycliffe's message dovetailed with the political aspirations of the English aristo-crats. He called for a church without possessions or political involvement run by humble priests who imitated Christ. In his writings, he says that the Bible should be the only religious authority and damned the Pope as the Antichrist. Wycliffe also called for the king to confiscate the property of the Catholic Church.

Although the nobility thought it too risky to take on the church directly at that time, Wycliffe was protected from the church's inevitably hostile reaction. On several occasions, Catholic officials called for the renegade theologian's activities to be restricted, but each time powerful friends came to his aid. In 1381, Catholic officials at Oxford condemned his attack on the transubstantiation doctrine; at a Catholic council the following year, the archbishop of Canterbury declared Wycliffe's teach-ings to be heresy.

Wycliffe's ideas were well received by the poor, who liked the notion that poverty is associated with holiness. In 1381, there was a peasant uprising against the ruling classes. Wycliffe's enemies blamed his teachings for stirring the masses. In fact, however, Wycliffe had always rejected violence as alien to the way of Christ. Alarmed at the uprising, his aristocratic protectors abandoned him, and he was forced to retire. He died three years later.

Wycliffe left a potent legacy. In order to make the message of the Bible available to everyone, he commissioned the first English translation of the Bible, known as "Wycliffe's Bible" (although he was not the actual translator); this book continued to be in great demand for many years after his death. His dream of a church freed from its materialistic obsessions and its pope was kept alive by the Lollards; they proved less shy about violence than their teacher and attempted to overthrow the English government in 1414. Wycliffe's stand on reforming the church resembled that of Martin Luther much later, and helped Luther's ideas take root when they arrived in England during the sixteenth century. A Bohemian scholar who studied with Wycliffe at Oxford brought his writings back to Prague. There, they inspired the last great heretic of the Middle Ages, JAN HUS.

Brigham YOUNG   The man who established the MORMONS in the state of Utah, Brigham Young was an early disciple of the faith's founder, JOSEPH SMITH. Young was born in 1801 and joined the Mormons in Ohio in the early 1830s. He was a natural leader, quickly ascending to the upper levels of the organization. Young was chosen to head the Mormons' first international mission to Great Britain in 1840.

Following Smith's murder in 1844, the movement fragmented. The majority of Mormons wanted Young to be the new leader. Three years later, he declared that the Mormons should leave their settlement at Nauvoo, Illinois, and travel west to a "promised land" in order to escape persecution. The arduous trek of the Mormons to Utah has become legendary. When they arrived in the Salt Lake Valley, Young declared, "This is the place."

Young remained the head of the largest branch of the Mormons until his death in 1877. His leadership saw the movement grow to more than 140,000 members. One of his actions, however, the Mountain Meadows massacre of 1857, has remained an embarrassment to Mormons to this day. A group of travelers was passing through

Utah on their way to California. For reasons that remain unclear, Young ordered an attack, and 120 people were killed. The leader of the Mormon raiding party was executed by the United States government for murder, but Young, who gave the command, escaped prosecution.

Young had a lasting effect on the doctrines of the Mormons. He was an enthusiastic supporter of polygamy, taking twenty-five wives himself. He also championed the notion of blood atonement, which states that certain sins can be redeemed only by spilling the blood of the person who committed the sin. His memory is honored today in the name of the largest private institution of higher learning in North America, the Mormon-operated Brigham Young University.

ZENOBIA   Zenobia was a ruler of the region including the towns of Antioch and Samosata, which were under Roman domination during the mid-third century A.D. In the belief (which was probably correct) that the Roman emperor had arranged for the assassination of her husband, Prince Odenaethus, Zenobia briefly broke away from Roman control. During her independent rule, she supported PAUL OF SAMOSATA, her treasurer, in a power struggle within the Christian community at Antioch. Paul taught the heresy of ADOPTIONISM. After the Roman army reconquered Zenobia's lands and she was deposed, the orthodox church in Rome convinced pagan Emperor Aurelian to dismiss Paul and give control of the church in Antioch to the Catholics.

ZEPHYRINUS   Pope from A.D. 198 to 217, Zephyrinus presided over a time of turbulence within the Christian community of Rome. The heresy of ADOPTIONISM, which had arisen during the tenure of Pope VICTOR I, his predecessor, continued to flourish. The Adoptionists' claim that Christ was not God but was a man "adopted" by God, opposed the orthodox teaching that Christ was divine. Zephyrinus acted against the Adoptionists by excommunicating their leader, THEODOTUS THE MONEY CHANGER.

Another prominent debate at the time concerned the doctrine of MODALISM. In opposition to the Adoptionists, the Modalists believed that Christ the Son of God was the same Person as God the Father. Zephyrinus also taught this. The official Catholic view that subsequently developed considered Modalism to be a heresy. Orthodoxy defines Christ as a separate divine Person, although He and the Father have the same basic nature. Pope Zephyrinus's support of the Modalist heresy has been a thorny issue for the proponents of the doctrine of papal infallibility.

Shabbatai ZEVI   In the seventeenth century, Shabbatai Zevi's claim to be the Messiah rocked the Jewish world. Modern historians agree that, in fact, he suffered from a mental illness known now as bipolar disorder, or manic depression. The bipolar sufferer can pass through alternating phases of excitement and depression and today is often treated with lithium to stabilize the mood swings. In Zevi's case, these disturbances were convincingly presented to the Jewish public as a sign of his divinity.

Zevi was born in the city of Smyrna (in what is now Turkey) in 1626. His was a family of wealthy merchants, but his interest in religion led him to training for a career as a rabbi. By his teen years, he was studying the mysteries of the KAB-

BALAH. Zevi wondered if he had a special part to play in the unfolding of God's secret will.

By the time he was twenty-two, the young scholar began to experience severe mood changes. During his periods of excitement, the urge to violate the restrictions of Jewish religious law gripped him. Zevi shouted the name of God (YHVH), which should never be pronounced in public; he also celebrated the three major festivals of the Jewish calendar within a single week and conducted a wedding ceremony in which he married the Torah, the sacred scriptures. Zevi also believed that he could levitate and proclaimed that he was the Messiah.

Few took the new savior seriously. Most people recognized that Zevi was affected by something other than divine illumination and pitied him. However, his scandalous behavior led to his expulsion by Jewish community leaders, first from his hometown of Smyrna, then from Salonika, and finally from Constantinople. For several years, Zevi wandered around the eastern Mediterranean region. During his calmer periods, he thought that he was afflicted with demons. He prayed to God and practiced Kabbalistic meditations to rid himself of his emotional problems.

While living in Jerusalem, Zevi heard rumors concerning a young holy man named NATHAN, who lived in nearby Gaza. In 1665, Zevi sought Nathan out, hoping that he might receive a cure for his ailment. Instead, to Zevi's amazement, Nathan insisted that Zevi actually *was* the long-awaited Messiah. Nathan had studied the Kabbalistic system of ISAAC LURIA, which emphasizes that Jewish people are working toward a restoration of perfection in the universe. But he had modified Luria's ideas, magnifying the role of a savior in this restoration. Nathan's eccentric visitor fulfilled his expectations concerning the savior.

Zevi's encounter with Nathan triggered another episode of excitement, during which he convinced himself of his Messianic status. Nathan became the Messiah's prophet and promoter. Nathan's writings and Zevi's public appearances began to attract serious attention at this time. Jewish communities became polarized over the issue of Zevi's claims, and members of the uneducated classes flocked to the new savior. Nathan developed a complex explanation for Zevi's behavior that impressed many rabbis and other intellectuals as well. The SHABBATEAN movement was born.

During the months that followed, Zevi traveled north through Jerusalem, Safed, and Aleppo, eventually arriving in Smyrna. His following grew. Nathan called on the people of Israel to repent and devised new religious practices to this end. Zevi continued to violate the norms of Jewish life, uttering the sacred name, consuming forbidden foods, and urged his devotees to do likewise. As the Shabbateans grew in number, they also became more aggressive: if a rabbi publicly opposed the new Messiah, he could expect a mob to harass him and perhaps to burn down his house.

News and rumors about these events spread to Jewish communities throughout Europe and Africa. Believers in Zevi's divinity appeared far from the sites of his activities. Groups of Shabbateans would fall into trances, experiencing visions of the new Messiah or babbling prophecies. Evidently, the stories about Zevi had tapped the deep yearning of the Jews for their deliverance—a yearning that had been fanned by the recent massacres in Poland and Russia, during which hundreds of thousands of Jews were slaughtered.

The stories about Zevi were so convincing that some people were willing to bet on their authenticity. An entry in the diary of English writer Samuel Pepys reads: "I am told for certain . . . of a Jew in town, that in the name of the rest do offer to give any man ten pounds to be paid one hundred pounds if a certain person, now at Smyrna, be within these two years crowned . . . as the King of the World and that this man is the true Messiah."

The Turkish authorities became concerned that Zevi might attempt to lead a Jewish uprising against the Ottoman Empire. In February 1666, he was arrested at sea while approaching Constantinople, where mass demonstrations of Shabbatean devotion had broken out among the Jews. Zevi remained in jail for several months. During his imprisonment, the bribes of his followers ensured that the Messiah was comfortable. He was able to hold court, receiving delegations of his disciples, and continued to issue assurances that he was the savior. Nathan wrote letters explaining how Zevi's detention was part of the divine plan.

What happened next, however, must have strained Nathan's explanatory powers to the limit. After a rival prophet denounced Zevi to the Turkish authorities, the sultan decided that Zevi's activities could not be permitted to continue. The sultan issued an ultimatum: Zevi had to choose between conversion to Islam and immediate execution. The savior donned a turban, accepted the Moslem faith, and was renamed Aziz Mehmed Effendi.

After his adoption of Islam, Zevi lived for nine more years. The Turkish government granted him a pension in the hope that he would act as a Moslem missionary among the Jews. He continued to experience dramatic shifts in mood; during his excited periods, he would again proclaim himself the Messiah. Zevi died in 1676 in the town of Dulcino on the Adriatic coast.

Meanwhile, Nathan devised an explanation for Zevi's conversion. The savior, having delivered the Jewish people, now had to save the Moslems. In order to accomplish this, he had to disguise himself as a Moslem. While many Shabbateans had renounced Zevi—or pretended that they had always opposed him—after his conversion, others accepted Nathan's face-saving idea. Some of the remaining Shabbateans followed the example of their savior and publicly converted to Islam while secretly maintaining their adoration of Zevi. Another Shabbatean group insisted that only the savior was supposed to become a Moslem. They remained within the Jewish community, often keeping their adherence to Zevi a private matter.

The impact of the Zevi affair on the Jewish world continued long after his death. His association with the Kabbalah tainted that mystical tradition; many came to regard it as too dangerous for public knowledge, and many others condemned it altogether. The Shabbatean movement itself persisted in various forms, both Jewish and Moslem. In the eighteenth century, JACOB FRANK, who viewed himself as a reincarnation of Zevi, seriously disrupted the Jewish community in Poland. Disciples of Zevi have survived into the twentieth century. In 1943, the Nazis murdered a group of Shabbateans in occupied Greece; a Shabbatean community endures to this day in the Iranian city of Mashhad.

Jan ZIZKA   Jan Zizka was the leader of the violent TABORITE heretics in Bohemia during the Hussite Wars of the early fifteenth century. The Taborites destroyed churches and murdered Catholics, which provoked a Crusade against them. Against the numerically superior enemy, Jan Zizka engineered a string of unlikely military victories despite his blindness. He invented a primitive type of tank for battlefield use, which can still be viewed in a museum in the Czech town of Tabor. In addition to attacking Catholics, Zizka also pursued other heretics; he arranged for fifty members of the ADAMITE sect to be burned at the stake. He died of the plague in 1424.

ZOHAR   The name of this text is an Aramaic word meaning "splendor" or "radiance"; hence, it is usually called *The Book of Splendor*. The *Zohar* is the most important work in the literature of the Jewish mystical tradition called KABBALAH. *The Book of Splendor* is immense: in print, it occupies five large volumes. Most of the text concerns the teachings of Simeon bar Yochai, a famous rabbi of the second century A.D. Since the *Zohar*'s appearance in Europe at the end of the thirteenth century, controversy has raged over its authorship. Most Kabbalists traditionally accepted the claim that Rabbi Simeon or an immediate disciple wrote it. However, modern scholars have established that the author of the *Zohar* was the man who first presented it to the world, Rabbi Moses de Leon, a Spanish Kabbalist who died in 1305.

According to de Leon, a sage named Nachmanides discovered the writings of Simeon, concealed since ancient times, in Palestine. De Leon claimed that Nachmanides sent the *Zohar* to him for editing. De Leon wrote it himself, around 1270. The practice of attributing the authorship of a document to a famous historical figure in order to increase its authority is an old Jewish custom dating back at least to the PSEUDEPIGRAPHA.

The *Zohar* brings together ideas from many earlier Kabbalistic works, such as the SEFER YETZIRAH. A central theme in the text is a call to awareness: "Man, whilst in this world, considers not and reflects not what he is standing on, and each day as it passes he regards as though it has vanished into nothingness." In order to live a holy life, people must first become aware of their present situation: "O, ye terrestrial beings who are sunk deep in slumber, awake!"

The Book of Splendor teaches that each person has three souls. The *nefesh*, or vital soul, is closely associated with the physical body and its instincts. The *nefesh* ordinarily remains near the grave after death, although it can sometimes wander the earth, providing invisible help to the living. The *neshamah* is the inner soul, the "costly pearl" of light God sent into this world. If people care for the *neshamah*, it will guide them. After death, this soul can ascend to the throne of God, from whence it came. The third soul is the *ruach* or spirit, which mediates between the *nefesh* and the *neshamah*. Following death, the *ruach* dwells in the "earthly Garden of Eden." People can achieve a healthy and holy life by promoting harmony among the three souls, so that after death they can reach their appropriate destinations. Like many other Kabbalistic works, the *Zohar* also teaches a doctrine of REINCARNATION.

The *Zohar* does not, however, contain systematic instructions for the development of awareness or the balancing of the three souls. Rather, suggestions and hints are scattered throughout the text. Much emphasis is placed on meditating upon the image of the Tree of Life. Later students of the *Zohar* practiced elaborate visualizations of the Tree, representing the emanations of God.

The Book of Splendor became well known—indeed notorious—because of the importance it places on the spiritual aspects of sexuality. God is described using both male and female imagery, and the creation of the universe is said to have occurred through sexual intercourse. Humans are split into two sexes, but spiritual wholeness can be achieved only by their reunification. This doctrine seems to have been understood literally. The *Zohar* recommends that one should make love (within marriage) once a week, except during the woman's menstrual period. In this way, a couple becomes "one without blemish." God is present during these sacred sex acts and is driven away when they are prevented.

The study of dreams is another crucial facet of the spiritual life, according to the *Zohar*: "A dream uninterpreted is like a letter undeciphered." Dreams contain information about the future, as well as about hidden aspects of the present, mixed with falsehood. Therefore, one must analyze each object and color in the dream carefully, using a specific set of interpretations. Some historians believe that the *Zohar* may have inspired Sigmund Freud to develop his method of dream analysis.

The Book of Splendor also regards the domain of sound as a pathway to awakening. Every object in the universe is singing the praises of its Creator. The *Zohar* encourages people to listen to the world in order to overhear its songs. Certain hymns are regarded as the containers of powerful spiritual secrets, as are the Hebrew names of God.

Throughout its history, the *Zohar* has been both revered and reviled. Most Kabbalists accepted the work as a great resource for spiritual development. For example, great sixteenth century Kabbalist ISAAC LURIA derived many of his doctrines and meditation techniques from the *Zohar*. Some Kabbalists even claimed that it contained the inner truth of the Jewish tradition. Such extreme claims provoked the opposition of Jewish authorities who were not attracted to Kabbalah, and the *Zohar* was sometimes condemned as unorthodox. Interest in the text carried over into the Christian version of the tradition, the CABALA. Leading promoters of the *Cabala*, such as CHRISTIAN KNORR VON ROSENROTH, translated portions of the *Zohar* into more accessible languages.

In more recent times, as the Kabbalah became alienated from the Jewish mainstream, the *Zohar* was viewed with increasing hostility. Leading nineteenth century Jewish historian, Heinrich Graetz, thought that the *Zohar* had harmed the course of Judaism by introducing a muddled sort of mysticism: "Its contents are as curious, confused and chaotic as its form and external dress." In the present century, with the rehabilitation of the Kabbalistic tradition within Judaism, interest in the riches of *The Book of Splendor* has again returned.

ZWICKAU PROPHETS   The German town of Zwickau became a center of heresy during the first years of the Protestant Reformation in the sixteenth century. Radical Protestant THOMAS MÜNZER preached there, calling for the Holy Spirit to inspire the violent overthrow of the existing social order. The authorities chased Münzer from Zwickau, but many followers remained.

In 1521, the nearby town of Wittenberg was visited by "prophets" from Zwickau. The prophets were probably a group of Münzerites who sought to establish a Christian community that would reject all forms of authority except for obedience to the Holy Spirit. At first, the prophets were welcomed as fellow Protestants. Martin

Luther, Wittenberg's most famous citizen, was abroad when the Zwickau prophets arrived. When he returned the following year, he regarded the group from Zwickau as a threat. The Reformation movement would disintegrate without obedience to its leaders, he feared, and the prophets obeyed no one but God. Luther used his influence to drive them from the town. Their subsequent fate is unknown, but they likely merged with other radical Protestant groups.

LISTING OF ENTRIES ORGANIZED BY TOPIC

A. MEANINGS OF HERESY (*Definitions and Related Terms*)

Apostasy
Blasphemy
Heathenism
Infidels

Perfectionism
Pantheism
Paganism
Polytheism

Profanity
Schism
Tritheism

See also: INTRODUCTION.

B. CHRISTIAN HERESIES AND HERETICS BY HISTORICAL PERIOD (*Heresies that span more than one period are listed under the period in which they originated or in which they were most prominent.*)

1. Ancient (First–Sixth Centuries)

Acacius of Caesarea
Adoptionism
Aesclypedotus
Aetius
Anastasius
Anomoeans
Apelles
Aphthartodocetae
Apollinarianism
Apollinaris of Laodicea
Arianism
Arius
Armenian Christians
Artemas
Assyrian Christians
Asterius
Barsumas (1)
Barsumas (2)
Basil of Ancyra
Basilidean Gnosticism
Basilides

Borborites
Cainites
Carpocrates
Carpocratian Gnosticism
Cassian, John
Celestius
Cerinthus
Cleomenes
Constantius II
Crypto-Sabellianism
Dionysius of Alexandria
Dioscurus
Docetism
Donatism
Donatus
Dynamic Monarchianism
Ebionites
Elkesaites
Epigonus
Epiphanes
Eudoxius

Eunomius
Eusebius of Nicomedia
Eutyches
Faustus of Riez
Gaianus of Alexandria
Glaucas
Gnosticism
Homoeans
Homoiousians
Ibas
Isochrists
Jacob Baradaeus
Jacobites
Jovinian
Julian of Eclanum
Julian of Halicarnassus
Lucian of Antioch
Majorinus
Marcellina
Marcellus of Ancyra
Marcion

2. Pagan Competitors of Ancient Christianity

3. Medieval (Seventh–Fourteenth Centuries)

Monteforte Heretics
Nicetas
Olivi, Peter
Orleans Heretics
Pastoureaux
Paulicians
Paul the Armenian
Petrobruscians

Pierre de Bruys
Ratramnus
Segarelli, Gerard
Sergio
Sergius
Spanish Adoptionism
Speroni, Hugo

Spiritual Franciscans
Symeon
Tanchelm of Flanders
Theophilus
Waldensians
Waldo, Peter
Wycliffe, John

4. Renaissance and Reformation (Fifteenth–Seventeenth Centuries)

Adamites
Ammann, Jacobus
Anabaptists
Anti-Trinitarianism
Arminianism
Arminius, Jacobus
Arnault, Henri
Blandrata, Giorgio
Bockelson, Jan
Bohemian Brethren
Bruno, Giordano
Budny, Simon
Cabala
Campanella, Tommasso
Cranmer, Thomas
Crell, Nicholas
Czechowic, Martin
David, Ferencz
Dee, John
Diggers
Fenelon, François
Fifth Monarchy Men
Filippov, Danila
Galileo
George of Podebrady
Gribaldi, Matteo
Guibourg, Abbé
Guyon, Madame
Hamilton, Patrick

Hoffmann, Melchior
Hooper, John
Horebites
Hus, Jan
Huska, Martin
Hussites
Hutchinson, Anne
Hutterites
Hutter, Jacob
Jansen, Cornelius
Jansenism
Joan of Arc
John of Wesel
Knipperdolling, Bernt
La Voisin
Latimer, Hugh
Levellers
Lilburne, John
Lukas of Prague
Matthys, Jan
Melchiorites
Mennonites
Molinos, Miguel de
Morton, Thomas
Muggletonians
Münster Heretics
Münzer, Thomas
Nayler, James
Oldcastle, Sir John

Paleologus, Jacob
Pico Della Mirandola,
    Giovanni
Pikarts
Purvey, John
Quietism
Ranters
Ridley, Nicholas
Riedemann, Peter
Rothmann, Bernt
Savonarola, Girolamo
Schwenkfelder Church
Servetus, Michael
Simons, Menno
Socinianism
Socinus, Faustus
Stancari, Francesco
Taborites
Trithemius of Sponheim
Unitas Fratrum
Utraquists
Von Schwenkfeld, Carl
Williams, Roger
Winstanley, Gerrard
Wishart, George
Zizka, Jan
Zwickau Prophets

5. Modern (Eighteenth–Twentieth Centuries)

Amish
Binggeli, Johannes
Blavatsky, Madame Helena
    Petrovna
Boullan, Abbé
Camisards

Church of Carmel
Dashwood, Sir Francis
Doukhobors
Ferrette, Jules
Forest Brotherhood
Fox, Matthew

Frank, Jacob
Hensley, George
Hermanos Penitentes
Jehovah's Witnesses
Khlysty
Kolesnikov, Sylvan

Kung, Hans
Lee, Ann
Mathew, Arnold
Medmenham Monks
Miller, William
Millerism
Modernism
Mormons
Noyes, John Humphrey
Old Catholics
Oneida Community
Rasputin, Grigori Efimovich

Russell, Charles
Russellites
Rutherford, Joseph
Selivanov, Kondrati
Seventh Day Adventists
Shakers
Skoptsy
Smith, Joseph
Snake Handlers
Society for the Reparation
    of Souls
Spiritualism

Swedenborg, Emanuel
Swedenborgianism
Theosophy
Unitarianism
Unternahrer, Anton
Verigin, Peter
Vilatte, Joseph
Vintras, Eugene
Wandering Bishops
White, Ellen G.
Young, Brigham

C. HERETICAL AND ESOTERIC JUDAISM

Abraham the Jew
Abulafia, Abraham
Frank, Jacob
Kabbalah
Luria, Isaac

Merkabah Mysticism
Molcho, Solomon
Nathan of Gaza
Pseudepigrapha
Reubeni, David

Sefer Yetzirah
Shabbateans
Zevi, Shabbatai
Zohar

D. HERESIES IN THE EAST (*Byzantine and Russian Territories*)

Acacius of Caesarea
Anastasius
Apollinarianism
Arianism
Armenian Christians
Assyrian Christians
Babai the Great
Barsumas (1)
Barsumas (2)
Basil of Ancyra
Basil the Bogomil
Bogomil
Bogomilism
Chrysocheir
Constans II
Constantine V
Constantine of Armenia
Constantius II
Coptic Christians
Doukhobors
Ebedjesus
Filippov, Danila

Gurdjieff, George
Hutterites
Iconoclasm
Isochrists
Jacob Baradaeus
Jacobites
Jacob of Edessa
Julian of Halicarnassus
Karbeas
Khlysty
Kolesnikov, Sylvan
Leo V
Leo IV
Leo III
Lucian of Antioch
Malabar Christians
Marcellus of Ancyra
Maronites
Messalians
Michael II
Monenergism
Monophysitism

Monotheletism
Nestorianism
Nestorius
Nicetas
Origenism
Paulianists
Paulicians
Paul of Samosata
Paul the Armenian
Rasputin, Grigori
    Efimovich
Selivanov, Kondrati
Sergio
Sergius
Skoptsy
Symeon
Theodore of Mopsuestia
Theodoret
Theopaschites
Theophilus
Valens
Zenobia

E. HERESIES IN NORTH AMERICA *(The following individuals and groups have been particularly prominent in North America; many European heresies not listed under this heading have also been represented in North America.)*

Adamites	Millerism	Shakers
Brother Twelve	Miller, William	Smith, Joseph
Doukhobors	Mormons	Snake Handlers
Fox, Matthew	Morton, Thomas	Spiritualism
Hensley, George	Noyes, John Humphrey	Theosophy
Hutchinson, Anne	Oneida Community	Unitarianism
Hutterites	Russell, Charles	Verigin, Peter
Jehovah's Witnesses	Russellites	White, Ellen G.
Lee, Ann	Rutherford, Joseph	Williams, Roger
Mennonites	Seventh Day Adventists	Young, Brigham

F. HERESIES BY DOCTRINAL THEME *(Entries concerning individuals are not listed here, unless their views are not subsumed under the heading of a heretical group. Many heresies addressed more than one doctrinal theme. Each heresy is listed in this section only once under its most distinctive theme.)*

1. Human Nature and Potential
(Unorthodox views of human powers and destiny; self-perfectability; self-deification)

Abelard, Peter	Julian of Eclanum	Pikarts
Eudes de l'Etoile	Khlysty	Paleologus, Jacob
Forest Brotherhood	Modernism	Paracelsus
Frank, Jacob	Molcho, Solomon	Ranters
Free Spirit, Heresy of the	Mormons	Reincarnation
Gottschalk	Oneida Community	Reubeni, David
Gurdjieff, George	Origenism	Schwenkfelder Church
Gnosis	Paracelsus	Semi-Pelagianism
Gnosticism	Pelagianism	Skoptsy
Jansenism	Pico Della Mirandola,	Zevi, Shabbatai
Jovinian	Giovanni	

2. Relations with Social and Material Worlds
(Unorthodox definitions and valuations of matter; rejection of money, property, conventional authority, and social structures)

Adamites	Cornelius, Wilhelm	Knights Templar
Alchemy	Diggers	Levellers
Amish	Donatism	Lollards
Apostolici	Fraticelli	Melitus of Lycopolis
Arnoldists	Galileo	Morton, Thomas
Astrology	Henry of Lausanne	Novatianism
Beghards	Horebites	Old Catholics
Beguines	Humiliati	Orleans Heretics
Bruno, Giordano	Hutterites	Pastoureaux
Camisards	Joan of Arc	Petrobruscians

Rosicrucians
Spiritual Franciscans
Taborites

Tanchelm of Flanders
Unitas Fratrum
Waldensians

Wandering Bishops
Williams, Roger
Zwickau Prophets

3. Relations with Spirit Worlds

Angel Magic
Angels
Demon Magic
Demons
Enochian Magic
Golden Dawn, Hermetic
   Order of the

Magic
Magonia
Natural Magic
Necromancy
Ordo Templi Orientis

Qabalah
Spiritualism
Swedenborgianism
Theosophy

4. Relations with Divinity
(Unorthodox forms of mysticism; rejection, inversion, or replacement of conventional sacraments)

Abulafia, Abraham
Amatory Mass
Anabaptists
Arras Heretics
Berengar
Black Mass
Cabala
Church of Carmel

Flagellants
Hussites
Hutchinson, Anne
Iconoclasm
Kabbalah
Medmenham Monks
Mennonites
Merkabah Mysticism

Montanism
Monteforte Heretics
Quietism
Ratramnus
Shakers
Snake Handlers
Utraquists

5. Time
(Unorthodox views concerning history or calendrical observances)

Fifth Monarchy Men
Joachim of Fiore
Millerism

Quartodecimanism
Russellites
Savonarola, Girolamo

Seventh Day Adventists
Shabbateans
Vintrasianism

6. Nature of God
(The following list includes unorthodox views of Christ in the context of the Trinity.)

Amalric of Bena
Anomoeans
Anti-Trinitarianism
Arianism
Bogomilism
Cathars
David of Dinant

John of Wesel
John Scotus Erigena
Manichaeism
Marcionism
Modalism
Muggletonians
Patripassianism

Paulicians
Priscillianism
Socinianism
Sabellianism
Satanism
Unitarianism

7. Nature of Christ
(Unorthodox views on Christ's divinity, humanity, powers of salvation)

Adoptionism
Aphthartodocetae
Apollinarianism
Arminianism
Docetism
Ebionites

Elkesaites
Jesus
Monenergism
Monophysitism
Monotheletism

Nestorianism
Pantera, Tiberius
Paulianists
Spanish Adoptionism
Theopaschites

G. UNORTHODOX AND ESOTERIC TEXTS

Almadel
Arbatel of Magic
Black Pullet
The Book of Elkesai
The Book of Enoch
The Book of Mormon
The Book of the Secrets
    of Enoch
Chaldean Oracles
Corpus Hermeticum

Emerald Tablet
The Gospel of Philip
The Gospel of Thomas
The Gospel of Truth
Grand Grimoire
Grimoire of Honorius
Grimoires
Grimorium Verum
Hermetica
The Hymn of the Pearl

The Key of Solomon
The Lemegeton
Nag Hammadi Library
Pseudepigrapha
Sacred Magic of
    Abramelin the Mage
Sefer Yetzirah
Treatise on Angel Magic
The Voynich Manuscript
Zohar

H. BIOGRAPHIES OF HERETICS

Abelard, Peter
Abraham the Jew
Abulafia, Abraham
Acacius of Caesarea
Aesclypedotus
Aetius
Agrippa, Cornelius
Amalric of Bena
Ammann, Jakob
Anastasius
Apelles
Apollinaris of Laodicea
Arius
Arminius, Jacobus
Arnaud, Henri
Arnold of Brescia
Artemas
Asterius
Babai the Great
Barsumas (1)
Barsumas (2)
Basilides
Basil of Ancyra
Basil the Bogomil

Bentivenga of Gubbio
Berengar
Binggeli, Johannes
Blandrata, Giorgio
Blavatsky, Madame Helena
    Petrovna
Bockelson, Jan
Bogomil
Boniface VIII
Boullan, Abbè
Brother Twelve
Bruno, Giordano
Budny, Simon
Campanella, Tommasso
Carpocrates
Cassian, John
Cecco d'Ascoli
Celestius
Celsus
Cerinthus
Clementius of Bucy
Cleomenes
Constans II
Constantine V

Constantine of Armenia
Constantius II
Cornelius, Wilhelm
Cranmer, Thomas
Crell, Nicholas
Crowley, Aleister
Czechowic, Martin
Dashwood, Sir Francis
David, Ferencz
David of Dinant
Dee, John
Dionysius of Alexandria
Dioscurus
Donatus
Dolcino, Friar
Ebedjesus
Ebion
Eckhart (von Hocheim),
    Meister
Elipandus
Epigonus
Epiphanes
Eudes de l'Etoile
Eudoxius

I. SUPPRESSION OF HERESY (*Legislation and Persecution*)

SUGGESTIONS FOR FURTHER READING

HERESIES (*General Works and Major Themes*)

Bainton, R. H. *Concerning Heresies: A Collection of the Opinions of Learned Men Both Ancient and Modern.* New York, 1933.

Baker, D. *Schism, Heresy and Religious Protest.* New York, 1972.

Belloc, H. *The Great Heresies.* Freeport, NY, 1968.

Berger, P. L. *The Heretical Imperative,* New York, 1979.

Berman, M. *The Reenchantment of the World.* Ithaca, NY, 1981.

———. *Coming to Our Senses: Body and Spirit in the Hidden History of the West.* New York, 1989.

Brown, H. O. J. *Heresies: The Image of Christ in the Mirror of Heresy and Orthodoxy from the Apostles to the Present.* Grand Rapids, MI, 1988.

Cavendish, R. *The Powers of Darkness.* New York, 1975.

Chamberlin, E. R. *The Bad Popes.* New York, 1993.

Christie-Murray, D. *A History of Heresy.* London, 1976.

Clifton, C. S. *Encyclopedia of Heresies and Heretics.* Santa Barbara, 1992.

Couliano, I. P. *The Tree of Gnosis: Gnostic Mythology From Early Christianity to Modern Nihilism.* San Francisco, 1992.

Cristiani, L. *Heresies and Heretics.* New York, 1959.

Cross, F. L. *The Oxford Dictionary of the Christian Church.* Oxford, 1957.

Daraul, A. *A History of Secret Societies.* New York, 1990.

De Rosa, P. *Vicars of Christ: The Dark Side of the Papacy.* New York, 1988.

Endleman, R. *Deviance and Psychopathology: The Sociology and Psychology of Outsiders.* Malabar, FL, 1990.

Head, J., and S. L. Cranston. *Reincarnation in World Thought.* New York, 1967.

Lawton, D. *Blasphemy.* Philadelphia, 1993.

Levy, L. W. *Blasphemy: Verbal Offense Against the Sacred, From Moses to Salman Rushdie.* New York, 1993.

Liguori, A. M. *The History of Heresies and Their Refutation: Or the Triumph of the Church.* Dublin, 1847.

MacGregor, G. *Dictionary of Religion and Philosophy.* New York, 1991.

Mather, G. A., and L. A. Nichols. *Dictionary of Cults, Sects, Religions and the Occult.* Grand Rapids, MI, 1993.

Nigg, W. *The Heretics: Heresy Through the Ages.* New York, 1990.

Pressense, E. *Heresy and Christian Doctrine.* London, 1873.

Rhodes, H. T. F. *The Satanic Mass.* London, 1954.

Schultz, T., ed. *The Fringes of Reason: A Whole Earth Catalog.* New York, 1989.

Trismegistus, R. *Birth of a Heretic.* Toronto, 1957.

Walter, N. *Blasphemy: Ancient and Modern.* London, 1990.

Webster, R. *A Brief History of Blasphemy.* Southwold, U.K., 1990.

ANCIENT CHRISTIAN HERESIES AND COMPETITORS (*First–Sixth Centuries*)

Amidon, P. R., ed. *The Panarion of St. Epiphanius, Bishop of Salamis.* New York, 1990.

Barnes, T. D. *Tertullian: A Historical and Literary Study.* Oxford, 1971.

Barnstone, W., ed. *The Other Bible: A Collection of Ancient, Esoteric Texts, Excluded from the Official Canon of the Old and New Testaments.* New York, 1984.

Bauer, W. *Orthodoxy and Heresy in Earliest Christianity.* Philadelphia, 1971.

Blackman, E. C. *Marcion and His Influence.* London, 1948.

Burkitt, F. C. *The Religion of the Manichees.* New York, 1925.

Chuvin, P. *A Chronicle of the Last Pagans.* Cambridge, MA, 1989.

Dart, J. *The Jesus of Heresy and History.* San Francisco, 1988.

Evans, R. F. *Pelagius: Inquiries and Reappraisals.* London, 1968.

Filoramo, G. *A History of Gnosticism.* Cambridge, MA, 1990.

Fowden, G. *The Egyptian Hermes: A Historical Approach to the Late Pagan Mind.* New York, 1986.

Fox, R. L. *Pagans and Christians.* San Francisco, 1987.

Frend, W. H. C. *The Donatist Church: A Movement of Protest in Roman North Africa.* Oxford, 1952.

————. *The Rise of the Monophysite Movement: Chapters in the History of the Church in the Fifth and Sixth Centuries.* New York, 1972.

Grant, R. M. *Gnosticism: A Source Book of Heretical Writings from the Early Christian Period.* New York, 1961.

Gregg, R. C. *Early Arianism: A View of Salvation.* Philadelphia, 1981.

Gwatkin, H. M. *Studies of Arianism: Chiefly Referring to the Character and Chronology of the Reaction Which Followed the Council of Nicaea.* Cambridge, U.K., 1900.

Hedrick, C. W., and R. Hodgson, eds. *Nag Hammadi, Gnosticism, and Early Christianity.* Peabody, MA, 1986.

Jonas, H. *The Gnostic Religion: The Message of the Alien God and the Beginnings of Christianity.* Boston, 1958.

Jones, A. H. M. *Were Ancient Heresies Disguised Social Movements?* Philadelphia, 1966.

Koijn, A. F. J., and G. J. Reinijk. *Patristic Evidence for Jewish-Christian Sects.* Leiden, 1973.

Layton, B. *The Gnostic Scriptures.* New York, 1987.

Legreton, J. *History of the Dogma of the Trinity from its Origins to the Council of Nicaea.* London, 1939.

Luck, G. *Arcana Mundi: Magic and the Occult in the Greek and Roman Worlds.* Baltimore, 1985.

MacMullen, R. *Enemies of the Roman Order: Treason, Unrest, and Alienation in the Empire.* London, 1992.

Newman, J. H. C. *The Arians of the Fourth Century.* London, 1919.

Pagels, E. *The Gnostic Gospels.* New York, 1979.

————. *Adam, Eve and the Serpent.* New York, 1988.

Pelikan, J. *The Emergence of the Catholic Tradition (100–600).* Chicago, 1971.

Prestige, G. L. *St. Basil the Great and Apollinaris of Laodicea.* London, 1956.

Quispel, G. *Gnostic Studies.* Istanbul, 1974.

Raven, C. E. *Apollinarianism: An Essay on the Christology of the Early Church.* New York, 1923.

Roberts, A., and J. Donaldson, eds. *The Writings of Irenaeus.* Edinburgh, 1868.

Robinson, J. M., ed. *The Nag Hammadi Library.* San Francisco, 1989.

Rudolph, K. *Gnosis: The Nature and History of Gnosticism.* New York, 1983.

Smith, M. *Jesus the Magician.* San Francisco, 1978.

Trigg, J. W. *Origen: The Bible and Philosophy in the Third Century Church.* Atlanta, 1983.

Turner, H. E. W. *The Pattern of Christian Truth: A Study in the Relations Between Orthodoxy and Heresy in the Early Church.* London, 1954.

Vine, A. R. *The Nestorian Churches.* London, 1937.

Wallis, R. T., ed. *Neoplatonism and Gnosticism.* Albany, NY, 1992.

Widengren, G. *Mani and Manichaeism.* London, 1965.

Willis, G. G. *Saint Augustine and the Donatist Controversy.* London, 1950.

MEDIEVAL CHRISTIAN HERESIES *(Seventh–Fourteenth Centuries)*

Barber, M. *The Trial of the Templars.* New York, 1978.

Berkhout, C. T., and J. B. Russell. *Medieval Heresies: A Bibliography 1960–1979.* Toronto, 1981.

Bett, H. *Joachim of Flora.* Richwood, NY, 1976.

Birks, W., and R. A. Gilbert. *The Treasure of Montsegur.* London, 1987.

Bussell, F. W. *Religious Thought and Heresy in the Middle Ages.* Port Washington, NY, 1971.

Cohn, N. *The Pursuit of the Millennium: Revolutionary Millenarians and Mystical Anarchists of the Middle Ages.* London, 1970.

Comba, E. *History of the Waldenses of Italy, from Their Origin to the Reformation*. New York, 1978.

Crowder, C. M. D., ed. *Unity, Heresy and Reform, 1378–1460: The Conciliar Response to the Great Schism*. London, 1977.

Erbstösser, M. *Heretics in the Middle Ages*. Leipzig, 1984.

Fahey, J. F. *The Eucharistic Teaching of Ratramnus of Corbie*. Mundelein, IL, 1951.

Fine, J. V. A. *The Bosnian Church: A New Interpretation. A Study of the Bosnian Church and Its Place in State and Society from the 13th to the 15th Centuries*. New York, 1975.

Garsoian, N. G. *The Paulician Heresy*. The Hague, 1968.

Greenaway, G. W. *Arnold of Brescia*. New York, 1931.

Hyma, A. *The Brethren of the Common Life*. Grand Rapids, MI, 1950.

Lambert, M. D. *Medieval Heresy: Popular Movements from Bogomil to Hus*. London, 1977.

Leff, G. *Heresy in the Later Middle Ages: The Relation of Heterodoxy to Dissent c. 1250–1450*. New York, 1967.

Lerner, R. E. *The Heresy of the Free Spirit in the Later Middle Ages*. Berkeley, 1972.

Levitov, L. *Solution of the Voynich Manuscript*. Laguna Hills, CA, 1987.

Loos, M. *Dualist Heresy in the Middle Ages*. The Hague, 1974.

Lourdaux, W., and D. Verhelst, eds. *The Concept of Heresy in the Middle Ages (11th–13th Centuries)*. The Hague, 1976.

Macdonald, A. J. *Berengar and the Reform of Sacramental Doctrine*. New York, 1930.

Marks, C. *Pilgrims, Heretics, and Lovers: A Medieval Journey*. New York, 1975.

Martin, E. J. *A History of the Iconoclastic Controversy*. London, 1930.

McDonnell, E. W. *The Beguines and Beghards in Medieval Culture*. New Brunswick, NJ, 1954.

McFarlane, K. B. *John Wycliffe and the Beginnings of English Nonconformity*. London, 1952.

McGinn, B. *The Calabrian Abbot: Joachim of Fiore in the History of Western Thought*. New York, 1985.

Melia, P., ed. *The Origin, Persecutions, and Doctrines of the Waldenses*. New York, 1978.

Molnar, A. *A Challenge to Constantinianism: The Waldensian Theology in the Middle Ages*. Geneva, 1976.

Moore, R. I. *The Birth of Popular Heresy*. London, 1975.

———. *The Origins of European Dissent*. London, 1977.

Obolensky, D. *The Bogomils: A Study of Balkan Neo-Manichaeism*. New York, 1948.

Partner, P. *The Murdered Magicians: The Templars and Their Myth*. London, 1981.

Pelikan, J. *The Spirit of Eastern Christendom (600–1700)*. Chicago, 1974.

———. *The Growth of Medieval Theology (600–1300)*. Chicago, 1978.

Peters, E., ed. *Heresy and Authority in Medieval Europe*. Philadelphia, 1980.

Reeves, M. *Joachim of Fiore and the Prophetic Future*. San Francisco, 1977.

Runciman, S. *The Medieval Manichee: A Study of the Christian Dualist Heresy*. Cambridge, U.K., 1947.

Russell, J. B. *Dissent and Reform in the Early Middle Ages*. Berkeley, 1965.

———. *Religious Dissent in the Middle Ages*. New York, 1971.

Tashkovski, D. *Bogomilism in Macedonia*. Skopje, 1975.

Tobin, F. *Meister Eckhart: Thought and Language*. Philadelphia, 1986.

Wakefield, W. L. *Heresy, Crusade and Inquisition in Southern France, 1100–1250*. New York, 1974.

Wakefield, W. L., and A. P. Evans. *Heresies of the High Middle Ages: Selected Sources Translated and Annotated*. New York, 1969.

Warner, H. J. *The Albigensian Heresy*. New York, 1967.

CHRISTIAN HERESIES OF THE RENAISSANCE AND REFORMATION
(Fifteenth–Seventeenth Centuries)

Bainton, R. H. *Hunted Heretic: The Life and Death of Michael Servetus, 1511–1553*. Boston, 1953.

Davis, K. R. *Anabaptism and Asceticism: A Study in Intellectual Origins*. Scottdale, PA, 1974.

Erikson, K. T. *Wayward Puritans: A Study in the Sociology of Deviance*. New York, 1966.

Fenlon, D. *Heresy and Obedience in Tridentine Italy: Cardinal Pole and the Counter-Reformation*. Cambridge, U.K., 1972.

Friedman, J. *Michael Servetus: A Case Study in Total Heresy*. Geneva, 1978.

Gairdner, J. *Lollardy and the Reformation in England*. London, 1908–1913.

Goertz, H. J. *Profiles of Radical Reformers: Biographical Sketches from Thomas Muntzer to Paracelsus*. Scottdale, PA, 1982.

Gritsch, E. W. *Reformer Without a Church: The Life and Thought of Thomas Muntzer, 1488?–1525*. Philadelphia, 1967.

Gross, L. *The Golden Years of the Hutterites*. Scottdale, PA, 1980.

Heymann, F. G. *George of Bohemia: King of Heretics*. Princeton, 1965.

Hillerbrand, H. J. ed. *A Bibliography of Anabaptism*. Elkhart, IN, 1962.

———. *A Bibliography of Menno Simons (c. 1520–1630)*. Elkhart, IN, 1962.

Hopton, A. *Digger Tracts, 1649–50*. London, 1989.

Horsch, J. *The Hutterian Brethren, 1528–1931*. Scottdale, PA, 1931.

Klaasen, W. *Anabaptism: Neither Catholic Nor Protestant*. Waterloo, 1973.

Kaminsky, H. *A History of the Hussite Revolution*. Berkeley, 1967.

Kot, S. *Socinianism in Poland: The Social and Political Ideas of the Polish Antitrinitarians in the Sixteenth and Seventeenth Centuries*. Boston, 1957.

McKnight, S. A. *Sacralizing the Secular: The Renaissance Origins of Modernity*. Baton Rouge, LA, 1989.

Mladonovic, P. *John Hus at the Council of Constance*. New York, 1965.

Mullett, M. *Radical Religious Movements in Early Modern Europe*. London, 1980.

Ozment, S. *Mysticism and Dissent: Religious Ideology and Social Protest in the Sixteenth Century*. New Haven, 1973.

Pelikan, J. *Reformation of Church and Dogma (1300–1700)*. Chicago, 1984.

Redondi, P. *Galileo: Heretic*. Princeton, 1987.

Spinka, M. *John Hus: A Biography*. Princeton, 1968.

Spitz, L. W. *The Protestant Reformation: 1517–1559*. New York, 1985.

Stayer, J. *Anabaptists and the Sword*. Lawrence, KS, 1974.

Thomson, J. A. F. *The Later Lollards, 1414–1520*. Oxford, 1965.

Wilbur, E. M. *A History of Unitarianism, Socinianism and Its Antecedents*. Cambridge, MA, 1945.

Williams, G. H. *Spiritual and Anabaptist Writers: Documents Illustrative of the Radical Reformation*, Philadelphia, 1957.

———. *The Radical Reformation*. Philadelphia, 1962.

———. *The Polish Brethren: Documentation of the History and Thought of Unitarianism in the Polish-Lithuanian Commonwealth and in the Diaspora, 1601–1685*. Chico, CA, 1980.

Yates, F. A. *Giordano Bruno and the Hermetic Tradition*. Chicago, 1964.

Zeman, J. K. *The Anabaptists and Czech Brethren in Moravia, 1526–1628*. The Hague, 1969.

Zuck, L. P. *Christianity and Revolution: Radical Christian Testimonies, 1520–1650*. Philadelphia, 1975.

MODERN CHRISTIAN HERESIES AND OTHER UNORTHODOX MOVEMENTS *(Eighteenth–Twentieth Centuries)*

Allen, T. T. *Selections from the Autobiography of Madame Guyon*. New Canaan, CT, 1980.

Andrews, E. D. *The People Called Shakers*. New York, 1953.

Bach, M. *Strange Sects and Curious Cults*. Westport, CT, 1961.

Blandreth, H. R. T. *Episcopi Vagantes and the Anglican Church*. London, 1961.

Blavatsky, H. P. *The Secret Doctrine*. London, 1888.

Botting, H. and G. *The Orwellian World of the Jehovah's Witnesses*. Toronto, 1984.

Braden, C. S. *These Also Believe: A Study of Modern American Cults and Minority Religious Movements*. New York, 1949.

Brandon, R. *The Spiritualists*. Buffalo, 1984.

Brodie, F. M. *No Man Knows My History*. London, 1965.

Carlson, S., and G. Larue. *Satanism in America: How the Devil Got Much More Than His Due*. El Cerrito, CA, 1989.

Cockshut, A. O. J. *Religious Controversies of the Nineteenth Century: Selected Documents*. Lincoln, NE, 1966.

Cohen, D. *Waiting for the Apocalypse*. Buffalo, 1983.

De Jonge, A. *The Life and Times of Grigorii Rasputin*. New York, 1982.

Ellwood, R. S. *Alternative Altars*. Chicago, 1979.

Fuller, J. O. *Blavatsky and Her Teachers*. London, 1988.

Goodspeed, E. T. *Modern Apocrypha*. Boston, 1956.

Green, M. *Prophets of a New Age: The Politics of Hope From the Eighteenth Through the Twenty-First Centuries.* New York, 1992.

Gutierrez, G. *A Theology of Liberation.* Maryknoll, NY, 1973.

Holt, S. *Terror in the Name of God: The Story of the Freedom Doukhobors.* Toronto, 1965.

Judah, J. S. *The History and Philosophy of the Metaphysical Movements in America.* Philadelphia, 1967.

Keizer, L. S. *The Wandering Bishops.* Santa Cruz, CA, 1976.

Kirvan, J., ed. *The Infallibility Debate.* New York, 1971.

Knox, R. A. *Enthusiasm: A Chapter in the History of Religion with Special Reference to the Seventeenth and Eighteenth Centuries.* Oxford, 1950.

Kung, H. *Infallible?* London, 1971.

Larsen, E. *Strange Sects and Cults: A Study of Their Origins and Influence.* New York, 1971.

Martin, W. *The Kingdom of the Cults.* Minneapolis, 1985.

May, J. L. *Father Tyrrell and the Modernist Movement.* London, 1932.

McKenzie, J. L. *Authority in the Church.* New York, 1966.

Melton, J. G. *Encyclopedic Handbook of Cults in America.* New York, 1986.

Nelson, G. L. *Spiritualism and Society.* New York, 1969.

O'Dea, T. *The Mormons.* Chicago, 1957.

Oliphant, J. *Brother Twelve: The Incredible Story of Canada's False Prophet.* Toronto, 1991.

Podmore, F. *Modern Spiritualism.* London, 1902.

Rahner, K. *On Heresy.* New York, 1964.

Raschke, C. A. *The Interruption of Eternity: Modern Gnosticism and the Origins of the New Religious Consciousness.* Chicago, 1980.

Rogerson, A. *Millions Now Living Will Never Die.* London, 1969.

Sakolsky, R., and J. Koehnline, eds. *Gone to Croatan: Origins of North American Dropout Culture.* Brooklyn, NY, 1993.

Sigstedt, C. *The Swedenborg Epic.* New York, 1952.

Speeth, K. R. *The Gurdjieff Work.* New York, 1976.

Sweet, W. W. *Religion in the Development of American Culture, 1765–1840.* New York, 1952.

WITCH HUNTS AND PERSECUTIONS OF HERETICS

Ankarloo, B., and G. Henningsen, eds. *Early Modern European Witchcraft: Centers and Peripheries.* Oxford, 1990.

Anonymous. *A Short History of the Inquisition.* New York, 1907.

Burman, E. *The Inquisition: The Hammer of Heresy.* Wellingborough, U.K., 1984.

Cohn, N. *Europe's Inner Demons: An Enquiry Inspired by the Great Witch-Hunt.* London, 1975.

Coulton, G. G. *Inquisition and Liberty.* Gloucester, MA, 1969.

———. *The Inquisition.* Folcroft, PA, 1974.

Douglas, M., ed. *Witchcraft Confession and Accusations.* London, 1970.

Easlea, B. *Witch Hunting, Magic and the New Philosophy: An Introduction to the Debates of the Scientific Revolution, 1450–1750.* Brighton, 1980.

Ginzburg, C. *The Night Battles.* London, 1983.

———. *Ecstasies: Deciphering the Witches' Sabbath.* New York, 1991.

Guiley, R. E. *The Encyclopedia of Witches and Witchcraft.* New York, 1989.

Hamilton, B. *The Medieval Inquisition.* London, 1981.

Haught, J. A. *Holy Horrors: An Illustrated History of Religious Murder and Madness.* Buffalo, 1990.

Hayward, F. *The Inquisition.* New York, 1966.

Hazard, H. W., ed. *A History of the Crusades.* Madison, WI, 1975.

Henningsen, G. *The Witches' Advocate: Basque Witchcraft and the Spanish Inquisition.* Reno, 1980.

Hicks, R. A. *In Pursuit of Satan: The Police and the Occult.* Buffalo, 1991.

Hinckeldey, C. *Criminal Justice Through the Ages: From Divine Judgement to Modern German Legislation.* Rothenburg, 1981.

Jameson, J. F., ed. *Persecution and Liberty.* New York, 1931.

Kamen, H. *The Spanish Inquisition.* London, 1965.

Kieckhefer, R. *European Witch Trials: Their Foundations in Popular and Learned Culture, 1300–1500*. Berkeley, 1976.

———. *Repression of Heresy in Medieval Germany*. Philadelphia, 1979.

Kittredge, G. L. *Witchcraft in Old and New England*. Cambridge, MA, 1929.

Klaits, J. *Servants of Satan: The Age of the Witch Hunts*. Bloomington, IN, 1985.

Kors, A. C., and E. Peters. *Witchcraft in Europe, 1100–1700: A Documentary History*. Philadelphia, 1972.

Larner, C. *Enemies of God: The Witch Hunt in Scotland*. London, 1981.

Lea, H. C. *The Inquisition of the Middle Ages: Its Organization and Operation*. New York, 1969.

Levack, B. P. *The Witch-Hunt in Early Modern Europe*. London, 1987.

Midelfort, H. C. E. *Witch Hunting in Southwestern Germany, 1562–1684*. Stanford, 1972.

Monter, E. W. *Witchcraft in France and Switzerland: The Borderlands During the Reformation*. Ithaca, NY, 1976.

Moore, R. I. *The Formation of a persecuting society: Power and Deviance in Western Europe, 950–1250*. Oxford, 1987.

Newall, V., ed. *The Witch–figure*. London, 1973.

Notestein, W. *A History of Witchcraft in England from 1558 to 1718*. New York, 1968.

O'Brien, J. A. *The Inquisition*. New York, 1973.

Oldenbourg, Z. *Massacre at Montsegur: A History of the Albigensian Crusade*. London, 1961.

Peters, E. *The Magician, the Witch, and the Law*. Philadelphia, 1982.

———. *Torture*. Oxford, 1985.

———. *Inquisition*. New York, 1988.

Robbins, R. H. *The Encyclopedia of Witchcraft and Demonology*. New York, 1981.

Russell, J. B. *Witchcraft in the Middle Ages*. Ithaca, NY, 1972.

Strayer, J. R. *The Albigensian Crusades*. New York, 1971.

Summers, M., ed. *Compendium Maleficarum*. London, 1970.

———. *Malleus Maleficarum*. New York, 1971.

Sumption, J. *The Albigensian Crusade*. London, 1978.

Trevor-Roper, H. R. *The European Witch-Craze of the Sixteenth and Seventeenth Centuries*. New York, 1956.

Turberville, A. S. *Mediaeval Heresy and the Inquisition*. Hamden, CT, 1964.

HERETICAL AND ESOTERIC JUDAISM

Bakan, D. *Sigmund Freud and the Jewish Mystical Tradition*. New York, 1958.

Bokser, B. Z. *The Jewish Mystical Tradition*. New York, 1981.

Halevi, Z. S. *Tree of Life: An Introduction to the Kabbalah*. London, 1986.

———. *Kabbalah and Psychology*. York Beach, ME, 1987.

Hoffman, E. *The Way of Splendor: Jewish Mysticism and Modern Psychology*. Boulder, 1981.

Idel, M. *Kabbalah: New Perspectives*. New Haven, 1988.

———. *The Mystical Experience in Abraham Abulafia*. Albany, NY, 1988.

Kaplan, A. *Meditation and Kabbalah*. New York, 1982.

———. *Sefer Yetzirah: The Book of Creation*. York Beach, ME, 1990.

Scholem, G. *Major Trends in Jewish Mysticism*. New York, 1974.

———. *Sabbatai Sevi—The Mystical Messiah*. Princeton, NJ, 1981.

———. *Kabbalah*. New York, 1987.

———. *Origins of the Kabbalah*. Princeton, 1987.

Sperling, H., and M. Simon, tr. *Zohar*. London, 1931–1934.

Trachtenberg, J. *Jewish Magic and Superstition*. New York, 1975.

Weiner, H. *9½ Jewish Mystics*. New York, 1969.

OCCULT TRADITIONS: *Alchemy, Astrology, Magic*

Adler, M. *Drawing Down the Moon: Witches, Druids, Goddess--worshippers and Other Pagans in America Today*. Boston, 1987.

Agrippa, H. C. *The Philosophy of Natural Magic*. Secaucus, NJ, 1974.

Blau, J. *The Christian Interpretation of Cabala in the Renaissance*. Port Washington, 1965.

Burland, C. *The Arts of the Alchemists*. New York, 1968.

Butler, E. M. *Ritual Magic*. New York, 1959.

Butler, W. E. *The Magician, His Training and Work*. York Beach, ME, 1969.

Cavendish, R. *The Black Arts*. London, 1969.

Cavendish, R., ed. *Man, Myth and Magic: An Illustrated Encyclopedia of the Supernatural*. London, 1970.

Cavendish, R. *A History of Magic*. New York, 1977.

Clulee, N. H. *John Dee's Natural Philosophy: Between Science and Religion*. New York, 1988.

Coudert, A. *Alchemy: The Philosopher's Stone*. Boulder, 1980.

Couliano, I. P. *Eros and Magic in the Renaissance*. Chicago, 1987.

Crowley, A. *Magick in Theory and Practice*. New York, 1976.

De Givry, G. *Witchcraft, Magic and Alchemy*. New York, 1971.

Dobbs, B. J. T. *The Foundations of Newton's Alchemy: Or, "The Hunting of the Greene Lyon."* Cambridge, U.K., 1975.

Eliade, M. *The Forge and the Crucible: The Origins and Structures of Alchemy*. New York, 1971.

Fabricius, J. *Alchemy: The Medieval Alchemists and Their Royal Art*. Wellingborough, UK, 1989.

Flint, V. *The Rise of Magic in Early Medieval Europe*. Princeton, 1991.

Gettings, F. *Dictionary of Occult, Hermetic and Alchemical Sigils*. London, 1981.

Gilchrist, C. *The Elements of Alchemy*. Rockport, MA, 1991.

Goodrick-Clarke, N. *Paracelsus: Essential Writings*. Wellingborough, 1990.

Grant, K. *The Magical Revival*. New York, 1972.

Graubard, M. A. *Astrology and Alchemy: Two Fossil Sciences*. New York, 1953.

Haeffner, M. *The Dictionary of Alchemy: From Maria Prophetissa to Isaac Newton*. London, 1991.

Holmyard, E. J. *Alchemy*. Harmondsworth, UK, 1968.

Howe, E. *The Magicians of the Golden Dawn: A Documentary History of a Magical Order, 1887–1923*. York Beach, ME, 1972.

Jacobi, J., ed. *Paracelsus: Selected Writings*. Princeton, 1979.

Kenton, W. *Astrology: The Celestial Mirror*. London, 1974.

Kieckhefer, R. *Magic in the Middle Ages*. Cambridge, U.K., 1990.

King, F. *Sexuality, Magic and Perversion*. Secaucus, NJ, 1972.

———. *Magic: The Western Tradition*. London, 1975.

Klossowski de Rola, S. *Alchemy: The Secret Art*. London, 1973.

———. *The Golden Game: Alchemical Engravings of the Seventeenth Century*. New York, 1988.

Knight, G. *A Practical Guide to Qabalistic Symbolism*. York Beach, ME, 1978.

———. *The History of White Magic*. London, 1978.

Lindsay, J. *The Origins of Alchemy in Graeco-Roman Egypt*. New York, 1970.

Luhrmann, T. M. *Persuasions of the Witch's Craft: Ritual Magic in Contemporary England*. Cambridge, MA, 1989.

Mathers, S. L. M., ed. *The Book of the Sacred Magic of Abramelin the Mage, as Delivered Unto His Son Lamech, A.D. 1458*. New York, 1975.

———. *The Key of Solomon the King (Clavicula Salomonis)*. York Beach, ME, 1989.

McIntosh, C. *The Astrologers and Their Creed: An Historical Outline*. New York, 1969.

———. *The Rosicrucians: The History, Mythology and Rituals of an Occult Order*. Wellingborough, UK, 1987.

McLean, A., ed. *A Treatise on Angel Magic*. Grand Rapids, MI, 1989.

Moore, T. *The Planets Within: The Astrological Psychology of Marsilio Ficino*. Great Barrington, MA, 1990.

O'Keefe, D. L. *Stolen Lightning: The Social Theory of Magic*. New York, 1983.

Raine, K. J. *Yeats, the Tarot, and the Golden Dawn*. Dublin, 1972.

Regardie, I. *The Golden Dawn*. St. Paul, MN, 1985.

Schueler, G. J. *Enochian Magic: A Practical Guide*. St. Paul, MN, 1985.

Scott, W., ed. *Hermetica: The Ancient Greek and Latin Writings which Contain Religious or Philosophic Teachings Ascribed to Hermes Trismegistus*. Boston, 1985.

Seligmann, K. *The History of Magic and the Occult*. New York, 1983.

Shah, S. I. *The Secret Lore of Magic: Books of the Sorcerers*. London, 1972.

Shumaker, W. *The Occult Sciences in the Renaissance: A Study in Intellectual Patterns*. Berkeley, 1972.

Spence, L. *The Encyclopedia of the Occult*. London, 1988.

Suster, G. *John Dee: Essential Readings*. Wellingborough, UK: 1986.

Symonds, J. *The Great Beast: The Life and Magick of Aleister Crowley.* St. Albans, UK, 1973.

Tester, J. *A History of Western Astrology.* New York, 1987.

Thomas, K. *Religion and the Decline of Magic.* London, 1970.

Turner, R. *Elizabethan Magic.* Shaftesbury, UK, 1989.

Waite, A. E. *The Book of Ceremonial Magic: The Secret Tradition in Goetia, Including the Rites and Mysteries of Goetic Theurgy, Sorcery and Infernal Necromancy.* Secaucus, NJ, 1961.

Walker, D. P. *Spiritual and Demonic Magic: From Ficino to Campanella.* Notre Dame, 1975.

Webb, J. *The Occult Underground.* LaSalle, IL, 1974.

———. *The Occult Establishment.* LaSalle, IL, 1976.

Yates, F. *The Occult Philosophy in the Elizabethan Age.* New York, 1979.

PERIODICALS ON ALTERNATIVE-REALITY TRADITIONS

Alexandria: The Journal of the Western Cosmological Tradition. Phanes Press, P.O. 6114, Grand Rapids, MI 49516.

Cauda Pavonis: Studies in Hermeticism. c/o Stanton J. Linden, Dept. of English, Washington State University, Pullman, WA 99164.

Gnosis: A Journal of the Western Inner Traditions, P.O. 14217, San Francisco, CA 94114.

The Hermetic Journal, P.O. 375, Headington, Oxford OX3 5PW, UK.